Understanding Media and Culture: An Introduction to Mass Communication

Understanding Media and Culture: An Introduction to Mass Communication

UNIVERSITY OF MINNESOTA LIBRARIES PUBLISHING EDITION, 2016. THIS EDITION ADAPTED FROM A WORK ORIGINALLY PRODUCED IN 2010 BY A PUBLISHER WHO HAS REQUESTED THAT IT NOT RECEIVE ATTRIBUTION.
MINNEAPOLIS, MN

Contents

Chapter 4: Newspapers

Chapter 5: Magazines

Chapter 6: Music

Chapter 7: Radio

Chapter 8: Movies

Chapter 14: Ethics of Mass Media

Chapter 15: Media and Government

Chapter 16: The Future of Mass Media

About this Book

Understanding Media and Culture: An Introduction to Mass Communication is adapted from a work produced and distributed under a Creative Commons license (CC BY-NC-SA) in 2010 by a publisher who has requested that they and the original author not receive attribution. This adapted edition is produced by the University of Minnesota Libraries Publishing through the eLearning Support Initiative.

This adaptation has reformatted the original text, and replaced some images and figures to make the resulting whole more shareable. This adaptation has not significantly altered or updated the original 2010 text. This work is made available under the terms of a Creative Commons Attribution-NonCommercial-ShareAlike license.

Distributed by State University of New York Press.

On the cover: Cover image authored by: Jakob Owens Located at: https://unsplash.com/photos/WUmb_eBrpjs

ISBN: 978-1-64176-027-0

Chapter 1: Media and Culture

1.1 Media and Culture

Pop Culture Mania

Figure 1.1

Paul Townsend – 1960s Beatlemania Fashion – CC BY-ND 2.0.

Just as fans could purchase Jerry Lind hats, Beatles fans could purchase Beatle wigs
(as pictured above).

In 1850, an epidemic swept America—but instead of leaving victims sick with fever or flu, this epidemic involved a rabid craze for the music of Swedish soprano Jenny Lind. American showman P. T. Barnum (who would later go on to found the circus now known as Ringling Bros. and Barnum & Bailey), a shrewd marketer and self-made millionaire, is credited with spreading "Lindomania" through a series of astute show-business moves. Barnum promised Lind an unprecedented $1,000-a-night fee (the equivalent of $28,300 in 2009) for her entire 93-performance tour of the United States. Ever the savvy self-promoter, Barnum turned his huge investment to his advantage by using it to create publicity—and it paid off. When the Swedish soprano's ship docked on U.S. shores, she was greeted by 40,000 ardent fans; another 20,000 swarmed her hotel (Barnum). Congress was adjourned specifically for Lind's visit to Washington, DC, where the National Theatre had to be enlarged to accommodate her audiences. A town in California and an island in Canada were named in her honor. Enthusiasts could purchase Jenny Lind hats, chairs, boots, opera glasses, and even pianos. Barnum's marketing expertise made Lind a household name and created an overwhelming demand for a singer previously unknown to American audiences.

The "Jenny rage" that the savvy Barnum was able to create was not a unique phenomenon, however; a little more than a century later, a new craze transformed some American teenagers into screaming, fainting Beatlemaniacs. Though other performers like Frank Sinatra and Elvis Presley were no strangers to manic crowds, the Beatles attracted an unprecedented amount of attention when they first arrived in the United States. When the British foursome touched down at New York's Kennedy Airport in 1964, they were met by more than 3,000 frenzied fans. Their performance on *The Ed Sullivan Show* was seen by 73 million people, or 40 percent of the U.S. population. The crime rate that night dropped to its lowest level in 50 years (Ehrenreich, et. al., 1992). Beatlemania was at such a fever pitch that *Life* magazine cautioned that "a Beatle who ventures out unguarded into the streets runs the very real peril of being dismembered or crushed to death by his fans." The BBC publicized the trend and perhaps added to it by highlighting the paraphernalia for fans to spend their money on: "T-shirts, sweat shirts, turtle-neck sweaters, tight-legged trousers, night shirts, scarves, and jewelry inspired by the Beatles" were all available, as were Beatles-style mop-top wigs.

In the 21st century, rabid fans could turn their attention to a whole swath of pop stars in the making when the reality TV program *American Idol* hit the airwaves in 2002. The show was the only television program ever to have snagged the top spot in the Nielsen ratings for six seasons in a row, often averaging more than 30 million nightly viewers. Rival television network executives were alarmed, deeming the pop giant "the ultimate schoolyard bully," "the Death Star," or even "the most impactful show in the history of television," according to former NBC Universal CEO Jeff Zucker (Carter, 2007). New cell phone technologies allowed viewers to have a direct role in the program's star-making enterprise through casting votes, signing up for text alerts, or playing trivia games on their phones. In 2009, AT&T estimated that *Idol*-related text traffic amounted to 178 million messages (Poniewozik, 2009).

These three crazes all relied on various forms of media to create excitement. Whether through newspaper advertisements, live television broadcasts, or integrated Internet marketing, media industry tastemakers help shape what we care about. For as long as mass media has existed in the United States, it's helped to create and fuel mass crazes, skyrocketing celebrities, and pop culture manias of all kinds. Even in our era of seemingly limitless entertainment options, mass hits like *American Idol* still have the ability to dominate the public's attention. In the chapters to come, we'll look at different kinds of mass media and how they have been changed by—and are changing—the world we live in.

References

Barnum, P. T." Answers.com, http://www.answers.com/topic/p-t-barnum.

Carter, Bill. "For Fox's Rivals, 'American Idol' Remains a 'Schoolyard Bully,'" *New York Times*, February 20, 2007, Arts section.

Ehrenreich, Barbara, Elizabeth Hess, and Gloria Jacobs, "Beatlemania: Girls Just Want to Have Fun," in *The Adoring Audience: Fan Culture and Popular Media*, ed. Lisa A. Lewis (New York: Routledge, 1992), 84–106.

Poniewozik, James. "American Idol's Voting Scandal (Or Not)," *Tuned In* (blog), *Time*, May 28, 2009, http://tunedin.blogs.time.com/2009/05/28/american-idols-voting-scandal-or-not/.

1.2 Intersection of American Media and Culture

Learning Objectives

1. Distinguish between mass communication and mass media.
2. Identify key points in American media and culture.

Pop culture and American media are inextricably linked. Consider that Jenny Lind, the Beatles, and *American Idol* were each promoted using a then-new technology (photography for Lind, television for the Beatles, and the Internet and text messaging for *American Idol*).

Mass Communication, Mass Media, and Culture

The chapters to come will provide an in-depth look at many kinds of media, at how media trends are reshaping the United States' cultural landscape, and at how that culture shapes media in turn. These topics will be explored through an examination of mass media and mass communication both past and present—and speculation about what the future might look like.

First, it is important to distinguish between mass communication and mass media and to attempt a working definition of culture. Mass communication refers to information transmitted to large segments of the population. The transmission of mass communication may happen using one or many different kinds of media (singular medium), which is the means of transmission, whether print, digital, or electronic. Mass media specifically refers to a means of communication that is designed to reach a wide audience. Mass media platforms are commonly considered to include radio, newspapers, magazines, books, video games, and Internet media such as blogs, podcasts, and video sharing. Another way to consider the distinction is that a mass media message may be disseminated through several forms of mass media, such as an ad campaign with television, radio, and Internet components. Culture generally refers to the shared values, attitudes, beliefs, and practices that characterize a social group, organization, or institution. Just as it is difficult to pin down an exact definition of culture, cultures themselves can be hard to draw boundaries around, as they are fluid, diverse, and often overlapping.

Figure 1.2

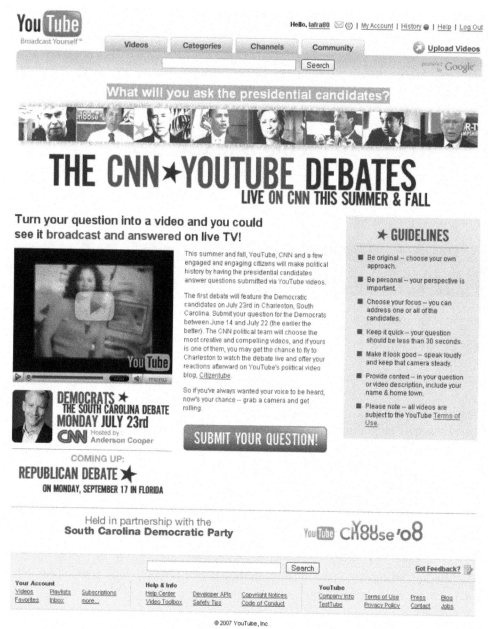

Advances in media technology allowed for unprecedented voter participation in the 2007 CNN/YouTube® presidential debates.

Iafra – The CNN + YouTube Debates – CC BY-NC-ND 2.0.

Throughout U.S. history, evolving media technologies have changed the way we relate socially, economically, and politically. In 2007, for example, a joint venture between the 24-hour news network CNN and the video-sharing site YouTube allowed voters to pose questions directly to presidential candidates in two televised debates. Voters could record their questions and upload them to YouTube, and a selection of these videos were then chosen by the debate moderators and played directly to the presidential candidates. This new format opened up the presidential debates to a much wider array of people, allowing for greater voter participation than has been possible in the past, where questions were posed solely by journalists or a few carefully chosen audience members.

In today's wired world of smartphones and streaming satellite feeds, our expectations of our leaders, celebrities, teachers, and even ourselves are changing in even more drastic ways. This book provides you with the context, tools, and theories to engage with the world of mass media through an examination of the history, theory, and effects of media practices and roles in America. This book also provides you with the framework to consider some of the crucial issues affecting media and culture in today's world.

Key Takeaways

- Mass communication refers to a message transmitted to a large audience; the means of transmission is known as mass media. Many different kinds of mass media exist and have existed for centuries. Both the messages and the media affect culture, which is a diffused collection of behaviors, practices, beliefs, and values that are particular to a group, organization, or institution. Culture and media exert influence on each other in subtle, complex ways.

- The 2008 election is an example of how changes in media technology have had a major impact on society. But the influence goes both ways, and sometimes cultural changes impact how media evolves.

Exercises

Read the following questions about media and culture:

1. The second half of the 20th century included a huge increase in forms of media available, including radio, cinema, television, and the Internet. But some form of mass communication has always been a part of U.S. history. What were the dominant forms of media present in the United States during the Industrial Revolution? World Wars I and II? Other important historical eras? How did these forms of media differ from the ones we have today? How did they help shape the way people interacted with and understood the world they lived in? How does mass communication differ from mass media?

2. Contemporary Americans have more means of getting information and entertainment than ever before. What are the major media present in the United States today? How do these forms of media interact with one another? How do they overlap? How are they distinct?

3.
What is the role of media in American culture today?

   - Some people argue that high-profile cases in the 1990s, such as the criminal trial of O. J. Simpson, Bill Clinton's impeachment proceedings, and the first Persian Gulf War helped fuel the demand for 24-hour news access. What are some other ways that culture affects media?

   - Conversely, how does mass media affect culture? Do violent television shows and video games influence viewers to become more violent? Is the Internet making our culture more open and democratic or more shallow and distracted?

4. Though we may not have hover cars and teleportation, today's electronic gadgets would probably

leave Americans of a century ago breathless. How can today's media landscape help us understand what might await us in years to come? What will the future of American media and culture look like?

5. Write down some of your initial responses or reactions, based on your prior knowledge or intuition. Each response should be a minimum of one paragraph. Keep the piece of paper somewhere secure and return to it on the last day of the course. Were your responses on target? How has your understanding of media and culture changed? How might you answer questions differently now?

1.3 The Evolution of Media

Learning Objectives

1. Identify four roles the media performs in our society.
2. Recognize events that affected the adoption of mass media.
3. Explain how different technological transitions have shaped media industries.

In 2010, Americans could turn on their television and find 24-hour news channels as well as music videos, nature documentaries, and reality shows about everything from hoarders to fashion models. That's not to mention movies available on demand from cable providers or television and video available online for streaming or downloading. Half of U.S. households receive a daily newspaper, and the average person holds 1.9 magazine subscriptions (State of the Media, 2004) (Bilton, 2007). A University of California, San Diego study claimed that U.S. households consumed a total of approximately 3.6 zettabytes of information in 2008—the digital equivalent of a 7-foot high stack of books covering the entire United States—a 350 percent increase since 1980 (Ramsey, 2009). Americans are exposed to media in taxicabs and buses, in classrooms and doctors' offices, on highways, and in airplanes. We can begin to orient ourselves in the information cloud through parsing what roles the media fills in society, examining its history in society, and looking at the way technological innovations have helped bring us to where we are today.

What Does Media Do for Us?

Media fulfills several basic roles in our society. One obvious role is entertainment. Media can act as a springboard for our imaginations, a source of fantasy, and an outlet for escapism. In the 19th century, Victorian readers disillusioned by the grimness of the Industrial Revolution found themselves drawn into fantastic worlds of fairies and other fictitious beings. In the first decade of the 21st century, American television viewers could peek in on a conflicted Texas high school football team in *Friday Night Lights*; the violence-plagued drug trade in Baltimore in *The Wire*; a 1960s-Manhattan ad agency in *Mad Men*; or the last surviving band of humans in a distant, miserable future in *Battlestar Galactica*. Through bringing us stories of all kinds, media has the power to take us away from ourselves.

Media can also provide information and education. Information can come in many forms, and it may sometimes be difficult to separate from entertainment. Today, newspapers and news-oriented television and radio programs make available stories from across the globe, allowing readers or viewers in London to access voices and videos from Baghdad, Tokyo, or Buenos Aires. Books and magazines provide a more in-depth look at a wide range of subjects. The free online encyclopedia *Wikipedia* has articles on topics from presidential nicknames to child prodigies to tongue twisters in various languages. The Massachusetts Institute of Technology (MIT) has posted free lecture notes, exams, and audio and video recordings of classes on its OpenCourseWare website, allowing anyone with an Internet connection access to world-class professors.

Another useful aspect of media is its ability to act as a public forum for the discussion of important issues. In newspapers or other periodicals, letters to the editor allow readers to respond to journalists or to voice their opinions on the issues of the day. These letters were an important part of U.S. newspapers even when the nation was a British colony, and they have served as a means of public discourse ever since. The Internet is a fundamentally democratic medium that allows everyone who can get online the ability to express their opinions through, for example, blogging or podcasting—though whether anyone will hear is another question.

Similarly, media can be used to monitor government, business, and other institutions. Upton Sinclair's 1906 novel *The Jungle* exposed the miserable conditions in the turn-of-the-century meatpacking industry; and in the early 1970s, *Washington Post* reporters Bob Woodward and Carl Bernstein uncovered evidence of the Watergate break-in and subsequent cover-up, which eventually led to the resignation of President Richard Nixon. But purveyors of mass media may be beholden to particular agendas because of political slant, advertising funds, or ideological bias, thus constraining their ability to act as a watchdog. The following are some of these agendas:

1. Entertaining and providing an outlet for the imagination

2. Educating and informing

3. Serving as a public forum for the discussion of important issues

4. Acting as a watchdog for government, business, and other institutions

It's important to remember, though, that not all media are created equal. While some forms of mass communication are better suited to entertainment, others make more sense as a venue for spreading information. In terms of print media, books are durable and able to contain lots of information, but are relatively slow and expensive to produce; in contrast, newspapers are comparatively cheaper and quicker to create, making them a better medium for the quick turnover of daily news. Television provides vastly more visual information than radio and is more dynamic than a static printed page; it can also be used to broadcast live events to a nationwide audience, as in the annual State of the Union address given by the U.S. president. However, it is also a one-way medium—that is, it allows for very little direct person-to-person communication. In contrast, the Internet encourages public discussion of issues and allows nearly everyone who wants a voice to have one. However, the Internet is also largely unmoderated. Users may have to wade through thousands of inane comments or misinformed amateur opinions to find quality information.

The 1960s media theorist Marshall McLuhan took these ideas one step further, famously coining the phrase "the medium is the message (McLuhan, 1964)." By this, McLuhan meant that every medium delivers information in a different way and that content is fundamentally shaped by the medium of transmission. For example, although television news has the advantage of offering video and live coverage, making a story come alive more vividly, it is also a faster-paced medium. That means more stories get covered in less depth. A story told on television will probably be flashier, less in-depth, and with less context than the same story covered in a monthly magazine; therefore, people who get the majority of their news from television may have a particular view of the world shaped not by the *content* of what they watch but its *medium*. Or, as computer scientist Alan Kay put it, "Each medium has a special way of representing ideas that emphasize particular ways of thinking and de-emphasize others (Kay, 1994)." Kay was writing in 1994, when the Internet was just transitioning from an academic research network to an open public system. A decade and a half later, with the Internet firmly ensconced in our daily lives, McLuhan's intellectual descendants are the media analysts who claim that the Internet is making us better at associative thinking, or more democratic, or shallower. But McLuhan's claims don't leave much space for individual autonomy or resistance. In an essay about television's effects on contemporary fiction, writer David Foster Wallace scoffed at the "reactionaries who regard TV as some malignancy visited on an innocent populace, sapping IQs and compromising SAT scores while we all sit there on ever fatter bottoms with little mesmerized spirals revolving in our eyes.... Treating television as evil is just as reductive and silly as treating it like a toaster with pictures (Wallace, 1997)." Nonetheless, media messages and technologies affect us in countless ways, some of which probably won't be sorted out until long in the future.

A Brief History of Mass Media and Culture

Until Johannes Gutenberg's 15th-century invention of the movable type printing press, books were painstakingly handwritten and no two copies were exactly the same. The printing press made the mass production of print media possible. Not only was it much cheaper to produce written material, but new transportation technologies also made it easier for texts to reach a wide audience. It's hard to overstate the importance of Gutenberg's invention, which helped usher in massive cultural movements like the European Renaissance and the Protestant Reformation. In 1810, another German printer, Friedrich Koenig, pushed media production even further when he essentially hooked the steam engine up to a printing press, enabling the industrialization of printed media. In 1800, a hand-operated printing press could produce about 480 pages per hour; Koenig's machine more than doubled this rate. (By the 1930s, many printing presses could publish 3,000 pages an hour.)

This increased efficiency went hand in hand with the rise of the daily newspaper. The newspaper was the perfect medium for the increasingly urbanized Americans of the 19th century, who could no longer get their local news merely through gossip and word of mouth. These Americans were living in unfamiliar territory, and newspapers and other media helped them negotiate the rapidly changing world. The Industrial Revolution meant that some people had more leisure time and more money, and media helped them figure out how to spend both. Media theorist Benedict Anderson has argued that newspapers also helped forge a sense of national identity by treating readers across the country as part of one unified community (Anderson, 1991).

In the 1830s, the major daily newspapers faced a new threat from the rise of penny papers, which were low-priced broadsheets that served as a cheaper, more sensational daily news source. They favored news of murder and adventure over the dry political news of the day. While newspapers catered to a wealthier, more educated audience, the penny press attempted to reach a wide swath of readers through cheap prices and entertaining (often scandalous) stories. The penny press can be seen as the forerunner to today's gossip-hungry tabloids.

Figure 1.3

The penny press appealed to readers' desires for lurid tales of murder and scandal.

Wikimedia Commons – public domain.

In the early decades of the 20th century, the first major nonprint form of mass media—radio—exploded in popularity. Radios, which were less expensive than telephones and widely available by the 1920s, had the unprecedented ability of allowing huge numbers of people to listen to the same event at the same time. In 1924, Calvin Coolidge's preelection speech reached more than 20 million people. Radio was a boon for advertisers, who now had access to a large and captive audience. An early advertising consultant claimed that the early days of radio were "a glorious opportunity for the advertising man to spread his sales propaganda" because of "a countless audience, sympathetic, pleasure seeking, enthusiastic, curious, interested, approachable in the privacy of their homes (Briggs & Burke, 2005)." The reach of radio also meant that the medium was able to downplay regional differences and encourage a unified sense of the American lifestyle—a lifestyle that was increasingly driven and defined by consumer purchases. "Americans in the 1920s were the first to wear ready-made, exact-size clothing…to play electric phonographs, to use electric vacuum cleaners, to listen to commercial radio broadcasts, and to drink fresh orange juice year round (Mintz, 2007)." This boom in consumerism put its stamp on the 1920s and also helped contribute to the Great Depression of the 1930s (Library of Congress). The consumerist impulse drove production to unprecedented levels, but when the Depression began and consumer demand dropped dramatically, the surplus of production helped further deepen the economic crisis, as more goods were being produced than could be sold.

The post–World War II era in the United States was marked by prosperity, and by the introduction of a seductive new form of mass communication: television. In 1946, about 17,000 televisions existed in the United States; within 7 years, two-thirds of American households owned at least one set. As the United States' gross national product (GNP) doubled in the 1950s, and again in the 1960s, the American home became firmly ensconced as a consumer unit; along with a television, the typical U.S. household owned a car and a house in the suburbs, all of which contributed to the nation's thriving consumer-based economy (Briggs & Burke, 2005). Broadcast television was the dominant form of mass media, and the three major networks controlled more than 90 percent of the news programs, live events, and sitcoms viewed by Americans. Some social critics argued that television was fostering a homogenous, conformist culture by reinforcing ideas about what "normal" American life looked like. But television also contributed to the counterculture of the 1960s. The Vietnam War was the nation's first televised military conflict, and nightly images of war footage and war protesters helped intensify the nation's internal conflicts.

Broadcast technology, including radio and television, had such a hold on the American imagination that newspapers and other print media found themselves having to adapt to the new media landscape. Print media was more durable and easily archived, and it allowed users more flexibility in terms of time—once a person had purchased a magazine, he or she could read it whenever and wherever. Broadcast media, in contrast, usually aired programs on a fixed schedule, which allowed it to both provide a sense of immediacy and fleetingness. Until the advent of digital video recorders in the late 1990s, it was impossible to pause and rewind a live television broadcast.

The media world faced drastic changes once again in the 1980s and 1990s with the spread of cable television. During the early decades of television, viewers had a limited number of channels to choose from—one reason for the charges of homogeneity. In 1975, the three major networks accounted for 93 percent of all television viewing. By 2004, however, this share had dropped to 28.4 percent of total viewing, thanks to the spread of cable television. Cable providers allowed viewers a wide menu of choices, including channels specifically tailored to people who wanted to watch only golf, classic films, sermons, or videos of sharks. Still, until the mid-1990s, television was dominated by the three large networks. The Telecommunications Act of 1996, an attempt to foster competition by deregulating the industry, actually resulted in many mergers and buyouts that left most of the control of the broadcast spectrum in the hands of a few large corporations. In 2003, the Federal Communications Commission (FCC) loosened regulation even further, allowing a single company to own 45 percent of a single market (up from 25 percent in 1982).

Technological Transitions Shape Media Industries

New media technologies both spring from and cause social changes. For this reason, it can be difficult to neatly sort the evolution of media into clear causes and effects. Did radio fuel the consumerist boom of the 1920s, or did the radio become wildly popular because it appealed to a society that was already exploring consumerist tendencies? Probably a little bit of both. Technological innovations such as the steam engine, electricity, wireless communication, and the Internet have all had lasting and significant effects on American culture. As media historians Asa Briggs and Peter Burke note, every crucial invention came with "a change in historical perspectives." Electricity altered the way people thought about time because work and play were no longer dependent on the daily rhythms of sunrise and sunset; wireless communication collapsed distance; the Internet revolutionized the way we store and retrieve information.

Figure 1.4

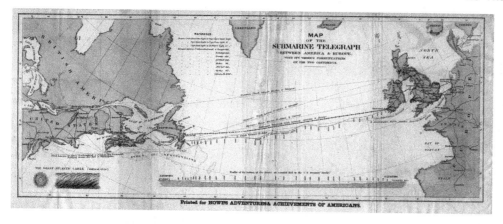

The transatlantic telegraph cable made nearly instantaneous communication between the United States and Europe possible for the first time in 1858.

Amber Case – 1858 trans-Atlantic telegraph cable route – CC BY-NC 2.0.

The contemporary media age can trace its origins back to the electrical telegraph, patented in the United States by Samuel Morse in 1837. Thanks to the telegraph, communication was no longer linked to the physical transportation of messages; it didn't matter whether a message needed to travel 5 or 500 miles. Suddenly, information from distant places was nearly as accessible as local news, as telegraph lines began to stretch across the globe, making their own kind of World Wide Web. In this way, the telegraph acted as the precursor to much of the technology that followed, including the telephone, radio, television, and Internet. When the first transatlantic cable was laid in 1858, allowing nearly instantaneous communication from the United States to Europe, the *London Times* described it as "the greatest discovery since that of Columbus, a vast enlargement…given to the sphere of human activity."

Not long afterward, wireless communication (which eventually led to the development of radio, television, and other broadcast media) emerged as an extension of telegraph technology. Although many 19th-century inventors, including Nikola Tesla, were involved in early wireless experiments, it was Italian-born Guglielmo Marconi who is recognized as the developer of the first practical wireless radio system. Many people were fascinated by this new invention. Early radio was used for military communication, but soon the technology entered the home. The burgeoning interest in radio inspired hundreds of applications for broadcasting licenses from newspapers and other news outlets, retail stores, schools, and even cities. In the 1920s, large media networks—including the National Broadcasting Company (NBC) and the Columbia Broadcasting System (CBS)—were launched, and they soon began to dominate the airwaves. In 1926, they owned 6.4 percent of U.S. broadcasting stations; by 1931, that number had risen to 30 percent.

Figure 1.5

Gone With the Wind defeated *The Wizard of Oz* to become the first color film ever to win the Academy Award for Best Picture in 1939.

In addition to the breakthroughs in audio broadcasting, inventors in the 1800s made significant advances in visual media. The 19th-century development of photographic technologies would lead to the later innovations of cinema and television. As with wireless technology, several inventors independently created a form of photography at the same time, among them the French inventors Joseph Niépce and Louis Daguerre and the British scientist William Henry Fox Talbot. In the United States, George Eastman developed the Kodak camera in 1888, anticipating that Americans would welcome an inexpensive, easy-to-use camera into their homes as they had with the radio and telephone. Moving pictures were first seen around the turn of the century, with the first U.S. projection-hall opening in Pittsburgh in 1905. By the 1920s, Hollywood had already created its first stars, most notably Charlie Chaplin; by the end of the 1930s, Americans were watching color films with full sound, including *Gone With the Wind* and *The Wizard of Oz*.

Television—which consists of an image being converted to electrical impulses, transmitted through wires or radio waves, and then reconverted into images—existed before World War II, but gained mainstream popularity in the 1950s. In 1947, there were 178,000 television sets made in the United States; 5 years later, 15 million were made. Radio, cinema, and live theater declined because the new medium allowed viewers to be entertained with sound and moving pictures in their homes. In the United States, competing commercial stations (including the radio powerhouses of CBS and NBC) meant that commercial-driven programming dominated. In Great Britain, the government managed broadcasting through the British Broadcasting Corporation (BBC). Funding was driven by licensing fees instead of advertisements. In contrast to the U.S. system, the BBC strictly regulated the length and character of commercials that could be aired. However, U.S. television (and its increasingly powerful networks) still dominated. By the beginning of 1955, there were around 36 million television sets in the United States, but only 4.8 million in all of Europe. Important national events, broadcast live for the first time, were an impetus for consumers to buy sets so they could witness the spectacle; both England and Japan saw a boom in sales before important royal weddings in the 1950s.

Figure 1.6

In the 1960s, the concept of a useful portable computer was still a dream; huge mainframes were required to run a basic operating system.

In 1969, management consultant Peter Drucker predicted that the next major technological innovation would be an electronic appliance that would revolutionize the way people lived just as thoroughly as Thomas Edison's light bulb had. This appliance would sell for less than a television set and be "capable of being plugged in wherever there is electricity and giving immediate access to all the information needed for school work from first grade through college." Although Drucker may have underestimated the cost of this hypothetical machine, he was prescient about the effect these machines—personal computers—and the Internet would have on education, social relationships, and the culture at large. The inventions of random access memory (RAM) chips and microprocessors in the 1970s were important steps to the Internet age. As Briggs and Burke note, these advances meant that "hundreds of thousands of components could be carried on a microprocessor." The reduction of many different kinds of content to digitally stored information meant that "print, film, recording, radio and television and all forms of telecommunications [were] now being thought of increasingly as part of one complex." This process, also known as convergence, is a force that's affecting media today.

Key Takeaways

- Media fulfills several roles in society, including the following:

    ◦ entertaining and providing an outlet for the imagination,

    ◦ educating and informing,

    ◦ serving as a public forum for the discussion of important issues, and

    ◦ acting as a watchdog for government, business, and other institutions.

- Johannes Gutenberg's invention of the printing press enabled the mass production of media, which was then industrialized by Friedrich Koenig in the early 1800s. These innovations led to the daily newspaper, which united the urbanized, industrialized populations of the 19th century.

- In the 20th century, radio allowed advertisers to reach a mass audience and helped spur the consumerism of the 1920s—and the Great Depression of the 1930s. After World War II, television boomed in the United States and abroad, though its concentration in the hands of three major networks led to accusations of homogenization. The spread of cable and subsequent deregulation in the 1980s and 1990s led to more channels, but not necessarily to more diverse ownership.

- Transitions from one technology to another have greatly affected the media industry, although it is difficult to say whether technology caused a cultural shift or resulted from it. The ability to make technology small and affordable enough to fit into the home is an important aspect of the popularization of new technologies.

Exercises

Choose two different types of mass communication—radio shows, television broadcasts, Internet sites, newspaper advertisements, and so on—from two different kinds of media. Make a list of what role(s) each one fills, keeping in mind that much of what we see, hear, or read in the mass media has more than one aspect. Then, answer the following questions. Each response should be a minimum of one paragraph.

1. To which of the four roles media plays in society do your selections correspond? Why did the creators of these particular messages present them in these particular ways and in these particular mediums?

2. What events have shaped the adoption of the two kinds of media you selected?

3. How have technological transitions shaped the industries involved in the two kinds of media you have selected?

References

Anderson, Benedict *Imagined Communities: Reflections on the Origin and Spread of Nationalism*, (London: Verso, 1991).

Bilton, Jim. "The Loyalty Challenge: How Magazine Subscriptions Work," *In Circulation*, January/February 2007.

Briggs and Burke, *Social History of the Media*.

Briggs, Asa and Peter Burke, *A Social History of the Media: From Gutenberg to the Internet* (Malden, MA: Polity Press, 2005).

Kay, Alan. "The Infobahn Is Not the Answer," *Wired*, May 1994.

Library of Congress, "Radio: A Consumer Product and a Producer of Consumption," Coolidge-Consumerism Collection, http://lcweb2.loc.gov:8081/ammem/amrlhtml/inradio.html.

McLuhan, Marshall. *Understanding Media: The Extensions of Man*, (New York: McGraw-Hill, 1964).

Mintz, Steven "The Jazz Age: The American 1920s: The Formation of Modern American Mass Culture," *Digital History*, 2007, http://www.digitalhistory.uh.edu/database/article_display.cfm?hhid=454.

Ramsey, Doug. "UC San Diego Experts Calculate How Much Information Americans Consume" UC San Diego News Center, December 9, 2009, http://ucsdnews.ucsd.edu/newsrel/general/12-09Information.asp.

State of the Media, project for Excellence in Journalism, *The State of the News Media 2004*, http://www.stateofthemedia.org/2004/.

Wallace, David Foster "E Unibus Pluram: Television and U.S. Fiction," in *A Supposedly Fun Thing I'll Never Do Again* (New York: Little Brown, 1997).

1.4 Convergence

It's important to keep in mind that the implementation of new technologies doesn't mean that the old ones simply vanish into dusty museums. Today's media consumers still watch television, listen to radio, read newspapers, and become immersed in movies. The difference is that it's now possible to do all those things through one device—be it a personal computer or a smartphone—and through the Internet. Such actions are enabled by media convergence, the process by which previously distinct technologies come to share tasks and resources. A cell phone that also takes pictures and video is an example of the convergence of digital photography, digital video, and cellular telephone technologies. An extreme, and currently nonexistent, example of technological convergence would be the so-called black box, which would combine all the functions of previously distinct technology and would be the device through which we'd receive all our news, information, entertainment, and social interaction.

Kinds of Convergence

But convergence isn't just limited to technology. Media theorist Henry Jenkins argues that convergence isn't an end result (as is the hypothetical black box), but instead a process that changes how media is both consumed and produced. Jenkins breaks convergence down into five categories:

1. Economic convergence occurs when a company controls several products or services within the same industry. For example, in the entertainment industry a single company may have interests across many kinds of media. For example, Rupert Murdoch's News Corporation is involved in book publishing (HarperCollins), newspapers (*New York Post*, *The Wall Street Journal*), sports (Colorado Rockies), broadcast television (Fox), cable television (FX, National Geographic Channel), film (20th Century Fox), Internet (MySpace), and many other media.

2. Organic convergence is what happens when someone is watching a television show online while exchanging text messages with a friend and also listening to music in the background—the "natural" outcome of a diverse media world.

3. Cultural convergence has several aspects. Stories flowing across several kinds of media platforms is one component—for example, novels that become television series (*True Blood*); radio dramas that become comic strips (*The Shadow*); even amusement park rides that become film franchises (*Pirates of the Caribbean*). The character Harry Potter exists in books, films, toys, and amusement park rides. Another aspect of cultural convergence is participatory culture—that is, the way media consumers are able to annotate, comment on, remix, and otherwise influence culture in unprecedented ways. The video-sharing website YouTube is a prime example of participatory culture. YouTube gives anyone with a video camera and an Internet connection the opportunity to communicate with people around the world and create and shape cultural trends.

4. Global convergence is the process of geographically distant cultures influencing one another despite the distance that physically separates them. Nigeria's cinema industry, nicknamed Nollywood, takes its cues from India's Bollywood, which is in turn inspired by Hollywood in the United States. *Tom and Jerry* cartoons are popular on Arab satellite television channels. Successful American horror movies *The Ring* and *The Grudge* are remakes of Japanese hits. The advantage of global convergence is access to a wealth of cultural influence; its downside, some critics posit, is the threat of cultural imperialism, defined by Herbert Schiller as the way developing countries are "attracted, pressured, forced, and sometimes bribed into shaping social institutions to correspond to, or even promote, the values and structures of the dominating centre of the system (White, 2001)." Cultural imperialism can be a formal policy or can happen more subtly, as with the spread of outside influence through television, movies, and other cultural projects.

5. Technological convergence is the merging of technologies such as the ability to watch TV shows online on sites like Hulu or to play video games on mobile phones like the Apple iPhone. When more and more different kinds of media are transformed into digital content, as Jenkins notes, "we expand the potential relationships between them and enable them to flow across platforms (Jenkins, 2001)."

Figure 1.7

Nigeria's Nollywood produces more films annually than any other country besides India.

Effects of Convergence

Jenkins's concept of organic convergence is perhaps the most telling. To many people, especially those who grew up in a world dominated by so-called old media, there is nothing organic about today's media-dominated world. As a *New York Times* editorial recently opined, "Few objects on the planet are farther removed from nature—less, say, like a rock or an insect—than a glass and stainless steel smartphone (New York Times, 2010)." But modern American culture is plugged in as never before, and today's high school students have never known a world where the Internet didn't exist. Such a cultural sea change causes a significant generation gap between those who grew up with new media and those who didn't.

A 2010 study by the Kaiser Family Foundation found that Americans aged 8 to 18 spend more than 7.5 hours with electronic devices each day—and, thanks to multitasking, they're able to pack an average of 11 hours of media content into that 7.5 hours (Lewin, 2010). These statistics highlight some of the aspects of the new digital model of media consumption: participation and multitasking. Today's teenagers aren't passively sitting in front of screens, quietly absorbing information. Instead, they are sending text messages to friends, linking news articles on Facebook, commenting on YouTube videos, writing reviews of television episodes to post online, and generally engaging with the culture they consume. Convergence has also made multitasking much easier, as many devices allow users to surf the Internet, listen to music, watch videos, play games, and reply to e-mails on the same machine.

However, it's still difficult to predict how media convergence and immersion are affecting culture, society, and individual brains. In his 2005 book *Everything Bad Is Good for You*, Steven Johnson argues that today's television and video games are mentally stimulating, in that they pose a cognitive challenge and invite active engagement and problem solving. Poking fun at alarmists who see every new technology as making children stupider, Johnson jokingly cautions readers against the dangers of book reading: It "chronically understimulates the senses" and is "tragically isolating." Even worse, books "follow a fixed linear path. You can't control their narratives in any fashion—you simply sit back and have the story dictated to you…. This risks instilling a general passivity in our children, making them feel as though they're powerless to change their circumstances. Reading is not an active, participatory process; it's a submissive one (Johnson, 2005)."

A 2010 book by Nicholas Carr, *The Shallows: What the Internet Is Doing to Our Brains* is more pessimistic. Carr worries that the vast array of interlinked information available through the Internet is eroding attention spans and making contemporary minds distracted and less capable of deep, thoughtful engagement with complex ideas and arguments. "Once I was a scuba diver in a sea of words," Carr reflects ruefully. "Now I zip along the surface like a guy on a Jet Ski (Carr, 2010)." Carr cites neuroscience studies showing that when people try to do two things at once, they give less attention to each and perform the tasks less carefully. In other words, multitasking makes us do a greater number of things poorly. Whatever the ultimate cognitive, social, or technological results, convergence is changing the way we relate to media today.

Video Killed the Radio Star: Convergence Kills Off Obsolete Technology—or Does It?

When was the last time you used a rotary phone? How about a street-side pay phone? Or a library's card catalog? When you need brief, factual information, when was the last time you reached for a volume of *Encyclopedia Britannica*? Odds are it's been a while. All of these habits, formerly common parts of daily life, have been rendered essentially obsolete through the progression of convergence.

But convergence hasn't erased old technologies; instead, it may have just altered the way we use them. Take cassette tapes and Polaroid film, for example. Influential musician Thurston Moore of the band Sonic Youth recently claimed that he only listens to music on cassette. Polaroid Corporation, creators of the once-popular instant-film cameras, was driven out of business by digital photography in 2008, only to be revived 2 years later—with pop star Lady Gaga as the brand's creative director. Several Apple iPhone apps allow users to apply effects to photos to make them look more like a Polaroid photo.

Cassettes, Polaroid cameras, and other seemingly obsolete technologies have been able to thrive—albeit in niche markets—both despite and because of Internet culture. Instead of being slick and digitized, cassette tapes and Polaroid photos are physical objects that are made more accessible and more human, according to enthusiasts, because of their flaws. "I think there's a group of people—fans and artists alike—out there to whom music is more than just a file on your computer, more than just a folder of MP3s," says Brad Rose, founder of a Tulsa, Oklahoma-based cassette label (Hogan, 2010). The distinctive Polaroid look—caused by uneven color saturation, underdevelopment or overdevelopment, or just daily atmospheric effects on the developing photograph—is emphatically analog. In an age of high resolution, portable printers, and camera phones, the Polaroid's appeal to some has something to do with ideas of nostalgia and authenticity. Convergence has transformed who uses these media and for what purposes, but it hasn't eliminated these media.

Key Takeaways

- Twenty-first century media culture is increasingly marked by convergence, or the coming together of previously distinct technologies, as in a cell phone that also allows users to take video and check e-mail.

- Media theorist Henry Jenkins identifies the five kinds of convergence as the following:

   1. Economic convergence is when a single company has interests across many kinds of media.

   2. Organic convergence is multimedia multitasking, or the natural outcome of a diverse media world.

   3. Cultural convergence is when stories flow across several kinds of media platforms and when readers or viewers can comment on, alter, or otherwise talk back to culture.

   4. Global convergence is when geographically distant cultures are able to influence one another.

   5. Technological convergence is when different kinds of technology merge. The most extreme example of technological convergence would be one machine that controlled every media function.

- The jury is still out on how these different types of convergence will affect people on an individual and societal level. Some theorists believe that convergence and new-media technologies make people smarter by requiring them to make decisions and interact with the media they're consuming; others fear the digital age is giving us access to more information but leaving us shallower.

Exercises

Review the viewpoints of Henry Jenkins, Steven Johnson, and Nicholas Carr. Then, answer the following questions. Each response should be a minimum of one paragraph.

   1. Define convergence as it relates to mass media and provide some examples of convergence you've observed in your life.

   2. Describe the five types of convergence identified by Henry Jenkins and provide an example of each type that you've noted in your own experience.

   3. How do Steven Johnson and Nicholas Carr think convergence is affecting culture and society? Whose argument do you find more compelling and why?

References

Carr, Nicholas *The Shallows: What the Internet Is Doing to Our Brains* (New York: Norton, 2010).

Hogan, Marc. "This Is Not a Mixtape," *Pitchfork*, February 22, 2010, http://pitchfork.com/features/articles/7764-this-is-not-a-mixtape/2/.

Jenkins, Henry. "Convergence? I Diverge," *Technology Review*, June 2001, 93.

Johnson, Steven *Everything Bad Is Good for You* (Riverhead, NY: Riverhead Books, 2005).

Lewin, Tamar "If Your Kids Are Awake, They're Probably Online," *New York Times*, January 20, 2010, http://www.nytimes.com/2010/01/20/education/20wired.html.

New York Times, editorial, "The Half-Life of Phones," *New York Times*, June 18, 2010, http://www.nytimes.com/2010/06/20/opinion/20sun4.html1.

White, Livingston A. "Reconsidering Cultural Imperialism Theory," *TBS Journal* 6 (2001), http://www.tbsjournal.com/Archives/Spring01/white.html.

1.5 The Role of Social Values in Communication

Learning Objectives

1. Identify two limitations on free speech that are based on social values.

2. Identify examples of propaganda in mass media.

3. Explain the role of the gatekeeper in mass media.

In a 1995 *Wired* magazine article, "The Age of Paine," Jon Katz suggested that the Revolutionary War patriot Thomas Paine should be considered "the moral father of the Internet." The Internet, Katz wrote, "offers what Paine and his revolutionary colleagues hoped for—a vast, diverse, passionate, global means of transmitting ideas and opening minds." In fact, according to Katz, the emerging Internet era is closer in spirit to the 18th-century media world than to the 20th-century's "old media" (radio, television, print). "The ferociously spirited press of the late 1700s…was dominated by individuals expressing their opinions. The idea that ordinary citizens with no special resources, expertise, or political power—like Paine himself—could sound off, reach wide audiences, even spark revolutions, was brand-new to the world (Creel, 1920)." Katz's impassioned defense of Paine's plucky independence speaks to the way social values and communication technologies are affecting our adoption of media technologies today. Keeping Katz's words in mind, we can ask ourselves additional questions about the role of social values in communication. How do they shape our ideas of mass communication? How, in turn, does mass communication change our understanding of what our society values?

Figure 1.8

Thomas Paine is regarded by some as the "moral father of the Internet" because his independent spirit is reflected in the democratization of mass communication via the Internet.

Marion Doss – Thomas Paine, Engraving – CC BY-SA 2.0.

Free Speech and Its Limitations

The value of free speech is central to American mass communication and has been since the nation's revolutionary founding. The U.S. Constitution's very first amendment guarantees the freedom of the press. Because of the First

Amendment and subsequent statutes, the United States has some of the broadest protections on speech of any industrialized nation. However, there are limits to what kinds of speech are legally protected—limits that have changed over time, reflecting shifts in U.S. social values.

Figure 1.9

Artist Shepard Fairey, creator of the iconic Obama HOPE image, was sued by the Associated Press for copyright infringement; Fairey argued that his work was protected by the fair use exception.

Wikimedia Commons – public domain; Cliff – National Portrait Gallery Hangs Shepard Fairey's Portrait of Barack Obama – CC BY 2.0.

Definitions of obscenity, which is not protected by the First Amendment, have altered with the nation's changing social attitudes. James Joyce's *Ulysses*, ranked by the Modern Library as the best English-language novel of the 20th century, was illegal to publish in the United States between 1922 and 1934 because the U.S. Customs Court declared the book obscene because of its sexual content. The 1954 Supreme Court case *Roth v. the United States* defined obscenity more narrowly, allowing for differences depending on community standards. The sexual revolution and social changes of the 1960s made it even more difficult to pin down just what was meant by community standards—a question that is still under debate to this day. The mainstreaming of sexually explicit content like *Playboy* magazine, which is available in nearly every U.S. airport, is another indication that obscenity is still open to interpretation.

Regulations related to obscene content are not the only restrictions on First Amendment rights; copyright law also puts limits on free speech. Intellectual property law was originally intended to protect just that—the proprietary rights, both economic and intellectual, of the originator of a creative work. Works under copyright can't be reproduced without the authorization of the creator, nor can anyone else use them to make a profit. Inventions, novels, musical tunes, and even phrases are all covered by copyright law. The first copyright statute in the United States set 14 years as the maximum term for copyright protection. This number has risen exponentially in the 20th century; some works are now copyright-protected for up to 120 years. In recent years, an Internet culture that enables file sharing, musical mash-ups, and YouTube video parodies has raised questions about the fair use exception to copyright law. The exact line between what types of expressions are protected or prohibited by law are still being set by courts, and as the changing values of the U.S. public evolve, copyright law—like obscenity law—will continue to change as well.

Propaganda and Other Ulterior Motives

Sometimes social values enter mass media messages in a more overt way. Producers of media content may have vested interests in particular social goals, which, in turn, may cause them to promote or refute particular viewpoints. In its most heavy-handed form, this type of media influence can become propaganda, communication that intentionally attempts to persuade its audience for ideological, political, or commercial purposes. Propaganda often (but not always) distorts the truth, selectively presents facts, or uses emotional appeals. During wartime, propaganda often includes caricatures of the enemy. Even in peacetime, however, propaganda is frequent. Political campaign commercials in which one candidate openly criticizes the other are common around election time, and some negative ads deliberately twist the truth or present outright falsehoods to attack an opposing candidate.

Other types of influence are less blatant or sinister. Advertisers want viewers to buy their products; some news sources, such as Fox News or *The Huffington Post*, have an explicit political slant. Still, people who want to exert media influence often use the tricks and techniques of propaganda. During World War I, the U.S. government created the Creel Commission as a sort of public relations firm for the United States' entry into the war. The Creel Commission used radio, movies, posters, and in-person speakers to present a positive slant on the U.S. war effort and to demonize the opposing Germans. Chairman George Creel acknowledged the commission's attempt to influence the public but shied away from calling their work propaganda:

In no degree was the Committee an agency of censorship, a machinery of concealment or repression…. In all things, from first to last, without halt or change, it was a plain publicity proposition, a vast enterprise in salesmanship, the world's greatest adventures in advertising…. We did not call it propaganda, for that word, in German hands, had come to be associated with deceit and corruption. Our effort was educational and informative throughout, for we had such confidence in our case as to feel that no other argument was needed than the simple, straightforward presentation of the facts (Creel, 1920).

Of course, the line between the selective (but "straightforward") presentation of the truth and the manipulation of propaganda is not an obvious or distinct one. (Another of the Creel Commission's members was later deemed the father of public relations and authored a book titled *Propaganda*.) In general, however, public relations is open about presenting one side of the truth, while propaganda seeks to invent a new truth.

Figure 1.10

World War I propaganda posters were sometimes styled to resemble movie posters in an attempt to glamorize the war effort.

Wikimedia Commons – public domain.

Gatekeepers

In 1960, journalist A. J. Liebling wryly observed that "freedom of the press is guaranteed only to those who own one." Liebling was referring to the role of gatekeepers in the media industry, another way in which social values influence mass communication. Gatekeepers are the people who help determine which stories make it to the public, including reporters who decide what sources to use and editors who decide what gets reported on and which stories make it to the front page. Media gatekeepers are part of society and thus are saddled with their own cultural biases, whether consciously or unconsciously. In deciding what counts as newsworthy, entertaining, or relevant, gatekeepers pass on their own values to the wider public. In contrast, stories deemed unimportant or uninteresting to consumers can linger forgotten in the back pages of the newspaper—or never get covered at all.

In one striking example of the power of gatekeeping, journalist Allan Thompson lays blame on the news media for its sluggishness in covering the Rwandan genocide in 1994. According to Thompson, there weren't many outside reporters in Rwanda at the height of the genocide, so the world wasn't forced to confront the atrocities happening there. Instead, the nightly news in the United States was preoccupied by the O. J. Simpson trial, Tonya Harding's attack on a fellow figure skater, and the less bloody conflict in Bosnia (where more reporters were stationed). Thompson went on to argue that the lack of international media attention allowed politicians to remain complacent (Thompson, 2007). With little media coverage, there was little outrage about the Rwandan atrocities, which contributed to a lack of political will to invest time and troops in a faraway conflict. Richard Dowden, Africa editor for the British newspaper *The Independent* during the Rwandan genocide, bluntly explained the news media's larger reluctance to focus on African issues: "Africa was simply not important. It didn't sell newspapers. Newspapers have to make profits. So it wasn't important (Thompson, 2007)." Bias on the individual and institutional level downplayed the genocide at a time of great crisis and potentially contributed to the deaths of hundreds of thousands of people.

Gatekeepers had an especially strong influence in old media, in which space and time were limited. A news broadcast could only last for its allotted half hour, while a newspaper had a set number of pages to print. The Internet, in contrast, theoretically has room for infinite news reports. The interactive nature of the medium also minimizes the gatekeeper function of the media by allowing media consumers to have a voice as well. News aggregators like Digg allow readers to decide what makes it on to the front page. That's not to say that the wisdom of the crowd is always wise—recent top stories on Digg have featured headlines like "Top 5 Hot Girls Playing Video Games" and "The girl who must eat every 15 minutes to stay alive." Media expert Mark Glaser noted that the digital age hasn't eliminated gatekeepers; it's just shifted who they are: "the editors who pick featured artists and apps at the Apple iTunes store, who choose videos to spotlight on YouTube, and who highlight Suggested Users on Twitter," among others (Glaser, 2009). And unlike traditional media, these new gatekeepers rarely have public bylines, making it difficult to figure out who makes such decisions and on what basis they are made.

Observing how distinct cultures and subcultures present the same story can be indicative of those cultures' various social values. Another way to look critically at today's media messages is to examine how the media has functioned in the world and in the United States during different cultural periods.

Key Takeaways

- American culture puts a high value on free speech; however, other societal values sometimes take precedence. Shifting ideas about what constitutes obscenity, a kind of speech that is not legally protected by the First Amendment, is a good example of how cultural values impact mass communication—and of how those values change over time. Copyright law, another restriction put on free speech, has had a similar evolution over the nation's history.

- Propaganda is a type of communication that attempts to persuade the audience for ideological, political, or social purposes. Some propaganda is obvious, explicit, and manipulative; however, public relations professionals borrow many techniques from propaganda and they try to influence their audience.

- Gatekeepers influence culture by deciding which stories are considered newsworthy. Gatekeepers can promote social values either consciously or subconsciously. The digital age has lessened the power of gatekeepers somewhat, as the Internet allows for nearly unlimited space to cover any number of events and stories; furthermore, a new gatekeeper class has emerged on the Internet as well.

Exercises

Please answer the following questions. Each response should be a minimum of one paragraph.

1. Find an advertisement—either in print, broadcast, or online—that you have recently found to be memorable. Now find a nonadvertisement media message. Compare the ways that the ad and the nonad express social values. Are the social values the same for each of them? Is the influence overt or covert? Why did the message's creators choose to present their message in this way? Can this be considered propaganda?

2. Go to a popular website that uses user-uploaded content (YouTube, Flickr, Twitter, Metafilter, etc.). Look at the content on the site's home page. Can you tell how this particular content was selected to be featured? Does the website list a policy for featured content? What factors do you think go into the selection process?

3. Think of two recent examples where free speech was limited because of social values. Who were the gatekeepers in these situations? What effect did these limitations have on media coverage?

References

Creel, George. *How We Advertised America* (New York: Harper & Brothers, 1920).

Glaser, Marc. "New Gatekeepers Twitter, Apple, YouTube Need Transparency in Editorial Picks," *PBS Mediashift*, March 26, 2009, http://www.pbs.org/mediashift/2009/03/new-gatekeepers-twitter-apple-youtube-need-transparency-in-editorial-picks085.html.

Thompson, Allan. "The Media and the Rwanda Genocide" (lecture, Crisis States Research Centre and POLIS at the London School of Economics, January 17, 2007), http://www2.lse.ac.uk/publicEvents/pdf/20070117_PolisRwanda.pdf.

1.6 Cultural Periods

Table 1.1 Cultural Periods

Modern Era	Early Modern Period (late 1400s–1700s)	Began with Johannes Gutenberg's invention of the movable type printing press; characterized by improved transportation, educational reform, and scientific inquiry.
	Late Modern Period (1700s–1900s)	Sparked by the Industrial Revolution; characterized by technical innovations, increasingly secular politics, and urbanization.
Postmodern Age (1950s–present)	Marked by skepticism, self-consciousness, celebration of differences, and the digitalization of culture.	

After exploring the ways technology, culture, and mass media have affected one another over the years, it may also be helpful to look at recent cultural eras more broadly. A cultural period is a time marked by a particular way of understanding the world through culture and technology. Changes in cultural periods are marked by fundamental switches in the way people perceive and understand the world. In the Middle Ages, truth was dictated by authorities like the king and the church. During the Renaissance, people turned to the scientific method as a way to reach truth through reason. And, in 2008, *Wired* magazine's editor in chief proclaimed that Google was about to render the scientific method obsolete (Anderson, 2008). In each of these cases, it wasn't that the nature of truth changed, but the way humans attempted to make sense of a world that was radically changing. For the purpose of studying culture and mass media, the post-Gutenberg modern and postmodern ages are the most relevant ones to explore.

The Modern Age

The Modern Age, or **modernity**, is the postmedieval era, a wide span of time marked in part by technological innovations, urbanization, scientific discoveries, and globalization. The Modern Age is generally split into two parts: the early and the late modern periods.

The *early modern period* began with Gutenberg's invention of the movable type printing press in the late 15th century and ended in the late 18th century. Thanks to Gutenberg's press, the European population of the early modern period saw rising literacy rates, which led to educational reform. As noted in preceding sections, Gutenberg's machine also greatly enabled the spread of knowledge and, in turn, spurred the Renaissance and the Protestant Reformation. During the early modern period, transportation improved, politics became more secularized, capitalism spread, nation-states grew more powerful, and information became more widely accessible. Enlightenment ideals of reason, rationalism, and faith in scientific inquiry slowly began to replace the previously dominant authorities of king and church.

Huge political, social, and economic changes marked the end of the 18th century and the beginning of the *late modern period*. The Industrial Revolution, which began in England around 1750, combined with the American Revolution in 1776 and the French Revolution in 1789, marked the beginning of massive changes in the world.

The French and American revolutions were inspired by a rejection of monarchy in favor of national sovereignty and representative democracy. Both revolutions also heralded the rise of secular society as opposed to church-based authority systems. Democracy was well suited to the so-called Age of Reason, with its ideals of individual rights and progress.

Though less political, the Industrial Revolution had equally far-reaching consequences. It did not merely change the way goods were produced—it also fundamentally changed the economic, social, and cultural framework of its time. The Industrial Revolution doesn't have clear start or end dates. However, during the 19th century, several crucial inventions—the internal combustion engine, steam-powered ships, and railways, among others—led to innovations in various industries. Steam power and machine tools increased production dramatically. But some of the biggest changes coming out of the Industrial Revolution were social in character. An economy based on manufacturing instead of agriculture meant that more people moved to cities, where techniques of mass production led people to value efficiency both in and out of the factory. Newly urbanized factory laborers could no longer produce their own food, clothing, or supplies, and instead turned to consumer goods. Increased production led to increases in wealth, though income inequalities between classes also started to grow.

These overwhelming changes affected (and were affected by) the media. As noted in preceding sections, the fusing of steam power and the printing press enabled the explosive expansion of books and newspapers. Literacy rates rose, as did support for public participation in politics. More and more people lived in the city, had an education, got their news from the newspaper, spent their wages on consumer goods, and identified as citizens of an industrialized nation. Urbanization, mass literacy, and new forms of mass media contributed to a sense of mass culture that united people across regional, social, and cultural boundaries.

Modernity and the Modern Age, it should be noted, are distinct from (but related to) the cultural movement of modernism. The Modern Era lasted from the end of the Middle Ages to the middle of the 20th century; modernism, however, refers to the artistic movement of late 19th and early 20th centuries that arose from the widespread changes that swept the world during that period. Most notably, modernism questioned the limitations of traditional forms of art and culture. Modernist art was in part a reaction against the Enlightenment's certainty of progress and rationality. It celebrated subjectivity through abstraction, experimentalism, surrealism, and sometimes pessimism or even nihilism. Prominent examples of modernist works include James Joyce's stream-of-consciousness novels, cubist paintings by Pablo Picasso, atonal compositions by Claude Debussy, and absurdist plays by Luigi Pirandello.

The Postmodern Age

Modernism can also be seen as a transitional phase between the modern and postmodern eras. While the exact definition and dates of the Postmodern Age are still being debated by cultural theorists and philosophers, the general consensus is that the Postmodern Age began during the second half of the 20th century and was marked by skepticism, self-consciousness, celebration of difference, and the reappraisal of modern conventions. The Modern Age took for granted scientific rationalism, the autonomous self, and the inevitability of progress; the Postmodern Age questioned or dismissed many of these assumptions. If the Modern Age valued order, reason, stability, and absolute truth, the Postmodern Age reveled in contingency, fragmentation, and instability. The effect of technology on culture, the rise of the Internet, and the Cold War are all aspects that led to the Postmodern Age.

The belief in objective truth that characterized the Modern Age is one of the major assumptions overturned in the Postmodern Age. Postmodernists instead took their cues from Erwin Schrödinger, the quantum physicist who famously devised a thought experiment in which a cat is placed inside a sealed box with a small amount of radiation that may or may not kill it. While the box remains sealed, Schrödinger proclaimed, the cat exists simultaneously in both states, dead and alive. Both potential states are equally true. Although the thought experiment was devised to explore issues in quantum physics, it appealed to postmodernists in its assertion of radical uncertainty. Rather than there being an absolute objective truth accessible by rational experimentation, the status of reality was contingent and depended on the observer.

This value of the relative over the absolute found its literary equivalent in the movement of deconstruction. While Victorian novelists took pains to make their books seem more realistic, postmodern narratives distrusted professions of reality and constantly reminded readers of the artificial nature of the story they were reading. The emphasis was not on the all-knowing author, but instead on the reader. For the postmodernists, meaning was not injected into a work by its creator, but depended on the reader's subjective experience of the work. The poetry of Sylvia Plath and Allen Ginsberg exemplify this, as much of their work is emotionally charged and designed to create a dialogue with the reader, oftentimes forcing the reader to confront controversial issues such as mental illness or homosexuality.

Another way the Postmodern Age differed from the Modern Age was in the rejection of what philosopher Jean-François Lyotard deemed "grand narratives." The Modern Age was marked by different large-scale theories that attempted to explain the totality of human experience, such as capitalism, Marxism, rationalism, Freudianism, Darwinism, fascism, and so on. However, increasing globalization and the rise of subcultures called into question the sorts of theories that claimed to explain everything at once. Totalitarian regimes during the 20th century, such as Adolf Hitler's Third Reich and the USSR under Joseph Stalin, led to a mistrust of power and the systems held up by power. The Postmodern Age, Lyotard theorized, was one of micronarratives instead of grand narratives—that is, a multiplicity of small, localized understandings of the world, none of which can claim an ultimate or absolute truth. An older man in Kenya, for example, does not view the world in the same way as a young woman from New York. Even people from the same cultural backgrounds have different views of the world—when you were a teenager, did your parents understand your way of thinking? The diversity of human experience is a marked feature of the postmodern world. As Lyotard noted, "Eclecticism is the degree zero of contemporary general culture; one listens to reggae, watches a Western, eats McDonald's food for lunch and local cuisine for dinner, wears Paris perfume in Tokyo and retro clothes in Hong Kong; knowledge is a matter for TV games (Lyotard, 1984)."

Postmodernists also mistrusted the idea of originality and freely borrowed across cultures and genres. William S. Burroughs gleefully proclaimed a sort of call to arms for his generation of writers in 1985: "Out of the closets and into the museums, libraries, architectural monuments, concert halls, bookstores, recording studios and film studios of the world. Everything belongs to the inspired and dedicated thief (Burroughs,1993)." The feminist artist Barbara Kruger, for example, creates works of art from old advertisements, and writers, such as Kathy Acker, reconstructed existing texts to form new stories. The rejection of traditional forms of art and expression embody the Postmodern Age.

From the early Modern Age through the Postmodern Age, people have experienced the world in vastly different ways. Not only has technology rapidly become more complex, but culture itself has changed with the times. When reading further, it's important to remember that forms of media and culture are hallmarks of different eras, and the different ways in which media are presented often tell us a lot about the culture and times.

Key Takeaways

- A cultural period is a time marked by a particular way of understanding the world through culture and technology. Changes in cultural periods are marked by fundamental changes in the way we perceive and understand the world. The Modern Age began after the Middle Ages and lasted through the early decades of the 20th century, when the Postmodern Age began.

- The Modern Age was marked by Enlightenment philosophy, which focused on the individual and placed a high value on rational decision making. This period saw the wide expansion of capitalism, colonialism, democracy, and science-based rationalism. The Renaissance, the Protestant Reformation, the American and French Revolutions, and World War I were all significant events that took place during the Modern Age. One of the most significant, however, was the Industrial Revolution; its emphasis on routinization and efficiency helped society restructure itself similarly.

- Postmodernity differed from modernity in its questioning of reason, rejection of grand narratives, and emphasis on subcultures. Rather than searching for one ultimate truth that could explain all of history, the postmodernists focused on contingency, context, and diversity.

Exercises

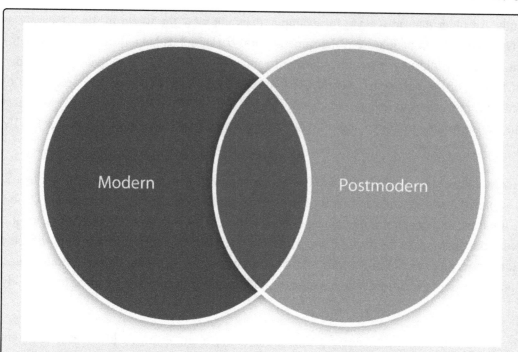

Draw a Venn diagram of the two cultural periods discussed at length in this chapter. Make a list of the features, values, and events that mark each period. Then, answer the questions below. Each response should be a minimum of one paragraph.

1. What defines a cultural period?

2. How do the two periods differ? Do they overlap in any ways?

3. What do you predict the next cultural era has in store? When will it begin?

References

Anderson, Chris. "The End of Theory: The Data Deluge Makes the Scientific Method Obsolete," *Wired*, June 23, 2008, http://www.wired.com/science/discoveries/magazine/16-07/pb_theory.

Burroughs, William S. "Les Velours," *The Adding Machine*, (New York: Arcade Publishing, 1993), 19–21.

Lyotard, Jean-François *The Postmodern Condition: A Report on Knowledge,* trans. Geoff Bennington and Brian Massumi (Minneapolis: University of Minnesota Press, 1984).

1.7 Mass Media and Popular Culture

<table>
<tr><td align="center">**Learning Objectives**</td></tr>
</table>

1. Determine the influence of tastemakers in traditional media.

2. Identify the ways the digital age is undermining the traditional role of tastemakers.

3. Determine how Internet culture now allows creators to bypass gatekeepers and determine the potential effects this will have.

Burroughs's jubilant call to bring art "out of the closets and into the museums" spoke to postmodernism's willingness to meld high and low culture (Leonard, 1997). And although the Postmodern Age specifically embraced popular culture, mass media and pop culture have been entwined from their very beginnings. In fact, mass media often determines what does and does not make up the pop culture scene.

Tastemakers

Historically, mass pop culture has been fostered by an active and tastemaking mass media that introduces and encourages the adoption of certain trends. Although they are similar in some ways to the widespread media gatekeepers discussed in Section 1.4.3 "Gatekeepers", tastemakers differ in that they are most influential when the mass media is relatively small and concentrated. When only a few publications or programs reach millions of people, their writers and editors are highly influential. *The New York Times*'s restaurant reviews used to be able to make a restaurant successful or unsuccessful through granting (or withdrawing) its rating.

Or take the example of Ed Sullivan's variety show, which ran from 1948 to 1971, and is most famous for hosting the first U.S. appearance of the Beatles—a television event that was at the time the most-watched TV program ever. Sullivan hosted musical acts, comedians, actors, and dancers and had the reputation of being able to turn an act on the cusp of fame into full-fledged stars. Comedian Jackie Mason compared being on *The Ed Sullivan Show* to "an opera singer being at the Met. Or if a guy is an architect that makes the Empire State Building.…This was the biggest (Leonard, 1997)." Sullivan was a classic example of an influential tastemaker of his time. A more modern example is Oprah Winfrey, whose book club endorsements often send literature, including old classics like Leo Tolstoy's *Anna Karenina*, skyrocketing to the top of *The New York Times* Best Sellers list.

Figure 1.11

For Elvis Presley's third appearance on *The Ed Sullivan show*, he was shown only from the waist up; Sullivan considered his dancing too scandalous for family viewing.

Wikimedia Commons – public domain.

Along with encouraging a mass audience to see (or skip) certain movies, television shows, video games, books, or fashion trends, people use tastemaking to create demand for new products. Companies often turn to advertising firms to help create public hunger for an object that may have not even existed 6 months before. In the 1880s, when George Eastman developed the Kodak camera for personal use, photography was most practiced by professionals. "Though the Kodak was relatively cheap and easy to use, most Americans didn't see the need for a camera; they had no sense that there was any value in visually documenting their lives," noted *New Yorker* writer James Surowiecki (Surowiecki, 2003). Kodak became a wildly successful company not because Eastman was good at selling cameras, but because he understood that what he really had to sell was photography. Apple Inc. is a modern master of this technique. By leaking just enough information about a new product to cause curiosity, the technology company ensures that people will be waiting excitedly for an official release.

Tastemakers help keep culture vital by introducing the public to new ideas, music, programs, or products, but tastemakers are not immune to outside influence. In the traditional media model, large media companies set aside large advertising budgets to promote their most promising projects; tastemakers buzz about "the next big thing," and obscure or niche works can get lost in the shuffle.

A Changing System for the Internet Age

In retrospect, the 20th century was a tastemaker's dream. Advertisers, critics, and other cultural influencers had access to huge audiences through a number of mass-communication platforms. However, by the end of the century, the rise of cable television and the Internet had begun to make tastemaking a more complicated enterprise. While *The Ed Sullivan Show* regularly reached 50 million people in the 1960s, the most popular television series of 2009—*American Idol*—averaged around 25.5 million viewers per night, despite the fact that the 21st-century United States could claim more people and more television sets than ever before (Wikipedia, 2012). However, the proliferation of TV channels and other competing forms of entertainment meant that no one program or channel could dominate the attention of the American public as in Sullivan's day.

Table 1.2 Viewings of Popular Television Broadcasts

Show/Episode	Number of Viewers	Percent of Households	Year
The Ed Sullivan Show / The Beatles' first appearance	73 million	45.1%	1964
The Ed Sullivan Show / Elvis Presley's first appearance	60 million	82.6%	1956
I Love Lucy / "Lucy Goes to the Hospital"	44 million	71.7%	1953
*M*A*S*H / Series finale*	106 million	60.2%	1983
Seinfeld / Series finale	76 million	41.3%	1998
American Idol / Season 5 finale	36 million	17%	2006

Meanwhile, a low-tech home recording of a little boy acting loopy after a visit to the dentist ("David After Dentist") garnered more than 37 million YouTube viewings in 2009 alone. The Internet appears to be eroding some of the tastemaking power of the traditional media outlets. No longer is the traditional mass media the only dominant force in creating and promoting trends. Instead, information spreads across the globe without the active involvement of traditional mass media. Websites made by nonprofessionals can reach more people daily than a major newspaper. Music review sites such as Pitchfork keep their eyes out for the next big thing, whereas review aggregators like Rotten Tomatoes allow readers to read hundreds of movie reviews by amateurs and professionals alike. Blogs make it possible for anyone with Internet access to potentially reach an audience of millions. Some popular bloggers have transitioned from the traditional media world to the digital world, but others have become well known without formal institutional support. The celebrity-gossip chronicler Perez Hilton had no formal training in journalism when he started his blog, PerezHilton.com, in 2005; within a few years, he was reaching millions of readers a month.

E-mail and text messages allow people to transmit messages almost instantly across vast geographic expanses. Although personal communications continue to dominate, e-mail and text messages are increasingly used to directly transmit information about important news events. When Barack Obama wanted to announce his selection of Joe Biden as his vice-presidential running mate in the 2008 election, he bypassed the traditional televised press conference and instead sent the news to his supporters directly via text message—2.9 million text messages, to be exact (Covey). Social networking sites, such as Facebook, and microblogging services, such as Twitter, are another source of late-breaking information. When Michael Jackson died of cardiac arrest in 2009, "RIP Michael Jackson" was a top trending topic on Twitter before the first mainstream media first reported the news.

Thanks to these and other digital-age media, the Internet has become a pop culture force, both a source of amateur talent and a source of amateur promotion. However, traditional media outlets still maintain a large amount of control and influence over U.S. pop culture. One key indicator is the fact that many singers or writers who first make their mark on the Internet quickly transition to more traditional media—YouTube star Justin Bieber was signed by a mainstream record company, and blogger Perez Hilton is regularly featured on MTV and VH1. New-media stars are quickly absorbed into the old-media landscape.

Getting Around the Gatekeepers

Not only does the Internet give untrained individuals access to a huge audience for their art or opinions, but it also allows content creators to reach fans directly. Projects that may not have succeeded through traditional mass media may get a second chance through newer medias. The profit-driven media establishment has been surprised by the success of some self-published books. For example, dozens of literary agents rejected first-time author Daniel Suarez's novel *Daemon* before he decided to self-publish in 2006. Through savvy self-promotion through influential bloggers, Suarez garnered enough attention to land a contract with a major publishing house.

Figure 1.12

E-readers offer authors a way to get around the traditional publishing industry, but their thousands of options can make choosing hard on readers.

Edvvc – eReader Comparison – CC BY 2.0.

Suarez's story, though certainly exceptional, reaches some of the questions facing creators and consumers of pop culture in the Internet age. Without the influence of an agent, editor, or PR company, self-published content may be able to hew closer to the creator's intention. However, much of the detailed marketing work must be performed by the work's creator instead of by a specialized public relations team. And with so many self-published, self-promoted works uploaded to the Internet every day, it's easy for things—even good things—to get lost in the shuffle.

Critic Laura Miller spells out some of the ways in which writers in particular can take control of their own publishing: "Writers can upload their works to services run by Amazon, Apple and… Barnes & Noble, transforming them into e-books that are instantly available in high-profile online stores. Or they can post them on services like Urbis.com, Quillp.com, or CompletelyNovel.com and coax reviews from other hopeful users (Miller, 2010)." Miller also points out that many of these companies can produce hard copies of books as well. While such a system may be a boon for writers who haven't had success with the traditional media establishment, Miller notes that it may not be the best option for readers, who "rarely complain that there isn't enough of a selection on Amazon or in their local superstore; they're more likely to ask for help in narrowing down their choices (Miller, 2010)."

The question remains: Will the Internet era be marked by a huge and diffuse pop culture, where the power of traditional mass media declines and, along with it, the power of the universalizing blockbuster hit? Or will the

Internet create a new set of tastemakers—influential bloggers—or even serve as a platform for the old tastemakers to take on new forms?

Democratizing Tastemaking

In 1993, *The New York Times* restaurant critic Ruth Reichl wrote a review about her experiences at the upscale Manhattan restaurant Le Cirque. She detailed the poor service she received when the restaurant staff did not know her and the excellent service she received when they realized she was a professional food critic. Her article illustrated how the power to publish reviews could affect a person's experience at a restaurant. The Internet, which turned everyone with the time and interest into a potential reviewer, allowed those ordinary people to have their voices heard. In the mid-2000s, websites such as Yelp and TripAdvisor boasted hundreds of reviews of restaurants, hotels, and salons provided by users. Amazon allows users to review any product it sells, from textbooks to bathing suits. The era of the democratized review had come, and tastemaking was now everyone's job.

By crowdsourcing (harnessing the efforts of a number of individuals online to solve a problem) the review process, the idea was, these sites would arrive at a more accurate description of the service in choice. One powerful reviewer would no longer be able to wield disproportionate power; instead, the wisdom of the crowd would make or break restaurants, movies, and everything else. Anyone who felt treated badly or scammed now had recourse to tell the world about it. By 2008, Yelp had 4 million reviews

However, mass tastemaking isn't as perfect as some people had promised. Certain reviewers can overly influence a product's overall rating by contributing multiple votes. One study found that a handful of Amazon users were casting hundreds of votes, while most rarely wrote reviews at all. Online reviews also tend to skew to extremes—more reviews are written by the ecstatic and the furious, while the moderately pleased aren't riled up enough to post online about their experiences. And while traditional critics are supposed to adhere to ethical standards, there's no such standard for online reviews. Savvy authors or restaurant owners have been known to slyly insert positive reviews or attempt to skew ratings systems. To get an accurate picture, potential buyers may find themselves wading through 20 or 30 online reviews, most of them from nonprofessionals. And sometimes those people aren't professionals for a reason. Consider these user reviews on Amazon of William Shakespeare's *Hamlet*: "There is really no point and it's really long," "I really didn't enjoy reading this book and I wish that our English teacher wouldn't force my class to read this play," and "don't know what Willy Shakespeare was thinking when he wrote this one play tragedy, but I thought this sure was boring! Hamlet does too much talking and not enough stuff." While some may argue that these are valid criticisms of the play, these comments are certainly a far cry from the thoughtful critique of a professional literary critic.

These and other issues underscore the point of having reviews in the first place—that it's an advantage to have certain places, products, or ideas examined and critiqued by a trusted and knowledgeable source. In an article about Yelp, *The New York Times* noted that one of the site's elite reviewers had racked up more than 300 reviews in 3 years, and then pointed out that "By contrast, a *New York Times* restaurant critic might take six years to amass 300 reviews. The critic visits a restaurant several times, strives for anonymity and tries to sample every dish on the menu (McNeil, 2008)." Whatever your vantage point, it's clear that old-style tastemaking is still around and still valuable—but the democratic review is here to stay.

Key Takeaways

- Traditionally, pop culture hits were initiated or driven by the active support of media tastemakers. When mass media is concentrated, people with access to platforms for mass communication wield quite a bit of power in what becomes well known, popular, or even infamous. Ed Sullivan's wildly popular variety TV show in the 1950s and 1960s served as a star-making vehicle and a tastemaker of that period.

- The digital age, with its proliferation of accessible media, has undermined the traditional role of the tastemaker. In contrast to the traditional media, Internet-based mass media are not limited by time or space, and they allow bloggers, critics, or aspiring stars to potentially reach millions without the backing of the traditional media industry.

- However, this democratization has its downsides. An abundance of mass communication without some form of filtration can lead to information overload. Additionally, online reviews can be altered or biased.

Exercises

Find a popular newspaper or magazine that discusses popular culture. Look through it to determine what pop culture movements, programs, or people it seems to be covering. Then, answer the following questions. Each response should be a minimum of one paragraph.

1. What is the overall tone of this periodical? What messages does it seem to be promoting, either implicitly or explicitly?

2. What are tastemakers? How might they be influencing the articles in this newspaper or magazine?

Next, find a website that deals with popular culture and answer the questions below.

1. Are there differences between the traditional media's and the new media's approach to popular culture?

2. How does the website you chose undermine tastemakers and gatekeepers?

References

Covey, Nic. "Flying Fingers," Nielsen, http://en-us.nielsen.com/main/insights/consumer_insight/issue_12/flying_fingers.

Leonard, John. "The Ed Sullivan Age," *American Heritage*, May/June 1997.

McNeil, Donald G. "Eat and Tell," *New York Times*, November 4, 2008, Dining & Wine section.

Miller, Laura. "When Anyone Can Be a Published Author," Salon, June 22, 2010, http://www.salon.com/books/laura_miller/2010/06/22/slush.

Surowiecki, James. "The Tastemakers," *New Yorker*, January 13, 2003.

Wikipedia, , s.v. "The Ed Sullivan Show," last modified June 26, 2012, http://en.wikipedia.org/wiki/The_Ed_Sullivan_Show; *Wikipedia*, s.v. "American Idol," last modified June 26, 2012, http://en.wikipedia.org/wiki/American_Idol.

1.8 Media Literacy

Learning Objectives

1. Define media literacy.

2. Describe the role of individual responsibility and accountability when responding to pop culture.

3. List the five key considerations about any media message.

In Gutenberg's age and the subsequent modern era, literacy—the ability to read and write—was a concern not only of educators, but also of politicians, social reformers, and philosophers. A literate population, many reasoned, would be able to seek out information, stay informed about the news of the day, communicate effectively, and make informed decisions in many spheres of life. Because of this, literate people made better citizens, parents, and workers. Several centuries later, as global literacy rates continued to grow, there was a new sense that merely being able to read and write was not enough. In a media-saturated world, individuals needed to be able to sort through and analyze the information they were bombarded with every day. In the second half of the 20th century, the skill of being able to decode and process the messages and symbols transmitted via media was named media literacy. According to the nonprofit National Association for Media Literacy Education (NAMLE), a person who is media literate can access, analyze, evaluate, and communicate information. Put another way by John Culkin, a pioneering advocate for media literacy education, "The new mass media—film, radio, TV—are new languages, their grammar as yet unknown (Moody, 1993)." Media literacy seeks to give media consumers the ability to understand this new language. The following are questions asked by those that are media literate:

1. Who created the message?

2. What are the author's credentials?

3. Why was the message created?

4. Is the message trying to get me to act or think in a certain way?

5. Is someone making money for creating this message?

6. Who is the intended audience?

7. How do I know this information is accurate?

Why Be Media Literate?

Culkin called the pervasiveness of media "the unnoticed fact of our present," noting that media information was as omnipresent and easy to overlook as the air we breathe (and, he noted, "some would add that it is just as polluted") (Moody, 1993). Our exposure to media starts early—a study by the Kaiser Family Foundation found that 68 percent of children ages 2 and younger spend an average of 2 hours in front of a screen (either computer or television) each day, while children under 6 spend as much time in front of a screen as they do playing outside (Lewin). U.S. teenagers are spending an average of 7.5 hours with media daily, nearly as long as they spend in school. Media literacy isn't merely a skill for young people, however. Today's Americans get much of their information from various media sources—but not all that information is created equal. One crucial role of media literacy education is to enable us to skeptically examine the often-conflicting media messages we receive every day.

Advertising

Many of the hours people spend with media are with commercial-sponsored content. The Federal Trade Commission (FTC) estimated that each child aged 2 to 11 saw, on average, 25,629 television commercials in 2004 alone, or more than 10,700 minutes of ads. Each adult saw, on average, 52,469 ads, or about 15.5 days' worth of television advertising (Holt, 2007). Children (and adults) are bombarded with contradictory messages—newspaper articles about the obesity epidemic run side by side with ads touting soda, candy, and fast food. The American Academy of Pediatrics maintains that advertising directed to children under 8 is "inherently deceptive" and exploitative because young children can't tell the difference between programs and commercials (Shifrin, 2005). Advertising often uses techniques of psychological pressure to influence decision making. Ads may appeal to vanity, insecurity, prejudice, fear, or the desire for adventure. This is not always done to sell a product—antismoking public service announcements may rely on disgusting images of blackened lungs to shock viewers. Nonetheless, media literacy involves teaching people to be guarded consumers and to evaluate claims with a critical eye.

Bias, Spin, and Misinformation

Advertisements may have the explicit goal of selling a product or idea, but they're not the only kind of media message with an agenda. A politician may hope to persuade potential voters that he has their best interests at heart. An ostensibly objective journalist may allow her political leanings to subtly slant her articles. Magazine writers might avoid criticizing companies that advertise heavily in their pages. News reporters may sensationalize stories to boost ratings—and advertising rates.

Mass-communication messages are created by individuals, and each individual has his or her own set of values, assumptions, and priorities. Accepting media messages at face value could lead to confusion because of all the contradictory information available. For example, in 2010, a highly contested governor's race in New Mexico led to conflicting ads from both candidates, Diane Denish and Susana Martinez, each claiming that the other agreed to policies that benefited sex offenders. According to media watchdog site FactCheck.org, the Denish team's ad "shows a preteen girl—seemingly about 9 years old—going down a playground slide in slow-motion, while ominous music plays in the background and an announcer discusses two sex crime cases. It ends with an empty swing, as the announcer says: 'Today we don't know where these sex offenders are lurking, because

Susana Martinez didn't do her job.'" The opposing ad proclaims that "a department in Denish's cabinet gave sanctuary to criminal illegals, like child molester Juan Gonzalez (Robertson & Kiely, 2010)." Both claims are highly inflammatory, play on fear, and distort the reality behind each situation. Media literacy involves educating people to look critically at these and other media messages and to sift through various messages and make sense of the conflicting information we face every day.

New Skills for a New World

In the past, one goal of education was to provide students with the information deemed necessary to successfully engage with the world. Students memorized multiplication tables, state capitals, famous poems, and notable dates. Today, however, vast amounts of information are available at the click of a mouse. Even before the advent of the Internet, noted communications scholar David Berlo foresaw the consequences of expanding information technology: "Most of what we have called formal education has been intended to imprint on the human mind all of the information that we might need for a lifetime." Changes in technology necessitate changes in how we learn, Berlo noted, and these days "education needs to be geared toward the handling of data rather than the accumulation of data (Shaw, 2003)."

Wikipedia, a hugely popular Internet encyclopedia, is at the forefront of the debate on the proper use of online sources. In 2007, Middlebury College banned the use of *Wikipedia* as a source in history papers and exams. One of the school's librarians noted that the online encyclopedia "symbolizes the best and worst of the Internet. It's the best because everyone gets his/her say and can state their views. It's the worst because people who use it uncritically take for truth what is only opinion (Byers, 2007)." Or, as comedian and satirist Stephen Colbert put it, "Any user can change any entry, and if enough other users agree with them, it becomes true (Colbert, 2006)." A computer registered to the U.S. Democratic Party changed the *Wikipedia* page for Rush Limbaugh to proclaim that he was "racist" and a "bigot," and a person working for the electronic voting machine manufacturer Diebold was found to have erased paragraphs connecting the company to Republican campaign funds (Fildes, 2007). Media literacy teaches today's students how to sort through the Internet's cloud of data, locate reliable sources, and identify bias and unreliable sources.

Individual Accountability and Popular Culture

Ultimately, media literacy involves teaching that images are constructed with various aims in mind and that it falls to the individual to evaluate and interpret these media messages. Mass communication may be created and disseminated by individuals, businesses, governments, or organizations, but it is always received by an individual. Education, life experience, and a host of other factors make each person interpret constructed media in different ways; there is no correct way to interpret a media message. But on the whole, better media literacy skills help us function better in our media-rich environment, enabling us to be better democratic citizens, smarter shoppers, and more skeptical media consumers. When analyzing media messages, consider the following:

1. **Author:** Consider who is presenting the information. Is it a news organization, a corporation, or an individual? What links do they have to the information they are providing? A news station might be owned by the company it is reporting on; likewise, an individual might have financial reasons for supporting a certain message.

2. **Format:** Television and print media often use images to grab people's attention. Do the visuals only present one side of the story? Is the footage overly graphic or designed to provoke a specific reaction? Which celebrities or professionals are endorsing this message?

3. **Audience:** Imagine yourself in another's shoes. Would someone of the opposite gender feel the same way as you do about this message? How might someone of a different race or nationality feel about it? How might an older or younger person interpret this information differently? Was this message made to appeal to a specific audience?

4. **Content:** Even content providers that try to present information objectively can have an unconscious slant. Analyze who is presenting this message. Does he or she have any clear political affiliations? Is he or she being paid to speak or write this information? What unconscious influences might be at work?

5. **Purpose:** Nothing is communicated by mass media without a reason. What reaction is the message trying to provoke? Are you being told to feel or act a certain way? Examine the information closely and look for possible hidden agendas.

With these considerations as a jumping-off place, we can ensure that we're staying informed about where our information comes from and why it is being sent—important steps in any media literacy education (Center for Media Literacy).

Key Takeaways

- Media literacy, or the ability to decode and process media messages, is especially important in today's media-saturated society. Media surrounds contemporary Americans to an unprecedented degree and from an early age. Because media messages are constructed with particular aims in mind, a media-literate individual will interpret them with a critical eye. Advertisements, bias, spin, and misinformation are all things to look for.

- Individual responsibility is crucial for media literacy because, while media messages may be produced by individuals, companies, governments, or organizations, they are always received and decoded by individuals.

- When analyzing media messages, consider the message's author, format, audience, content, and purpose.

Exercises

List the considerations for evaluating media messages and then search the Internet for information on a current event. Choose one blog post, news article, or video about the topic and identify the author, format, audience, content, and purpose of your chosen subject. Then, respond to the following questions. Each response should be a minimum of one paragraph.

1. How did your impression of the information change after answering the five questions? Do you think other questions need to be asked?

2. Is it difficult or easy to practice media literacy on the Internet? What are a few ways you can practice media literacy for television or radio shows?

3. Do you think the public has a responsibility to be media literate? Why or why not?

End-of-Chapter Assessment

Review Questions

1.
Section 1

   a. What is the difference between mass communication and mass media?

   b. What are some ways that culture affects media?

   c. What are some ways that media affect culture?

2.
Section 2

   a. List four roles that media plays in society.

   b. Identify historical events that have shaped the adoption of various mass-communication platforms.

   c. How have technological shifts affected the media over time?

3.
Section 3

   a. What is convergence, and what are some examples of it in daily life?

   b. What were the five types of convergence identified by Jenkins?

   c. How are different kinds of convergence shaping the digital age on both an individual and a social level?

4.
Section 4

   a. How does the value of free speech affect American culture and media?

   b. What are some of the limits placed on free speech, and how do they reflect social values?

   c. What is propaganda, and how does it reflect and/or impact social values?

   d. Who are gatekeepers, and how do they influence the media landscape?

5.
Section 5

a. What is a cultural period?

b. How did events, technological advances, political changes, and philosophies help shape the Modern Era?

c. What are some of the major differences between the modern and postmodern eras?

6.
Section 6

a. What is media literacy, and why is it relevant in today's world?

b. What is the role of the individual in interpreting media messages?

c. What are the five considerations for evaluating media messages?

Critical Thinking Questions

1. What does the history of media technology have to teach us about present-day America? How might current and emerging technologies change our cultural landscape in the near future?

2. Are gatekeepers and tastemakers necessary for mass media? How is the Internet helping us to reimagine these roles?

3. The idea of cultural periods presumes that changes in society and technology lead to dramatic shifts in the way people see the world. How have digital technology and the Internet changed how people interact with their environment and with each other? Are we changing to a new cultural period, or is contemporary life still a continuation of the Postmodern Age?

4. U.S. law regulates free speech through laws on obscenity, copyright infringement, and other things. Why are some forms of expression protected while others aren't? How do you think cultural values will change U.S. media law in the near future?

5. Does media literacy education belong in U.S. schools? Why or why not? What might a media literacy curriculum look like?

Career Connection

In a media-saturated world, companies use consultants to help analyze and manage the interaction between their organizations and the media. Independent consultants develop projects, keep abreast of media trends, and provide advice based on industry reports. Or, as writer, speaker, and media consultant Merlin Mann put it, the "primary job is to stay curious about everything, identify the points where two forces might clash, then enthusiastically share what that might mean, as well as why you might care (Mann)."

Read the blog post "So what do consultants do?" at http://www.consulting-business.com/so-what-do-consultants-do.html.

Now, explore writer and editor Merlin Mann's website (http://www.merlinmann.com). Be sure to take a look at the "Bio" and "FAQs" sections. These two pages will help you answer the following questions:

1. Merlin Mann provides some work for free and charges a significant amount for other projects. What are some of the indications he gives in his biography about what he values? How do you think this impacts his fees?

2. Check out Merlin Mann's projects. What are some of the projects Merlin is or has been involved with? Now look at the "Speaking" page. Can you see a link between his projects and his role as a prominent writer, speaker, and consultant?

3. Check out Merlin's FAQ section. What is his attitude about social networking sites? What about public relations? Why do you think he holds these opinions?

4. Think about niches in the Internet industry where a consultant might be helpful. Do you have expertise, theories, or reasonable advice that might make you a useful asset for a business or organization? Find an example of an organization or group with some media presence. If you were this group's consultant, how would you recommend they better reach their goals?

References

Byers, Meredith "Controversy Over Use of *Wikipedia* in Academic Papers Arrives at Smith," *Smith College Sophian*, News section, March 8, 2007.

Center for Media Literacy, "Five Key Questions Form Foundation for Media Inquiry," http://www.medialit.org/reading-room/five-key-questions-form-foundation-media-inquiry.

Colbert, Stephen. "The Word: Wikiality," *The Colbert Report*, July 31, 2006.

Fildes, Jonathan. "*Wikipedia* 'Shows CIA Page Edits,'" *BBC News*, Science and Technology section, August 15, 2007.

Holt, Debra. and others, Children's Exposure to TV Advertising in 1977 and 2004, Federal Trade Commission Bureau of Economics staff report, June 1, 2007.

Lewin. "If Your Kids Are Awake."

Mann, Merlin. http://www.merlinmann.com/projects/.

Moody, Kate. "John Culkin, SJ: The Man Who Invented Media Literacy: 1928–1993," Center for Media Literacy, http://www.medialit.org/reading_room/article408.html.

Robertson, Lori and Eugene Kiely, "Mudslinging in New Mexico: Gubernatorial Candidates Launch Willie Horton-Style Ads, Each Accusing the Other of Enabling Sex Offenders to Strike Again," *FactCheck.org*, June 24, 2010, http://factcheck.org/2010/06/mudslinging-in-new-mexico/.

Shaw, David. "A Plea for Media Literacy in our Nation's Schools," *Los Angeles Times*, November 30, 2003.

Shifrin, Donald. "Perspectives on Marketing, Self-Regulation and Childhood Obesity" (remarks, Federal Trade Commission Workshop, Washington, DC, July 14–15, 2005).

Chapter 2: Media Effects

2.1 Mass Media and Its Messages

Learning Objectives

1. Explain the different ways mass media affects culture.
2. Analyze cultural messages that the media send.
3. Explain the ways new media have affected culture.

When media consumers think of media messages, they may think of televised public service announcements or political advertisements. These obvious examples provide a venue for the transfer of a message through a medium, whether that message is a plea for fire safety or the statement of a political position. But what about more abstract political advertisements that simply show the logo of a candidate and a few simple words? Media messages can range from overt statements to vague expressions of cultural values.

Disagreements over the content of media messages certainly exist. Consider the common allegations of political bias against various news organizations. Accusations of hidden messages or agenda-driven content have always been an issue in the media, but as the presence of media grows, the debate concerning media messages increases. This dialogue is an important one; after all, mass media have long been used to persuade. Many modern persuasive techniques stem from the use of media as a propaganda tool. The role of propaganda and persuasion in the mass media is a good place to start when considering various types of media effects.

Propaganda and Persuasion

Encyclopedia Britannica defines propaganda simply as the "manipulation of information to influence public opinion (Britannica Concise Encyclopedia)." This definition works well for this discussion because the study and use of propaganda has had an enormous influence on the role of persuasion in modern mass media. In his book *The Creation of the Media*, Paul Starr argues that the United States, as a liberal democracy, has favored employing an independent press as a public guardian, thus putting the media in an inherently political position (Starr, 2004). The United States—in contrast to other nations where media are held in check—has encouraged an independent commercial press and thus given the powers of propaganda and persuasion to the public (Starr, 2004).

Figure 2.2

Benjamin Franklin used a powerful image of a severed snake to emphasize the importance of the colonies joining together during the American Revolution.

Wikimedia Commons – public domain.

Like any type of communication, propaganda is not inherently good or bad. Whether propaganda has a positive or negative effect on society and culture depends on the motivations of those who use it. People promoting movements as wide-ranging as Christianity, the American Revolution, and the communist revolutions of the 20th century have all used propaganda to disseminate their messages (Jowett & O'Donnell, 2006). Newspapers and pamphlets that glorified the sacrifices at Lexington and Concord and trumpeted the victories of George Washington's army greatly aided the American Revolution. For example, Benjamin Franklin's famous illustration of a severed snake with the caption "Join or Die" serves as an early testament to the power and use of print propaganda (Jowett & O'Donnell, 2006).

As you will learn in Chapter 4 "Newspapers", the penny press made newspapers accessible to a mass audience and became a force for social cohesion during the 1830s (Jowett & O'Donnell, 2006). Magazines adopted a similar format later in the 19th century, and print media's political and social power rose. In an infamous example of the new power of print media, some newspapers encouraged the Spanish-American War of 1898 by fabricating stories of Spanish atrocities and sabotage (Jowett & O'Donnell, 2006). For example, after the USS *Maine* sunk off the coast of Havana, Cuba, some newspapers blamed the Spanish—even though there was no evidence—fueling the public's desire for war with Spain.

The present-day, pejorative connotation of propaganda stems from the full utilization of mass media by World War I–era governments to motivate the citizenry of many countries to go to war. Some media outlets characterized the war as a global fight between Anglo civilization and Prussian barbarianism. Although some of those fighting the war had little understanding of the political motivations behind it, wartime propaganda convinced them to enlist (Miller, 2005). As you will read in Chapter 12 "Advertising and Public Relations", World War I legitimized the advertising profession in the minds of government and corporate leaders because its techniques were useful in patriotic propaganda campaigns. Corporations quickly adapted to this development and created an advertising boom in the 1920s by using World War I propaganda techniques to sell products (Miller, 2005).

In modern society, the persuasive power of the mass media is well known. Governments, corporations, nonprofit organizations, and political campaigns rely on both new and old media to create messages and to send them to the general public. The comparatively unregulated nature of U.S. media has made, for better or worse, a society in which the tools of public persuasion are available to everyone.

Media and Behavior

Although the mass media send messages created specifically for public consumption, they also convey messages that are not properly defined as propaganda or persuasion. Some argue that these messages influence behavior, especially the behavior of young people (Beatty, 2006). Violent, sexual, and compulsive behaviors have been linked to media consumption and thus raise important questions about the effects of media on culture.

Violence and the Media

On April 20, 1999, students Eric Harris and Dylan Klebold entered their Denver-area high school, Columbine High School, armed with semiautomatic weapons and explosives. Over the next few hours, the pair killed 12 classmates and one faculty member before committing suicide (Lamb, 2008). The tragedy and its aftermath captured national attention, and in the weeks following the Columbine High School shootings, politicians and pundits worked to assign blame. Their targets ranged from the makers of the first-person shooter video game *Doom* to the Hollywood studios responsible for *The Matrix* (Brook, 1999).

However, in the years since the massacre, research has revealed that the perpetrators were actually attempting a terrorist bombing rather than a first-person shooter style rampage (Toppo, 1999). But did violent video games so desensitize the two teenagers to violence that they could contemplate such a plan? Did movies that glorify violent solutions create a culture that would encourage people to consider such methods? Because modern culture is so immersed in media, the issue becomes a particularly complex one, and it can be difficult to understand the types of effects that violent media produce.

Figure 2.3

The 1999 Columbine High School shooting led to greater debate and criticism over violent video games.

Mentat Kilbernes – Columbine Massacre RPG – CC BY-NC 2.0.

A number of studies have verified certain connections between violent video games and violent behavior in young people. For example, studies have found that some young people who play violent video games reported angry thoughts and aggressive feelings immediately after playing. Other studies, such as one conducted by Dr. Chris A. Anderson and others, point to correlations between the amount of time spent playing violent video games and increased incidence of aggression (Anderson, 2003). However, these studies do not prove that video games cause violence. Video game defenders argue that violent people can be drawn to violent games, and they point to lower overall incidence of youth violence in recent years compared to past decades (Adams, 2010). Other researchers admit that individuals prone to violent acts are indeed drawn to violent media; however, they claim that by keeping these individuals in a movie theater or at home, violent media have actually contributed to a reduction in violent social acts (Goodman, 2008).

Whether violent media actually cause violence remains unknown, but unquestionably these forms of media send an emotional message to which individuals respond. Media messages are not limited to overt statements; they can also use emotions, such as fear, love, happiness, and depression. These emotional reactions partially account for the intense power of media in our culture.

Sex and the Media

In many types of media, sexual content—and its strong emotional message—can be prolific. A recent study by researchers at the University of North Carolina entitled "Sexy Media Matter: Exposure to Sexual Content in Music, Movies, Television, and Magazines Predicts Black and White Adolescents' Sexual Behavior" found that young people with heavy exposure to sexually themed media ranging from music to movies are twice as likely to engage in early sexual behavior as young people with light exposure. Although the study does not prove a conclusive link between sexual behavior and sexually oriented media, researchers concluded that media acted as an influential source of information about sex for these youth groups (Dohney, 2006). Researcher Jane Brown thinks part of the reason children watch sexual content is related to puberty and their desire to learn about sex. While many parents are hesitant to discuss sex with their children, the media can act like a "super peer," providing information in movies, television, music, and magazines (Dohney, 2006). You will learn more about the impact of sexual content in the media in Chapter 14 "Ethics of Mass Media".

Cultural Messages and the Media

The media sends messages that reinforce cultural values. These values are perhaps most visible in celebrities and the roles that they adopt. Actors such as John Wayne and Marilyn Monroe came to represent aspects of masculinity and femininity that were adopted into mainstream culture during the mid-20th century. Throughout the 1990s, basketball player Michael Jordan appeared in television, film, magazines, and advertising campaigns as a model of athleticism and willpower. Singers such as Bob Dylan have represented a sense of freedom and rebellion against mainstream culture.

Figure 2.4

Tonto from *The Lone Ranger* reinforced cultural stereotypes about Native Americans. Do you think this type of characterization would be acceptable in modern television?

Although many consider celebrity culture superficial and a poor reflection of a country's values, not all celebrities are simply entertainers. Civil rights leaders, social reformers, and other famous public figures have come to represent important cultural accomplishments and advancements through their representations in the media. When images of Abraham Lincoln or Susan B. Anthony appear in the media, they resonate with cultural and historical themes greatly separated from mere fame.

Celebrities can also reinforce cultural stereotypes that marginalize certain groups. Television and magazines from the mid-20th century often portrayed women in a submissive, domestic role, both reflecting and reinforcing the cultural limitations imposed on women at the time. Advertising icons developed during the early 20th century, such as Aunt Jemima and the Cream of Wheat chef, similarly reflected and reinforced a submissive, domestic servant role for African Americans. Other famous stereotypes—such as the Lone Ranger's Native American sidekick, Tonto, or Mickey Rooney's Mr. Yunioshi role in *Breakfast at Tiffany's*—also reinforced American preconceptions about ethnic predispositions and capabilities.

Whether actual or fictional, celebrities and their assumed roles send a number of different messages about cultural values. They can promote courageous truth telling, hide and prolong social problems, or provide a concrete example of an abstract cultural value.

New Media and Society

New media—the Internet and other digital forms of communication—have had a large effect on society. This communication and information revolution has created a great deal of anguish about digital literacy and other issues that inevitably accompany such a social change. In his book on technology and communication, *A Better Pencil*, Dennis Baron discusses this issue:

For Plato, only speech, not writing, can produce the kind of back-and-forth—the dialogue—that's needed to get at the truth…the text, orphaned by its author once it's on the page, cannot defend itself against misreading…. These are strong arguments, but even in Plato's day they had been rendered moot by the success of the written word. Although the literacy rate in classical Greece was well below 10 percent, writing had become an important feature of the culture. People had learned to trust and use certain kinds of writing—legal texts, public inscriptions, business documents, personal letters, and even literature—and as they did so, they realized that writing, on closer examination, turned out to be neither more nor less reliable or ambiguous than the spoken word, and it was just as real (Baron, 2009).

Baron makes the point that all communication revolutions have created upheavals and have changed the standards of literacy and communication. This historical perspective gives a positive interpretation to some otherwise ominous developments in communication and culture.

Information

The Internet has made an incredible amount of new information available to the general public. Both this wealth of information and the ways people process it are having an enormous effect on culture. New perceptions of information have emerged as access to it grows. Older-media consumption habits required in-depth processing of information through a particular form of media. For example, consumers read, watched, or viewed a news report in its entirety, typically within the context of a news publication or program. Fiction appeared in book or magazine form.

Today, information is easier to access, thus more likely to traverse several forms of media. An individual may read an article on a news website and then forward part of it to a friend. That person in turn describes it to a coworker without having seen the original context. The ready availability of information through search engines may explain how a clearly satirical *Onion* article on the *Harry Potter* phenomenon came to be taken as fact. Increasingly, media outlets cater to this habit of searching for specific bits of information devoid of context. Information that will attract the most attention is often featured at the expense of more important stories. At one point on March 11, 2010, for example, *The Washington Post* website's most popular story was "Maintaining a Sex Life (Kakutani, 2010)."

Another important development in the media's approach to information is its increasing subjectivity. Some analysts have used the term cyberbalkanization to describe the way media consumers filter information. Balkanization is an allusion to the political fragmentation of Eastern Europe's Balkan states following World War I, when the Ottoman Empire disintegrated into a number of ethnic and political fragments. Customized news feeds allow individuals to receive only the kinds of news and information they want and thus block out sources that report unwanted stories or perspectives. Many cultural critics have pointed to this kind of information filtering as the source of increasing political division and resulting loss of civic discourse. When media consumers hear only the information they want to, the common ground of public discourse that stems from general agreement on certain principles inevitably grows smaller (Kakutani, 2010).

Literacy

On one hand, the growth of the Internet as the primary information source exposes the public to increased levels of text, thereby increasing overall literacy. Indeed, written text is essential to the Internet: Web content is overwhelmingly text-based, and successful participation in Internet culture through the use of blogs, forums, or a personal website requires a degree of textual literacy that is not necessary for engagement in television, music, or movies.

Critics of Internet literacy, however, describe the majority of forum and blog posts as subliterate, and argue that the Internet has replaced the printed newspapers and books that actually raised the standards of literacy. One nuanced look at the Internet's effect on the way a culture processes and perceives information states that literacy will not simply increase or decrease, but will change qualitatively (Choney, 2010). Perhaps the standards for literacy will shift to an emphasis on simplicity and directness, for example, rather than on elaborate uses of language.

News

Figure 2.5

President Barack Obama fired General Stanley McChrystal after a controversial *Rolling Stone* story in which McChrystal spoke poorly of the Obama administration was leaked on the Internet.

Wikimedia Commons – public domain.

Certainly, the Internet has affected the way that cultures consume news. The public expects to receive information quickly, and news outlets respond rapidly to breaking stories. On Monday, June 21, 2010, for example, a spokesperson for *Rolling Stone* magazine first released quotes from a story featuring General Stanley McChrystal publicly criticizing members of the Obama administration on matters of foreign policy. By that evening, the story had become national news despite the fact *Rolling Stone* didn't even post it to its website until Tuesday morning—some time after several news outlets had already posted the entire story on their own sites. Later that same day, McChrystal issued a public apology, and on Wednesday flew to Washington where President Barack Obama fired him. The printed *Rolling Stone* issue featuring the article hit newsstands Friday, 2 days after McChrystal had been replaced (Timpane, 2010).

Convergence Culture

The term *convergence* can hold several different meanings. In his book *Convergence Culture: Where Old and New Media Collide,* Henry Jenkins offers a useful definition of convergence as it applies to new media:

"By convergence, I mean the flow of content across multiple media platforms, the cooperation between multiple media industries, and the migratory behavior of media audiences who will go almost anywhere in search of the kinds of entertainment experiences they want (Jenkins, 2006)."

A self-produced video on the YouTube website that gains enormous popularity and thus receives the attention of a news outlet is a good example of this migration of both content and audiences. Consider this flow: The video appears and gains notoriety, so a news outlet broadcasts a story about the video, which in turn increases its popularity on YouTube. This migration works in a number of ways. Humorous or poignant excerpts from television or radio broadcasts are often posted on social media sites and blogs, where they gain popularity and are seen by more people than had seen the original broadcast.

Thanks to new media, consumers now view all types of media as participatory. For example, the massively popular talent show *American Idol* combines an older-media format—television—with modern media consumption patterns by allowing the home audience to vote for a favorite contestant. However, *American Idol* segments regularly appear on YouTube and other websites, where people who may never have seen the show comment on and dissect them. Phone companies report a regular increase in phone traffic following the show, presumably caused by viewers calling in to cast their votes or simply to discuss the program with friends and family. As a result, more people are exposed to the themes, principles, and culture of *American Idol* than the number of people who actually watch the show (Jenkins, 2006).

New media have encouraged greater personal participation in media as a whole. Although the long-term cultural consequences of this shift cannot yet be assessed, the development is undeniably a novel one. As audiences become more adept at navigating media, this trend will undoubtedly increase.

Bert Is Evil

Figure 2.6

Jughead – evil bert – CC BY-NC-ND 2.0.

In 2001, high school student Dino Ignacio created a collage of *Sesame Street* character Bert with terrorist Osama bin Laden as part of a series for his website. Called "Bert Is Evil," the series featured the puppet engaged in a variety of illicit activities. A Bangladesh-based publisher looking for images of bin Laden found the collage on the Internet and used it in an anti-American protest poster, presumably without knowledge of who Bert was. This ended up in a CNN report on anti-American protests, and public outrage over the use of Bert made Ignacio's original site a much-imitated cult phenomenon.

The voyage of this collage from a high school student's website to an anti-American protest poster in the Middle East to a cable television news network and finally back to the Internet provides a good illustration of the ways in which content migrates across media platforms in the modern era. As the collage crossed geographic and cultural boundaries, it grew on both corporate and grassroots media. While this is not the norm for media content, the fact that such a phenomenon is possible illustrates the new directions in which media is headed (Jenkins, 2006).

Key Takeaways

- Propaganda and persuasion have long been a part of the interactions between media and culture.
- Most studies on media and behavior do not establish direct links between the two but do reveal important correlations among media, violence, and sexual behavior.
- Through the media, celebrities have come to signify important cultural values and tendencies, and they transmit specific cultural messages.
- New digital forms of media have revolutionized the way people access and consume media content. Rather than simply replacing old media, however, new forms of media encourage participatory media consumption and content migration.

Exercises

1. Celebrities can represent cultural values and principles when they are portrayed in the media. The same celebrity can represent very different things depending on the form of media and its portrayal of that person. Find a celebrity magazine, such as *People* or *Us Weekly*, either online or in print, and choose one of the celebrities mentioned. Then, answer the following questions:

   ◦ How is this celebrity portrayed in the magazine?
   ◦ What kind of roles does the celebrity take in other forms of media, such as television or film?
   ◦ How do these portrayals associate with specific cultural values?

2.
Explain how the media has affected culture. Be sure to discuss the following topics and to provide examples of each.

   ◦ Propaganda and persuasion
   ◦ Behavior
   ◦ Cultural messages

3. How has new media affected literacy and information consumption? How is this different from

older forms of media?

References

Adams, Jill U. "Effects of Violent Video Games," *Los Angeles Times*, May 3, 2010, http://articles.latimes.com/2010/may/03/health/la-he-closer-20100503.

Anderson, Craig A. and others, "The Influence of Media Violence on Youth," *Psychological Science in the Public Interest* 4, no. 3 (2003): 81–110.

Baron, Dennis. *A Better Pencil: Readers, Writers, and the Digital Revolution* (New York: Oxford University Press, 2009), 5.

Beatty, Alexandra. "Studying Media Effects on Children and Youth: Improving Methods and Measures, Workshop Summary," March 2–3, 2006, The National Academies Press, http://www.nap.edu/openbook.php?record_id=11706; "Media Influence on Youth," Crisis Connection, http://www.crisisconnectioninc.org/teens/media_influence_on_youth.htm.

Britannica Concise Encyclopedia, s.v. "Propaganda."

Brook, Tom. "Is Hollywood to Blame?" *BBC News*, April 23, 1999, http://news.bbc.co.uk/2/hi/special_report/1999/03/99/tom_brook/326529.stm.

Choney, Suzanne. "Internet Making Our Brains Different, Not Dumb," *MSNBC*, Feb. 19, 2010, http://www.msnbc.msn.com/id/35464896/ns/technology_and_science-tech_and_gadgets/.

Doheny, Kathleen "Mass Media May Prompt Kids to Try Sex: Study," *Health Scout*, April 3, 2006, http://www.healthscout.com/news/1/531862/main.html.

Garth S. Jowett and Victoria O'Donnell, *Propaganda and Persuasion* (Thousand Oaks, CA: Sage, 2006), 60–61.

Goodman, Peter. "Violent Films May Cut Real Crime, Study Finds," *New York Times*, January 7, 2008, http://www.nytimes.com/2008/01/07/technology/07iht-violence.4.9058958.html.

Jenkins, Henry *Convergence Culture: Where Old and New Media Collide* (New York: New York University Press, 2006), 2.

Kakutani, Michiko. "Texts Without Context," *New York Times*, March 17, 2010, http://www.nytimes.com/2010/03/21/books/21mash.html.

Lamb, Gina. "Columbine High School," Times Topics, *New York Times*, April 17, 2008, http://topics.nytimes.com/topics/reference/timestopics/organizations/c/columbine_high_school/index.html.

Miller, Mark Crispin. introduction to *Propaganda*, by Edward Bernays (Brooklyn, NY: IG Publishing, 2005), 11.

Starr, Paul. *Creation of the Media* (New York: Basic Books, 2004), 394–395.

Timpane, Jim. "New Media Too Speedy to Outflank," *Philly.com*, June 24, 2010, http://www.philly.com/philly/entertainment/20100624_New_media_too_speedy_to_outflank.html.

Toppo, Greg. "10 Years Later, the Real Story Behind Columbine," *USA Today*, April 13, 2009, http://www.usatoday.com/news/nation/2009-04-13-columbine-myths_N.htm.

2.2 Media Effects Theories

Learning Objectives

1. Identify the basic theories of media effects.
2. Explain the uses of various media effects theories.

Early media studies focused on the use of mass media in propaganda and persuasion. However, journalists and researchers soon looked to behavioral sciences to help figure out the effect of mass media and communications on society. Scholars have developed many different approaches and theories to figure this out. You can refer to these theories as you research and consider the media's effect on culture.

Widespread fear that mass-media messages could outweigh other stabilizing cultural influences, such as family and community, led to what is known as the direct effects model of media studies. This model assumed that audiences passively accepted media messages and would exhibit predictable reactions in response to those messages. For example, following the radio broadcast of *War of the Worlds* in 1938 (which was a fictional news report of an alien invasion), some people panicked and believed the story to be true.

Challenges to the Direct Effects Theory

The results of the *People's Choice Study* challenged this model. Conducted in 1940, the study attempted to gauge the effects of political campaigns on voter choice. Researchers found that voters who consumed the most media had generally already decided for which candidate to vote, while undecided voters generally turned to family and community members to help them decide. The study thus discredited the direct effects model and influenced a host of other media theories (Hanson, 2009). These theories do not necessarily give an all-encompassing picture of media effects but rather work to illuminate a particular aspect of media influence.

Marshall McLuhan's Influence on Media Studies

During the early 1960s, English professor Marshall McLuhan wrote two books that had an enormous effect on the history of media studies. Published in 1962 and 1964, respectively, the *Gutenberg Galaxy* and *Understanding Media* both traced the history of media technology and illustrated the ways these innovations had changed both individual behavior and the wider culture. *Understanding Media* introduced a phrase that McLuhan has become known for: "The medium is the message." This notion represented a novel take on attitudes toward media—that the media themselves are instrumental in shaping human and cultural experience.

His bold statements about media gained McLuhan a great deal of attention as both his supporters and critics responded to his utopian views about the ways media could transform 20th-century life. McLuhan spoke of a media-inspired "global village" at a time when Cold War paranoia was at its peak and the Vietnam War was a hotly debated subject. Although 1960s-era utopians received these statements positively, social realists found them cause for scorn. Despite—or perhaps because of—these controversies, McLuhan became a pop culture icon, mentioned frequently in the television sketch-comedy program *Laugh-In* and appearing as himself in Woody Allen's film *Annie Hall*.

The Internet and its accompanying cultural revolution have made McLuhan's bold utopian visions seem like prophecies. Indeed, his work has received a great deal of attention in recent years. Analysis of McLuhan's work has, interestingly, not changed very much since his works were published. His supporters point to the hopes and achievements of digital technology and the utopian state that such innovations promise. The current critique of McLuhan, however, is a bit more revealing of the state of modern media studies. Media scholars are much more numerous now than they were during the 1960s, and many of these scholars criticize McLuhan's lack of methodology and theoretical framework.

Despite his lack of scholarly diligence, McLuhan had a great deal of influence on media studies. Professors at Fordham University have formed an association of McLuhan-influenced scholars. McLuhan's other great achievement is the popularization of the concept of media studies. His work brought the idea of media effects into the public arena and created a new way for the public to consider the influence of media on culture (Stille, 2000).

Agenda-Setting Theory

In contrast to the extreme views of the direct effects model, the agenda-setting theory of media stated that mass media determine the issues that concern the public rather than the public's views. Under this theory, the issues that receive the most attention from media become the issues that the public discusses, debates, and demands action on. This means that the media is determining what issues and stories the public thinks about. Therefore, when the media fails to address a particular issue, it becomes marginalized in the minds of the public (Hanson).

When critics claim that a particular media outlet has an agenda, they are drawing on this theory. Agendas can range from a perceived liberal bias in the news media to the propagation of cutthroat capitalist ethics in films. For example, the agenda-setting theory explains such phenomena as the rise of public opinion against smoking. Before the mass media began taking an antismoking stance, smoking was considered a personal health issue. By promoting antismoking sentiments through advertisements, public relations campaigns, and a variety of media outlets, the mass media moved smoking into the public arena, making it a public health issue rather than a personal health issue (Dearing & Rogers, 1996). More recently, coverage of natural disasters has been prominent in the news. However, as news coverage wanes, so does the general public's interest.

Figure 2.7

Through a variety of antismoking campaigns, the health risks of smoking became a public agenda.

Quinn Dombrowski – Weapons of mass destruction – CC BY-SA 2.0.

Media scholars who specialize in agenda-setting research study the salience, or relative importance, of an issue and then attempt to understand what causes it to be important. The relative salience of an issue determines its place within the public agenda, which in turn influences public policy creation. Agenda-setting research traces public policy from its roots as an agenda through its promotion in the mass media and finally to its final form as a law or policy (Dearing & Rogers, 1996).

Uses and Gratifications Theory

Practitioners of the uses and gratifications theory study the ways the public consumes media. This theory states that consumers use the media to satisfy specific needs or desires. For example, you may enjoy watching a show like *Dancing With the Stars* while simultaneously tweeting about it on Twitter with your friends. Many people use the Internet to seek out entertainment, to find information, to communicate with like-minded individuals, or to pursue self-expression. Each of these uses gratifies a particular need, and the needs determine the way in which media is used. By examining factors of different groups' media choices, researchers can determine the motivations behind media use (Papacharissi, 2009).

A typical uses and gratifications study explores the motives for media consumption and the consequences associated with use of that media. In the case of *Dancing With the Stars* and Twitter, you are using the Internet as a way to be entertained and to connect with your friends. Researchers have identified a number of common motives for media consumption. These include relaxation, social interaction, entertainment, arousal, escape, and a host of interpersonal and social needs. By examining the motives behind the consumption of a particular form of media, researchers can better understand both the reasons for that medium's popularity and the roles that the medium fills in society. A study of the motives behind a given user's interaction with Facebook, for example, could explain the role Facebook takes in society and the reasons for its appeal.

Uses and gratifications theories of media are often applied to contemporary media issues. The analysis of the relationship between media and violence that you read about in preceding sections exemplifies this. Researchers employed the uses and gratifications theory in this case to reveal a nuanced set of circumstances surrounding violent media consumption, as individuals with aggressive tendencies were drawn to violent media (Papacharissi, 2009).

Symbolic Interactionism

Another commonly used media theory, symbolic interactionism, states that the self is derived from and develops through human interaction. This means the way you act toward someone or something is based on the meaning you have for a person or thing. To effectively communicate, people use symbols with shared cultural meanings. Symbols can be constructed from just about anything, including material goods, education, or even the way people talk. Consequentially, these symbols are instrumental in the development of the self.

This theory helps media researchers better understand the field because of the important role the media plays in creating and propagating shared symbols. Because of the media's power, it can construct symbols on its own. By using symbolic interactionist theory, researchers can look at the ways media affects a society's shared symbols and, in turn, the influence of those symbols on the individual (Jansson-Boyd, 2010).

One of the ways the media creates and uses cultural symbols to affect an individual's sense of self is advertising. Advertisers work to give certain products a shared cultural meaning to make them desirable. For example, when you see someone driving a BMW, what do you think about that person? You may assume the person is successful or powerful because of the car he or she is driving. Ownership of luxury automobiles signifies membership in a certain socioeconomic class. Equally, technology company Apple has used advertising and public relations to attempt to become a symbol of innovation and nonconformity. Use of an Apple product, therefore, may have a symbolic meaning and may send a particular message about the product's owner.

Media also propagate other noncommercial symbols. National and state flags, religious images, and celebrities gain shared symbolic meanings through their representation in the media.

Spiral of Silence

The spiral of silence theory, which states that those who hold a minority opinion silence themselves to prevent social isolation, explains the role of mass media in the formation and maintenance of dominant opinions. As minority opinions are silenced, the illusion of consensus grows, and so does social pressure to adopt the dominant position. This creates a self-propagating loop in which minority voices are reduced to a minimum and perceived popular opinion sides wholly with the majority opinion. For example, prior to and during World War II, many Germans opposed Adolf Hitler and his policies; however, they kept their opposition silent out of fear of isolation and stigma.

Because the media is one of the most important gauges of public opinion, this theory is often used to explain the interaction between media and public opinion. According to the spiral of silence theory, if the media propagates a particular opinion, then that opinion will effectively silence opposing opinions through an illusion of consensus. This theory relates especially to public polling and its use in the media (Papacharissi).

Media Logic

The media logic theory states that common media formats and styles serve as a means of perceiving the world. Today, the deep rooting of media in the cultural consciousness means that media consumers need engage for only a few moments with a particular television program to understand that it is a news show, a comedy, or a reality show. The pervasiveness of these formats means that our culture uses the style and content of these shows as ways to interpret reality. For example, think about a TV news program that frequently shows heated debates between opposing sides on public policy issues. This style of debate has become a template for handling disagreement to those who consistently watch this type of program.

Media logic affects institutions as well as individuals. The modern televangelist has evolved from the adoption of television-style promotion by religious figures, while the utilization of television in political campaigns has led candidates to consider their physical image as an important part of a campaign (Altheide & Snow, 1991).

Cultivation Analysis

The cultivation analysis theory states that heavy exposure to media causes individuals to develop an illusory perception of reality based on the most repetitive and consistent messages of a particular medium. This theory most commonly applies to analyses of television because of that medium's uniquely pervasive, repetitive nature. Under this theory, someone who watches a great deal of television may form a picture of reality that does not correspond to actual life. Televised violent acts, whether those reported on news programs or portrayed on television dramas, for example, greatly outnumber violent acts that most people encounter in their daily lives. Thus, an individual who watches a great deal of television may come to view the world as more violent and dangerous than it actually is.

Cultivation analysis projects involve a number of different areas for research, such as the differences in perception between heavy and light users of media. To apply this theory, the media content that an individual normally watches must be analyzed for various types of messages. Then, researchers must consider the given media consumer's cultural background of individuals to correctly determine other factors that are involved in his or her perception of reality. For example, the socially stabilizing influences of family and peer groups influence children's television viewing and the way they process media messages. If an individual's family or social life plays a major part in her life, the social messages that she receives from these groups may compete with the messages she receives from television.

Key Takeaways
• The now largely discredited direct effects model of media studies assumes that media audiences passively accept media messages and exhibit predictable reactions in response to those messages.

- Credible media theories generally do not give as much power to the media, such as the agenda-setting theory, or give a more active role to the media consumer, such as the uses and gratifications theory.

- Other theories focus on specific aspects of media influence, such as the spiral of silence theory's focus on the power of the majority opinion or the symbolic interactionism theory's exploration of shared cultural symbolism.

- Media logic and cultivation analysis theories deal with how media consumers' perceptions of reality can be influenced by media messages.

Exercises

1.
Media theories have a variety of uses and applications. Research one of the following topics and its effect on culture. Examine the topic using at least two of the approaches discussed in this section. Then, write a one-page essay about the topic you've selected.

- Media bias

- Internet habits

- Television's effect on attention span

- Advertising and self-image

- Racial stereotyping in film

2. Many of the theories discussed in this section were developed decades ago. Identify how each of these theories can be used today? Do you think these theories are still relevant for modern mass media? Why?

References

David Altheide and Robert Snow, *Media Worlds in the Postjournalism Era* (New York: Walter de Gruyter, 1991), 9–11.

Dearing, James and Everett Rogers, *Agenda-Setting* (Thousand Oaks, CA: Sage, 1996), 4.

Hanson, Ralph. *Mass Communication: Living in a Media World* (Washington, DC: CQ Press, 2009), 80–81.

Hanson, Ralph. *Mass Communication*, 92.

Jansson-Boyd, Catherine. *Consumer Psychology* (New York: McGraw-Hill, 2010), 59–62.

Papacharissi, Zizi. "Uses and Gratifications," 153–154.

Papacharissi, Zizi. "Uses and Gratifications," in *An Integrated Approach to Communication Theory and Research*, ed. Don Stacks and Michael Salwen (New York: Routledge, 2009), 137.

Stille, Alexander. "Marshall McLuhan Is Back From the Dustbin of History; With the Internet, His Ideas Again Seem Ahead of Their Time," *New York Times*, October 14, 2000, http://www.nytimes.com/2000/10/14/arts/marshall-mcluhan-back-dustbin-history-with-internet-his-ideas-again-seem-ahead.html.

2.3 Methods of Researching Media Effects

Learning Objectives

1. Identify the prominent media research methods.
2. Explain the uses of media research methods in a research project.

Media theories provide the framework for approaching questions about media effects ranging from as simple as how 10-year-old boys react to cereal advertisements to as broad as how Internet use affects literacy. Once researchers visualize a project and determine a theoretical framework, they must choose actual research methods. Contemporary research methods are greatly varied and can range from analyzing old newspapers to performing controlled experiments.

Content Analysis

Content analysis is a research technique that involves analyzing the content of various forms of media. Through content analysis, researchers hope to understand both the people who created the content and the people who consumed it. A typical content analysis project does not require elaborate experiments. Instead, it simply requires access to the appropriate media to analyze, making this type of research an easier and inexpensive alternative to other forms of research involving complex surveys or human subjects.

Content analysis studies require researchers to define what types of media to study. For example, researchers studying violence in the media would need to decide which types of media to analyze, such as television, and the types of formats to examine, such as children's cartoons. The researchers would then need to define the terms used in the study; media violence can be classified according to the characters involved in the violence (strangers, family members, or racial groups), the type of violence (self-inflicted, slapstick, or against others), or the context of the violence (revenge, random, or duty-related). These are just a few of the ways that media violence could be studied with content-analysis techniques (Berger, 1998).

Archival Research

Any study that analyzes older media must employ archival research, which is a type of research that focuses on reviewing historical documents such as old newspapers and past publications. Old local newspapers are often available on microfilm at local libraries or at the newspaper offices. University libraries generally provide access to archives of national publications such as *The New York Times* or *Time*; publications can also increasingly be found in online databases or on websites.

Older radio programs are available for free or by paid download through a number of online sources. Many television programs and films have also been made available for free download, or for rent or sale through online distributors. Performing an online search for a particular title will reveal the options available.

Resources such as the Internet Archive (www.archive.org) work to archive a number of media sources. One important role of the Internet Archive is website archiving. Internet archives are invaluable for a study of online media because they store websites that have been deleted or changed. These archives have made it possible for Internet content analyses that would have otherwise been impossible.

Surveys

Surveys are ubiquitous in modern life. Questionaires record data on anything from political preferences to personal hygiene habits. Media surveys generally take one of the following two forms.

A descriptive survey aims to find the current state of things, such as public opinion or consumer preferences. In media, descriptive surveys establish television and radio ratings by finding the number of people who watch or listen to particular programs. An analytical survey, however, does more than simply document a current situation. Instead, it attempts to find out why a particular situation exists. Researchers pose questions or hypotheses about media, and then conduct analytical surveys to answer these questions. Analytical surveys can determine the relationship between different forms of media consumption and the lifestyles and habits of media consumers.

Surveys can employ either open-ended or closed-ended questions. Open-ended questions require the participant to generate answers in their own words, while closed-ended questions force the participant to select an answer from a list. Although open-ended questions allow for a greater variety of answers, the results of closed-ended questions are easier to tabulate. Although surveys are useful in media studies, effective use requires keeping their limitations in mind.

Social Role Analysis

As part of child rearing, parents teach their children about social roles. When parents prepare children to attend school for example, they explain the basics of school rules and what is expected of a student to help the youngsters understand the role of students. Like the role of a character in a play, this role carries specific expectations that differentiate school from home. Adults often play a number of different roles as they navigate between their responsibilities as parents, employees, friends, and citizens. Any individual may play a number of roles depending on his or her specific life choices.

Social role analysis of the media involves examining various individuals in the media and analyzing the type of role that each plays. Role analysis research can consider the roles of men, women, children, members of a racial minority, or members of any other social group in specific types of media. For example, if the role children play in cartoons is consistently different from the role they play in sitcoms, then certain conclusions might be drawn about both of these formats. Analyzing roles used in media allows researchers to gain a better understanding of the messages that the mass media sends (Berger, 1998).

Depth Interviews

The depth interview is an anthropological research tool that is also useful in media studies. Depth interviews take surveys one step further by allowing researchers to directly ask a study participant specific questions to gain a fuller understanding of the participant's perceptions and experiences. Depth interviews have been used in research projects that follow newspaper reporters to find out their reasons for reporting certain stories and in projects that attempt to understand the motivations for reading romance novels. Depth interviews can provide a deeper understanding of the media consumption habits of particular groups of people (Priest, 2010).

Rhetorical Analysis

Rhetorical analysis involves examining the styles used in media and attempting to understand the kinds of messages those styles convey. Media styles include form, presentation, composition, use of metaphors, and reasoning structure. Rhetorical analysis reveals the messages not apparent in a strict reading of content. Studies involving rhetorical analysis have focused on media such as advertising to better understand the roles of style and rhetorical devices in media messages (Gunter, 2000).

Focus Groups

Like depth interviews, focus groups allow researchers to better understand public responses to media. Unlike a depth interview, however, a focus group allows the participants to establish a group dynamic that more closely resembles that of normal media consumption. In media studies, researchers can employ focus groups to judge the reactions of a group to specific media styles and to content. This can be a valuable means of understanding the reasons for consuming specific types of media.

Figure 2.8

Focus groups are effective ways to obtain a group opinion on media.

Experiments

Media research studies also sometimes use controlled experiments that expose a test group to an experience involving media and measure the effects of that experience. Researchers then compare these measurements to those of a control group that had key elements of the experience removed. For example, researchers may show one group of children a program with three incidents of cartoon violence and another control group of similar children the same program without the violent incidents. Researchers then ask the children from both groups the same sets of questions, and the results are compared.

Participant Observation

In participant observation, researchers try to become part of the group they are studying. Although this technique is typically associated with anthropological studies in which a researcher lives with members of a particular culture to gain a deeper understanding of their values and lives, it is also used in media research.

Media consumption often takes place in groups. Families or friends gather to watch favorite programs, children may watch Saturday morning cartoons with a group of their peers, and adults may host viewing parties for televised sporting events or awards shows. These groups reveal insights into the role of media in the lives of the public. A researcher might join a group that watches football together and stay with the group for an entire season. By becoming a part of the group, the researcher becomes part of the experiment and can reveal important influences of media on culture (Priest).

Researchers have studied online role-playing games, such as *World of Warcraft,* in this manner. These games reveal an interesting aspect of group dynamics: Although participants are not in physical proximity, they function as a group within the game. Researchers are able to study these games by playing them. In the book *Digital Culture, Play, and Identity: A World of Warcraft Reader*, a group of researchers discussed the results of their participant observation studies. The studies reveal the surprising depth of culture and unwritten rules that exist in the *World of Warcraft* universe and give important interpretations of why players pursue the game with such dedication (Corneliussen & Rettberg, 2008).

Key Takeaways

- Media research methods are the practical procedures for carrying out a research project. These methods include content analysis, surveys, focus groups, experiments, and participant observation.

- Research methods generally involve either test subjects or analysis of media. Methods involving test subjects include surveys, depth interviews, focus groups, and experiments. Analysis of media can include content, style, format, social roles, and archival analysis.

Exercises

Media research methods offer a variety of procedures for performing a media study. Each of these methods varies in cost; thus, a project with a lower budget would be prohibited from using some of the more costly methods. Consider a project on teen violence and video game use. Then answer the following short-response questions. Each response should be a minimum of one paragraph.

1. Which methods would a research organization with a low budget favor for this project? Why?

2. How might the results of the project differ from those of one with a higher budget?

References

Berger, Arthur Asa. *Media Research Techniques* (Thousand Oaks, CA: Sage, 1998), 23–24.

Corneliussen, Hilde and Jill Walker Rettberg, "Introduction: 'Orc ProfessorLFG,' or Researching in Azeroth," in *Digital Culture, Play, and Identity: A World of Warcraft Reader*, ed. Hilde Corneliussen and Jill Walker Rettberg (Cambridge, MA: Massachusetts Institute of Technology, 2008), 6–7.

Gunter, Barrie. *Media Research Methods: Measuring Audiences, Reactions and Impact* (Thousand Oaks, CA: Sage, 2000), 89.

Priest, Susanna Hornig *Doing Media Research: An Introduction* (Thousand Oaks, CA: Sage, 2010), 16–22.

Priest, Susanna Hornig *Doing Media Research*, 96–98.

2.4 Media Studies Controversies

Learning Objectives

1. Explain some of the major objections to specific media theories.
2. Identify ways media studies are used to support political opinions.
3. Differentiate between proper and improper use of media studies.

Important debates over media theory have questioned the foundations and hence the results of media research. Within academia, theories and research can represent an individual's lifework and livelihood. As a result, issues of tenure and position, rather than issues of truth and objectivity, can sometimes fuel discussion over theories and research.

Problems With Methodology and Theory

Although the use of advanced methodologies can resolve many of the questions raised about various theories, the fact remains that the use of these theories in public debate generally follows a broader understanding. For example, if a hypothetical study found that convicted violent offenders had aggressive feelings after playing the video game *Doom*, many would take this as proof that video games cause violent acts without considering other possible explanations. Often, the nuances of these studies are lost when they enter the public arena.

Active versus Passive Audience

A significant division among media studies theorists is the belief that audiences are passive or active. A passive audience, in the most extreme statement of this position, passively accepts the messages that media send it. An active audience, on the other hand, is fully aware of media messages and makes informed decisions about how to process and interact with media. Newer trends in media studies have attempted to develop a more complex view of media audiences than the active versus passive debate affords, but in the public sphere, this opposition frames many of the debates about media influence (Heath & Bryant, 2000).

Arguments against Agenda-Setting Theory

A number of criticisms have dogged agenda-setting theory. Chief among these is that agenda-setting studies are unable to prove cause and effect; essentially, no one has truly shown that the media agenda sets the public agenda and not the other way around. An agenda-setting study could connect the prevalence of a topic in the media with later changes in public policy and may conclude that the media set this agenda. However, policy makers and lobbyists often conduct public relations efforts to encourage the creation of certain policies. In addition, public concern over issues generates media coverage as well, making it difficult to tell if the media is responding to public desire for coverage of an issue or if it is pushing an issue on its own agenda (Kwansah-Aidoo, 2005).

Arguments Against Uses and Gratifications Theory

The general presuppositions of the uses and gratifications theory have drawn criticism. By assuming that media fulfill a functional purpose in an individual's life, the uses and gratifications theory implicitly justifies and reaffirms the place of media in the public sphere. Furthermore, because it focuses on personal, psychological aspects of media, the theory cannot question whether media is artificially imposed on an individual. Studies involving the uses and gratifications theory are often sound methodologically, but the overall assumptions of the studies are left unquestioned (Grossberg, et. al., 2006).

Arguments Against Spiral of Silence Theory

Although many regard the spiral of silence theory as useful when applying its broadest principles, it is weak when dealing with specifics. For example, the phenomenon of the spiral of silence is most visible in individuals who are fearful of social isolation. Those who are less fearful are less likely to be silent if public opinion turns against them. Nonconformists contradict the claims of the spiral of silence theory.

Critics have also pointed out that the spiral of silence theory relies heavily on the values of various cultural groups. A public opinion trend in favor of gun control may not silence the consensus within National Rifle Association meetings. Every individual is a part of a larger social group with specific values. Although these values may differ from widespread public opinion, individuals need not fear social isolation within their particular social group (Gastil, 2008).

Arguments Against Cultivation Analysis Theory

Critics have faulted cultivation analysis theory for relying too heavily on a broad definition of violence. Detractors argue that because violence means different things to different subgroups and individuals, any claim that a clear message of violence could be understood in the same way by an entire culture is false. This critique would necessarily extend to other studies involving cultivation analysis. Different people understand media messages in varying ways, so broad claims can be problematic. Cultivation analysis is still an important part of media studies, but critics have questioned its unqualified validity as a theory (Shanahan & Morgan, 1999).

Politics and Media Studies

Media theories and studies afford a variety of perspectives. When proponents of a particular view employ those theories and studies, however, they are often oversimplified and can result in contradictory claims. In fact, when politicians and others employ media studies to validate a political perspective, this is a common result.

Media Bias

A good example of the ways that media can bolster political opinion is through coverage, which leads to the debate over media bias. One 1985 study found that journalists were more likely to hold liberal views than were members of the public. Over the years, many have cited this study to support the opinion that the media holds a liberal bias. However, another study found that between the years of 1948 and 1990, 78 percent of newspaper presidential endorsements were for Republicans (Hanson).

Media favoritism again became a source of contention during the 2008 presidential race. A random sampling of campaign coverage in the run-up to the election found that 82 percent of stories featured Barack Obama, while only 52 percent discussed John McCain (Raasch, 2008). Allegations that the media favored Obama seemed to bolster the idea of a liberal bias. But other studies belied this belief. Research conducted during the election showed that favorable media coverage of Obama occurred only after his poll numbers rose, hinting that the media were reacting to public opinion rather than attempting to influence it (Reuters, 2008).

Figure 2.9

Allegations of media bias are a recurring theme in political debates.

The Weekly Bull – BBC – Report the Truth on Gaza protest – CC BY-NC-ND 2.0.

Media Decency

Decency standards in media have long been an issue, and they continue to change in ways that are not necessarily predictable. Once banned in the United States for obscenity, James Joyce's *Ulysses* is now considered a classic of modern literature, while many schools have banned children's classic *Adventures of Huckleberry Finn* for its use of ethnic slurs. Because of the regulatory powers that government possesses over the media, decency is also an inherently political issue. As media studies have progressed, they have increasingly appeared in the debates over decency standards. Although media studies cannot prove a word or image is indecent, they can help discern the impact of that word or image and, thus, greatly influence the debate.

Organizations or figures with stated goals often use media studies to support those aims. For example, the Parents Television Council reported on a study that compared the ratio of comments about nonmarital sex to comments about marital sex during the hours of 8 p.m. to 9 p.m. The study employed content analysis to come up with specific figures; however, the Parents Television Council then used those findings to make broad statements, such as "the institution of marriage is regularly mocked and denigrated (Rayworth, 2008)." Because content analysis does not analyze the effect on audiences or analyze how material is presented, it does not offer a scientific way to judge whether a comment is mocking and denigrating marriage, so such interpretations are arguably unsupported by the research. For example, researchers performing a content analysis by documenting the amount of sex or violence on television are not analyzing how this content is interpreted by the audience. They are simply noting the number of instances. Equally, partisan groups can use a number of different linguistic turns to make media studies fit their agenda.

Media studies involving violence, pornography, and profanity are inherently politically charged, and politicians have also conducted their own media studies. In 2001, for example, a Senate bill aimed at Internet decency that had little support in Congress came to the floor. One of the sponsoring senators attempted to increase interest by bringing a file full of some of the most egregious pornographic images he could find to the Senate floor. The bill passed 84 to 16 (Elmer-Dewitt, 2001).

Jack Thompson versus Violent Video Games

One of the most outspoken critics of violent video games is the now-disbarred lawyer Jack Thompson. Despite questionable use of media research, Thompson has made many claims referencing research. In an interview with *CBS News*, Thompson stated that "hundreds of studies" existed that proved the link between violent video games and real violence. Later in the interview, he listed increasing school murder statistics as proof of the effects of violent video games (Vitka, 2005). In light of the media effects theories elucidated in this chapter, Thompson was obviously not being honest about the findings of video game–violence research and was making claims that no media effects scholar could confidently make.

Thompson initiated several lawsuits against *Grand Theft Auto* video game developer Take 2 Interactive, claiming that the company should be held liable for encouraging violent actions by minors. His lawsuits were thrown out of court, and he eventually came to a settlement with Take 2 Interactive—who had countersued—to drop all litigation (Jones, 2007). Thompson's frivolous use of the legal system caused the state of Alabama to revoke his license to practice law in 2005, and, in 2008, the Florida Supreme Court disbarred him for life (Hefflinger, 2008).

Jack Thompson's actions may seem extreme, but he represents a common pattern of media study misrepresentation. Pundits, social reformers, and politicians frequently use the results of media studies to support their agenda without regard for accuracy. The use of media research to lend credence to a political opinion is widespread even as the public struggles to understand the effects of new media on culture.

Media Consolidation

Although media consolidation will be discussed in more depth in later chapters, the topic's intersection with media studies results deserves a place here. Media consolidation occurs when large media companies buy up smaller media outlets. Although government regulation has historically stymied this trend by prohibiting ownership of a large number of media outlets, the Federal Communications Commission (FCC) has loosened many of the restrictions on large media companies in recent years.

Media studies often prove vital to decisions regarding media consolidation. These studies measure the impact that consolidation has had on the media's public role and on the content of local media outlets to compare it with that of conglomerate-owned outlets. The findings often vary depending on the group conducting the test. Other times tests are ignored entirely.

In 2003, the FCC loosened restrictions on owning multiple media outlets in the same city, citing studies that the agency had developed to weigh the influence of particular media outlets such as newspapers and television stations (Ahrens, 2003). In 2006, however, reports surfaced that a key study had been discarded during the 2003 decision. The study showed an increase in time allocated for news when TV stations were owned locally, thus raising questions about whether media consolidation was a good thing for local news (MSNBC, 2006).

Key Takeaways

- Audience interpretation is vital to media studies. Media theories generally fall between the active and passive audience interpretations. Agenda-setting theory favors the passive audience interpretation, and consequently must prove that the public is affected by media agendas. The uses and gratifications theory favors the active audience, and consequently justifies the place of media in the public sphere.

- In politics, media studies are often used to support various opinions. Among the more prominent media studies employed are those that deal with media bias, violence in the media, and indecency.

- The use of media studies in public debate has led to subjective studies that have a predetermined outcome. Many studies conducted by special interest groups use definitions that favor their perspectives. Politicians often copy the style, rather than the substance, of a media study in an attempt to give authority to their points of view.

Exercises

Media studies are often used to support specific opinions, regardless of whether their results justify such a use. Studies are also conducted with predetermined outcomes that support a specific view. With this in mind, answer the following short-response questions. Each response should be a minimum of one paragraph.

1. How are media studies used to support political opinions? Give two examples.

2. What kind of guidelines should be used to ensure clear and objective use of media studies?

3. Identify weaknesses of popular media theories discussed in this section.

End-of-Chapter Assessment

Review Questions

1.
Section 1

    a. List three historical events that have relied on propaganda.

    b. Provide three examples of cultural messages that the media sends.

    c. How have new media affected older forms of media?

2.
Section 2

    a. How does agenda-setting theory differ from direct effects theory?

    b. Use the spiral of silence to explain an actual lapse in media coverage.

    c. Why would uses and gratifications theory be an appropriate theory for a study of Internet purchasing habits?

3.
Section 3

    a. Name the different types of media analysis techniques and explain their uses.

    b. Explain the differences among a survey, a depth interview, and a focus group.

    c. What resources would be important for a project analyzing the historical representation of women in advertising?

4.
Section 4

    a. Explain the opposition between theories of passive and active media audiences.

b. How are media studies commonly misused to support political opinions?

c. How might media studies be used in a study on indecency?

Critical Thinking Questions

1. The media has become an ever-increasing part of modern life. How do you think the media and its messages have affected you personally?

2. Media studies attempt to understand the role that the media plays in culture and in individual lives. Given the criticisms of particular media theories, what do you think the limitations of media studies are? Consider the media theories discussed in this chapter. Which ones do you find the most convincing and why? Which ones do you find least convincing?

3. Among the methods used to analyze audiences, which do you think would guarantee the most accurate results? How does this affect your opinion of studies that use other results?

Career Connection

Media studies are used in a variety of professions and capacities. These range from university researchers to small-time music groups that want to assess their online presence. A number of online research tools exist that can help organizations and individuals learn more about the effect of media on important issues and topics.

List two or three prospective careers and think of one way that media studies could be beneficial in each. Search for online media research tools that would assist you in a media research project involving your chosen careers. Answer the following questions:

- What kind of project would be beneficial to you in this field?

- How would you set up the project to ensure usable and accurate results?

- How would you present the results of your studies to clients, employees, and investors?

References

Ahrens, Frank "FCC Eases Media Ownership Rules," *Washington Post*, June 3, 2003, http://www.washingtonpost.com/ac2/wp-dyn?pagename=article&contentId=A5555-2003Jun2.

Elmer-Dewitt, Philip "On a Screen Near You," *Time*, June 24, 2001, http://www.time.com/time/magazine/article/0,9171,1101950703-134361,00.html.

Gastil, John. *Political Communication and Deliberation* (Thousand Oaks, CA: Sage, 2008), 61–62.

Grossberg, Lawrence and others, *Mediamaking: Mass Media in a Popular Culture* (Thousand Oaks, CA: Sage, 2006), 266–267.

Hanson. *Mass Communication*, 101–102.

Heath, Robert and Jennings Bryant, *Human Communication Theory and Research: Concepts, Contexts, and Challenges* (Mahwah, NJ: Lawrence Erlbaum Associates, 2000), 385–386.

Hefflinger, Mark "Controversial Game Lawsuit Attorney Jack Thompson Disbarred," *Digital Media Wire*, September 26, 2008, http://www.dmwmedia.com/news/2008/09/26/controversial-game-lawsuit-attorney-jack-thompson-disbarred.

Jones, K. C. "Grand Theft Auto Company Settles With Jack Thompson," *InformationWeek*, April 20, 2007, http://www.informationweek.com/news/global-cio/showArticle.jhtml?articleID=199200271.

Kwansah-Aidoo, Kwamena "Prospects for Agenda-Setting Research in the 21st Century," in *Topical Issues in Communications and Media Research*, ed. Kwamena Kwansah-Aidoo (New York: Nova Science Publishers, 2005), 40–41.

MSNBC, Associated Press, "Powell Denies Seeing Media Ownership Study," *MSNBC*, September 15, 2006, http://msnbc.msn.com/id/14850729/.

Raasch, Chuck. "Media Bias Aside, Obama's Trip an Important Test," *USA Today*, July 24, 2008, http://www.usatoday.com/news/opinion/columnist/raasch/2008-07-24-newpolitics_N.htm.

Rayworth, Melissa. "TV Decency Standards Challenge Parents," *Cape Cod Times*, August 10, 2008, http://www.capecodonline.com/apps/pbcs.dll/article?AID=/20080810/LIFE/808100317.

Reuters. "Despite Republican Complaints, Media Bias Largely Missing From US Campaign: Study," *Canada.com*, November 6, 2008, http://www.canada.com/vancouversun/news/story.html?id=97db2fe0-4b4f-4524-b265-57a0e0c3a38f.

Shanahan, James and Michael Morgan, *Television and its Viewers: Cultivation Theory and Research* (New York: Cambridge University Press, 1999), 59–60.

Vitka, William "Gamespeak: Jack Thompson," GameCore, *CBS News*, February 25, 2005, http://www.cbsnews.com/stories/2005/02/24/tech/gamecore/main676446.shtml.

Chapter 3: Books

3.1 Books

A Lost Generation of Readers?

Figure 3.1

In 2004, the National Endowment for the Arts (NEA) released a report that it said represented "a national crisis." What was under such dire peril that it threatened to "impoverish both cultural and civic life," as NEA Chairman Dana Gioia put it? Reading—or, more aptly put, not reading. According to the report, *Reading at Risk: A Survey of Literary Reading in America*, less than half the population engaged in any literary reading in 2002, a record low since the survey's beginnings in 1982 (National Endowment for the Arts, 2004).

The report, which asked respondents whether they had read any literary fiction (novels, short stories, plays, or poetry) over the past year showed especially stark numbers among the youngest adults. Those aged 18–24 saw a rate of decline 55 percent greater than the total adult population. (Books read for school or work weren't counted in the survey, which was examining Americans' leisure reading habits.) According to the NEA, the overall 10 percent drop in literary readers represented a loss of 20 million potential readers, most of them young. In 1982, young adults (people aged 18–34) were most likely to engage in literary reading; by 2002, they were the least likely group. Based on this, the report asks, "Are we losing a generation of readers (National Endowment for the Arts, 2004)?"

Despite these facts, the publishing industry's releasing more books than ever before. In 2003, just 1 year after the NEA issued its gloomy warning about the state of reading, 175,000 new titles were published in the United States—a 19 percent jump from the year before (Bowker, 2004). Since the early part of the 21st century, the U.S. publishing industry has had an average annual monetary growth rate of 1.1 percent; however, net sales have dropped from $26 billion to $23 billion in the past year (Association of American Publishers, 2009). Meanwhile, as the NEA report notes, 24 percent of Americans' recreational spending went to electronics, while books accounted for only 5.6 percent in 2002. Perhaps unsurprisingly, the households that watched television more read less. The report warned that "at the current rate of loss, literary reading as a leisure activity will virtually disappear in half a century (National Endowment for the Arts)."

As a response to the alarming statistics, in 2006 the NEA launched its Big Read program, essentially a city-wide book club in which community members are encouraged to read the same book at the same time. The NEA provided publicity, funding for kickoff parties, and readers' guides. The residents of Tampa, Florida, read *The Joy Luck Club* and were accorded a visit by author Amy Tan, and the residents of Washington, DC, chose Ernest J. Gaines's *A Lesson Before Dying* with hopes that it would spur conversations about race, justice, and violence. The Big Read's DC program director said that he hoped the book got young people talking, noting that the book raises all sorts of relevant questions, such as "Do we offer second chances for people after making mistakes, especially youth in DC? What about youth in the justice system? So many people who have been through the juvenile justice system will testify a book set them free," he claimed (Brown, 2010).

When the NEA's 2008 numbers were released, many people were again surprised. The statistics showed that the decline in reading had reversed, the first such increase in 26 years. Once again, the change was most significant among young adults, who had a 21 percent increase from 2002 (Rich, 2009). The NEA credited the "millions of parents, teachers, librarians, and civic leaders [who] took action… [to ensure that] reading became a higher priority in families, schools, and communities (Rich, 2009)." Another factor may have been in play, however; the 2008 study was the first to include online reading. To understand what books mean in the present world of e-readers and digital libraries, it helps to examine how they functioned in the past and to consider how they might change in the future.

References

Association of American Publishers, "Industry Statistics 2009: AAP Reports Book Sales Estimated at $23.9 Billion in 2009," http://www.publishers.org/main/IndustryStats/indStats_02.htm.

Bowker. "U.S. Book Production Soars to 175,000 New Titles in 2003; Trade Up, University Presses Down," news release, May 27, 2004, http://www.bowker.com/press/bowker/2004_0527_bowker.htm.

Brown, DeNeen. "Ernest J. Gaines's 'Lesson' Prompts Teens to Grapple With Stark Realities," *Washington Post*, May 10, 2010, Arts section.

National Endowment for the Arts, *Reading at Risk: A Survey of Literary Reading in America* (New York: Author, 2004).

National Endowment for the Arts, *Reading at Risk*.

Rich, Mokoto "Fiction Reading Increases for Adults," *New York Times*, January 11, 2009, Arts section.

3.2 History of Books

Ancient Books

Most historians trace the origins of the book back to the ancient Egyptians, whose papyrus scrolls looked very different from the books we're accustomed to today. From the time they first developed a written script, around 3000 BCE, Egyptians wrote on many different surfaces, including metal, leather, clay, stone, and bone. Most prominent, though, was the practice of using reed pens to write on papyrus scrolls. In many ways, papyrus was an ideal material for the Egyptians. It was made using the tall reeds that grew plentifully in the Nile Valley. Individual sheets of papyrus were glued or sewn together to make scrolls. A standard scroll was around 30 feet long and 7 to 10 inches wide, while the longest Egyptian scroll ever found stretched over 133 feet, making it almost as long as the Statue of Liberty when it was rolled all the way out (Harry Ransom Center).

By the 6th century BCE, papyrus was the most common writing surface throughout the Mediterranean and was used by the Greeks and Romans. Because papyrus grew in Egypt, the Egyptians had a virtual monopoly over the papyrus trade. Many ancient civilizations housed their scrolls in large libraries, which acted as both repositories of knowledge and displays of political and economic power. The Royal Library of Alexandria boasted around half a million scrolls in its collection; some scholars claim that this was between 30 and 70 percent of all books in existence at the time (Kelly, 2006). But other powerful entities in the ancient world were growing tired of the Egyptians' monopoly over the papyrus trade.

Parchment was made from treated animal skins that were scraped thin to create a flexible, even surface. Parchment had several advantages over papyrus: It was more durable, both sides could be written on, and its trade wasn't monopolized by the Egyptians. Its spread coincided with another crucial development in the history of the book. Between the 2nd and 4th centuries, the Romans began sewing folded sheets of papyrus or parchment together, and binding them between wooden covers. This form, called the codex, has essentially the same structure as today's books. The codex was much more user-friendly than was the papyrus scroll: more portable, easier to store and handle, and less expensive to produce. It also allowed readers to quickly flip between sections. While reading a scroll was a two-handed activity, a codex could be propped open in front of a reader, allowing for note taking. Traditions changed slowly in the ancient world, however, and the scroll remained the dominant form for secular works for several centuries. The codex was the preferred form for early Christian texts, and the spread of Christianity eventually brought about the dominance of the codex; by the 6th century CE, it had almost entirely replaced the scroll.

Figure 3.2

The earliest known printed books were created using woodblock printing.

The next major innovation in the history of books, the use of block printing on paper, began in Tang Dynasty China around 700 CE, though it wouldn't arrive in Europe for nearly 800 years. The first known examples of text printed on paper are tiny, 2.5-inch-wide scrolls of Buddhist prayers commissioned by Japan's Empress Shōtoku in 764 CE. The earliest example of a dated, printed book is a Buddhist text called the *Diamond Sutra* (868 CE). Woodblock printing was a meticulous process that involved carving an entire page of text onto a wooden block, then inking and pressing the block to print a page.

In medieval Europe, however, scribes were still laboriously copying texts by hand. Book culture in the Middle Ages was dominated by monasteries, which became centers of intellectual life. The largest monasteries had rooms called scriptoria where monks copied, decorated, and preserved both religious and secular volumes. Many of the classical texts we have today owe their preservation to diligent medieval monks, who thought of scholarship, even the study of secular and pre–Christian writers, as a way to become closer to God. The hand-copied books produced in the Middle Ages were much more ornate than the mass-produced books of today. These were illuminated manuscripts that included painted embellishments that were added on to the handwritten books. The word *illuminate* comes from the Latin *illuminare*, which means to *light up*, and some medieval books were literally made to shine through applications of gold or silver decorations. Other ornate additions included illustrations, decorative capital letters, and intricately drawn borders. The degree of embellishment depended on the book's intended use and the wealth of its owner. Medieval manuscripts were so highly valued that some scribes placed so-called book curses at the front of their manuscripts, warning that anyone who stole or defaced the copy would be cursed. Written in a copy of the Vulgate Bible, for example, is this warning: "Whoever steals this book let him die the death; let be him be frizzled in a pan; may the falling sickness rage within him; may he be broken on the wheel and be hanged (Virginia Commonwealth University Libraries)."

Though illuminated books were highly prized, they were also expensive and labor-intensive to create. By the end of the Middle Ages, the papal library in Avignon, France, held only a few thousand manuscripts compared to the nearly half-million texts found at the Library of Alexandria in ancient times (Fischer, 2004). Bookmaking in the Western world became somewhat less expensive when paper emerged as the primary writing surface. Making paper from rags and other fibers, a technique that originated in 2nd-century China, reached the Islamic world in the 8th century and led to a flowering of book culture there. By the 12th century, Marrakesh, in modern-day Morocco, was said to have had a street lined with a hundred booksellers. But it wasn't until the 14th century that paper manufacturing began in earnest in Europe.

Gutenberg's Industry-Changing Invention

Papermaking coincided with another crucial step forward in the history of books: Johannes Gutenberg's invention of mechanical movable type in 1448. Though the simple act of crafting small, movable letters may seem mundane in the contemporary world of digital devices and microchips, it is difficult to overstate the importance of Gutenberg's invention and the effect it had on the world. The Biography Channel and A&E both named Gutenberg as the single most influential person of the second millennium, ahead of Shakespeare, Galileo, and Columbus, and *Time* magazine cited movable type as the single most important invention of the past 1,000 years. Through his invention, Gutenberg indisputably changed the world.

Much of Gutenberg's life is shrouded in mystery. It is known that he was a German goldsmith and book printer and that he spent the 1440s collecting investors for a mysterious project. That invention turned out to be the printing press, which combined existing technologies—such as the screw press, which was already used for papermaking—with his own innovation—individual metal letters and punctuation marks that could be independently rearranged—to revolutionize how books were made. Though Gutenberg probably printed other, earlier materials, it was the Bible he printed in 1455 that brought him renown. In his small print shop in his hometown of Mainz, Germany, Gutenberg used his movable type press to print 180 copies of the Bible, 135 on paper and 45 on vellum (Harry Ransom Center). This book, commonly called the Gutenberg Bible, ushered in Europe's so-called Gutenberg Revolution and paved the way for the commercial mass printing of books. In 1978, the Harry Ransom Humanities Research Center of the University of Texas at Austin purchased a complete copy of the Gutenberg Bible for $2.4 million.

Over the next few centuries, the printing press changed nearly everything about how books were made, distributed, and read. Printing books was a vastly swifter system than handwriting books was, and paper was much less expensive to produce than parchment. Before the printing press, books were generally commissioned and then copied. The printing press meant that multiple identical editions of the same book could be printed in a relatively short time, while it probably would've taken a scribe at least a year to handwrite the Bible. As Gutenberg's invention led to more and more printing shops springing up all over Europe, the very idea of what a book looked like began to change. In medieval times, books were the valuable, rare product of hundreds (if not thousands) of hours of work, and no two were the same. After Gutenberg, books could be standardized, plentiful, and relatively cheap to produce and disseminate. Early printed books were made to look like illuminated manuscripts, complete with hand-drawn decorations. However, printers soon realized the economic potential of producing multiple identical copies of one text, and book printing soon became a speculative business, with printers trying to guess how many copies a particular book could sell. By the end of the 15th century, 50 years after Gutenberg's invention of movable type, printing shops had sprung up throughout Europe, with an estimated 300 in Germany alone. Gutenberg's invention was a resounding success, and the printing and selling of books boomed. The Harry Ransom Humanities Research Center estimates that before the invention of the printing press, the total number of books in all of Europe was around 30,000. By 1500 CE, the book was thriving as an industrial object, and the number of books in Europe had grown to as many as 10 to 12 million (Jones, 2000).

Effects of the Mass Production of Books

The post–Gutenberg world was revolutionized by the advent of the printed book. One thing that did not substantially change, however, was the form of the book itself. Despite minor tweaks and alterations, the ancient form of the codex remained relatively intact. What did rapidly evolve was the way books were produced and distributed and the way information circulated through the world.

Simply put, the mechanical reproduction of books meant that there were more books available at a lower cost, and the growth of international trade allowed these books to have a wider reach. The desire for knowledge among the growing middle class and the new availability of classical texts from ancient Greece and Rome helped fuel the Renaissance, a period of celebration of the individual and of a turn toward humanism. For the first time, texts could be widely dispersed, allowing political, intellectual, religious, and cultural ideas to spread widely. Also for the first time, many people could read the same books and be exposed to the same ideas at the same time, giving rise to mass media and mass culture. Science was revolutionized as well. For example, standardized, widely dispersed texts meant that scientists in Italy were exposed to the theories and discoveries of scientists in England. Because of improved communication, technological and intellectual ideas spread more quickly, enabling scientists from disparate areas to more easily build on the breakthroughs and successes of others.

As the Renaissance progressed, the size of the middle class grew, as did literacy rates. Rather than a few hundred precious volumes housed in monastery or university libraries, books were available to people outside monastic or university settings, which meant that more books were available to women. In effect, the mass production of books helped knowledge become democratized. However, this spread of information didn't proceed without resistance. Thanks in part to the spread of dissenting ideas, the Roman Catholic Church, the dominant institution of medieval Europe, found its control slipping. In 1487, only a few decades after Gutenberg first printed his Bible, Pope Innocent VIII insisted that all books be prescreened by church authorities before they were allowed to be printed (Green & Karolides, 2005). One book the church banned was the Bible printed in any language other than Latin—a language that few people outside of clerical or scholarly circles understood. In 1517, Martin Luther instigated the Protestant Reformation. He challenged the church's authority by insisting that people had the right to read the Bible in their own language. The church rightly feared the spread of vernacular Bibles; the more people who had access to the text, the less control the church was able to exert over how it was interpreted. Since the church's interpretation of the Bible dictated in no small part the way many people lived their lives, the church's sway over the hearts and minds of the faithful was severely undermined by accessible printed Bibles and the wave of Protestantism they encouraged. The Catholic Church's attempt to control the printing industry proved impossible to maintain, and over the next few centuries, the church would see its power decline significantly, as it was no longer the sole keeper of religious knowledge as it had been throughout the Middle Ages.

The Bible wasn't the only text that was beginning to be published in languages other than Latin. The Renaissance saw a growing interest in texts published in the vernacular, the speech of the "common people." As books became more available to the middle class, people wanted to read books written in their native tongue. Early well-known works in the vernacular included Dante's *Divine Comedy* (first printed in Italian in 1472) and Chaucer's *Canterbury Tales* (published in Middle English in the 15th century). Genres with popular appeal, such as plays and poetry, became increasingly widespread. In the 16th and 17th centuries, inexpensive chapbooks (the name derives, appropriately enough, from *cheap books*) became popular. Chapbooks were small and cheaply printed, and they often included popular ballads, humorous stories, or religious tracts. The proliferation of chapbooks showed just how much the Gutenberg Revolution had transformed the written word. In just a few hundred years, many people had access to reading material, and books would no longer be considered sacred objects.

Because of the high value placed on human knowledge during the Renaissance, libraries flourished during this time period. As they had been in ancient Egypt, libraries were once again a way of displaying national power and wealth. The German State Library in Berlin was founded in 1661, and other European centers soon followed, such as the National Library of Spain in Madrid in 1711 and the British Library (the world's largest) in London in 1759. Libraries were also associated with universities, clubs, and museums; however, these were often only for subscribers. The United Kingdom's Public Libraries Act of 1850 fostered the development of free, public lending libraries. After the American Civil War, public libraries flourished in the newly reunified United States, helped by fundraising and lobbying by women's clubs. Philanthropist Andrew Carnegie helped bring the Renaissance ideals of artistic patronage and democratized knowledge into the 20th century when he helped found more than 1,700 public libraries between 1881 and 1919 (Krasner-Khait, 2001).

History of Document Control

While Gutenberg's invention of the printing press ushered in an age of democratized knowledge and incipient mass culture, it also transformed the act of authorship, making writing a potentially profitable enterprise. Before the mass production of books, authorship had few financial rewards (unless a generous patron got involved). As a consequence, pre-Renaissance texts were often collaborative, and many books didn't even list an author. The earliest concept of the copyright, from the time of the scriptoria, was who had the right to copy a book by hand. The printed book, however, was a speculative commercial enterprise, in that large numbers of identical copies could be sold. The explosive growth of the European printing industry meant that authors could potentially profit from the books they made and then wrote if their legal rights were recognized. In contemporary terms, copyright allows a person the right to exclude others from copying, distributing, and selling a work. This is a right usually given to the creator, although that right can be sold or otherwise transferred. Works not covered by copyright or for which the copyright has expired are part of the public domain, which means that they are essentially public property and can be used freely by anyone without permission or royalty payments.

The origins of contemporary copyright law are usually traced back to the Statute of Queen Anne. This law, enacted in England in 1710, was the first to recognize the legal rights of authors, though in an incomplete manner. It granted a book's publisher 14 years of exclusive rights and legal protection, renewable for another 14-year term if the author was still living. Anyone who infringed on a copyrighted work paid a fine, half of which went to the author and half to the government. Early copyright was intended to limit monopoly and censorship, to provide a sense of stability to authors, and to promote learning by ensuring that documents would be widely accessible.

The United States established its first copyright law not long after the Declaration of Independence. The U.S. Constitution granted Congress the power "to promote the progress of science and useful arts, by securing for limited times to authors and inventors the exclusive right to their respective writings and discoveries" in Article I, Section 8, Clause 8. The first federal copyright law, the Copyright Law of 1790, was modeled on the Statute of Queen Anne and it similarly granted exclusive rights for 14 years, renewable for 14 more if the author was living at the end of the first term.

The "limited times" mentioned in the Constitution have steadily lengthened since the 18th century. The Copyright Act of 1909 allowed for an initial 28-year term of copyright, which was renewable for one additional 28-year term. The Copyright Act of 1976, which preempted the 1909 act, extended copyright protection to "a term consisting of the life of the author and 50 years after the author's death," was substantially longer than the original law's potential 56-year term. In 1998, copyright was extended even further, to 70 years after the author's death. The 1998 law, called the Copyright Term Extension Act, also added a 20-year extension to all currently copyrighted works. This automatic extension meant that no new works would enter the public domain until 2019 at the earliest. Critics of the Copyright Term Extension Act called it the "Mickey Mouse Protection Act" because the Walt Disney Company lobbied for the law (Krasniewicz, 2010). Because of the 20-year copyright extension, Mickey Mouse and other Disney characters remained out of the public domain, which meant that they were still the exclusive property of Disney.

The 1976 law also codified the terms of fair use for the first time. Fair-use law specifies the ways in which a work (or parts of a work) under copyright could legally be used by someone other than the copyright holder for "purposes such as criticism, comment, news reporting, teaching (including multiple copies for classroom use), scholarship, or research, is not an infringement of copyright." That is, a book review quoting snippets of a book, or a researcher citing someone else's work is not infringing on copyright. Given an Internet culture that thrives on remixes, linking, and other creative uses of source material, the boundaries of the legal definition of fair use have met with many challenges in recent years.

History of the Book-Publishing Industry

With the exception of self-published works, the author isn't the person in charge of producing the book or sending it out into the world. These days, the tasks of editing, designing, printing, promoting, and distributing a book generally fall to the book's publisher. Although authors are usually the ones with their names prominently displayed on the spine, a published book is actually the product of many different kinds of labor by many different people.

Early book printers acted as publishers, because they produced pages and sold them commercially. In England, the Stationer's Company, which was essentially a printer's guild, had a monopoly over the printing industry and was also allowed to censor texts. The Statute of Queen Anne, the 1710 copyright law, came about partially as a result of some of these early publishers overstepping their bounds.

In the 19th-century United States, publishers fulfilled many roles, and it was not uncommon for one company to print, wholesale, and even retail their own books. Although bookstores and printers existed in the United States, the Northeast emerged as the nation's publishing epicenter, with hotspots in Philadelphia, New York, and Boston. During the 1800s, the U.S. book industry swiftly expanded. In 1820, the books manufactured and sold in the United States totaled about $2.5 million; by 1850, even though the price of books had dropped substantially, sales figures had quintupled (Howe, 2007). Technological advances in the 19th century, including machine-made paper and the Linotype typesetting machine, made book publishing simpler and more profitable. Many of today's large publishing companies were created in the 19th century; for example, Houghton Mifflin originated in 1832; Little, Brown & Company formed in 1837; and Macmillan was founded in Scotland in 1843 and opened its U.S. branch in 1869. By the turn of the century, New York was the center of publishing in the United States.

The rapid growth of the publishing industry and evolving intellectual property laws meant that authors could make money from their writing during this period. Perhaps it's no surprise, then, to learn that the first literary agents also emerged in the late 19th century. Literary agents act as intermediaries between the author and the publisher, negotiating contracts and parsing difficult legal language. The world's first literary agent, A. P. Watt, worked in London in 1881 and essentially defined the role of the contemporary literary agent—he got paid to negotiate on behalf of the author. A former advertising agent, Watt decided to charge based on commission, meaning that he would take in a set percentage of his clients' earnings. Watt set the fee as 10 percent, which is still considered standard today.

The biggest change to hit publishing in the first half of the 20th century was the increasing popularity of the paperback book. Books covered in less expensive, less durable paper existed since Renaissance chapbooks were invented, but they were usually crudely printed works that were meant only as passing entertainment. In 1935, the publishing industry was changed forever when Penguin Books Ltd., a paperback publisher, launched in England, ushered in the so-called paperback revolution. Instead of being crude and cheaply made, Penguin titles were simple but well designed. Though Penguin sold paperbacks for only 25¢, it concentrated on providing works of literary merit, thus fundamentally changing the idea of what quality books should look like. Some early Penguin titles included Ernest Hemingway's *A Farewell to Arms* and Dashiell Hammett's *The Thin Man*. In the decades that followed, more and more paperback publishing companies were launched by people hoping to capitalize on Penguin's success. The first U.S.-based paperback company was Pocket Books, founded in 1939. By 1960, paperbacks were outselling hardbacks in the United States (Ogle, 2003).

The second half of the 20th century was marked by the consolidation of the U.S. book-publishing industry and by a larger trend toward media consolidation. Between 1960 and 1989, about 578 mergers and acquisitions occurred in the U.S. book industry; between 1990 and 1995, 300 occurred; and between 1996 and 2000, nearly 380 occurred (Greco, 2005). This was just a part of the larger international trend toward mass media consolidation, where large international media empires acquired smaller companies in many different industries. For example, the German media company Bertelsmann AG had acquired Bantam Books, Doubleday, and Random House; London-based Pearson owned Viking, Penguin, Putnam, and the Dutton Group; and AOL Time Warner owned Little, Brown and Company and Warner Books. Because publicly traded companies have obligations to their shareholders, the publishing industry found itself pressured to turn increasingly high profits. By 2010, roughly 60 percent of all books sold in the United States were published by six large publishing houses, often referred to as the Big Six (see Figure 3.3) (Hyatt, 2010). In the first years of the third millennium, book publishing was an increasingly centralized, profit-driven industry.

Figure 3.3

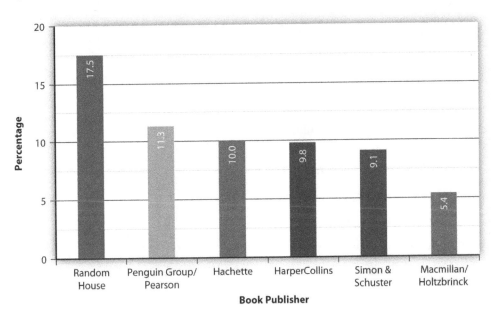

The Big Six control more than 60 percent of the book market (Hyatt, 2010).

Key Takeaways

- Papyrus scrolls were the earliest forms of books, superseded in the 6th century by the codex. The codex was more portable, sturdier, and easier to store, which made it a more popular format. During the Middle Ages, books were handwritten on parchment and then painstakingly decorated. At this time, monasteries were the centers of intellectual life, and most book copying happened in their scriptoria. Until the invention of mechanical movable type, books were expensive and not widely available.

- The Gutenberg Revolution changed how information circulated around the globe. The invention of mechanical movable type made books much cheaper and quicker to produce, which led to the swifter spread of ideas. Access to classical texts spurred the European Renaissance and led to higher literacy rates among women. With millions of books circulating in the world, popular literature soon emerged, sometimes in the form of inexpensive chapbooks.

- Copyright law was originally meant to protect authors from censorship and to allow them to profit from their work. The first copyright law was England's Statute of Queen Anne in 1710. In the 20th century, American copyright law steadily increased the terms of protection for works under copyright.

- The publishing industry arose to help authors produce and distribute copies of their work. Early printers acted as wholesale booksellers. In the 20th century, paperback books revived the publishing industry by making high literature available in an inexpensive, portable format. By the turn of the century, book publishing was dominated by six publishing companies, themselves part of large media conglomerations.

Exercises

Questions about the exact extent of fair use of copyrighted materials have been especially relevant in recent years because of the popularity of using and manipulating copyrighted materials on the Internet. Go on a website with user-uploaded content (such as YouTube or *Wikipedia*) and find examples of works that use copyrighted content in a way that you think is justified under fair use. Then, find examples of works that you think do not use copyrighted content in a way permitted by fair use. Answer the following questions when you have completed your research:

- What is the difference between the two examples you found?

- What criteria did you use to make your decision?

- What objections might be made by someone who could classify the works differently than you did?

- How does current fair-use law differ from ancient, medieval, and modern copyright laws?

References

Fischer, Steven Roger *A History of Reading* (New York: Reaktion Books, 2004).

Greco, Albert N. *The Book Publishing Industry* (New York: Routledge, 2005).

Green, Jonathan and Nicholas J. Karolides, *The Encyclopedia of Censorship* (Facts on File, 2005), 111.

Harry Ransom Center, "The Gutenberg Bible at the Ransom Center," University of Texas at Austin, http://www.hrc.utexas.edu/educator/modules/gutenberg/books/early/.

Harry Ransom Center, "The Gutenberg Bible."

Howe, Daniel Walker. *What Hath God Wrought: The Transformation of America, 1815–1848* (New York: Oxford University Press, 2007).

Hyatt, Michael. "Top Ten U.S. Book Publishers for 2009," January 15, 2010, http://michaelhyatt.com/2010/01/top-ten-u-s-book-publishers-for-2009.html.

Jones, Bruce. "Manuscripts, Books, and Maps: The Printing Press and a Changing World," September 5, 2000, http://communication.ucsd.edu/bjones/Books/booktext.html.

Kelly, Kevin. "Scan This Book!" *New York Times Magazine*, May 14, 2006.

Krasner-Khait, Barbara. "Survivor: The History of the Library," *History Magazine*, October/November 2001.

Krasniewicz, Louise. *Walt Disney: A Biography* (Santa Barbara, CA: Greenwood, 2010), 43.

Ogle, Matthew. "The Paperback Revolution," CRC Studio, 2003, http://www.crcstudio.org/paperbacks/revolution.php.

Virginia Commonwealth University Libraries, "Book Curses," http://www.library.vcu.edu/preservation/curse.html.

3.3 Books and the Development of U.S. Popular Culture

Learning Objectives

1. Identify the change in women's roles after the American Revolution and how it impacted early U.S. literature.

2. Name some distinctive aspects of American style used by 19th-century writers.

3. Identify popular works of 20th-century fiction.

Figure 3.4

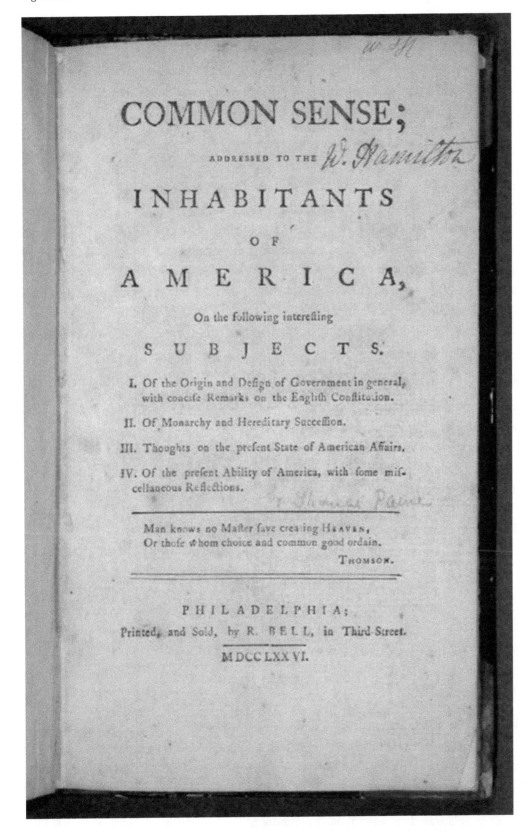

Common Sense, a pamphlet published anonymously in 1776, argued for the American colonies'
independence from Britain.

At the turn of the 18th century, the American colonies could only claim about 250 published books (Baym, 2007). In 2010 alone, more than 288,000 new titles were published. As the United States has grown and developed, books have grown and developed along with it. Sometimes books have amplified differences within the nation, sometimes their authors have worked to proclaim a distinctive American style; sometimes the authors have tried to expose hypocrisies in government and society, and sometimes the authors have celebrated America's multifaceted population. Throughout the history of the United States, books have influenced American popular culture and have been influenced by it as well.

In the years leading up to the American Revolution, newspapers and pamphlets were the publication method of choice because they could be quickly printed and were ideal for circulating short political and news items at a moment of rapid change. Thomas Paine's *Common Sense*, first published anonymously in 1776, could be considered America's first best seller. As literacy rates soared in post-independence America and the nation became more stable, the market for longer books increased. William Hill Brown's *The Power of Sympathy: or, The Triumph of Nature*, published in 1789, is considered the first American novel. Brown's epistolary novel, which is a novel made up of letters of correspondence, warned about the dangers of seduction. Brown's novel shares some features with a novel published 2 years later, *Charlotte Temple* by Susannah Rowson, another cautionary tale about a woman falling prey to seduction.

Though women were often the subjects of popular novels, they were increasingly the audience as well. Eighteenth-century Americans were influenced by Enlightenment values, which maintained that a strong nation needed an educated, moral population. Although the public realm of education, employment, and politics was dominated by men, women had control over the domestic sphere and the education of the next generation. The 18th-century idea that American women should educate their children for the good of the emerging nation, sometimes called republican motherhood, helped to legitimize, expand, and improve women's education. Women's literacy rates rose sharply during this period, and more and more books were tailored to women's interests, as women tended to have more leisure time for reading. Authors such as Frances Burney and Mary Wollstonecraft wrote about issues facing women of the period, and openly criticized the fixed role of females in society.

However, in these early years of the American novel, some people found the form potentially dangerous and subversive because it was too entertaining and it appealed to people's, especially women's, imaginations. A character in *The Boarding School* by Hannah Webster Foster, a popular writer of the time period, espouses this particular viewpoint:

Novels, are the favorite and the most dangerous kind of reading, now adopted by the generality of young ladies…. Their romantic pictures of love, beauty, and magnificence, fill the imagination with ideas which lead to impure desires, a vanity of exterior charms, and a fondness for show and dissipation, by no means consistent with that simplicity, modesty, and chastity, which should be the constant inmates of the female breast (Foster, 2010).

Part of the perceived threat of novels was their widespread popularity with many different kinds of people. An early biography of Susannah Rowson characterized the wide readership of her novel:

It has stolen its way alike into the study of the divine and into the workshop of the mechanic, into the parlor of the accomplished lady and the bed-chamber of her waiting maid, into the log-hut on the extreme border of modern civilization and into the forecastle of the whale ship on the lonely ocean. It has been read by the grey bearded professor after his 'divine Plato'; by the beardless clerk after balancing his accounts at night, by the traveler waiting for the next conveyance at the village inn; by the school girl stealthfully in her seat at school (Darnton, 1996).

These popular 18th-century novels were preoccupied with providing moral guidance and cautionary tales to the citizens of the newly formed United States. Questions of freedom and responsibility were paramount as the emerging nation attempted to establish a uniquely American literature.

Books in the 1800s—How *Uncle Tom's Cabin* Helped Start a War

Rowson's *Charlotte Temple* became the most popular book in the 1800s until *Uncle Tom's Cabin* was published (Winship, 2009). Written by abolitionist and preacher Harriet Beecher Stowe in 1852—9 years before the beginning of the Civil War—*Uncle Tom's Cabin* was a smash hit by any definition. An impassioned critique of slavery that tugged on readers' emotions, the novel sold 300,000 copies in its first year and became the century's second-best-selling book after the Bible (PBS, 1862). Stowe's novel has been credited with heightening tensions between the North and the South. The novel was not only popular domestically. The first London edition sold 200,000 copies in a year, and the book was the first American novel to be translated into Chinese (PBS, 1862). The absence of international copyright law meant that Stowe was not compensated for most of these translations. Many unauthorized stage versions of the play were produced as well, causing historians to theorize that more people saw theatrical adaptations of the play than read the book. As with today's stage and film adaptations of books, some of these versions of Stowe's story were faithful to the novel, while others changed the story's ending or even twisted the story to make it pro-slavery. In the early 1900s, nine silent film versions of the novel were released, making *Uncle Tom's Cabin* the most-filmed story of the silent film era. With her book, Stowe helped establish the political novel as an important touchstone of American literature.

Figure 3.5

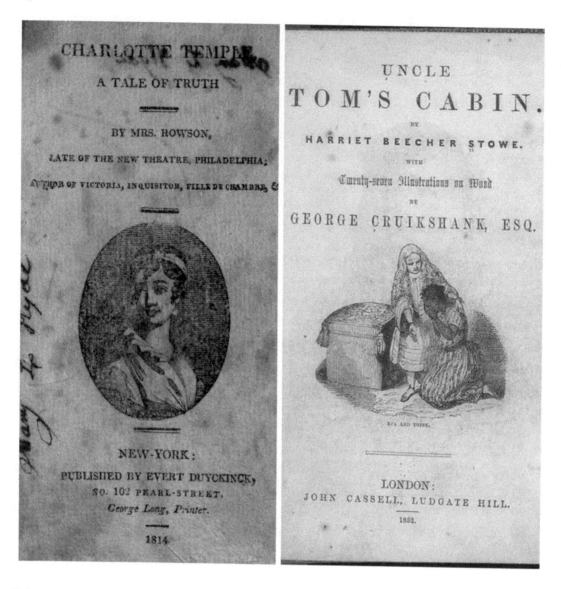

Before strict copyright law, many different versions of Stowe's novel cropped up.

Wikimedia Commons – public domain.

Other 19th-century writers in the United States concentrated on developing a uniquely American style, a mode of self-expression distinct from European models. James Fenimore Cooper, author of *The Last of the Mohicans* (1826), wrote adventure stories that celebrated the American frontier, championing a theme that would intrigue U.S. writers for centuries to come. Poet Walt Whitman wrote *Leaves of Grass* (1855), a collection of poems that shocked readers with its frank sexuality and fresh use of language. In contrast to most other English-language poets at the time, Whitman wrote in free verse, mimicking the rhythms of actual speech in his poems. He was purposefully informal; he valued everyday speech; he spoke openly about sexual themes; and he was an important figure in establishing an American idiom that was open, informal, and focused on the experiences of common people. Washington Irving, author of the now-iconic short stories "Rip Van Winkle" (1819) and "The Legend of Sleepy Hollow" (1820), helped establish satire and wit as important aspects of the emerging American style.

Mark Twain famously used humor in his many works of journalism, travel writing, and fiction. Twain's characters' voices are funny, irreverent, and full of off-the-wall idioms and odd regional coinages. This passage, from the first chapter of *The Adventures of Huckleberry Finn* (1884), shows Twain's use of distinctively American speech patterns: "The Widow Douglas she took me for her son, and allowed she would sivilize me; but it was rough living in the house all the time, considering how dismal regular and decent the widow was in all her ways; and so when I couldn't stand it no longer I lit out (Twain, 1912)." Twain was also one of the first writers to use a then-newfangled invention—the typewriter.

Edgar Allan Poe is best known for writing macabre stories and poems like "The Raven" (1845), "The Cask of Amontillado" (1846), and "The Tell-Tale Heart" (1843). A master of the Gothic genre, Poe is also credited with writing the first detective story, 1841's "The Murders in the Rue Morgue." (Some people also credit Poe with the invention of the horror story and the science fiction story.) In this and other stories, Poe established many of the classic features of detective stories, including Arthur Conan Doyle's Sherlock Holmes tales: a brilliant, crime-solving detective who works outside the standard police system; the detective's assistant or friend, who serves as narrator; and an emphasis on analysis and solving a crime through reason. Poe had such a strong effect on the mystery genre that the Mystery Writers of America annually give out the Edgar Awards, named in honor of Poe.

At the end of the 1800s, American literature could be broadly categorized as reflecting an interest in the natural landscape, preoccupation with questions of identity (both of the individual and the nation), an interest in humor or satire, a pride in common speech, and an interest in politics. An emerging interest in what we now call genre fiction was increasing and would become a fully fledged movement as the 20th century progressed.

Twentieth Century and Beyond

The production of books in the 1900s was cheaper than ever because of improved technology. The 20th century saw a multiplicity of genres that began to better reflect the diversity of experiences and interests in the United States. Furthermore, the paperback revolution eroded the distinction between high and low art. By the end of the century, however, books were facing competition for attention with films, television, video games, and the Internet.

Figure 3.6

L. Frank Baum's *The Wonderful Wizard of Oz* was the basis
for the famous 1939 movie *The Wizard of Oz*.

Wikimedia Commons – public domain.

In 1900, L. Frank Baum published *The Wonderful Wizard of Oz*, a novel set in the fantastical world of Oz. It became the best-selling children's book for the next 2 years and went on to spawn 13 sequels. Baum's book is considered part of the so-called golden age of children's literature, which is considered to have begun with Lewis Carroll's *Adventures of Alice in Wonderland* (1865) and ended with A. A. Milne's Winnie-the-Pooh books (1924–1928). Along with children's literature, other kinds of genre fiction saw their birth or growth in the 20th century. Owen Wister's *The Virginian* (1902) and Zane Grey's *Riders of the Purple Sage* (1912) established the Western as a uniquely American genre that would influence the popular Wild West films of the 1920s and beyond. Other genres including science fiction, horror, mystery, and romance sprung up out of the late-19th and early-20th dime novels, named for their cheap cost and known for their sensational, quickly written stories. The dime novel gave way to the even-cheaper pulp magazines and books, inexpensive publications named for the cheap pulp paper they were printed on. Pulp stories were generally sensational and featured sordid tales of murder, prostitution, and gangster violence; others told fantastical stories of aliens or monsters. The pulps were gleefully low culture and were quite popular with readers. Conan the Barbarian, Tarzan, Zorro, and The Shadow all made their first appearances as characters in early pulps. The paperback revolution of the 1930s, 40s, and 50s gave genre stories a wider reach in a more durable format.

While many 19th-century U.S. writers worked to create a distinctive American style, some 20th-century writers aimed to debunk American myths. After World War II, the United States' emerged as a dominant world power.

Some writers became preoccupied with critiquing American society and government. Dissatisfied with the widespread 1950s ideals of conformity and homogeneity, Beat Generation authors wrote in a freewheeling, informal style and proudly described their drug use and sexual exploits. Touchstone works of the Beat Generation include Allen Ginsberg's *Howl and Other Poems* (1956), Jack Kerouac's *On the Road* (1957), and William S. Burroughs's *Naked Lunch* (1959). These books celebrated road trips, drug trips, spiritual yearning, distrust of the mass media, and gleeful obscenity, and they helped pave the way for the hippie movement of the 1960s.

After the end of the Cold War in 1991, American literature saw an upswing in books that expressed the diversity of voices and experiences of late-20th-century America. Jhumpa Lahiri and Amy Tan wrote about the immigrant experience; Sherman Alexie and Louise Erdrich penned acclaimed novels about Native American life; and Toni Morrison explored the political and historical dimensions of slavery and race in the United States. Sometimes called multicultural literature, these and other books were celebrated as a way to promote cross-cultural understanding by examining the different value systems, histories, traditions, and speech patterns of people in America.

The 21st-century market has so far been dominated by several massively popular novel franchises—such as *Left Behind*, *Harry Potter*, *The Twilight Saga*, and *The Da Vinci Code*—that have collectively sold hundreds of millions of copies. These haven't only been popular as books; they've also spawned equally lucrative films and merchandise tie-ins. Consumers who are so inclined can purchase *Twilight Saga* wall decals, *Harry Potter* earrings, or *Da Vinci Code* board games. In some ways, such novel franchises harken back to *Uncle Tom's Cabin* in the 19th century, which was a multiplatform success popular on the page, stage, and screen.

Figure 3.7

Pulp publications captured readers with their lurid, colorful covers.

Defining Obscenity: "Howl" Goes on Trial

Figure 3.8

"Howl" marked a turning point in United States obscenity laws.

Maddie Keating – two – CC BY-NC-ND 2.0.

Allen Ginsberg's poem "Howl" met with strong reactions, both positive and negative, when it was released by City Lights Books in 1956. Ginsberg's poem was instantly notorious for its descriptions of sexual acts, both heterosexual and homosexual, drug use, mental hospitals, and antiestablishment conspiracies. Many readers were shocked by Ginsberg's words; however, that was precisely his intent. He once described "Howl" as "an emotional time bomb that would continue exploding in U.S. consciousness in case our military-industrial-nationalist complex solidified (Ginsberg, 1995)." In 1957, U.S. customs officials seized a shipment of copies of the book on the grounds of obscenity, but soon after dropped their charges. However, the poem's legal struggles weren't over; that same year, the California police sent plainclothes officers to City Lights Bookstore to buy a copy and then promptly arrested the salesclerk and the store owner on charges of obscenity.

The "Howl" trial came in the same year as several other landmark Supreme Court cases that liberalized the legal definition of obscenity in the United States. Before 1957, a more strict definition held that any material with a possible immoral influence was obscene. This stance led to a ban on works by authors such as James Joyce and D. H. Lawrence. Under the new law, a work would be judged by "community standards" and could only be judged obscene if its "dominant theme taken as a whole appeals to the prurient interest." In other words, books could no longer be deemed obscene on the basis of a single four-letter word. It also meant that the poem's obscenity would have to be judged against the relatively liberal standards of San Francisco, where the police sting operation had taken place.

The American Civil Liberties Union (ACLU) leapt to City Lights' defense, and the presiding judge overturned the obscenity charge, citing the poem's "redeeming social importance." In hindsight, the judge seems undoubtedly correct about the poem's social importance. "Howl" and the obscenity rulings of 1957 marked a crucial bridge between the post–World War II years of enthusiastic patriotism and social conformity and the 1960s ethos of free love and antigovernment sentiment. By the time of Ginsberg's death in 1997, *Howl and Other Poems* had sold more than 800,000 copies (Raskin, 2006).

Key Takeaways

- After the Revolutionary War, the United States was preoccupied with questions of self-determination. Many popular books reflected similar concerns about freedom through stories that explored the dangers of seduction for women. During this time, the ideals of republican motherhood also boosted literacy rates for women, although reading novels was still seen by some as a potentially subversive activity.

- During the 19th century, *Uncle Tom's Cabin* was a national sensation that heightened divisions between the North and South and that may have hastened the outbreak of the Civil War. The book was also popular as a stage play and, later, as a silent film. Other American writers of this period tried to establish a distinctive American voice, whether through political engagement, satire, interest in the natural world, or use of regional dialects and idioms.

- In the 20th century, genre fiction came to prominence through popular, sensational pulp novels. Genres such as children's literature, science fiction, mystery, and romance were given a boost beginning in the 1930s by the spread of the paperback book. The second half of the 20th century was marked by writers who challenged conformist ideas of the United States. The Beat Generation risked jail time for obscenity, while multicultural literature celebrated a multiplicity of voices and viewpoints.

- The 21st century has so far been dominated by a number of novel franchises with massive sales and multiple marketing tie-ins.

Exercises

Consider a novel or book from any era in U.S. history that has made an impression on you. Research this book on the Internet to discover how it played a part in shaping U.S. popular culture, how culture shaped the book in question, or both. Then, answer the following questions:

- What was the social or cultural climate at the time of its publication?

- What was the initial critical reception? Did opinions of the book change over time?

- At what point was the book most popular?

- Does the book belong to a larger movement? Was it a reaction against a political moment or literary movement that came before?

References

Baym, Nina. introduction to *The Norton Anthology of American Literature* (New York: W. W. Norton & Company, 2007) A:1–14.

Darnton, Robert. *The Kiss of Lamourette: Reflections in Cultural History* (New York: W. W. Norton & Company, 1996).

Foster, Hannah Webster. *The Boarding School; or, Lessons of a Preceptress to Her Pupils* (1829; repr., Whitefish, MT: Kessinger Publishing, 2010).

Ginsberg, Allen. *Howl*, ed. Miles Barry, (New York: Harper Perennial, 1995).

PBS, Africans in America Resource Bank, "Slave Narratives and *Uncle Tom's Cabin*, 1845–1862," PBS, http://www.pbs.org/wgbh/aia/part4/4p2958.html.

Raskin, Johan. *American Scream: Allen Ginsberg's "Howl" and the Making of the Beat Generation* (Berkeley: University of California Press, 2006).

Twain, Marc. *The Adventures of Huckleberry Finn* (1885; repr., New York: Harper & Brothers, 1912).

Winship, Micheal. "Two Early American Bestsellers," *Common-place* 9, no. 3 (2009), http://www.common-place.org/vol-09/no-03/winship/.

3.4 Major Book Formats

Learning Objectives

1. Determine the role of hardcover books in the publishing industry.
2. Identify the differences in the two major formats of paperback books.
3. Recognize the changes that e-books bring to the publishing industry.

From ancient Egyptian papyrus scrolls to scrollable 21st-century e-books, a book can come in many different formats. However, in some ways, it seems like the more things change, the more they stay the same. In the same way that early printed books were painstakingly illuminated to look more like medieval books, today's e-books use e-paper technology to mimic the look of a printed page. Even the hardcover books we're familiar with today are direct descendants of the ancient codex.

Hardcover

While the first codices enclosed bound papers between wooden covers (the word *codex* means *block of wood* in Latin), contemporary hardcover book covers are usually made of cardboard sheathed in cloth, paper, or leather. The printed pages of the book are either sewn or glued to the cover. Until the early 1800s, most books were sold unbound. A buyer would purchase a sheath of printed papers that would be bound either by the bookseller or by a commissioned bindery. British publisher William Pickering is considered the first publisher to issue books in uniform cloth bindings in 1820. About a decade later, dust jackets, the detachable outer covers that sheathe most hardback books today, arrived on the scene. Dust jackets were initially meant only as a protective covering for the binding, but soon they became a place where designers could create a colorful and distinctive cover for a book.

Figure 3.9

Original dust jackets are especially important for book collectors—a first edition of F. Scott Fitzgerald's *The Great Gatsby* without the dust jacket sells for around $3000; with the dust jacket intact, it can go for more than $30,000.

yoppy – The Great Gatsby – CC BY 2.0.

The durability of hardcover books makes them attractive to both authors and book purchasers. However, the competitive economics of today's publishing industry means that some books are never issued in hardcover. Because hardcover books are more expensive to produce and almost always cost more than their paperback equivalents, publishers tend to reserve the format for books that they expect will sell well.

Based on projected sales, publishers must decide how big of a print run to order for a new hardcover book. A book's print run refers to all the copies made in one setup of the printing apparatus. A failed book may only have one, while a successful book may have 50 or more printings. Figuring out how many copies of a book to print is an inexact science, as publishers must essentially guess how well a book will sell. There is no standard size for a print run. The U.K. edition of the first *Harry Potter* book had an initial print run of only 500 copies; the U.S. print run of the seventh and final book in the series was a record-breaking 12 million. When an initial print run is sold out, the book is either reprinted (these copies are considered a second printing) or is considered out of print. The contemporary publishing industry will often issue a first-run hardcover printing, followed by subsequent paperback editions.

Paperback

Inexpensive paper-bound books have been around for centuries in formats like the chapbook, the British penny dreadful, and the American dime novel. However, the hardcover book, whether as an ancient codex or its contemporary equivalent, was the dominant format in the book world for thousands of years. The introduction of a new format in the 1930s, the paperback, was considered revolutionary. The so-called paperback revolution began during the Great Depression, when paperbacks were marketed as inexpensive alternatives to hardcover editions. Penguin Books, Ltd., the first majorly successful paperback publishing company, kept prices low by ordering large print runs and selling books in nontraditional retailers, such as Woolworth's drugstores. Penguin also broke the traditional paperback mold by avoiding pulp fiction entertainment novels and instead printing books that were both cheap and intellectually stimulating. Donald Porter Geddes, the editor of Pocket Books, the first paperback publishing house in the United States, spelled out this new approach to bookselling in 1944: "The best books apparently have the greatest appeal to the greatest number of people…the larger American public need no longer suffer from the delusion that it is intellectually inferior, or, from a literary point of view, lacking in any aspect in good taste, judgment, and appetite (Ogle, 1960)." By 1960, when paperback books first outsold hardcovers, these early paperback innovators were proved right.

While paperback publishing first issued only reprints of books that had already been issued in hardcover, paperback originals, books that had their initial print run as a paperback edition, emerged in the 1950s. Paperback originals were another step in helping to remove the stigma from the paperback book. In 1999, Jhumpa Lahiri's *The Interpreter of Maladies* was the first paperback original to win the Pulitzer Prize for fiction.

Today's books published in paperback are traditionally divided into two broad categories: mass-market paperbacks and trade paperbacks. Mass-market paperbacks are small, inexpensive editions that are sometimes issued after a hardcover edition, although many genre novels are printed only in mass-market paperback editions. Trade paperbacks are larger and generally of better quality. They're often printed on higher-quality paper (sometimes acid-free paper). If the trade paperback follows a hardcover release, the paperback will be the same size as the hardcover and will have the same pagination and page layout as the hardcover edition.

Traditionally, hardcover books have been seen as more prestigious than paperbacks, though that stereotype may be beginning to change. In recent years, some publishers of literary fiction were seeing 50 to 75 percent of the hardcover books they shipped to bookstores returned to them unsold. As a response, certain publishers opted to release books with uncertain sales potential as trade paperbacks, bypassing the hardcover format entirely. "Getting somebody to spend $22 on a book by an author who they've never heard of is hard, but getting them to spend $13.95 on a paperback is much easier," Random House's Jane von Mehren told *The New York Times* in 2006 (Wyatt, 2006). Some publishers are concerned that book reviewers don't take trade paperback editions as seriously, but that too may be slowly changing. Another publishing strategy is to release hardcover and trade paperback editions simultaneously rather than delaying the paperback edition for several months (or even years, in the case of exceptionally popular books). Such a technique is intended to drive up sales, taking advantage of initial publicity to capture readers who may be unwilling to pay the full hardcover price for a book.

Whatever the concerns that publishers may have about issuing paperbacks, the format is still dominant in the U.S. publishing industry. According to the American Association of Publishers (AAP), 35 percent of the books sold in 2009 were trade paperbacks; 35 percent hardcovers; 21 percent mass market paperbacks; 2 percent audio books; 2 percent e-books; and 5 percent "other (Eco-Libris)."

E-Books

The hardcover book's expensive, durable binding seemed to say that it was an object intended for posterity. If paperback books disrupted the traditional concept of books by making them cheaper and more portable, then the e-book is poised to cause an even greater change in how readers interact with a text. E-books, also known as electronic or digital books, are the digital media equivalent of printed books. That is, they are books read on the screen of an electronic device, whether a cell phone, personal computer, or dedicated e-book reader.

E-books differ from their print equivalents in many significant ways. For one, there's no physical production cost, which means that e-books are generally less expensive than traditional books. There's also no cost to store or transport e-books. Because an e-book's publisher doesn't need to order a set print run, a text issued as an e-book doesn't ever have to go out of print. E-books also appeal to readers who want instant gratification. Instead of having to travel to a brick-and-mortar bookstore or wait for a delivery, a reader can download an e-book in a matter of minutes.

Early e-books were mostly technical manuals or digitized versions of works in the public domain. As the Internet took off and as electronic devices became increasingly mobile, book publishers began to issue digital editions of their works. In the first decade of the 21st century, various companies began issuing software and hardware platforms for electronic books, each competing for dominance in this emerging market.

Although e-books make up only a small percentage of total book sales, that number is growing. Dan Brown's *The Lost Symbol*, the follow up to his massively popular novel *The Da Vinci Code*, sold more copies as a Kindle e-book than as a hardcover in the first few days after its September 2009 release. However, e-book successes have led to a threat that faces many kinds of digital content: online piracy. Only a few days after its initial release, Brown's novel had been illegally downloaded more than 100,000 times. Some authors and publishers are concerned that Internet users expect free content and will find a way around spending money on e-books. American novelist Sherman Alexie recently voiced some of these anxieties, "With the open-source culture on the Internet, the idea of ownership—of artistic ownership—goes away (Frisch, 2010)." Other prominent authors have reacted to the e-book in various ways. In 2000, Stephen King published his novella *Riding the Bullet* as a digital file that could only be read on a computer; in contrast, J. K. Rowling has stated that the *Harry Potter* novels won't ever be released as e-books (McHugh, 2005). However, piracy has struck Rowling's novels as well. Every *Harry Potter* novel is available in pirated form, either as a scanned copy or one that was manually typed out by fans.

Another concern with e-books is the possibility of digital decay. All an e-book is, after all, is a collection of data saved to a disk. It turns out that digital formats tend to decay much faster than their physical counterparts (Bollacker, 2010). The swift turnover of digital devices is another concern; the possibility exists that a book bought on a Kindle device in 2010 will be not be compatible with an equivalent device in 2035 or even 2015.

E-book sales still make up a small part of the overall book market, 3 to 5 percent by most estimates, but their sales increased by 177 percent in 2009. *The New Yorker* cites a projection that e-books will someday account for between 25 and 50 percent of all book sales (Auletta, 2010). And with newer models of e-book readers, such as the iPad, boasting full color screens and the ability to embed web links and video in a book's text, e-books may fundamentally reshape how people read in the future.

Key Takeaways

- Hardcover books are a direct descendant of the ancient codex. Because they are more durable and more expensive, they are considered more prestigious than paperback books. Traditionally, publishers order an initial print run in hardcover, followed by a paperback release.

- Paperback books are popular because they are more portable and less expensive than their hardcover equivalents are. Books issued in paperback can be either mass market paperbacks or trade paperbacks, which are pricier and higher quality. To stay competitive and to attract customers, publishers are releasing some novels simultaneously in hardcover and paperback; other books skip hardcover and are released as paperback originals.

- Although they make up only 3 to 5 percent of current sales, e-books have the potential to transform the book market. Gaining currency with customers only in recent years, the e-book has the advantage of being cheaper and more portable than even most paperbacks. Some concerns with e-books include the prevalence of piracy and the potential for digital decay.

Exercises

Create a list of the three book formats mentioned in this section, and then answer the following questions:

- What are the features, advantages, and drawbacks of each format?
- How do they differ? How are they the same?
- What type of person might each format appeal to?
- Which format do you prefer the most, and why?

References

Auletta, Ken. "Publish or Perish," Annals of Communication, *New Yorker*, April 26, 2010.

Bollacker, Kurt D. "Avoiding a Digital Dark Age," *American Scientist* 98, no. 3 (2010): 106.

Eco-Libris, "Some Facts About the Book Publishing Industry," Eco-Libris, http://www.ecolibris.net/bookpublish.asp.

Frisch, Matt. "Digital Piracy Hits the E-book Industry," *CNN*, January 1, 2010, http://www.cnn.com/2010/TECH/01/01/ebook.piracy/index.html.

McHugh, John B. "J. K. Rowling Refuses E-books for Potter," *USA Today*, June 14, 2005, http://www.usatoday.com/life/books/news/2005-06-14-rowling-refuses-ebooks_x.htm.

Ogle, "The Paperback Revolution."

Wyatt, Edward. "Literary Novels Going Straight to Paperback," *New York Times*, March 22, 2006, Books section.

3.5 Current Publishing Trends

Learning Objectives

1. Indicate the effect of blockbuster syndrome on the publishing industry.
2. Recognize how book superstores have changed the business of bookselling.
3. Identify the causes and results of price wars in the book industry.

The last few decades have seen a sharp rise in electronic entertainment. In 2009, the average American spent 56 percent of his or her free time watching TV, and less than 7 percent of his or her free time reading (Bureau of Labor Statistics, 2010). Video game sales rose 19 percent in 2008 alone and have continued to climb (MSNBC, 2009). In a world full of diverting entertainments, each clamoring for people's time, the publishing industry is endeavoring to do everything it can to capture readers' attention.

Blockbuster Syndrome

Imagine this scenario: A young author has spent the last few years slaving over his novel, rewriting and revising until the whole thing is polished, exciting, and fresh. He sends out his manuscript and is lucky enough to find a literary agent eager to support his work. The agent sells the book to a publisher, netting the author a decent advance; the book goes on to get great reviews, win some awards, and sell 20,000 copies. To most people, this situation sounds like a dream come true. But in an increasingly commercialized publishing industry, with a focus on finding the next blockbuster, this burgeoning author could be at risk of not getting his contract renewed.

In an industry increasingly dominated by large media corporations with obligations to stockholders, publishers feel pressured to turn a profit. As a result, they tend to bank on sure-fire best sellers, books that are expected to sell millions (or tens of millions) of copies, regardless of literary merit. The industry's growing focus on a few best-selling authors, called blockbuster syndrome, often means less support and less money for the vast majority of writers who don't sell millions of copies.

An advance is a sum of money paid to the author in expectation of future royalties. Royalties are a percentage of the book's sale price. So if a publisher gives an author a $10,000 advance, the author has immediate access to that money, but the first $10,000 worth of royalties goes to the publisher. After that, the author accumulates royalties for every book sold. In this way, an advance is a cross between a loan and a gamble. If the book doesn't sell well, the author doesn't have to pay back the advance; however, he or she won't earn any additional money from royalties. However, as many as three-quarters of books don't earn back their advances, meaning that their authors aren't making any money from sales at all.

Publishers and writers are notoriously hush-hush about the actual sums of advances. A recent *New York Times* article estimated an average advance to be around $30,000, though actual figures vary widely. Keeping in mind that a book may take years to write, it's clear that many authors are barely eking out a living from their books.

Figure 3.10 All Advances Aren't Equal

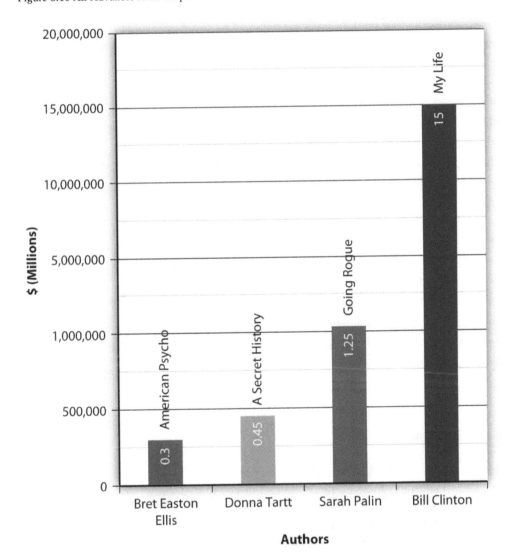

Bret Easton Ellis, *American Psycho*: $300,000 (Benatar, 1990).

Donna Tartt, *A Secret History*: $450,000 (Allen, 1992)

Sarah Palin, *Going Rogue*: $1.25 million (Rosen, 2009)

Bill Clinton, *My Life*: $15 million (McIntire, 2008)

These days, though, most of the media attention is focused on the few books each year that earn their authors huge advances and go on to sell massive numbers of copies—the blockbusters. But the focus on blockbusters can have a damaging effect on emerging writers. Because publishing is a gamble, advances to new or unproven writers are generally low. Additionally, because a publishing house wants to recoup its initial investment, a book that earned an author a big advance will probably get a big publicity budget. Unfortunately, the flip side is also true; a small advance equals a small publicity budget, which can trap many authors in a vicious circle. In most cases, a book without much promotion won't have the chance to become a hit. If the book isn't a hit, the publisher can justify an even lower advance for the next book and a lower budget for promotion. The result is that many books by emerging authors get lost in the shuffle. "It used to be that the first book earned a modest advance, then you would build an audience over time and break even on the third or fourth book," Morgan Entrekin, the publisher of Grove/Atlantic, told *The New York Times*. "Now the first book is expected to land a huge advance and huge sales.... Now we see a novelist selling 9,000 hardcovers and 15,000 paperbacks, and they see themselves as a failure (Bureau of Labor Statistics)."

Potential blockbusters come at a high price for the publisher as well. They threaten to eat up publicity budgets and dominate publishers' attention. An extremely large advance will only pay off if a massive number of copies sell, which makes the publishing houses less likely to take a gamble on unconventional books. This can also lead to a glut of similar books being pushed by publishers. After Dan Brown's huge success with *The Da Vinci Code* in 2003, publishers rushed to capitalize on its success by releasing similar art history–conspiracy–mystery thrillers, few of which interested readers.

To a certain extent, focusing on blockbusters has worked for the publishing industry. Today's best sellers sell more copies than best sellers did 10 years ago and make up a larger share of the market. However, overall book sales have remained relatively flat over the past 8 years (Association of American Publisher, 2011). In other words, it's not that more books are being sold; it's just that more of the sales are taken up by a few heavily promoted blockbusters. However, the blockbuster syndrome threatens to damage the industry in other ways. In a best-seller-driven system, literature becomes a commodity, with little value placed on a book's artistic merit. Instead, the primary concern is whether or not it will sell.

Authors Say "No" to Blockbuster Syndrome

Discontented with the industry's focus on blockbusters at the expense of other books, some authors are taking control of publishing their materials. John Edgar Wideman, a celebrated author who has been a finalist for the National Book Award and is the only writer to have twice won the International PEN/Faulkner Award, had published more than 20 books through the traditional publishing system. But by the time he was looking for a home for his new collection of short stories, *Briefs: Stories for the Palm of the Mind*, he was ready for something new. "The blockbuster syndrome is a feature of our social landscape that has gotten out of hand," Wideman said. "Unless you become a blockbuster, your book disappears quickly. It becomes not only publish or perish, but sell or perish (Reid, 2010)." Wideman eventually decided to team up with self-publishing service Lulu, which meant that he gave up a traditional contract and advance payment in favor of greater control and a higher percentage of royalties. Other authors are turning away from the Big Six publishers and seeking out independent publishing houses, which often offer a different model. McSweeney's offers low advances and splits all profits with the author evenly. Vanguard offers no advances, but gives authors high royalties and guarantees a high marketing budget. These nontraditional systems allow authors more flexibility at a time when the publishing industry is facing rapid change. As Wideman puts it, "I like the idea of being in charge. I have more control over what happens to my book. And I have more control over whom I reach (Reid, 2010)."

Rise (and Fall?) of Book Superstores

Figure 3.11

Small independent bookstores find it hard to compete with multibillion-dollar corporations.

library_mistress – My first library workplace – CC BY-SA 2.0; Mike Mozart – Barnes & Noble Book Store – CC BY 2.0.

In the late 20th century, a new group of colossal bookstores reshaped the retail sale of books in the United States. Two of the most well-known and prevalent book retailers, Barnes & Noble and Borders (the largest and second-largest book retailers in the United States, respectively) expanded extensively by building book superstores in the late 1980s and early 1990s. These large retail outlets were different from traditional, smaller bookstores in several ways. They often sold many products other than books, including calendars, paper goods, and gifts. Many also housed in-store cafes, allowing patrons to browse books and sip lattes under the same roof. They were also physically bigger, and such megastores drew customers because of their wide selection and their ability to offer books at deeply discounted prices.

Many independent bookstores couldn't compete with the large chains' discounts, wide selection, and upscale atmosphere. According to *Publishers Weekly*, independent booksellers' share of the book market fell from 58 percent in 1972 to 15.2 percent in 1999. The American Booksellers Association (ABA), a trade association of bookstores, notes that its membership peaked at 5,200 in 1991; by 2005, that number had declined by 65 percent to 1,791. The decline of the independent bookstore coincided with the consolidation of the publishing industry, and some supporters of independent bookstores see a link between the two. Richard Howorth—owner of Square Books—an independent bookstore in Oxford, Mississippi, told *Mother Jones* magazine that "when the independent bookselling market was thriving in the '70s and '80s, more books were being published, more people were reading books, the sales of books were higher, and publishers' profit margins were much greater. With the rise of the corporate retailing powers and the consolidation in publishing, all of those things have declined (Gurwitt, 2000)." Book superstores emphasized high turnover and high-volume sales, placing a higher emphasis on best sellers and returning some mass market paperbacks to publishers after only 6 weeks on the shelves.

In more recent years, the book superstores have been under threat themselves. In 2009, large retailers like Target, Wal-Mart, and Costco sold more books than both independent and chain bookstores combined: nearly 45 percent of the market (Auletta). These stores didn't specialize in books and tended to offer only a few heavily promoted blockbuster titles. Large discount stores were able to negotiate favorable deals with publishers, allowing them to discount books even further than the book superstores in some cases. In more recent years, book superstores have also faced a threat from the increasing number of books purchased online. By 2010, Amazon, the largest online bookseller, accounted for around 15 to 20 percent of book sales in the United States.

The shift away from independent bookstores and toward bigger retailers, such as book superstores or nonspecialized retailers like Wal-Mart, has benefited the industry in some ways, most notably by making books cheaper and more widely available. Mega best sellers, such as the *Harry Potter* and *Twilight* series, were able to set sales records at least in part because the books were available for purchase in malls, convenience stores, supermarkets, and other nontraditional venues. However, overall book sales have not risen. And though consumers may be paying less for the books they're buying through these retailers, something may be lost as well. Jonathan Burnham, a publisher from HarperCollins, discussed the value of independent bookstores with *The New Yorker*, noting how they are similar to community centers: "There's a serendipitous element involved in browsing…. We walk in and know the people who work there and like to hear their reading recommendations."

Price Wars

Part of the reason book superstores were able to crowd out smaller, independent retailers was their ability to offer significant discounts on a book's cover price. Because the big chains sell more books, they can negotiate better deals with publishers and then pass the discounts to their customers. Not surprisingly, deep discounts appeal to customers, which is one reason the book superstores gained such a large share of the market in the 1990s. The superstores are able to sell books at such a sharp discount, sometimes even half of the listed price, because their higher sales numbers gives them bargaining power with the publishers. Independent bookstores buying the books at a normal wholesale rate (usually half the list price) are at a disadvantage; they can't offer deep discounts and, as a result, they must charge higher prices than the superstores. This deep discount policy is one reason best-seller sales have risen over the past decade (book superstores usually slash the prices of best sellers and new releases only). However, large discounts encourage high-volume selling, and emphasizing on high-volume selling encourages safe publishing choices. That is, the bookstores are able to make up for the big discounts only by selling tons of copies, and the books most likely to sell this well are blockbuster works by known-quantity authors. The threat of deep discounting to independent bookstores and its effect on the publishing industry has led some European countries to regulate prices. For example, bookstores in France are prohibited from discounting more than 5 percent, and in Germany, price slashing can only happen 9 months after a book's release.

Figure 3.12

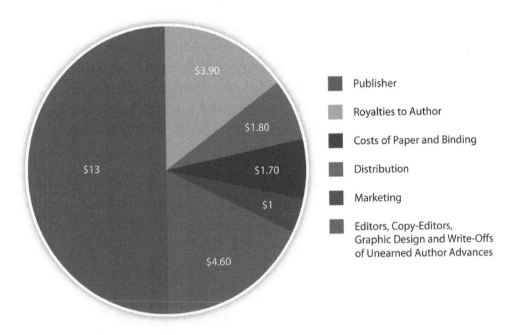

Why do books cost so much?

The brick-and-mortar bookstores aren't the only book discounters in the mix. Wal-Mart and other discount retailers sell more copies of the few books they offer at their stores, so they can negotiate even more favorable terms with publishers. Amazon, which dominates online book sales, routinely discounts books 20 percent or more.

Recently, other online retailers have been battling with Amazon for online bookselling profits. In October 2009, as retailers were preparing for the holiday season, Amazon and Wal-Mart were preparing to compete for sales. When Wal-Mart announced that it would lower preorder prices for 10 highly anticipated hardcover books to only $10, Amazon responded by matching that price the next day. Wal-Mart then lowered its price to $9, and Amazon followed. Unwilling to give up the fight, Wal-Mart lowered its prices by a penny, listing the 10 books at $8.99. Then another online retailer, Target, joined the fray, matching Wal-Mart's price. Wal-Mart dropped its list prices again by a penny, listing the books at $8.98 (Gregory, 2009).

While there's something almost comical about major retailers duking it out over pennies, it's also a situation that looked quite sobering to book retailers, from the independents to the large chains. The startling thing about the price wars among Amazon, Target, and Wal-Mart was that no one involved expected to make any money from these deeply discounted books. At $9 or less, these books were almost certainly selling at below retail value, perhaps by quite a lot.

If a book's list price is $35, its wholesale price is usually around half of that, in this case $17. If that book is priced at $9, that means an $8 loss to the retailer per copy. Although at first this seems like blatantly bad business, it works because all of these retailers are in the business of selling much more than just books. Large online retailers use the deep discounts to lure customers to their websites in hopes that these customers will purchase other items. These book sales are valuable as a way to drive traffic to the retailer's website. However, booksellers whose main business is still selling books, such as local independent bookstores, don't have this luxury.

E-books have also entered into the retail struggle. Because there are no printing costs, e-books are relatively cheap to make, and consumers expect to see the savings on their end. However, book publishers still sell the books to distributors at wholesale prices—about half of the retail value of the hardcover version. To tempt buyers, companies such as Amazon charge only $9.99 for the average e-title, once again taking a loss (Stone & Rich, 2009). Many hope to make up for it with device sales—consumers are more likely to spend hundreds of dollars on an inexpensive reader to access cheaper books. While major retailers may eventually profit from this method of sales, many wonder how long it will last. Author David Baldacci argues that a book industry based solely on profit isn't sustainable. In the end, he argues, "there won't be anyone selling [books] anymore because you just can't make any money (Rich, 2009)."

The inclination to focus only on net profits is indicative of a larger trend in the book industry. Retailers are getting larger, consumer prices are getting lower, and popular books are receiving the majority of attention. While this has positive short-term results for consumers and large retailers, the effects are devastating for most authors and smaller bookstores. Although, in the end, the introduction of e-books may be no more harmful to the industry than the explosion of paperbacks was in the early 1900s, the larger emphasis on quantity over quality threatens the literary value and sustainability of books.

Key Takeaways

- Blockbuster syndrome refers to the publishing industry's focus on books with best-seller potential at the expense of works that may not sell as well. Fueled by high advances that depend on high publicity budgets for high sales, less-popular authors often get lost in the shuffle. Such a system evaluates books on the basis of their commercial potential instead of their literary merit. Fed up with what they see as the industry's exclusive focus on blockbusters, some authors are turning away from the Big Six publishers and are opting for different publishing models.

- Book superstores rose to prominence in the 1990s because their low prices, large selection, and upscale atmosphere made them popular with book buyers. As a result, large numbers of independent bookstores closed. In recent years, the book superstores have been losing market share to large retailers such as Wal-Mart and Costco. These stores don't focus on selling books, and so they only have the shelf space for a few best sellers, thus helping to fuel the blockbuster syndrome. Additionally, brick-and-mortar stores are coming under threat from Amazon and other online retailers.

- Stores that sell a large volume of books are able to negotiate favorable terms with book publishers and they are then able to pass along deep discounts to their customers. Smaller independent bookstores are not able to do this, and so are less economically competitive. Recent price wars have erupted among online retailers like Amazon, Wal-Mart, and Target, who competed to sell books and e-books at prices so low they amounted to a net loss per sale. Retailers used these sales to drive business to their websites and to encourage customers to buy other products.

Exercises

Examine a recent list of best sellers (some lists to consider include those by *The New York Times, USA Today*, Book Sense, or *The Washington Post*). Complete a web search for the top-10 authors to see if they have published books previously and if their previous books were also on best-seller lists. Some questions to consider: Are the books part of a series or novel franchise? Do the books have film tie-ins? What conclusions can you draw from your research?

Write down two books, one a current or recent best seller and the other a book that was published at least 5 years ago. Look up the books' prices on Amazon and note both the list price and Amazon's sale price. Then find the price of the same book at a local chain bookstore and an independent bookseller. What factors might account for any differences in pricing? How might these prices have changed in recent years?

References

Allen, Brooke. "Panpipes and Preppies," review of *The Secret History,* by Donna Tartt, *New Criterion*, October 1992, Books, http://www.newcriterion.com/articles.cfm/Panpipes—preppies-4619.

Association of American Publishers, "AAP Publishers Report Strong Growth in Year-to-Year, Year-End Book Sales," press release, February 16, 2011.

Auletta, "Publish or Perish."

Benatar, Giselle. "American Psychodrama," *Entertainment Weekly*, November 30, 1990, http://www.ew.com/ew/article/0,,318714,00.html.

Gregory, Sean. "Walmart, Target, Amazon: Book Price War Heats Up," *Time*, October 27, 2009, http://www.time.com/time/business/article/0,8599,1932426,00.html.

Gurwitt, Rob. "Light in Oxford," *Mother Jones*, May/June 2000.

McIntire, Mike. "Clintons Made $109 Million in Last 8 Years," *New York Times*, April 5, 2008, http://www.nytimes.com/2008/04/05/us/politics/05clintons.html?_r=2.

MSNBC, Associated Press, "Video Game Sales Top $21 Billion in 2008," *Games on msnbc.com*, January

15, 2009, http://www.msnbc.msn.com/id/28682836/ns/technology_and_science-games/t/video-game-sales-top-billion/.

Reid, Calvin. "John Edgar Wideman to Self-Publish New Book Via Lulu.com," *Publishers Weekly*, March 5, 2010.

Rich, Mokoto. "Steal This Book (for $9.99)," *New York Times*, May 16, 2009, http://www.nytimes.com/2009/05/17/weekinreview/17rich.html.

Rosen, Yereth. "Palin's Financial Disclosure: $1.25 mln advance for 'Going Rouge'," *Reuters*, October 27, 2009, http://blogs.reuters.com/frontrow/2009/10/27/palins-financial-disclosure-125-mln-advance-for-going-rogue/.

Stone, Brad and Motoko Rich, "Sony to Cut E-Book Prices and Offer New Readers," *New York Times*, August 4, 2009, http://www.nytimes.com/2009/08/05/technology/personaltech/05sony.html.

U.S. Department of Labor, Bureau of Labor Statistics, *American Time Use Survey*, Table 11, "Time spent in leisure and sports activities for the civilian population by selected characteristics, 2009 annual averages," June 22, 2010, http://www.bls.gov/news.release/atus.t11.htm.

U.S. Department of Labor, Bureau of Labor Statistics, *American Time Use Survey*, Table 11.

3.6 The Influence of New Technology

Learning Objectives

1. Determine the benefits and drawbacks of digital libraries.
2. Define *print-on-demand* and *self-publishing*.

The book industry has changed enormously since its creation. From the invention of the papyrus scroll to the introduction of the e-book, new technologies continuously affect how people view and experience literature. With the advent of digital media, old-media industries, such as the book industry, must find ways to adapt. Some fear that this new technology will destroy the industry, while others maintain that it works to the industry's advantage. However, one thing is clear—digital technology promises to reshape the publishing industry as we know it.

E-Books

The first e-book readers were related to the personal digital assistant (PDA) devices, pocket-sized electronics that could store and display large amounts of text, that became popular in the 1990s. However, early e-book readers lingered on the market, popular in certain techy niches but unable to gain traction with the wider population. Early e-readers had minimal battery life and text that was difficult to read. Through the 2000s, technological advances allowed for smaller and sleeker models, the Apple iPhone and the iPad helped make readers more comfortable with reading on a small screen. The second half of the decade saw the release of many e-readers. The technology got a boost when Oprah Winfrey praised the Kindle on her show in October 2008. By that holiday season, e-book reader sales were booming, and it wasn't just the technologically savvy individuals who were interested anymore. Despite being criticized by some as providing an inferior reading experience to dedicated e-readers, the Apple iPad has been a powerful driving force behind e-book sales—more than 1.5 million books were downloaded on the Apple iPad during its first month of release in 2010 (Maneker, 2010).

E-books make up less than 5 percent of the current book market, but that number is growing. At the beginning of 2010, Amazon had about 400,000 titles available for the Kindle device. Some devices offer wireless accessibility, meaning that an e-reader doesn't have to be connected to a computer to access titles; an open Wi-Fi connection is all it needs. With access to a dazzling array of books available with just a few clicks, it's no wonder the contemporary consumer seems enamored with the e-book. An e-book reader has the space to store thousands of titles in an object smaller and lighter than the average hardcover novel. And though the devices themselves can be expensive, e-books are usually cheaper than their hardcopy equivalents; sometimes they're even free. Thanks to efforts like the Gutenberg Project and Google Books (see the following section), more than a million public domain titles are available as free e-books.

Anything that gets people excited about books and reading should be good for the publishing industry, right? Unfortunately for U.S. publishers, it's not that simple. Some publishers worry that e-book sales may actually end up hurting their bottom lines. During the Kindle's first year, Amazon essentially set the standard price for bestselling or new release e-books at $9.99. Since Amazon was acting as a wholesaler and buying these books for half the publisher's list price—generally around $25 for a new hardcover—the company was selling these titles at a loss. However, for Amazon, a short-term loss might have had long-term payoffs. At the start of 2010, the company controlled a 90 percent share of the e-book market. Faced with e-books that cost less than $10, traditional publishers worried that consumers would avoid purchasing a new hardcover priced at $25 (or even a $13 trade paperback).

Figure 3.13

Most e-readers are the size and shape of one hardcover book.

ndh – Kobo eReader – CC BY-NC 2.0.

In January 2010, the conflict between Amazon and the publishing establishment came to a head. Macmillan, one of the six major publishing companies in the United States, suggested a new business model to Amazon, one that resembled the deal that the Big Six publishers had worked out with Apple for e-book sales on the Apple iPad. Essentially, Amazon had been able to buy books from publishers at wholesale rates—half the hardcover list price—and then set whatever retail price it wanted. This allowed Amazon to choose to sell books at a loss in the hope of convincing more people to buy Kindles. Macmillan proposed a system in which Amazon would act more as a commission-earning agent than a wholesaler. In Macmillan's proposed model, the publisher would set the retail price and take 70 percent of each sale, leaving 30 percent for the retailer. Macmillan couldn't force Amazon to agree to this deal, but the publisher could strike a hard bargain: If Amazon refused Macmillan's offer, it could still sell Macmillan titles under the wholesale model, but the publisher would delay e-book editions for 7 months after hardcover releases. What followed was a standoff. Amazon didn't just reject Macmillan's proposal; it removed the "buy" button from all Macmillan books listed on its website (including print books), essentially refusing to sell Macmillan titles. However, after a few days, Amazon capitulated and agreed to Macmillan's terms, but not before issuing a strongly worded press release claiming that they agreed to sell Macmillan's titles "at prices we believe are needlessly high for e-books," because "Macmillan has a monopoly over their own titles (Rich & Stone, 2010)." Still, Macmillan and the other publishers seem to have won this battle: Amazon agreed that e-books for most new fiction and nonfiction books for adults will be priced at $12.99 to $14.99, though best sellers will still be $9.99 (Rich & Stone, 2010).

But the $10 book may be the least of the publishing industry's worries. At the start of 2010, more than half of the bestselling titles on Kindle were free. Some of these were public domain novels such as *Pride and Prejudice*, but many others were books by living authors being promoted by publishers by giving away the book. The industry hasn't yet come to a consensus about the utility of free e-books. Some publishers consider it a practice that devalues books in the eyes of customers. "At a time when we are resisting the $9.99 price of e-books," David Young of the Hachette Book Group told *The New York Times*, "it is illogical to give books away for free (Rich, 2010)." Other publishers consider free e-books a promotional tool to build word-of-mouth and to introduce readers to new authors.

Other e-books emerge from outside the traditional publishing system. Four of the five bestselling novels in Japan in 2007 were cell phone novels, books that were both written and intended to be read on cell phones. Cell-phone novels are traditionally written by amateurs who post them on free websites. Readers can download copies at no cost, which means no one is making much of a profit from this new genre. Although the phenomenon has not caught on in the United States yet, the cell phone novel is feared by some publishers as a further sign of the devaluation of books in a world where browsers expect content to be free.

With e-book sales expected to triple by 2015, it's hard to say what such a quickly growing industry will look like in the future (McQuivy, 2010). Some people have theorized that e-readers will lead to an increasing popularity of the short story, which can be bought and read in short increments. Others have claimed that they'll destroy the book industry as we know it. Whatever the future of books looks like, everything—from the way books are produced to the way we read them—continues to change rapidly because of new technologies.

Digitizing Libraries

The idea of a digitized library has been around since the early years of the Internet. A digital library stores its materials in a digital format, accessible by computers. Some digital libraries can be accessed locally; others can be accessed remotely through a computer network. Michael Hart founded Project Gutenberg, the oldest digital library, in 1971, 3 years before the Internet went live. Hart's initial goal was to make 10,000 of the most-consulted books publicly available and free by the end of the century. The forward-thinking Hart named his project after the inventor of the movable type printing press, perhaps realizing that book digitization had the potential to revolutionize the way humans produce and read books as much as Gutenberg's invention had centuries earlier. At first, the process was slow for Hart and his fellow book-digitizing volunteers because they were forced to copy text manually until 1989. In the early 1990s, scanners and text-recognition software allowed them to somewhat automate the process.

Fast-forward to 2010. Project Gutenberg's free online library boasts more than 30,000 public domain works available for free download. Stanford University uses a robotic page-turning scanner machine to digitize 1,000 book pages an hour. Stanford's partner in digital library production is Google Books, which has scanned over 10 million books since it began Google Books in 2004. A Chinese company claims to have digitized more than half of all books that have been published in Chinese since 1949. In 2006, *The New York Times* estimated that humans have published at least 32 million books throughout history; the huge push for book digitization makes it seem entirely possible that nearly all known books could be digitized within 50 years (Kelly).

Some liken the prospect of these widely accessible, easily searchable, free libraries to the proliferation of free libraries in the 19th century, which led to a surge in literacy rates. One of Project Gutenberg's stated goals is "to break down the bars of ignorance and illiteracy" through its library of digitized books (Hart & Newby, 2004). Digital libraries make a huge selection of texts available to people with Internet access, giving them the amazing potential to democratize knowledge. As Bill McCoy, the general manager of Adobe's e-publishing business, told *The New York Times* in 2006, "Some of us have thousands of books at home, can walk to wonderful big-box bookstores and well-stocked libraries and can get Amazon.com to deliver next day. The most dramatic effect of digital libraries will be not on us, the well-booked, but on the billions of people worldwide who are underserved by ordinary paper books (Hart & Newby, 2004)." Digitized libraries can make fragile materials available to browsers without damaging originals; academic libraries are also able to share important texts without shipping books across the country.

Google Books, the largest online library, is not run by an academic institution, though it does claim several as partners. The bulk of free digital books available from Google Books or elsewhere come from the public domain, which constitutes approximately 15 percent of all books. Google Books has made over a million of these titles fully and freely searchable and downloadable. Other works in the Google Books digital library include in-print texts whose publishers have worked out a deal with Google. Some of these titles have their full text available online; others allow only a limited number of page previews. As part of its partnership with publishers, a Google Books search result will often provide links to the publisher's website and to booksellers.

Google Books ran into trouble, however, when it began to digitize the millions of books with unclear legal status, such as out-of-print works that weren't yet in the public domain. Many of these are considered orphan works, meaning that no one is exactly sure who owns their copyright. In 2004, the site announced plans to scan these texts and to make them searchable, but it would only show sentence-long snippets to searchers. Copyright holders could ask Google to remove these snippets at any time. Google claimed that this digitization plan would benefit authors, whose books would no longer linger in out-of-print limbo; it would also help researchers and readers, who would be able to locate (and perhaps purchase) previously unavailable works.

Publishers and authors did not agree with Google. Many objected to Google's plan to scan first and look into copyright ownership later; others saw Google's profiting from works still under copyright as a clear violation of intellectual property law. In 2005, the Authors Guild of America and the American Association of Publishers (AAP) sued Google for "massive copyright infringement." Google argued that it was essentially creating a massive online card catalog; the Authors Guild and AAP alleged that Google was attempting to monopolize information and profit from it. In 2008, Google agreed to a $125 million settlement with the publishers and the Authors Guild. Some of that money would go directly to copyright holders; some would pay for legal fees; and some would go to found the Book Rights Registry, an independent nonprofit association that would ensure content users (like Google) are paying copyright owners. Copyright owners would get money from Google and from potential book sales; Google would get money from advertisers, book sales, and institutional subscriptions by libraries.

Still, not everyone agreed with the decision. The Open Book Alliance was formed by a diverse partnership of organizations, including Amazon, Internet Archive, and the National Writers Union, who fear that Google's proprietary control of so much copyrighted material was an antitrust violation. As the group states on its website:

We will assert that any mass book digitization and publishing effort be open and competitive. The process of achieving this promise must be undertaken in the open, grounded in sound public policy and mindful of the need to promote long-term benefits for consumers rather than isolated commercial interests. The Open Book Alliance will counter Google, the Association of American Publishers and the Authors' [sic] Guild's scheme to monopolize the access, distribution and pricing of the largest digital database of books in the world.

Another concern, which was mentioned earlier, in the digital library world is digital decay. One librarian at Harvard University told *The New York Times* that "we don't really have any methodology [to preserve digital material] as of yet…. We just store the disks in our climate-controlled stacks, and we're hoping for some kind of universal Harvard guidelines (Cohen, 2010)."

Print-on-Demand and Self-Publishing

Part of what made Gutenberg's printing press so revolutionary was that it allowed books to be mass produced. In medieval times, readers often commissioned a scribe to copy a text by hand, a process that could take months or even years. But despite their many conveniences, printed books carry their own risks for authors and publishers. Producing books in bulk means that publishers are taking a gamble, attempting to publish enough books to satisfy demand, but not so many that unwanted copies linger in warehouses. When a book doesn't sell as much as expected, the publisher may end up taking a loss if the costs of publishing the book exceed the revenue from its sale. Interestingly, modern technology has made it feasible for some authors and publishers to turn to an updated version of the medieval model of producing books on demand for specific customers, allowing them to avoid the risk of carrying a large inventory of books that may or may not sell. Print-on-demand, a system in which a book is printed only after an order is received, and the increasing trend of self-publishing may reshape the industry in the 21st century.

Self-publishing—a system that involves an author, not a third-party company, being in charge of producing and publishing a work—is not a new concept. Many authors self-published works in their lifetimes, including Virginia Woolf and Oscar Wilde. More recently, popular books like *The Joy of Cooking* and the *Chicken Soup for the Soul* series had their origins in self-publishing. Many authors also self-publish when they're unable to get support from the traditional publishing world. Daniel Suarez's techno-thriller *Daemon* was rejected by 48 agents before he opted for self-publishing. After creating interest on blogs, Suarez eventually got a two-book deal with Dutton, an imprint of Random House (McHugh, 2008). Additionally, self-publishing can be an attractive option for authors who want control over their own content. Instead of leaving decisions up to the publisher, authors can control their own editing, designing, and marketing.

One major challenge for authors who choose to strike out on their own is the stigma that's sometimes attached to self-published books. Until recent years, most self-published authors went through the so-called vanity presses, which charge writers a premium for published copies of their books. As the name implies, these types of self-publishing ventures were often seen as preying on writers' need to see their own work in print. To justify the cost of printing, a minimum order of a thousand copies was standard, and unless authors were able to find an audience, they had little hope of selling them all. Because there was no quality control and vanity presses would usually publish anyone with money, some readers were skeptical of self-published books. Major retailers and distributors generally refused to carry them, meaning that authors had to rely on their own marketing efforts to sell the books. Before the advent of the Internet, this usually meant either selling copies in person or relying on mail-order catalogs, neither of which is a very reliable way to sell enough copies to recoup costs.

However, beginning in the early 2000s, self-publishing has changed dramatically. Advances made in publishing technology have made it easier for self-published books to more closely resemble traditionally published ones. Free professional typesetting software has allowed writers to format their text for the page; Adobe Photoshop and similar programs have made image editing and graphic design feasible for amateurs and professionals. The Internet has revolutionized marketing and distribution, allowing authors of books about niche subjects to reach a worldwide audience. As a result, many new Internet-based self-publishing companies have sprung up, offering a variety of services. Some companies, such as Lulu Enterprises and CreateSpace, feature a low-cost service without many bells and whistles; others offer a package of services that may include professional editing, cover design, and marketing. The process has become streamlined as well. For example, to publish a book with Lulu, an author just has to upload a PDF of a properly formatted text file; decide what size, paper, and binding options to use; and make a cover using a premade template. Self-published books are generally quicker to produce and allow an author a higher share of the royalties, though it usually costs more on a per-book basis. As a result, self-published books often have a higher list price.

Whereas vanity publishers were stigmatized for charging authors sometimes thousands of dollars to publish their books, creating a book using the services of Lulu or CreateSpace doesn't cost the author anything. That's because users who upload their content aren't creating an actual, physical copy of a book; instead, they're essentially making a potential volume. With print-on-demand technology, books aren't printed until an order is placed, which significantly lowers the financial risk for self-publishers. Print-on-demand is especially useful for books with a limited or niche audience. Print-on-demand isn't only being used by self-publishers; both small presses and academic publishers are using the technology for older books without much of an audience. With print-on-demand, books that may only sell a few dozen copies a year can stay in print without the publisher having to worry about printing a full run of copies and being stuck with unsold inventory.

Although some self-published authors manage to find a huge audience, most don't. Bob Young, the founder of Lulu, told the *London Times* that his goal is to publish 1 million books that each sell 100 copies, rather than 100 books that sell 1 million copies each (Whitworth, 2006). Lulu and other enterprising self-publishers disrupt the traditional notion of the publishing house, which acted as a sort of gatekeeper for the book industry—ushering a few talented, lucky writers in and keeping others out. In the world of self-publishing, there are no barriers—anyone with a book in a PDF file can whip up a nice-looking paperback in under 1 hour. This has democratized the industry, allowing writers who had been rejected by the traditional publishers to find their own audience. But it has also meant that a lot of writing with little literary merit has been published as well. Additionally, if a best seller in the Lulu world is a book that sells 500 copies, as Bob Young told the *London Times*, then few authors are going to be able to make a living through self-publishing. Indeed, most of the self-publishing success stories involve writers whose self-published efforts sold well enough to get them a book deal with one of the traditional publishing houses, a sign that for better or for worse, the traditional publishing model still has the social cachet and sales to dominate the industry.

Key Takeaways

- E-books have been increasing in popularity with customers since the 1990s. However, the publishing industry is worried that setting the price for e-books at $9.99, as Amazon initially did for most titles, would turn consumers away from buying more expensive physical books. Amazon lost money on every $9.99 e-book but hoped that the low prices would act as an incentive to buy its e-book reader, the Kindle device. In 2010, Macmillan and other publishers forced Amazon to change its pricing model to give publishers more control over e-book prices.

- Digital libraries began with Project Gutenberg in 1971. Digitized books allow anyone with an Internet connection access to millions of volumes, and some advocates hope that digital libraries will lead to a rise in global literacy rates. Millions of books in the public domain are available for free download. Google Books, the largest digital library, has run into trouble with its plan to digitize as many books as possible, even books under current copyright. The Open Book Alliance accuses Google of monopolizing copyrighted content to make a profit.

- Self-publishing used to carry a social stigma as well as a high cost. Thanks to print-on-demand services, self-publishing is an increasingly popular option for amateur and professional writers. It appeals to authors who may have a niche audience or who want more control over their work. Print-on-demand makes it possible for books to never go out of print.

Exercises

Go to the website of a company that specializes in print-on-demand or self-publishing services and examine some of the books featured there. Then, answer the following questions:

- How do these books look similar in form and content to books you'd expect to find in your local bookstore? How do they look different?

- How do prices differ from some of the major retail chains? Are the prices more similar to e-book, paperback, or hardcover prices?

- Would you be willing to purchase a book on one of these sites? Why or why not?

End-of-Chapter Assessment

Review Questions

1.
Section 1

   a. What ancient book form did the codex replace, and why was the codex an improvement on that form?

   b. What is mechanical movable type, and how did it lead to the Gutenberg Revolution?

   c. What is copyright, and how has its legal interpretation changed over time?

   d. How has the publishing industry evolved since the invention of the printing press?

2.
Section 2

   a. How was 18th-century literature affected by the changing role of women during this period?

   b. What are some of the ways that authors tried to create a distinctive American style in the 19th century?

   c. What changes in American society were reflected by 20th-century literature?

3.
Section 3

   a. What are some of the advantages and disadvantages of hardcover books?

   b. What are the two kinds of paperback books, and how do they differ?

   c. What is an e-book, and how is it different from hardcopy books?

4.
Section 4

   a. What is blockbuster syndrome, and how does it affect the publishing industry?

   b. What factors led to the rise and decline of book superstores?

   c. How do price wars affect the publishing industry?

5.
Section 5

   a. What are some ways that e-books are changing the publishing industry?

   b. What are the benefits and drawbacks of digital libraries?

   c. What is print-on-demand, and how does it influence the book industry?

Critical Thinking Questions

1. One of the initial intentions of copyright law was to protect artists while also allowing a free market of ideas. Is copyright a good way to protect authors and their control over their work? Do you think copyright law means the same now as it did in the past? What are some concerns that are changing the meaning of copyright protection?

2. If the Gutenberg Revolution was a time when advances in technology led to rapid changes in culture and society, will e-books and digital libraries lead to a similarly revolutionary change in the way we live our lives? Why or why not?

3. The publishing industry is facing a time of rapid change. What are some factors threatening the traditional publishing mode, and what are some ways the industry could respond to these potential dangers?

4. What impact do blockbuster books have on the book industry? And on readers?

5. Some people argue that e-books will destroy the publishing industry, while others think that they'll be its savior. How have e-books begun to transform the publishing industry, and what impact do you think they will have in the future?

Career Connection

Publishing a book is no longer a simple thing. Authors have to contend with questions about copyright, movie rights, e-books, and blog publicity. In confusing times, literary agents act as writers' sidekicks. They discover new writers and then help those writers negotiate an increasingly complex market.

Read the article "A Book in You" from *The New Yorker* (http://www.newyorker.com/archive/2004/05/31/040531ta_talk_radosh), which discusses a literary agent who specializes in signing book deals with bloggers. Now, explore literary agent Betsy Lerner's blog at http://betsylerner.wordpress.com. After exploring for a bit, read the "About Me" section (the link is at the top). These two sites will help you answer the following questions:

1. Why does Kate Lee think that blogs are a good place to look for new authors to represent?

2. What can you tell about Betsy Lerner's attitude about the publishing industry from her blog? What about her attitude toward the writers she works with? What does she appear to find rewarding about her job?

3. Based on Betsy Lerner's blog, identify the daily work required to be an agent. What aspects of the job appear challenging and engaging? What seems to take up the most time?

References

Cohen, Patricia. "Fending Off Digital Decay, Bit by Bit," *New York Times*, March 15, 2010, Arts section.

Hart, Michael S. and Gregory B. Newby, "Project Gutenberg Principle of Minimal Regulation," Project

Gutenberg, 2004, http://www.gutenberg.org/wiki/ Gutenberg:Project_Gutenberg_Principle_of_Minimal_Regulation_ /_Administration_by_Michael_Hart_and_Greg_Newby.

Kelly, "Scan This Book!"

Maneker, Marion. "Parsing the iPad's Book Sale Numbers," *The Big Money*, May 4, 2010, http://www.thebigmoney.com/blogs/goodnight-gutenberg/2010/05/04/ibooks-vs-app-books-ipad.

McHugh, Josh. "How the Self-Published Debut *Daemon* Earned Serious Geek Cred," *Wired*, April 21, 2008.

McQuivy, James L. "eBook Buying Is About to Spiral Upward," Forrester Research: Making Leaders Successful Every Day, 2010, http://www.forrester.com/rb/Research/ebook_buying_is_about_to_spiral_upward/q/id/57664/t/ 2.

Rich, Mokoto. "With Kindle, the Best Sellers Don't Need to Sell," *New York Times*, January 23, 2010, Books section.

Rich, Mokoto. and Brad Stone, "Publisher Wins Fight With Amazon Over E-books," *New York Times*, January 31, 2010, Technology section.

Whitworth, Damian. "Publish and Be Downloaded," *Times* (London), March 8, 2006, Life and Style section.

Chapter 4: Newspapers

4.1 Newspapers

Newspaper Wars

Figure 4.1

The two major newspapers, the *The Wall Street Journal* and the *The New York Times*, battle for their place in the print world.

dennis crowley – Wall Street Journal – CC BY 2.0; Aaron Edwards – no-more-war – CC BY-NC 2.0.

On April 26, 2010, *Wired* magazine proclaimed that a "clash of the titans" between two major newspapers, *The Wall Street Journal* and *The New York Times*, was about to take place in the midst of an unprecedented downward spiral for the print medium (Burskirk, 2010). Rupert Murdoch, owner of *The Wall Street Journal*, had announced that his paper was launching a new section, one covering local stories north of Wall Street, something that had been part of *The New York Times'* focus since it first began over a century before. *New York Times* Chairman Arthur Sultzberger Jr. and CEO Janet Robinson pertly responded to the move, welcoming the new section and acknowledging the difficulties a startup can face when competing with the well-established *New York Times* (Burskirk, 2010).

Despite *The New York Times'* droll response, Murdoch's decision to cover local news indeed presented a threat to the newspaper, particularly as the two publications continue their respective moves from the print to the online market. In fact, some believe that *The Wall Street Journal*'s decision to launch the new section has very little to do with local coverage and everything to do with the Internet. Newspapers are in a perilous position: Traditional readership is declining even as papers are struggling to create a profitable online business model. Both *The Wall Street Journal* and *The New York Times* are striving to remain relevant as competition is increasing and the print medium is becoming unprofitable.

In light of the challenges facing the newspaper industry, *The Wall Street Journal*'s new section may have a potentially catastrophic effect on *The New York Times*. *Wired* magazine described the decision, calling it "two-pronged" to "starve the enemy and capture territory (Burskirk, 2010)." By offering advertising space at a discount in the new Metro section, *The Journal* would make money while partially cutting *The Times* off from some of its primary support. *Wired* magazine also noted that the additional material would be available to subscribers through the Internet, on smartphones, and on the iPad (Burskirk, 2010).

Attracting advertising revenue from *The New York Times* may give *The Wall Street Journal* the financial edge it needs to lead in the online news industry. As newspapers move away from print publications to online publications, a strong online presence may secure more readers and, in turn, more advertisers—and thus more revenue—in a challenging economic climate.

This emerging front in the ongoing battle between two of the country's largest newspapers reveals a problem the newspaper industry has been facing for some time. New York has long been a battleground for other newspapers, but before Murdoch's decision, these two papers coexisted peacefully for over 100 years, serving divergent readers by focusing on different stories. However, since the invention of radio, newspapers have worried about their future. Even though readership has been declining since the 1950s, the explosion of the Internet and the resulting accessibility of online news has led to an unprecedented drop in subscriptions since the beginning of the 21st century. Also hit hard by the struggling economy's reluctant advertisers, most newspapers have had to cut costs. Some have reinvented their style to appeal to new audiences. Some, however, have simply closed. As this struggle for profit continues, it's no surprise that *The Wall Street Journal* is trying to outperform *The New York Times*. But how did newspapers get to this point? This chapter provides historical context of the newspaper medium and offers an in-depth examination of journalistic styles and trends to illuminate the mounting challenges for today's industry.

References

Burskirk, Eliot Van "Print War Between *NYT* and *WSJ* Is Really About Digital," *Wired*, April 26, 2010, http://www.wired.com/epicenter/2010/04/print-war-between-nyt-and-wsj-is-really-about-digital.

4.2 History of Newspapers

Learning Objectives

1. Describe the historical roots of the modern newspaper industry.

2. Explain the effect of the penny press on modern journalism.

3. Define sensationalism and yellow journalism as they relate to the newspaper industry.

Over the course of its long and complex history, the newspaper has undergone many transformations. Examining newspapers' historical roots can help shed some light on how and why the newspaper has evolved into the multifaceted medium that it is today. Scholars commonly credit the ancient Romans with publishing the first newspaper, *Acta Diurna*, or *daily doings*, in 59 BCE. Although no copies of this paper have survived, it is widely believed to have published chronicles of events, assemblies, births, deaths, and daily gossip.

In 1566, another ancestor of the modern newspaper appeared in Venice, Italy. These *avisi*, or gazettes, were handwritten and focused on politics and military conflicts. However, the absence of printing-press technology greatly limited the circulation for both the *Acta Diurna* and the Venetian papers.

The Birth of the Printing Press

Figure 4.2

Johannes Gutenberg's printing press exponentially increased the rate at which printed materials could be reproduced.

Milestoned – Printing press – CC BY 2.0.

Johannes Gutenberg's printing press drastically changed the face of publishing. In 1440, Gutenberg invented a movable-type press that permitted the high-quality reproduction of printed materials at a rate of nearly 4,000 pages per day, or 1,000 times more than could be done by a scribe by hand. This innovation drove down the price of printed materials and, for the first time, made them accessible to a mass market. Overnight, the new printing press transformed the scope and reach of the newspaper, paving the way for modern-day journalism.

European Roots

The first weekly newspapers to employ Gutenberg's press emerged in 1609. Although the papers—*Relations: Aller Furnemmen*, printed by Johann Carolus, and *Aviso Relations over Zeitung*, printed by Lucas Schulte—did not name the cities in which they were printed to avoid government persecution, their approximate location can be identified because of their use of the German language. Despite these concerns over persecution, the papers were a success, and newspapers quickly spread throughout Central Europe. Over the next 5 years, weeklies popped up in Basel, Frankfurt, Vienna, Hamburg, Berlin, and Amsterdam. In 1621, England printed its first paper under the title *Corante, or weekly newes from Italy, Germany, Hungary, Poland, Bohemia, France and the Low Countreys*. By 1641, a newspaper was printed in almost every country in Europe as publication spread to France, Italy, and Spain.

Figure 4.3

Newspapers are the descendants of the Dutch *corantos* and the German pamphlets of the 1600s.

These early newspapers followed one of two major formats. The first was the Dutch-style *corantos*, a densely packed two- to four-page paper, while the second was the German-style pamphlet, a more expansive 8- to 24-page paper. Many publishers began printing in the Dutch format, but as their popularity grew, they changed to the larger German style.

Government Control and Freedom of the Press

Because many of these early publications were regulated by the government, they did not report on local news or events. However, when civil war broke out in England in 1641, as Oliver Cromwell and Parliament threatened and eventually overthrew King Charles I, citizens turned to local papers for coverage of these major events. In

November 1641, a weekly paper titled *The Heads of Severall Proceedings in This Present Parliament* began focusing on domestic news (Goff, 2007). The paper fueled a discussion about the freedom of the press that was later articulated in 1644 by John Milton in his famous treatise *Areopagitica*.

Figure 4.4

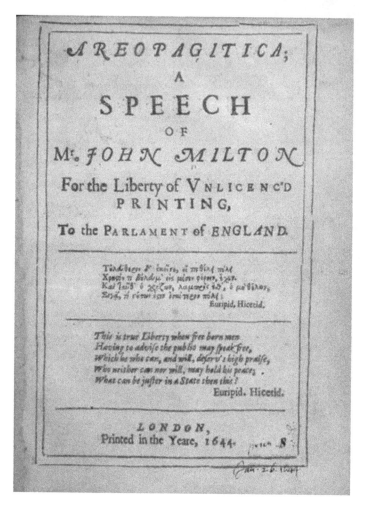

John Milton's 1644 *Areopagitica*, which criticized the British Parliament's role in regulating texts and helped pave the way for the freedom of the press.

Wikimedia Commons – public domain.

Although the *Areopagitica* focused primarily on Parliament's ban on certain books, it also addressed newspapers. Milton criticized the tight regulations on their content by stating, "Who kills a man kills a reasonable creature, God's image; but he who destroys a good book, kills reason itself, kills the image of God, as it were in the eye (Milton, 1644)." Despite Milton's emphasis on texts rather than on newspapers, the treatise had a major effect on printing regulations. In England, newspapers were freed from government control, and people began to understand the power of free press.

Papers took advantage of this newfound freedom and began publishing more frequently. With biweekly publications, papers had additional space to run advertisements and market reports. This changed the role of journalists from simple observers to active players in commerce, as business owners and investors grew to rely on the papers to market their products and to help them predict business developments. Once publishers noticed the growing popularity and profit potential of newspapers, they founded daily publications. In 1650, a German publisher began printing the world's oldest surviving daily paper, *Einkommende Zeitung*, and an English publisher followed suit in 1702 with London's *Daily Courant*. Such daily publications, which employed the relatively new format of headlines and the embellishment of illustrations, turned papers into vital fixtures in the everyday lives of citizens.

Colonial American Newspapers

Newspapers did not come to the American colonies until September 25, 1690, when Benjamin Harris printed *Public Occurrences, Both FORREIGN and DOMESTICK*. Before fleeing to America for publishing an article about a purported Catholic plot against England, Harris had been a newspaper editor in England. The first article printed in his new colonial paper stated, "The Christianized Indians in some parts of Plimouth, have newly appointed a day of thanksgiving to God for his Mercy (Harris, 1690)." The other articles in *Public Occurrences*, however, were in line with Harris's previously more controversial style, and the publication folded after just one issue.

Fourteen years passed before the next American newspaper, *The Boston News-Letter*, launched. Fifteen years after that, *The Boston Gazette* began publication, followed immediately by the *American Weekly Mercury* in Philadelphia. Trying to avoid following in Harris's footsteps, these early papers carefully eschewed political discussion to avoid offending colonial authorities. After a lengthy absence, politics reentered American papers in 1721, when James Franklin published a criticism of smallpox inoculations in the *New England Courant*. The following year, the paper accused the colonial government of failing to protect its citizens from pirates, which landed Franklin in jail.

After Franklin offended authorities once again for mocking religion, a court dictated that he was forbidden "to print or publish *The New England Courant*, or any other Pamphlet or Paper of the like Nature, except it be first Supervised by the Secretary of this Province (Massachusetts Historical Society)." Immediately following this order, Franklin turned over the paper to his younger brother, Benjamin. Benjamin Franklin, who went on to become a famous statesman and who played a major role in the American Revolution, also had a substantial impact on the printing industry as publisher of *The Pennsylvania Gazette* and the conceiver of subscription libraries.

The Trial of John Peter Zenger

Figure 4.5

The New York Weekly Journal founder John Peter Zenger brought controversial political discussion to the New York press.

Wikimedia Commons – public domain.

Boston was not the only city in which a newspaper discussed politics. In 1733, John Peter Zenger founded *The New York Weekly Journal*. Zenger's paper soon began criticizing the newly appointed colonial governor, William Cosby, who had replaced members of the New York Supreme Court when he could not control them. In late 1734, Cosby had Zenger arrested, claiming that his paper contained "divers scandalous, virulent, false and seditious reflections (Archiving Early America)." Eight months later, prominent Philadelphia lawyer Andrew Hamilton defended Zenger in an important trial. Hamilton compelled the jury to consider the truth and whether or not what was printed was a fact. Ignoring the wishes of the judge, who disapproved of Zenger and his actions, the jury returned a not guilty verdict to the courtroom after only a short deliberation. Zenger's trial resulted in two significant movements in the march toward freedom of the press. First, the trial demonstrated to the papers that they could potentially print honest criticism of the government without fear of retribution. Second, the British became afraid that an American jury would never convict an American journalist.

With Zenger's verdict providing more freedom to the press and as some began to call for emancipation from England, newspapers became a conduit for political discussion. More conflicts between the British and the colonists forced papers to pick a side to support. While a majority of American papers challenged governmental authorities, a small number of Loyalist papers, such as James Rivington's *New York Gazetteer*, gave voice to the pro-British side. Throughout the war, newspapers continued to publish information representing opposing viewpoints, and the partisan press was born. After the revolution, two opposing political parties—the Federalists and the Republicans—emerged, giving rise to partisan newspapers for each side.

Freedom of the Press in the Early United States

In 1791, the nascent United States of America adopted the First Amendment as part of the Bill of Rights. This act states that "Congress shall make no law respecting an establishment of religion, or prohibiting the free exercise thereof; or abridging the freedom of speech, or of the press; or the right of the people peaceable to assemble, and to petition the government for a redress of grievances (Cornell University Law School)." In this one sentence, U.S. law formally guaranteed freedom of press.

However, as a reaction to harsh partisan writing, in 1798, Congress passed the Sedition Act, which declared that "writing, printing, uttering, or publishing any false, scandalous and malicious writing or writings against the government of the United States" was punishable by fine and imprisonment (Constitution Society, 1798). When Thomas Jefferson was elected president in 1800, he allowed the Sedition Act to lapse, claiming that he was lending himself to "a great experiment…to demonstrate the falsehood of the pretext that freedom of the press is incompatible with orderly government (University of Virginia)." This free-press experiment has continued to modern times.

Newspapers as a Form of Mass Media

As late as the early 1800s, newspapers were still quite expensive to print. Although daily papers had become more common and gave merchants up-to-date, vital trading information, most were priced at about 6 cents a copy—well above what artisans and other working-class citizens could afford. As such, newspaper readership was limited to the elite.

The Penny Press

All that changed in September 1833 when Benjamin Day created *The Sun*. Printed on small, letter-sized pages, *The Sun* sold for just a penny. With the Industrial Revolution in full swing, Day employed the new steam-driven, two-cylinder press to print *The Sun*. While the old printing press was capable of printing approximately 125 papers per hour, this technologically improved version printed approximately 18,000 copies per hour. As he reached out to new readers, Day knew that he wanted to alter the way news was presented. He printed the paper's motto at the top of every front page of *The Sun*: "The object of this paper is to lay before the public, at a price within the means of every one, all the news of the day, and at the same time offer an advantageous medium for advertisements (Starr, 2004)."

The *Sun* sought out stories that would appeal to the new mainstream consumer. As such, the paper primarily published human-interest stories and police reports. Additionally, Day left ample room for advertisements. Day's adoption of this new format and industrialized method of printing was a huge success. The *Sun* became the first paper to be printed by what became known as the penny press. Prior to the emergence of the penny press, the most popular paper, New York City's *Courier and Enquirer*, had sold 4,500 copies per day. By 1835, *The Sun* sold 15,000 copies per day.

Figure 4.6

Benjamin Day's *Sun*, the first penny paper. The emergence of the penny press helped turn newspapers into a truly mass medium.

Another early successful penny paper was James Gordon Bennett's *New York Morning Herald*, which was first published in 1835. Bennett made his mark on the publishing industry by offering nonpartisan political reporting. He also introduced more aggressive methods for gathering news, hiring both interviewers and foreign correspondents. His paper was the first to send a reporter to a crime scene to witness an investigation. In the 1860s, Bennett hired 63 war reporters to cover the U.S. Civil War. Although the *Herald* initially emphasized sensational news, it later became one of the country's most respected papers for its accurate reporting.

Growth of Wire Services

Another major historical technological breakthrough for newspapers came when Samuel Morse invented the telegraph. Newspapers turned to emerging telegraph companies to receive up-to-date news briefs from cities across the globe. The significant expense of this service led to the formation of the Associated Press (AP) in 1846 as a cooperative arrangement of five major New York papers: the *New York Sun*, the *Journal of Commerce*, the *Courier and Enquirer*, the *New York Herald*, and the *Express*. The success of the Associated Press led to the development of wire services between major cities. According to the AP, this meant that editors were able to "actively collect news as it [broke], rather than gather already published news (Associated Press)." This collaboration between papers allowed for more reliable reporting, and the increased breadth of subject matter lent subscribing newspapers mass appeal for not only upper- but also middle- and working-class readers.

Yellow Journalism

In the late 1800s, *New York World* publisher Joseph Pulitzer developed a new journalistic style that relied on an intensified use of sensationalism—stories focused on crime, violence, emotion, and sex. Although he made major strides in the newspaper industry by creating an expanded section focusing on women and by pioneering the use of advertisements as news, Pulitzer relied largely on violence and sex in his headlines to sell more copies. Ironically, journalism's most prestigious award is named for him. His *New York World* became famous for such headlines as "Baptized in Blood" and "Little Lotta's Lovers (Fang, 1997)." This sensationalist style served as the forerunner for today's tabloids. Editors relied on shocking headlines to sell their papers, and although investigative journalism was predominant, editors often took liberties with how the story was told. Newspapers often printed an editor's interpretation of the story without maintaining objectivity.

At the same time Pulitzer was establishing the *New York World*, William Randolph Hearst—an admirer and principal competitor of Pulitzer—took over the *New York Journal*. Hearst's life partially inspired the 1941 classic film *Citizen Kane*. The battle between these two major New York newspapers escalated as Pulitzer and Hearst attempted to outsell one another. The papers slashed their prices back down to a penny, stole editors and reporters from each other, and filled their papers with outrageous, sensationalist headlines. One conflict that inspired particularly sensationalized headlines was the Spanish-American War. Both Hearst and Pulitzer filled their papers with huge front-page headlines and gave bloody—if sometimes inaccurate—accounts of the war. As historian Richard K. Hines writes, "The American Press, especially 'yellow presses' such as William Randolph Hearst's *New York Journal* [and] Joseph Pulitzer's *New York World* … sensationalized the brutality of the reconcentrado and the threat to American business interests. Journalists frequently embellished Spanish atrocities and invented others (Hines, 2002)."

Comics and Stunt Journalism

As the publishers vied for readership, an entertaining new element was introduced to newspapers: the comic strip. In 1896, Hearst's *New York Journal* published R. F. Outcault's the *Yellow Kid* in an attempt to "attract immigrant readers who otherwise might not have bought an English-language paper (Yaszek, 1994)." Readers rushed to buy papers featuring the successful yellow-nightshirt-wearing character. The cartoon "provoked a wave of 'gentle hysteria,' and was soon appearing on buttons, cracker tins, cigarette packs, and ladies' fans—and even as a character in a Broadway play (Yaszek, 1994)." Another effect of the cartoon's popularity was the creation of the term *yellow journalism* to describe the types of papers in which it appeared.

Figure 4.7

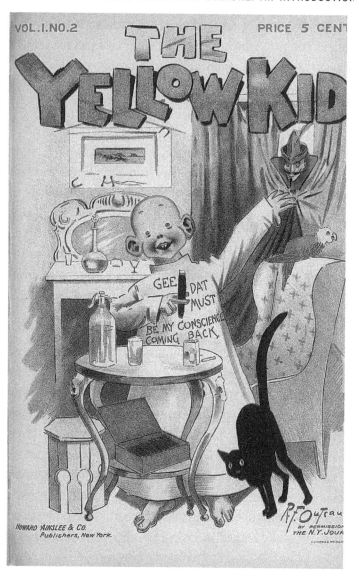

R. F. Outcault's the *Yellow Kid*, first published in William Randolf Hearst's
New York Journal in 1896.

Pulitzer responded to the success of the *Yellow Kid* by introducing stunt journalism. The publisher hired journalist Elizabeth Cochrane, who wrote under the name Nellie Bly, to report on aspects of life that had previously been ignored by the publishing industry. Her first article focused on the New York City Lunatic Asylum on Blackwell Island. Bly feigned insanity and had herself committed to the infamous asylum. She recounted her experience in her first article, "Ten Days in a Madhouse." "It was a brilliant move. Her madhouse performance inaugurated the performative tactic that would become her trademark reporting style (Lutes, 2002)." Such articles brought Bly much notoriety and fame, and she became known as the first stunt journalist. Although stunts such as these were considered lowbrow entertainment and female stunt reporters were often criticized by more traditional journalists, Pulitzer's decision to hire Bly was a huge step for women in the newspaper business. Bly and her fellow stunt reporters "were the first newspaperwomen to move, as a group, from the women's pages to the front page, from society news into political and criminal news (Lutes, 2002)."

Despite the sometimes questionable tactics of both Hearst and Pulitzer, each man made significant contributions to the growing journalism industry. By 1922, Hearst, a ruthless publisher, had created the country's largest media-holding company. At that time, he owned 20 daily papers, 11 Sunday papers, 2 wire services, 6 magazines, and a newsreel company. Likewise, toward the end of his life, Pulitzer turned his focus to establishing a school of journalism. In 1912, a year after his death and 10 years after Pulitzer had begun his educational campaign, classes opened at the Columbia University School of Journalism. At the time of its opening, the school had approximately 100 students from 21 countries. Additionally, in 1917, the first Pulitzer Prize was awarded for excellence in journalism.

Key Takeaways

- Although newspapers have existed in some form since ancient Roman times, the modern newspaper primarily stems from German papers printed in the early 1600s with Gutenberg's printing press. Early European papers were based on two distinct models: the small, dense Dutch *corantos* and the larger, more expansive German weeklies. As papers began growing in popularity, many publishers started following the German style.

- The *Sun*, first published by Benjamin Day in 1833, was the first penny paper. Day minimized paper size, used a new two-cylinder steam-engine printing press, and slashed the price of the paper to a penny so more citizens could afford a newspaper. By targeting his paper to a larger, more mainstream audience, Day transformed the newspaper industry and its readers.

- Joseph Pulitzer and William Randolph Hearst were major competitors in the U.S. newspaper industry in the late 1800s. To compete with one another, the two employed sensationalism—the use of crime, sex, and scandal—to attract readers. This type of journalism became known as yellow journalism. Yellow journalism is known for misleading stories, inaccurate information, and exaggerated detail.

Exercises

Please respond to the following writing prompts. Each response should be a minimum of one paragraph.

1. Examine one copy of a major daily newspaper and one copy of a popular tabloid. Carefully examine each publication's writing style. In what ways do the journals employ similar techniques, and in what ways do they differ?

2. Do you see any links back to the early newspaper trends that were discussed in this section? Describe them.

3. How do the publications use their styles to reach out to their respective audiences?

References

Archiving Early America, "Peter Zenger and Freedom of the Press," http://www.earlyamerica.com/earlyamerica/bookmarks/zenger/.

Associated Press, "AP History," http://www.ap.org/pages/about/history/history_first.html.

Constitution Society, "Sedition Act, (July 14, 1798)," http://www.constitution.org/rf/sedition_1798.htm.

Cornell University Law School, "Bill of Rights," http://topics.law.cornell.edu/constitution/billofrights.

Fang, Irving E. *A History of Mass Communication*: *Six Information Revolutions* (Boston: Focal PressUSA, 1997), 103.

Goff, Moira. "Early History of the English Newspaper," *17th-18th Century Burney Collection Newspapers*, Gale, 2007, http://find.galegroup.com/bncn/topicguide/bbcn_03.htm.

Harris, Benjamin. *Public Occurrences, Both FORREIGN and DOMESTICK*, September 25, 1690.

Hines, Richard K. "'First to Respond to Their Country's Call': The First Montana Infantry and the Spanish-American War and Philippine Insurrection, 1898–1899," *Montana: The Magazine of Western History* 52, no. 3 (Autumn 2002): 46.

Lutes, Jean Marie "Into the Madhouse with Nellie Bly: Girl Stunt Reporting in Late Nineteenth-Century America," *American Quarterly* 54, no. 2 (2002): 217.

Massachusetts Historical Society, "Silence DoGood: Benjamin Franklin in the New England Courant," http://www.masshist.org/online/silence_dogood/essay.php?entry_id=204.

Milton, John. *Areopagitica*, 1644, http://oll.libertyfund.org/index.php?option=com_content&task=view&id=23&Itemid=275.

Starr, Paul. *The Creation of the Media: Political Origins of Modern Communications* (New York: Basic Books, 2004), 131.

University of Virginia, "Thomas Jefferson on Politics & Government," http://etext.virginia.edu/jefferson/quotations/jeff1600.htm.

Yaszek, Lisa. "'Them Damn Pictures': Americanization and the Comic Strip in the Progressive Era," *Journal of American Studies* 28, no. 1 (1994): 24.

4.3 Different Styles and Models of Journalism

Learning Objectives

1. Explain how objective journalism differs from story-driven journalism.

2. Describe the effect of objectivity on modern journalism.

3. Describe the unique nature of literary journalism.

Location, readership, political climate, and competition all contribute to rapid transformations in journalistic models and writing styles. Over time, however, certain styles—such as sensationalism—have faded or become linked with less serious publications, like tabloids, while others have developed to become prevalent in modern-day reporting. This section explores the nuanced differences among the most commonly used models of journalism.

Objective versus Story-Driven Journalism

In the late 1800s, a majority of publishers believed that they would sell more papers by reaching out to specific groups. As such, most major newspapers employed a partisan approach to writing, churning out political stories and using news to sway popular opinion. This all changed in 1896 when a then-failing paper, *The New York Times*, took a radical new approach to reporting: employing objectivity, or impartiality, to satisfy a wide range of readers.

The Rise of Objective Journalism

At the end of the 19th century, *The New York Times* found itself competing with the papers of Pulitzer and Hearst. The paper's publishers discovered that it was nearly impossible to stay afloat without using the sensationalist headlines popularized by its competitors. Although *The New York Times* publishers raised prices to pay the bills, the higher charge led to declining readership, and soon the paper went bankrupt. Adolph Ochs, owner of the once-failing *Chattanooga Times*, took a gamble and bought *The New York Times* in 1896. On August 18 of that year, Ochs made a bold move and announced that the paper would no longer follow the sensationalist style that made Pulitzer and Hearst famous, but instead would be "clean, dignified, trustworthy and impartial (New York Times, 1935)."

This drastic change proved to be a success. *The New York Times* became the first of many papers to demonstrate that the press could be "economically as well as ethically successful (New York Times, 1935)." With the help of managing editor Carr Van Anda, the new motto "All the News That's Fit to Print," and lowered prices, *The New York Times* quickly turned into one of the most profitable impartial papers of all time. Since the newspaper's successful turnaround, publications around the world have followed *The New York Times'* objective journalistic style, demanding that reporters maintain a neutral voice in their writing.

The Inverted Pyramid Style

One commonly employed technique in modern journalism is the inverted pyramid style. This style requires objectivity and involves structuring a story so that the most important details are listed first for ease of reading. In the inverted pyramid format, the most fundamental facts of a story—typically the who, what, when, where, and why—appear at the top in the lead paragraph, with nonessential information in subsequent paragraphs. The style arose as a product of the telegraph. The inverted pyramid proved useful when telegraph connections failed in the middle of transmission; the editor still had the most important information at the beginning. Similarly, editors could quickly delete content from the bottom up to meet time and space requirements (Scanlan, 2003).

The reason for such writing is threefold. First, the style is helpful for writers, as this type of reporting is somewhat easier to complete in the short deadlines imposed on journalists, particularly in today's fast-paced news business. Second, the style benefits editors who can, if necessary, quickly cut the story from the bottom without losing vital information. Finally, the style keeps in mind traditional readers, most of who skim articles or only read a few paragraphs, but they can still learn most of the important information from this quick read.

Figure 4.8

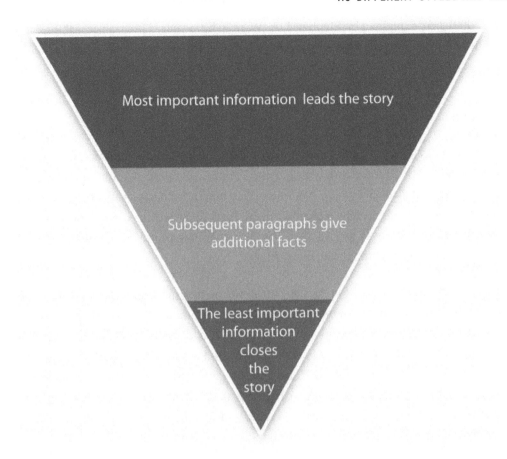

Interpretive Journalism

During the 1920s, objective journalism fell under critique as the world became more complex. Even though *The New York Times* continued to thrive, readers craved more than dry, objective stories. In 1923, *Time* magazine launched as the first major publication to step away from simple objectivity to try to provide readers with a more analytical interpretation of the news. As *Time* grew, people at some other publications took notice, and slowly editors began rethinking how they might reach out to readers in an increasingly interrelated world.

During the 1930s, two major events increased the desire for a new style of journalism: the Great Depression and the Nazi threat to global stability. Readers were no longer content with the who, what, where, when, and why of objective journalism. Instead, they craved analysis and a deeper explanation of the chaos surrounding them. Many papers responded with a new type of reporting that became known as interpretive journalism.

Interpretive journalism, following *Time*'s example, has grown in popularity since its inception in the 1920s and 1930s, and journalists use it to explain issues and to provide readers with a broader context for the stories that they encounter. According to Brant Houston, the executive director of Investigative Reporters and Editors Inc., an interpretive journalist "goes beyond the basic facts of an event or topic to provide context, analysis, and possible consequences (Houston, 2008)." When this new style was first used, readers responded with great interest to the new editorial perspectives that newspapers were offering on events. But interpretive journalism posed a new problem for editors: the need to separate straight objective news from opinions and analysis. In response, many papers in the 1930s and 1940s "introduced weekend interpretations of the past week's events…and interpretive columnists with bylines (Ward, 2008)." As explained by Stephen J. A. Ward in his article, "Journalism Ethics," the goal of these weekend features was to "supplement objective reporting with an informed interpretation of world events (Ward, 2008)."

Competition From Broadcasting

The 1930s also saw the rise of broadcasting as radios became common in most U.S. households and as sound–picture recordings for newsreels became increasingly common. This broadcasting revolution introduced new dimensions to journalism. Scholar Michael Schudson has noted that broadcast news "reflect[ed]…a new journalistic reality. The journalist, no longer merely the relayer of documents and messages, ha[d] become the interpreter of the news (Schudson, 1982)." However, just as radio furthered the interpretive journalistic style, it also created a new problem for print journalism, particularly newspapers.

Suddenly, free news from the radio offered competition to the pay news of newspapers. Scholar Robert W. McChesney has observed that, in the 1930s, "many elements of the newspaper industry opposed commercial broadcasting, often out of fear of losing ad revenues and circulation to the broadcasters (McChesney, 1992)." This fear led to a media war as papers claimed that radio was stealing their print stories. Radio outlets, however, believed they had equal right to news stories. According to Robert W. McChesney, "commercial broadcasters located their industry next to the newspaper industry as an icon of American freedom and culture (McChesney, 1992)." The debate had a major effect on interpretive journalism as radio and newspapers had to make decisions about whether to use an objective or interpretive format to remain competitive with each other.

The emergence of television during the 1950s created even more competition for newspapers. In response, paper publishers increased opinion-based articles, and many added what became known as op-ed pages. An op-ed page—short for *opposite the editorial page*—features opinion-based columns typically produced by a writer or writers unaffiliated with the paper's editorial board. As op-ed pages grew, so did interpretive journalism. Distinct from news stories, editors and columnists presented opinions on a regular basis. By the 1960s, the interpretive style of reporting had begun to replace the older descriptive style (Patterson, 2002).

Literary Journalism

Stemming from the development of interpretive journalism, literary journalism began to emerge during the 1960s. This style, made popular by journalists Tom Wolfe (formerly a strictly nonfiction writer) and Truman Capote, is often referred to as *new journalism* and combines factual reporting with sometimes fictional narration. Literary journalism follows neither the formulaic style of reporting of objective journalism nor the opinion-based analytical style of interpretive journalism. Instead, this art form—as it is often termed—brings voice and character to historical events, focusing on the construction of the scene rather than on the retelling of the facts.

Important Literary Journalists

Figure 4.9

The works of Tom Wolfe are some of the best examples of literary journalism of the 1960s.

Tom Wolfe was the first reporter to write in the literary journalistic style. In 1963, while his newspaper, New York's *Herald Tribune,* was on strike, *Esquire* magazine hired Wolfe to write an article on customized cars. Wolfe gathered the facts but struggled to turn his collected information into a written piece. His managing editor, Byron Dobell, suggested that he type up his notes so that *Esquire* could hire another writer to complete the article. Wolfe typed up a 49-page document that described his research and what he wanted to include in the story and sent it to Dobell. Dobell was so impressed by this piece that he simply deleted the "Dear Byron" at the top of the letter and published the rest of Wolfe's letter in its entirety under the headline "There Goes (Varoom! Varoom!) That Kandy-Kolored Tangerine-Flake Streamline Baby." The article was a great success, and Wolfe, in time, became known as the father of new journalism. When he later returned to work at the *Herald Tribune,* Wolfe brought with him this new style, "fusing the stylistic features of fiction and the reportorial obligations of journalism (Kallan, 1992)."

Truman Capote responded to Wolfe's new style by writing *In Cold Blood,* which Capote termed a "nonfiction novel," in 1966 (Plimpton, 1966). The tale of an actual murder that had taken place on a Kansas farm some years earlier, the novel was based on numerous interviews and painstaking research. Capote claimed that he wrote the book because he wanted to exchange his "self-creative world…for the everyday objective world we all inhabit (Plimpton, 1966)." The book was praised for its straightforward, journalistic style. *New York Times* writer George Plimpton claimed that the book "is remarkable for its objectivity—nowhere, despite his involvement, does the author intrude (Plimpton, 1966)." After *In Cold Blood* was finished, Capote criticized Wolfe's style in an interview, commenting that Wolfe "[has] nothing to do with creative journalism," by claiming that Wolfe did not have the appropriate fiction-writing expertise (Plimpton, 1966). Despite the tension between these two writers, today they are remembered for giving rise to a similar style in varying genres.

The Effects of Literary Journalism

Although literary journalism certainly affected newspaper reporting styles, it had a much greater impact on the magazine industry. Because they were bound by fewer restrictions on length and deadlines, magazines were more likely to publish this new writing style than were newspapers. Indeed, during the 1960s and 1970s, authors simulating the styles of both Wolfe and Capote flooded magazines such as *Esquire* and *The New Yorker* with articles.

Literary journalism also significantly influenced objective journalism. Many literary journalists believed that objectivity limited their ability to critique a story or a writer. Some claimed that objectivity in writing is impossible, as all journalists are somehow swayed by their own personal histories. Still others, including Wolfe, argued that objective journalism conveyed a "limited conception of the 'facts,'" which "often effected an inaccurate, incomplete story that precluded readers from exercising informed judgment (Kallan)."

Advocacy Journalism and Precision Journalism

The reactions of literary journalists to objective journalism encouraged the growth of two more types of journalism: advocacy journalism and precision journalism. Advocacy journalists promote a particular cause and intentionally adopt a biased, nonobjective viewpoint to do so effectively. However, serious advocate journalists adhere to strict guidelines, as "an advocate journalist is not the same as being an activist" according to journalist Sue Careless (Careless, 2000). In an article discussing advocacy journalism, Careless contrasted the role of an advocate journalist with the role of an activist. She encourages future advocate journalists by saying the following:

A journalist writing for the advocacy press should practice the same skills as any journalist. You don't fabricate or falsify. If you do you will destroy the credibility of both yourself as a working journalist and the cause you care so much about. News should never be propaganda. You don't fudge or suppress vital facts or present half-truths (Careless, 2000).

Despite the challenges and potential pitfalls inherent to advocacy journalism, this type of journalism has increased in popularity over the past several years. In 2007, *USA Today* reporter Peter Johnson stated, "Increasingly, journalists and talk-show hosts want to 'own' a niche issue or problem, find ways to solve it, and be associated with making this world a better place (Johnson, 2007)." In this manner, journalists across the world are employing the advocacy style to highlight issues they care about.

Oprah Winfrey: Advocacy Journalist

Television talk-show host and owner of production company Harpo Inc., Oprah Winfrey is one of the most successful, recognizable entrepreneurs of the late-20th and early-21st centuries. Winfrey has long been a news reporter, beginning in the late 1970s as a coanchor of an evening television program. She began hosting her own show in 1984, and in 2010, the *Oprah Winfrey Show* was one of the most popular TV programs on the air. Winfrey had long used her show as a platform for issues and concerns, making her one of the most famous advocacy journalists. While many praise Winfrey for using her celebrity to draw attention to causes she cares about, others criticize her techniques, claiming that she uses the advocacy style for self-promotion. As one critic writes, "I'm not sure how Oprah's endless self-promotion of how she spent millions on a school in South Africa suddenly makes her 'own' the 'education niche.' She does own the trumpet-my-own-horn niche. But that's not 'journalism (Schlussel, 2007).'"

Yet despite this somewhat harsh critique, many view Winfrey as the leading example of positive advocacy journalism. Sara Grumbles claims in her blog "Breaking and Fitting the Mold": "Oprah Winfrey obviously practices advocacy journalism…. Winfrey does not fit the mold of a 'typical' journalist by today's standards. She has an agenda and she voices her opinions. She ha[d] her own op-ed page in the form of a million dollar television studio. Objectivity is not her strong point. Still, in my opinion she is a journalist (Grumbles, 2007)."

Regardless of the arguments about the value and reasoning underlying her technique, Winfrey unquestionably practices a form of advocacy journalism. In fact, thanks to her vast popularity, she may be the most compelling example of an advocacy journalist working today.

Precision journalism emerged in the 1970s. In this form, journalists turn to polls and studies to strengthen the accuracy of their articles. Philip Meyer, commonly acknowledged as the father of precision journalism, says that his intent is to "encourage my colleagues in journalism to apply the principles of scientific method to their tasks of gathering and presenting the news (Meyer, 2002)." This type of journalism adds a new layer to objectivity in reporting, as articles no longer need to rely solely on anecdotal evidence; journalists can employ hard facts and figures to support their assertions. An example of precision journalism would be an article on voting patterns in a presidential election that cites data from exit polls. Precision journalism has become more popular as computers have become more prevalent. Many journalists currently use this type of writing.

Consensus versus Conflict Newspapers

Another important distinction within the field of journalism must be made between consensus journalism and conflict journalism. Consensus journalism typically takes place in smaller communities, where local newspapers generally serve as a forum for many different voices. Newspapers that use consensus-style journalism provide community calendars and meeting notices and run articles on local schools, events, government, property crimes, and zoning. These newspapers can help build civic awareness and a sense of shared experience and responsibility among readers in a community. Often, business or political leaders in the community own consensus papers.

Conversely, conflict journalism, like that which is presented in national and international news articles in *The New York Times*, typically occurs in national or metropolitan dailies. Conflict journalists define news in terms of societal discord, covering events and issues that contravene perceived social norms. In this style of journalism, reporters act as watchdogs who monitor the government and its activities. Conflict journalists often present both sides of a story and pit ideas against one another to generate conflict and, therefore, attract a larger readership. Both conflict and consensus papers are widespread. However, because they serve different purposes and reach out to differing audiences, they largely do not compete with each other.

Niche Newspapers

Niche newspapers represent one more model of newspapers. These publications, which reach out to a specific target group, are rising in popularity in the era of Internet. As Robert Courtemanche, a certified journalism educator, writes, "In the past, newspapers tried to be everything to every reader to gain circulation. That outdated concept does not work on the Internet where readers expect expert, niche content (Courtemanche, 2008)." Ethnic and minority papers are some of the most common forms of niche newspapers. In the United States—particularly in large cities such as New York—niche papers for numerous ethnic communities flourish. Some common types of U.S. niche papers are papers that cater to a specific ethnic or cultural group or to a group that speaks a particular language. Papers that cover issues affecting lesbians, gay men, and bisexual individuals—like the *Advocate*—and religion-oriented publications—like *The Christian Science Monitor*—are also niche papers.

The Underground Press

Some niche papers are part of the underground press. Popularized in the 1960s and 1970s as individuals sought to publish articles documenting their perception of social tensions and inequalities, the underground press typically caters to alternative and countercultural groups. Most of these papers are published on small budgets. Perhaps the most famous underground paper is New York's Pulitzer Prize–winning *Village Voice*. This newspaper was founded in 1955 and declares its role in the publishing industry by saying:

The *Village Voice* introduced free-form, high-spirited and passionate journalism into the public discourse. As the nation's first and largest alternative newsweekly, the Voice maintains the same tradition of no-holds-barred reporting and criticism it first embraced when it began publishing fifty years ago (Village Voice).

Despite their at-times shoestring budgets, underground papers serve an important role in the media. By offering an alternative perspective to stories and by reaching out to niche groups through their writing, underground-press newspapers fill a unique need within the larger media marketplace. As journalism has evolved over the years, newspapers have adapted to serve the changing demands of readers.

Key Takeaways

- Objective journalism began as a response to sensationalism and has continued in some form to this day. However, some media observers have argued that it is nearly impossible to remain entirely objective while reporting a story. One argument against objectivity is that journalists are human and are, therefore, biased to some degree. Many newspapers that promote objectivity put in place systems to help their journalists remain as objective as possible.

- Literary journalism combines the research and reporting of typical newspaper journalism with the writing style of fiction. While most newspaper journalists focus on facts, literary journalists tend to focus on the scene by evoking voices and characters inhabiting historical events. Famous early literary journalists include Tom Wolfe and Truman Capote.

- Other journalistic styles allow reporters and publications to narrow their editorial voice. Advocacy journalists encourage readers to support a particular cause. Consensus journalism encourages social and economic harmony, while conflict journalists present information in a way that focuses on views outside of the social norm.

- Niche newspapers—such as members of the underground press and those serving specific ethnic groups, racial groups, or speakers of a specific language—serve as important media outlets for distinct voices. The rise of the Internet and online journalism has brought niche newspapers more into the mainstream.

Exercises

Please respond to the following writing prompts. Each response should be a minimum of one paragraph.

1. Find an objective newspaper article that includes several factual details. Rewrite the story in a literary journalistic style. How does the story differ from one genre to the other?

2. Was it difficult to transform an objective story into a piece of literary journalism? Explain.

3. Do you prefer reading an objective journalism piece or a literary journalism piece? Explain.

References

Careless, Sue. "Advocacy Journalism," *Interim*, May 2000, http://www.theinterim.com/2000/may/10advocacy.html.

Courtemanche, Robert. "Newspapers Must Find Their Niche to Survive," Suite101.com, December 20, 2008, http://newspaperindustry.suite101.com/article.cfm/newspapers_must_find_their_niche_to_survive.

Grumbles, Sara. "Breaking and Fitting the Mold," *Media Chatter* (blog), October 3, 2007, http://www.commajor.com/?p=1244.

Houston, Brant. "Interpretive Journalism," *The International Encyclopedia of Communication*, 2008, http://www.blackwellreference.com/public/tocnode?id=g9781405131995_chunk_g978140513199514_ss82-1.

Johnson, Peter. "More Reporters Embrace an Advocacy Role," *USA Today*, March 5, 2007, http://www.usatoday.com/life/television/news/2007-03-05-social-journalism_N.htm.

Kallan, Richard A. "Tom Wolfe."

Kallan, Richard K. "Tom Wolfe," in *A Sourcebook of American Literary Journalism: Representative Writers in an Emerging Genre*, ed. Thomas B. Connery (Santa Barbara: Greenwood Press, 1992).

McChesney, Robert W. "Media and Democracy: The Emergence of Commercial Broadcasting in the United States, 1927–1935," in "Communication in History: The Key to Understanding" *OAH Magazine of History* 6, no. 4 (1992): 37.

Meyer, Phillip. *Precision Journalism: A Reporter's Introduction to Social Science Methods*, 4th ed. (Oxford: Rowman & Littlefield Publishers, 2002), vii.

New York Times, "Adolph S. Ochs Dead at 77; Publisher of Times Since 1896," *New York Times*, April 9, 1935, http://www.nytimes.com/learning/general/onthisday/bday/0312.html.

Patterson, Thomas. "Why Is News So Negative These Days?" *History News Network*, 2002, http://hnn.us/articles/1134.html.

Plimpton, George. "The Story Behind a Nonfiction Novel," *New York Times*, January 16, 1966, http://www.nytimes.com/books/97/12/28/home/capote-interview.html.

Scanlan, Chip. "Writing from the Top Down: Pros and Cons of the Inverted Pyramid," Poynter, June 20, 2003, http://www.poynter.org/how-tos/newsgathering-storytelling/chip-on-your-shoulder/12754/writing-from-the-top-down-pros-and-cons-of-the-inverted-pyramid/.

Schlussel, Debbie. "USA Today Heralds 'Oprah Journalism,'" *Debbie Schlussel* (blog), March 6, 2007, http://www.debbieschlussel.com/497/usa-today-heralds-oprah-journalism/.

Schudson, Michael. "The Politics of Narrative Form: The Emergence of News Conventions in Print and Television," in "Print Culture and Video Culture," *Daedalus* 111, no. 4 (1982): 104.

Village Voice, "About Us," http://www.villagevoice.com/about/index.

Ward, Stephen J. A. "Journalism Ethics," in *The Handbook of Journalism Studies*, ed. Karin Wahl-Jorgensen and Thomas Hanitzsch (New York: Routledge, 2008): 298.

4.4 How Newspapers Control the Public's Access to Information and Impact American Pop Culture

---

Learning Objectives

1. Describe two ways that newspapers control stories.
2. Define watchdog journalism.
3. Describe how television has impacted journalistic styles.

Since 1896, *The New York Times* has printed the phrase "All the News That's Fit to Print" as its masthead motto. The phrase itself seems innocent enough, and it has been published for such a long time now that many probably skim over it without giving it a second thought. Yet, the phrase represents an interesting phenomenon in the newspaper industry: control. Papers have long been criticized for the way stories are presented, yet newspapers continue to print—and readers continue to buy them.

"All the News That's Fit to Print"

In 1997, *The New York Times* publicly claimed that it was "an independent newspaper, entirely fearless, free of ulterior influence and unselfishly devoted to the public welfare (Herman, 1998)." Despite this public proclamation of objectivity, the paper's publishers have been criticized for choosing which articles to print based on personal financial gain. In reaction to that statement, scholar Edward S. Herman wrote that the issue is that *The New York Times* "defin[es] public welfare in a manner acceptable to their elite audience and advertisers (Herman, 1998)." *The New York Times* has continually been accused of determining what stories are told. For example, during the 1993 debate over the North American Free Trade Agreement (NAFTA), *The New York Times* clearly supported the agreement. In doing so, the newspaper exercised editorial control over its publication and the information that went out to readers.

However, *The New York Times* is not the only newspaper to face accusations of controlling which stories are told. In his review of *Read All About It: The Corporate Takeover of America's Newspapers*, Steve Hoenisch, editor of *Criticism.com*, offers these harsh words about what drives the stories printed in today's newspapers:

I've always thought of daily newspapers as the guardians of our—meaning the public's—right to know. The guardians of truth, justice, and public welfare and all that. But who am I fooling? America's daily newspapers don't belong to us. Nor, for that matter, do they even seek to serve us any longer. They have more important concerns now: appeasing advertisers and enriching stockholders (Hoenisch).

More and more, as readership declines, newspapers must answer to advertisers and shareholders as they choose which stories to report on.

However, editorial control does not end there. Journalists determine not only what stories are told but also how those stories are presented. This issue is perhaps even more delicate than that of selection. Most newspaper readers still expect news to be reported objectively and demand that journalists present their stories in this manner. However, careful public scrutiny can burden journalists, while accusations of controlling information affect their affiliated newspapers. However, this scrutiny takes on importance as the public turns to journalists and newspapers to learn about the world.

Journalists are also expected to hold themselves to high standards of truth and originality. Fabrication and plagiarism are prohibited. If a journalist is caught using these tactics, then his or her career is likely to end for betraying the public's trust and for damaging the publication's reputation. For example, *The New York Times* reporter Jayson Blair lost his job in 2003 when his plagiary and fabrication were discovered, and *The New Republic* journalist Stephen Glass was fired in 1998 for inventing stories, quotes, and sources.

Despite the critiques of the newspaper industry and its control over information, the majority of newspapers and journalists take their roles seriously. Editors work with journalists to verify sources and to double-check facts so readers are provided accurate information. In this way, the control that journalists and newspapers exert serves to benefit their readers, who can then be assured that articles printed are correct.

The New York Times Revisits Old Stories

Despite the criticism of *The New York Times*, the famous newspaper has been known to revisit their old stories to provide a new, more balanced view. One such example occurred in 2004 when, in response to criticism on their handling of the Iraq War, *The New York Times* offered a statement of apology. The apology read:

We have found a number of instances of coverage that was not as rigorous as it should have been. In some cases, information that was controversial then, and seems questionable now, was insufficiently qualified or allowed to stand unchallenged. Looking back, we wish we had been more aggressive in re-examining the claims as new evidence emerged—or failed to emerge (New York Times, 2004). Although the apology was risky—it essentially admitted guilt in controlling a controversial story—*The New York Times* demonstrated a commitment to ethical journalism.

Watchdog Journalism

One way that journalists control stories for the benefit of the public is by engaging in watchdog journalism. This form of journalism provides the public with information about government officials or business owners while holding those officials to high standards of operation. Watchdog journalism is defined as:

(1) independent scrutiny by the press of the activities of government, business and other public institutions, with an aim toward (2) documenting, questioning, and investigating those activities, to (3) provide publics and officials with timely information on issues of public concern (Bennett & Serrin, 2005).

One of the most famous examples of watchdog journalism is the role that Bob Woodward and Carl Bernstein of *The Washington Post* played in uncovering information about the Watergate break-in and scandal that ultimately resulted in President Richard Nixon's resignation. Newspapers and journalists often laud watchdog journalism, one of the most important functions of newspapers, yet it is difficult to practice because it requires rigorous investigation, which in turn demands more time. Many journalists often try to keep up with news as it breaks, so journalists are not afforded the time to research the information—nor to hone the skills—required to write a watchdog story. "Surviving in the newsroom—doing watchdog stories—takes a great deal of personal and political skill. Reporters must have a sense of guerilla warfare tactics to do well in the newsroom (Bennett & Serrin, 2005)."

To be successful, watchdog journalists must investigate stories, ask tough questions, and face the possibility of unpopularity to alert the public to corruption or mismanagement while elevating the public's expectations of the government. At the same time, readers can support newspapers that employ this style of journalism to encourage the press to engage in the challenging watchdog form of journalism. As scholars have observed, "Not surprisingly, watchdog journalism functions best when reporters understand it and news organizations and their audiences support it (Bennett & Serrin, 2005)."

Impact of Television and the Internet on Print

Newspapers have control over which stories are told and how those stories are presented. Just as the newspaper industry has changed dramatically over the years, journalistic writing styles have been transformed. Many times, such changes mirrored a trend shift in readership; since the 1950s, however, newspapers have had to compete with television journalism and, more recently, the Internet. Both television and the Internet have profoundly affected newspaper audiences and journalistic styles.

Case Study: *USA Today*

USA Today, founded in 1982 and known for its easy-to-read stories, is but one example of a paper that has altered its style to remain competitive with television and the Internet. In the past, newspapers placed their primary focus on the written word. Although some newspapers still maintain the use of written narration, many papers have shifted their techniques to attract a more television-savvy audience. In the case of *USA Today*, the emphasis lies on the second track—the visual story—dominated by large images accompanied by short written stories. This emphasis mimics the television presentation format, allowing the paper to cater to readers with short attention spans.

A perhaps unexpected shift in journalistic writing styles that derives from television is the more frequent use of present tense, rather than past tense, in articles. This shift likely comes from television journalism's tendency to allow a story to develop as it is being told. This subtle but noticeable shift from past to present tense in narration sometimes brings a more dramatic element to news articles, which may attract readers who otherwise turn to television news programs for information.

Like many papers, *USA Today* has redesigned its image and style to keep up with the sharp immediacy of the Internet and with the entertainment value of television. In fact, the paper's management was so serious about their desire to compete with television that from 1988 to 1990 they mounted a syndicated television series titled *USA Today: The Television Show* (later retitled *USA Today on TV*) (Internet Movie Database). Despite its short run, the show demonstrated the paper's focus on reaching out to a visual audience, a core value that it has maintained to this day. Today, *USA Today* has established itself as a credible and reliable news source, despite its unorthodox approach to journalism.

Key Takeaways

- Newspapers control which stories are told by selecting which articles make it to print. They also control how stories are told by determining the way in which information is presented to their readers.

- Watchdog journalism is an investigative approach to reporting that aims to inform citizens of occurrences in government and businesses.

- Television has not only contributed to the decline of readership for newspapers but has also impacted visual and journalistic styles. Newspapers, such as *USA Today*, have been profoundly affected by the television industry. *USA Today* caters to television watchers by incorporating large images and short stories, while primarily employing the present tense to make it seem as though the story is unfolding before the reader.

Exercises

Please respond to the following writing prompts. Each response should be a minimum of one paragraph.

1. Compare the journalistic styles of *USA Today* and *The Wall Street Journal*. Examine differences in the visual nature of the newspapers as well as in the journalistic style.

2. How has television affected these particular newspapers?

3. What noticeable differences do you observe? Can you find any similarities?

4. How did each newspaper cover events differently? How did each newspaper's coverage change the focus and information told? Did you find any watchdog stories, and, if so, what were they?

References

Bennett, W. Lance and William Serrin, "The Watchdog Role," in *The Institutions of American Democracy: The Press*, ed. Geneva Overholser and Kathleen Hall Jamieson (New York: Oxford University Press, 2005), 169.

Herman, Edward S. "All the News Fit to Print: Structure and Background of the New York Times," *Z Magazine*, April 1998, http://www.thirdworldtraveler.com/Herman%20/AllNewsFit_Herman.html.

Hoenisch, Steven. "Corporate Journalism," review of *Read All About It: The Corporate Takeover of America's Newspapers*, by James D. Squires, http://www.criticism.com/md/crit1.html#section-Read-All-About-It.

Internet Movie Database, "U.S.A Today: The Television Series," Internet Movie Database, http://www.imdb.com/title/tt0094572/.

New York Times, Editorial, "The Times and Iraq," *New York Times*, May 26, 2004, http://www.nytimes.com/2004/05/26/international/middleeast/26FTE_NOTE.html.

4.5 Current Popular Trends in the Newspaper Industry

Learning Objectives

1. Identify newspapers with high circulations.
2. Describe the decline of the newspaper industry.

Popular media such as television and the Internet have forever changed the newspaper industry. To fully understand the impact that current technology is having on the newspaper industry, it is necessary to first examine the current state of the industry.

Major Publications in the U.S. Newspaper Industry

Although numerous papers exist in the United States, a few major publications dominate circulation and, thus, exert great influence on the newspaper industry. Each of these newspapers has its own unique journalistic and editorial style, relying on different topics and techniques to appeal to its readership.

USA Today

USA Today currently tops the popularity chart with a daily circulation of 2,281,831 (Newspapers). This national paper's easy-to-read content and visually focused layout contribute to its high readership numbers. Although the paper does not formally publish on weekends, it does have a partner paper titled *USA Weekend. USA Today* consists of four sections: news, money, sports, and life; for the ease of its readers, the newspaper color-codes each section. Owned by the Gannett Company, the paper caters to its audience by opting for ease of comprehension over complexity.

The Wall Street Journal

Established in the late 1800s, *The Wall Street Journal* closely trails *USA Today*, with a circulation of 2,070,498 (Newspapers). In fact, *USA Today* and *The Wall Street Journal* have competed for the top circulation spot for many years. An international paper that focuses on business and financial news, *The Wall Street Journal* primarily uses written narration with few images. Recent changes to its layout, such as adding advertising on the front page and minimizing the size of the paper slightly to save on printing costs, have not dramatically shifted this long-standing focus. The paper runs between 50 and 96 pages per issue and gives its readers up-to-date information on the economy, business, and national and international financial news.

The New York Times

The New York Times is another major publication, with circulation at 1,121,623 (Newspapers). Founded in 1851, the New York City–based paper is owned by the New York Times Company, which also publishes several smaller regional papers. The flagship paper contains three sections: news, opinion, and features. Although its articles tend to be narrative-driven, the paper does include images for many of its articles, creating a balance between the wordier layout of *The Wall Street Journal* and the highly visual *USA Today*. *The New York Times* publishes international stories along with more local stories in sections such as Arts, Theater, and Metro. The paper has also successfully established itself on the Internet, becoming one of the most popular online papers today.

Los Angeles Times

The *Los Angeles Times*—currently the only West Coast paper to crack the top 10 circulation list—has also contributed much to the newspaper industry. First published in 1881, the California-based paper has a distribution of 907,977 (Newspapers). Perhaps the most unique feature of the paper is its Column One, which focuses on sometimes-bizarre stories meant to engage readers. Known for its investigative journalistic approach, the *Los Angeles Times* demands that its journalists "provide a rich, nuanced account" of the issues they cover (Los Angeles Times, 2007). By 2010, the paper had won 39 Pulitzer Prizes, including five gold medals for public service (Los Angeles Times).

The Washington Post

First published in 1877, *The Washington Post* is Washington, DC's oldest and largest paper, with a daily circulation of 709,997 (Top 10 US Newspapers by Circulation). According to its editors, the paper aims to be "fair and free and wholesome in its outlook on public affairs and public men (Washington Post)." In this vein, *The Washington Post* has developed a strong investigative journalism style, perhaps most exemplified by its prominent investigation of the Watergate Scandal.

The paper also holds the principle of printing articles fit "for the young as well as the old (Washington Post)." In 2003, *The Washington Post* launched a new section called the *Sunday Source* which targets the 18- to 34-year-old age group in an attempt to increase readership among younger audiences. This weekend supplement section focused on entertainment and lifestyle issues, like style, food, and fashion. Although it ceased publication in 2008, some of its regular features migrated to the regular paper. Like the *Los Angeles Times*, *The Washington Post* holds numerous Pulitzer Prizes for journalism.

Chicago Tribune

One other major publication with a significant impact on the newspaper industry is the *Chicago Tribune*, wielding a circulation of 643,086. First established in 1847, the paper is often remembered for famously miscalling the 1948 presidential election with the headline of "Dewey Defeats Truman."

Figure 4.10

The *Chicago Tribune*'s inaccurate declaration of the results of the tight 1948 presidential election has become one of the most famous headlines of all time.

Despite this error, the *Chicago Tribune* has become known for its watchdog journalism, including a specific watchdog section for issues facing Chicago, like pollution, politics, and more. It proudly proclaims its commitment "to standing up for your interests and serving as your watchdog in the corridors of power (Chicago Tribune)."

Dave Winer – Dewey Defeats Truman – CC BY-SA 2.0.

Declining Readership and Decreasing Revenues

Despite major newspapers' large circulations, newspapers as a whole are experiencing a dramatic decline in both subscribers and overall readership. For example, on February 27, 2009, Denver's *Rocky Mountain News* published its final issue after nearly 150 years in print. The front-page article "Goodbye, Colorado" reflected on the paper's long-standing history with the Denver community, observing that "It is with great sadness that we say goodbye to you today. Our time chronicling the life of Denver and Colorado, the nation and the world, is over (Rocky Mountain News, 2009)."

Readership Decline

The story of *Rocky Mountain News* is neither unique nor entirely unexpected. For nearly a half-century, predictions of the disappearance of print newspapers have been an ongoing refrain. The fear of losing print media began in the 1940s with the arrival of the radio and television. Indeed, the number of daily papers has steadily decreased since the 1940s; in 1990, the number of U.S. dailies was just 1,611. By 2008, that number had further shrunk to 1,408 (Newspaper Association of America). But the numbers are not as clear-cut as they appear. As one report observed, "The root problems go back to the late 1940s, when the percentage of Americans reading newspapers began to drop. But for years the U.S. population was growing so much that circulation kept rising and then, after 1970s, remained stable (State of the Media, 2004)." During the 1970s when circulation stopped rising, more women were entering the workforce. By the 1990s when "circulation began to decline in absolute numbers," the number of women in the workforce was higher than had ever been previously experienced (State of the Media, 2004). With women at work, there were fewer people at home with leisure time for reading daily papers for their news. This, combined with television journalism's rising popularity and the emergence of the Internet, meant a significant decrease in newspaper circulation. With newer, more immediate ways to get news, the disconnect between newspapers and consumers deepened.

Compounding the problem is newspapers' continuing struggle to attract younger readers. Many of these young readers simply did not grow up in households that subscribed to daily papers and so they do not turn to newspapers for information. However, the problem seems to be more complex "than fewer people developing the newspaper habit. People who used to read every day now read less often. Some people who used to read a newspaper have stopped altogether (State of the Media, 2004)."

Yet the most significant challenge to newspapers is certainly the Internet. As print readership declines, online readership has grown; fast, free access to breaking information contributes to the growing appeal of online news. Despite the increase in online news readers, that growth has not offset the drop in print readership. In 2008, the Pew Research Center conducted a news media consumption survey in which only

39 percent of participants claimed to having read a newspaper (either print or online) the day before, showing a drop from 43 percent in 2006. Meanwhile, readership of print newspapers fell from 34 percent to 25 percent in that time period (Dilling, 2009).

The study also observed that younger generations are primarily responsible for this shift to online reading. "The changes in reader habits seem to be similar amongst both Generation X and Y demographics, where marked increases in consulting online news sources were observed (Dilling, 2009)." Baby boomers and older generations do, for the most part, still rely on printed newspapers for information. Perhaps this distinction between generations is not surprising. Younger readers grew up with the Internet and have developed different expectations about the speed, nature, and cost of information than have older generations. However, this trend suggests that online readership along with the general decline of news readers may make printed newspapers all but obsolete in the near future.

Joint Operating Agreements

As readership began to decline in the 1970s and newspapers began experiencing greater competition within individual cities, Congress issued the Newspaper Preservation Act authorizing the structure of joint operating agreements (JOAs). The implementation of JOAs means that two newspapers could "share the cost of business, advertising, and circulation operations," which helped newspapers stay afloat in the face of an ever-shrinking readership (Milstead, 2009). The Newspaper Preservation Act also ensured that two competing papers could keep their distinct news divisions but merge their business divisions.

At its peak, 28 newspaper JOAs existed across the United States, but as the industry declines at an increasingly rapid rate, JOAs are beginning to fail. With today's shrinking pool of readers, two newspapers simply cannot effectively function in one community. In 2009, only nine JOAs continued operations, largely because JOAs "don't eliminate the basic problem of one newspaper gaining the upper hand in circulation and, hence, advertising revenue (Milstead, 2009)." With advertising playing a key role in newspapers' financial survival, revenue loss is a critical blow. Additionally, "in recent years, of course, the Internet has thrown an even more dramatic wrench into the equation. Classified advertising has migrated to Internet sites like craigslist.org while traditional retail advertisers…can advertise via their own web sites (Milstead, 2009)." As more advertisers move away from the newspaper industry, more JOAs will likely crumble. The destruction of JOAs will, in turn, result in the loss of more newspapers.

Newspaper Chains

As newspapers diminish in number and as newspaper owners find themselves in financial trouble, a dramatic increase in the consolidation of newspaper ownership has taken place. Today, many large companies own several papers across the country, buying independently owned papers to help them stay afloat. The change has been occurring for some time; in fact, "since 1975, more than two-thirds of independently owned newspapers…have disappeared (Free Press)." However, since 2000, newspaper consolidation has increased markedly as more papers are turning over control to larger companies.

In 2002, the 22 largest newspaper chains owned 39 percent of all the newspapers in the country (562 papers). Yet those papers represent 70 percent of daily circulation and 73 percent of Sunday. And their influence appears to be growing. These circulation percentages are a full percentage point higher than 2001 (State of the Media, 2004).

Among the 22 companies that own the largest percentage of the papers, four chains stand out: Gannett, the Tribune Company, the New York Times Company, and the McClatchy Company. Not only do these companies each own several papers across the country, but they also enjoy a higher-than-normal profit margin relative to smaller chains.

Recent Ownership Trends

In addition to consolidation, the decline of print newspapers has brought about several changes in ownership as companies attempt to increase their revenue. In 2007, media mogul Rupert Murdoch's News Corporation purchased *The Wall Street Journal* with an unsolicited $5 billion bid, promising to "pour money into the *Journal* and its website and use his satellite television networks in Europe and Asia to spread *Journal* content the world over (Ahrens, 2007)." Murdoch has used the buyout to move the paper into the technological world, asking readers and newspapers to embrace change. In 2009, he published an article in *The Wall Street Journal* assuring his readers that "the future of journalism is more promising than ever—limited only by editors and producers unwilling to fight for their readers and viewers, or government using its heavy hand either to overregulate or subsidize us (Murdoch, 2009)." Murdoch believes that the hope of journalism lies in embracing the changing world and how its inhabitants receive news. Time will tell if he is correct.

Despite changes in power, the consolidation trend is leveling off. Even large chains must cut costs to avoid shuttering papers entirely. In January 2009, the newspaper industry experienced 2,252 layoffs; in total, the U.S. newspaper industry lost 15,114 jobs that year (Murdoch, 2009). With the dual challenges of layoffs and decreasing readership, some in the journalism industry are beginning to explore other options for ownership, such as nonprofit ownership. As one article in the *Chronicle of Philanthropy* puts it, "It may be time for a more radical reinvention of the daily newspaper. The answer for some newspapers may be to adopt a nonprofit ownership structure that will enable them to seek philanthropic contributions and benefit from tax exemptions (Stehle, 2009)."

It is clear that the newspaper industry is on the brink of major change. Over the next several years, the industry will likely continue to experience a complete upheaval brought on by dwindling readership and major shifts in how individuals consume news. As newspapers scramble to find their footing in an ever-changing business, readers adapt and seek out trustworthy information in new ways.

Key Takeaways

- Some key players in the U.S. newspaper market include the *USA Today*, *The Wall Street Journal*, *The New York Times*, the *Los Angeles Times*, *The Washington Post*, and the *Chicago Tribune*.

- Although readership has been declining since the invention of the radio, the Internet has had the most profound effect on the newspaper industry as readers turn to free online sources of information.

- Financial challenges have led to the rise of ever-growing newspaper chains and the creation of JOAs. Nevertheless, newspapers continue to fold and lay off staff.

Exercises

Please respond to the following writing prompts. Each response should be a minimum of one paragraph.

1. Pick a major national event that interests you. Then, select two papers of the six discussed in this section and explore the differences in how those newspapers reported on the story. How does the newspaper's audience affect the way in which a story is presented?

2. Spend some time exploring websites of several major newspapers. How have these papers been responding to growing online readership?

References

Ahrens, Frank. "Murdoch Seizes Wall St. Journal in $5 Billion Coup," *Washington Post*, August 1, 2007, http://www.washingtonpost.com/wp-dyn/content/article/2007/07/31/AR2007073100896.html.

Chicago Tribune, "On Guard for Chicago," http://www.chicagotribune.com/news/chi-on-guard-for-chicago,0,3834517.htmlpage.

Dilling, Emily. "Study: Newspaper Readership Down, Despite Online Increase," *Shaping the Future of the Newspaper* (blog), March 3, 2009, http://www.sfnblog.com/circulation_and_readership/2009/03/study_newspaper_readership_down_despite.php.

Free Press, "Media Consolidation," http://www.freepress.net/policy/ownership/consolidation.

Los Angeles Times, "L.A. Times Ethics Guidelines," *Readers' Representative Journal* (blog), http://latimesblogs.latimes.com/readers/2007/07/los-angeles-tim.html.

Los Angeles Times, "Times' Pulitzer Prizes," http://www.latimes.com/about/mediagroup/latimes/la-mediagroup-pulitzers,0,1929905.htmlstory.

Milstead, David. "Newspaper Joint Operating Agreements Are Fading," *Rocky Mountain News*, January 22, 2009, http://www.rockymountainnews.com/news/2009/jan/22/newspaper-joas-fading/.

Murdoch, Rupert. "Journalism and Freedom," *Wall Street Journal*, December 8, 2009, http://online.wsj.com/article/SB10001424052748704107104574570191223415268.html.

Newspaper Association of American, "Total Paid Circulation," http://www.naa.org/TrendsandNumbers/Total-Paid-Circulation.aspx.

Newspaper, "Top 10 US Newspapers by Circulation," Newspapers.com, http://www.newspapers.com/top10.html.

Rocky Mountain News, "Goodbye, Colorado," February 7, 2009, http://www.rockymountainnews.com/news/2009/feb/27/goodbye-colorado/.

State of the Media, project for Excellence in Journalism, "Newspapers: Audience" in *The State of the News Media 2004*, http://www.stateofthemedia.org/2004/narrative_newspapers_audience.asp?cat=3&media=2.

State of the Media, project for Excellence in Journalism, "Newspapers: Ownership" in *The State of the News Media 2004*, http://www.stateofthemedia.org/2004/narrative_newspapers_ownership.asp?cat=5&media=2.

Stehle, Vince. "It's Time for Newspapers to Become Nonprofit Organizations," *Chronicle of Philanthropy*, March 12, 2009, http://gfem.org/node/492.

Washington Post, "General Information: Post Principles," https://nie.washpost.com/gen_info/principles/index.shtml.

4.6 Online Journalism Redefines News

Learning Objectives

1. Describe two ways in which online reporting may outperform traditional print reporting.

2. Explain the greatest challenges newspapers face as they transition to online journalism.

The proliferation of online communication has had a profound effect on the newspaper industry. As individuals turn to the Internet to receive news for free, traditional newspapers struggle to remain competitive and hold onto their traditional readers. However, the Internet's appeal goes beyond free content. This section delves further into the Internet and its influence on the print industry. The Internet and its role in media are explored in greater detail in Chapter 11 "The Internet and Social Media" of this textbook.

Competition From Blogs

Weblogs, or blogs, have offered a new take on the traditional world of journalism. Blogs feature news and commentary entries from one or more authors. However, journalists differ on whether the act of writing a blog, commonly known as blogging, is, in fact, a form of journalism.

Indeed, many old-school reporters do not believe blogging ranks as formal journalism. Unlike journalists, bloggers are not required to support their work with credible sources. This means that stories published on blogs are often neither verified nor verifiable. As Jay Rosen, New York University journalism professor, writes, "Bloggers are speakers and writers of their own invention, at large in the public square. They're *participating* in the great game of influence called public opinion (Rosen, 2004)." Despite the blurry lines of what constitutes "true" journalism—and despite the fact that bloggers are not held to the same standards as journalists—many people still seek out blogs to learn about news. Thus, blogs have affected the news journalism industry. According to longtime print journalist and blogger Gina Chen, "Blogging has changed journalism, but it is not journalism (Chen, 2009)."

Advantages Over Print Media

Beyond the lack of accountability in blogging, blogs are free from the constraints of journalism in other ways that make them increasingly competitive with traditional print publications. Significantly, Internet publication allows writers to break news as soon as it occurs. Unlike a paper that publishes only once a day, the Internet is constantly accessible, and information is ready at the click of a mouse.

In 1998, the Internet flexed its rising journalistic muscle by breaking a story before any major print publication: the Bill Clinton/Monica Lewinsky scandal. The *Drudge Report*, an online news website that primarily consists of links to stories, first made the story public, claiming to have learned of the scandal only after *Newsweek* magazine failed to publish it. On January 18, 1998, the story broke online with the title "*Newsweek* Kills Story on White House Intern. Blockbuster Report: 23-year-old, Former White House Intern, Sex Relationship with President." The report gave some details on the scandal, concluding the article with the phrase "The White House was busy checking the *Drudge Report* for details (Australian Politics, 1998)." This act revealed the power of the Internet because of its superiority in timeliness, threatening the relevancy of slower newspapers and news magazines.

Print media also continuously struggle with space constraints, another limit that the Internet is spared. As newspapers contemplate making the transition from print to online editions, several editors see the positive effect of this particular issue. N. Ram, editor in chief of *The Hindu*, claims, "One clear benefit online editions can provide is the scope this gives for accommodating more and longer articles…. There need be no space constraints, as in the print edition (Viswanathan, 2010)." With the endless writing space of the Internet, online writers have the freedom to explore topics more fully, to provide more detail, and to print interviews or other texts in their entirety—opportunities that many print journalists have longed for since newspapers first began publishing.

Online writing also provides a forum for amateurs to enter the professional realm of writing. With cost-cutting forcing newspapers to lay off writers, more and more would-be journalists are turning to the Internet to find ways to enter the field. Interestingly, the blogosphere has launched the careers of journalists who otherwise may never have pursued a career in journalism. For example, blogger Molly Wizenberg founded the blog *Orangette* because she didn't know what to do with herself: "The only thing I knew was that, whatever I did, it had to involve food and writing (Wyke, 2009)." After *Orangette* became a successful food blog, Wizenberg transitioned into writing for a traditional media outlet: food magazine *Bon Appetit*.

Online Newspapers

With declining readership and increasing competition from blogs, most newspapers have embraced the culture shift and have moved to online journalism. For many papers, this has meant creating an online version of their printed paper that readers will have access to from any location, at all times of the day. By 2010, over 10,000 newspapers had gone online. But some smaller papers—particularly those in two-paper communities—have not only started websites, but have also ceased publication of their printed papers entirely.

One such example is Seattle's *Post-Intelligencer*. In 2009, the newspaper stopped printing, "leaving the rival *Seattle Times* as the only big daily in town (Folkenflik, 2009)." As Steve Swartz, president of Hearst Newspapers and owner of the *Post-Intelligencer*, commented about the move to online-only printing, "Being the second newspaper in Seattle didn't work. We are very enthusiastic, however, about this experiment to create a digital-only business in Seattle with a robust community website at its core (Folkenflik, 2009)." For the *Post-Intelligencer*, the move meant a dramatic decrease in its number of staff journalists. The printed version of the paper employed 135 journalists, but the online version, Seattlepi.com, employs only two dozen. For Seattlepi.com, this shift has been doubly unusual because the online-only newspaper is not really like a traditional newspaper at all. As Swartz articulated, "Very few people come to our website and try to re-create the experience of reading a newspaper—in other words, spending a half-hour to 45 minutes and really reading most of the articles. We don't find people do that on the Web (Folkenflik, 2009)." The online newspaper is, in reality, still trying to figure out what it is. Indeed, this is an uncomfortable position familiar to many online-only papers: trapped between the printed news world and the online world of blogs and unofficial websites.

During this transitional time for newspapers, many professional journalists are taking the opportunity to enter the blogosphere, the realm of bloggers on the Internet. Journalist bloggers, also known as beatbloggers, have begun to utilize blogs as "tool[s] to engage their readers, interact with them, use them as sources, crowdsource their ideas and invite them to contribute to the reporting process," says beatblogger Alana Taylor (Taylor, 2009). As beatblogging grows, online newspapers are harnessing the popularity of this new phenomenon and taking advantage of the resources provided by the vast Internet audience through crowdsourcing (outsourcing problem solving to a large group of people, usually volunteers). Blogs are becoming an increasingly prominent feature on news websites, and nearly every major newspaper website displays a link to the paper's official blogs on its homepage. This subtle addition to the web pages reflects the print industry's desire to remain relevant in an increasingly online world.

Even as print newspapers are making the transformation to the digital world with greater or less success, Internet news sites that were never print papers have begun to make waves. Sites such as *The Huffington Post, The Daily Beast*, and the *Drudge Report* are growing in popularity. For example, *The Huffington Post* displays the phrase "The Internet Newspaper: News, Blogs, Video, Community" as its masthead, reiterating its role and focus in today's media-savvy world (Huffington Post). In 2008, former *Vanity Fair* editor Tina Brown cofounded and began serving as editor in chief of *The Daily Beast*. On *The Daily Beast*'s website, Brown has noted its success: "I revel in the immediacy, the responsiveness, the real-time-ness. I used to be the impatient type. Now I'm the serene type. Because how can you be impatient when everything happens right now, instantly (Brown, 2009)?"

Some newspapers are also making even more dramatic transformations to keep up with the changing online world. In 2006, large newspaper conglomerate GateHouse Media began publishing under a Creative Commons license, giving noncommercial users access to content according to the license's specifications. The company made the change to draw in additional online viewers and, eventually, revenue for the newspapers. Writer at the Center for Citizen Media, Lisa Williams, explains in her article published by *PressThink.org*:

GateHouse's decision to CC license its content may be a response to the cut-and-paste world of weblogs, which frequently quote and point to newspaper stories. Making it easier—and legal—for bloggers to quote stories at length means that bloggers are pointing their audience at that newspaper. Getting a boost in traffic from weblogs may have an impact on online advertising revenue, and links from weblogs also have an impact on how high a site's pages appear in search results from search engines such as Google. Higher traffic, and higher search engine rankings build a site's ability to make money on online ads (Williams, 2006).

GateHouse Media's decision to alter its newspapers' licensing agreement to boost advertising online reflects the biggest challenge facing the modern online newspaper industry: profit. Despite shrinking print-newspaper readership and rising online readership, print revenue remains much greater than digital revenue because the online industry is still determining how to make online newspapers profitable. As one article notes:

The positive news is that good newspapers like *The New York Times*, *The Guardian*, *The Financial Times*, and *The Wall Street Journal* now provide better, richer, and more diverse content in their Internet editions…. The bad news is that the print media are yet to find a viable, let alone profitable, revenue model for their Internet journalism (Viswanathan, 2010).

The issue is not only that information on the Internet is free but also that advertising is far less expensive online. As National Public Radio (NPR) reports, "The online-only plan for newspapers remains an unproven financial model; there are great savings by scrapping printing and delivery costs, but even greater lost revenues, since advertisers pay far more money for print ads than online ads (Folkenflik)."

Figure 4.11

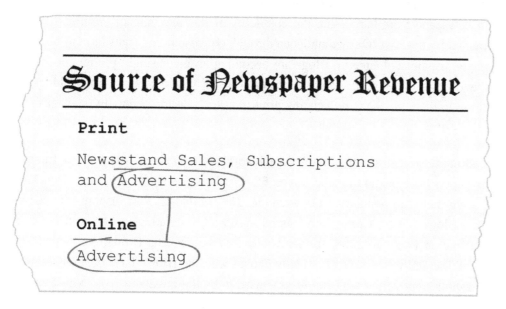

Sources of Newspaper Revenue

Despite these challenges, newspapers both in print and online continue to seek new ways to provide the public with accurate, timely information. Newspapers have long been adapting to cultural paradigm shifts, and in the face of losing print newspapers altogether, the newspaper industry continues to reinvent itself to keep up with the digital world.

Key Takeaways

- Print newspapers face increasing challenges from online media, particularly amateur blogs and professional online news operations.

- Internet reporting outperforms traditional print journalism both with its ability to break news as it happens and through its lack of space limitations. Still, nonprofessional Internet news is not subject to checks for credibility, so some readers and journalists remain skeptical.

- As newspapers move to online journalism, they must determine how to make that model profitable. Most online newspapers do not require subscriptions, and advertising is significantly less expensive online than it is in print.

Exercises

Please respond to the following writing prompts. Each response should be a minimum of one paragraph.

1. Choose a topic on which to conduct research. Locate a blog, a print newspaper, and an online-only newspaper that have information about the topic.

2. What differences do you notice in style and in formatting?

3. Does one appeal to you over the others? Explain.

4. What advantages does each source have over the others? What disadvantages?

5. Consider the changes the print newspaper would need to make to become an online-only paper. What challenges would the print newspaper face in transitioning to an online medium?

End-of-Chapter Assessment

Review Questions

1.
Section 1

   a. Which European technological advancement of the 1400s forever changed the print industry?

   b. Which country's "weeklies" provided a stylistic format that many other papers followed?

   c. In what ways did the penny paper transform the newspaper industry?

   d. What is sensationalism and how did it become a prominent style in the journalism industry?

2.
Section 2

   a. What are some challenges of objective journalism?

   b. What are the unique features of the inverted pyramid style of journalistic writing?

   c. How does literary journalism differ from traditional journalism?

   d. What are the differences between consensus journalism and conflict journalism?

3.
Section 3

   a. In what two ways do newspapers control information?

b. What are some of the defining features of watchdog journalism?

c. Using *USA Today* as a model, in what tangible ways has television affected the newspaper industry and styles of journalism?

4.
Section 4

a. What are a few of the country's most prominent newspapers, and what distinguishes them from one another?

b. Name and briefly describe three technological advances that have affected newspaper readership.

5.
Section 5

a. In what ways might online reporting benefit readers' access to information?

b. Why are print newspapers struggling as they transition to the online market?

Critical Thinking Questions

1. Have sensationalism or yellow journalism retained any role in modern journalism? How might these styles impact current trends in reporting?

2. Do a majority of today's newspapers use objective journalism or interpretive journalism? Why might papers tend to favor one style of journalism over another?

3. In what ways has watchdog journalism transformed the newspaper industry? What are the potential benefits and pitfalls of watchdog journalism?

4. Explore the challenges that have arisen due to the growing number of newspaper chains in the United States.

5. How has the Internet altered the way in which newspapers present news? How are print newspapers responding to the decline of subscribers and the rise of online readers?

Career Connection

Although modern print newspapers increasingly face economic challenges and have reduced the number of journalists they have on staff, career opportunities still exist in newspaper journalism. Those desiring to enter the field may need to explore new ways of approaching journalism in a transforming industry.

Read the articles "Every Newspaper Journalist Should Start a Blog," written by Scott Karp, found at http://publishing2.com/2007/05/22/every-newspaper-journalist-should-start-a-blog/, and "Writing the

Freelance Newspaper Article," by Cliff Hightower, at http://www.fmwriters.com/Visionback/Issue32/Writefreenewspaper.htm.

Think about these two articles as you answer the following questions.

1. What does Scott Karp mean when he says that a blog entails "embracing the power and accepting the responsibility of *being* a publisher"? What should you do on your blog to do just that?

2. According to Karp, what is "the fundamental law of the web"?

3. Karp lists two journalists who have shown opposition to his article. What are the criticisms or caveats to Karp's main article that are discussed?

4. Describe the three suggestions that Cliff Hightower provides when thinking about a career as a freelance writer. How might you be able to begin incorporating those suggestions into your own writing?

5. What two texts does Hightower recommend as you embark on a career as a freelance writer?

References

Australian Politics, "Original Drudge Reports of Monica Lewinsky Scandal (January 17, 1998)," AustralianPolitics.com, http://australianpolitics.com/usa/clinton/impeachment/drudge.shtml.

Brown, Tina. "The Daily Beast Turns One," *Daily Beast*, October 5, 2009, http://www.thedailybeast.com/blogs-and-stories/2009-10-05/the-daily-beast-turns-one/full/.

Chen, Gina. "Is Blogging Journalism?" Save the Media, March 28, 2009, http://savethemedia.com/2009/03/28/is-blogging-journalism/.

Folkenflik, "Newspapers Wade Into an Online-Only Future."

Folkenflik, David. "Newspapers Wade Into an Online-Only Future," NPR, March 20, 2009, http://www.npr.org/templates/story/story.php?storyId=102162128.

Huffington Post, http://www.huffingtonpost.com/.

Rosen, Jay. "Brain Food for BloggerCon," *PressThink* (blog), April 16, 2004, http://journalism.nyu.edu/pubzone/weblogs/pressthink/2004/04/16/con_prelude.html.

Taylor, Alana. "What It Takes to Be a Beatblogger," BeatBlogging.org (blog), March 5, 2009, http://beatblogging.org/2009/03/05/what-it-takes-to-be-a-beatblogger/.

Viswanathan, S. "Internet Media: Sky's the Limit," *Hindu*, March 28, 2010, http://beta.thehindu.com/opinion/Readers-Editor/article318231.ece.

Viswanathan, S. "Internet Media: Sky's the Limit," *Hindu*, March 28, 2010, http://beta.thehindu.com/opinion/Readers-Editor/article318231.ece.

Williams, Lisa. "Newspaper Chain Goes Creative Commons: GateHouse Media Rolls CC Over 96 Newspaper Sites," *PressThink* (blog), December 15, 2006, http://journalism.nyu.edu/pubzone/weblogs/pressthink/2006/12/15/newspaper_chain.html.

Wyke, Nick. "Meet the Food Bloggers: Orangette," *Times* (London), May 26, 2009, http://www.timesonline.co.uk/tol/life_and_style/food_and_drink/real_food/article6364590.ece.

Chapter 5: Magazines

5.1 Magazines

Changing Times, Changing Tastes

Figure 5.1

On October 5, 2009, publisher Condé Nast announced that the November 2009 issue of respected food magazine *Gourmet* would be its last. The decision came as a shock to many readers who, since 1941, had believed that "*Gourmet* was to food what *Vogue* is to fashion, a magazine with a rich history and a perch high in the publishing firmament (Clifford, 2009)." Although Condé Nast folded three other publications—parenting magazine *Cookie* and bridal magazines *Elegant Bride* and *Modern Bride*—the elimination of *Gourmet* received the most attention because of the publication's long history and popularity. Although some readers were angry about the sudden print halt, some understood that the closure was simply a reflection of a changing market.

Magazine publishers have been struggling with competition for advertising dollars for years. The magazine industry took a dramatic hit from the financial crisis that began in the fall of 2007, with many publications folding altogether, several moving to online-only models, and nearly all implementing mass layoffs to cut costs (Vocus Research). The crisis forced the high-end retailers that support Condé Nast magazines to slash their advertising budgets, and the subsequent decline in advertising revenue put the Condé Nast publications in jeopardy (Gross, 2009).

Although this appears to be grim news for an industry that has survived since the 17th century, magazines may not be truly obsolete. Many analysts are hopeful that the magazine industry, with its long, complex past, is simply in a slump. According to the Magazine Publishers of America, some 7,383 magazines appeared in publication in 2008 (Association of Magazine Media). The following year, media private-equity firm Veronis Suhler Stevenson predicted that magazine ad revenues would stabilize in 2013 (Clifford, 2009). Former *Newsweek* financial writer Daniel Gross—though admittedly biased—believes that the industry will strengthen. He describes the panic of some who refer to the demise of print media as symptoms of an "irrational depression surrounding print (Gross)." Yet even he admits that he may be mistaken in his belief that the current downward trend is just a bump in the road. As Gross stated, "If I'm wrong, I may have to eat my words. And I'll be doubly sad because I won't have *Gourmet* to tell me what wine goes best with them (Gross)." So, many have begun to wonder, what will the future of the magazine business hold?

If *Gourmet*'s closure is any indication, the magazines of the future will be a product of cross-media integration, particularly between print and television. "Advertising support for luxurious magazines like *Gourmet* has dwindled, while grocery store advertisers have continued to buy pages at more accessible, celebrity-driven magazines like *Every Day with Rachel Ray*, which specializes in 30-minute meals, and *Food Network Magazine* (Clifford)." This trend suggests that the best—and perhaps only—way for magazines to remain viable is to gain an audience via another medium and then use that celebrity-driven status to sell the print product.

The magazine industry may change drastically over the next several years. This evolution may be affected by a number of variables, such as the Internet, a new generation of readers, the fluctuation of advertising costs, and the recovery from the 2008 recession. What remains to be seen is whether the magazine industry can continue to be a dominant force in American culture in the midst of these changes.

References

Association of Magazine Media, "Clearing up Misperceptions about Magazine Closings," white paper, August 2009, http://www.magazine.org/ASSETS/ACC5AFCF184843B9B8A4CE13080DB232/misperceptions-about-magazine-closings-082009.pdf.

Clifford, "Condé Nast Closes *Gourmet*."

Clifford, Stephanie. "A Look Ahead at the Money in the Communications Industry," *New York Times*, August 3, 2009, http://www.nytimes.com/2009/08/04/business/media/04adco.html.

Clifford, Stephanie. "Condé Nast Closes *Gourmet* and 3 Other Magazines," *New York Times*, October 6, 2009, http://www.nytimes.com/2009/10/06/business/media/06gourmet.html.

Gross, "Don't Make Me Eat My Words."

Gross, Daniel. "Don't Make Me Eat My Words," *Newsweek*, October 7, 2009, http://www.newsweek.com/2009/10/06/don-t-make-me-eat-my-words.html.

Vocus Research, *State of the Media Report 2011: Adapting, Surviving, and Reviving,* http://www.vocus.com/resources/state-of-media/2011-report-adapting-surviving-reviving.pdf.

5.2 History of Magazine Publishing

Learning Objectives
1. Describe the European roots of the modern magazine.
2. Identify the changes that took place in magazine printing in the 1830s United States.
3. Describe the trends in journalism that arose during the 20th century.

Like the newspaper, the magazine has a complex history shaped by the cultures in which it developed. Examining the industry's roots and its transformation over time can contribute to a better understanding of the modern industry.

Early Magazines

After the printing press became prevalent in Europe, early publishers began to conceptualize the magazine. Forerunners of the familiar modern magazine first appeared during the 17th century in the form of brochures, pamphlets, and almanacs. Soon, publishers realized that irregular publication schedules required too much time and energy. A gradual shift then occurred as publishers sought regular readers with specific interests. But the early magazine was unlike any other previous publication. It was not enough of a news source to be a newspaper, but it could not be considered pleasure reading either. Instead, early magazines occupied the middle ground between the two (Encyclopedia Britannica).

Germany, France, and the Netherlands Lead the Way

German theologian and poet Johann Rist published the first true magazine between 1663 and 1668. Titled *Erbauliche Monaths-Unterredungen*, or *Edifying Monthly Discussions*, Rist's publication inspired a number of others to begin printing literary journals across Europe: Denis de Sallo's French *Journal des Sçavans* (1665), the Royal Society's English *Philosophical Transactions* (1665), and Francesco Nazzari's Italian *Giomale de'letterati* (1668). In 1684, exiled Frenchman Pierre Bayle published *Novelles de la République des Lettres* in the Netherlands to escape French censorship. Profoundly affected by a general revival of learning during the 1600s, the publications inspired enthusiasm for education.

Another Frenchman, Jean Donneau de Vizé, published the first "periodical of amusement," *Le Mercure Galant* (later renamed *Mercure de France*), in 1672, which contained news, short stories, and poetry. This combination of news and pleasurable reading became incredibly popular, causing other publications to imitate the magazine (Encyclopedia Britannica). This lighter magazine catered to a different reader than did the other, more intellectual publications of the day, offering articles for entertainment and enjoyment rather than for education.

With the arrival of the 18th century came an increase in literacy. Women, who enjoyed a considerable rise in literacy rates, began reading in record numbers. This growth affected the literary world as a whole, inspiring a large number of female writers to publish novels for female readers (Wolf). This influx of female readers also helped magazines flourish as more women sought out the publications as a source of knowledge and entertainment. In fact, many magazines jumped at the chance to reach out to women. The *Athenian Mercury*, the first magazine written specifically for women, appeared in 1693.

British Magazines Appear

Much as in newspaper publication, Great Britain closely followed continental Europe's lead in producing magazines. During the early 18th century, three major influential magazines published regularly in Great Britain: *Robinson Crusoe* author Daniel Defoe's the *Review*, Sir Richard Steele's the *Tatler*, and Joseph Addison and Steele's the *Spectator*.

All three of these publications were published either daily or several times a week. While they were supplied as frequently as newspapers, their content was closer to that of magazines. The *Review* focused primarily on domestic and foreign affairs and featured opinion-based political articles. The *Spectator* replaced the *Tatler*, which published from 1709 to 1711. Both *Tatler* and *Spectator* emphasized living and culture and frequently used humor to promote virtuous behavior (Wolf). *Tatler* and *Spectator*, in particular, drew a large number of female readers, and both magazines eventually added female-targeted publications: *Female Tatler* in 1709 and *Female Spectator* in 1744.

American Magazines

The first American magazines debuted in 1741, when Andrew Bradford's *American Magazine* and Benjamin Franklin's *General Magazine* began publication in Philadelphia a mere 3 days apart from each other. Neither magazine lasted long, however; *American Magazine* folded after only 3 months and *General Magazine* after 6. The short-lived nature of the publications likely had less to do with the outlets themselves and more to do with the fact that they were "limited by too few readers with leisure time to read, high costs of publishing, and expensive distribution systems (Straubbhaar, et. al., 2009)." Regardless of this early setback, magazines began to flourish during the latter half of the 18th century, and by the end of the 1700s, more than 100 magazines had appeared in the nascent United States. Despite this large publication figure, typical colonial magazines still recorded low circulation figures and were considered highbrow.

Mass-Appeal Magazines

All this changed during the 1830s when publishers began taking advantage of a general decline in the cost of printing and mailing publications and started producing less-expensive magazines with a wider audience in mind.

Magazine style also transformed. While early magazines focused on improvement and reason, later versions focused on amusement. No longer were magazines focused on the elite class. Publishers took advantage of their freshly expanded audience and began offering family magazines, children's magazines, and women's magazines. Women's publications again proved to be a highly lucrative market. One of the earliest American women's magazines was *Godey's Lady's Book*, a Philadelphia-based monthly that printed between 1830 and 1898. This particular magazine reached out to female readers by employing nearly 150 women.

The Saturday Evening Post

The first truly successful mass circulation magazine in the United States was *The Saturday Evening Post*. This weekly magazine first began printing in 1821 and remained in regular print production until 1969, when it briefly ceased circulation. However, in 1971 a new owner remodeled the magazine to focus on health and medical breakthroughs. From the time of its first publication in the early 1800s, *The Saturday Evening Post* quickly grew in popularity; by 1855, it had a circulation of 90,000 copies per year (Saturday Evening Post). Widely recognized for transforming the look of the magazine, the publication was the first to put artwork on its cover, a decision that *The Saturday Evening Post* has said "connected readers intimately with the magazine as a whole (Saturday Evening Post)." Certainly, *The Saturday Evening Post* took advantage of the format by featuring the work of famous artists such as Norman Rockwell. Using such recognizable artists boosted circulation as "Americans everywhere recognized the art of the *Post* and eagerly awaited the next issue because of it (Saturday Evening Post)."

Figure 5.3

The Saturday Evening Post popularized the use of artwork on its cover, setting a standard for other publications to follow.

Wikimedia Commons – public domain.

But *The Saturday Evening Post* did not only feature famous artists; it also published works by famous authors including F. Scott Fitzgerald, Sinclair Lewis, and Ring Lardner. The popularity of these writers contributed to the continuing success of the magazine.

Youth's Companion

Another early U.S. mass magazine was *Youth's Companion*, which published between 1827 and 1929 when it merged with *The American Boy*. Based in Boston, Massachusetts, this periodical featured fairly religious content and developed a reputation as a wholesome magazine that encouraged young readers to be virtuous and pious. Eventually, the magazine sought to reach a larger, adult audience by including tame entertainment pieces. Nevertheless, the magazine in time began featuring the work of prominent writers for both children and adults and became "a literary force to be reckoned with (Nineteenth-Century American Children and What They Read)."

Price Decreases Attract Larger Audiences

While magazines such as *The Saturday Evening Post* and *Youth's Companion* were fairly popular, the industry still struggled to achieve widespread circulation. Most publications cost the then-hefty sum of 25 or 35 cents per issue, limiting readership to the relative few who could afford them. This all changed in 1893 when Samuel Sidney McClure began selling *McClure's Magazine*, originally a literary and political magazine, at the bargain price of only 15 cents per issue. The trend caught on. Soon, *Cosmopolitan* (founded 1886) began selling for 12.5 cents, while *Munsey Magazine* (1886–1929) sold for only 10 cents. All three of these periodicals were widely successful. Frank A. Munsey, owner of *Munsey Magazine*, estimated that between 1893 and 1899 "the ten-cent magazine increased the magazine-buying public from 250,000 to 750,000 persons (Encycopaedia Britannica)." For the first time, magazines could be sold for less than they cost to produce. Because of greater circulation, publications could charge more for advertising space and decrease the cost to the customer.

By 1900, advertising had become a crucial component of the magazine business. In the early days of the industry, many publications attempted to keep advertisements out of their issues because of publishers' natural fondness toward literature and writing (Encycopaedia Britannica). However, once circulation increased, advertisers sought out space in magazines to reach the larger audience. Magazines responded by raising advertising rates, ultimately increasing their profitability. By the turn of the 20th century, advertising became the norm in magazines, particularly in some women's magazines, where advertisements accounted for nearly half of all content.

Early 20th-Century Developments

The arrival of the 20th century brought with it new types of magazines, including news, business, and picture magazines. In time, these types of publications came to dominate the industry and attract vast readerships.

Newsmagazines

As publishers became interested in succinctly presenting the fresh increase of worldwide information that technology made available during the late 19th and early 20th centuries, they designed the newsmagazine. In 1923, *Time* became the first newsmagazine that focused on world news. *Time* first began publication with the proposition that "people are uninformed because no publication has adapted itself to the time which busy men are able to spend simply keeping informed (Encycopaedia Britannica)." Although the periodical struggled during its early years, *Time* hit its stride in 1928 and its readership grew. The magazine's signature style of well-researched news presented in a succinct manner contributed greatly to its eventual success.

Several other newsmagazines came onto the market during this era as well. *Business Week* was founded in 1929 with a focus on the global market. *Forbes,* currently one of the most popular financial magazines, began printing in 1917 as a biweekly publication. In 1933, a former *Time* foreign editor founded *Newsweek,* which now has a circulation of nearly 4 million readers. Today, *Newsweek* and *Time* continue to compete with each other, furthering a trend that began in the early years of *Newsweek.*

Picture Magazines

Photojournalism, or the telling of stories through photography, also became popular during the early 20th century. Although magazines had been running illustrations since the 19th century, as photography grew in popularity so did picture magazines. The most influential picture magazine was Henry Luce's *Life,* which regularly published between 1936 and 1972. Within weeks of its initial publication, *Life* had a circulation of 1 million. In Luce's words, the publication aimed "to see life; to see the world; to witness great events; to watch the faces of the poor and the gestures of the proud; to see strange things (Encyopaedia Britannica)." It did not disappoint. Widely credited with establishing photojournalism, *Life* captured the attention of many on first read. With 96 large-format glossy pages, even the inaugural issue sold out. The opening photograph depicted an obstetrician holding a newborn baby with the caption "Life begins."

While *Life* was the most influential picture magazine, it was certainly not the only photo-centric publication. Popular biweekly picture magazine *Look* printed between 1937 and 1971, claiming to compete with *Life* by reaching out to a larger audience. Although *Look* offered *Life* stiff competition during their almost identical print runs, the latter magazine is widely considered to have a greater legacy. Several other photo magazines—including *Focus, Peek, Foto, Pic,* and *Click*—also took their inspiration from *Life.*

Into the 21st Century

During the late 20th and early 21st centuries, the advent of online technology began to greatly affect both the magazine industry and the print media as a whole. Much like newspaper publishers, magazine publishers have had to rethink their structure to reach out to an increasingly online market. The specifics of the changes made to the magazine industry will be discussed in further detail later in this chapter.

Key Takeaways

- The first magazine was published in Germany during the 17th century. The success of this publication led to the introduction of magazines across Europe. During the 17th and 18th centuries, publishers founded several different types of periodicals aimed at diverse audiences, including the elite and women.

- The 1830s triggered the arrival of mass circulation magazines in the United States. Publishers began offering less expensive magazines to a wider audience, promoting greater consumption of the print media.

- The introduction of newsmagazines and picture magazines dramatically changed the U.S. magazine industry during the early 20th century. Today, newsmagazines such as *Time* and *Newsweek* continue to dominate the magazine industry.

Exercises

Select a magazine that you enjoy reading and research its history. Then, answer the following writing prompts.

1. When was it founded, and by whom? Is the magazine similar to the early European and U.S. magazines? Why or why not?

2. How have its articles, photographs, and advertisements changed over the years? What changes in printing technologies in the 1830s had a direct influence on the way the magazine looks now?

3. Based on the way the magazine has adapted to trends in journalism during the 20th century, how do you predict the magazine will evolve in the future?

5.3 The Role of Magazines in the Development of American Popular Culture

Learning Objectives
1. Identify the change in regional and widespread advertising that occurred in the early 1900s.
2. Describe the backlash against pulp magazines in the 1930s.

Although magazines' great contributions to the development of culture and popular trends are today widely acknowledged, the industry has not always been influential. Because of the significant costs associated with printing and mailing publications, magazines originally reached out only to regional audiences. Not until these expenses declined and advertising revenues increased were magazines able to justify the cost of mass circulation.

Advertising for a National Market

The late 19th century brought with it an increase in mass circulation for the U.S. magazine industry. This meant that magazines that had once targeted only a small part of the country suddenly began reaching a nationwide audience. In addition to the obvious benefit of increased magazine revenue, this shift to broad circulation caused an interesting phenomenon: the introduction of national trends. For the first time in U.S. history, mass circulation allowed news, stories, consumer goods, and fashions to be diffused and advertised to widespread, rather than regional, audiences. Mass circulation of magazines united the country as geographically diverse consumers read the same stories and saw the same advertisements.

Due to this growth in readership, advertisements became increasingly vital to the magazine industry. Advertisers sought to reach a large audience, and magazines willingly afforded them that opportunity, selling advertising space at higher rates. One business manager of *Scribner's Monthly*, an early popular magazine, solicited advertisements by discussing the readership boom:

The publishers of *Scribner's Monthly* will insert in each number of the magazine certain pages devoted to advertisements of a character likely to interest magazine readers. These will not increase the postage, while they will add materially to the ability of the publishers to render their magazines readable and attractive. The press of advertisements upon our first number shows how quickly the claims of the new monthly upon the business public are recognized. Our edition will be very large, and it will have a national circulation. It is now well understood that a first-class popular magazine furnishes to all men who seek a national market the very best medium for advertising that exists (Ohmann, 1996).

That national market was an entirely new one for publishers and advertisers. By the 1930s, market research had become the norm for periodicals as magazines—and advertisers—worked to better understand what readers wanted in their publications. However, market research has its limits; many publishers instead embraced the potential of magazines to simply tell people what they want or need, thus solidifying the role of the magazine as a driver of popular culture. As one editor of *Vogue* articulated: "If we find out what people want, it's already too late (Encyclopaedia Britannica)."

Popular Literature in Magazines

Magazines offered a place not only for advertisers but also for authors and poets to reach a large audience. Several publications regularly hired both new and established authors to write stories. As circulation increased, so did the desire for these authors to publish their work.

Literary magazines enjoyed a boom during the 19th century, publishing some of the period's most important fiction. At one point or another, nearly every important American writer contributed to literary magazines; for example, Edgar Allan Poe, Mark Twain, Walt Whitman, and Ernest Hemingway all published in periodicals throughout their careers. Even writers working outside the country such as Ezra Pound and James Joyce sought out U.S. magazines to publish works that had been banned elsewhere.

Just as magazines offered authors a chance to display their writing to a large audience, they also allowed readers a taste of available literature. Even today, magazines print portions of books, which give readers a preview of the complete text. Portions of literary classics including *Uncle Tom's Cabin, Walden, Moby-Dick, Tom Sawyer, Huckleberry Finn,* and *Ulysses* all made their debuts in magazines. Some novels—such as Edgar Rice Burroughs's *Tarzan of the Apes,* John Hersey's *Hiroshima,* and Ernest Hemingway's *The Old Man and the Sea*—even appeared in magazines in full before being published in book form. The opportunity to publish in magazines has been invaluable for authors, but literary publications have also proved essential for the development of American culture. In publishing literary texts, journals have promoted now-classic stories, like the previously mentioned examples, that have defined American literary history and have shaped the U.S. story.

Pulp Magazines

During the late 1800s, a new type of magazine was established: the pulp magazine, an all-fiction publication named for its rough wood-pulp paper. At the time, dime novels did not qualify for the same inexpensive postal rates that magazines did—but the pulps did. Suddenly, individuals had the opportunity to read popular genre fiction in these cheap magazines, like *Adventure, Horror Stories, Startling Stories,* and *Weird Tales.*

Figure 5.4

Although pulp magazines first began publishing in 1896, they truly gained popularity during the early 20th century.

Terry McCombs – Pulp Heroes III: The Ladies – CC BY-NC 2.0.

Commonly acknowledged to be the invention of Frank Munsey, the pulps got their start as adventure magazines, but they eventually diverged into several categories such as love, detective, and western. The fiction stories did remarkably well until the mid-1930s, when newspaper comics first offered competition by printing collections on the same pulp paper. In 1937, however, the two genres collided with *Detective Comics* (where Batman made his first appearance), and the industry experienced a major boom. Although intended for children, the violent, horror-soaked comics drew a large adult audience. However, the graphic content of the pulp strips caused a stir, with the public divided on the nature of this new media. Defenders of the comics called them harmless, while critics thought they would provoke people to mimic the violent subject matter (Encyclopaedia Britannica). Just as legislators struggle today with debates over censorship of TV, music, and the Internet, they did so with pulp comics as well. Negative backlash against pulp comics was encouraged through several articles published by child psychologist Fredric Wertham, who alleged that comics were leading children into lives of crime (Coville). In response to the controversy, an industry group known as the Association of Comics Magazine Publishers established a Publishers Code in 1948 with the aim of regulating the content of pulp comics. The Publishers Code was not well enforced, however; many publishers chose to ignore the code, and thus the controversy continued to rage. When Senate hearings raised the threat of government regulation in 1954, the pulp comics industry opted for self-censorship, and as a result the much stricter Comics Code Authority was established to control what material reached consumers.

In spite of the controversy surrounding the magazines, the industry flourished, and eventually new forms of pulp magazines emerged. *Amazing Stories* offered science fiction, and hand-drawn pinups filled so-called "Girlie Pulps," which found an audience despite experiencing a setback in 1934 when police seized 10,000 copies and burned them. Even though both new genres attracted outcry from the public for their indecency, the pulps continued to grow in popularity. Many have argued that the difficulties of the Great Depression and the uncertainty of a looming world war made 1930s audiences ripe for the entertainment offered by fictional heroes, giving the pulp genre a ready audience.

Entertainment Magazines

The success of the pulps encouraged another major transformation in mainstream journalism: the rise of entertaining fan magazines. Typically focused on television, film, and music, fan magazines emerged as national entertainment during the early 20th century. During the early years of motion pictures, magazines such as *Photoplay, Picture Play, Movie Mirror,* and *Movieland* began publication, offering subscribers behind-the-scenes glimpses of well-known films. These periodicals were so successful that, as radio and television became popular, similar magazines came into existence to cover these new media. Television- and radio-focused magazines also provided weekly timetables of programs for their viewers and listeners. Although the emphasis of the fan magazine has changed over the years, even today much of the magazine industry is dominated by entertainment publications, like *Entertainment Weekly, Rolling Stone,* and *TV Guide.* In addition to providing entertainment news to readers, these publications are also useful to celebrities and media producers as a platform to market their new products.

Teen Magazines

During the 1940s, many publishers began pursuing teenagers, a previously ignored demographic. *Seventeen* magazine hit shelves in 1944, setting the stage for later publications such as *Tiger Beat* and *Teen People.* These magazines targeted young women, offering stories on fashion, makeup, celebrity news, and lifestyles. Since their beginnings, teen magazines have kept their articles relatively brief, instead reaching their target audiences with bright and bold photos. *Tiger Beat,* for example, is known for its collaged covers featuring a popular teen celebrity of the moment. Teen magazines influence popular culture not only through their reporting on celebrities, but also through their articles on celebrity fashion, which readers use to adopt fashion trends worn by celebrities. Like entertainment magazines, teen magazines are also useful marketing tools for celebrities and other media producers.

During their early years, most teen magazines sought out readers in their late teens, even offering articles on colleges. Today, however, to reach a wider audience, these same magazines intentionally target the preteen market by featuring younger actors and including more teenage celebrity gossip. In doing so, the magazine industry continues to influence younger and younger audiences, thus making a greater impact on American popular culture.

Figure 5.5

First popularized during the 1940s, teen magazines today target both tween and teenage audiences, bringing popular culture to the young.

shuttergrl – September 1975 – CC BY-NC-ND 2.0.

Do Magazine Images Negatively Influence Teenage Girls?

In 2006, the Madrid fashion show made headlines by banning overly thin models to project an image of beauty and health. According to fashion show organizers, "models had to be within a healthy weight range. That means a 5-foot-9 woman would need to be at least 125 pounds (Hellmich, 2006)." The debate over thin models has been around since the 1960s when model Twiggy entered the field. Since then, extremely thin models have ruled the runway despite claims to the contrary: Most American runway models measure within an inch or two of 6 feet tall, but weigh between just 120 and 124 pounds. With images of these models everywhere, many are growing concerned about their effect on American youths, especially teen girls.

Studies have shown that images of ultra-thin models distort women's views of health and beauty, leading to depression, extreme dieting, and eating disorders. In one study, 69 percent of girls said that fashion models influence their idea of the perfect body shape, despite the fact that most models weigh 23 percent less than the average female (Healthy Place). Another study showed that 68 percent of Stanford University undergraduate and graduate students felt worse about themselves after looking through a women's magazine (Healthy Place). Even more worrisome is the fact that young girls are being negatively affected by magazine images. "The number one wish for girls 11 to 17 is to be thinner, and girls as young as 5 have expressed fears of getting fat. Eighty percent of 10-year-old girls have dieted (Healthy Place)."

Some companies are fighting the trend of using super-thin models in their advertising. In 2004, Dove launched its Dove Campaign for Real Beauty; the company claims the goal of the ad campaign is to "help free ourselves and the next generation from beauty stereotypes (Dove)." Dove's ads feature women of many shapes, sizes, and ethnicities in little more than their undergarments. Dove has stated that it plans to continue using "real women" in marketing campaigns (Morrell, 2007).

Celebrity Magazines

Celebrity gossip is not just reserved for teen audiences. A stroll through a supermarket checkout lane reveals the vast assortment of celebrity magazines—also known as gossip magazines—that target adults. First popularized during the 1970s, these celebrity magazines offer readers an inside perspective on the lives of the famous. Many magazines publish gossip stories that humanize celebrities by featuring them in a negative light. Despite the best efforts of celebrities and their agents, placement in these magazines can make or break celebrities' reputations and foster much drama within the celebrity community. Because of intense competition for stories, celebrity magazines may pay large sums of money to celebrities or other sources for exclusive stories and photos. Celebrity magazines will be discussed in detail later in this chapter.

Key Takeaways

- When magazines began distributing nationwide, advertising underwent significant changes. Advertisers took advantage of the widespread audience and started marketing national trends. Advertising costs skyrocketed, as individuals across the country would now see and be influenced by the ads in magazines.

- During the 20th century, new types of magazines—such as literary magazines, pulp magazines, fan magazines, teen magazines, and celebrity magazines—all contributed to shared pop culture.

Exercises

Look through a teen magazine like *Seventeen* or *CosmoGIRL!* and examine the models present in them. Then, answer the following writing prompts.

1. Do you see any images that might negatively affect young readers? Do you see any images that promote a healthy body image? How might magazines alter their advertisements and articles to more positively affect young audiences?

2. How does this magazine differ from the magazines in the early 1900s? What advertising differences do you see?

3. How might the backlash against pulp magazines in the 1930s have contributed to the rise of teen magazines?

References

Coville, Jamie. "The Comic Book Villain, Dr. Fredric Wertham, M.D.," Seduction of the Innocents and the Attack on Comic Books, http://www.psu.edu/dept/inart10_110/inart10/cmbk4cca.html.

Dove, "Campaign for Real Beauty," http://www.dove.us/#/cfrb/about_cfrb.aspx.

Encyclopaedia Britannica, s.v. "History of Publishing."

Healthy Place, "Eating Disorders: Body Image and Advertising," December 11, 2008, http://www.healthyplace.com/eating-disorders/main/eating-disorders-body-image-and-advertising/menu-id-58/.

Hellmich, Nanci. "Do Thin Models Warp Girls' Body Image?" *USA Today*, September 26, 2006, http://www.usatoday.com/news/health/2006-09-25-thin-models_x.htm.

Morrell, Sophia. "Is the Use of Eating-Disorder Sufferers in Dove's Ad Campaign an Act of Desperation?" *Marketing Week*, August 16, 2007, http://www.marketingweek.co.uk/analysis/is-the-use-of-eating-disorder-sufferers-in-doves-ad-campaign-an-act-of-desperation?/2057515.article.

Ohmann, Richard. *Selling Culture: Magazines, Markets, and Class at the Turn of the Century* (New York: Verso, 1996), 26.

5.4 Major Publications in the Magazine Industry

Magazines have evolved significantly since their inception. Magazines have affected the world by bringing news, entertainment, literature, and photography to their readers. Additionally, the magazine industry has profoundly affected U.S. popular culture. As magazines have developed over time, individual publications have targeted specific groups and have found particular niches. This section explores a number of popular periodicals and their effect on their target audiences.

High-Circulation Magazines

The top 10 highest circulating magazines in the United States differ greatly in style and audience. From *AARP* to *Better Homes and Gardens*, from *National Geographic* to *Family Circle*, the list demonstrates the wide pool of readers and interests attracted to the medium. This section will explore the top three publications: *AARP The Magazine*, *AARP Bulletin*, and *Reader's Digest*.

AARP The Magazine and *AARP Bulletin*

Some may be surprised to learn that the two magazines with the highest circulation in the United States are not ones readily available to buy at a newsstand or grocery store: *AARP The Magazine* and *AARP Bulletin*. Published by the nonprofit organization AARP (formerly known as the American Association of Retired Persons), both are automatically sent to the organization's more than 40 million members.

A bimonthly publication that is "geared exclusively towards 50+ Americans seeking to enhance their quality of life as they age (AARP)," *AARP The Magazine* publishes lifestyle articles and includes sections dedicated to health, money, work, relationships, and travel, among others. Its mission statement reads:

AARP The Magazine provides three editorial versions targeted to different life stages (50–59, 60–69, 70+) to empower readers with editorial written just for them. Annual editorial packages, strong service journalism, and celebrity profiles will be presented in a warm, vibrant and inviting format to encourage readers to reflect, engage and enjoy (AARP).

AARP also publishes *AARP Bulletin*, which is "a monthly news publication that reaches influential consumers and policymakers (AARP)." Rather than presenting lifestyle stories, this publication focuses on news stories of interest to its target audience.

AARP Bulletin chronicles and interprets important social issues that affect 50+ Americans. News, balanced analysis and concise stories, in an accessible format, motivates these influential readers to engage in public policy on health care, financial well-being and consumer protection (AARP).

Reader's Digest

Reader's Digest boasts the third-highest circulation among U.S. magazines. First published in 1922 as a "digest of condensed articles of topical interest and entertainment value taken from other periodicals (Encyclopaedia Britannica)," this famous pocket-sized journal was first produced on a low budget by a husband and wife team who believed the magazine would sell despite numerous rejections from magazine publishers (Encyclopaedia Britannica). They were right. *Reader's Digest* was an almost immediate success and now regularly outsells competitors. The monthly magazine has subscribers around the globe and seeks to "create products that inform, enrich, entertain and inspire people of all ages and cultures around the world (Reader's Digest)."

News Magazines

As discussed earlier in this chapter, newsmagazines became popular during the 1920s. Today, newsmagazines make up a large portion of magazine sales, with multiple news periodicals ranking in the top 30 for circulation. Over time, a number of newsmagazines have established themselves in the industry, including *Time*, *Newsweek*, and *U.S. News & World Report*.

Newsweek

Newsweek's initial February 1933 issue was called *News-Week* and featured seven different photographs from the week's news on its cover. The weekly publication currently "offers comprehensive coverage of world events with a global network of correspondents, reporters and editors covering national and international affairs, business, science and technology, society and the arts and entertainment (Newsweek, 2007)." Relying on a wide array of reporters, *Newsweek* also uniquely publishes a reader-penned section titled "My Turn." The magazine has been hugely successful over the years and holds more prestigious National Magazine Awards than any other newsweekly.

The magazine has not been without its trials, however. In November of 2009 *Newsweek* published an article discussing Sarah Palin's book, *Going Rogue: An American Life*. The cover of that issue featured a photo of Palin that had been used in an issue of *Runner's World* with Palin in running attire. The words "How Do You Solve a Problem Like Sarah?" were splayed across the photograph.

Figure 5.6

Sarah Palin was the subject of a controversial cover of *Newsweek*, published in November 2009, that earned the magazine much criticism.

FairbanksMike – Saying Goodbye – CC BY 2.0.

The cover caused a popular backlash, with readers calling it sexist and unfair. One reader suggested that *Newsweek* would never print a photograph of Barack Obama in such attire. In response, *Newsweek* published a photo of President Obama in his swim trunks in its following issue, although this photo was smaller and on an inside page rather than on the cover.

Time

Time has remained an influential publication during the decades since its inception. Today, the publication prides itself on its "rare convergence of incisive reporting, lively writing and world-renowned photography," which combined have earned it the praise of being "journalism at its best (Time)." The magazine is divided into four main sections: Briefing, The Well, Life, and Arts. Briefing includes concise stories on major news events in the United States and other countries. The Well section features longer articles, including the cover story and articles on world and business. Life contains stories on health, science, technology, and the environment. Finally, Arts consists of reviews of theater, film, literature, music, exhibits, and architecture. Like *Newsweek*, *Time* has won numerous awards and prides itself on being "the guide through chaos" in an era of information overload (Time).

U.S. News & World Report

Created through the merger of a newspaper and a magazine, *U.S. News & World Report* has gained great prestige over the years. In 1933—the same year that *Newsweek* debuted—journalist David Lawrence began publishing a weekly newspaper called the *United States News*. Six years later, he founded a weekly magazine titled *World Report*. In 1948, the two weeklies merged to create the new *U.S. News & World Report*. The magazine's focus is similar to those of *Time* and *Newsweek*, but *U.S. News & World Report* concentrates more on political, economic, health, and education stories, perhaps in part because it is based in Washington, DC. Although for most of its long history the magazine published weekly, in 2008 it announced its transition to a monthly printing schedule, vowing to concentrate on its website.

The magazine is perhaps best known for its annual ranking of U.S. colleges. This ranking began in 1983 and has since evolved to include newsstand books of *America's Best Colleges* and *America's Best Graduate Schools*. Since the ranking system began, students turn to the publication for information about the strengths and weaknesses of institutions of higher learning.

Women's Magazines

Female readers have been important to the magazine industry since the early 19th century, initially because women were not traditionally part of the workforce and were believed to have more leisure time to read. This lucrative market has only grown over time. In an increasingly online era, many magazines have sought ways to expand their scope to reach a larger audience. Yet others, such as *Ladies' Home Journal*, *Good Housekeeping*, and *Better Homes and Gardens*, have maintained their original scope and have still managed to turn profits. These three periodicals are part of the "Seven Sisters," a group of magazines traditionally targeted at women.

Ladies' Home Journal

Ladies' Home Journal began in 1879 as a column for women published in the *Tribune and Farmer* newspaper. The wife of the publisher was not entirely impressed with her husband's column and so began writing it herself (Aliperti). The column grew in popularity so rapidly that, by 1883, Louisa Knapp Curtis had published her first major supplement called the *Ladies Home Journal and Practical Housekeeper*. Today, the publishers of the *Ladies' Home Journal* state that it is "a unique lifestyle magazine dedicated to the millions of American women who want to look good, do good and feel great (Meredith)." Ranked twelfth in circulation, the magazine presently has a readership of nearly 4 million (Echo Media). *Ladies' Home Journal* focuses on style, health, relationships, and food. Perhaps its most recognizable feature is a column titled "Can This Marriage Be Saved?", which made its debut in 1953. The regular column features stories of real-life couples struggling in their marriages, offers advice from marriage and family therapists, and projects the outcomes.

Good Housekeeping

In May of 1885, *Good Housekeeping* began publishing with the intention of providing "information about running a home, a broad range of literary offerings, and opportunities for reader input (Library of Congress)." Fifteen years later, the magazine founded the Good Housekeeping Research Institute. The research institute includes a product-evaluation laboratory where a staff of scientists, engineers, nutritionists, and researchers evaluate a wide variety of products. The magazine then reports their findings to its readers to "improve the lives of consumers and their families through education and product evaluation (Good Housekeeping)." The magazine describes itself as:

Devoted to contemporary women. Monthly articles focus on food, fitness, beauty, and childcare using the resources of the Good Housekeeping Institute. From human interest stories and social issues to money management and travel, the magazine will encourage positive living for today's woman (Good Housekeeping Magazine, 2010).

With over 4.6 million readers, *Good Housekeeping* currently ranks ninth highest in U.S. circulation (Echo Media).

Better Homes and Gardens

Making its print debut in 1922, *Better Homes and Gardens* entered the industry later than its counterparts. Currently, the magazine is ranked fifth in circulation in the United States with a readership of more than 7.6 million (Echo Media). Since its inception, the publication has focused on home and gardening style and decorations. Its positioning statement reads:

For the woman who reads *Better Homes and Gardens*, home is where she creates her life story. It's her haven, where she raises her family, entertains friends, and celebrates life's big—and small—accomplishments. It's where she indulges her dreams and builds a world of her own. Home is her emotional center—it's where life happens. *Better Homes and Gardens* recognizes this and inspires her with infinite possibilities for creativity and self-expression. Each issue delivers smart, approachable editorial on design and individual style, decorating and gardening, food and entertaining, and personal and family well-being. *Better Homes and Gardens* helps her bridge the gap between dreaming and doing (Meredith).

The monthly magazine is divided into six sections: Food and Nutrition, Home, Health, Family, Gardening, and Lifestyle.

Cosmopolitan

First published in 1886, the female-targeted *Cosmopolitan* has changed dramatically over time from its original intent of being a "first-class family magazine (Mott, 1957)." In the first issue, the editor told readers that "there will be a department devoted exclusively to the interests of women, with articles on fashions, on household decoration, on cooking, and the care and management of children, etc., also a department for the younger members of the family (Mott, 1957)." Just 2 years later, however, the original publishing company went out of business, and after several publisher changes *Cosmopolitan* was eventually purchased by newspaper mogul William Randolph Hearst in 1905.

The magazine became more successful during the 1960s when Helen Gurley Brown "transformed an antiquated general-interest mag called *Cosmopolitan* into the must-read for young, sexy single chicks (Benjamin)." Brown transformed the magazine from the family-focused publication it was to the somewhat controversial read with an emphasis on sex, work, and fashion that it is today. The magazine describes the transformation saying:

Over the years, *Cosmo* has not only become the number-one-selling monthly magazine on the newsstand, but it has also served as an agent for social change, encouraging women everywhere to go after what they want (whether it be in the boardroom or the bedroom) (Benjamin).

In 1965, *Cosmopolitan* revamped its journal with Brown's vision in mind. The first retooled issue had an article about birth-control pills, then a relatively new and controversial innovation. The magazine's provocative articles attracted a large readership, but many found it offensive. Conservatives believed that the content was too racy, while some feminists thought it was too focused on beauty and pleasing men (Benjamin). Yet the publishers of *Cosmopolitan* believed that they were introducing a new form of feminism (Benjamin). Brown argued that "*Cosmo* is feminist in that we believe women are just as smart and capable as men are and can achieve anything men can. But it also acknowledges that while work is important, men are too. The *Cosmo* girl absolutely loves men (Benjamin)!"

Today, *Cosmopolitan* continues to attract readers by maintaining the same ideals that Brown put forth in the 1960s. Nearly 30 percent of every issue is dedicated to relationships, sex especially. The rest provides articles on beauty, fashion, entertainment, health and fitness, and self-improvement.

Men's Magazines

Just as women's magazines have existed for much of the history of the medium, over the years many magazines have been devoted to male readers. One of the most enduring and popular of those magazines is *Sports Illustrated*.

Sports Illustrated

When *Time* cocreator Henry Luce launched *Sports Illustrated* in 1954, his staff was doubtful about its chances. Spectator sports had not yet reached the level of popularity they have today, and the new magazine failed to make a profit for its first 12 years of publication. As television brought spectator sports to the growing suburbs, however, their popularity quickly rose, and *Sports Illustrated* became a success. Managing editor Andre Laguerre assembled a staff of talented, loyal writers and instituted the extensive use of color photographs, developing the basis for the format the magazine still uses.

In 1964, Laguerre initiated the *Sports Illustrated* Swimsuit Edition as a way of increasing sales during the winter months when there are fewer developments in sports. Putting model Babette March on the cover in a bikini helped the magazine sell, and the swimsuit edition became an annual tradition. Filled with pictures of models in revealing swimwear, the issue generates its share of controversy but is consistently the best-selling issue of the magazine each year.

Celebrity Magazines

Despite being criticized at times for their less-than-sophisticated approach to journalism, celebrity magazines bring in enormous profits and help shape U.S. pop culture, fueling the obsession some Americans have with the mundane day-to-day details of the lives of celebrities. Three of the most prominent celebrity magazines currently publishing are *People*, *OK!*, and *Us Weekly*.

People

Since it first began publishing as a spin-off of *Time* magazine's "People" section in 1974, *People* has been a leading celebrity magazine. The publication sets itself apart from other celebrity gossip magazines by publishing human-interest stories alongside photos and articles about celebrities. The publishers of *People* state that they avoid pure Hollywood gossip articles and they refuse to publish stories without some sort of verification (Moni). This editorial slant is unique among celebrity magazines, and, as such, the publication frequently receives exclusive interviews and photo shoots with celebrities. The somewhat more respectful relationship between the publishers and some celebrities has helped *People* become the most popular celebrity magazine in circulation, ranking thirteenth overall with a verified readership of over 3.6 million in 2010 (Moni).

OK!

A British-run magazine that began publishing in 1993, *OK!* claims to "bring you the truth and the inside scoop about celebrities (OK Magazine)." Known for its exclusive interviews that often lead to public announcements on pregnancies and engagements, *OK!* initially had a policy to print only positive celebrity profiles (Search). That policy changed in 2007 thanks to an erratic interview with pop singer Britney Spears, which was so surprising that the magazine decided to break with tradition and publish it anyway (Search). In 2008, Spears agreed to a second interview with the publication in which she discussed her previous behavior, leading to a more positive profile of the singer. The widely successful magazine has readers around the world along with several branch publications.

Us Weekly

Founded in 1977, *Us Weekly* followed the format of a bimonthly entertainment news and review magazine until 2000, when it switched formats to become a weekly leader in celebrity news and style. The publication "delivers a mass audience of young, educated, and affluent adults who are compelled by breaking celebrity news, Hollywood style and the best in entertainment (Us Weekly)." *Us Weekly* has become known for its fashion sections such as "Who Wore It Best?," a reader poll comparing two celebrities wearing the same outfit, and "Fashion Police," in which comedians comment on celebrity fashion mishaps and successes. With a circulation of nearly 2 million in December 2010, *Us Weekly* prides itself on being a leader in the celebrity magazine industry (Us Weekly).

Key Takeaways

- *AARP The Magazine*, *AARP Bulletin*, and *Reader's Digest* boast the three highest U.S. circulations among contemporary magazines.
- Women's magazines, such as *Cosmopolitan*, make up a large portion of the medium.

Exercises

Study the top 10 highest circulating magazines, which were outlined in this section: http://www.magazine.org/CONSUMER_MARKETING/CIRC_TRENDS/ABC2009TOTALrank.aspx. Then, answer the following writing prompts.

1. Why might these magazines rank higher in circulation than others? What themes, audiences, and differences set these apart?

2. Is any controversy surrounding them comparable to the controversy surrounding the modern *Cosmopolitan*?

References

AARP, "AARP Bulletin," http://aarpmedia.org/bulletin.

AARP, "AARP The Magazine," http://aarpmedia.org/atm.

Aliperti, Cliff. "The Ladies' Home Journal: Development under Louisa Knapp Curtis and Edward W. Bok," http://www.things-and-other-stuff.com/magazines/ladies-home-journal.html.

Benjamin, Jennifer "How Cosmo Changed the World," *Cosmopolitan,* http://www.cosmopolitan.com/about/about-us_how-cosmo-changed-the-world.

Echo Media, "Better Homes and Gardens," http://www.echo-media.com/mediaDetail.php?ID=4227&filterUsed=FALSE;Audit Bureau of Circulations, http://www.accessabc.com/.

Echo Media, "Good Housekeeping," http://www.echo-media.com/mediaDetail.php?ID=4155&filterUsed=FALSE; Audit Bureau of Circulations, http://www.accessabc.com/.

Echo Media, "Ladies' Home Journal," http://www.echo-media.com/mediaDetail.php?ID=4162.

Encyclopaedia Britannica, s.v. "Reader's Digest," http://www.britannica.com/EBchecked/topic/492829/Readers-Digest.

Good Housekeeping Magazine," http://worldmags.net/women/2022-good-housekeeping-september-2010-us.html.

Good Housekeeping, "About the Good Housekeeping Research Institute," http://www.goodhousekeeping.com/product-testing/history/about-good-housekeeping-research-institute.

Library of Congress, "Today in History: *Good Housekeeping*," American Memory Project, http://memory.loc.gov/ammem/today/may02.html.

Meredith, Better Homes and Gardens, "Positioning Statement," http://www.meredith.com/mediakit/bhg/index.html.

Meredith, Ladies' Home Journal, "Mission Statement," http://www.meredith.com/mediakit/lhj/print/index.htm.

Moni, Alyssa. "An Inside Look at People Magazine," March 31, 2011, http://www.hercampus.com/school/bu/inside-look-people-magazine.

Mott, Frank Luthor. *A History of American Magazines: 1885–1905* (Cambridge, MA: Harvard University Press, 1957), 480.

Newsweek, "History of *Newsweek*," http://www.newsweek.com/2007/10/10/history-of-newsweek.html.

OK Magazine!, "About," http://www.okmagazine.com/about/.

Reader's Digest, "Customer Care," http://www.rd.com/customer-care/.

Search, "OK!" http://www.search.com/reference/OK!.

Time, "National Editorial," http://205.188.238.181/time/mediakit/1/us/timemagazine/national/.

Us Weekly, "Us Weekly Circulation Strength," http://srds.com/mediakits/UsWeekly-print/Circulation.html.

Us Weekly, "Us Weekly Media Kit," http://www.srds.com/mediakits/us_weekly/index.html.

5.5 How Magazines Control the Public's Access to Information

Learning Objectives

1. Describe how the formats of newspapers and magazines differ.
2. Explain the impact of advertisements on story.

Magazines control the public's access to information in a variety of ways. Like the newspaper industry, the magazine industry not only dictates which stories get told, but also how those stories are presented. Although significant similarities between the newspaper and magazine industries' control over information exist, some notable differences within the industries themselves deserve exploration.

Format

In general, the format of most magazines allows for a more in-depth discussion of a topic than is possible in the relatively constrained space available in newspapers. Most large newspapers, such as *The Washington Post* or the *Los Angeles Times*, generally cap even their longest articles at 1,000 words (State of the Media, 2004). Magazines, however, frequently allow for double that word count when publishing articles of great interest (State of the Media, 2004). Length, however, varies from magazine to magazine and story to story. Coverage of the war in Iraq offers a good example of this variance. Researchers studied magazine coverage of Iraq over a period of 4 weeks in 2003 by examining the difference in reporting among *Time, Newsweek,* and *U.S. News & World Report.*

In these four issues, the war in Iraq accounted for more than a fifth (22 percent) of all stories and roughly a third (32 percent) of all the space. These stories were also more likely than others to be long and in depth…. There were also differences in the way that the three magazines covered the situation. *Time* devoted the most space to the war, 37 percent, compared to the 34 percent for *Newsweek* and 24 percent for *U.S. News.* And again, *Time* had more long stories (seven stories in the four issues studied were more than 2,000 words). *Newsweek* ran six long stories in the four issues studied and *U.S. News* ran two long stories (State of the Media, 2004).

Although these differences might not appear that great, the results reflect editorial choice and, therefore, the power the magazine industry has over information control.

Choice to Publish

Just as newspapers do, magazines control which stories reach the public by deciding which articles to include in their publications. As might be expected, the choice of stories depends on the political climate and on global events.

Leading newsmagazines *Time* and *Newsweek* both underwent major transitions in their content during the late 20th century. Between the 1970s and 1990s, both greatly increased science articles, entertainment articles, and stories on personal health. Interestingly, despite both publications' stated commitment to news, a dramatic decrease took place in articles on domestic- and foreign-government affairs. Whether these changes reflected a change in reader interest or an alteration in the editors' perspectives remains unclear; however, these shifts demonstrate that what is published is entirely up to the magazine and its editorial staff, as they are the ones who have the final word.

Advertisers' Influence

Magazines derive approximately half of their income from advertisers (Cyber College, 2010). With such a large stake in the magazine industry, advertisers can play a major role in deciding which stories are printed. Because magazines are so dependent on advertisers for their revenue, they are cautious about the content they place in their pages.

Magazines tend to shy away from controversial content that can turn off advertisers. Recently, a large American auto manufacturer sent a memo to about 50 magazines asking that their ad agency be notified if future issues of the magazine contained articles that addressed political, sexual, or social issues that might be seen as provocative, controversial, or offensive (Cyber College, 2010).

The balance that magazines must maintain to keep advertisers happy is a delicate one. With ad prices driving the magazine industry, many publications are forced to satisfy advertisers by avoiding potentially controversial stories.

Another anecdote about advertisers controlling stories illustrates how some publishers must conform to advertiser demands.

In an even more blatant attempt to influence magazine content, another large corporation informed a number of magazine publishers that the content of their magazines would be carefully monitored for several months and that a large advertising contract would be awarded to the publication that portrayed their industry in the most favorable light (Cyber College).

With stories such as these, it may seem easy to paint the advertising industry as an evil, controlling entity that seeks to keep stories from the public. While advertisers may exhibit some control over stories, they also have a lot at stake.

As online media grows, today many advertisers are pulling their expensive print ads in favor of cheaper, web-based advertisements (Knarr). Advertising revenue has decreased steadily since the 1990s, mirroring the rise in online readership (HighBeam Business). This drop in advertising may, in fact, force magazines to give advertisers more control over their content to avoid losing further funding. While it may be difficult to precisely pin down the level of influence advertisers exert over magazine content, evidence suggests they do exert some control.

Editorial Leanings

Each magazine has its own editorial slant, which helps determine which stories get published and how those stories are presented. A 2003 study examining leading newsmagazines *Time, Newsweek, and U.S. News & World Report* verified these differences by demonstrating variations in how the publications presented their articles to the reading public.

U.S. News & World Report…is the most information-laden, the most likely to publish highly traditional hard news topics and the most likely to report in a neutral manner—a more straightforward accounting of the facts of events with less of a writer's "take" or opinion on what those events mean. *Newsweek* is lighter, more oriented toward lifestyle and celebrity coverage, and more likely to publish stories that contain an emotional component. *Time* magazine is something of a hybrid between the two. Its content is more like *U.S. News'*—neutral and information driven. Its covers, on the other hand, look a good deal more like *Newsweek's*—highlighting lifestyle and entertainment(State of the Media).

These distinctions among the three publications may seem slight, but they have an effect on the information contained between their covers. However, these editorial leanings do not make one magazine more prestigious or valid than the others; *U.S. News & World Report* may offer facts and figures about a particular event, while *Newsweek* may provide the human side of the story. Readers should understand, though, that several variables affect the articles that they see in each publication.

Online News Sources

The Internet has significantly changed the way that the public receives information. The advent of online news sources has somewhat lessened the control that magazines have over information. Today, several online-only magazines provide, for little to no cost, news and coverage that would have previously been available only through print publications. Online-only magazines include *Slate*, which offers a daily digest of information from newspapers around the globe, and *Salon*, which provides readers many stories for free and more in-depth coverage for a subscription cost. Like their print counterparts, online magazines rely on revenue from advertisers, but because that advertising is less costly, advertisers may have less of a stake in online content. All these factors contribute to changing perspectives on the way that information is being controlled in the journalism industry.

Key Takeaways

- In general, magazine formats offer more space for coverage than newspapers. This increased space permits greater coverage and can give readers more in-depth information about events.

- Advertisers, which provide approximately half of all magazine revenue, maintain some control over the magazine industry by threatening to pull ads from magazines that print stories that are considered too racy, too political, or not consistent with their beliefs.

Exercises

Select a current major news event that interests you. Read an article from a major newspaper and an article from a magazine on the event. Then, answer the following writing prompts.

1. How do the articles differ? How are they similar?

2. What advertisements surround the article? How might they affect the story or reveal who the target audience is?

3. Do you think that this audience has an effect on the way the story is covered? Why or why not?

References

Cyber College, "Magazines: Economics and Careers," March 20, 2010, http://www.cybercollege.com/frtv/mag3.htm.

HighBeam Business, "Periodicals: Publishing, or Publishing and Printing" http://business.highbeam.com/industry-reports/wood/periodicals-publishing-publishing-printing.

Knarr, David. "Magazine Advertising – Trade Secrets," http://www.studio1productions.com/Articles/MagAds.htm.

State of the Media, Project for Excellence in Journalism, "Magazines" in *The State of the News Media 2004*, http://www.stateofthemedia.org/2004/narrative_magazines_contentanalysis.asp?cat=2&media=7.

State of the Media, Project for Excellence in Journalism, "Magazines" in *The State of the News Media 2004*.

State of the Media, Project for Excellence in Journalism, "Newspapers" in *The State of the News Media 2004*, http://www.stateofthemedia.org/2004/narrative_newspapers_contentanalysis.asp?cat=2&media=2.

5.6 Specialization of Magazines

Learning Objectives

1. Identify different types of specialized magazines.
2. Recognize ways that advertisers benefit from the specialization of magazines.

Over the last century, magazines have slowly moved into more specialized, fragmented groupings. This transformation from general-interest to niche publications began with the popularization of television. To survive the threat posed by the success of broadcast media, print publications worked to stand out from their competitors by developing market niches. During this transition, magazine editors found that by specializing they were also appealing to advertisers hoping to reach specific audiences. No longer were ads just going out to the general public. Instead, advertisers could target groups by gender, age, race, class, and social and cultural interests (Cambell, et. al.).

From the medical field to the auto industry, specialization has become necessary to compete in an ever-growing market. Yet the trend is perhaps most obvious in mass media and in the publishing industry in particular. "In 2006, the Magazine Publishers of America trade organization listed more than 40 special categories of consumer magazines (Cambell, et. al.)." This wide variety of niche publications reflects the increasing specificity of markets and audiences. "In publishing, demand for specialized magazines and books can be evidenced by looking at the magazine rack. [There are] magazines focusing on photography to cars, to economics and foreign affairs and more (Hess, 2007)." Specialization is likely to increase, rather than decrease. "Market fragmentation has and probably will continue to proliferate. Customization and individualization will probably be the continuing trend (Hess, 2007)."

Professional Trade Publications

Nearly every trade group produces some sort of professional publication for its members. Many trade organizations even have their own libraries that house publications solely dedicated to their specific groups. For example, if a person wishes to find information on agriculture, forestry, fishing, and hunting organizations, the National Agricultural Library in Beltsville, Maryland, near Washington, DC, might offer a starting point. This library is one of four national libraries of the United States and has one of the world's largest agricultural information collections and links a nationwide network of state land-grant and U.S. Department of Agriculture field libraries (Career Resource Library). This is but one example of the array of trade-group publications available. Resources such as the Career Resource Library are also available to those who wish to browse publications by trade groups.

Scholarly Publications

Academic journals have, in some form, been around since the early years of magazine publication. During the 17th century, the *Universal Historical Bibliothèque* became the first journal to invite scholarly contributions. Today, hundreds of scholarly journals exist, such as the *American Economic Review* and *The Journal of Marriage and Families*, and every academic field has its own array of journals to which scholars can contribute. Most university libraries allow students and faculty access to these journals via library databases.

In every academic field, journals are ranked based on the types of articles they publish and on their selectiveness. Most academic journals use a peer-reviewing process to determine which articles are printed. During this process, a panel of readers reviews an anonymous article and then decides whether to accept the paper, accept with changes, or reject it altogether. Scholarly publication is essential for graduate students and university faculty members alike as they seek to disseminate their ideas and progress in their careers.

Religious Groups

With faith at the center of many individuals' lives, it is hardly surprising that there are hundreds of magazines dedicated to religious groups. From *Christianity Today* to *Catholic Digest*, Christian publications make up the largest group of religious magazines. But Christianity is not the only faith represented in periodicals. *Kashrus Magazine* targets the Jewish community, and *Shambhala Sun* is affiliated with the Buddhist faith. Additionally, certain magazines, such as *CrossCurrents*, are designed for people of all faiths. The magazine's publishers state that *CrossCurrents* serves as "a global network for people of faith and intelligence who are committed to connecting the wisdom of the heart and the life of the mind (Cross Currents)."

Political Groups

Political groups also have capitalized on the magazine industry. Whether liberal or conservative, most people can find a publication that reflects their political opinions. Two such magazines are *The American Prospect* and *The American Conservative*. *The American Prospect* targets Democrats with "thoughtful views of America's progressive liberal Democratic issues, ideas, politics and policy (All You Can Read)." Conversely, *the American Conservative* is aimed at right-leaning individuals. Edited by well-known conservatives Pat Buchanan and Taki Theodoracopulos, this biweekly "is dedicated to reigniting the conservative conversation, engaging the neo-conservative agenda through its espousal of traditional conservative themes (All You Can Read)."

Pulp and Genre Fiction Magazines

Although today not as many pulp magazines publish as did at the style's height of popularity, during the 1930s, this unique niche still plays an important role in the magazine industry. One such example is *Asimov's Science*

Fiction, a science fiction magazine founded in 1977 and still popular today. Founded because "one of science fiction's most influential and prolific writers, Isaac Asimov wanted to provide a home for new SF (science fiction) writers—a new magazine that young writers could break into. *Asimov's Science Fiction* remains that home, as well as the publisher of some of the field's best known authors (Asimov's Science Fiction)." True to its original intention, the magazine publishes stories of varying lengths for the avid science fiction fan.

Figure 5.7

Asmiov's Science Fiction is a modern pulp magazine reaching out to sci-fi readers around the globe.

Another modern example of a genre magazine is *Ellery Queen's Mystery Magazine*. First launched in 1941 to "raise the sights of mystery writers generally to a genuine literary form," to "encourage good writing among our colleagues by offering a practical market not otherwise available," and to "develop new writers seeking expression in the genre (The Mystery Place)," the journal has published a large number of now famous writers including Rudyard Kipling, William Faulkner, Ernest Hemingway, Norman Mailer, and Alice Walker. Today, the publication prides itself on being "on the cutting edge of crime and mystery fiction, offering readers the very best stories being written in the genre anywhere in the world (The Mystery Place)." Though pulp and genre fiction magazines tend to have a fairly low circulation—*Asimov's* circulation in 2009 was about 17,000—the caliber of the authors they often attract gives these publications a great degree of influence within their respective niches (Anders, 2009).

Hobby and Interest Magazines

Perhaps the most populated classification is that of hobby and special-interest magazines, a reflection of the wide array of hobbies and interests that different individuals enjoy. Within this classification of journals, one can find magazines on such topics as sports (*Sports Illustrated*), wellness (*Health)*, cooking (*Bon Appétit*), home decoration and renovation (*This Old House*), and travel and geography (*National Geographic*).

Readers interested in specific hobbies can generally find a magazine that caters to them. Photographers, for example, can subscribe to the *British Journal of Photography*, the world's longest-running photography magazine, in publication since 1854. This journal prints "profiles of emerging talent alongside star names, a picture-led Portfolio section, business analysis and detailed technology reviews (British Journal of Photography)." Music enthusiasts can choose from an array of publications ranging from more general ones such as *Spin* and the *International Early Music Review* to highly specific such as the *Journal of the International Double Reed Society* and *Just Jazz Guitar*. There are also magazines entirely devoted to crafting, such as *Creating Keepsakes* for scrapbook enthusiasts, and for pet ownership, such as the appropriately named *Pet*.

Fashion has provided a highly lucrative and visible interest magazine market. Founded in 1892, the most famous fashion magazine is *Vogue*. "*Vogue* has been America's cultural barometer, putting fashion in the context of the larger world we live in—how we dress, live, socialize; what we eat, listen to, watch; who leads and inspires us (Vogue)." The magazine has a huge following, with a circulation topping 1.2 million readers. *Vogue*'s mission statement declares an intent to lead the way in the fashion magazine industry, reading:

Vogue's story is the story of women, of culture, of what is worth knowing and seeing, of individuality and grace, and of the steady power of earned influence. For millions of women each month, *Vogue* is the eye of the culture, inspiring and challenging them to see things differently, in both themselves and the world (Vogue).

Despite *Vogue*'s high circulation, most special-interest magazines have a smaller readership. This can be worrisome for editors charged with adding more subscriptions to make a larger profit. However, the appeal of such specific audiences generates more revenue from advertisers, who can purchase magazine space knowing that their ads are reaching a targeted audience.

Vogue Crosses Media Lines

In recent years, *Vogue* has served as inspiration for two major films: *The Devil Wears Prada* (2006) and *The September Issue* (2009). Based on Lauren Weisberger's novel of the same name, *The Devil Wears Prada* is a feature film about a young woman living in New York dreaming of becoming a magazine writer. She lands a job as the assistant to the city's most ruthless magazine editor, Miranda Priestly—played by Meryl Streep—who runs *Runway* magazine, a fictionalized version of *Vogue*. This coming-of-age story highlights the work that goes into producing a magazine of such prestige. Streep was nominated for an Oscar award for her performance and, appropriately for a film about fashion, the costume designer was also nominated for Best Achievement in Costume Design.

The September Issue is a documentary chronicling *Vogue* editor in chief Anna Wintour's preparation for the 2007 fall fashion issue. Wintour, the editor upon whom Streep's character in *The Devil Wears Prada* was loosely based (Zeitchik, 2011), is well known for being a powerful influence on the fashion industry and a demanding editor. The film, however, humanizes her, while still demonstrating her obsession with fashion and with perfection in her magazine.

The success of both films reveals a fascination with the fashion and publishing industries. The fact that these two films would be released as the magazine industry is in decline is surprising but perhaps reflects an interest in journalism from a younger audience. The use of publishing as a topic in the film medium shows how magazines, though struggling, remain relevant and how special-interest magazines, like those in fashion, can transcend the medium and cross over into other mass media.

Key Takeaways

- Niche publications include magazines that cater to hobbyists in such diverse fields as sports, crafts, music, and even pets. Some modern niche publications hearken back to the pulp magazines of the 1930s.

- Although niche markets for magazines mean fewer readers, advertisers often prefer to publish ads in these more specialized publications because their ads will reach a more targeted demographic, thus ensuring that nearly everyone reading the journal will have an interest in their product.

Exercises

Consider the specialized magazines discussed in this section, as well as others you are familiar with, and identify whether or not you are among the target audience for each. Then, read a copy of a magazine targeting a specialized group or demographic you are not a part of. For example, if you're a man, examine a copy of *Cosmopolitan*, or if you have no interest in fashion, look through an issue of *Vogue*. Then, answer the following writing prompts.

1. What do you learn about the subject from one edition of one magazine?

2. How do the articles reach out to the target demographic?

3. How are the advertisements doing the same?

References

All You Can Read, "Top 10 Political Magazines," AllYouCanRead.com, http://www.allyoucanread.com/top-10-political-magazines/.

Anders, Charlie Jane "Has The Print Magazine Circulation Crash Started To Level Off?" *io9*, June 25, 2009, http://io9.com/5302638/has-the-print-magazine-circulation-crash-started-to-level-off.

Asimov's Science Fiction, http://www.asimovs.com/201007/index.shtml.

British Journal of Photography, "About Us," http://www.bjp-online.com/static/about-us.

Campbell, Richard. Christopher R Martin, Bettina Fabos, "Magazines in the Age of Specialization: Chapter Nine," pp. 255–284, *Media and Culture: An Introduction to Mass Communication*, http://www.profbob.com/MCOM%2072/Media%20Culture%20TEXT/Media%20Culture%20PPTs/Chapter%209.ppt.

Career Resource Library, CareerOneStop, http://www.acinet.org/crl/library.aspx?LVL2=99&LVL3=n&LVL1=58&CATID=744&PostVal=9.

CrossCurrents, http://www.aril.org/.

Hess, Jennifer. "Specialization Trends in Business," Helium.com, October 5, 2007, http://www.helium.com/items/664459-specialization-trends-in-business.

The Mystery Place, "About *EQMM*: A Brief History of *Ellery Queen's Mystery Magazine*," The Mystery Place, http://www.themysteryplace.com/eqmm/about/history.aspx.

Vogue, "Mission Statement," http://www.condenastmediakit.com/vog/index.cfm.

Zeitchik, Steven. "Meryl Streep and her 'Devil Wears Prada' Director Jump Into New Springs," *24 Frames* (blog), *Los Angeles Times*, February 8, 2011, http://latimesblogs.latimes.com/movies/2011/02/meryl-streep-david-frankel-hope-springs-prada.html.

5.7 Influence of the Internet on the Magazine Industry

Learning Objectives

1. Describe how print magazines have adapted to an online market.
2. Indicate a unique benefit of print magazines archiving back issues on their websites.

In March of 2010, *Consumerist* published a story titled "Print edition of *TV Guide* tells me to go online to read most of cover story." According to the article, *TV Guide* printed a story listing "TV's Top 50 Families," but shocked readers by including only the top 20 families in its print version. To discover the rest of the list, readers needed to go online (Villarreal, 2010). As dismayed as some readers were, this story reflects an ongoing trend in magazine journalism: the move toward online reporting.

Just like their newspaper cousins, magazines have been greatly affected by the influence of the Internet. With so much information available online, advertisers and readers are accessing content on the Internet, causing declines in both revenue and readership. These changes are forcing magazines to adapt to an increasingly online market.

Online-Only Magazines

In 1995, *Salon* launched the first major online-only magazine at http://www.salon.com. "Salon, the award-winning online news and entertainment website, combines original investigative stories, breaking news, provocative personal essays and highly respected criticism along with popular staff-written blogs about politics, technology and culture (Salon)." Like many print magazines, the site divides content into sections including entertainment, books, comics, life, news and politics, and technology and business. With an average of 5.8 million monthly unique visitors, this online magazine demonstrates the potential successes of Internet-based publications (Salon).

Other online-only magazines include *Slate* and *PC Magazine*. All three magazines, like most online publications, support themselves in part through ads that appear alongside articles and other content. Founded in 1996, *Slate* is a "general interest publication offering analysis and commentary about politics, news, and culture (Slate)." Considering itself "a daily magazine on the Web," *Slate* offers its readers information on news and politics, arts, life, business, technology, and science via online articles, podcasts, and blogs (Slate). The successful magazine has been recognized with numerous awards for its contributions to journalism.

PC Magazine differs somewhat from *Slate* or *Salon* in that it was originally a print publication. First published in 1982, the computer magazine published hard-copy issues for over 15 years before announcing in 2008 that its January 2009 issue would be its last printed edition. In an open letter to its readers, *PC Magazine* discussed the transition:

Starting in February 2009, *PC Magazine* will become a 100-percent digital publication. So, in addition to our popular network of Websites…we'll offer *PC Magazine Digital Edition* to all of our print subscribers. The *PC Magazine Digital Edition* has actually been available since 2002. So for thousands of you, the benefits of this unique medium are already clear. And those benefits will continue to multiply in the coming months, as we work hard to enhance your digital experience (Ulanoff, 2008).

While it is perhaps fitting that this computer-focused publication is one of the first print magazines to move to an entirely online form, its reasons for the transition were financial rather than creative. In describing the decision, Jason Young, chief executive of Ziff Davis Media, said, "The viability for us to continue to publish in print just isn't there anymore (Clifford, 2008)." Unfortunately for the magazine industry, Young's sentiment reflects a trend that has been building for some time. Several other publications have followed in *PC Magazine*'s footsteps, making the move from print to online-only. Journals such as *Elle Girl* and *Teen People* that were once available in print can now be viewed only via the Internet. As printing costs rise and advertising and subscription revenues decrease, more magazines will likely be making similar shifts.

Magazine-Like Websites

In recent years, websites that function much as magazines once did without officially being publications themselves have become an increasingly popular online model. For example, Pitchfork Media is an Internet publication on the music industry. Established in 1995, the site offers readers criticism and commentary on contemporary music and has many of the same features as a traditional music magazine: reviews, news, articles, and interviews. Whether the site is capitalizing on the success of print magazines by following their format or if it is simply responding to its readers by providing them with an accessible online experience is a debatable point. Of course, the website also has many features that would not be available in print, such as a streaming playlist of music and music videos. This hybrid of magazine-like content with new-media content offers a possible vision of the digital future of print publications.

Print Magazines With Online Presences

Indeed, most print magazines have created websites. Nearly every major print publication has a site available either for free or through subscription. Yet there are intrinsic differences between the print and online media. Bernadette Geyer, author of a poetry chapbook, *What Remains*, discusses the practical contrasts between online and print journals saying:

I will read a print journal cover to cover because I can bookmark where I left off…. Simply taking all of the content of what would have been a print issue and putting it online with links from a Table of Contents is all well and good in theory, but I have to ask, how many people actually sit and read all of the contents of an online journal that publishes several authors/genres per issue (Geyer, 2010)?

Her question is a good one, and one which most magazines have already asked themselves. In light of this dilemma, magazines with online editions have sought ways to attract readers who may not, in fact, read much. Most websites also include online-only content such as blogs, podcasts, and daily news updates that, naturally, are not available in print form. The additional features on magazines' websites likely stem from a need to attract audiences with shorter attention spans and less time to devote to reading entire articles.

Another way that magazines court online readers is by offering back-issue content. Readers can browse old articles without having to remember in which issue the content first appeared. The cost for this varies from publication to publication. For example, CooksIllustrated.com reprints recipes from previous issues as part of a paid online membership service, while CookingLight.com offers back issues for free. Some magazines have online archive collections, though those collections generally do not print entire articles or complete issues. *Time*, for example, offers "hand-picked covers and excerpts from the best articles on a wide variety of subjects (Time)." *Time* suggests that one should "use them as chronological guides to *Time*'s past coverage of a person, event, or topic (Time)." Still, even without the entire collection online, there is a distinct benefit of being able to search back for articles from 1923 from a computer.

Is Print Dead?

The question *Is print dead?* has dominated the magazine and newspaper industries for several years. In 2008, *The New York Times* printed an article titled "Mourning Old Media's Decline," in which author David Carr describes multiple announcements of job loss in the print industry. Thousands of individuals working at magazines and newspapers faced layoffs because of reduced subscriber and advertiser demand. "Clearly the sky is falling," he writes, "The question now is how many people will be left to cover it (Carr, 2008)." At the same time, Carr articulates the shift in readership from print to web, saying, "The paradox of all these announcements is that newspapers and magazines do not have an audience problem—newspaper Web sites are a vital source of news, and growing—but they do have a consumer problem (Carr, 2008)." With a majority of magazines and newspapers now available for free online, one has to wonder how the industry will stay afloat. Although advertisements pay for a portion of the cost of running a magazine, it may not be enough.

The debate over whether print is still viable is a heated one that is infiltrating the magazine industry. At a 2006 magazine editorial meeting, *Glamour*'s editor in chief, Cindi Leive, claimed that she "loves this question…. Is print dead? Discuss (Benkoil & Stableford, 2006)!" The editor in chief of *More* magazine responded to the statement saying, "It's what we talk about all day long (Benkoil & Stableford, 2006)." But for as many people who are fighting for the print industry to remain profitable, there is an equally vocal group arguing for the elimination of the print medium altogether. In a 2005 published debate on the topic, former print editor-turned-blogger Jeff Jarvis squared off against John Griffin, president of the National Geographic Society's magazine group. Jarvis claimed, "Print is not dead. Print is where words go to die." But Griffin countered, "Actually print is where words go to live—we're still reading the ancient Greeks (Jarvis & Griffin, 2005)."

Regardless of your position, the fact that the print industry is facing hardships is unquestionable. Magazines are rethinking their marketing strategies to remain viable in an increasingly online world. But many are hopeful that journals will find a way to publish both in print and on the Internet. After all, "There's something special and unique, even luxurious about reading a big, glossy magazine…. Or, in the words of *Marie Claire* editor Joanna Coles, 'As long as people take baths, there will always be a monthly magazine (Benkoil & Stableford).'"[1]

Key Takeaways

- Print journals are adapting to an increasingly online market by offering web-only features such as blogs, podcasts, and daily news updates. Regularly updating websites may help publications remain relevant as more readers turn to the Internet to receive information.

- As more magazines archive back issues on their websites, readers benefit by being able to search for old articles and, sometimes, entire editions. Many back issues are offered for free, but some publications require a subscription fee for this perk.

Exercises

Explore the website of one of your favorite magazines. Consider how the site maintains the look and feel of its print edition, and how the site distinguishes itself from its original print version. Then, answer the following writing prompts.

1. Has it successfully adapted to the online market? Why or why not?

2. Does the website offer an archive of back issues? If so, describe the archive's features and identify its pros and cons.

End-of-Chapter Assessment

Review Questions

1.
Section 1

    a. What medium "came to occupy the large middle groups…between the book and the newspaper (Encyclopaedia Britannica)"?

    b. How did magazines first evolve and diffuse?

    c. How and why did early magazines target women?

    d. What was the first truly successful U.S. mass magazine?

    e. Name one early successful newsmagazine and one successful picture magazine.

2.
Section 2

---

1. Benkoil and Stableford, "Is Print Dead? Discuss!"

a. How did the advent of nationwide magazine circulation affect American culture?

b. Describe the controversy surrounding early pulp magazines.

3.
Section 3

a. What are the three highest circulating magazines in the United States today?

b. What are some long-running, influential women's magazines?

c. Why did feminists speak out against the 1960s transformation of *Cosmopolitan* magazine?

4.
Section 4

a. How does format play a role in the way stories are presented?

b. Why do advertisers attempt to control which stories are published and how they are presented?

5.
Section 5

a. List four specializations in the magazine industry.

b. How do advertisers benefit from specialization?

6.
Section 6

a. Explain *PC Magazine*'s move to an online-only market.

b. How do print magazines remain relevant in an increasingly online world?

c. What role do advertisers play in the way the Internet is affecting the magazine industry?

Critical Thinking Questions

1. What major contributions did *The Saturday Evening Post* offer to the magazine industry?

2. How did pulp magazines move the U.S. journalism industry forward? Are there any modern examples of publications that are doing the same?

3. Describe the differences among current celebrity magazines. How might so many journals of similar style and repute remain competitive in today's declining market?

4. What is an editorial slant and how does it play a role in industry control?

5. Describe what brought about the need for niche magazines and discuss how niche magazines stay afloat despite smaller audiences.

6. Discuss the debate over the question *Is print dead*? Explain both sides of the argument.

> ### Career Connection
>
> Specialization in the magazine industry has provided magazines and advertisers the ability to seek out target audiences, bettering a publication's chances of remaining competitive in a declining market. Choose a specialization that interests you. Select two magazines where you might like to work within that specialization. Look through the website for each magazine, looking specifically at job opportunities and staff positions. Use the information you find to answer the following questions.
>
> 1. What entry-level positions are available at each magazine?
>
> 2. How might one move up within the company?
>
> 3. What is the company's mission statement and how might you use that information to better prepare yourself for a job in the industry?
>
> 4. What tools might you need to acquire before applying for a position?
>
> 5. What surprised you in your research?

References

Benkoil and Stableford, "Is Print Dead? Discuss!"

Benkoil, Dorian and Dylan Stableford, "Is Print Dead? Discuss!" Mediabistro.com, November 17, 2006, http://www.mediabistro.com/articles/cache/a9077.asp.

Carr, David. "Mourning Old Media's Decline," *New York Times*, October 28, 2008, http://www.nytimes.com/2008/10/29/business/media/29carr.html.

Clifford, Stephanie. "*PC Magazine*, a Flagship for Ziff Davis, Will Cease Printing a Paper Version," *New York Times*, November 19, 2008, http://www.nytimes.com/2008/11/20/business/media/20mag.html.

Encyclopaedia Britannica, s.v. "History of Publishing," http://www.britannica.com/EBchecked/topic/482597/publishing/28679/Magazine-publishing.

Geyer, Bernadette "Online vs. Print Journal Models," *Bernadette Geyer: Livin' the Literary Life in the Exiles of Suburbia* (blog), March 9, 2010, http://bernadettegeyer.blogspot.com/2010/03/online-vs-print-journal-models.html.

Jarvis, Jeff. and John Griffin, "Is Print Doomed?" *Fast Company*, December 1, 2005, http://www.fastcompany.com/magazine/101/open-debate-extra.html.

Salon, "Salon Fact Sheet," http://www.salon.com/press/fact/.

Slate, "About Us: Everything you need to know about *Slate*," http://www.slate.com/id/2147070/.

Time, "*Time* Magazine Archives," http://www.time.com/time/archive/.

Ulanoff, Lance. "*PC Magazine* Goes 100% Digital," (2008), *PC Magazine,* http://www.pcmag.com/article2/0,2817,2335009,00.asp.

Villarreal, Phil. "Print Edition of *TV Guide* Tells Me to Go Online to Read Most of Cover Story," *Consumerist* (blog), March 30, 2010, http://consumerist.com/2010/03/print-edition-of-tv-guide-tells-me-to-go-online-to-read-most-of-cover-story.html.

Chapter 6: Music

6.1 Music

From Social Networking to Stardom

Figure 6.1

In 2006, Californian vocalist Colbie Caillat was an aspiring singer-songwriter. Although her audio engineer father, Ken Caillat, coproduced one of the biggest selling albums of all time, Fleetwood Mac's *Rumours*, Colbie had never considered booking a studio, much less campaigning for a record deal. She considered her music to be a hobby rather than a career choice (Waco Tribune-Herald, 2010). Fast-forward a year later and Caillat's debut album, *Coco*, was at No. 5 on the *Billboard 200* album chart, on its way to achieving platinum status. How did an unknown artist from Malibu, California, become a best-selling star in so little time? Caillat's success can be attributed, in part, to the social networking website MySpace.

Hugely popular among teens and young adults in the mid-2000s, MySpace enables people to set up a personal profile on which they can post original music for the public to listen to and comment on. One of Caillat's friends thought that her music merited a wider audience and set up a page on which Caillat could post her tunes. Six months later, Caillat was the MySpace website's top unsigned artist (Colbie Caillat). The site enables people to "friend" artists or performers whose music they enjoy. As Caillat's friend count climbed to 100,000, music labels began to notice. In 2007, she signed with Universal Records and released her debut album, *Coco*. Boosted by the online success of the single "Bubbly," *Coco* reached No. 5 on the Billboard chart and established Caillat as a bona fide pop star. She has since won a Grammy award for "Lucky," her duet with Jason Mraz, toured with artists such as the Goo Goo Dolls and John Mayer, and in 2009, released a second successful album, *Breakthrough*. The combined sales of Caillat's first two albums are upward of 4 million copies worldwide.

Caillat's story highlights one area in which the Internet is changing the face of the music industry. Aspiring artists no longer need to rely on expensive publicists, recording studios, or contacts within the industry; they can connect directly with fans to sell their music. Social networking sites, like MySpace, and virtual worlds, like Second Life, make it easier for fans to search for new music and easier for artists to communicate with fans. In fact, MySpace has been so influential that it teamed with several major labels to create the MySpace music website. Generating a buzz on social networking sites is sometimes enough to achieve fame and stardom. Of course, for every Colbie Caillat, there are thousands of unknown singers and bands trying to promote their music online with little or no success. Despite this, it's clear that social networking sites have taken some control away from record labels and placed it in the hands of the artists themselves.

Artists are also using social networking sites to develop a more intimate relationship with fans. In the past couple of years, the Twitter social networking website has become hugely popular among musicians and fans alike. The microblogging service enables users to send a tweet message—a short post of 140 characters or less that is displayed on the author's profile page and delivered to his or her subscribers. Musicians such as John Mayer, Alicia Keys, Britney Spears, and Lily Allen regularly post on Twitter, providing their fans with real-time updates about their daily lives and promoting their musical endeavors.

Social networking sites are just the latest technological development in the music business. An in-depth look at the history and evolution of popular music throughout the last century will help explain some of the current processes and trends in the industry.

References

Colbie Caillat, *ColbieCaillat.com*, http://www.colbiecaillat.com/colbie.

Waco Tribune-Herald, "Colbie Caillat Turns Hobby into Billboard Success, Will Perform at Baylor's Diadeloso," *Waco Tribune-Herald*, April 15, 2010, http://www.wacotrib.com/accesswaco/arts/Colbie-Caillat-turns-hobby-into-Billboard-success-will-perform-at-Baylors-Diadeloso.html.

6.2 The Evolution of Popular Music

The first stirrings of popular or pop music—any genre of music that appeals to a wide audience or subculture—began in the late 19th century, with discoveries by Thomas Edison and Emile Berliner. In 1877, Edison discovered that sound could be reproduced using a strip of tinfoil wrapped around a rotating metal cylinder. Edison's phonograph provided ideas and inspiration for Berliner's gramophone, which used flat discs to record sound. The flat discs were cheaper and easier to produce than were the cylinders they replaced, enabling the mass production of sound recordings. This would have a huge impact on the popular music industry, enabling members of the middle class to purchase technology that was previously available only to an elite few. Berliner founded the Berliner Gramophone Company to manufacture his discs, and he encouraged popular operatic singers such as Enrico Caruso and Dame Nellie Melba to record their music using his system. Opera singers were the stars of the 19th century, and their music generated most of the sheet music sales in the United States. Although the gramophone was an exciting new development, it would take 20 years for disc recordings to rival sheet music in commercial importance (Shepherd, 2003).

In the late 19th century, the lax copyright laws that existed in the United States at the beginning of the century were strengthened, providing an opportunity for composers, singers, and publishers to work together to earn money by producing as much music as possible. Numerous publishers began to emerge in an area of New York that became known as Tin Pan Alley. Allegedly named because the cacophony of many pianos being played in the publishers' demo rooms sounded like people pounding on tin pans, Tin Pan Alley soon became a prolific source of popular music, with its publishers mass-producing sheet music to satisfy the demands of a growing middle class. Whereas classical artists were exalted for their individuality and expected to differ stylistically from other classical artists, popular artists were praised for conforming to the tastes of their intended audience. Popular genres expanded from opera to include vaudeville—a form of variety entertainment containing short acts featuring singers, dancers, magicians, and comedians that opened new doors for publishers to sell songs popularized by the live shows—and ragtime, a style of piano music characterized by a syncopated melody.

Figure 6.2

For most of the 20th century, gramophone records were the primary medium used for commercial music reproduction.

Science Museum London – EMG Mark Xb handmade gramophone, c 1934. – CC BY-SA 2.0.

The Tin Pan Alley tradition of song publishing continued throughout the first half of the 20th century with the show tunes and soothing ballads of Irving Berlin, Cole Porter, and George Gershwin, and songwriting teams of the early 1950s, such as Jerry Leiber and Mike Stoller. By hiring songwriters to compose music based on public demand and mainstream tastes, the Tin Pan Alley publishers introduced the concept of popular music as we know it.

The Roaring 1920s: Radio versus Records

In the 1920s, Tin Pan Alley's dominance of the popular music industry was threatened by two technological developments: the advent of electrical recording and the rapid growth of radio.

During the early days of its development, the gramophone was viewed as a scientific novelty that posed little threat to sheet music because of its poor sound quality. However, as inventors improved various aspects of the device, the sales of gramophone records began to affect sheet music sales. The Copyright Act of 1911 had imposed a royalty on all records of copyrighted musical works to compensate for the loss in revenue to composers and authors. This loss became even more prominent during the mid-1920s, when improvements in electrical recording drastically increased sales of gramophones and gramophone records. The greater range and sensitivity of the electrical broadcasting microphone revolutionized gramophone recording to such an extent that sheet music sales plummeted. From the very beginning, the record industry faced challenges from new technology.

Composers and publishers could deal with the losses caused by an increase in gramophone sales because of the provisions made in the Copyright Act. However, when radio broadcasting emerged in the early 1920s, both gramophone sales and sheet-music sales began to suffer. Radio was an affordable medium that enabled listeners to experience events as they took place. Better yet, it offered a wide range of free music that required none of the musical skills, expensive instruments, or sheet music necessary for creating one's own music in the home, nor the expense of purchasing records to play on the gramophone. This development was a threat to the entire recording industry, which began to campaign for, and was ultimately granted, the right to collect license fees from broadcasters. With the license fees in place, the recording industry eventually began to profit from the new technology.

Figure 6.3

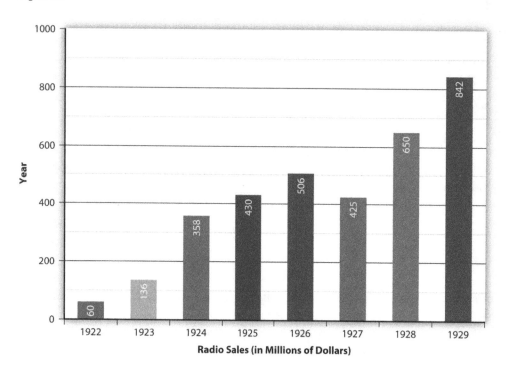

Radio sales dramatically increased throughout the 1920s because radios were an affordable way to listen to free music and live events.

The 1930s: The Rise of Jazz and Blues

The ascendance of Tin Pan Alley coincided with the emergence of jazz in New Orleans. An improvisational form of music that was primarily instrumental, jazz incorporated a variety of styles, including African rhythms, gospel, and blues. Established by New Orleans musicians such as King Oliver and his protégé, Louis Armstrong, who is considered by many to be one of the greatest jazz soloists in history, jazz spread along the Mississippi River by the bands that traveled up and down the river playing on steamboats. During the Prohibition era in the 1920s and early 1930s, some jazz bands played in illegal speakeasies, which helped generate the genre's reputation for being immoral and for threatening the country's cultural values. However, jazz became a legitimate form of entertainment during the 1930s, when White orchestras began to incorporate jazz style into their music. During this time, jazz music began to take on a big band style, combining elements of ragtime, Black spirituals, blues, and European music. Key figures in developing the big jazz band included bandleaders Duke Ellington, Coleman Hawkins, and Glenn Miller. These big band orchestras used an arranger to limit improvisation by assigning parts of a piece of music to various band members. Although improvisation was allowed during solo performances, the format became more structured, resulting in the swing style of jazz that became popular in the 1930s. As the decade progressed, social attitudes toward racial segregation relaxed and big bands became more racially integrated.

At the heart of jazz, the blues was a creation of former Black slaves who adapted their African musical heritage to the American environment. Dealing with themes of personal adversity, overcoming hard luck, and other emotional turmoil, the blues is a 12-bar musical form with a call-and-response format between the singer and his guitar. Originating in the Mississippi Delta, just upriver from New Orleans, blues music was exemplified in the work of W. C. Handy, Ma Rainey, Robert Johnson, and Lead Belly, among others. Unlike jazz, the blues did not spread significantly to the Northern states until the late 1930s and 1940s. Once Southern migrants introduced the blues to urban Northern cities, the music developed into distinctive regional styles, ranging from the jazz-oriented Kansas City blues to the swing-based West Coast blues. Chicago blues musicians such as Muddy Waters were the first to electrify the blues through the use of electric guitars and to blend urban style with classic Southern blues. The electric guitar, first produced by Adolph Rickenbacker in 1931, changed music by intensifying the sound and creating a louder volume that could cut through noise in bars and nightclubs (Rickenbacker, 2010). By focusing less on shouting, singers could focus on conveying more emotion and intimacy in their performances. This electrified form of blues provided the foundations of rock and roll.

Figure 6.4

The Chicago blues, characterized by the use of electric guitar and harmonica, provided the foundations of rock and roll. Muddy Waters was one of the most famous Chicago blues musicians.

Nesster – Muddy Waters at Newport 1960 – CC BY-SA 2.0.

The 1920s through the 1950s is considered the golden age of radio. During this time, the number of licensed radio stations in the United States exploded from five in 1921 to over 600 by 1925 (Salmon, 2010). The introduction of radio broadcasting provided a valuable link between urban city centers and small, rural towns. Able to transmit music nationwide, rural radio stations broadcasted local music genres that soon gained popularity across the country.

The 1940s: Technology Progresses

Technological advances during the 1940s made it even easier for people to listen to their favorite music and for artists to record it. The introduction of the reel-to-reel tape recorder paved the way for several innovations that would transform the music industry. The first commercially available tape recorders were monophonic, meaning that they only had one track on which to record sound onto magnetic tape. This may seem limiting today, but at the time it allowed for exciting innovations. During the 1940s and 1950s, some musicians—most notably guitarist Les Paul, with his song "Lover (When You're Near Me)"—began to experiment with overdubbing, in which they played back a previously recorded tape through a mixer, blended it with a live performance, and recorded the composite signal onto a second tape recorder. By the time four-track and eight-track recorders became readily available in the 1960s, musicians no longer had to play together in the same room; they could record each of their individual parts and combine them into a finished recording.

Figure 6.5

Reel-to-reel tape recorders and magnetic tape not only helped artists experiment with overdubbing, but they also were a compact method for reproducing and preserving audio.

Stuart Blacklock – Leevers Rich series D2B – CC BY-ND 2.0.

While the reel-to-reel recorders were in the early stages of development, families listened to records on their gramophones. The 78 revolutions per minute (rpm) disc had been the accepted recording medium for many years despite the necessity of changing the disc every 5 minutes. In 1948, Columbia Records perfected the 12-inch 33 rpm long-playing (LP) disc, which could play up to 25 minutes per side and had a lower level of surface noise than the earlier (and highly breakable) shellac discs (Lomax, 2003). The 33 rpm discs became the standard form for full albums and would dominate the recorded music industry until the advent of the compact disc (CD).

During the 1940s, a mutually beneficial alliance between sound recording and radio existed. Artists such as Frank Sinatra and Ella Fitzgerald profited from radio exposure. Until this time, music had primarily been recorded for adults, but the popularity of Sinatra and his contemporaries revealed an entirely untapped market: teenagers. The postwar boom of the 1930s and early 1940s provided many teenagers spending money for records. Radio airplay helped to promote and sell records and the recording artists themselves, which in turn stabilized the recording industry. The near riots caused by the appearance of New Jersey crooner Frank Sinatra in concert paved the way for mass hysteria among Elvis Presley and Beatles fans during the rock and roll era.

The 1950s: The Advent of Rock and Roll

New technology continued to develop in the 1950s with the introduction of television. The new medium spread rapidly, primarily because of cheaper mass-production costs and war-related improvements in technology. In 1948, only 1 percent of America's households owned a television; by 1953 this figure had risen to nearly 50 percent, and by 1978 nearly every home in the United States owned a television (Genova). The introduction of television into people's homes threatened the existence of the radio industry. The radio industry adapted by focusing on music, joining forces with the recording industry to survive. In an effort to do so, it became somewhat of a promotional tool. Stations became more dependent on recorded music to fill airtime, and in 1955 the Top 40 format was born. Playlists for radio stations were based on popularity (usually the *Billboard* Top 40 singles chart), and a popular song might be played as many as 30 or 40 times a day. Radio stations began to influence record sales, which resulted in increased competition for spots on the playlist. This ultimately resulted in payola—the illegal practice of receiving payment from a record company for broadcasting a particular song on the radio. The payola scandal came to a head in the 1960s, when Cleveland, Ohio, DJ Alan Freed and eight other disc jockeys were accused of taking money for airplay. Following Freed's trial, an antipayola statute was passed, making payola a misdemeanor crime.

Technology wasn't the only revolution that took place during the 1950s. The urban Chicago blues typified by artists such as Muddy Waters, Howlin' Wolf, and B. B. King surged in popularity among White and Black teenagers alike. Marketed under the name rhythm and blues, or **R&B**, the sexually suggestive lyrics in songs such as "Sexy Ways" and "Sixty Minute Man" and the electrified guitar and wailing harmonica sounds appealed to young listeners. At the time, R&B records were classified as "race music" and their sales were segregated from the White music records tracked on the pop charts (Szatmary, 2010). Nonetheless, there was a considerable amount of crossover among audiences. In 1952, the Dolphin's of Hollywood record store in Los Angeles, which specialized in R&B music, noted that 40 percent of its sales were to White individuals (Szatmary, 2010).

Although banned from some stations, others embraced the popular new music. In 1951, Freed started a late-night R&B show called *The Moondog Rock & Roll House Party* and began referring to the music he played as rock and roll (History Of Rock). Taking its name from a blues slang term for sex, the music obtained instant notoriety, gaining widespread support among teenage music fans and widespread dislike among the older generation (History Of Rock). Frenetic showmen Little Richard and Chuck Berry were early pioneers of rock and roll, and their wild stage performances became characteristic of the genre. As the integration of White and Black individuals progressed in the 1950s with the repeal of segregation laws and the initiation of the civil rights movement, aspects of Black culture, including music, became more widely accepted by many White individuals. However, it was the introduction of a White man who sang songs written by Black musicians that helped rock and roll really spread across state and racial lines. Elvis Presley, a singer and guitarist, the "King of Rock and Roll," further helped make music written by Black individuals acceptable to mainstream White audiences and also helped popularize rockabilly—a blend of rock and country music—with Black audiences during the mid-1950s. Heavily influenced by his rural Southern roots, Presley combined the R&B music of bluesmen B. B. King, John Lee Hooker, and Howlin' Wolf with the country-western tradition of Roy Acuff, Ernest Tubb, and Jimmie Rodgers, and added a touch of gospel (Elvis). The reaction Presley inspired among hordes of adolescent girls—screaming, crying, rioting—solidified his reputation as the first true rock and roll icon.

Figure 6.6

Elvis Presley brought the style of R&B bluesmen to mainstream audiences in the 1950s.

The 1960s: Rock and Roll Branches Out From R&B

Prior to 1964, rock and roll was primarily an American export. Although U.S. artists frequently reached the top of the charts overseas, few European artists achieved success on this side of the Atlantic. This situation changed almost overnight with the arrival of British pop phenomenon the Beatles. Combining elements of skiffle—a type of music played on rudimentary instruments, such as banjos, guitars, or homemade instruments—doo-wop, and soul, the four mop-haired musicians from Liverpool, England, created a genre of music known as Merseybeat, named after the River Mersey. The Beatles' genial personalities and catchy pop tunes made them an instant success in the United States, and their popularity was heightened by several appearances on *The Ed Sullivan Show*. When the Beatles arrived in New York in 1964, they were met by hundreds of reporters and police officers and thousands of fans. Their appearance on *The Ed Sullivan Show* a few days later was the largest audience for an American television program, with approximately one in three Americans (74 million) tuning in (Gould, 2007). *Beatlemania*—the term coined to describe fans' wildly enthusiastic reaction to the band—extended to other British bands, and by the mid-1960s, the Kinks, the Zombies, the Animals, Herman's Hermits, and the Rolling Stones were all making appearances on the U.S. charts. The Rolling Stones' urban rock sound steered away from pop music and remained more true to the bluesy, R&B roots of rock and roll. During their first appearance on *The Ed Sullivan Show*, the Stones were lewd and vulgar, prompting host Ed Sullivan to denounce their behavior (although he privately acknowledged that the band had received the most enthusiastic applause he had ever seen) (Ed Sullivan). The British Invasion transformed rock and roll into the all-encompassing genre of rock, sending future performers in two different directions: the melodic, poppy sounds of the Beatles, on the one hand, and the gritty, high-volume power rock of the Stones on the other.

Figure 6.7

After the Rolling Stones' first appearance on *The Ed Sullivan Show*, host Ed Sullivan apologized to the viewing audience for the band's lewd behavior.

The branching out of rock and roll continued in several other directions throughout the 1960s. Surf music, embodied by artists such as the Beach Boys, Jan and Dean, and Dick Dale, celebrated the aspects of youth culture in California. With their twanging electric guitars and glossy harmonies, the surf groups sang of girls, beaches, and convertible cars cruising along the West Coast. In Detroit, some Black performers were developing a sound that would have crossover appeal with both Black and White audiences. Combining R&B, pop, gospel, and blues into a genre known as soul, vocalists such as James Brown, Aretha Franklin, Otis Redding, and Wilson Pickett sang about the lives of Black Americans. Producer and songwriter Berry Gordy Jr. developed soul music through the creation of his Motown label, which would become one of the most successful businesses owned by a Black individual in American history (Notable Biographies). Capitalizing on the 1960s girl-group craze, Gordy produced hits by the Marvelettes, Martha and the Vandellas, and, most successfully, Diana Ross and the Supremes. For his bands, he created a slick, polished image designed to appeal to the American mainstream.

In the late 1960s, supporters of the civil rights movement—along with feminists, environmentalists, and Vietnam War protesters—were gravitating toward folk music, which would become the sound of social activism. Broadly referring to music that is passed down orally through the generations, folk music retained an unpolished, amateur quality that inspired participation and social awareness. Carrying on the legacy of the 1930s labor activist Woody Guthrie, singer-songwriters such as Joan Baez; Peter, Paul, and Mary; and Bob Dylan sang social protest songs about civil rights, discrimination against Black Americans, and the Cuban Missile Crisis. Having earned himself a reputation as a political spokesperson, Dylan was lambasted by traditional folk fans for playing an electric guitar at the 1965 Newport Folk Festival. However, his attempt to reach a broader crowd inspired the folk rock genre, pioneered by the Los Angeles band the Byrds (PBS). Even though many fans questioned his decision to go electric, Dylan's poetic and politically charged lyrics were still influential, inspiring groups like the Beatles and the Animals. Protest music in the 1960s was closely aligned with the hippie culture, in which some viewed taking drugs as a form of personal expression and free speech. Artists such as Jimi Hendrix, Jefferson Airplane, the Grateful Dead, and the Doors believed that the listening experience could be enhanced using mind-altering drugs (Rounds, 2007). This spirit of freedom and protest culminated in the infamous Woodstock festival in the summer of 1969, although the subsequent deaths of many of its stars from drug overdoses cast a shadow over the psychedelic culture.

The 1970s: From Glam Rock to Punk

After the Vietnam War ended, college students began to settle down and focus on careers and families. For some, selfish views took the place of concern with social issues and political activism, causing writer Tom Wolfe to label the 1970s the "me" decade (Wolfe, 1976). Musically, this ideological shift resulted in the creation of glam rock, an extravagant, self-indulgent form of rock that incorporated flamboyant costumes, heavy makeup, and elements of hard rock and pop. A primarily British phenomenon, glam rock was popularized by acts such as Slade, David Bowie, the Sweet, Elton John, and Gary Glitter. It proved to be a precursor for the punk movement in the late 1970s. Equally flamboyant, but rising out of a more electronic sound, disco also emerged in the 1970s. Popular disco artists included KC and the Sunshine Band, Gloria Gaynor, the Bee Gees, and Donna Summer, who helped to pioneer its electronic sound. Boosted by the success of 1977 film *Saturday Night Fever*, disco's popularity spread across the country. Records were created especially for discos, and record companies churned out tunes that became huge hits on the dance floor.

Reacting against the commercialism of disco and corporate rock, punk artists created a minimalist, angry form of rock that returned to rock and roll basics: simple chord structures, catchy tunes, and politically motivated lyrics. Like the skiffle bands of the 1950s, the appeal of punk rock was that anyone with basic musical skills could participate. The punk rock movement emerged out of CBGB, a small bar in New York City that featured bands such as Television, Blondie, and the Ramones. Never a huge commercial success in the United States, punk rock exploded in the United Kingdom, where high unemployment rates and class divisions had created angry, disenfranchised youths (BBC). The Sex Pistols, fronted by Johnny Rotten, developed an aggressive, pumping sound that appealed to a rebellious generation of listeners, although the band was disparaged by many critics at the time. In 1976, British music paper *Melody Maker* complained that "the Sex Pistols do as much for music as World War II did for the cause of peace (Gray, 2001)." Punk bands began to abandon their sound in the late 1970s, when the punk style became assimilated into the rock mainstream.

Figure 6.8

Even though the Sex Pistols were severely criticized in the 1970s, their music went on to inspire countless acts and helped develop the underground music scene in England and the United States.

nico7martin – Sex Pistols – CC BY 2.0.

The 1980s: The Hip-Hop Generation

Whereas many British youths expressed their displeasure through punk music, many disenfranchised Black American youths in the 1980s turned to hip-hop—a term for the urban culture that includes break dancing, graffiti art, and the musical techniques of rapping, sampling, and scratching records. Reacting against the extravagance of disco, many poor urban rappers developed their new street culture by adopting a casual image consisting of T-shirts and sportswear, developing a language that reflected the everyday concerns of the people in low-income, urban areas, and by embracing the low-budget visual art form of graffiti. They described their new culture as hip-hop, after a common phrase chanted at dance parties in New York's Bronx borough.

The hip-hop genre first became popular among Black youths in the late 1970s, when record spinners in the Bronx and Harlem started to play short fragments of songs rather than the entire track (known as sampling) (Demers, 2003). Early hip-hop artists sampled all types of music, like funk, soul, and jazz, later adding special effects to the samples and experimenting with techniques such as rotating or scratching records back and forth to create a rhythmic pattern. For example, Kool Moe Dee's track "How Ya Like Me Now" includes samples from James Brown's classic funk song "Papa's Got a Brand New Bag." The DJs would often add short raps to their music to let audiences know who was playing the records, a trend that grew more elaborate over time to include entire spoken verses. Artists such as Grandmaster Flash and the Furious Five added political and social commentary on the realities of life in low-income, high-crime areas—a trend that would continue with later rappers such as Public Enemy and Ice-T.

Figure 6.9

Early hip-hop artists, like Run-D.M.C., opposed the clean-cut, polished world of soul and pop by embracing political lyrics that were inspired by everyday life.

SoulRider.222 – RUN DMC – CC BY-ND 2.0.

In the early 1980s, a second wave of rap artists brought inner-city rap to American youths by mixing it with hard guitar rock. Pioneered by groups such as Run-D.M.C. and the Beastie Boys, the new music appealed to Black and White audiences alike. Another subgenre that emerged was gangsta rap, a controversial brand of hip-hop epitomized by West Coast rappers such as Ice Cube and Tupac Shakur. Highlighting violence and gang warfare, gangsta rappers faced accusations that they created violence in inner cities—an argument that gained momentum with the East Coast–West Coast rivalry of the 1990s.

The 1990s: New Developments in Hip-Hop, Rock, and Pop

Hip-hop and gangsta rap maintained their popularity in the early 1990s with artists such as Tupac Shakur, the Notorious B.I.G., Dr. Dre, Eazy-E, Ice Cube, and Snoop Dogg at the top of the charts. West Coast rappers such as Tupac Shakur and Snoop Dogg favored gangsta rap, while East Coast rappers, like the Notorious B.I.G. and Sean Combs, stuck to a traditional hip-hop style. The rivalry culminated with the murders of Shakur in 1996 and B.I.G. in 1997.

Figure 6.10

The shooting deaths of gangsta rappers Tupac Shakur and the Notorious B.I.G. caused a shift in the hip-hop industry toward less violent music.

Tupac Amaru Shakur – Notorious BIG & 2Pac – CC BY-NC-ND 2.0.

Along with hip-hop and gangsta rap, alternative rock came to the forefront in the 1990s with grunge. The grunge scene emerged in the mid-1980s in the Seattle area of Washington State. Inspired by hardcore punk and heavy metal, this subgenre of rock was so-called because of its messy, sludgy, distorted guitar sound, the disheveled appearance of its pioneers, and the disaffected nature of the artists. Initially achieving limited success with Seattle band Soundgarden, Seattle independent label Sub Pop became more prominent when it signed another local band, Nirvana. Fronted by vocalist and guitarist Kurt Cobain, Nirvana came to be identified with Generation X—the post–baby boom generation, many of whom came from broken families and experienced violence both on television and in real life. Nirvana's angst-filled lyrics spoke to many members of Generation X, launching the band into the mainstream. Ironically, Cobain was uncomfortable and miserable, and he would eventually commit suicide in 1994. Nirvana's success paved the way for other alternative rock bands, including Green Day, Pearl Jam, and Nine Inch Nails. More recently, alternative rock has fragmented into even more specific subgenres.

Figure 6.11

Britney Spears was one of the driving forces behind the teen-pop phenomenon of the late 1990s, paving the way for pop stars Christina Aguilera and Pink.

Britney Spears – Britney Spears toxic (Bbspears) – CC BY-SA 2.0.

By the end of the 1990s, mainstream tastes leaned toward pop music. A plethora of boy bands, girl bands, and pop starlets emerged, sometimes evolving from gospel choir groups, but more often than not created by talent scouts. The groups were aggressively marketed to teen audiences. Popular bands included the Backstreet Boys, 'N Sync, and the Spice Girls. Meanwhile, individual pop acts from the MTV generation such as Madonna, Michael Jackson, and Prince continued to generate hits.

The 2000s: Pop Stays Strong as Hip-Hop Overtakes Rock in Popularity

The 2000s began right where the 1990s left off, with young singers such as Christina Aguilera and Destiny's Child ruling the pop charts. Pop music stayed strong throughout the decade with Gwen Stefani, Mariah Carey, Beyoncé, Katy Perry, and Lady Gaga achieving mainstream success. By the end of the decade, country artists, like Carrie Underwood and Taylor Swift, transitioned from country stars to bona fide pop stars. While rock music started the decade strong, by the end of the 2000s, rock's presence in mainstream music had waned, with a few exceptions such as Nickelback, Linkin Park, and Green Day.

Figure 6.12

Taylor Swift's 2008 album *Fearless* went multiplatinum, and hits like "You Belong to Me" and "Love Story" helped her go from country star to mainstream pop star.

VersusLiveQuizShow – Taylor Swift (2007) – CC BY-SA 2.0.

Unlike rock music, hip-hop maintained its popularity, with more commercial, polished artists such as Kanye West, Jay-Z, Lupe Fiasco, and OutKast achieving enormous success. While some gangsta rappers from the 1990s—like Dr. Dre and Snoop Dogg—softened their images, other rappers—such as 50 Cent and Eminem—continued to project a tough image and to use violent lyrics. An alternative style of hip-hop emerged in the 2000s that infused positive messages and an element of social conscience to the music that was missing from early hip-hop tracks. Artists such as Common, Mos Def, and the Black Eyed Peas found success even though they didn't represent traditional stereotypes of hip-hop.

Key Takeaways

- Popular music as we know it originated out of the Tin Pan Alley tradition that emerged at the beginning of the 20th century in which composers, singers, and publishers worked together to create hit songs. The primary difference between popular music and classical music is that, whereas classical artists were exalted for their individuality and expected to differ stylistically from other classical composers, popular artists were praised for conforming to the tastes of their intended audience.

- Technological developments played a vital role in bringing popular music to people's homes. The invention of the phonograph and gramophone in the late 19th century enabled the reproduction and mass distribution of sound recordings for the first time. The invention of the reel-to-reel tape recorder and the development of vinyl records in the 1940s drastically improved this process. The postwar prevalence of radio hugely impacted popular music, with radio airplay of popular songs promoting record sales.

- Throughout the last century, tastes in popular music have evolved to encompass a wide variety of styles. People who enjoyed opera at the turn of the 20th century saw the rise of vaudeville and ragtime in the Tin Pan Alley era. Jazz and blues emerged from New Orleans and the Mississippi Delta during the 1930s, and musical styles adapted as people migrated to Northern urban areas. Rhythm and blues laid the groundwork for rock and roll that shook up popular music in the 1950s. Popular music diversified in the 1960s to encompass surf, folk, and soul music. In the 1970s, glam rock and disco became popular, and punk rockers revolted against the excesses of these styles. Hip-hop dominated the 1980s, and its popularity continued into the 1990s and 2000s. Pop was also successful in the 1990s and 2000s, while mainstream interest in alternative rock waned at the end of the 2000s.

Exercise

Choose a decade between 1900 and 2010. Research a technological development that took place during this time that influenced pop music—for example, the development of the electric guitar and its influence on rock and roll. Consider how this development influenced trends within the industry.

References

BBC, "Making ends meet in the 70s," *BBC News Magazine*, June 7, 2007, http://news.bbc.co.uk/2/hi/uk_news/magazine/6729847.stm.

Demers, Joanna. "Sampling the 1970s in Hip-Hop," *Popular Music* 21 (2003): 41–56.

Ed Sullivan, "The Rolling Stones," The Official Ed Sullivan Site, http://www.edsullivan.com/artists/the-rolling-stones.

Elvis, "Biography," Elvis Presley: Official Site of the King of Rock 'n' Roll, http://www.elvis.com/about-the-king/biography_.aspx.

Genova, Tom. "Number of TV Households in America," Television History – The First 75 Years, http://www.tvhistory.tv/Annual_TV_Households_50-78.JPG.

Gould, Jonathan. *Can't Buy Me Love: The Beatles, Britain, and America* (New York: Harmony Books, 2007), 3–4.

Gray, Marcus. *The Clash: Return of the Last Gang in Town* (London: Helter Skelter, 2001), 147.

History of Rock, "Alan Freed" History-of-rock.com, http://www.history-of-rock.com/freed.htm.

Lomax, Alan. Alan Lomax: Selected Writings 1934–1997, ed. Ronald D. Cohen (New York: Routledge, 2003), 102.

Notable Biographies, "Berry Gordy Jr. Biography," *Encyclopedia of World Biography*, http://www.notablebiographies.com/Gi-He/Gordy-Jr-Berry.html.

PBS, "Bob Dylan," PBS.org: American Roots Music: The Songs & the Artists, http://www.pbs.org/americanrootsmusic/pbs_arm_saa_bobdylan.html.

Rickenbacker, "Early Years: The Earliest Days of the Electric Guitar," Rickenbacker International Corporation, June 22, 2010, http://www.rickenbacker.com/history_early.asp; Mary Bellis, "The History of Guitar and Electric Guitar," About.com Guide, http://inventors.about.com/od/gstartinventions/a/guitar_2.htm.

Rounds, Dwight. *The Year the Music Died: 1964–1972: A Commentary on the Best Era of Pop Music, and an Irreverent Look at the Musicians and Social Movements of the Time* (Austin: Bridgeway Books, 2007), 292.

Salamon, Ed. *Pittsburgh's Golden Age of Radio* (Chicago: Arcadia, 2010), 8.

Shepherd, John. *Continuum Encyclopedia of Popular Music of the World* (New York: Continuum, 2003), 483.

Szatmary, David. *Rockin' in Time: A Social History of Rock and Roll* (Upper Saddle River, NJ: Prentice Hall, 2010), 16.

Wolfe, Tom. "The 'Me' Decade and the Third Great Awakening," *New York Magazine*, August 23, 1976, http://nymag.com/news/features/45938/.

6.3 The Reciprocal Nature of Music and Culture

The tightknit relationship between music and culture is almost impossible to overstate. For example, policies on immigration, war, and the legal system can influence artists and the type of music they create and distribute. Music may then influence cultural perceptions about race, morality, and gender that can, in turn, influence the way people feel about those policies.

Cultural Influences on Music

The evolution of popular music in the United States in the 20th century was shaped by a myriad of cultural influences. Rapidly shifting demographics brought previously independent cultures into contact and also created new cultures and subcultures, and music evolved to reflect these changes. Among the most important cultural influences on music are migration, the evolution of youth culture, and racial integration.

Migration

One of the major cultural influences on the popular music industry over the past century is migration. In 1910, 89 percent of Black Americans still lived in the South, most of them in rural farming areas (Weingroff, 2011). Three years later, a series of disastrous events devastated the cotton industry. World cotton prices plummeted, a boll weevil beetle infestation destroyed large areas of crops, and in 1915, flooding destroyed many of the houses and crops of farmers along the Mississippi River. Already suffering from the restrictive "Jim Crow" laws that segregated schools, restaurants, hotels, and hospitals, Black sharecroppers began to look to the North for a more prosperous lifestyle. Northern states were enjoying an economic boom as a result of an increased demand for industrial goods because of the war in Europe. They were also in need of labor because the war had slowed the rate of foreign immigration to Northern cities. Between 1915 and 1920, as many as 1 million Black individuals moved to Northern cities in search of jobs, closely followed by another million throughout the following decade (Nebraska Studies, 2010). The mass exodus of Black farmers from the South became known as the Great Migration, and by 1960, 75 percent of all Black Americans lived in cities (Emerging Minds, 2005).

The Great Migration had a huge impact on political, economic, and cultural life in the North, and popular music reflected this cultural change.

Figure 6.13

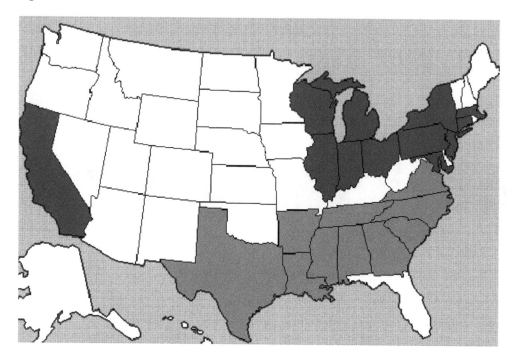

During the Great Migration, the 12 states in blue had the largest population growth of Black individuals, while the states in red had the 10 largest net losses (Martin).

Some of the Black individuals who moved to Northern cities came from the Mississippi Delta, home of the blues. The most popular destination was Chicago. Delta-born pianist Eddie Boyd later told *Living Blues* magazine, "I thought of coming to Chicago where I could get away from some of that racism and where I would have an opportunity to, well, do something with my talent…. It wasn't peaches and cream, man, but it was a hell of a lot better than down there where I was born (Szatmary)." At first, the migrants brought their style of country blues to the city. Characterized by the guitar and the harmonica, the Delta blues was identified by its rhythmic structure and strong vocals. Migrant musicians were heavily influenced by Delta blues musicians such as Charley Patton and legendary guitarist Robert Johnson. However, as the urban setting began to influence the migrants' style, they started to record a hybrid of blues, vaudeville, and swing, including the boogie-woogie and rolling-bass piano. Mississippi-born guitarist Muddy Waters, who moved to Chicago in the early 1940s, revolutionized the blues by combining his Delta roots with an electric guitar and amplifier. He did so partly out of necessity, since he could barely make himself heard in crowded Chicago clubs with an acoustic guitar (Chicago Blues Guitar). Waters's style was peppier and more buoyant than the sullen country blues. His plugged-in electric blues became the hallmark of the Chicago blues style, influencing countless other musicians and creating the underpinnings of rock and roll. Other migrant bluesmen helped to create regional variations of the blues all around the country, including John Lee Hooker in Detroit, Michigan, and T-Bone Walker in Los Angeles, California.

Youth Culture

Prior to 1945, most music was created with adults in mind, and teenage musical tastes were barely a consideration.

Young adults had few freedoms—most males were expected to join the military or get a job to support their fledgling families, while most females were expected to marry young and have children. Few young adults attended college, and personal freedom was limited. Following World War II, this situation changed drastically. A booming economy helped create an American middle class, which created an opening for a youth consumer culture. Unsavory memories of the war discouraged some parents from forcing their children into the military, and many emphasized enjoying life and having a good time. As a result, teenagers found they had a lot more freedom. This new liberalized culture allowed teenagers to make decisions for themselves, and, for the first time, many had the financial means to do so. Whereas many adults enjoyed the traditional sounds of Tin Pan Alley, teens were beginning to listen to rhythm and blues songs played by radio disc jockeys such as Alan Freed. Increased racial integration within the younger generation made them more accepting of Black musicians and their music, which was considered "cool," and provided a welcome escape from the daunting political and social tension caused by Cold War anxieties. The wide availability of radios, juke boxes, and 45 rpm records exposed this new style of rock and roll music to a broad teenage audience.

Figure 6.14

The popularity of *American Bandstand* made host Dick Clark an influential tastemaker in pop music.

Wikimedia Commons – public domain.

Once teenagers had the buying power to influence record sales, record companies began to notice. Between 1950 and 1959, record sales in the United States skyrocketed from $189 million to nearly $600 million (Szatmary). The 45 rpm vinyl records that were introduced in the late 1940s were an affordable option for teens with allowances. Dick Clark, a radio presenter in Philadelphia, soon tuned in to the new teenage tastes. Sensing an opportunity to tap in to a potentially lucrative market, he acquired enough advertising support to turn local hit music telecast *Bandstand* into a national television phenomenon.

Figure 6.15

Teen heartthrob Fabian was molded to fit teenage musical tastes in order to maximize record sales.

Otto Caldwell – Fabian Forte – CC BY-NC 2.0.

The result was the launch of *American Bandstand* in 1957, a music TV show that featured a group of teenagers dancing to current hit records. The show's popularity prompted record producers to create a legion of rock and roll acts specifically designed to appeal to a teenage audience, including Fabian and Frankie Avalon (Grimes, 2011). During its almost 40-year run, *American Bandstand* was a prominent influence on teenage fashions and musical tastes and, in turn, reflected the contemporary youth culture.

Racial Integration

Following the Great Migration, racial tensions increased in Northern cities. Whereas many Northerners had previously been unconcerned with the issue of race relations in the South, they found themselves confronted with the very real issue of having to compete for jobs with Black migrant workers. Black workers found themselves pushed into undesirable neighborhoods, often living in crowded, unsanitary slums where they were charged exorbitant rates by unscrupulous landlords. During the 1940s, racial tensions boiled over into race riots, most notably in Detroit. The city's 1943 riot caused the deaths of 34 people, 25 of whom were Black (Gilcrest, 1993).

Frustrated with inequalities in the legal system that distinguished Black and White individuals, members of the civil rights movement pushed for racial equality. In 1948, an executive order granted by President Harry Truman integrated the military. The move toward equality gained further momentum in 1954, with the U.S. Supreme Court decision to end segregation in public schools in the landmark case *Brown v. Board of Education*. The civil rights movement escalated throughout the late 1950s and early 1960s, aided by highly publicized events such as Rosa Parks's refusal to give up her seat on a bus to a White passenger in Montgomery, Alabama, in 1955. In 1964, Congress passed the most sweeping civil rights legislation since the Civil War, forbidding discrimination in public places and authorizing financial aid to enable school desegregation.

Although racist attitudes did not change overnight, the cultural changes brought on by the civil rights movement laid the groundwork for the creation of an integrated society. The Motown sound developed by Berry Gordy Jr. in the 1960s both reflected and furthered this change. Gordy believed that by coaching talented but unpolished Black artists, he could make them acceptable to mainstream culture. He hired a professional to head an in-house finishing school, teaching his acts how to move gracefully, speak politely, and use proper posture (Michigan Rock and Roll Legends). Gordy's commercial success with gospel-based pop acts such as the Supremes, the Temptations, the Four Tops, and Martha and the Vandellas reflected the extent of racial integration in the mainstream music industry. Gordy's most successful act, the Supremes, achieved 12 No. 1 singles on the *Billboard Hot 100* chart.

Figure 6.16

The commercial success of Motown girl group the Supremes reflected changing attitudes toward race in the United States.

Wikimedia Commons – public domain.

Musical Influences on Culture

Even though pop music is frequently characterized as a negative influence on society, particularly with respect to youth culture, it also has positive effects on culture. Many artists in the 1950s and 1960s pushed the boundaries of socially acceptable behavior with sexually charged movements and androgynous appearances. Without these precedents, acts like the Rolling Stones or David Bowie may have never made the transition into mainstream success.

On the other hand, over the past 50 years, critics have blamed rock and roll for juvenile delinquency, heavy metal for increased teenage aggression, and gangsta rap for a rise in gang warfare among young urban males. One recent study claimed that youths who listen to music with sexually explicit lyrics were more likely to have sex at an early age, stating that exposure to lots of sexually degrading music gives teens "a specific message about sex (MSNBC, 2006)." In addition to its effects on youth culture, popular music has contributed to shifting cultural values regarding race, morality, and gender.

Race

As the music of Chuck Berry and Little Richard gained popularity among White teens in the United States during the 1950s, most of the new rock acts were signed to independent labels, and larger companies such as RCA were losing their share of the market.

To capitalize on the public's enthusiasm for rock and roll and to prevent the loss of further potential profits, big record companies signed White artists to cover the songs of Black artists. The songs were often censored for the mainstream market by the removal of any lyrics that referenced sex, alcohol, or drugs. Pat Boone was the most successful cover artist of the era, releasing songs originally sung by artists such as Fats Domino, the El Dorados, Little Richard, and Big Joe Turner. Releasing a cover of a Black performer's song by a White performer was known as hijacking a hit, and this practice usually left black artists signed to independent labels broke. Because large companies such as RCA could widely promote and distribute their records—six of Boone's recordings reached the No. 1 spot on the Billboard chart—their records frequently outsold the original versions. Many White artists and producers would also take writing credit for the songs they covered and would buy the rights to songs from Black writers without giving them royalties or songwriting credit. This practice fueled racism within the music industry. Independent record producer Danny Kessler of Okeh Records said, "The odds for a black record to crack through were slim. If the black record began to happen, the chances were that a white artist would cover—and the big stations would play the white records…. There was a color line, and it wasn't easy to cross (Szatmary)."

Although cover artists profited from the work of Black R&B singers, occasionally they also helped to promote the original recordings. Many teenagers who heard covers on mainstream radio stations sought out the original artists' versions, increasing sales and prompting Little Richard to refer to Pat Boone as "the man who made me a millionaire (Crane, 2005)." Benefiting from covers also worked both ways. In 1962, soul singer Ray Charles covered Don Gibson's hit "I Just Can't Stop Loving You," which became a hit on country and western charts and furthered mainstream acceptance of Black musicians. Other Black artists to cover hits by White performers included Otis Redding, who performed the Rolling Stones hit "Satisfaction," and Jimi Hendrix, who covered Bob Dylan's "All Along the Watchtower."

Hijacking Hits

Releasing cover versions of hit songs was fairly standard practice before the 1950s because it was advantageous for songwriters and producers to have as many artists as possible sing their records to maximize royalties. Several versions of the same song often appeared in the music charts at the same time. However, the practice acquired racial connotations during the 1950s when larger music labels hijacked R&B hits, using their financial strength to promote the cover version at the expense of the original recording, which often exploited Black talent. As a result, many 1950s R&B artists lost out on royalties.

Two contemporary Black performers who were victims of this practice were R&B singer LaVern Baker and blues singer Arthur "Big Boy" Crudup. Baker, who was signed with then small-time label Atlantic Records, had been promoted as a pop singer. Because her songs appealed to mainstream audiences, they were ideal for covering, and industry giant Mercury Records took full advantage of this. When Baker released her 1955 hit "Tweedle Dee," Mercury immediately put out its own version, a note-for-note cover sung by White pop singer Georgia Gibbs. Atlantic could not match Mercury's marketing budget, and Gibbs's version outsold Baker's recording, causing her to lose an estimated $15,000 in royalties (Parales, 1997).

Around the same time, Arthur Crudup was producing hits such as "So Glad You're Mine," "Who's Been Foolin' You," "That's All Right Mama," and "My Baby Left Me," which were subsequently released by performers such as Elvis Presley, Creedence Clearwater Revival, and Rod Stewart for huge financial gain,

Crudup's songs made everybody rich—except him. This realization caused him to quit playing altogether in the late 1950s. A later attempt to collect back royalties was unsuccessful (Stanton, 1998). Baker filed a lawsuit in an attempt to revise the Copyright Act of 1909, making it illegal to copy an arrangement verbatim without permission. The lawsuit was unsuccessful, and Gibbs continued to cover Baker's songs (Dahl).

Morality

When Elvis Presley burst onto the rock and roll scene in the mid-1950s, many conservative parents of teenagers all over the United States were horrified. With his gyrating hips and sexually suggestive body movements, Presley was viewed as a threat to the moral well-being of young women. Television critics denounced his performances as vulgar, and on a 1956 appearance on the *Ed Sullivan Show*, cameras filmed him only from the waist up. One critic for the *New York Daily News* wrote that popular music "has reached its lowest depths in the 'grunt and groin' antics of one Elvis Presley (Collins, 2002)." Despite the critics' opinions, Presley immediately gained a fan base among teenage audiences, particularly adolescent girls, who frequently broke into hysterics at his concerts. Rather than tone down his act, Presley defended his movements as manifestations of the music's rhythm and beat and continued to gyrate on stage. Liberated from the constraints imposed by morality watchdogs, Presley set a precedent for future rock and roll performers and marked a major transition in popular culture.

In addition to decrying raunchy onstage performances by rock and roll artists, moralists in the conservative Eisenhower era objected to the sexually suggestive lyrics found in original rock and roll songs. Big Joe Turner's version of "Shake, Rattle, and Roll" used sexual phrases and referred to the bedroom, while Little Richard's original version of "Tutti Frutti" contained the phrase "tutti frutti, loose booty (Hall & Hall, 2006)." Although many of these lyrics were sanitized for mainstream White audiences when they were rereleased as cover versions, the idea that rock and roll was a threat to morality had been firmly implanted in many people's minds.

Ironically, many of the controversial key figures in the rock and roll era came from extremely religious backgrounds. Presley was a member of the evangelical First Assembly of God Church, where he acquired his love of gospel music (History Of Rock). Similarly, Ray Charles soaked up gospel influences from his local Baptist church (Walk Of Fame). Jerry Lee Lewis came from a strict Christian background and often struggled to reconcile his religious beliefs with the moral implications of the music he created. During a recording session in 1957, Lewis argued with manager Sam Phillips that the hit song "Great Balls of Fire" was too "sinful" for him to record (History, 1957). The religious backgrounds of the rock and roll pioneers both influenced and challenged moral norms. When Ray Charles recorded "I Got a Woman" in 1955, he reworded the gospel tune "Jesus Is All the World to Me," drawing criticism that the song was sacrilegious. Despite the objections, Charles's style caught on with other musicians, and his experimentation with merging gospel and R&B resulted in the birth of soul music.

Gender

While Presley was revolutionizing people's notions of sexual freedom and expression, other performers were changing cultural norms regarding gender identity. Dressed in flamboyant clothing with a pompadour hairstyle and makeup, Little Richard was an exotic, androgynous performer who blurred traditional gender boundaries and shocked 1950s audiences with his blatant campiness. Between his wild onstage antics, bisexual tendencies, and love of post-concert orgies, the self-proclaimed "King and Queen of Rock and Roll" challenged many social conventions of the time (Buckley, 2003). Little Richard's flamboyant, gender-bending appearance was so outrageous that it was not taken seriously during the 1950s—he was considered an entertainer whose androgynous look bore no relevance to the real world. However, Richard paved the way for future entertainers to shift cultural perceptions of gender. Later musicians such as David Bowie, Prince, and Boy George adopted his outrageous style, frequently appearing on stage wearing glittery costumes and heavy makeup. The popularity of these 1970s and 1980s pop idols, along with other gender-bending performers such as Annie Lennox and Michael Jackson, helped make androgyny more acceptable in mainstream society.

Figure 6.17

Gender-bending performers such as Little Richard, David Bowie, Boy George, and Prince helped to change social attitudes toward androgyny.

Key Takeaways

- The relationship between music and culture is reciprocal. Cultural influences on music include factors such as migration, youth culture, and racial integration. Musical influences on culture include factors such as racism within the music industry, content of particular genres of music that push conventional ideas of morality, and the physical appearance of individual performers.

- The mass migration of Southern Black individuals to urban areas during the early 20th century brought the blues to the North. Influenced by their new urban setting, migrant musicians incorporated new styles, including vaudeville and swing, into their music. Muddy Waters began playing electric guitar to make himself heard in the Chicago clubs and inadvertently created a new style known as Chicago blues.

- Young people in the 1950s had increased financial and personal freedom, giving them the power to influence record sales. Record companies began marketing rock and roll records specifically to teens, and the popularity of the new genre was enhanced by radio airplay and TV shows such as *American Bandstand*.

- The civil rights movement helped bring about desegregation in the 1950s. Although racial tensions persisted and race riots occurred in several Northern cities, racial integration gradually took place. The move toward integration was furthered and reflected by the Motown sound created by Berry Gordy Jr. Motown had crossover appeal among Black and White audiences, illustrated by the mainstream success of groups such as the Supremes.

- Large record companies fueled racism in the music industry by hijacking the hits of Black performers and releasing censored cover versions by White artists. The practice cost Black artists royalties. Although many performers were angered by the trend, some believed it helped popularize their original recordings.

- Rock and roll music was denounced for its negative impact on morality. Elvis Presley's "vulgar" onstage gyrations outraged critics in the conservative Eisenhower era. Sexually suggestive song lyrics were also held responsible by many for a decline in moral values, although they were often censored cover versions.

- Gender-bending performers such as Little Richard, David Bowie, and Annie Lennox helped normalize androgyny in American culture.

Exercise

Choose a genre of popular music from the last century. Using the ideas in this section as a starting point, examine ways in which your chosen genre has influenced aspects of culture and ways in which cultural aspects have affected the genre's development.

- Which factors have played the biggest roles? Are they interrelated?

References

Buckley, Peter. *The Rough Guide to Rock* (Rough Guides, 2003), 603–604.

Chicago Blues Guitar, "Chicago Blues Guitar Story," ChicagoBluesGuitar.com, http://www.chicagobluesguitar.com.

Collins, Dan. "How Big Was the King?" *CBS News*, August 7, 2002, http://www.cbsnews.com/stories/2002/08/07/entertainment/main517851.shtml.

Crane, Dan. "Cover Me: Introducing the Instant Tribute," *New York Times*, March 27, 2005, http://www.nytimes.com/2005/03/27/arts/music/27cran.html.

Dahl, Bill. "LaVern Baker," allmusic, http://www.allmusic.com/artist/lavern-baker-p3619/biography.

Emerging Minds, "The Great Migration," Emerging Minds, January 31, 2005, http://emergingminds.org/The-Great-Migration.html.

Gilcrest, Brenda J. "Detroit's 1943 Race Riot, 50 Years Ago Today, Still Seems Too Near," *Detroit Free Press*, June 20, 1993.

Grimes, William. "Bob Marcucci, 81, Backer of Fabian and Frankie Avalon," *New York Times*, March 18, 2011, http://query.nytimes.com/gst/fullpage.html?res=9A01EEDA1E3EF93BA25750C0A9679D8B63.

Hall, Dennis and Susan G. Hall, *American Icons: An Encyclopedia of the People, Places, and Things That Have Shaped Our Culture Volume 1* (Greenwood, 2006), 134.

History Of Rock, "Elvis Presley," History-of-rock.com, http://www.history-of-rock.com/elvis_presley.htm.

History, "Jerry Lee Lewis Records 'Great Balls of Fire' in Memphis, Tennessee," *History.com: This Day in History*: October 8, 1957, http://www.history.com/this-day-in-history/jerry-lee-lewis-records-quotgreat-balls-of-firequot-in-memphis-tennessee.

Martin, Elizabeth Anne. "Detroit and the Great Migration, 1916–1929," Bentley Historical Library, University of Michigan, http://bentley.umich.edu/research/publications/migration/ch1.php.

Michigan Rock and Roll Legends, "Berry Gordy Jr.," Michigan Rock and Roll Legends," http://www.michiganrockandrolllegends.com/Default.aspx?name=BERRYGORDY.

MSNBC, Associated Press, "Dirty Song Lyrics Can Prompt Early Teen Sex," *MSNBC*, August 7, 2006, http://www.msnbc.msn.com/id/14227775/.

Nebraska Studies, "Racial Tensions in Omaha: African American Migration" Nebraskastudies.org, June 25, 2010, http://www.nebraskastudies.org/0700/stories/0701_0131.html.

Parales, Jon. "LaVern Baker is Dead at 67; A Rhythm-and-Blues Veteran," *New York Times*, March 12, 1997, http://www.nytimes.com/1997/03/12/arts/lavern-baker-is-dead-at-67-a-rhythm-and-blues-veteran.html.

Stanton, Scott. *The Tombstone Tourist; Musicians* (New York: Simon & Schuster, 1998), 67.

Szatmary, *Rockin' in Time*, 26.

Szatmary, *Rockin' in Time*, 4.

Szatmary, *Rockin' in Time*, 57.

Walk Of Fame, "Ray Charles," *Hollywood Walk of Fame*, http://www.walkoffame.com/ray-charles.

Weingroff, Richard. "Highway History: The Road to Civil Rights: The Black Migration," U.S. Department of Transportation Federal Highway Administration, April 7, 2011, http://www.fhwa.dot.gov/highwayhistory/road/s10.cfm.

6.4 Current Popular Trends in the Music Industry

Learning Objectives

1. Assess the influence of the major record labels in the music industry.
2. Describe the role played by independent labels in the music industry.

In Weezer's 2008 song "Pork and Beans," vocalist Rivers Cuomo sings, "Timbaland knows the way to reach the top of the charts/Maybe if I work with him I can perfect the art (AOL Music Sessions)." The lyrics, a reference to hip-hop producer Timbaland's multiple high-profile collaborations, are an angry reaction to a meeting between Cuomo and record executives at the band's Geffen label. During the meeting, the executives told the band members they needed to write more commercial material, prompting a defiant (though commercially successful) response (Reesman, 2008). The incident is a reflection of the balance between commercial success and artistic expression in the music industry. Record labels need artists that inspire the record-buying public, while artists need the financial backing and expertise of record labels and their marketing teams. In recent years, tensions between artists and their labels have been heightened by the cost-cutting measures that have taken place at many companies due to the impact of online file sharing on profits.

The Influence of Major Record Labels

During the 1990s, the record industry was booming. Music lovers were busy replacing their cassette tapes and vinyl records with CDs, and sales were high. In 1999, the total revenue from music sales and licensing peaked at $14.6 billion (Goldman, 2010). Ten years later, record label executives were not as successful. Revenue had plunged to $6.3 billion, with the Recording Industry Association of America (RIAA) reporting declining revenue in nine of the 10 previous years, with album sales dropping an average of 8 percent every year (Goldman, 2010). Why the drastic decline? Experts agree that the primary culprit is the growing popularity of digital music, which initially began through peer-to-peer file sharing—the process of swapping media files over the Internet—such as the Napster service.

Despite a massive loss in profits over the past decade, the global music business still comprises a powerful oligopoly—a market condition in which a few firms dominate most of an industry's production and distribution. The global reach of these few companies means that they have the promotion and marketing muscle to determine which types of music reach listeners' ears and which become obsolete. Each of the major record labels has a strong infrastructure that oversees every aspect of the music business, from production, manufacture, and distribution to marketing and promotion.

Between 1950 and 1980, a large number of major record labels and numerous independent labels competed for a share of the musical pie. Gradually, the larger labels began buying up the independent labels, and then started trying to purchase each other. By the late 1990s, only six major labels remained: Warner, Universal, Sony, BMG, EMI, and Polygram. In 1998, Universal acquired Polygram, and 6 years later Sony and BMG merged. Sony later bought out BMG to obtain sole ownership of the company. Currently, the music industry is dominated by the so-called Big Four: Sony Music Entertainment, EMI, Universal Music Group, and Warner Music Group. The Big Four control over 85 percent of the U.S. recording music industry (Copynot). Figure 6.11 shows a graph of the current distribution of market share.

Figure 6.18

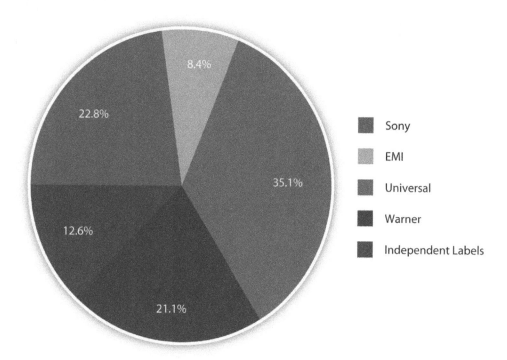

Four major music labels control over 85 percent of the U.S. recording music industry.

Data courtesy of The Nielsen Company

Sony Music Entertainment

In 2004, Japanese-owned Sony Music Entertainment (part of Sony) and German-owned BMG Entertainment (part of Bertelsmann) merged to create Sony BMG. The joint venture was a bid to overcome weak retail sales, online file sharing, and fierce competition from rival forms of media (Reuters, 2003). Independent music companies opposed the merger in Europe, arguing that it created a market imbalance, but the European Commission upheld its decision to allow the consolidation. In 2008, Sony bought out BMG's 50 percent stake for $1.2 billion (Kaplan). The company now has full ownership of the second-largest record label in the world. Subsidiary labels owned by Sony include Arista, Columbia, Epic, Jive, RCA, and Zomba, and the company represents numerous artists, including Alicia Keys, Ke$ha, and Sade.

EMI Group

The EMI Group is a British company, most famous for introducing the Beatles to the world through its Parlaphone subsidiary. Originally formed in 1931, through a merger of the UK Columbia Gramophone Company and the Gramophone Company, the money-losing company was taken over in 2007 by private equity firm Terra Firma Capital Partners Ltd. for $6.5 billion (Chassany, 2009). In an attempt to return the company to profit following the deal, Terra Firma head Guy Hands began slashing costs, eliminating more than 1,000 jobs in the process (Finch, et. al., 2008). Following the takeover, several high-profile artists quit the label, including Radiohead, who described the new management structure as "a confused bull in a china shop (Chassany, 2009)." As of 2010, the struggling company, which represents artists such as Coldplay, Lily Allen, and Pink Floyd, faces being taken over by its bankers after failing to secure a deal to sell its North American distribution rights to one of the other major labels (Dailynews, 2010).

Warner Music Group

Originally launched as Warner Bros. Records in 1958, the Warner Music Group gained momentum during the 1960s and 1970s with the purchase of several important new labels, including Elektra and Atlantic. Like the other major labels, the company began to suffer from declining sales due to the advent of free online music swapping. In 2004, Time Warner decided to abandon its record label and offloaded its music division to an investor group so that it could focus on more profitable areas, such as Time Warner Cable. The $2.6 billion deal included more than 800 artists, including Linkin Park, Metallica, and Kid Rock, as well as the group's publishing arm, Warner/Chapell Music, which owned more than a million copyrights (Vise, 2003).

After a brief period of independence, Warner Music Group went public in 2005, making the company the only stand-alone music company to be publically traded in the United States. To prepare for its public offering, the company made around $250 million in cuts through layoffs and consolidation (Leeds, 2005). The move caused concern among the label's artists that investors' interests would take priority over performers' interests and prompted rock-rap group Linkin Park to demand an early release from its contract with Warner. Guitarist Brad Delson characterized the company as "bad news," adding, "We don't want to be around to see what happens (Leeds, 2005)." The band eventually worked out a lucrative new deal with the company. As of 2010, Warner Music Group is considering the possibility of purchasing EMI should the struggling company fail to meet its debt repayments (Sibun, 2010).

Universal Music Group

The largest of the Big Four record labels, Universal Music Group established itself as an industry giant in 1998, with the merger of PolyGram and Universal. Both companies already owned numerous subsidiaries, and the merger of the two entertainment conglomerates created the largest music company in the world. Wholly owned by French international media firm Vivendi since 2006, the company has gone on to acquire BMG Music Publishing and Univision Music Group, among smaller labels. Its acquisition of U.K. labels Sanctuary Music Group and V2 in 2007 drew criticisms from the independent sector that the recording giant was heading toward a monopoly (Sherwin, 2007). The Association of Independent Music claimed that the deals would "further marginalize a vibrant independent sector, serving to stifle competition and narrow consumer choice (Sibun, 2010)." Despite the objections, both deals went ahead.

Universal Music Group's catalog of artists includes U2, Amy Winehouse, Lady Gaga, Taylor Swift, and the Black Eyed Peas. Despite its powerful status, the company has suffered from declining sales of physical products along with the rest of the music industry. As of 2010, UMG plans to lure customers back to purchasing physical CDs by lowering prices to under $10 (the average price of a digitally purchased album) (Swindle, 2010).

Independent Record Labels: A Smaller Share of the Pie

In addition to the four major record labels, independent production companies, or indie record labels, operate without the financial assistance of one of the Big Four (although in recent years, the definition has shifted to incorporate indies that are partially owned by one of the major labels). Ranging from small grassroots or garage labels to large, profitable businesses, indie labels typically produce music that is less commercially viable and more eclectic than the music produced by the larger mainstream companies.

Indie Origins

Independent labels have played a small but significant role in the music industry for as long as there has been a market. When patents held on sound recording technologies entered the public market in the 1920s, opportunities arose for small recording companies to enter the business. To avoid competing with larger firms such as RCA and Edison, the new independent companies focused on neglected areas of the music industry, such as folk, gospel, and rural blues. When the major labels decided during World War II to abandon then-unprofitable music recorded by Black artists, the independent labels quickly rushed in to fill the void, enjoying a boom during the rock and roll era when R&B music soared in popularity. Between 1955 and 1959, the U.S. market share of the major companies had dropped from 78 percent to 44 percent, while the market share of independent companies rose from 22 percent to 56 percent (History Of Rock, 2009). Sun Records played a particularly important role in the development of both rock and roll and country music by releasing records by Elvis Presley, Jerry Lee Lewis, Johnny Cash, and Roy Orbison.

During the 1970s punk era, indie labels profited from the antimainstream, anticorporate attitude of many punk rock bands, which disassociated themselves from the major labels. The indie-rock movement grew throughout the 1980s and 1990s, with labels such as Sub Pop, I.R.S., and Epitaph and epitomized by the music of the Smiths, the Stone Roses, R.E.M., and the Jesus and Mary Chain. This movement was known as "college rock," which would later become alternative rock. However, as alternative rock grew in popularity, grunge bands such as Nirvana, Soundgarden, and Pearl Jam broke into the mainstream. This attracted the attention of major record labels, which began to look at the music with a commercially oriented approach. Many artists found themselves faced with a dilemma: stay true to their indie roots or "sell out" to a major record label in the hope of financial gain.

The Pressure to Sell Out: Nirvana

When Seattle grunge band Nirvana began to achieve success in the late 1980s, they were signed to independent label Sub Pop. Popular among college students, the band's 1989 album *Bleach* sold well enough for the band to consider moving to a bigger label. Amid rumors that Sub Pop was planning on signing as a subsidiary of a major record company because of financial difficulties, the band decided to cut out the middleman and seek a new contract itself (Norris, 2004). Signing with DGC Records (an imprint of Geffen), Nirvana released *Nevermind* in 1991 and found itself thrust into the mainstream. Within 9 months of its release, the album had sold more than 4 million copies (compared to 30,000 copies of *Bleach*), knocked Michael Jackson's *Dangerous* from the top of the *Billboard* chart, and placed Nirvana at the forefront of public attention.

For Sub Pop, Nirvana's success was both a blessing and a curse. Under severe financial stress, the label had begun layoffs in the spring of 1991, reducing its staff of 25 to a core group of five employees (Sub Pop Records, 2008). With the royalties it received from *Nevermind*, along with the buyout from Nirvana's contract, and potential royalties from any future albums, Sub Pop was pulled back from the brink of collapse. However, the carefully crafted niche that Sub Pop had found in the music industry vanished. Eager to discover the next big thing in grunge, major labels began scoping out Seattle bands, offering them large advances against which the smaller independent companies could not compete. Sub Pop chief Bruce Pavitt said of one band, "I was told by our head A&R agent that they would be happy with a $5,000 advance. Two months later we were giving them a check for $150,000 (Sub Pop Records, 2008)." In 1995, the company sold 49 percent of its shares to Warner Bros in exchange for financial backing.

Nirvana had equally ambivalent feelings about the transition from a small independent label to a major record company. At a concert shortly after the band signed their deal with DGC, lead singer Kurt Cobain declared to the crowd, "Hello, we're major-label corporate rock sellouts (Kunkel, 2007)." Having spent several years among the anticommercial, do-it-yourself grunge crowd in Seattle, the band's members were uncomfortable with their new position as wealthy rock stars.

Advantages of Indie Labels

Although they frequently lose their talent to industry heavyweights, indie labels hold several advantages over major record companies. They are generally smaller, enabling them to respond to changing popular musical tastes more quickly than can large companies with more cumbersome processes and procedures in place. This enables them to pick up on emerging trends and bring them to market quickly. Although unable to compete with the distribution and promotion power of the major labels, indie labels can focus on niche markets, tapping into regional trends. For example, hip-hop's initial commercial successes in the late 1970s and early 1980s came through small independent labels such as Tommy Boy and Sugar Hill. Realizing that record executives would find the raw street version of hip-hop unworkable, the labels came up with the idea of using house bands to play with emcees to improve the commercial viability of the genre. An early example of this process was Sugarhill Gang's "Rapper's Delight," which was a worldwide hit (Anderson, 2006).

Figure 6.19

Artists who have switched from an independent label to a major label midway through their careers include Green Day, Nirvana, and Death Cab for Cutie.

FoolOnTheHill301 – Green Day Background – CC BY 3.0; José Luis Merizalde – Nirvana Set Box – CC BY-NC 2.0; Wikimedia Commons – public domain.

The nature of the independent production process may also prove advantageous. A shorter path from creation of the music to distribution and promotion makes it easier to maintain the artist's original vision. For this reason, many artists prefer to work with independent labels, believing the final product to be more authentic. This argument is also used by some fans of independent labels, who trust companies that only produce one brand of music to adhere to a consistent sound and musical style.

Vanity Labels

A popular trend among major record labels is to allow high-profile recording artists to front their own indie labels with the financial backing of the larger company. Frequently referred to as vanity labels, these are spin-offs of the parent company that enable artists to run "a label within a label" and release music by other performers that they admire. Examples include Madonna's Maverick, Trent Reznor's Nothing, and Michael Jackson's MJJ. Allowing an artist to create a vanity label benefits a major record label in several ways: It encourages artists to remain with the parent company for longer than they may have otherwise done, it reduces the amount of promotional effort required by the label because fans are likely to be attracted to new music based on the recommendation of favorite artists, and it increases the likelihood that bands in niche genres will become big moneymakers for the company.

However, vanity label projects often prove risky and unsuccessful because the label provides all of the money while the proven artist is responsible for developing new acts, and recent losses in the music industry have caused major labels to cut funding for artist-run ventures. For example, Mariah Carey's label, Crave, ended up dissolving less than a year after it opened. In 2004, Universal Records President Monte Lipman commented, "Back in the day, when the industry was a lot healthier, it was 'OK, here's $2–$3million. Go start your label and let us know when you're ready to start your first act.' Those days are absolutely over (First Coast News, 2004)."

Key Takeaways

- The global music business constitutes a powerful oligopoly—a market condition in which a few firms dominate most of an industry's production and distribution. Major record labels make up over 85 percent of the music industry. Currently, the four major record labels (known as the Big Four) are EMI, Sony Music Entertainment, Universal Music Group, and Warner Music Group.

- Indie record labels are smaller labels that operate without financial assistance from the Big Four and typically produce less commercially viable music. Although they do not have the marketing and promotional power of the major labels, indies have several advantages. They are smaller and more flexible than major labels, enabling them to respond more quickly to trends in the industry. Indies are also able to tap into niche markets, and their simple structure often means that the music stays closer to the artist's original vision. Major labels often allow high-profile stars to set up their own indie labels, known as vanity labels because they reflect the personal musical tastes of the high-profile artist.

Exercise

Draw a T-chart. Label the left-hand column *Major Record Labels* and the right-hand column *Independent Record Labels*. Using the information in this chapter, your own knowledge, and further Internet research, list the advantages held by each type of label in the music industry. Consider the size and structure of each type of company, financial issues, artist preferences, and the impact of digital distribution.

Major Record Labels	Independent Record Labels
• Larger labels have money for wider promotion and distribution.	• Smaller labels can react quickly to emerging trends.

References

Anderson, Rhome. "Hip to Hip-Hop," *Washington Post*, February 19, 2006, http://www.washingtonpost.com/wp-dyn/content/article/2006/02/16/AR2006021602077.html.

AOL Music Sessions, "Weezer, '(If You're Wondering If I Want You To) I Want You' Sessions," AOL Music Sessions, http://music.aol.com/sessions/weezer-if-youre-wondering-if-i-want-you-to-i-want-you-sessions/.

Chassany, Anne-Sylvaine. "Terra Firma Sues Citi over EMI Takeover," *Bloomberg Businessweek*, December 18, 2009, http://www.businessweek.com/globalbiz/content/dec2009/gb20091218_584654.htm.

Copynot, "The Big Four Record Companies," Copyright Law, Treaties and Advice, http://www.copynot.org/Pages/The%20big%20four%20Record%20Companies.html.

Dailynews, Associated Press, "Music Group EMI Facing Bank Takeover After Talks Fall Apart," *Los Angeles Daily News*, April 2, 2010, http://www.dailynews.com/business/ci_14805128.

Finch, Julia, Owen Gibson, and Alex Needham, "Radiohead Quit, Robbie Williams on Strike—and Now 1,000 Jobs Cut," *Guardian* (London), January 12, 2008, http://www.guardian.co.uk/media/2008/jan/12/robbiewilliams.emi.

First Coast News, Associated Press, "Record Cos. Wary of Vanity Label Deals," *Jacksonville (FL) First Coast News*, June 28, 2004, http://www.firstcoastnews.com/news/strange/news-article.aspx?storyid=20660.

Goldman, David. "Music's Lost Decade: Sales Cut in Half," *CNN*, February 3, 2010, http://money.cnn.com/2010/02/02/news/companies/napster_music_industry/index.htm.

History Of Rock, "Rock and Roll Timeline," The History of Rock 'n' Roll, October 15, 2009, http://www.history-of-rock.com/rock_and_roll_timeline.htm.

Kaplan, David. "Sony Buys Bertelsmann's 50 Percent Stake In Sony BMG for $1.2 Billion," PaidContent.org: The Economics of Digital Content, http://paidcontent.org/article/419-sony-buys-back-bertelsmanns-50-percent-stake-in-sony-bmg-company-rename/.

Kunkel, Benjamin. "Stupid and Contagious," *New York Times*, May 6, 2007, http://www.nytimes.com/2007/05/06/books/review/Kunkel.t.html.

Leeds, Jeff. "A Band Makes Its Case Against Record Label," *New York Times*, May 9, 2005, http://www.nytimes.com/2005/05/09/arts/music/09linkin.html.

Norris, Chris. "Ghost of Saint Kurt," *Spin*, April 2004, 57–63.

Reesman, Bryan. "Weezer Goes into the Red on New CD," *Mix*, September 1, 2008, http://mixonline.com/recording/tracking/music-weezer/.

Reuters, "Sony, BMG Agree on Music Merger," *CNN World Business*, November 7, 2003, http://edition.cnn.com/2003/BUSINESS/11/06/sony.bmg.reut/.

Sherwin, Adam. "Indies Accuse Universal of Gaining Monopoly" *Times* (London), October 1, 2007, http://business.timesonline.co.uk/tol/business/industry_sectors/media/article2563208.ece.

Sibun, Jonathan. "KKR and Warner Music Talk Over Break-Up Bid for EMI," *Telegraph* (London), March 14, 2010, http://www.telegraph.co.uk/finance/newsbysector/retailandconsumer/7443456/KKR-and-Warner-Music-talk-over-break-up-bid-for-EMI.html.

Sub Pop Records, "About Us," April 2, 2008, http://www.subpop.com/about.

Swindle, Anna. "Universal Music Group Plans to Lower CD Prices," *Paste*, March 23, 2010, http://www.pastemagazine.com/articles/2010/03/post-69.html.

Vise, David. "Time Warner Sells Music Unit to Bronfman for $2.6B," *Washington Post*, November 24, 2003, http://www.washingtonpost.com/ac2/wp-dyn/A9806-2003Nov24.

6.5 Influence of New Technology

Learning Objectives

1. Determine the difference between illegal file sharing and legitimate digital downloads.

2. Identify ways in which digital music sales have influenced the music industry.

3. Identify ways in which the Internet has enabled artists to sell music directly to fans.

In the mid-1990s, CD sales were booming. Cassette tapes were all but obsolete, and record companies were reaping the benefits of sales to consumers who wanted their music collections in the latest technological format. This boom was a familiar step in the evolution of technology. In past decades, records seemed to have an ironclad lock on sales, but they were eventually passed by cassette sales. Cassettes, as previously mentioned, were then passed by CD sales. However, despite a few advantages in quality and convenience, there were several areas in which CDs were lacking. They were expensive for consumers to purchase, and consumers had to buy a full album even if they were only interested in listening to one or two songs on it because every album came as a complete package.

At the height of the CD revolution, new digital technology was being developed that would eliminate these disadvantages and revolutionize digital music storage. In 1989, German company Fraunhofer-Gesellshaft discovered how to compress digital audio to approximately one-tenth the size of the original audio with almost no discernible loss in quality to the average listener. Small enough to be transmitted over a modem, the so-called MP3 files (the *MP* stands for *Moving Pictures Experts Group*, which is the group that sets the standard for audio and video compression and transmission, and the *3* refers to the most popular layer or scheme with the standard) could be downloaded onto a website or FTP site in a relatively short amount of time. Initially done only by a tech-savvy elite, the process of downloading and sharing audio files was a painstaking process because MP3 files were not in one centralized location. Peer-to-peer file sharing—the process in which two or more computer systems are connected over the Internet for the purpose of sharing music or video files—became a worldwide phenomenon in 1999 with the development of centralized online file-sharing system Napster.

File Sharing: From Illegal Downloading to Digital Music Stores

In 1999, Northeastern University student Shawn Fanning dropped out of school to complete work on a software project that would simplify finding and downloading MP3 files on the Internet (Doyle, 2000). The result was a free downloadable Napster program that transformed PCs into servers for exchanging music files over the Internet. The program also sported a chat-room feature that served a community of music fans eager to discuss their favorite bands. Originally an experiment between Fanning and his friends, the program's popularity spread through word of mouth. By the end of the first week, 15,000 people had downloaded the program (Riedel, 2006).

Although music fans were thrilled by their newfound ability to download free songs (albeit illegally), the record industry was not happy. In December 1999, all four major record labels, together with the Recording Industry Association of America (RIAA), launched a series of lawsuits against Fanning and his site for copyright infringement. Citing the nonpayment of royalties and the loss of revenue through lost CD sales, the RIAA also claimed that artists would be unwilling to create new songs now that they could be obtained for free. In response, Napster argued that it merely provided the software for people to share music files and no copyrighted material appeared on the site itself. In addition, Fanning claimed that the site encouraged people to go out and buy CDs based on the exposure artists received from Napster (Riedel, 2006).

As the number of the Napster program users grew, the lawsuit began to garner publicity. Some Napster supporters, many of them college students, viewed the legal battle as a David versus Goliath situation and rooted for Fanning to beat the corporate music giants. Most recording artists sided with the record labels, with heavy metal rock group Metallica and rap artist Dr. Dre launching their own separate lawsuits against Napster in April 2000. However, some bands discovered a way to use the site to their advantage. Alternative rock group Radiohead promoted its album *Kid A* by secretly releasing the record to Napster 3 weeks before its street release date, creating a wave of publicity that launched the album to the No. 1 spot on the *Billboard 200* chart in October 2000 (Menta, 2000). Reggae-rock band Dispatch poured free recordings onto the site, increasing its fan base to such an extent that it sold out multiple nights at Madison Square Garden in early 2007 (Knopper, 2009). Dispatch bassist Pete Heimbold said, "What we found was it really didn't deter kids from coming to shows and buying CDs. In fact, I think it had the opposite effect—people heard songs off Napster and had a lot of merchandise and CDs (Knopper, 2009)."

Despite the Napster program's many advantages, including a built-in user base of 26.4 million people, the major record labels were unable to reach a deal with the site to create any form of fee-based service. In 2007, former EMI Executive Ted Cohen said, "The record labels had an opportunity to create a digital ecosystem and infrastructure to sell music online, but they kept looking at the small picture instead of the big one. They wouldn't let go of CDs (Mnookin, 2007)." A court injunction in 2000 ordered Napster to remove all copyrighted material from its servers, and within two days the website was effectively shut down. Following a bankruptcy liquidation, the Napster program was reinvented as a paid subscription service in 2003. Under its new terms, users pay a fee to access music.

The Post-Napster Universe: Gnutella and Kazaa

Napster's initial success resulted in a wave of similar sites emerging throughout 2000. The creators of these new services recognized that Napster's legal problems were the result of maintaining a central file server. By keeping a list of all the users on the network, Napster was able to control its users' activities by blocking illegal downloads. When the court ordered the service to halt illegal downloading, the absence of a central database destroyed the entire Napster network.

To avoid a similar fate, new peer-to-peer (P2P) systems adopted two different approaches. The Gnutella network, which serves clients such as LimeWire, BearShare, and WinMX, avoided maintaining a central database. Instead, it dispersed information about file locations across computer "nodes" around the world. Users were able to find each other, but the service could disclaim the ability to prevent copyright infringements. The lack of a centralized server and multiple client base meant that, unlike Napster, it would be impossible to shut down the entire Gnutella network through a simple court order. Courts would need to block all Gnutella network traffic at the Internet service provider (ISP) level of the Internet, a far trickier prospect than simply shutting down a central database.

In addition to a lack of a central database, some P2P providers set up in offshore locations to take advantage of less-restrictive copyright laws and weaker enforcement. Kazaa was initially based in the Pacific island nation of Vanuata and operated out of Australia. However, the company's offshore location did not protect it from copyright infringement laws. After a series of legal wrangles, Kazaa was ordered to modify its software in Australia in 2005 and agreed to pay $100 million in damages to the record industry. In 2006, the site became a legal music download service (BBC News, 2006).

Not content with pursuing providers of illegal music downloads, the RIAA also took legal action against the users of sites such as LimeWire and Kazaa. In 2003, the recording industry sued 261 American music fans for illegally sharing songs on P2P networks (Kravets, 2008). Although fines under U.S. copyright law can rise to up to $150,000 per illegally downloaded track, most of the cases were settled for much less. As of 2008, the RIAA had sued or threatened to sue more than 30,000 individuals for copyright infringement (Kravets, 2008).

Busted! Woman Fined $1.92 Million

In an ongoing legal battle with the RIAA, Minnesota woman Jammie Thomas was found guilty of copyright infringement for a second time in 2009 and fined $1.92 million for illegally downloading 24 songs on file-sharing Kazaa website. First fined $222,000 for using the Kazaa service, the 30-year-old single mother of four refused to settle with the recording industry out of court. Thomas claimed her innocence, maintaining that she was not the Kazaa service user whose files had been detected by RIAA investigators (Kravets, 2008).

The case became the first of its kind to go before a jury in 2007, and Thomas faced fines ranging from $18,000 to $3.6 million under the Copyright Act of 1976. After deliberating for 5 hours, a jury found her guilty of copyright infringement and awarded the RIAA $222,000 in damages. The verdict was thrown out a year later when a federal judge declared a mistrial. However, jurors in Thomas's second trial found her guilty again, upping the fine to $1.92 million. A federal judge later reduced the damages to $50,000. In January 2010, the RIAA offered to close the case for $25,000, but Thomas continued to refuse to pay (Kravets, 2010).

Thomas's case has provoked strong reactions on both sides of the debate. RIAA spokeswoman Cara Duckwork said, "It is a shame that Ms. Thomas-Rasset continues to deny any responsibility for her actions rather than accept a reasonable settlement offer and put this case behind her (Kravets, 2010)." Joe Sibley, one of Thomas's lawyers, argued, "They want to use this case as a bogeyman to scare people into doing what they want, to pay exorbitant damages (Kravets, 2010)." The RIAA is currently winding down its 6-year campaign against illegal downloaders, approximately 30,000 lawsuits in all. Instead the RIAA is focusing on creating a program with Internet providers to discontinue service to users who continue to break online copyright laws (Kravets, 2010).

The Advent of Digital Music Stores

With the closure of the Napster program and the crackdown on illegal downloading, a void in the music distribution market opened and was almost immediately filled by fee-based online music providers. This void helped to resurrect one company many feared was declining. Apple launched iTunes—a free application for the Mac computer that converted audio CDs into digital music files, organized digital music collections, and played Internet radio—and the iPod—a portable media player compatible with the iTunes software—in 2001, and both products have dominated the market ever since. In 2003, the company signed deals with all of the major record labels and launched the iTunes Store, a virtual store that enabled people to buy and download digital music on demand. Initially featuring 200,000 songs at a cost of $0.99 each to download, the store quickly revolutionized the digital music industry. Within a week, iTunes Store customers purchased 1 million songs (Apple). Six months later, Apple convinced the record labels to expand the service to Microsoft Windows operating system users, and by the following year, the iTunes Store had gone international. Within 5 years of its launch, the iTunes Store was the top music seller in the United States, and in February 2010, Apple celebrated its 10 billionth download (Williams, 2010).

Several companies have attempted to cash in on the success of iTunes, with varying results. In 2007, Internet giant Amazon.com launched the Amazon MP3 digital music download store that initially offered more than 2 million songs priced between $0.89 and $0.99 (Richardson, 2007). Amazon's major selling point was its lack of digital rights management (DRM) software, which enabled music downloads to be played on any hardware device. In contrast, songs downloaded through the iTunes appliance program could only be played on Apple products. Apple removed these restrictions in 2009 after negotiating an agreement with the major record labels. Despite its efforts to topple Apple from the top spot in the digital music arena, the Amazon MP3 service only commanded 8 percent of the digital music market in 2009, compared with Apple's 69 percent of the market (NPD Group, 2009). Napster has also stayed in the game by releasing a new design plan in 2009 after being purchased by Best Buy. The plan requires users to pay a fee to access all the music in its catalog. This plan has kept Napster in business; however, the company only had 1 percent to 2 percent of the market share at the beginning of 2010 (Weintraub, 2010). Other online music stores are operated by Wal-Mart, Rhapsody, and Yahoo! Music.

The Impact of Digital Music Technology

Once digital music technology was introduced to the world, its domination of the music industry was almost instantaneous. MP3 players have several key advantages over CD players. They are smaller and more portable, eliminating the necessity of lugging around bulky CD carrying cases. Whereas CDs can only hold a relatively small amount of data, MP3 players are able to compress thousands of songs onto a single device (this lack of packaging and manufacturing has caused disputes between artists and labels over royalties, which will be discussed later on). The lack of moving parts means MP3 players can be taken jogging or cycling without the risk of a song skipping every time the user hits a bumpy patch of road. Users are also no longer obligated to buy entire albums; instead, they can pick and choose their favorite songs from a catalog of online music.

Of the many brands of MP3 player currently available on the market, Apple's iPod has been the dominant force in the digital music industry since its launch in 2001 (see Figure 6.15). Apple CEO Steve Jobs attributes the success of his product to its simple design. In a 2005 interview he said, "One of the biggest insights we have was that we decided not to try to manage your music library on the iPod, but to manage it in iTunes. Other companies tried to do everything on the device itself and made it so complicated that it was useless (levy, 2006)." The iPod has also reaped the benefits of a successful marketing campaign and constant reinvention of its original format. Customers now have the choice of several different iPod models according to their need for storage space and desire for additional services such as Internet access and video-playing capability.

Figure 6.20

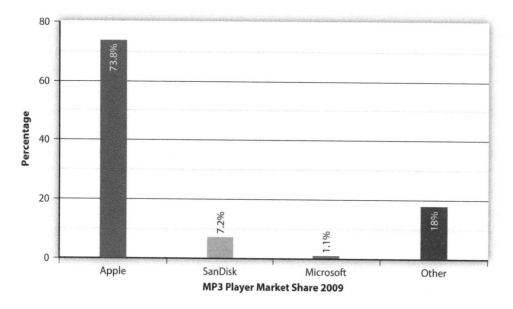

Since its launch in 2001, Apple's iPod has remained the biggest-selling brand of MP3 player (Nusca, 2009).

Profit Division

One effect that Apple iTunes and other online retailers have had on the music industry is to shake up the way that profits are divided among artists and record labels. Because of the unanticipated boom in digital record sales, recording artists and their publishers were unprepared for the possibility that they might need to renegotiate their contracts to include digital downloads. Many artists discovered to their cost that their contracts predated the digital download era, leaving them open to exploitative royalty rates for digital downloads of songs and ringtones.

The very definition of digital royalties is still under negotiation—should a download be classified as licensed use of an artist's music (which nets the artist approximately 50 percent of the download fee in royalties), or should it be classified as a retail sale (which nets the artist approximately 12 percent of the download fee in royalties) (Michaels, 2009)? The answer depends on the contractual agreement between artists and record labels. In 2009, rapper Eminem's publishing company FBT Productions sued Universal Music Group for $1.6 million of unpaid royalties, arguing that the downloads should fall under the "licensing" agreements that cover physical releases such as CDs, rather than the "distribution" agreements put forth by Universal Music Group (Michaels, 2009). A jury agreed that a song sold online is no different from a song bought in a store and ruled in favor of the record label.

Because online retailers such as Apple are responsible for the marketing, management, and delivery of downloaded music, record labels' overheads are much lower. This new industry trend has prompted many artists and publishers to demand a bigger share of labels' profits. As of 2010, a $0.99 download from the iTunes appliance program generates $0.30 for Apple and $0.70 for the record label, of which $0.09 goes to the songwriter and publisher as a standard mechanical royalty (Albanesius, 2008).

CD Sales

The burgeoning popularity of digital music has drastically reduced revenue brought in from CD sales since 2001. Although many people have switched from illegally downloading to purchasing music on digital stores, paid digital downloads have not yet begun to make up for the loss of revenue from CD sales, and illegal downloads remain a problem for the recording industry. According to online download tracker BigChampagne Media Measurement, unauthorized downloads still represent about 90 percent of the market (Goldman). With album sales declining at a rate of 8 percent a year, music executives are trying to figure out how to stem the flow of money flooding out of the CD sales market. Former head of Yahoo! Music David Goldberg said, "The digital music business is a war of attrition that nobody seems to be winning. The CD is still disappearing, and nothing is replacing it in entirety as a revenue generator (Goldman)." In 2009, digital revenue sales rose and were well on the way to equaling CD sales, which were on the decline (see Figure 6.21).

Figure 6.21

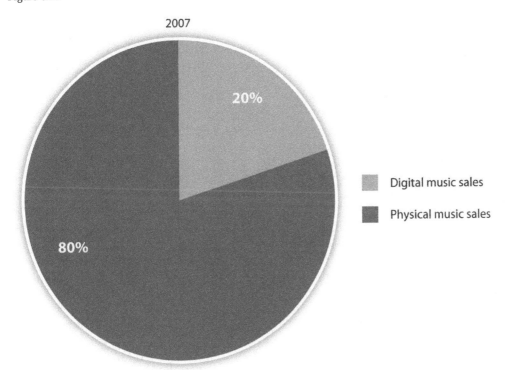

2007

Digital music sales

Physical music sales

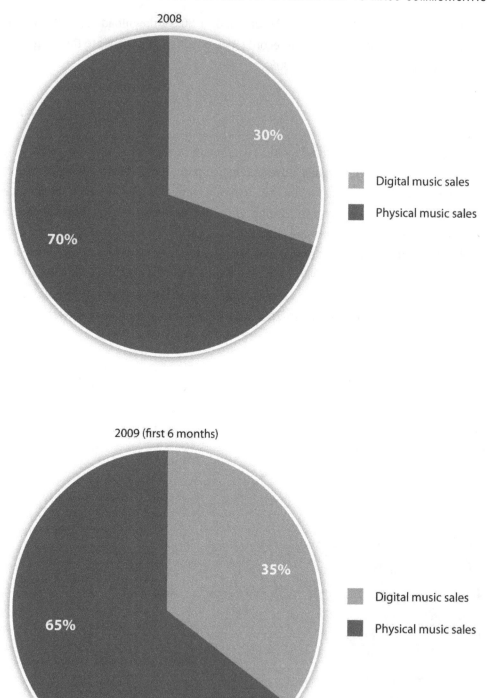

Digital Music Sales versus Physical Music Sales (Graham, 2009).

To partially make up for lost sales, the music industry has been generating revenue through licensing fees, including fees for ringtones, music played on Internet radio stations such as MySpace Music and Pandora, and music videos on the YouTube video-sharing website that is owned by Google. In 2009, digital licensing revenue reached $84 million and continues to grow (Goldman). Meanwhile, recording artists are focusing their attention on live performances and merchandise, which have become their main source of revenue. Demand for concert tickets rose at least 7 percent in 2008 to $4.2 billion, according to touring industry trade magazine *Pollstar* (Sisario, 2008).

Utilizing the Internet: A New Level of Indie

Artists such as Nine Inch Nails and Radiohead are abandoning the traditional music industry model in favor of marketing their songs directly to fans.

Over the past few years, the Internet has begun to level the proverbial playing field between major and independent record labels. Exemplifying how smaller indie labels are able to latch on to trends more quickly than the Big Four, indies have embraced new technology, including blogging, online video sites, and online social networking sites, as a means of promoting their music, while the major labels have fallen behind the curve. With social networking sites enabling artists to communicate directly with their fans, the need for extensive financial backing or an industry middleman is all but eliminated. Now, artists can upload their music onto a social networking site for free and generate record sales purely through word of mouth.

Although a few indie artists have become household names entirely through the buzz generated on social networking sites, many others find that they need some guidance. The direct-to-fan business model has created opportunities for web-based companies such as Nimbit and ReverbNation, which provide software that enables independent artists and record labels to market their music online, keep track of sales, create demand for their music, and communicate with fans. The companies offer social networking applications that enable fans to purchase music directly from the artists rather than being redirected to a third-party website. Other advantages for bands include automatic updates to fans across a variety of networking sites, digital distribution through the iTunes appliance program and other stores, and real-time sales updates.

Many established artists have also embraced the direct-to-fan business model. In 2007, Nine Inch Nails frontman Trent Reznor announced that the band was splitting from its contractual obligations to Universal Music Group to distribute its next albums independently. Well known for his vocal distaste of major record labels and their profiteering, Reznor encouraged fans in Australia to steal his album *Year Zero* because he believed it was priced too highly there (SPIN, 2007). Commenting on the state of the music industry in a 2007 interview he said, "I've got a battle where I'm trying to put out quality material that matters and I've got fans that feel it's their right to steal it and I've got a company that's so bureaucratic and clumsy and ignorant and behind the times they don't know what to do, so they rip the people off (Johnson, 2007)." Following the band's split with Universal, they released studio album *The Slip* as a free digital download in 2008. Reznor stated, "This one's on me," on his website, thanking fans for their loyalty. The album was downloaded 1.4 million times within the first 6 weeks of its release (Kent, 2011). A similar technique used by tech-savvy alternative band Radiohead reaped even higher rewards in 2007, when its retail release of *In Rainbows* entered the album chart at No. 1 even though the digital version had been offered online at a price of the customer's choosing several months earlier (see Chapter 11 "The Internet and Social Media" for more information about Radiohead's *In Rainbows* release) (Brandle, 2008). The web-based direct release model allows bands such as Radiohead and Nine Inch Nails to obtain vital information about their fan bases—including e-mail addresses—that they can use for future promotions. Whether or not the practice proves to be a passing fad, the traditional music industry model is shifting as new technology makes it easier for artists to communicate directly with their fans.

Key Takeaways

- The introduction of digital music technology and peer-to-peer file sharing in 1999 changed the nature of the music industry. Websites, such as the Napster service, which enabled users to share free music, negatively impacted CD sales. Although the RIAA successfully shut down Napster, other sites emerged throughout the early 2000s, such as the Gnutella network and the Kazaa service. Rather than figuring out a way to make money from digital music, the recording industry focused its efforts on bringing lawsuits against illegal downloaders. By the time iTunes and other fee-based music sites became available, irreversible damage had been done to the industry's sales figures.

- Apple's iTunes Store is the dominant digital music retailer in the United States, commanding almost 70 percent of the digital music market. The boom in digital music sales has affected the music industry in several ways: It has changed the way that profits are distributed among recording artists and labels, it has caused a massive decline in CD sales, and it has prompted industry executives to seek profits elsewhere (for example, through licensing fees).

- The Internet has proved advantageous for smaller indie labels that take advantage of blogging, social networking sites, and video websites as a means to promote their music. Companies such as Nimbit and ReverbNation are replacing some of the functions performed by major record labels, enabling artists to promote and distribute their own music directly to fans. Established bands such as Radiohead and Nine Inch Nails have separated from major labels and used the Internet to successfully distribute their music at little or no cost to fans. The ready availability and low cost of this new technology is changing the music industry, and the Big Four companies may need to adapt traditional business models to return to profit.

Exercise

Visit the Apple website (http://www.apple.com/) and compare its digital music services and products with those of its nearest competitors. For music, look at Amazon (http://www.amazon.com/), Yahoo! Music (http://new.music.yahoo.com/), and Napster (http://www.napster.com). How do the prices and experiences differ? For MP3 players, look at Sony (http://www.sony.com), Philips (http://www.usa.philips.com/), and RCA (http://www.rca.com).

- How do the various MP3 players differ?

- After comparing Apple to its competitors, why do you think Apple commands a larger share of the digital music market?

- Conduct a survey among your peers to research consumer opinions. How have these sites been influenced by digital music sales?

End-of-Chapter Assessment

Review Questions

1.
Section 1

   a. How did Tin Pan Alley influence the development of popular music, and how did the music that came out of Tin Pan Alley differ from classical music?

   b. What are some of the technological developments that influenced the growth of popular music, and how did they assist its progress?

   c. What genres of music developed throughout the 20th century? What musical elements characterize each genre?

2.
Section 2

   a. What cultural factors influenced the popular music industry in the 20th century?

   b. How did music influence culture in the 20th century? How are music and culture interrelated?

3.
Section 3

a. What are the Big Four record labels? In what ways do they influence the music industry?

b. What are the main differences between major labels and indie labels? What are the advantages and disadvantages of each?

c. What three steps are involved in the music production process? What factors are currently affecting the ways in which music is produced and distributed?

4.
Section 4

a. How did peer-to-peer sharing networks affect the music business when they were first introduced? How did digital music progress from users downloading music illegally to purchasing from online music stores?

b. What are some of the impacts that digital music has had on the industry? How are industry executives responding to these impacts?

c. What is the direct-to-fan business model, and how has new technology enabled its progression?

Critical Thinking Questions

1. Does music primarily reflect or influence cultural and social change?

2. How did the major record labels' reaction to peer-to-peer file sharing place them at a strategic disadvantage in the music industry?

3. What are the potential implications of the direct-to-fan business model for the future of the music industry?

4. Music critics frequently proclaim the "death of rock and roll." How might the corporate influence of the Big Four over the modern music industry be related to these claims?

5. How have social and political factors influenced musical tastes throughout the past century?

Career Connection

Although many traditional music industry careers are in decline as a result of poor CD sales and the impact of new technology, changes within the industry have created new opportunities. As artists turn away from recorded music and focus on live performances, demand for concert tickets continues to rise. One possible career path in the music industry is that of a concert promoter. Read about the demands and expectations of a concert promoter at http://entertainment.howstuffworks.com/concert-tour2.htm. Once you have familiarized yourself with the material, read about the personal experiences of concert promoter David Werlin at http://www.bankrate.com/brm/news/advice/19990701a.asp and answer the following questions:

1. What advantages and disadvantages does Werlin give for working for a big promotion company versus working for a small organization?

2. How do both the HowStuffWorks website and Werlin's experiences emphasize the need for flexibility when working as a concert promoter?

3. As with many careers, working as a concert promoter usually involves starting at the bottom and working your way to the top. Think about how you might promote an event on your college campus or in your neighborhood. Use the tips from both websites to make a list of things you would need to consider to prepare for the event.

References

Albanesius, Chloe. "Music-Download Royalty Rates Left Unchanged," *PC Magazine*, October 2, 2008, http://www.pcmag.com/article2/0,2817,2331598,00.asp.

Apple, "iPod + iTunes Timeline," Apple Press Info, http://www.apple.com/pr/products/ipodhistory/.

BBC News, "Kazaa Site Becomes Legal Service," July 27, 2006, http://news.bbc.co.uk/2/hi/science/nature/5220406.stm.

Brandle, Lars. "'In Rainbows' Looms for U.K. No. 1," *Billboard*, January 2, 2008, http://www.billboard.com/news/in-rainbows-looms-for-u-k-no-1-1003690356.story#/news/in-rainbows-looms-for-u-k-no-1-1003690356.story.

Doyle, T. C. "Shawn Fanning, Founder, Napster," *CRN*, November 10, 2000, http://www.crn.com/news/channel-programs/18834885/shawn-fanning-founder-napster.htm;jsessionid=nqMTTQpakxKozxhpf778kw**.ecappj01.

Goldman, "Music's Lost Decade."

Goldman, "Music's Lost Decade."

Graham, Lee. "Digital Music Increases Share of Overall Music Sales Volume in the U.S.," news release, NPD Group, August 18, 2009, http://www.npd.com/press/releases/press_090818.html.

Johnson, Neala. "Q & A with Trent Reznor of Nine Inch Nails," *Herald Sun* (Melbourne), May 17, 2007, http://www.heraldsun.com.au/entertainment/music/q-a-with-trent-reznor-of-nine-inch-nails/story-e6frf9hf-1111113550202.

Kent, F. Daniel. "The Upward Spiral of Trent Reznor," *Dishmag*, April 2011, http://dishmag.com/issue120/music-film/13777/the-upward-spiral-of-trent-reznor/.

Knopper, Steve. "Napster Wounds the Giant," *Rocky Mountain News*, January 2, 2009, http://www.rockymountainnews.com/news/2009/jan/02/napster-wounds-the-giant/.

Kravets, David. "File Sharing Lawsuits at a Crossroads, After 5 Years of RIAA Litigation," *Wired*, September 4, 2008, http://www.wired.com/threatlevel/2008/09/proving-file-sh/.

Kravets, David. "Settlement Rejected in 'Shocking' RIAA File Sharing Verdict," *Wired*, January 27, 2010, http://www.wired.com/threatlevel/2010/01/settlement-rejected-in-shocking-riaa-file-sharing-verdict/.

Kravets, David. "Verizon Terminating Copyright Infringers' Internet Access," *Wired*, January 20, 2010, http://www.wired.com/threatlevel/2010/01/verizon-terminating-internet-accessinternet-access/.

Levy, Steven. "Q&A: Jobs on iPod's Cultural Impact," *Newsweek*, October 15, 2006, http://www.msnbc.msn.com/id/15262121/site/newsweek/print/1/displaymode/1098/.

Menta, Richard. "Did Napster Take Radiohead's New Album to Number 1?" MP3newswire.net, October 28, 2000, http://www.mp3newswire.net/stories/2000/radiohead.html.

Michaels, Sean. "Eminem Sues Universal Over Digital Royalties," *Guardian* (London), February 25, 2009, http://www.guardian.co.uk/music/2009/feb/25/eminem-universal-digital-royalties-lawsuit.

Mnookin, Seth. "Universal's CEO Once Called iPod Users Thieves. Now He's Giving Songs Away,' *Wired*, November 27, 2007, http://www.wired.com/entertainment/music/magazine/15-12/mf_morris?currentPage=2.

NPD Group, "Digital Music Increases Share of Overall Music Sales Volume in the U.S.," news release, August 18, 2009, http://www.npd.com/press/releases/press_090818.html.

Nusca, Andrew. "Apples Announces New iPod Touch, Nano, Shuffle, Classic; iTunes 9," *The Toy Box Blog*, ZDNet, September 9, 2009, http://www.zdnet.com/blog/gadgetreviews/apple-announces-new-ipod-touch-nano-shuffle-classic-itunes-9/7240.

Richardson, Adam. "Quick Take on Amazon's MP3 Download Store," *Matter/Anti-Matter* (blog), October 3, 2007, http://news.cnet.com/8301-13641_3-9790970-44.html.

Riedel, Sarah. "A Brief History of Filesharing: From Napster to Legal Music Downloads," Associated Content from Yahoo, February 24, 2006, http://www.associatedcontent.com/article/20644/a_brief_history_of_filesharing_from_pg2.html?cat=15.

Sisario, Ben. "Music Sales Fell in 2008, but Climbed on the Web," *New York Times*, December 31, 2008, http://www.nytimes.com/2009/01/01/arts/music/01indu.html.

SPIN, "Trent Reznor Blasts Label," *SPIN*, May 15, 2007, http://www.spin.com/articles/trent-reznor-blasts-label.

Weintraub, Seth. "Android Helps Amazon Triple Online Music Marketshare," *Fortune*, CNN Money, May 26, 2010, http://tech.fortune.cnn.com/2010/05/26/android-helps-amazon-triple-music-marketshare/.

Williams, Martyn. "Timeline: iTunes Store at 10 Billion," *Computerworld*, February 24, 2010, http://www.computerworld.com/s/article/9162018/Timeline_iTunes_Store_at_10_billion.

Chapter 7: Radio

7.1 Radio

Figure 7.1

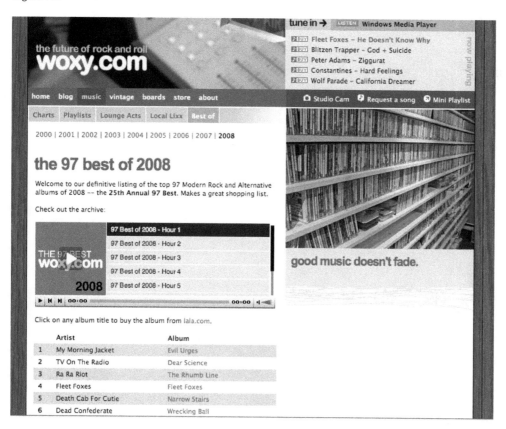

In 1983, radio station WOXY's new owners bought the station and changed its format from Top 40 to the up-and-coming alternative rock format, kicking off with U2's "Sunday Bloody Sunday (WOXY, 2009)." Then located in the basement of a fast-food restaurant in Ohio, the station was a risk for its purchasers, a husband and wife team who took a chance by changing the format to a relatively new one. Their investment paid off with the success of their station. By 1990, WOXY had grown in prestige to become one of *Rolling Stone* magazine's top 15 radio stations in the country, and had even been made famous by a reference in the 1988 film *Rain Man* (Bishop, 2004). In 1998, the station launched a web cast and developed a national following, ranking 12th among Internet broadcasters for listenership in 2004 (Bishop, 2004).

When the station's owners decided to retire and sell the frequency allocation in 2004, they hoped to find investors to continue the online streaming version of the station. After several months of unsuccessful searching, however, the station went off the air entirely—only to find a last-minute investor willing to fund an Internet version of the station (WOXY).

The online version of the station struggled to make ends meet until it was purchased by the online music firm Lala (Cheng, 2010). The now-defunct Lala sold WOXY to music company Future Sounds Inc., which moved the station and staff from Ohio to Austin, Texas. In March 2010, citing "current economic realities and the lack of ongoing funding," WOXY.com went off the air with only a day's notice (Cheng, 2010).

Taken in the context of the modern Internet revolution and the subsequent faltering of institutions such as newspapers and book publishers, the rise and fall of WOXY may seem to bode ill for the general fate of radio. However, taken in the larger context of radio's history, this story of the Internet's effect on radio could prove to be merely another leap in a long line of radio revolutions. From the shutting down of all broadcasts during World War I to the eclipse of radio by television during the 1950s, many arbiters of culture and business have prophesized the demise of radio for decades. Yet this chapter will show how the inherent flexibility and intimacy of the medium has allowed it to adapt to new market trends and to continue to have relevance as a form of mass communication.

References

Bishop, Lauren. "97X Farewell," *Cincinnati Enquirer*, May 10, 2004, http://www.enquirer.com/editions/2004/05/10/tem_tem1a.html.

Cheng, Jacqui. "Bad Luck, Funding Issues Shutter Indie Station WOXY.com," *Ars Technica* (blog), March 23, 2010, http://arstechnica.com/media/news/2010/03/bad-luck-funding-issues-shutter-indie-station-woxycom.ars.

WOXY, "The History of WOXY," 2009, http://woxy.com/about/.

WOXY, "The History."

7.2 Evolution of Radio Broadcasting

Learning Objectives

1. Identify the major technological changes in radio as a medium since its inception.
2. Explain the defining characteristics of radio's Golden Age.
3. Describe the effects of networks and conglomerates on radio programming and culture.

At its most basic level, radio is communication through the use of radio waves. This includes radio used for person-to-person communication as well as radio used for mass communication. Both of these functions are still practiced today. Although most people associate the term *radio* with radio stations that broadcast to the general public, radio wave technology is used in everything from television to cell phones, making it a primary conduit for person-to-person communication.

The Invention of Radio

Guglielmo Marconi is often credited as the inventor of radio. As a young man living in Italy, Marconi read a biography of Hienrich Hertz, who had written and experimented with early forms of wireless transmission. Marconi then duplicated Hertz's experiments in his own home, successfully sending transmissions from one side of his attic to the other (PBS). He saw the potential for the technology and approached the Italian government for support. When the government showed no interest in his ideas, Marconi moved to England and took out a patent on his device. Rather than inventing radio from scratch, however, Marconi essentially combined the ideas and experiments of other people to make them into a useful communications tool (Coe, 1996).

Figure 7.2

Guglielmo Marconi developed an early version of the wireless radio.

Wikimedia Commons – public domain.

In fact, long-distance electronic communication has existed since the middle of the 19th century. The telegraph communicated messages through a series of long and short clicks. Cables across the Atlantic Ocean connected even the far-distant United States and England using this technology. By the 1870s, telegraph technology had been used to develop the telephone, which could transmit an individual's voice over the same cables used by its predecessor.

When Marconi popularized wireless technology, contemporaries initially viewed it as a way to allow the telegraph to function in places that could not be connected by cables. Early radios acted as devices for naval ships to communicate with other ships and with land stations; the focus was on person-to-person communication. However, the potential for broadcasting—sending messages to a large group of potential listeners—wasn't realized until later in the development of the medium.

Broadcasting Arrives

The technology needed to build a radio transmitter and receiver was relatively simple, and the knowledge to build such devices soon reached the public. Amateur radio operators quickly crowded the airwaves, broadcasting messages to anyone within range and, by 1912, incurred government regulatory measures that required licenses and limited broadcast ranges for radio operation (White). This regulation also gave the president the power to shut down all stations, a power notably exercised in 1917 upon the United States' entry into World War I to keep amateur radio operators from interfering with military use of radio waves for the duration of the war (White).

Wireless technology made radio as it is known today possible, but its modern, practical function as a mass communication medium had been the domain of other technologies for some time. As early as the 1880s, people relied on telephones to transmit news, music, church sermons, and weather reports. In Budapest, Hungary, for example, a subscription service allowed individuals to listen to news reports and fictional stories on their telephones (White). Around this time, telephones also transmitted opera performances from Paris to London. In 1909, this innovation emerged in the United States as a pay-per-play phonograph service in Wilmington, Delaware (White). This service allowed subscribers to listen to specific music recordings on their telephones (White).

In 1906, Massachusetts resident Reginald Fessenden initiated the first radio transmission of the human voice, but his efforts did not develop into a useful application (Grant, 1907). Ten years later, Lee de Forest used radio in a more modern sense when he set up an experimental radio station, 2XG, in New York City. De Forest gave nightly broadcasts of music and news until World War I halted all transmissions for private citizens (White).

Radio's Commercial Potential

After the World War I radio ban lifted with the close of the conflict in 1919, a number of small stations began operating using technologies that had developed during the war. Many of these stations developed regular programming that included religious sermons, sports, and news (White). As early as 1922, Schenectady, New York's WGY broadcast over 40 original dramas, showing radio's potential as a medium for drama. The WGY players created their own scripts and performed them live on air. This same groundbreaking group also made the first known attempt at television drama in 1928 (McLeod, 1998).

Businesses such as department stores, which often had their own stations, first put radio's commercial applications to use. However, these stations did not advertise in a way that the modern radio listener would recognize. Early radio advertisements consisted only of a "genteel sales message broadcast during 'business' (daytime) hours, with no hard sell or mention of price (Sterling & Kittross, 2002)." In fact, radio advertising was originally considered an unprecedented invasion of privacy, because—unlike newspapers, which were bought at a newsstand—radios were present in the home and spoke with a voice in the presence of the whole family (Sterling & Kittross, 2002). However, the social impact of radio was such that within a few years advertising was readily accepted on radio programs. Advertising agencies even began producing their own radio programs named after their products. At first, ads ran only during the day, but as economic pressure mounted during the Great Depression in the 1930s, local stations began looking for new sources of revenue, and advertising became a normal part of the radio soundscape (Sterling & Kittross, 2002).

The Rise of Radio Networks

Not long after radio's broadcast debut, large businesses saw its potential profitability and formed networks. In 1926, RCA started the National Broadcasting Network (NBC). Groups of stations that carried syndicated network programs along with a variety of local shows soon formed its Red and Blue networks. Two years after the creation of NBC, the United Independent Broadcasters became the Columbia Broadcasting System (CBS) and began competing with the existing Red and Blue networks (Sterling & Kittross, 2002).

Although early network programming focused mainly on music, it soon developed to include other programs. Among these early innovations was the variety show. This format generally featured several different performers introduced by a host who segued between acts. Variety shows included styles as diverse as jazz and early country music. At night, dramas and comedies such as *Amos 'n' Andy*, *The Lone Ranger*, and *Fibber McGee and Molly* filled the airwaves. News, educational programs, and other types of talk programs also rose to prominence during the 1930s (Sterling & Kittross, 2002).

The Radio Act of 1927

In the mid-1920s, profit-seeking companies such as department stores and newspapers owned a majority of the nation's broadcast radio stations, which promoted their owners' businesses (ThinkQuest). Nonprofit groups such as churches and schools operated another third of the stations. As the number of radio stations outgrew the available frequencies, interference became problematic, and the government stepped into the fray.

The Radio Act of 1927 established the Federal Radio Commission (FRC) to oversee regulation of the airwaves. A year after its creation, the FRC reallocated station bandwidths to correct interference problems. The organization reserved 40 high-powered channels, setting aside 37 of these for network affiliates. The remaining 600 lower-powered bandwidths went to stations that had to share the frequencies; this meant that as one station went off the air at a designated time, another one began broadcasting in its place. The Radio Act of 1927 allowed major networks such as CBS and NBC to gain a 70 percent share of U.S. broadcasting by the early 1930s, earning them $72 million in profits by 1934 (McChesney, 1992). At the same time, nonprofit broadcasting fell to only 2 percent of the market (McChesney, 1992).

In protest of the favor that the 1927 Radio Act showed toward commercial broadcasting, struggling nonprofit radio broadcasters created the National Committee on Education by Radio to lobby for more outlets. Basing their argument on the notion that the airwaves—unlike newspapers—were a public resource, they asserted that groups working for the public good should take precedence over commercial interests. Nevertheless, the Communications Act of 1934 passed without addressing these issues, and radio continued as a mainly commercial enterprise (McChesney, 1992).

The Golden Age of Radio

The so-called Golden Age of Radio occurred between 1930 and the mid-1950s. Because many associate the 1930s with the struggles of the Great Depression, it may seem contradictory that such a fruitful cultural occurrence arose during this decade. However, radio lent itself to the era. After the initial purchase of a receiver, radio was free and so provided an inexpensive source of entertainment that replaced other, more costly pastimes, such as going to the movies.

Radio also presented an easily accessible form of media that existed on its own schedule. Unlike reading newspapers or books, tuning in to a favorite program at a certain time became a part of listeners' daily routine because it effectively forced them to plan their lives around the dial.

Daytime Radio Finds Its Market

During the Great Depression, radio became so successful that another network, the Mutual Broadcasting Network, began in 1934 to compete with NBC's Red and Blue networks and the CBS network, creating a total of four national networks (Cashman, 1989). As the networks became more adept at generating profits, their broadcast selections began to take on a format that later evolved into modern television programming. Serial dramas and programs that focused on domestic work aired during the day when many women were at home. Advertisers targeted this demographic with commercials for domestic needs such as soap (Museum). Because they were often sponsored by soap companies, daytime serial dramas soon became known as *soap operas*. Some modern televised soap operas, such as *Guiding Light*, which ended in 2009, actually began in the 1930s as radio serials (Hilmes, 1999).

The Origins of Prime Time

During the evening, many families listened to the radio together, much as modern families may gather for television's prime time. Popular evening comedy variety shows such as George Burns and Gracie Allen's *Burns and Allen*, the *Jack Benny Show*, and the *Bob Hope Show* all began during the 1930s. These shows featured a central host—for whom the show was often named—and a series of sketch comedies, interviews, and musical performances, not unlike contemporary programs such as *Saturday Night Live*. Performed live before a studio audience, the programs thrived on a certain flair and spontaneity. Later in the evening, so-called prestige dramas such as *Lux Radio Theater* and *Mercury Theatre on the Air* aired. These shows featured major Hollywood actors recreating movies or acting out adaptations of literature (Hilmes).

Figure 7.3

Many prime-time radio broadcasts featured film stars recreating famous films over the air.

Wikimedia Commons – public domain.

Instant News

By the late 1930s, the popularity of radio news broadcasts had surpassed that of newspapers. Radio's ability to emotionally draw its audiences in close to events made for news that evoked stronger responses and, thus, greater interest than print news could. For example, the infant son of famed aviator Charles Lindbergh was kidnapped and murdered in 1932. Radio networks set up mobile stations that covered events as they unfolded, broadcasting nonstop for several days and keeping listeners updated on every detail while tying them emotionally to the outcome (Brown, 1998).

As recording technology advanced, reporters gained the ability to record events in the field and bring them back to the studio to broadcast over the airwaves. One early example of this was Herb Morrison's recording of the *Hindenburg* disaster. In 1937, the *Hindenburg* blimp exploded into flames while attempting to land, killing 37 of its passengers. Morrison was already on the scene to record the descent, capturing the fateful crash. The entire event was later broadcast, including the sound of the exploding blimp, providing listeners with an unprecedented emotional connection to a national disaster. Morrison's exclamation "Oh, the humanity!" became a common phrase of despair after the event (Brown, 1998).

Radio news became even more important during World War II, when programs such as Norman Corwin's *This Is War!* sought to bring more sober news stories to a radio dial dominated by entertainment. The program dealt with the realities of war in a somber manner; at the beginning of the program, the host declared, "No one is invited to sit down and take it easy. Later, later, there's a war on (Horten, 2002)." In 1940, Edward R. Murrow, a journalist working in England at the time, broadcast firsthand accounts of the German bombing of London, giving Americans a sense of the trauma and terror that the English were experiencing at the outset of the war (Horten,

2002). Radio news outlets were the first to broadcast the attack on Pearl Harbor that propelled the United States into World War II in 1941. By 1945, radio news had become so efficient and pervasive that when Roosevelt died, only his wife, his children, and Vice President Harry S. Truman were aware of it before the news was broadcast over the public airwaves (Brown).

The Birth of the Federal Communications Commission

The Communications Act of 1934 created the Federal Communications Commission (FCC) and ushered in a new era of government regulation. The organization quickly began enacting influential radio decisions. Among these was the 1938 decision to limit stations to 50,000 watts of broadcasting power, a ceiling that remains in effect today (Cashman). As a result of FCC antimonopoly rulings, RCA was forced to sell its NBC Blue network; this spun-off division became the American Broadcasting Corporation (ABC) in 1943 (Brinson, 2004).

Another significant regulation with long-lasting influence was the Fairness Doctrine. In 1949, the FCC established the Fairness Doctrine as a rule stating that if broadcasters editorialized in favor of a position on a particular issue, they had to give equal time to all other reasonable positions on that issue (Browne & Browne, 1986). This tenet came from the long-held notion that the airwaves were a public resource, and that they should thus serve the public in some way. Although the regulation remained in effect until 1987, the impact of its core concepts are still debated. This chapter will explore the Fairness Doctrine and its impact in greater detail in a later section.

Radio on the Margins

Despite the networks' hold on programming, educational stations persisted at universities and in some municipalities. They broadcast programs such as *School of the Air* and *College of the Air* as well as roundtable and town hall forums. In 1940, the FCC reserved a set of frequencies in the lower range of the FM radio spectrum for public education purposes as part of its regulation of the new spectrum. The reservation of FM frequencies gave educational stations a boost, but FM proved initially unpopular due to a setback in 1945, when the FCC moved the FM bandwidth to a higher set of frequencies, ostensibly to avoid problems with interference (Longley, 1968). This change required the purchase of new equipment by both consumers and radio stations, thus greatly slowing the widespread adoption of FM radio.

One enduring anomaly in the field of educational stations has been the Pacifica Radio network. Begun in 1949 to counteract the effects of commercial radio by bringing educational programs and dialogue to the airwaves, Pacifica has grown from a single station—Berkeley, California's KPFA—to a network of five stations and more than 100 affiliates (Pacifica Network). From the outset, Pacifica aired newer classical, jazz, and folk music along with lectures, discussions, and interviews with public artists and intellectuals. Among Pacifica's major innovations was its refusal to take money from commercial advertisers, relying instead on donations from listeners and grants from institutions such as the Ford Foundation and calling itself listener-supported (Mitchell, 2005).

Another important innovation on the fringes of the radio dial during this time was the growth of border stations. Located just across the Mexican border, these stations did not have to follow FCC or U.S. regulatory laws. Because the stations broadcast at 250,000 watts and higher, their listening range covered much of North America. Their content also diverged—at the time markedly—from that of U.S. stations. For example, Dr. John Brinkley started station XERF in Del Rio, Mexico, after being forced to shut down his station in Nebraska, and he used the border station in part to promote a dubious goat gland operation that supposedly cured sexual impotence (Dash, 2008). Besides the goat gland promotion, the station and others like it often carried music, like country and western, that could not be heard on regular network radio. Later border station disc jockeys, such as Wolfman Jack, were instrumental in bringing rock and roll music to a wider audience (Rudel, 2008).

Television Steals the Show

A great deal of radio's success as a medium during the 1920s and 1930s was due to the fact that no other medium could replicate it. This changed in the late 1940s and early 1950s as television became popular. A 1949 poll of people who had seen television found that almost half of them believed that radio was doomed (Gallup, 1949). Television sets had come on the market by the late 1940s, and by 1951, more Americans were watching television during prime time than ever (Bradley). Famous radio programs such as *The Bob Hope Show* were made into television shows, further diminishing radio's unique offerings (Cox, 1949).

Surprisingly, some of radio's most critically lauded dramas launched during this period. *Gunsmoke*, an adult-oriented Western show (that later become television's longest-running show) began in 1952; crime drama *Dragnet*, later made famous in both television and film, broadcast between 1949 and 1957; and *Yours Truly, Johnny Dollar* aired from 1949 to 1962, when CBS canceled its remaining radio dramas. However, these respected radio dramas were the last of their kind (Cox, 2002). Although radio was far from doomed by television, its Golden Age was.

Transition to Top 40

As radio networks abandoned the dramas and variety shows that had previously sustained their formats, the soundscape was left to what radio could still do better than any other mass medium: play music. With advertising dollars down and the emergence of better recording formats, it made good business sense for radio to focus on shows that played prerecorded music. As strictly music stations began to rise, new innovations to increase their profitability appeared. One of the most notable and far-reaching of these innovations was the Top 40 station, a concept that supposedly came from watching jukebox patrons continually play the same songs (Brewster & Broughton, 2000). Robert Storz and Gordon McLendon began adapting existing radio stations to fit this new format with great success. In 1956, the creation of limited playlists further refined the format by providing about 50 songs that disc jockeys played repeatedly every day. By the early 1960s, many stations had developed limited playlists of only 30 songs (Walker, 2001).

Another musically fruitful innovation came with the increase of Black disc jockeys and programs created for Black audiences. Because its advertisers had nowhere to go in a media market dominated by White performers, Black radio became more common on the AM dial. As traditional programming left radio, disc jockeys began to develop as the medium's new personalities, talking more in between songs and developing followings. Early Black disc jockeys even began improvising rhymes over the music, pioneering techniques that later became rap and hip-hop. This new personality-driven style helped bring early rock and roll to new audiences (Walker, 2001).

FM: The High-Fidelity Counterculture

As music came to rule the airwaves, FM radio drew in new listeners because of its high-fidelity sound capabilities.

When radio had primarily featured dramas and other talk-oriented formats, sound quality had simply not mattered to many people, and the purchase of an FM receiver did not compete with the purchase of a new television in terms of entertainment value. As FM receivers decreased in price and stereo recording technology became more popular, however, the high-fidelity trend created a market for FM stations. Mostly affluent consumers began purchasing component stereos with the goal of getting the highest sound quality possible out of their recordings (Douglas, 2004). Although this audience often preferred classical and jazz stations to Top 40 radio, they were tolerant of new music and ideas (Douglas, 2004).

Both the high-fidelity market and the growing youth counterculture of the 1960s had similar goals for the FM spectrum. Both groups eschewed AM radio because of the predictable programming, poor sound quality, and over-commercialization. Both groups wanted to treat music as an important experience rather than as just a trendy pastime or a means to make money. Many adherents to the youth counterculture of the 1960s came from affluent, middle-class families, and their tastes came to define a new era of consumer culture. The goals and market potential of both the high-fidelity lovers and the youth counterculture created an atmosphere on the FM dial that had never before occurred (Douglas, 2004).

Between the years 1960 and 1966, the number of households capable of receiving FM transmissions grew from about 6.5 million to some 40 million. The FCC also aided FM by issuing its nonduplication ruling in 1964. Before this regulation, many AM stations had other stations on the FM spectrum that simply duplicated the AM programming. The nonduplication rule forced FM stations to create their own fresh programming, opening up the spectrum for established networks to develop new stations (Douglas, 2004).

The late 1960s saw new disc jockeys taking greater liberties with established practices; these liberties included playing several songs in a row before going to a commercial break or airing album tracks that exceeded 10 minutes in length. University stations and other nonprofit ventures to which the FCC had given frequencies during the late 1940s popularized this format, and, in time, commercial stations tried to duplicate their success by playing fewer commercials and by allowing their disc jockeys to have a say in their playlists. Although this made for popular listening formats, FM stations struggled to make the kinds of profits that the AM spectrum drew (Douglas, 2004).

In 1974, FM radio accounted for one-third of all radio listening but only 14 percent of radio profits (Douglas, 2004). Large network stations and advertisers began to market heavily to the FM audience in an attempt to correct this imbalance. Stations began tightening their playlists and narrowing their formats to please advertisers and to generate greater revenues. By the end of the 1970s, radio stations were beginning to play specific formats, and the progressive radio of the previous decade had become difficult to find (Douglas, 2004).

The Rise of Public Radio

After the Golden Age of Radio came to an end, most listeners tuned in to radio stations to hear music. The variety shows and talk-based programs that had sustained radio in early years could no longer draw enough listeners to make them a successful business proposition. One divergent path from this general trend, however, was the growth of public radio.

Groups such as the Ford Foundation had funded public media sources during the early 1960s. When the foundation decided to withdraw its funding in the middle of the decade, the federal government stepped in with the Public Broadcasting Act of 1967. This act created the Corporation for Public Broadcasting (CPB) and charged it with generating funding for public television and radio outlets. The CPB in turn created National Public Radio (NPR) in 1970 to provide programming for already-operating stations. Until 1982, in fact, the CPB entirely and exclusively funded NPR. Public radio's first program was *All Things Considered*, an evening news program that focused on analysis and interpretive reporting rather than cutting-edge coverage. In the mid-1970s, NPR attracted Washington-based journalists such as Cokie Roberts and Linda Wertheimer to its ranks, giving the coverage a more professional, hard-reporting edge (Schardt, 1996).

However, in 1983, public radio was pushed to the brink of financial collapse. NPR survived in part by relying more on its member stations to hold fundraising drives, now a vital component of public radio's business model. In 2003, Joan Kroc, the widow of McDonald's CEO and philanthropist Ray Kroc, bequeathed a grant of over $200 million to NPR that may keep it afloat for many years to come.

Figure 7.4

A Prairie Home Companion, hosted by Garrison Keillor (pictured here), is a long-standing
public radio tradition that hearkens back to the early days of radio variety shows.

Having weathered the financial storm intact, NPR continued its progression as a respected news provider. During the first Gulf War, NPR sent out correspondents for the first time to provide in-depth coverage of unfolding events. Public radio's extensive coverage of the 2001 terrorist bombings gained its member stations many new listeners, and it has since expanded (Clift, 2011). Although some have accused NPR of presenting the news with a liberal bias, its listenership in 2005 was 28 percent conservative, 32 percent liberal, and 29 percent moderate. Newt Gingrich, a conservative Republican and former speaker of the house, has stated that the network is "a lot less on the left" than some may believe (Sherman, 2005). With more than 26 million weekly listeners and 860 member stations in 2009, NPR has become a leading radio news source (Kamenetz, 2009).

Public radio distributors such as Public Radio International (PRI) and local public radio stations such as WBEZ in Chicago have also created a number of cultural and entertainment programs, including quiz shows, cooking shows, and a host of local public forum programs. Storytelling programs such as *This American Life* have created a new kind of free-form radio documentary genre, while shows such as PRI's variety show *A Prairie Home*

Companion have revived older radio genres. This variety of popular public radio programming has shifted radio from a music-dominated medium to one that is again exploring its vast potential.

Conglomerates

During the early 1990s, many radio stations suffered the effects of an economic recession. Some stations initiated local marketing agreements (LMAs) to share facilities and resources amid this economic decline. LMAs led to consolidation in the industry as radio stations bought other stations to create new hubs for the same programming. The Telecommunications Act of 1996 further increased consolidation by eliminating a duopoly rule prohibiting dual station ownership in the same market and by lifting the numerical limits on station ownership by a single entity.

As large corporations such as Clear Channel Communications bought up stations around the country, they reformatted stations that had once competed against one another so that each focused on a different format. This practice led to mainstream radio's present state, in which narrow formats target highly specific demographic audiences.

Ultimately, although the industry consolidation of the 1990s made radio profitable, it reduced local coverage and diversity of programming. Because stations around the country served as outlets for a single network, the radio landscape became more uniform and predictable (Keith, 2010). Much as with chain restaurants and stores, some people enjoy this type of predictability, while others prefer a more localized, unique experience (Keith, 2010).

Key Takeaways

- The Golden Age of Radio covered the period between 1930 and 1950. It was characterized by radio's overwhelming popularity and a wide range of programming, including variety, music, drama, and theater programs.

- Top 40 radio arose after most nonmusic programming moved to television. This format used short playlists of popular hits and gained a great deal of commercial success during the 1950s and 1960s.

- FM became popular during the late 1960s and 1970s as commercial stations adopted the practices of free-form stations to appeal to new audiences who desired higher fidelity and a less restrictive format.

- Empowered by the Telecommunications Act of 1996, media conglomerates have subsumed unprecedented numbers of radio stations by single companies. Radio station consolidation brings predictability and profits at the expense of unique programming.

Exercises

Please respond to the following short-answer writing prompts. Each response should be a minimum of one paragraph.

1. Explain the advantages that radio had over traditional print media during the 1930s and 1940s.

2. Do you think that radio could experience another golden age? Explain your answer.

3. How has the consolidation of radio stations affected radio programming?

4. Characterize the overall effects of one significant technological or social shift described in this section on radio as a medium.

References

Bradley, Becky. "American Cultural History: 1950–1959," *Lone Star College, Kingwood*, http://kclibrary.lonestar.edu/decade50.html.

Brewster, Bill and Frank Broughton, *Last Night a DJ Saved My Life: The History of the Disc Jockey*, (New York: Grove Press, 2000), 48.

Brinson, Susan. *The Red Scare, Politics, and the Federal Communications Commission, 1941–1960* (Westport, CT: Praeger, 2004), 42.

Brown, *Manipulating the Ether*, 123.

Brown, Robert. *Manipulating the Ether: The Power of Broadcast Radio in Thirties America* (Jefferson, NC: MacFarland, 1998), 134–137.

Browne, Ray and Glenn Browne, *Laws of Our Fathers: Popular Culture and the U.S. Constitution* (Bowling Green, OH: Bowling Green State University Popular Press, 1986), 132.

Cashman, *America in the Twenties and Thirties*, 327.

Cashman, Sean. *America in the Twenties and Thirties: The Olympian Age of Franklin Delano Roosevelt* (New York: New York University Press, 1989), 328.

Clift, Nick. "Viewpoint: Protect NPR, It Protects Us," *Michigan Daily*, February 15, 2011, http://www.michigandaily.com/content/viewpoint-npr.

Coe, Lewis. *Wireless Radio: A Brief History* (Jefferson, NC: MacFarland, 1996), 4–10.

Cox, Jim. *American Radio Networks: A History* (Jefferson, NC: MacFarland, 2009), 171–175.

Cox, Jim. *Say Goodnight, Gracie: The Last Years of Network Radio* (Jefferson, NC: MacFarland, 2002), 39–41.

Dash, Mike. "John Brinkley, the goat-gland quack," *The Telegraph*, April 18, 2008, http://www.telegraph.co.uk/culture/books/non_fictionreviews/3671561/John-Brinkley-the-goat-gland-quack.html.

Douglas, Susan. *Listening In: Radio and the American Imagination* (Minneapolis: University of Minnesota Press, 2004), 266–268.

Gallup, George. "One-Fourth in Poll Think Television Killing Radio," *Schenectady (NY) Gazette*, June 8, 1949, http://news.google.com/newspapers?id=d3YuAAAAIBAJ&sjid=loEFAAAAIBAJ&pg=840,1029432&dq=radio-is-doomed&hl=en.

Grant, John. Experiments and Results in Wireless Telegraphy (reprinted from *The American Telephone Journal*, 49–51, January 26, 1907), http://earlyradiohistory.us/1907fes.htm.

Hilmes, *Radio Voices*, 183–185.

Hilmes, Michele. *Radio Voices: American Broadcasting 1922–1952* (Minneapolis: University of Minnesota Press, 1999), 157.

Horten, Gerd. *Radio Goes to War: The Cultural Politics of Propaganda During World War II* (Los Angeles: University of California Press, 2002), 48–52.

Kamenetz, Anya. "Will NPR Save the News?" *Fast Company*, April 1, 2009, http://www.fastcompany.com/magazine/134/finely-tuned.html.

Keith, Michael. *The Radio Station: Broadcast, Satellite and Internet* (Burlington, MA: Focal Press, 2010), 17–24.

Longley, Lawrence D. "The FM Shift in 1945," *Journal of Broadcasting* 12, no. 4 (1968): 353–365.

McChesney, Robert W. "Media and Democracy: The Emergence of Commercial Broadcasting in the United States, 1927–1935," in "Communication in History: The Key to Understanding," *OAH Magazine of History* 6, no. 4 (1992).

McLeod, Elizabeth. "The WGY Players and the Birth of Radio Drama," 1998, http://www.midcoast.com/~lizmcl/wgy.html.

Mitchell, Jack. *Listener Supported: The Culture and History of Public Radio* (Westport, CT: Praeger, 2005), 21–24.

Museum, "Soap Opera," *The Museum of Broadcast Communications*, http://www.museum.tv/eotvsection.php?entrycode=soapopera.

Pacifica Network, "Pacifica Network Stations," *The Pacifica Foundation*, http://pacificanetwork.org/radio/content/section/7/42/.

PBS, "Guglielmo Marconi," *American Experience: People & Events*, http://www.pbs.org/wgbh/amex/rescue/peopleevents/pandeAMEX98.html.

Rudel, Anthony. *Hello, Everybody! The Dawn of American Radio* (Orlando, FL: Houghton Mifflin Harcourt, 2008), 130–132.

Schardt, Sue. "Public Radio—A Short History," Christian Science Monitor Publishing Company, 1996, http://www.wsvh.org/pubradiohist.htm.

Sherman, Scott. "Good, Gray NPR," *The Nation*, May 23, 2005, 34–38.

Sterling, Christopher and John Kittross, *Stay Tuned: A History of American Broadcasting*, 3rd ed. (New York: Routledge, 2002), 124.

ThinkQuest, "Radio's Emergence," *Oracle ThinkQuest: The 1920s*, http://library.thinkquest.org/27629/themes/media/md20s.html.

Walker, Jesse. *Rebels on the Air: An Alternative History of Radio in America* (New York: New York University Press, 2001), 56.

White, "Broadcasting After World War I (1919–1921)," *United States Early Radio History*, http://earlyradiohistory.us/sec016.htm.

White, "News and Entertainment by Telephone (1876–1925)," *United States Early Radio History*, http://earlyradiohistory.us/sec003.htm.

White, "Pre-War Vacuum Tube Transmitter Development 1914–1917)," *United States Early Radio History*, http://earlyradiohistory.us/sec011.htm.

White, Thomas. "Pioneering Amateurs (1900–1917)," *United States Early Radio History*, http://earlyradiohistory.us/sec012.htm.

7.3 Radio Station Formats

Learning Objectives

1. Describe the use of radio station formats in the development of modern stations.
2. Analyze the effects of formats on radio programming.

Early radio network programming laid the groundwork for television's format, with many different programs that appealed to a variety of people broadcast at different times of the day. As television's popularity grew, however, radio could not compete and so it turned to fresh programming techniques. A new type of format-driven station became the norm. Propelled by the development of new types of music such as psychedelic rock and smooth jazz, the evolution of radio station formats took place. Since the beginning of this shift, different stations have tended to focus on the music that certain demographics preferred. For example, many people raised on Top 40 radio of the 1950s and 1960s did not necessarily want to hear modern pop hits, so stations playing older popular songs emerged to meet their needs.

Modern formats take into account aging generations, with certain stations specifically playing the pop hits of the 1950s and early 1960s, and others focusing on the pop hits of the late 1960s, 1970s, and 1980s. These formats have developed to target narrow, defined audiences with predictable tastes and habits. Ratings services such as Arbitron can identify the 10-year age demographic, the education level, and even the political leanings of listeners who prefer a particular format. Because advertisers want their commercials to reach an audience likely to buy their products, this kind of audience targeting is crucial for advertising revenue.

Top Radio Formats

The following top radio formats and their respective statistics were determined by an Arbitron survey that was released in 2010 (Arbitron Inc., 2010). The most popular formats and subformats cover a wide range of demographics, revealing radio's wide appeal.

Country

Country music as a format includes stations devoted both to older and newer country music. In 2010, the country music format stood as the most popular radio format, beating out even such prominent nonmusic formats as news and talk. The format commanded the greatest listener share and the second largest number of stations dedicated to the style. Favored in rural regions of the country, the country music format—featuring artists like Keith Urban, the Dixie Chicks, and Tim McGraw—appeals to both male and female listeners from a variety of income levels (Arbitron Inc., 2010).

News/Talk/Information

The news/talk/information format includes AM talk radio, public radio stations with talk programming, network news radio, sports radio, and personality talk radio. This format reached nearly 59 million listeners in 2010, appealing particularly to those aged 65 and older; over 70 percent of its listeners had attended college. These listeners also ranked the highest among formats in levels of home ownership (Arbitron Inc., 2010).

Adult Contemporary

Generally targeted toward individuals over 30, the adult contemporary (AC) format favors pop music from the last 15 to 20 years as opposed to current hits. Different subformats, such as hot AC and modern AC, target younger audiences by playing songs that are more current. In 2010, the majority of AC audience were affluent, married individuals divided roughly along the national average politically. Adult contemporary listeners ranked highest by format in at-work listening. Hot AC, a subformat of AC that plays more current hits, ranked seventh in the nation. Urban AC, a version of AC that focuses on older R&B hits, ranked eighth in the nation in 2010 (Arbitron Inc., 2010).

Pop Contemporary Hit Radio

Pop contemporary hit radio, or pop CHR, is a subformat of contemporary hit radio (CHR). Other subformats of CHR include dance CHR and rhythmic CHR. Branded in the 1980s, this format encompasses stations that have a Top 40 orientation but draw on a wide number of formats, such as country, rock, and urban (Ford, 2008). In 2010, pop CHR ranked first among teenaged listeners, with 65 percent of its overall listeners aged under 35. This music, ranging from popular artists like Taylor Swift and Kanye West to Shakira, was played in the car more than at home or work, and saw its largest listening times in the evenings. Rhythmic CHR, a subformat focusing on a mix of rhythmic pop, R&B, dance, and hip-hop hits, also ranked high in 2010 (Arbitron).

Classic Rock

Classic rock stations generally play rock singles from the 1970s and 1980s, like "Stairway to Heaven," by Led Zeppelin, and "You Shook Me All Night Long," by AC/DC. Another distinct but similar format is album-oriented rock (AOR). This format focuses on songs that were not necessarily released as singles, also known as album cuts (Radio Station World). In 2010, classic rock stations ranked fifth in listener figures. These individuals were overwhelmingly men (70 percent) between the ages of 35 and 54 (54 percent). Classic rock was most often listened to in the car and at work, with only 26 percent of its listeners tuning in at home (Arbitron).

Urban Contemporary

The urban contemporary format plays modern hits from mainly Black artists—such as Lil Wayne, John Legend, and Ludacris—featuring a mix of soul, hip-hop, and R&B. In 2010, the format ranked eleventh in the nation. Urban contemporary focuses on listeners in the 18–34 age range (Arbitron).

Mexican Regional

The Mexican regional format is devoted to Spanish-language music, particularly Mexican and South American genres. In 2010, it ranked thirteenth in the nation and held the top spot in Los Angeles, a reflection of the rise in immigration from Mexico, Central America, and South America. Mexican regional's listener base was over 96 percent Hispanic, and the format was most popular in the Western and Southwestern regions of the country. However, it was less popular in the Eastern regions of the country; in New England, for example, the format held a zero percent share of listening. The rise of the Mexican regional format illustrates the ways in which radio can change rapidly to meet new demographic trends (Arbitron).

An increasingly Spanish language–speaking population in the United States has also resulted in a number of distinct Spanish-language radio formats. These include Spanish oldies, Spanish adult hits, Spanish religious, Spanish tropical, and Spanish talk among others. Tejano, a type of music developed in Hispanic Texan communities, has also gained enough of an audience to become a dedicated format (Arbitron).

Other Popular Formats

Radio formats have become so specialized that ratings group Arbitron includes more than 50 designations. What was once simply called rock music has been divided into such subformats as alternative and modern rock. Alternative rock began as a format played on college stations during the 1980s but developed as a mainstream format during the following decade, thanks in part to the popular grunge music of that era. As this music aged, stations began using the term modern rock to describe a format dedicated to new rock music. This format has also spawned the active rock format, which plays modern rock hits with older rock hits thrown in (Radio Station World).

Nostalgia formats have split into a number of different formats as well. Oldies stations now generally focus on hits from the 1950s and 1960s, while the classic hits format chooses from hits of the 1970s, 1980s, and 1990s. Urban oldies, which focuses on R&B, soul, and other urban music hits from the 1950s, 1960s, and 1970s, has also become a popular radio format. Formats such as adult hits mix older songs from the 1970s, 1980s, and 1990s with a small selection of popular music, while formats such as '80s hits picks mainly from the 1980s (Radio Station World).

Radio station formats are an interesting way to look at popular culture in the United States. The evolution of nostalgia formats to include new decades nods to the size and tastes of the nation's aging listeners. Hits of the 1980s are popular enough with their demographic to have entire stations dedicated to them, while other generations prefer stations with a mix of decades. The rise of the country format and the continued popularity of the classic rock format are potential indicators of cultural trends.

Key Takeaways

- Radio station formats target demographics that can generate advertising revenue.
- Contemporary hit radio was developed as a Top 40 format that expanded beyond strictly pop music to include country, rock, and urban formats.
- Spanish-language formats have grown in recent years, with Mexican regional moving into the top 10 formats in 2008.
- Nostalgia genres have developed to reflect the tastes of aging listeners, ranging from mixes of music from the 1970s, 1980s, and 1990s with current hits to formats that pick strictly from the 1980s.

Exercises

Please respond to the following writing prompts. Each response should be a minimum of one paragraph.

1. What is the purpose of radio station formats?
2. How have radio station formats affected the way that modern stations play music?
3. Pick a format, such as country or classic rock, and speculate on the reasons for its popularity.

References

Arbitron Inc., *Radio Today: How America Listens to Radio*, 2010.

Arbitron, *Radio Today*, 27–30.

Arbitron, *Radio Today*, 32–34.

Ford, John. "Contemporary Hit Radio," September 2, 2008, http://radioindustry.suite101.com/article.cfm/contemporary_hit_radio_history.

Radio Station World, "Oldies, Adult Hits, and Nostalgia Radio Formats," *Radio Station World*, 1996–2010, http://radiostationworld.com/directory/radio_formats/radio_formats_oldies.asp.

Radio Station World, "Rock and Alternative Music Formats," *Radio Station World*, 1996–2010, http://radiostationworld.com/directory/Radio_Formats/radio_formats_rock.asp.

Radio Station World, "Rock and Alternative Music Formats," *Radio Station World*.

7.4 Radio's Impact on Culture

Learning Objectives

1. Analyze radio as a form of mass media.

2. Describe the effects of radio on the spread of different types of music.

3. Analyze the effects of the Fairness Doctrine on political radio.

4. Formulate opinions on controversial issues in radio.

Since its inception, radio's impact on American culture has been immense. Modern popular culture is unthinkable without the early influence of radio. Entire genres of music that are now taken for granted, such as country and rock, owe their popularity and even existence to early radio programs that publicized new forms.

A New Kind of Mass Media

Mass media such as newspapers had been around for years before the existence of radio. In fact, radio was initially considered a kind of disembodied newspaper. Although this idea gave early proponents a useful, familiar way to think about radio, it underestimated radio's power as a medium. Newspapers had the potential to reach a wide audience, but radio had the potential to reach almost everyone. Neither illiteracy nor even a busy schedule impeded radio's success—one could now perform an activity and listen to the radio at the same time. This unprecedented reach made radio an instrument of social cohesion as it brought together members of different classes and backgrounds to experience the world as a nation.

Radio programs reflected this nationwide cultural aspect of radio. *Vox Pop*, a show originally based on person-in-the-street interviews, was an early attempt to quantify the United States' growing mass culture. Beginning in 1935, the program billed itself as an unrehearsed "cross-section of what the average person really knows" by asking random people an assortment of questions. Many modern television shows still employ this format not only for viewers' amusement and information but also as an attempt to sum up national culture (Loviglio, 2002). *Vox Pop* functioned on a cultural level as an acknowledgement of radio's entrance into people's private lives to make them public (Loviglio, 2002).

Radio news was more than just a quick way to find out about events; it was a way for U.S. citizens to experience events with the same emotions. During the Ohio and Mississippi river floods of 1937, radio brought the voices of those who suffered as well as the voices of those who fought the rising tides. A West Virginia newspaper explained the strengths of radio in providing emotional voices during such crises: "Thanks to radio…the nation as a whole has had its nerves, its heart, its soul exposed to the needs of its unfortunates…We are a nation integrated and interdependent. We are 'our brother's keeper (Brown).'"

Radio's presence in the home also heralded the evolution of consumer culture in the United States. In 1941, two-thirds of radio programs carried advertising. Radio allowed advertisers to sell products to a captive audience. This kind of mass marketing ushered in a new age of consumer culture (Cashman).

War of the Worlds and the Power of Radio

During the 1930s, radio's impact and powerful social influence was perhaps most obvious in the aftermath of the Orson Welles's notorious *War of the Worlds* broadcast. On Halloween night in 1938, radio producer Orson Welles told listeners of the *Mercury Theatre on the Air* that they would be treated to an original adaptation of H. G. Wells's classic science fiction novel of alien invasion *War of the Worlds*. The adaptation started as if it were a normal music show that was interrupted by news reports of an alien invasion. Many listeners had tuned in late and did not hear the disclaimer, and so were caught up by the realism of the adaptation, believing it to be an actual news story.

Figure 7.5

The WAR of the WORLDS
By H. G. Wells
Author of "Under the Knife," "The Time Machine," etc.

Orson Welles's *War of the Worlds* broadcast terrified listeners, many of whom actually believed a Martian invasion was actually occurring.

Wikimedia Commons – public domain.

According to some, an estimated 6 million people listened to the show, with an incredible 1.7 million believing it to be true (Lubertozzi & Holmsten, 2005). Some listeners called loved ones to say goodbye or ran into the street armed with weapons to fight off the invading Martians of the radio play (Lubertozzi

& Holmsten, 2005). In Grovers Mill, New Jersey—where the supposed invasion began—some listeners reported nonexistent fires and fired gunshots at a water tower thought to be a Martian landing craft. One listener drove through his own garage door in a rush to escape the area. Two Princeton University professors spent the night searching for the meteorite that had supposedly preceded the invasion (Lubertozzi & Holmsten, 2005). As calls came in to local police stations, officers explained that they were equally concerned about the problem (Lubertozzi & Holmsten, 2005).

Although the story of the *War of the Worlds* broadcast may be funny in retrospect, the event traumatized those who believed the story. Individuals from every education level and walk of life had been taken in by the program, despite the producers' warnings before, during the intermission, and after the program (Lubertozzi & Holmsten, 2005). This event revealed the unquestioning faith that many Americans had in radio. Radio's intimate communication style was a powerful force during the 1930s and 1940s.

Radio and the Development of Popular Music

One of radio's most enduring legacies is its impact on music. Before radio, most popular songs were distributed through piano sheet music and word of mouth. This necessarily limited the types of music that could gain national prominence. Although recording technology had also emerged several decades before radio, music played live over the radio sounded better than it did on a record played in the home. Live music performances thus became a staple of early radio. Many performance venues had their own radio transmitters to broadcast live shows—for example, Harlem's Cotton Club broadcast performances that CBS picked up and broadcast nationwide.

Radio networks mainly played swing jazz, giving the bands and their leaders a widespread audience. Popular bandleaders including Duke Ellington, Benny Goodman, and Tommy Dorsey and their jazz bands became nationally famous through their radio performances, and a host of other jazz musicians flourished as radio made the genre nationally popular (Wald, 2009). National networks also played classical music. Often presented in an educational context, this programming had a different tenor than did dance-band programming. NBC promoted the genre through shows such as the *Music Appreciation Hour*, which sought to educate both young people and the general public on the nuances of classical music (Howe, 2003). It created the NBC Symphony Orchestra, a 92-piece band under the direction of famed conductor Arturo Toscanini. The orchestra made its first performance in 1937 and was so popular that Toscanini stayed on as conductor for 17 years (Horowitz, 2005). The Metropolitan Opera was also popular; its broadcasts in the early 1930s had an audience of 9 million listeners (Horowitz, 2005).

Regional Sounds Take Hold

The promotional power of radio also gave regional music an immense boost. Local stations often carried their own programs featuring the popular music of the area. Stations such as Nashville, Tennessee's WSM played early country, blues, and folk artists. The history of this station illustrates the ways in which radio—and its wide range of broadcasting—created new perspectives on American culture. In 1927, WSM's program *Barn Dance*, which featured early country music and blues, followed an hour-long program of classical music. George Hay, the host of *Barn Dance*, used the juxtaposition of classical and country genres to spontaneously rename the show: "For the past hour we have been listening to music taken largely from Grand Opera, but from now on we will present 'The Grand Ole Opry (Kyriakoudes).'" NBC picked up the program for national syndication in 1939, and it is currently one of the longest-running radio programs of all time.

Figure 7.6

Country musician Dolly Parton sings a song on stage during a Grand Ole Opry live broadcast in Nashville, Tenn. as U.S. soldiers watch the show simultaneously in Iraq on April 23, 2005. Secretary of Defense Donald. H. Rumsfeld also visited Nashville to thank Dolly Parton, the Grand Ole Opry and the American people for their support of our troops. DoD photo by Tech. Sgt. Cherie A. Thurlby, U.S. Air Force.

The *Grand Ole Opry* gave a national stage to country and early rock musicians.

Wikimedia Commons – public domain.

Shreveport, Louisiana's KWKH aired an *Opry*-type show called *Louisiana Hayride*. This program propelled stars such as Hank Williams into the national spotlight. Country music, formerly a mix of folk, blues, and mountain music, was made into a genre that was accessible by the nation through this show. Without programs that featured these country and blues artists, Elvis Presley and Johnny Cash would not have become national stars, and country music may not have risen to become a popular genre (DiMeo, 2010).

In the 1940s, other Southern stations also began playing rhythm and blues records recorded by Black artists. Artists such as Wynonie Harris, famous for his rendition of Roy Brown's "Good Rockin' Tonight," were often played by White disc jockeys who tried to imitate Black Southerners (Laird, 2005). During the late 1940s, both Memphis, Tennessee's WDIA and Atlanta, Georgia's WERD were owned and operated by Black individuals. These disc jockeys often provided a measure of community leadership at a time when few Black individuals were in powerful positions (Walker).

Radio's Lasting Influences

Radio technology changed the way that dance and popular music were performed. Because of the use of microphones, vocalists could be heard better over the band, allowing singers to use a greater vocal range and create more expressive styles, an innovation that led singers to become an important part of popular music's image. The use of microphones similarly allowed individual performers to be featured playing solos and lead parts, features that were less encouraged before radio. The exposure of radio also led to more rapid turnover in popular music. Before radio, jazz bands played the same arrangement for several years without it getting old, but as radio broadcasts reached wide audiences, new arrangements and songs had to be produced at a more rapid pace to keep up with changing tastes (Wald).

The spotlight of radio allowed the personalities of artists to come to the forefront of popular music, giving them newfound notoriety. Phil Harris, the bandleader from the *Jack Benny Show*, became the star of his own program. Other famous musicians used radio talent shows to gain fame. Popular programs such as *Major Bowes and His Original Amateur Hour* featured unknown entertainers trying to gain fame through exposure to the show's large audience. Major Bowes used a gong to usher bad performers offstage, often contemptuously dismissing them, but not all the performers struck out; such successful singers as Frank Sinatra debuted on the program (Sterling & Kitross).

Television, much like modern popular music, owes a significant debt to the Golden Age of Radio. Major radio networks such as NBC, ABC, and CBS became—and remain—major forces in television, and their programming decisions for radio formed the basis for television. Actors, writers, and directors who worked in radio simply transferred their talents into the world of early television, using the successes of radio as their models.

Radio and Politics

Over the years, radio has had a considerable influence on the political landscape of the United States. In the past, government leaders relied on radio to convey messages to the public, such as President Franklin D. Roosevelt's "fireside chats." Radio was also used as a way to generate propaganda for World War II. The War Department established a Radio Division in its Bureau of Public Relations as early as 1941. Programs such as the *Treasury Hour* used radio drama to raise revenue through the sale of war bonds, but other government efforts took a decidedly political turn. Norman Corwin's *This Is War!* was funded by the federal Office of Facts and Figures (OFF) to directly garner support for the war effort. It featured programs that prepared listeners to make personal sacrifices—including death—to win the war. The program was also directly political, popularizing the idea that the New Deal was a success and bolstering Roosevelt's image through comparisons with Lincoln (Horten).

FDR's Fireside Chats

Figure 7.7

During his presidency, Franklin D. Roosevelt delivered fireside chats, a series of radio broadcasts in which he spoke directly to the American people.

UNC Greensboro Special Collections and University Archives – Franklin Roosevelt photograph, 1940s – CC BY-NC-ND 2.0.

President Franklin D. Roosevelt's Depression-era radio talks, or "fireside chats," remain one of the most famous uses of radio in politics. While governor of New York, Roosevelt had used radio as a political tool, so he quickly adopted it to explain the unprecedented actions that his administration was taking to deal with the economic fallout of the Great Depression. His first speech took place only 1 week after being inaugurated. Roosevelt had closed all of the banks in the country for 4 days while the government dealt with a national banking crisis, and he used the radio to explain his actions directly to the American people (Grafton, 1999).

Roosevelt's first radio address set a distinct tone as he employed informal speech in the hopes of inspiring confidence in the American people and of helping them stave off the kind of panic that could have destroyed the entire banking system. Roosevelt understood both the intimacy of radio and its powerful outreach (Grafton, 1999). He was thus able to balance a personal tone with a message that was meant for millions of people. This relaxed approach inspired a CBS executive to name the series the "fireside chats (Grafton, 1999)."

Roosevelt delivered a total of 27 of these 15- to 30-minute-long addresses to estimated audiences of 30 million to 40 million people, then a quarter of the U.S. population (Grafton, 1999). Roosevelt's use of radio was both a testament to his own skills and savvy as a politician and to the power and ubiquity of radio during this period. At the time, there was no other form of mass media that could have had the same effect.

Certainly, radio has been used by the government for its own purposes, but it has had an even greater impact on politics by serving as what has been called "the ultimate arena for free speech (Davis & Owen, 1998)." Such infamous radio firebrands as Father Charles Coughlin, a Roman Catholic priest whose radio program opposed the New Deal, criticized Jews, and supported Nazi policies, aptly demonstrated this capability early in radio's history (Sterling & Kitross). In recent decades, radio has supported political careers, including those of U.S. Senator Al Franken of Minnesota, former New York City mayor Rudy Giuliani, and presidential aspirant Fred Thompson. Talk show hosts such as Rush Limbaugh have gained great political influence, with some even viewing Limbaugh as the *de facto* leader of the Republican Party (Halloran, 2009).

The Importance of Talk Radio

An important contemporary convergence of radio and politics can be readily heard on modern talk radio programs. Far from being simply chat shows, the talk radio that became popular in the 1980s features a host who takes callers and discusses a wide assortment of topics. Talk radio hosts gain and keep their listeners by sheer force of personality, and some say shocking or insulting things to get their message across. These hosts range from conservative radio hosts such as Rush Limbaugh to so-called shock jocks such as Howard Stern.

Repeal of the Fairness Doctrine

While talk radio first began during the 1920s, the emergence of the format as a contemporary cultural and political force took place during the mid- to late-1980s following the repeal of the Fairness Doctrine (Cruz, 2007). As you read earlier in this chapter, this doctrine, established in 1949, required any station broadcasting a political point of view over the air to allow equal time to all reasonable dissenting views. Despite its noble intentions of safeguarding public airwaves for diverse views, the doctrine had long attracted a level of dissent. Opponents of the Fairness Doctrine claimed that it had a chilling effect on political discourse as stations, rather than risk government intervention, avoided programs that were divisive or controversial (Cruz, 2007). In 1987, the FCC under the Reagan administration repealed the regulation, setting the stage for an AM talk radio boom; by 2004, the number of talk radio stations had increased by 17-fold (Anderson, 2005).

The end of the Fairness Doctrine allowed stations to broadcast programs without worrying about finding an opposing point of view to balance the stated opinions of its host. Radio hosts representing all points of the political spectrum could say anything that they wanted to—within FCC limits—without fear of rebuttal. Media bias and its ramifications will be explored at greater length in Chapter 14 "Ethics of Mass Media".

The Revitalization of AM

The migration of music stations to the FM spectrum during the 1960s and 1970s provided a great deal of space on the AM band for talk shows. With the Fairness Doctrine no longer a hindrance, these programs slowly gained notoriety during the late 1980s and early 1990s. In 1998, talk radio hosts railed against a proposed congressional pay increase, and their listeners became incensed; House Speaker Jim Wright received a deluge of faxes protesting it from irate talk radio listeners from stations all over the country (Douglas). Ultimately, Congress canceled the pay increase, and various print outlets acknowledged the influence of talk radio on the decision. Propelled by events such as these, talk radio stations rose from only 200 in the early 1980s to more than 850 in 1994 (Douglas).

Coast to Coast AM

Although political programs unquestionably rule AM talk radio, that dial is also home to a kind of show that some radio listeners may have never experienced. Late at night on AM radio, a program airs during which listeners hear stories about ghosts, alien abductions, and fantastic creatures. It's not a fictional drama program, however, but instead a call-in talk show called *Coast to Coast AM*. In 2006, this unlikely success ranked among the top 10 AM talk radio programs in the nation—a stunning feat considering its 10 p.m. to 2 a.m. time slot and bizarre format (Vigil, 2006).

Originally started by host Art Bell in the 1980s, *Coast to Coast* focuses on topics that mainstream media outlets rarely treat seriously. Regular guests include ghost investigators, psychics, Bigfoot biographers, alien abductees, and deniers of the moon landing. The guests take calls from listeners who are allowed to ask questions or talk about their own paranormal experiences or theories.

Coast to Coast's current host, George Noory, has continued the show's format. In some areas, its ratings have even exceeded those of Rush Limbaugh's (Vigil, 2006). For a late-night show, these kinds of high ratings are rare. The success of *Coast to Coast* is thus a continuing testament to the diversity and unexpected potential of radio (Vigil, 2006).

On-Air Political Influence

As talk radio's popularity grew during the early 1990s, it quickly became an outlet for political ambitions. In 1992, nine talk show hosts ran for U.S. Congress. By the middle of the decade, it had become common for many former—or failed—politicians to attempt to use the format. Former California governor Jerry Brown and former New York mayor Ed Koch were among the mid-1990s politicians that had AM talk shows (Annenberg Public Policy Center, 1996). Both conservatives and liberals widely agree that conservative hosts dominate AM talk radio. Many talk show hosts, such as Limbaugh, who began his popular program 1 year after the repeal of the Fairness Doctrine, have made a profitable business out of their programs.

Figure 7.8

Talk radio shows increased dramatically in number and popularity in the wake of the 1987 repeal of the Fairness Doctrine.

JD Lasica – Blogworld Talk Radio – CC BY-NC 2.0.

During the 2000s, AM talk radio continued to build. Hosts such as Michael Savage, Sean Hannity, and Bill O'Reilly furthered the trend of popular conservative talk shows, but liberal hosts also became popular through the short-lived Air America network. The network closed abruptly in 2010 amid financial concerns (Stelter, 2010). Although the network was unsuccessful, it provided a platform for such hosts as MSNBC TV news host Rachel Maddow and Minnesota Senator Al Franken. Other liberal hosts such as Bill Press and Ron Reagan, son of President Ronald Reagan, have also found success in the AM political talk radio field (Stelter, 2010). Despite these successes, liberal talk radio is often viewed as unsustainable (Hallowell, 2010). To some, the failure of Air America confirms conservatives' domination of AM radio. In response to the conservative dominance of talk radio, many prominent liberals, including House Speaker Nancy Pelosi, have advocated reinstating the Fairness Doctrine and forcing stations to offer equal time to contrasting opinions (Stotts, 2008).

Freedom of Speech and Radio Controversies

While the First Amendment of the U.S. Constitution gives radio personalities the freedom to say nearly anything they want on the air without fear of prosecution (except in cases of obscenity, slander, or incitement of violence, which will be discussed in greater detail in Chapter 15 "Media and Government"), it does not protect them from being fired from their jobs when their controversial comments create a public outrage. Many talk radio hosts, such as Howard Stern, push the boundaries of acceptable speech to engage listeners and boost ratings, but sometimes radio hosts push too far, unleashing a storm of controversy.

Making (and Unmaking) a Career out of Controversy

Talk radio host Howard Stern has managed to build his career on creating controversy—despite being fined multiple times for indecency by the FCC, Stern remains one of highest-paid and most popular talk radio hosts in the United States. Stern's radio broadcasts often feature scatological or sexual humor, creating an "anything goes" atmosphere. Because his on-air antics frequently generate controversy that can jeopardize advertising sponsorships and drive away offended listeners—in addition to risking fines from the FCC—Stern has a history of uneasy relationships with the radio stations that employ him. In an effort to free himself of conflicts with station owners and sponsors, in 2005 Stern signed a contract with Sirius Satellite Radio, which is exempt from FCC regulation, so that he can continue to broadcast his show without fear of censorship.

Stern's massive popularity gives him a lot of clout, which has allowed him to weather controversy and continue to have a successful career. Other radio hosts who have gotten themselves in trouble with poorly considered on-air comments have not been so lucky. In April 2007, Don Imus, host of the long-running *Imus in the Morning*, was suspended for racist and sexist comments made about the Rutgers University women's basketball team (MSNBC, 2007). Though he publically apologized, the scandal continued to draw negative attention in the media, and CBS canceled his show to avoid further unfavorable publicity and the withdrawal of advertisers. Though he returned to the airwaves in December of that year with a different station, the episode was a major setback for Imus's career and his public image. Similarly, syndicated conservative talk show host Dr. Laura Schelssinger ended her radio show in 2010 due to pressure from radio stations and sponsors after her repeated use of a racial epithet on a broadcast incited a public backlash (MSNBC, 2007).

As the examples of these talk radio hosts show, the issue of freedom of speech on the airwaves is often complicated by the need for radio stations to be profitable. Outspoken or shocking radio hosts can draw in many listeners, attracting advertisers to sponsor their shows and bringing in money for their radio stations. Although some listeners may be offended by these hosts and may stop tuning in, as long as the hosts continue to attract advertising dollars, their employers are usually content to allow the hosts to speak freely on the air. However, if a host's behavior ends up sparking a major controversy, causing advertisers to withdraw their sponsorship to avoid tarnishing their brands, the radio station will often fire the host and look to someone who can better sustain advertising partnerships. Radio hosts' right to free speech does not compel their employer to give them the forum to exercise it. Popular hosts like Don Imus may find a home on the air again once the furor has died down, but for radio hosts concerned about the stability of their careers, the lesson is clear: there are practical limits on their freedom of speech.

Key Takeaways

- Radio was unique as a form of mass media because it had the potential to reach anyone, even the illiterate. Radio news in the 1930s and 1940s brought the emotional impact of traumatic events home to the listening public in a way that gave the nation a sense of unity.

- Radio encouraged the growth of national popular music stars and brought regional sounds to wider audiences. The effects of early radio programs can be felt both in modern popular music and in television programming.

- The Fairness Doctrine was created to ensure fair coverage of issues over the airwaves. It stated that radio stations must give equal time to contrasting points of view on an issue. An enormous rise in the popularity of AM talk radio occurred after the repeal of the Fairness Doctrine in 1987.

- The need for radio stations to generate revenue places practical limits on what radio personalities can say on the air. Shock jocks like Howard Stern and Don Imus test, and sometimes exceed, these limits and become controversial figures, highlighting the tension between freedom of speech and the need for businesses to be profitable.

Exercises

Please respond to the following writing prompts. Each response should be a minimum of one paragraph.

1. Describe the unique qualities that set radio apart from other forms of mass media, such as newspapers.

2. How did radio bring new music to places that had never heard it before?

3. Describe political talk radio before and after the Fairness Doctrine. What kind of effect did the Fairness Doctrine have?

4. Do you think that the Fairness Doctrine should be reinstated? Explain your answer.

5. Investigate the controversy surrounding Don Imus and the comments that led to his show's cancellation. What is your opinion of his comments and CBS's reaction to them?

References

Anderson, Brian. *South Park Conservatives: The Revolt Against Liberal Media Bias* (Washington D.C.: Regnery Publishing, 2005), 35–36.

Annenberg Public Policy Center, *Call-In Political Talk Radio: Background, Content, Audiences, Portrayal in Mainstream Media*, Annenberg Public Policy Center Report Series, August 7, 1996, http://www.annenbergpublicpolicycenter.org/Downloads/Political_Communication/Political_Talk_Radio /1996_03_political_talk_radio_rpt.PDF.

Brown, *Manipulating the Ether*, 140.

Cashman, *America in the Twenties and Thirties*, 329.

Cruz, Gilbert. "GOP Rallies Behind Talk Radio," *Time*, June 28, 2007, http://www.time.com/time/politics/article/ 0,8599,1638662,00.html.

Davis, Richard. and Diana Owen, *New Media and American Politics* (New York: Oxford University Press, 1998), 54.

DiMeo, Nate. "New York Clashes with the Heartland," Hearing America: A Century of Music on the Radio, *American Public Media*, 2010, http://americanradioworks.publicradio.org/features/radio/b1.html.

Douglas, *Listening In*, 287.

Grafton, John. ed., *Great Speeches—Franklin Delano Roosevelt* (Mineola, NY: Dover, 1999), 34.

Halloran, Liz. "Steele-Limbaugh Spat: A Battle for GOP's Future?" *NPR*, March 2, 2009, http://www.npr.org/templates/story/story.php?storyId=101430572.

Hallowell, Billy. "Media Matters' Vapid Response to Air America's Crash," *Big Journalism*, January 26, 2010, http://bigjournalism.com/bhallowell/2010/01/26/media-matters-vapid-response-to-air-americas-crash.

Horowitz, Joseph. *Classical Music in America: A History of Its Rise and Fall* (New York: Norton, 2005), 399–404.

Horten, *Radio Goes to War*, 45–47.

Howe, Sondra Wieland "The NBC Music Appreciation Hour: Radio Broadcasts of Walter Damrosch, 1928–1942," *Journal of Research in Music Education* 51, no. 1 (Spring 2003).

Kyriakoudes, Louis. *The Social Origins of the Urban South*: *Race, Gender, and Migration in Nashville and Middle Tennessee, 1890–1930* (Chapel Hill: University of North Carolina Press, 2003), 7.

Laird, Tracey. *Louisiana Hayride: Radio and Roots Music Along the Red River* (New York: Oxford University Press, 2005), 4–10.

Loviglio, Jason. "Vox Pop: Network Radio and the Voice of the People" in *Radio Reader: Essays in the Cultural History of Radio*, ed. Michele Hilmes and Jason Loviglio (New York: Routledge, 2002), 89–106.

Lubertozzi, Alex and Brian Holmsten, *The War of the Worlds: Mars' Invasion of Earth, Inciting Panic and Inspiring Terror From H. G. Wells to Orson Welles and Beyond* (Naperville, IL: Sourcebooks, 2005), 7–9.

MSNBC, Imus in the Morning, MSNBC, April 4, 2007.

Stelter, Brian. "Liberal Radio, Even Without Air America," *New York Times*, January 24, 2010, http://www.nytimes.com/2010/01/25/arts/25radio.html.

Sterling and Kitross, *Stay Tuned*, 182.

Sterling and Kitross, *Stay Tuned*, 199.

Stotts, Bethany. "Pelosi Supports Return of Fairness Doctrine," *Accuracy in Media Column*, June 26, 2008, http://www.aim.org/aim-column/pelosi-support-return-of-fairness-doctrine.

Vigil, Delfin. "Conspiracy Theories Propel AM Radio Show Into the Top Ten," *San Francisco Chronicle*, November 12, 2006, http://articles.sfgate.com/2006-11-12/news/17318973_1_radio-show-coast-cold-war.

Wald, *Beatles Destroyed Rock 'n' Roll*, 95–96.

Wald, Elijah. *How the Beatles Destroyed Rock 'n' Roll: An Alternative History of American Popular Music* (New York: Oxford University Press, 2009), 100–104.

Walker, *Rebels on the Air*, 53–54.

7.5 Radio's New Future

Although the future of radio has been doubted many times throughout its history, it is still in existence. The inherent portability of the medium gives it an advantage over other types of media that require an individual's full attention, such as television or print. The simplicity of radio has leant itself to a variety of uses.

In recent years, new technologies have promised to expand the reach of radio and to expand the kinds of programming it offers. Satellite and HD radio have increased the amount and diversity of available programming by making more stations available. Internet radio has increased the accessibility of radio communication, and practically anyone who has access to a computer can create subscription podcasts to distribute around the world. These new technologies promise to make radio an enduring, innovative form of media.

Satellite Radio

In 1998, the FCC awarded licenses to two businesses interested in creating a radio version of cable television—without the cables. This act was the beginning of satellite radio, and the companies soon became XM and Sirius. These two networks sold special receivers that could pick up satellite transmissions broadcasting a wide range of formats on different channels to listeners who paid a monthly fee for the commercial-free programming.

Like cable television, satellite radio was not required to censor its disc jockeys or guests for profanity. This attracted somewhat controversial radio personalities known for their conflicts with the FCC, such as Howard Stern and Opie and Anthony. The networks also drew hosts such as NPR's Bob Edwards and Bruce Springsteen's guitarist "Little" Steven Van Zandt to create their own shows. Because listeners paid one price for access to all of the channels, disc jockeys experienced less pressure to adhere to the limited playlist style of programming that was the norm for terrestrial radio stations (Breen, 2005). In 2008, Sirius and XM merged to form Sirius XM. In 2010, the company recorded its first profits (Reuters, 2010).

Figure 7.9

Talk show host Howard Stern moved his controversial program to satellite radio in 2006, removing himself from FCC censorship rules and helping to popularize the medium.

HD Radio

Developed around 2001 to help terrestrial radio stations compete with emerging satellite radio technology, HD radio is essentially a digital transmission of radio signals resulting in less static and better sound quality, even for AM stations. Upgraded quality is not the major benefit of HD radio, however; the technology allows signals to be compressed so that one station can air so-called shadow stations on the same frequency as its regular broadcast.

Although listeners need an HD radio to receive these channels, they pay no subscription fee, as independent stations provide their own programming as they deem necessary (Pogue, 2009).

Stations such as NPR's WAMU in Washington, DC, broadcast different types of programming on their shadow channels. For example, the station's 88.5-1 broadcasts the regular analog schedule of WAMU, while 88.5-2 broadcasts bluegrass and country music programming, and 88.5-3 broadcasts public radio programs not available on the analog version of 88.5 (American Universe Radio).

HD radio allows current broadcasters to provide content that they would normally put aside in favor of more commercial programs. WAMU's bluegrass and country shadow station plays content originally played over the airwaves but relegated to the Internet in favor of more marketable programs. The innovation of HD radio allowed the station to reintroduce the programs without risking its financial stability. With this financial freedom, HD radio offers a host of programming possibilities for traditional radio.

Internet Radio and Podcasting

Broadcasting is both a strength and limitation of broadcasting. Although technological advances of the past 50 years, such as audio recorders and microphones, have made creating a radio program simple, finding a way to broadcast that program presents difficulties for the average person. The expansion of the Internet, however, has changed this limitation into a manageable hurdle for both businesses and individuals alike.

Internet Radio

At its core, Internet radio is simply the streaming of audio programs through the medium of the Internet. As early as 1994, radio stations such as Chapel Hill, North Carolina's WXYC were broadcasting their signal over the Internet, and so potentially gaining a worldwide audience (WXYC). Soon, online-only radio stations were created to broadcast programs. Services such as Live 365, founded in 1999, have acted as distributors for Internet radio programs, charging broadcasters fees to stream their programs to a large listening audience.

Another type of Internet radio service is Pandora radio. This radio website does not distribute existing programs but rather allows users to create their own custom music radio stations. A listener creates a Pandora account and types in a song, composer, or artist, and the service creates a station that plays songs that are similar to the user's selection. This analysis of music attempts to collect as many details about a song as possible, from lyrics to instrumentation to harmony, and then categorizes songs according to these attributes, making it possible for listeners to customize their own stations based on one or more of the cataloged attributes. The listener can delete unwanted songs from the playlist and create new stations as well. Pandora currently relies on on-screen advertising and has implemented audio advertisements as well (Beltrone, 2009). Other music services such as Yahoo! Music, AOL Radio, and Jango offer radio stations with multiple programmed genres.

Problems of Internet Broadcasting

Despite the rise of Internet radio over the past several years, its success has never been a sure thing. As the trend gained momentum, many inexperienced broadcasters confronted the issue of royalties, and many experienced broadcasters encountered new legal issues related to streaming. Stations that broadcast over the airwaves must pay publishing royalties to the musicians and songwriters behind the recordings. Rather than pay an individual musician or songwriter each time a recording is played, however, broadcasters—including radio station, coffee shops, and restaurants—pay for a blanket license that allows them to play any song. As Internet broadcasting grew, musicians and record labels began demanding royalties from Internet stations and specifying new licensing restrictions. For instance, Pandora radio's license specifies that users can buy a song, but they can't replay a song without purchasing it, nor can they skip more than six songs per hour.

Other issues arose as terrestrial stations began streaming on the Internet. Since its inception, the medium has struggled with such concerns as whether advertisers should pay for commercials played over the Internet as well as over the air and what types of licenses should be used for Internet radio stations. In time, the federal government mediated an agreement between broadcasters and record companies with the Webcasters Settlement Act of 2009. This legislation designated Internet-only stations as pure-play stations, dividing them according to the types of coverage they offer. Each category pays royalties in different ways, ensuring both fair compensation for artists and the future viability of Internet radio (Albenesius, 2009).

Podcasting

Unlike Internet radio, podcasting employs downloadable rather than streamed programs. The term *podcasting* itself stems from the use of MP3 players such as Apple's iPod to use programs on demand. Many terrestrial stations have employed podcasting to supplement their traditional over-the-air broadcasting. Because these are single programs rather than continuous stations, podcasts are an easier medium to produce than is Internet radio.

Some podcast producers, such as Mignon Fogarty, have created programs that led to book deals and a steady income. Fogarty's weekly *Grammar Girl: Quick and Dirty Tricks* podcast focuses on simple grammar rules. Within a year of its inception, this podcast racked up 1 million downloads and received national acclaim (Faherty, 2007). Nevertheless, podcasting does not fit neatly into the traditional concept of radio. Yet, there is no question that it is following in the footsteps of past radio programs, and that it provides a potential vision of the medium's place in the years to come. Just as radio evolved from a medium for soap operas and live music to talk shows and recorded music, podcasts are a window into what radio may evolve into in the future.

Key Takeaways

- Radio's flexibility as a medium has allowed it to adjust to the fluctuations of audience tastes and markets.
- Satellite radio is a subscription-based service, while HD radio is provided at no cost by current radio providers.
- Internet radio and podcasting have allowed many new programs and stations to be broadcast at low cost.

Exercises

Please respond to the following writing prompts. Each response should be a minimum of one paragraph.

1. Define satellite radio, HD radio, Internet radio, and podcasting.

2. How have each of these mediums fared in terms of popularity?

3. Pick one of these mediums and predict its future success given its current popularity.

End-of-Chapter Assessment

Review Questions

1.
Section 1

a. Name three major changes that have affected the development of radio.

b. What made the period from the 1930s to the 1950s radio's golden age?

c. How have large networks affected the development of radio?

d. Has the corporate consolidation of radio over the past decades made radio better or worse in your opinion? Explain your answer.

2.
Section 2

a. How and why do modern radio stations employ radio formats?

b. What is your opinion about the effects of formats on the current state of radio?

c. Describe your favorite radio format and explain how the advertising is marketed to you.

3.
Section 3

a. What makes radio unique among forms of mass media?

b. Explain the ways radio affected the development of your favorite genre of music.

c. How do you think popular music would be heard and spread if there was no radio?

d. What do you think political talk radio would presently be like if the Fairness Doctrine had not been repealed?

4.
Section 4

a. How do you think new radio technologies will affect traditional radio broadcasting over the next 10 years?

b. Of the four new radio technologies listed in Section 7.4 "Radio's New Future", which do you think has the most potential to succeed? Explain your answer.

Critical Thinking Questions

1. Taken as a whole, has government regulation been good or bad for radio? Explain your answer using specific examples.

2. Given the rise of tightly formatted radio stations, do you think it is still possible to have a truly popular music? Why or why not?

3. Do you think radio should be treated as a public resource or a private commodity? If your view was made law, how would it affect radio programming?

4. If radio is a public resource, how should issues of freedom of speech and censorship be handled?

5. Given the history of radio, do you think that new innovations in radio will make radio more democratic and accessible, or will regulatory and market forces control access?

Career Connection

New technologies in radio have created new radio career possibilities. As podcasting, Internet radio, satellite radio, and HD radio have fueled demand for new content, opportunities have emerged for self-starters to create and host their own radio programs or become freelance radio journalists.

Consider some of the uses for podcasting and radio journalism. Some useful links for researching careers in these areas, among others you may find through your own research, are (http://transom.org/) and (http://www.airmedia.org/). Based on your research and ideas, identify a career field in online radio that you may wish to pursue. Think about ways that people in this career field have employed radio. Now answer the following questions:

1. How have people used radio in your chosen career?

2. How have new technologies, such as podcasting and Internet radio, allowed for new uses of radio in this career?

3. How could you use radio in your career even if you weren't necessarily a radio producer or journalist?

4. What kinds of projects or initiatives could you undertake that would involve radio?

References

Albenesius, Chloe. "Internet Radio Reaches Deal on Royalty Rates," *PC Magazine*, July 7, 2009, http://www.pcmag.com/article2/0,2817,2349813,00.asp.

American Universe Radio, WAMU, "Schedules," http://wamu.org/programs/schedule/.

Beltrone, Gabriel. "Pandora's Back," *The Big Money*, July 23, 2009, http://www.thebigmoney.com/articles/monetize/2009/07/23/pandora-s-back.

Breen, Bill. "Written in the Stars," *Fast Company*, February 1, 2005, http://www.fastcompany.com/magazine/91/open_stars.html.

Faherty, John. "'Grammar Girl' Podcasts Rule Online," *USA Today*, March 8, 2007, http://www.usatoday.com/tech/webguide/internetlife/2007-03-08-grammar-girl_N.htm.

Pogue, David. "HD Radio Crying Out to Be Heard," *New York Times*, April 8, 2009, http://www.nytimes.com/2009/04/09/technology/personaltech/09pogue.html.

Reuters, "Sirius XM Posts Profit, Its First Since Merger, *New York Times*, February 25, 2010, http://www.nytimes.com/2010/02/26/technology/26radio.html.

WXYC, "Simulcast," http://wxyc.org/about/simulcast.

Chapter 8: Movies

8.1 Movies

Figure 8.1

NASA Goddard Space Flight Center – Viewing 3D IMAX clips – CC BY 2.0.

In 2009, many moviegoers were amazed by the three-dimensional (3-D) film *Avatar*. *Avatar* grossed over $1.8 billion in theaters worldwide, $1.35 billion from 3-D sales alone (Gray, 2010). Following in that vein, dozens of other movie studios released 3-D films, resulting in lesser box office successes such as *Alice in Wonderland*, *Clash of the Titans*, and *Shrek Forever After*. Many film reviewers and audiences seemed adamant—3-D movies were the wave of the future.

However, could this eye-popping technology actually ruin our moviegoing experience? Brian Moylan, a critic for Gawker.com, argues that it already has. The problem with 3-D, he says, is that "It is so mind-numbingly amazing that narrative storytelling hasn't caught up with the technology. The corporate screenwriting borgs are so busy trying to come up with plot devices to highlight all the newfangled whoosiwhatsits—objects being hurled at the audience, flying sequences, falling leaves, glowing Venus Flytraps—that no one is really bothering to tell a tale (Moylan)."

James Cameron, director of *Avatar*, agrees. "[Studios] think, 'what was the takeaway lessons from *Avatar*? Oh you should make more money with 3-D.' They ignore the fact that we natively authored the film in 3-D, and [they] decide that what we accomplished in several years of production could be done in an eight week (post-production 3-D) conversion [such as] with *Clash of the Titans* (Baig, 2010)." Cameron makes the following point: While recent films such as *Avatar* (2009) and *Beowulf* (2007) were created exclusively for 3-D, many other filmmakers have converted their movies to 3-D after filming was already complete. *Clash of the Titans* is widely criticized because its 3-D effects were quickly added in postproduction (Baig, 2010).

What effect does this have on audiences? Aside from the complaints of headaches and nausea (and the fact that some who wear glasses regularly can find it uncomfortable or even impossible to wear 3-D glasses on top of their own), many say that the new technology simply makes movies look worse. The film critic Roger Ebert has continuously denounced the technology, noting that movies such as *The Last Airbender* look like they're "filmed with a dirty sheet over the lens (Ebert, 2010)." 3-D technology can cause a movie to look fuzzier, darker, and generally less cinematically attractive. However, movie studios are finding 3-D films attractive for another reason.

Because seeing a movie in 3-D is considered a "premium" experience, consumers are expected to pay higher prices. And with the increasing popularity of IMAX 3D films, tickets may surpass $20 per person (Stewart & McClintock, 2010). This gives 3-D films an advantage over 2-D ones as audiences are willing to pay more.

The recent 3-D boom has often been compared to the rise of color film in the early 1950s. However, some maintain that it's just a fad. Will 3-D technology affect the future of filmmaking? With a host of new 3-D technologies for the home theater being released in 2010, many are banking on the fact that it will. Director James Cameron, however, is unsure of the technology's continuing popularity, arguing that "If people put bad 3-D in the marketplace they're going to hold back or even threaten the emerging of 3-D (Baig)." What is important, he maintains, is the creative aspect of moviemaking—no technology can replace good filmmaking. In the end, audiences will determine the medium's popularity. Throughout the history of film, Technicolor dyes, enhanced sound systems, and computer-generated graphics have boasted huge box-office revenues; however, it's ultimately the viewers who determine what a good movie is and who set the standard for future films.

References

Baig, "Cameron: 3D Promising, But Caution Needed."

Baig, Edward. "'Avatar' Director James Cameron: 3D Promising, but Caution Needed," *USA Today*, March 11, 2010, http://content.usatoday.com/communities/technologylive/post/2010/03/james-cameron/1.

Ebert, Roger, review of *The Last Airbender*, directed by M. Night Shyamalan, *Chicago Sun Times*, June 30, 2010, http://rogerebert.suntimes.com/apps/pbcs.dll/article?AID=/20100630/REVIEWS/100639999.

Gray, Brandon. "'Avatar' is New King of the World," Box Office Mojo, January 26, 2010, http://boxofficemojo.com/news/?id=2657.

Moylan, Brian. "3D is Going to Ruin Movies for a Long Time to Come," *Gawker*, http://gawker.com/#!5484085/3d-is-going-to-ruin-movies-for-a-long-time-to-come.

Stewart, Andrew and Pamela McClintock, "Big Ticket Price Increase for 3D Pics," *Variety*, March 24, 2010, http://www.variety.com/article/VR1118016878.html?categoryid=13&cs=1.

8.2 The History of Movies

Learning Objectives

1. Identify key points in the development of the motion picture industry.

2. Identify key developments of the motion picture industry and technology.

3. Identify influential films in movie history.

The movie industry as we know it today originated in the early 19th century through a series of technological developments: the creation of photography, the discovery of the illusion of motion by combining individual still images, and the study of human and animal locomotion. The history presented here begins at the culmination of these technological developments, where the idea of the motion picture as an entertainment industry first emerged. Since then, the industry has seen extraordinary transformations, some driven by the artistic visions of individual participants, some by commercial necessity, and still others by accident. The history of the cinema is complex, and for every important innovator and movement listed here, others have been left out. Nonetheless, after reading this section you will understand the broad arc of the development of a medium that has captured the imaginations of audiences worldwide for over a century.

The Beginnings: Motion Picture Technology of the Late 19th Century

While the experience of watching movies on smartphones may seem like a drastic departure from the communal nature of film viewing as we think of it today, in some ways the small-format, single-viewer display is a return to film's early roots. In 1891, the inventor Thomas Edison, together with William Dickson, a young laboratory assistant, came out with what they called the kinetoscope, a device that would become the predecessor to the motion picture projector. The kinetoscope was a cabinet with a window through which individual viewers could experience the illusion of a moving image (Gale Virtual Reference Library) (British Movie Classics). A perforated celluloid film strip with a sequence of images on it was rapidly spooled between a light bulb and a lens, creating the illusion of motion (Britannica). The images viewers could see in the kinetoscope captured events and performances that had been staged at Edison's film studio in East Orange, New Jersey, especially for the Edison kinetograph (the camera that produced kinetoscope film sequences): circus performances, dancing women, cockfights, boxing matches, and even a tooth extraction by a dentist (Robinson, 1994).

Figure 8.2

The Edison kinetoscope.

todd.vision – Kinetoscope – CC BY 2.0.

As the kinetoscope gained popularity, the Edison Company began installing machines in hotel lobbies, amusement parks, and penny arcades, and soon kinetoscope parlors—where customers could pay around 25 cents for admission to a bank of machines—had opened around the country. However, when friends and collaborators suggested that Edison find a way to project his kinetoscope images for audience viewing, he apparently refused, claiming that such an invention would be a less profitable venture (Britannica).

Because Edison hadn't secured an international patent for his invention, variations of the kinetoscope were soon being copied and distributed throughout Europe. This new form of entertainment was an instant success, and a number of mechanics and inventors, seeing an opportunity, began toying with methods of projecting the moving images onto a larger screen. However, it was the invention of two brothers, Auguste and Louis Lumière—photographic goods manufacturers in Lyon, France—that saw the most commercial success. In 1895, the brothers patented the cinématographe (from which we get the term *cinema*), a lightweight film projector that also functioned as a camera and printer. Unlike the Edison kinetograph, the cinématographe was lightweight enough for easy outdoor filming, and over the years the brothers used the camera to take well over 1,000 short films, most of which depicted scenes from everyday life. In December 1895, in the basement lounge of the Grand Café, Rue des Capucines in Paris, the Lumières held the world's first ever commercial film screening, a sequence of about 10 short scenes, including the brother's first film, *Workers Leaving the Lumière Factory*, a segment lasting less than a minute and depicting workers leaving the family's photographic instrument factory at the end of the day, as shown in the still frame here in Figure 8.3 (Encyclopedia of the Age of Industry and Empire).

Believing that audiences would get bored watching scenes that they could just as easily observe on a casual walk around the city, Louis Lumière claimed that the cinema was "an invention without a future (Menand, 2005)," but a demand for motion pictures grew at such a rapid rate that soon representatives of the Lumière company were traveling throughout Europe and the world, showing half-hour screenings of the company's films. While cinema initially competed with other popular forms of entertainment—circuses, vaudeville acts, theater troupes, magic shows, and many others—eventually it would supplant these various entertainments as the main commercial attraction (Menand, 2005). Within a year of the Lumières' first commercial screening, competing film companies were offering moving-picture acts in music halls and vaudeville theaters across Great Britain. In the United States, the Edison Company, having purchased the rights to an improved projector that they called the Vitascope, held their first film screening in April 1896 at Koster and Bial's Music Hall in Herald Square, New York City.

Film's profound impact on its earliest viewers is difficult to imagine today, inundated as many are by video images. However, the sheer volume of reports about the early audience's disbelief, delight, and even fear at what they were seeing suggests that viewing a film was an overwhelming experience for many. Spectators gasped at the realistic details in films such as Robert Paul's *Rough Sea at Dover*, and at times people panicked and tried to flee the theater during films in which trains or moving carriages sped toward the audience (Robinson). Even the public's perception of film as a medium was considerably different from the contemporary understanding; the moving image was an improvement upon the photograph—a medium with which viewers were already familiar—and this is perhaps why the earliest films documented events in brief segments but didn't tell stories. During this "novelty period" of cinema, audiences were more interested by the phenomenon of the film projector itself, so vaudeville halls advertised the kind of projector they were using (for example "The Vitascope—Edison's Latest Marvel") (Balcanasu, et. al.), rather than the names of the films (Britannica Online).

Figure 8.3

Workers Leaving the Lumière Factory: One of the first films viewed by an audience.

By the close of the 19th century, as public excitement over the moving picture's novelty gradually wore off, filmmakers were also beginning to experiment with film's possibilities as a medium in itself (not simply, as it had been regarded up until then, as a tool for documentation, analogous to the camera or the phonograph). Technical innovations allowed filmmakers like Parisian cinema owner Georges Méliès to experiment with special effects that produced seemingly magical transformations on screen: flowers turned into women, people disappeared with puffs of smoke, a man appeared where a woman had just been standing, and other similar tricks (Robinson).

Not only did Méliès, a former magician, invent the "trick film," which producers in England and the United States began to imitate, but he was also the one to transform cinema into the narrative medium it is today. Whereas before, filmmakers had only ever created single-shot films that lasted a minute or less, Méliès began joining these short films together to create stories. His 30-scene *Trip to the Moon* (1902), a film based on a Jules Verne novel, may have been the most widely seen production in cinema's first decade (Robinson). However, Méliès never developed his technique beyond treating the narrative film as a staged theatrical performance; his camera, representing the vantage point of an audience facing a stage, never moved during the filming of a scene. In 1912, Méliès released his last commercially successful production, *The Conquest of the Pole*, and from then on, he lost audiences to filmmakers who were experimenting with more sophisticated techniques (Encyclopedia of Communication and Information).

Figure 8.4

Georges Méliès's *Trip to the Moon* was one of the first films to incorporate fantasy elements and to use "trick" filming techniques, both of which heavily influenced future filmmakers.

Craig Duffy – Workers Leaving The Lumiere Factory – CC BY-NC 2.0.

The Nickelodeon Craze (1904–1908)

One of these innovative filmmakers was Edwin S. Porter, a projectionist and engineer for the Edison Company. Porter's 12-minute film, *The Great Train Robbery* (1903), broke with the stagelike compositions of Méliès-style films through its use of editing, camera pans, rear projections, and diagonally composed shots that produced a continuity of action. Not only did *The Great Train Robbery* establish the realistic narrative as a standard in cinema, it was also the first major box-office hit. Its success paved the way for the growth of the film industry, as investors, recognizing the motion picture's great moneymaking potential, began opening the first permanent film theaters around the country.

Known as nickelodeons because of their 5 cent admission charge, these early motion picture theaters, often housed in converted storefronts, were especially popular among the working class of the time, who couldn't afford live theater. Between 1904 and 1908, around 9,000 nickelodeons appeared in the United States. It was the nickelodeon's popularity that established film as a mass entertainment medium (Dictionary of American History).

The "Biz": The Motion Picture Industry Emerges

As the demand for motion pictures grew, production companies were created to meet it. At the peak of nickelodeon popularity in 1910 (Britannica Online), there were 20 or so major motion picture companies in the

United States. However, heated disputes often broke out among these companies over patent rights and industry control, leading even the most powerful among them to fear fragmentation that would loosen their hold on the market (Fielding, 1967). Because of these concerns, the 10 leading companies—including Edison, Biograph, Vitagraph, and others—formed the Motion Picture Patents Company (MPPC) in 1908. The MPPC was a trade group that pooled the most significant motion picture patents and established an exclusive contract between these companies and the Eastman Kodak Company as a supplier of film stock. Also known as *the Trust*, the MPPC's goal was to standardize the industry and shut out competition through monopolistic control. Under the Trust's licensing system, only certain licensed companies could participate in the exchange, distribution, and production of film at different levels of the industry—a shut-out tactic that eventually backfired, leading the excluded, independent distributors to organize in opposition to the Trust (Britannica Online).

The Rise of the Feature

In these early years, theaters were still running single-reel films, which came at a standard length of 1,000 feet, allowing for about 16 minutes of playing time. However, companies began to import multiple-reel films from European producers around 1907, and the format gained popular acceptance in the United States in 1912 with Louis Mercanton's highly successful *Queen Elizabeth*, a three-and-a-half reel "feature," starring the French actress Sarah Bernhardt. As exhibitors began to show more features—as the multiple-reel film came to be called—they discovered a number of advantages over the single-reel short. For one thing, audiences saw these longer films as special events and were willing to pay more for admission, and because of the popularity of the feature narratives, features generally experienced longer runs in theaters than their single-reel predecessors (Motion Pictures). Additionally, the feature film gained popularity among the middle classes, who saw its length as analogous to the more "respectable" entertainment of live theater (Motion Pictures). Following the example of the French *film d'art*, U.S. feature producers often took their material from sources that would appeal to a wealthier and better educated audience, such as histories, literature, and stage productions (Robinson).

As it turns out, the feature film was one factor that brought about the eventual downfall of the MPPC. The inflexible structuring of the Trust's exhibition and distribution system made the organization resistant to change. When movie studio, and Trust member, Vitagraph began to release features like *A Tale of Two Cities* (1911) and *Uncle Tom's Cabin* (1910), the Trust forced it to exhibit the films serially in single-reel showings to keep with industry standards. The MPPC also underestimated the appeal of the star system, a trend that began when producers chose famous stage actors like Mary Pickford and James O'Neill to play the leading roles in their productions and to grace their advertising posters (Robinson). Because of the MPPC's inflexibility, independent companies were the only ones able to capitalize on two important trends that were to become film's future: single-reel features and star power. Today, few people would recognize names like Vitagraph or Biograph, but the independents that outlasted them—Universal, Goldwyn (which would later merge with Metro and Mayer), Fox (later 20th Century Fox), and Paramount (the later version of the Lasky Corporation)—have become household names.

Hollywood

As moviegoing increased in popularity among the middle class, and as the feature films began keeping audiences in their seats for longer periods of time, exhibitors found a need to create more comfortable and richly decorated theater spaces to attract their audiences. These "dream palaces," so called because of their often lavish embellishments of marble, brass, guilding, and cut glass, not only came to replace the nickelodeon theater, but also created the demand that would lead to the Hollywood studio system. Some producers realized that the growing demand for new work could only be met if the films were produced on a regular, year-round system. However, this was impractical with the current system that often relied on outdoor filming and was predominately based in Chicago and New York—two cities whose weather conditions prevented outdoor filming for a significant portion of the year. Different companies attempted filming in warmer locations such as Florida, Texas, and Cuba, but the place where producers eventually found the most success was a small, industrial suburb of Los Angeles called Hollywood.

Hollywood proved to be an ideal location for a number of reasons. Not only was the climate temperate and sunny year-round, but land was plentiful and cheap, and the location allowed close access to a number of diverse topographies: mountains, lakes, desert, coasts, and forests. By 1915, more than 60 percent of U.S. film production was centered in Hollywood (Britannica Online).

The Art of Silent Film

While the development of narrative film was largely driven by commercial factors, it is also important to acknowledge the role of individual artists who turned it into a medium of personal expression. The motion picture of the silent era was generally simplistic in nature; acted in overly animated movements to engage the eye; and accompanied by live music, played by musicians in the theater, and written titles to create a mood and to narrate a story. Within the confines of this medium, one filmmaker in particular emerged to transform the silent film into an art and to unlock its potential as a medium of serious expression and persuasion. D. W. Griffith, who entered the film industry as an actor in 1907, quickly moved to a directing role in which he worked closely with his camera crew to experiment with shots, angles, and editing techniques that could heighten the emotional intensity of his scenes. He found that by practicing parallel editing, in which a film alternates between two or more scenes of action, he could create an illusion of simultaneity. He could then heighten the tension of the film's drama by alternating between cuts more and more rapidly until the scenes of action converged. Griffith used this technique to great effect in his controversial film *The Birth of a Nation*, which will be discussed in greater detail later on in this chapter. Other techniques that Griffith employed to new effect included panning shots, through which he was able to establish a sense of scene and to engage his audience more fully in the experience of the film, and tracking shots, or shots that traveled with the movement of a scene (Motion Pictures), which allowed the audience—through the eye of the camera—to participate in the film's action.

MPAA: Combating Censorship

As film became an increasingly lucrative U.S. industry, prominent industry figures like D. W. Griffith, slapstick comedian/director Charlie Chaplin, and actors Mary Pickford and Douglas Fairbanks grew extremely wealthy and influential. Public attitudes toward stars and toward some stars' extravagant lifestyles were divided, much as they are today: On the one hand, these celebrities were idolized and imitated in popular culture, yet at the same time, they were criticized for representing a threat, on and off screen, to traditional morals and social order. And much as it does today, the news media liked to sensationalize the lives of celebrities to sell stories. Comedian Roscoe "Fatty" Arbuckle, who worked alongside future icons Charlie Chaplin and Buster Keaton, was at the center of one of the biggest scandals of the silent era. When Arbuckle hosted a marathon party over Labor Day weekend in 1921, one of his guests, model Virginia Rapp, was rushed to the hospital, where she later died. Reports of a drunken orgy, rape, and murder surfaced. Following World War I, the United States was in the middle of significant social reforms, such as Prohibition. Many feared that movies and their stars could threaten the moral order of the country. Because of the nature of the crime and the celebrity involved, these fears became inexplicably tied to the Artbuckle case (Motion Pictures). Even though autopsy reports ruled that Rapp had died from causes for which Arbuckle could not be blamed, the comedian was tried (and acquitted) for manslaughter, and his career was ruined.

The Arbuckle affair and a series of other scandals only increased public fears about Hollywood's impact. In response to this perceived threat, state and local governments increasingly tried to censor the content of films that depicted crime, violence, and sexually explicit material. Deciding that they needed to protect themselves from government censorship and to foster a more favorable public image, the major Hollywood studios organized in 1922 to form an association they called the Motion Picture Producers and Distributers of America (later renamed the Motion Picture Association of America, or **MPAA**). Among other things, the MPAA instituted a code of self-censorship for the motion picture industry. Today, the MPAA operates by a voluntary rating system, which means producers can voluntarily submit a film for review, which is designed to alert viewers to the age-appropriateness of a film, while still protecting the filmmakers' artistic freedom (Motion Picture Association of America).

Silent Film's Demise

In 1925, Warner Bros. was just a small Hollywood studio looking for opportunities to expand. When representatives from Western Electric offered to sell the studio the rights to a new technology they called Vitaphone, a sound-on-disc system that had failed to capture the interest of any of the industry giants, Warner Bros. executives took a chance, predicting that the novelty of talking films might be a way to make a quick, short-term profit. Little did they anticipate that their gamble would not only establish them as a major Hollywood presence but also change the industry forever.

The pairing of sound with motion pictures was nothing new in itself. Edison, after all, had commissioned the kinetoscope to create a visual accompaniment to the phonograph, and many early theaters had orchestra pits to provide musical accompaniment to their films. Even the smaller picture houses with lower budgets almost always had an organ or piano. When Warner Bros. purchased Vitaphone technology, it planned to use it to provide prerecorded orchestral accompaniment for its films, thereby increasing their marketability to the smaller theaters that didn't have their own orchestra pits (Gochenour, 2000). In 1926, Warner debuted the system with the release of *Don Juan*, a costume drama accompanied by a recording of the New York Philharmonic Orchestra; the public responded enthusiastically (Motion Pictures). By 1927, after a $3 million campaign, Warner Bros. had wired more than 150 theaters in the United States, and it released its second sound film, *The Jazz Singer*, in which the actor Al Jolson improvised a few lines of synchronized dialogue and sang six songs. The film was a major breakthrough. Audiences, hearing an actor speak on screen for the first time, were enchanted (Gochenour). While radio, a new and popular entertainment, had been drawing audiences away from the picture houses for some time, with the birth of the "talkie," or talking film, audiences once again returned to the cinema in large numbers, lured by the promise of seeing and hearing their idols perform (Higham, 1973). By 1929, three-fourths of Hollywood films had some form of sound accompaniment, and by 1930, the silent film was a thing of the past (Gochenour).

"I Don't Think We're in Kansas Anymore": Film Goes Technicolor

Although the techniques of tinting and hand painting had been available methods for adding color to films for some time (Georges Méliès, for instance, employed a crew to hand-paint many of his films), neither method ever caught on. The hand-painting technique became impractical with the advent of mass-produced film, and the tinting process, which filmmakers discovered would create an interference with the transmission of sound in films, was abandoned with the rise of the talkie. However, in 1922, Herbert Kalmus's Technicolor company introduced a dye-transfer technique that allowed it to produce a full-length film, *The Toll of the Sea*, in two primary colors (Gale Virtual Reference Library). However, because only two colors were used, the appearance of *The Toll of the Sea* (1922), *The Ten Commandments* (1923), and other early Technicolor films was not very lifelike. By 1932, Technicolor had designed a three-color system with more realistic results, and for the next 25 years, all color films were produced with this improved system. Disney's *Three Little Pigs* (1933) and *Snow White and the Seven Dwarves* (1936) and films with live actors, like MGM's *The Wizard of Oz* (1939) and *Gone With the Wind* (1939), experienced early success using Technicolor's three-color method.

Despite the success of certain color films in the 1930s, Hollywood, like the rest of the United States, was feeling the impact of the Great Depression, and the expenses of special cameras, crews, and Technicolor lab processing made color films impractical for studios trying to cut costs. Therefore, it wasn't until the end of the 1940s that Technicolor would largely displace the black-and-white film (Motion Pictures in Color).

Rise and Fall of the Hollywood Studio

The spike in theater attendance that followed the introduction of talking films changed the economic structure of the motion picture industry, bringing about some of the largest mergers in industry history. By 1930, eight studios produced 95 percent of all American films, and they continued to experience growth even during the Depression. The five most influential of these studios—Warner Bros., Metro-Goldwyn-Mayer, RKO, 20th Century Fox, and Paramount—were vertically integrated; that is, they controlled every part of the system as it related to their films, from the production to release, distribution, and even viewing. Because they owned theater chains worldwide, these studios controlled which movies exhibitors ran, and because they "owned" a stock of directors, actors, writers, and technical assistants by contract, each studio produced films of a particular character.

The late 1930s and early 1940s are sometimes known as the "Golden Age" of cinema, a time of unparalleled success for the movie industry; by 1939, film was the 11th-largest industry in the United States, and during World War II, when the U.S. economy was once again flourishing, two-thirds of Americans were attending the theater at least once a week (Britannica Online). Some of the most acclaimed movies in history were released during this period, including *Citizen Kane* and *The Grapes of Wrath*. However, postwar inflation, a temporary loss of key foreign markets, the advent of the television, and other factors combined to bring that rapid growth to an end. In 1948, the case of the *United States v. Paramount Pictures*—mandating competition and forcing the studios to relinquish control over theater chains—dealt the final devastating blow from which the studio system would never recover. Control of the major studios reverted to Wall Street, where the studios were eventually absorbed by multinational corporations, and the powerful studio heads lost the influence they had held for nearly 30 years (Baers, 2000).

Figure 8.5

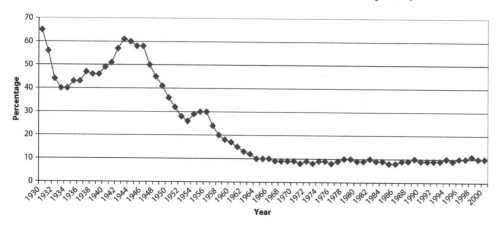

Percentage of the US Population That Went to the Cinema on Average Weekly

Rise and Decline of Movie Viewing During Hollywood's "Golden Age"

Graph from Pautz, Michelle C. 2002. The Decline in Average Weekly Cinema Attendance: 1930–2000. Issues in Political Economy, 11 (Summer): 54–65.

Post–World War II: Television Presents a Threat

While economic factors and antitrust legislation played key roles in the decline of the studio system, perhaps the most important factor in that decline was the advent of the television. Given the opportunity to watch "movies" from the comfort of their own homes, the millions of Americans who owned a television by the early 1950s were attending the cinema far less regularly than they had only several years earlier (Motion Pictures). In an attempt to win back diminishing audiences, studios did their best to exploit the greatest advantages film held over television. For one thing, television broadcasting in the 1950s was all in black and white, whereas the film industry had the advantage of color. While producing a color film was still an expensive undertaking in the late 1940s, a couple of changes occurred in the industry in the early 1950s to make color not only more affordable, but more realistic in its appearance. In 1950, as the result of antitrust legislation, Technicolor lost its monopoly on the color film industry, allowing other providers to offer more competitive pricing on filming and processing services. At the same time, Kodak came out with a multilayer film stock that made it possible to use more affordable cameras and to produce a higher quality image. Kodak's Eastmancolor option was an integral component in converting the industry to color. In the late 1940s, only 12 percent of features were in color; however, by 1954 (after the release of Kodak Eastmancolor) more than 50 percent of movies were in color (Britannica Online).

Another clear advantage on which filmmakers tried to capitalize was the sheer size of the cinema experience. With the release of the epic biblical film *The Robe* in 1953, 20th Century Fox introduced the method that would soon be adopted by nearly every studio in Hollywood: a technology that allowed filmmakers to squeeze a wide-angle image onto conventional 35-mm film stock, thereby increasing the aspect ratio (the ratio of a screen's width to its height) of their images. This wide-screen format increased the immersive quality of the theater experience. Nonetheless, even with these advancements, movie attendance never again reached the record numbers it experienced in 1946, at the peak of the Golden Age of Hollywood (Britannica Online).

Mass Entertainment, Mass Paranoia: HUAC and the Hollywood Blacklist

The Cold War with the Soviet Union began in 1947, and with it came the widespread fear of communism, not only from the outside, but equally from within. To undermine this perceived threat, the House Un-American Activities Committee (HUAC) commenced investigations to locate communist sympathizers in America who were suspected of conducting espionage for the Soviet Union. In the highly conservative and paranoid atmosphere of the time, Hollywood, the source of a mass-cultural medium, came under fire in response to fears that subversive, communist messages were being embedded in films. In November 1947, more than 100 people in the movie business were called to testify before the HUAC about their and their colleagues' involvement with communist affairs. Of those investigated, 10 in particular refused to cooperate with the committee's questions. These 10, later known as the Hollywood Ten, were fired from their jobs and sentenced to serve up to a year in prison. The studios, already slipping in influence and profit, were eager to cooperate in order to save themselves, and a number of producers signed an agreement stating that no communists would work in Hollywood.

The hearings, which recommenced in 1951 with the rise of Senator Joseph McCarthy's influence, turned into a kind of witch hunt as witnesses were asked to testify against their associates, and a blacklist of suspected communists evolved. Over 324 individuals lost their jobs in the film industry as a result of blacklisting (the denial of work in a certain field or industry) and HUAC investigations (Georgakas, 2004; Mills, 2007; Dressler, et. al., 2005).

Down With the Establishment: Youth Culture of the 1960s and 1970s

Movies of the late 1960s began attracting a younger demographic, as a growing number of young people were drawn in by films like Sam Peckinpah's *The Wild Bunch* (1969), Stanley Kubrick's *2001: A Space Odyssey* (1968), Arthur Penn's *Bonnie and Clyde* (1967), and Dennis Hopper's *Easy Rider* (1969)—all revolutionary in their genres—that displayed a sentiment of unrest toward conventional social orders and included some of the earliest instances of realistic and brutal violence in film. These four films in particular grossed so much money at the box offices that producers began churning out low-budget copycats to draw in a new, profitable market (Motion Pictures). While this led to a rise in youth-culture films, few of them saw great success. However, the new liberal attitudes toward depictions of sex and violence in these films represented a sea of change in the movie industry that manifested in many movies of the 1970s, including Francis Ford Coppola's *The Godfather* (1972), William Friedkin's *The Exorcist* (1973), and Steven Spielberg's *Jaws* (1975), all three of which saw great financial success (Britannica Online; Belton, 1994).

Blockbusters, Knockoffs, and Sequels

In the 1970s, with the rise of work by Coppola, Spielberg, George Lucas, Martin Scorsese, and others, a new breed of director emerged. These directors were young and film-school educated, and they contributed a sense of professionalism, sophistication, and technical mastery to their work, leading to a wave of blockbuster productions, including *Close Encounters of the Third Kind* (1977), *Star Wars* (1977), *Raiders of the Lost Ark* (1981), and *E.T.: The Extra-Terrestrial* (1982). The computer-generated special effects that were available at this time also contributed to the success of a number of large-budget productions. In response to these and several earlier blockbusters, movie production and marketing techniques also began to shift, with studios investing more money in fewer films in the hopes of producing more big successes. For the first time, the hefty sums producers and distributers invested didn't go to production costs alone; distributers were discovering the benefits of TV and radio advertising and finding that doubling their advertising costs could increase profits as much as three or four times over. With the opening of *Jaws*, one of the five top-grossing films of the decade (and the highest grossing film of all time until the release of *Star Wars* in 1977), Hollywood embraced the wide-release method of movie distribution, abandoning the release methods of earlier decades, in which a film would debut in only a handful of select theaters in major cities before it became gradually available to mass audiences. *Jaws* was released in 600 theaters simultaneously, and the big-budget films that followed came out in anywhere from 800 to 2,000 theaters nationwide on their opening weekends (Belton; Hanson & Garcia-Myers, 2000).

The major Hollywood studios of the late 1970s and early 1980s, now run by international corporations, tended to favor the conservative gamble of the tried and true, and as a result, the period saw an unprecedented number of high-budget sequels—as in the *Star Wars*, *Indiana Jones*, and *Godfather* films—as well as imitations and adaptations of earlier successful material, such as the plethora of "slasher" films that followed the success of the 1979 thriller *Halloween*. Additionally, corporations sought revenue sources beyond the movie theater, looking to the video and cable releases of their films. Introduced in 1975, the VCR became nearly ubiquitous in American homes by 1998 with 88.9 million households owning the appliance (Rosen & Meier, 2000). Cable television's growth was slower, but ownership of VCRs gave people a new reason to subscribe, and cable subsequently expanded as well (Rogers). And the newly introduced concept of film-based merchandise (toys, games, books, etc.) allowed companies to increase profits even more.

The 1990s and Beyond

The 1990s saw the rise of two divergent strands of cinema: the technically spectacular blockbuster with special, computer-generated effects and the independent, low-budget film. The capabilities of special effects were enhanced when studios began manipulating film digitally. Early examples of this technology can be seen in *Terminator 2: Judgment Day* (1991) and *Jurassic Park* (1993). Films with an epic scope—*Independence Day* (1996), *Titanic* (1997), and *The Matrix* (1999)—also employed a range of computer-animation techniques and special effects to wow audiences and to draw more viewers to the big screen. *Toy Story* (1995), the first fully computer-animated film, and those that came after it, such as *Antz* (1998), *A Bug's Life* (1998), and *Toy Story 2* (1999), displayed the improved capabilities of computer-generated animation (Sedman, 2000). At the same time, independent directors and producers, such as the Coen brothers and Spike Jonze, experienced an increased popularity, often for lower-budget films that audiences were more likely to watch on video at home (Britannica Online). A prime example of this is the 1996 Academy Awards program, when independent films dominated the Best Picture category. Only one movie from a big film studio was nominated—*Jerry Maguire*—while the rest were independent films. The growth of both independent movies and special-effects-laden blockbusters continues to the present day. You will read more about current issues and trends and the future of the movie industry later on in this chapter.

Key Takeaways

- The concept of the motion picture was first introduced to a mass audience through Thomas Edison's kinetoscope in 1891. However, it wasn't until the Lumière brothers released the cinématographe in 1895 that motion pictures were projected for audience viewing. In the United States, film established itself as a popular form of entertainment with the nickelodeon theater in the 1910s.

- The release of *The Jazz Singer* in 1927 marked the birth of the talking film, and by 1930 silent film was a thing of the past. Technicolor emerged for film around the same time and found early success with movies like *The Wizard of Oz* and *Gone With the Wind*. However, people would continue to make films in black and white until the late 1950s.

- By 1915 most of the major film studios had moved to Hollywood. During the Golden Age of Hollywood, these major studios controlled every aspect of the movie industry, and the films they produced drew crowds to theaters in numbers that have still not been surpassed. After World War II, the studio system declined as a result of antitrust legislation that took power away from studios and of the invention of the television.

- During the 1960s and 1970s, there was a rise in films—including *Bonnie and Clyde*, *The Wild Bunch*, *2001: A Space Odyssey*, and *Easy Rider*—that celebrated the emerging youth culture and a rejection of the conservatism of the previous decades. This also led to looser attitudes toward depictions of sexuality and violence in film. The 1970s and 1980s saw the rise of the blockbuster, with films like *Jaws*, *Star Wars*, *Raiders of the Lost Ark*, and *The Godfather*.

- The adoption of the VCR by most households in the 1980s reduced audiences at movie theaters but opened a new mass market of home movie viewers. Improvements in computer animation led to more special effects in film during the 1990s with movies like *The Matrix*, *Jurassic Park*, and the first fully computer-animated film, *Toy Story*.

Exercises

Identify four films that you would consider to be representative of major developments in the industry and in film as a medium that were outlined in this section. Imagine you are using these films to explain movie history to a friend. Provide a detailed explanation of why each of these films represents significant changes in attitudes, technology, or trends and situate each in the overall context of film's development. Consider the following questions:

1. How did this movie influence the film industry?

2. What has been the lasting impact of this movie on the film industry?

3. How was the film industry and technology different before this film?

References

Baers, Michael. "Studio System," in *St. James Encyclopedia of Popular Culture*, ed. Sara Pendergast and Tom Pendergast (Detroit: St. James Press, 2000), vol. 4, 565.

Balcanasu, Andrei Ionut, Sergey V. Smagin, and Stephanie K. Thrift, "Edison and the Lumiere Brothers," *Cartoons and Cinema of the 20th Century,* http://library.thinkquest.org/C0118600/index.phtml?menu=en%3B1%3Bci1001.html.

Belton, *American Cinema/American Culture,* 305.

Belton, John. *American Cinema/American Culture.* (New York: McGraw-Hill, 1994), 284–290.

Britannica Online, s.v. "History of the Motion Picture".

Britannica Online, s.v. "Kinetoscope," http://www.britannica.com/EBchecked/topic/318211/Kinetoscope/318211main/Article.

Britannica Online, s.v. "nickelodeon."

Britannica Online. s.v. "History of the Motion Picture." http://www.britannica.com/EBchecked/topic/394161/history-of-the-motion picture; Robinson, *From Peep Show to Palace,* 45, 53.

British Movie Classics, "The Kinetoscope," British Movie Classics, http://www.britishmovieclassics.com/thekinetoscope.php.

Dictionary of American History, 3rd ed., s.v. "Nickelodeon," by Ryan F. Holznagel, Gale Virtual Reference Library.

Dresler, Kathleen, Kari Lewis, Tiffany Schoser and Cathy Nordine, "The Hollywood Ten," Dalton Trumbo, 2005, http://www.mcpld.org/trumbo/WebPages/hollywoodten.htm.

Encyclopedia of Communication and Information (New York: MacMillan Reference USA, 2002), s.v. "Méliès, Georges," by Ted C. Jones, Gale Virtual Reference Library.

Encyclopedia of the Age of Industry and Empire, s.v. "Cinema."

Fielding, Raymond *A Technological History of Motion Pictures and Television* (Berkeley: California Univ. Press, 1967) 21.

Gale Virtual Reference Library, "Motion Pictures in Color," in *American Decades,* ed. Judith S. Baughman and others, vol. 3, Gale Virtual Reference Library.

Gale Virtual Reference Library, Europe 1789–1914: Encyclopedia of the Age of Industry and Empire, vol. 1, s.v. "Cinema," by Alan Williams, Gale Virtual Reference Library.

Georgakas, Dan. "Hollywood Blacklist," in *Encyclopedia of the American Left,* ed. Mari Jo Buhle, Paul Buhle, and Dan Georgakas, 2004, http://writing.upenn.edu/~afilreis/50s/blacklist.html.

Gochenour, "Birth of the 'Talkies,'" 578.

Gochenour, Phil. "Birth of the 'Talkies': The Development of Synchronized Sound for Motion Pictures," in *Science and Its Times,* vol. 6, *1900–1950,* ed. Neil Schlager and Josh Lauer (Detroit: Gale, 2000), 577.

Hanson, Steve and Sandra Garcia-Myers, "Blockbusters," in *St. James Encyclopedia of Popular Culture*, ed. Sara Pendergast and Tom Pendergast (Detroit: St. James Press, 2000), vol. 1, 282.

Higham, Charles. *The Art of the American Film: 1900–1971*. (Garden City: Doubleday & Company, 1973), 85.

Menand, Louis "Gross Points," *New Yorker*, February 7, 2005, http://www.newyorker.com/archive/2005/02/07/050207crat_atlarge.

Mills, Michael. "Blacklist: A Different Look at the 1947 HUAC Hearings," Modern Times, 2007, http://www.moderntimes.com/blacklist/.

Motion Picture Association of America, "History of the MPAA," http://www.mpaa.org/about/history.

Motion Pictures in Color, "Motion Pictures in Color."

Motion Pictures, "Griffith," *Motion Pictures*, http://www.uv.es/EBRIT/macro/macro_5004_39_6.html#0011.

Motion Pictures, "Post World War I US Cinema," *Motion Pictures*, http://www.uv.es/EBRIT/macro/macro_5004_39_10.html#0015.

Motion Pictures, "Pre World War II Sound Era: Introduction of Sound," *Motion Pictures*, http://www.uv.es/EBRIT/macro/macro_5004_39_11.html#0017.
Motion Pictures, "Pre World-War I US Cinema," *Motion Pictures: The Silent Feature: 1910-27*, http://www.uv.es/EBRIT/macro/macro_5004_39_4.html#0009.

Motion Pictures, "Recent Trends in US Cinema," *Motion Pictures*, http://www.uv.es/EBRIT/macro/macro_5004_39_37.html#0045.

Motion Pictures, "The War Years and Post World War II Trends: Decline of the Hollywood Studios," *Motion Pictures*, http://www.uv.es/EBRIT/macro/macro_5004_39_24.html#0030.

Robinson, *From Peep Show to Palace*, 135, 144.

Robinson, *From Peep Show to Palace*, 63.

Robinson, *From Peep Show to Palace*, 74–75; *Encyclopedia of the Age of Industry and Empire*, s.v. "Cinema."

Robinson, David. *From Peep Show to Palace: The Birth of American Film* (New York: Columbia University Press, 1994), 43–44.

Rogers, Everett. "Video is Here to Stay," *Center for Media Literacy*, http://www.medialit.org/reading-room/video-here-stay.

Rosen, Karen and Alan Meier, "Power Measurements and National Energy Consumption of Televisions and Video Cassette Recorders in the USA," *Energy*, 25, no. 3 (2000), 220.

Sedman, David. "Film Industry, Technology of," in *Encyclopedia of Communication and Information*, ed. Jorge Reina Schement (New York: MacMillan Reference, 2000), vol. 1, 340.

8.3 Movies and Culture

Movies Mirror Culture

The relationship between movies and culture involves a complicated dynamic; while American movies certainly influence the mass culture that consumes them, they are also an integral part of that culture, a product of it, and therefore a reflection of prevailing concerns, attitudes, and beliefs. In considering the relationship between film and culture, it is important to keep in mind that, while certain ideologies may be prevalent in a given era, not only is American culture as diverse as the populations that form it, but it is also constantly changing from one period to the next. Mainstream films produced in the late 1940s and into the 1950s, for example, reflected the conservatism that dominated the sociopolitical arenas of the time. However, by the 1960s, a reactionary youth culture began to emerge in opposition to the dominant institutions, and these antiestablishment views soon found their way onto the screen—a far cry from the attitudes most commonly represented only a few years earlier.

In one sense, movies could be characterized as America's storytellers. Not only do Hollywood films reflect certain commonly held attitudes and beliefs about what it means to be American, but they also portray contemporary trends, issues, and events, serving as records of the eras in which they were produced. Consider, for example, films about the September 11, 2001, terrorist attacks: *Fahrenheit 9/11*, *World Trade Center*, *United 93*, and others. These films grew out of a seminal event of the time, one that preoccupied the consciousness of Americans for years after it occurred.

Birth of a Nation

In 1915, director D. W. Griffith established his reputation with the highly successful film *The Birth of a Nation*, based on Thomas Dixon's novel *The Clansman*, a prosegregation narrative about the American South during and after the Civil War. At the time, *The Birth of a Nation* was the longest feature film ever made, at almost

3 hours, and contained huge battle scenes that amazed and delighted audiences. Griffith's storytelling ability helped solidify the narrative style that would go on to dominate feature films. He also experimented with editing techniques such as close-ups, jump cuts, and parallel editing that helped make the film an artistic achievement.

Griffith's film found success largely because it captured the social and cultural tensions of the era. As American studies specialist Lary May has argued, "[Griffith's] films dramatized every major concern of the day (May, 1997)." In the early 20th century, fears about recent waves of immigrants had led to certain racist attitudes in mass culture, with "scientific" theories of the time purporting to link race with inborn traits like intelligence and other capabilities. Additionally, the dominant political climate, largely a reaction against populist labor movements, was one of conservative elitism, eager to attribute social inequalities to natural human differences (Darity). According to a report by the New York *Evening Post* after the film's release, even some Northern audiences "clapped when the masked riders took vengeance on Negroes (Higham)." However, the outrage many groups expressed about the film is a good reminder that American culture is not monolithic, that there are always strong contingents in opposition to dominant ideologies.

While critics praised the film for its narrative complexity and epic scope, many others were outraged and even started riots at several screenings because of its highly controversial, openly racist attitudes, which glorified the Ku Klux Klan and blamed Southern Blacks for the destruction of the war (Higham). Many Americans joined the National Association for the Advancement of Colored People (NAACP) in denouncing the film, and the National Board of Review eventually cut a number of the film's racist sections (May). However, it's important to keep in mind the attitudes of the early 1900s. At the time the nation was divided, and Jim Crow laws and segregation were enforced. Nonetheless, *The Birth of a Nation* was the highest grossing movie of its era. In 1992, the film was classified by the Library of Congress among the "culturally, historically, or aesthetically significant films" in U.S. history.

Figure 8.6

The Birth of a Nation expressed racial tensions of the early 20th century.

"The American Way"

Until the bombing of Pearl Harbor in 1941, American films after World War I generally reflected the neutral, isolationist stance that prevailed in politics and culture. However, after the United States was drawn into the war in Europe, the government enlisted Hollywood to help with the war effort, opening the federal Bureau of Motion Picture Affairs in Los Angeles. Bureau officials served in an advisory capacity on the production of war-related films, an effort with which the studios cooperated. As a result, films tended toward the patriotic and were produced to inspire feelings of pride and confidence in being American and to clearly establish that America and its allies were forces of good. For instance, critically acclaimed *Casablanca* paints a picture of the ill effects of fascism, illustrates the values that heroes like Victor Laszlo hold, and depicts America as a place for refugees to find democracy and freedom (Digital History).

These early World War II films were sometimes overtly propagandist, intended to influence American attitudes rather than present a genuine reflection of American sentiments toward the war. Frank Capra's *Why We Fight* films, for example, the first of which was produced in 1942, were developed for the U.S. Army and were later shown to general audiences; they delivered a war message through narrative (Koppes & Black, 1987). As the war continued, however, filmmakers opted to forego patriotic themes for a more serious reflection of American sentiments, as exemplified by films like Alfred Hitchcock's *Lifeboat*.

Youth versus Age: From Counterculture to Mass Culture

In Mike Nichols's 1967 film *The Graduate*, Dustin Hoffman, as the film's protagonist, enters into a romantic affair with the wife of his father's business partner. However, Mrs. Robinson and the other adults in the film fail to understand the young, alienated hero, who eventually rebels against them. *The Graduate*, which brought in more than $44 million at the box office, reflected the attitudes of many members of a young generation growing increasingly dissatisfied with what they perceived to be the repressive social codes established by their more conservative elders (Dirks).

This baby boomer generation came of age during the Korean and Vietnam wars. Not only did the youth culture express a cynicism toward the patriotic, prowar stance of their World War II–era elders, but they displayed a fierce resistance toward institutional authority in general, an antiestablishmentism epitomized in the 1967 hit film *Bonnie and Clyde*. In the film, a young, outlaw couple sets out on a cross-country bank-robbing spree until they're killed in a violent police ambush at the film's close (Belton).

Figure 8.7

Bonnie and Clyde reflected the attitudes of a rising youth culture.

Wikimedia Commons – public domain.

Bonnie and Clyde's violence provides one example of the ways films at the time were testing the limits of permissible on-screen material. The youth culture's liberal attitudes toward formally taboo subjects like sexuality and drugs began to emerge in film during the late 1960s. Like *Bonnie and Clyde*, Sam Peckinpah's 1969 Western *The Wild Bunch*, displays an early example of aestheticized violence in film. The wildly popular *Easy Rider* (1969)—containing drugs, sex, and violence—may owe a good deal of its initial success to liberalized audiences. And in the same year, *Midnight Cowboy*, one of the first Hollywood films to receive an X rating (in this case for its sexual content), won three Academy Awards, including Best Picture (Belton). As the release and subsequently successful reception of these films attest, what at the decade's outset had been countercultural had, by the decade's close, become mainstream.

The Hollywood Production Code

When the MPAA (originally MPPDA) first banded together in 1922 to combat government censorship and to promote artistic freedom, the association attempted a system of self-regulation. However, by 1930—in part because of the transition to talking pictures—renewed criticism and calls for censorship from conservative groups made it clear to the MPPDA that the loose system of self-regulation was not enough protection. As a result, the MPPDA instituted the Production Code, or Hays Code (after MPPDA director William H. Hays), which remained in place until 1967. The code, which according to motion picture producers concerned itself with ensuring that movies were "directly responsible for spiritual or moral progress, for higher types of social life, and for much correct thinking (History Matters)," was strictly enforced starting in 1934, putting an end to most public complaints. However, many people in Hollywood resented its restrictiveness. After a series of Supreme Court cases in the 1950s regarding the code's restrictions to freedom of speech, the Production Code grew weaker until it was finally replaced in 1967 with the MPAA rating system (American Decades Primary Sources, 2004).

MPAA Ratings

As films like *Bonnie and Clyde* and *Who's Afraid of Virginia Woolf?* (1966) tested the limits on violence and language, it became clear that the Production Code was in need of replacement. In 1968, the MPAA adopted a ratings system to identify films in terms of potentially objectionable content. By providing officially designated categories for films that would not have passed Production Code standards of the past, the MPAA opened a way for films to deal openly with mature content. The ratings system originally included four categories: G (suitable for general audiences), M (equivalent to the PG rating of today), R (restricted to adults over age 16), and X (equivalent to today's NC-17).

The MPAA rating systems, with some modifications, is still in place today. Before release in theaters, films are submitted to the MPAA board for a screening, during which advisers decide on the most appropriate rating based on the film's content. However, studios are not required to have the MPAA screen releases ahead of time—some studios release films without the MPAA rating at all. Commercially, less restrictive ratings are generally more beneficial, particularly in the case of adult-themed films that have the potential to earn the most restrictive rating, the NC-17. Some movie theaters will not screen a movie that is rated NC-17. When filmmakers get a more restrictive rating than they were hoping for, they may resubmit the film for review after editing out objectionable scenes (Dick, 2006).

The New War Film: Cynicism and Anxiety

Unlike the patriotic war films of the World War II era, many of the films about U.S. involvement in Vietnam reflected strong antiwar sentiment, criticizing American political policy and portraying war's damaging effects on those who survived it. Films like *Dr. Strangelove* (1964), *M*A*S*H* (1970), *The Deer Hunter* (1978), and *Apocalypse Now* (1979) portray the military establishment in a negative light and dissolve clear-cut distinctions, such as the "us versus them" mentality, of earlier war films. These, and the dozens of Vietnam War films that were produced in the 1970s and 1980s—Oliver Stone's *Platoon* (1986) and *Born on the Fourth of July* (1989) and Stanley Kubrick's *Full Metal Jacket* (1987), for example—reflect the sense of defeat and lack of closure Americans felt after the Vietnam War and the emotional and psychological scars it left on the nation's psyche (Dirks, 2010; Anderegg, 1991). A spate of military and politically themed films emerged during the 1980s as

America recovered from defeat in Vietnam, while at the same time facing anxieties about the ongoing Cold War with the Soviet Union.

Fears about the possibility of nuclear war were very real during the 1980s, and some film critics argue that these anxieties were reflected not only in overtly political films of the time but also in the popularity of horror films, like *Halloween* and *Friday the 13th*, which feature a mysterious and unkillable monster, and in the popularity of the fantastic in films like *E.T.: The Extra-Terrestrial*, *Raiders of the Lost Ark*, and *Star Wars*, which offer imaginative escapes (Wood, 1986).

Movies Shape Culture

Just as movies reflect the anxieties, beliefs, and values of the cultures that produce them, they also help to shape and solidify a culture's beliefs. Sometimes the influence is trivial, as in the case of fashion trends or figures of speech. After the release of *Flashdance* in 1983, for instance, torn T-shirts and leg warmers became hallmarks of the fashion of the 1980s (Pemberton-Sikes, 2006). However, sometimes the impact can be profound, leading to social or political reform, or the shaping of ideologies.

Film and the Rise of Mass Culture

During the 1890s and up until about 1920, American culture experienced a period of rapid industrialization. As people moved from farms to centers of industrial production, urban areas began to hold larger and larger concentrations of the population. At the same time, film and other methods of mass communication (advertising and radio) developed, whose messages concerning tastes, desires, customs, speech, and behavior spread from these population centers to outlying areas across the country. The effect of early mass-communication media was to wear away regional differences and create a more homogenized, standardized culture.

Film played a key role in this development, as viewers began to imitate the speech, dress, and behavior of their common heroes on the silver screen (Mintz, 2007). In 1911, the Vitagraph company began publishing *The Motion Picture Magazine*, America's first fan magazine. Originally conceived as a marketing tool to keep audiences interested in Vitagraph's pictures and major actors, *The Motion Picture Magazine* helped create the concept of the film star in the American imagination. Fans became obsessed with the off-screen lives of their favorite celebrities, like Pearl White, Florence Lawrence, and Mary Pickford (Doyle, 2008).

American Myths and Traditions

American identity in mass society is built around certain commonly held beliefs, or myths about shared experiences, and these American myths are often disseminated through or reinforced by film. One example of a popular American myth, one that dates back to the writings of Thomas Jefferson and other founders, is an emphasis on individualism—a celebration of the common man or woman as a hero or reformer. With the rise of mass culture, the myth of the individual became increasingly appealing because it provided people with a sense of autonomy and individuality in the face of an increasingly homogenized culture. The hero myth finds embodiment in the Western, a film genre that was popular from the silent era through the 1960s, in which the lone cowboy, a seminomadic wanderer, makes his way in a lawless, and often dangerous, frontier. An example is 1952's *High Noon*. From 1926 until 1967, Westerns accounted for nearly a quarter of all films produced. In other films, like

Frank Capra's 1946 movie *It's a Wonderful Life*, the individual triumphs by standing up to injustice, reinforcing the belief that one person can make a difference in the world (Belton). And in more recent films, hero figures such as Indiana Jones, Luke Skywalker (*Star Wars*), and Neo (*The Matrix*) have continued to emphasize individualism.

Social Issues in Film

As D. W. Griffith recognized nearly a century ago, film has enormous power as a medium to influence public opinion. Ever since Griffith's *The Birth of a Nation* sparked strong public reactions in 1915, filmmakers have been producing movies that address social issues, sometimes subtly, and sometimes very directly. More recently, films like *Hotel Rwanda* (2004), about the 1994 Rwandan genocide, or *The Kite Runner* (2007), a story that takes place in the midst of a war-torn Afghanistan, have captured audience imaginations by telling stories that raise social awareness about world events. And a number of documentary films directed at social issues have had a strong influence on cultural attitudes and have brought about significant change.

In the 2000s, documentaries, particularly those of an activist nature, were met with greater interest than ever before. Films like *Super Size Me* (2004), which documents the effects of excessive fast-food consumption and criticizes the fast-food industry for promoting unhealthy eating habits for profit, and *Food, Inc.* (2009), which examines corporate farming practices and points to the negative impact these practices can have on human health and the environment, have brought about important changes in American food culture (Severson, 2009). Just 6 weeks after the release of *Super Size Me*, McDonald's took the supersize option off its menu and since 2004 has introduced a number of healthy food options in its restaurants (Sood, 2004). Other fast-food chains have made similar changes (Sood, 2004).

Other documentaries intended to influence cultural attitudes and inspire change include those made by director Michael Moore. Moore's films present a liberal stance on social and political issues such as health care, globalization, and gun control. His 2002 film *Bowling for Columbine*, for example, addressed the Columbine High School shootings of 1999, presenting a critical examination of American gun culture. While some critics have accused Moore of producing propagandistic material under the label of documentary because of his films' strong biases, his films have been popular with audiences, with four of his documentaries ranking among the highest grossing documentaries of all time. *Fahrenheit 9/11* (2004), which criticized the second Bush administration and its involvement in the Iraq War, earned $119 million at the box office, making it the most successful documentary of all time (Dirks, 2006).

Key Takeaways

- As products of mass culture, movies reflect cultural attitudes, trends, and concerns:

  1. D. W. Griffith's film *The Birth of a Nation*, presenting a racist perspective on the U.S. Civil War and its aftermath, reflected racist concerns of the era in which it was produced.

  2. During World War II, films reflected the patriotic, prowar sentiments of the time.

  3. In the 1960s and 1970s with the rise of an antiestablishment youth culture, movies adopted more liberal stances toward sexuality and violence and displayed a cynicism toward established

social structures.

- After the failure of the Vietnam War, films reflected a more ambivalent attitude toward war.

- The MPAA rating system, established in 1968, gave filmmakers greater freedom in the content they were able to portray on screen.

- Movies shape cultural attitudes and customs, as audiences adopt the attitudes and styles of the characters they watch on screen. Filmmakers may use their movies to influence cultural attitudes toward certain social issues, as in *Fahrenheit 9/11* and *Super Size Me*.

Exercises

1. Consider three films you have watched in the last year. In what ways have these films reflected current concerns, trends, or attitudes? Of these movies, which do you think have the most potential to shape cultural attitudes or bring about social change? How do you think these movies might bring about this change?

2. Locate a film that has been remade and watch the original and remade versions. Besides the obvious changes in fashion and technology, what other differences do you notice that reflect the cultural attitudes, trends, and events in which each film was produced?

References

American Decades Primary Sources, "The Production Code of the Motion Picture Producers and Distributers of America, Inc.—1930–1934," *American Decades Primary Sources*, ed. Cynthia Rose (Detroit: Gale, 2004), vol. 4, 12–15.

Anderegg, Michael. introduction to *Inventing Vietnam: The War in Film and Television*, ed. Michael Anderegg (Philadelphia: Temple University Press, 1991), 6–8.

Belton, *American Cinema/American Culture*, 286.

Belton, John. introduction to *Movies and Mass Culture*, ed. John Belton, 12.

Darity, William A. "Birth of a Nation," *Encyclopedia of the Social Sciences*, 2nd ed., ed. William A. Darity, Jr., Gale Virtual Reference Library, 1:305–306.

Dick, Kirby. interview by Terry Gross, *Fresh Air*, NPR, September 13, 2006, http://www.npr.org/templates/story/story.php?storyId=6068009.

Digital History, Review of *Casablanca*, directed by Michael Curtiz, Digital History, http://www.digitalhistory.uh.edu/historyonline/bureau_casablanca.cfm.

Dirks, Tim. "1980s Film History," Filmsite, 2010, http://www.filmsite.org.

Dirks, Tim. "Film History of the 2000s," *Filmsite; Washington Post*, "The 10 Highest-Grossing Documentaries," July 31, 2006, http://www.washingtonpost.com/wp-dyn/content/graphic/2006/07/31/GR2006073100027.html.

Dirks, Tim. review of *The Graduate*, directed by Mike Nichols, Filmsite, http://www.filmsite.org/grad.html.

Doyle, Jack. "A Star is Born: 1910s," *Pop History Dig*, 2008, http://www.pophistorydig.com/?tag=film-stars-mass-culture.

Higham, *Art of the American Film*, 13.

History Matters, "Complete Nudity is Never Permitted: The Motion Picture Code of 1930," http://historymatters.gmu.edu/d/5099/.

Koppes, Clayton R. and Gregory D. Black, *Hollywood Goes to War: How Politics, Profits and Propaganda Shaped World War II Movies* (Los Angeles: The Free Press, 1987), 122.

May, "Apocalyptic Cinema," 46.

May, Lary. "Apocalyptic Cinema: D. W. Griffith and the Aesthetics of Reform," in *Movies and Mass Culture*, ed. John Belton (New Brunswick, NJ: Rutgers University Press, 1997), 26.

Mintz, Steven. "The Formation of Modern American Mass Culture," *Digital History*, 2007, http://www.digitalhistory.uh.edu/database/article_display.cfm?HHID=455.

Pemberton-Sikes, Diana. "15 Movies That Inspired Fashion Trends," *The Clothing Chronicles*, March 3, 2006, http://www.theclothingchronicles.com/archives/217-03032006.htm.

Severson, Kim. "Eat, Drink, Think, Change," *New York Times*, June 3, 2009, http://www.nytimes.com/2009/06/07/movies/07seve.html.

Sood, Suemedha. "Weighing the Impact of 'Super Size Me,'" *Wiretap*, June 29, 2004. http://www.wiretapmag.org/stories/19059/.

Wood, Robin. *Hollywood from Vietnam to Reagan* (New York: Columbia University Press, 1986), 168.

8.4 Issues and Trends in Film

Learning Objectives

1. Recognize the role the major Hollywood studios have in shaping the movie industry today.
2. Identify the major economic concerns involved in the production and distribution of films.
3. Describe the effects of piracy on the movie industry.

Filmmaking is both a commercial and artistic venture. The current economic situation in the film industry, with increased production and marketing costs and lower audience turnouts in theaters, often sets the standard for the films big studios are willing to invest in. If you wonder why theaters have released so many remakes and sequels in recent years, this section may help you to understand the motivating factors behind those decisions.

The Influence of Hollywood

In the movie industry today, publicity and product are two sides of the same coin. Even films that get a lousy critical reception can do extremely well in ticket sales if their marketing campaigns manage to create enough hype. Similarly, two comparable films can produce very different results at the box office if they have been given different levels of publicity. This explains why the film *What Women Want*, starring Mel Gibson, brought in $33.6 million in its opening weekend in 2000, while a few months later, *The Million Dollar Hotel*, also starring Gibson, only brought in $29,483 during its opening weekend (Nash Information Services, 2000; Nash Information Services, 2001). Unlike in the days of the Hollywood studio system, no longer do the actors alone draw audiences to a movie. The owners of the nation's major movie theater chains are keenly aware that a film's success at the box office has everything to do with studio-generated marketing and publicity. *What Women Want* was produced by Paramount, one of the film industry's six leading studios, and widely released (on 3,000 screens) after an extensive marketing effort, while *The Million Dollar Hotel* was produced by Lionsgate, an independent studio without the necessary marketing budget to fill enough seats for a wide release on opening weekend (Epstein, 2005).

The Hollywood "dream factory," as Hortense Powdermaker labeled it in her 1950 book on the movie industry (Powdermaker), manufactures an experience that is part art and part commercial product (James, 1989). While the studios of today are less factory-like than they were in the vertically integrated studio system era, the coordinated efforts of a film's production team can still be likened to a machine calibrated for mass production. The films the studios churn out are the result of a capitalist enterprise that ultimately looks to the "bottom line" to guide most major decisions. Hollywood is an industry, and as in any other industry in a mass market, its success relies on control of production resources and "raw materials" and on its access to mass distribution and marketing strategies to maximize the product's reach and minimize competition (Belton). In this way, Hollywood has an enormous influence on the films to which the public has access.

Ever since the rise of the studio system in the 1930s, the majority of films have originated with the leading Hollywood studios. Today, the six big studios control 95 percent of the film business (Dick). In the early years, audiences were familiar with the major studios, their collections of actors and directors, and the types of films that each studio was likely to release. All of that changed with the decline of the studio system; screenwriters, directors, scripts, and cinematographers no longer worked exclusively with one studio, so these days, while moviegoers are likely to know the name of a film's director and major actors, it's unusual for them to identify a film with the studio that distributes it. However, studios are no less influential. The previews of coming attractions that play before a movie begins are controlled by the studios (Busis, 2010). Online marketing, TV commercials, and advertising partnerships with other industries—the name of an upcoming film, for instance, appearing on some Coke cans—are available tools for the big-budget studios that have the resources to commit millions to prerelease advertising. Even though studios no longer own the country's movie theater chains, the films produced by the big six studios are the ones the multiplexes invariably show. Unlike films by independents, it's a safe bet that big studio movies are the ones that will sell tickets.

The Blockbuster Standard

While it may seem like the major studios are making heavy profits, moviemaking today is a much riskier, less profitable enterprise than it was in the studio system era. The massive budgets required for the global marketing of a film are huge financial gambles. In fact, most movies cost the studios much more to market and produce—upward of $100 million—than their box-office returns ever generate. With such high stakes, studios have come to rely on the handful of blockbuster films that keep them afloat (New World Encyclopedia), movies like *Titanic*, *Pirates of the Caribbean*, and *Avatar* (New World Encyclopedia). The blockbuster film becomes a touchstone, not only for production values and story lines, but also for moviegoers' expectations. Because studios know they can rely on certain predictable elements to draw audiences, they tend to invest the majority of their budgets on movies that fit the blockbuster mold. Remakes, movies with sequel setups, or films based on best-selling novels or comic books are safer bets than original screenplays or movies with experimental or edgy themes.

James Cameron's *Titanic* (1997), the second highest grossing movie of all time, saw such success largely because it was based on a well-known story, contained predictable plot elements, and was designed to appeal to the widest possible range of audience demographics with romance, action, expensive special effects, and an epic scope—meeting the blockbuster standard on several levels. The film's astronomical $200 million production cost was a gamble indeed, requiring the backing of two studios, Paramount and 20th Century Fox (Hansen & Garcia-Meyers). However, the rash of high-budget, and high-grossing, films that have appeared since—*Harry Potter and the Sorcerer's Stone* and its sequels (2002–2011), *Avatar* (2009), *Alice in Wonderland* (2010), *The Lord of the Rings* films (2001–2003), *The Dark Knight* (2008), and others—are an indication that, for the time being, the blockbuster standard will drive Hollywood production.

The Role of Independent Films

While the blockbuster still drives the industry, the formulaic nature of most Hollywood films of the 1980s, 1990s, and into the 2000s has opened a door for independent films to make their mark on the industry. Audiences have welcomed movies like *Fight Club* (1999), *Lost in Translation* (2003), and *Juno* (2007) as a change from standard Hollywood blockbusters. Few independent films reached the mainstream audience during the 1980s, but a number of developments in that decade paved the way for their increased popularity in the coming years. The Sundance Film Festival (originally the U.S. Film Festival) began in Park City, Utah, in 1980 as a way for independent filmmakers to showcase their work. Since then, the festival has grown to garner more public attention, and now often represents an opportunity for independents to find market backing by larger studios. In 1989, Steven Soderbergh's *sex, lies, and videotape*, released by Miramax, was the first independent to break out of the art-house circuit and find its way into the multiplexes.

In the 1990s and 2000s, independent directors like the Coen brothers, Wes Anderson, Sofia Coppola, and Quentin Tarantino made significant contributions to contemporary cinema. Tarantino's 1994 film, *Pulp Fiction*, garnered attention for its experimental narrative structure, witty dialogue, and nonchalant approach to violence. It was the first independent film to break $100 million at the box office, proving that there is still room in the market for movies produced outside of the big six studios (Bergan, 2006).

The Role of Foreign Films

English-born Michael Apted, former president of the Director's Guild of America, once said, "Europeans gave me the inspiration to make movies…but it was the Americans who showed me how to do it (Apted, 2007)." Major Hollywood studio films have dominated the movie industry worldwide since Hollywood's golden age, yet American films have always been in a relationship of mutual influence with films from foreign markets. From the 1940s through the 1960s, for example, American filmmakers admired and were influenced by the work of overseas auteurs—directors like Ingmar Bergman (Sweden), Federico Fellini (Italy), François Truffaut (France), and Akira Kurosawa (Japan), whose personal, creative visions were reflected in their work (Pells, 2006). The concept of the auteur was particularly important in France in the late 1950s and early 1960s when French filmmaking underwent a rebirth in the form of the New Wave movement. The French New Wave was characterized by an independent production style that showcased the personal authorship of its young directors (Bergan). The influence of the New Wave was, and continues to be, felt in the United States. The generation of young, film school-educated directors that became prominent in American cinema in the late 1960s and early 1970s owe a good deal of their stylistic techniques to the work of French New Wave directors.

Figure 8.8

The French New Wave movement of the 1950s and 1960s showed that films could be both artistically and commercially successful. Jean-Luc Godard's *Breathless* is well known for its improvisatory techniques and use of jump cuts.

Vintage Breathless Movie Poster Detail – CC BY 2.0.

In the current era of globalization, the influence of foreign films remains strong. The rapid growth of the entertainment industry in Asia, for instance, has led to an exchange of style and influence with U.S. cinema. Remakes of a number of popular Japanese horror films, including *The Ring* (2005), *Dark Water* (2005), and *The Grudge* (2004), have fared well in the United States, as have Chinese martial arts films like *Crouching Tiger, Hidden Dragon* (2000), *Hero* (2002), and *House of Flying Daggers* (2004). At the same time, U.S. studios have recently tried to expand into the growing Asian market by purchasing the rights to films from South Korea, Japan, and Hong Kong for remakes with Hollywood actors (Lee, 2005).

Cultural Imperialism or Globalization?

With the growth of Internet technology worldwide and the expansion of markets in rapidly developing countries, American films are increasingly finding their way into movie theaters and home DVD players around the world. In the eyes of many people, the problem is not the export of a U.S. product to outside markets, but the export of American culture that comes with that product. Just as films of the 1920s helped to shape a standardized, mass culture as moviegoers learned to imitate the dress and behavior of their favorite celebrities, contemporary film is now helping to form a mass culture on the global scale, as the youth of foreign nations acquire the American speech, tastes, and attitudes reflected in film (Gienow-Hecht, 2006).

Staunch critics, feeling helpless to stop the erosion of their national cultures, accuse the United States of cultural imperialism through flashy Hollywood movies and commercialism—that is, deliberate conquest of one culture by another to spread capitalism. At the same time, others argue that the worldwide impact of Hollywood films is an inevitable part of globalization, a process that erodes national borders, opening the way for a free flow of ideas between cultures (Gienow-Hecht, 2006).

The Economics of Movies

With control of over 95 percent of U.S. film production, the big six Hollywood studios—Warner Bros., Paramount, 20th Century Fox, Universal, Columbia, and Disney—are at the forefront of the American film industry, setting the standards for distribution, release, marketing, and production values. However, the high costs of moviemaking today are such that even successful studios must find moneymaking potential in crossover media—computer games, network TV rights, spin-off TV series, DVD and releases on Blu-ray Disc format, toys and other merchandise, books, and other after-market products—to help recoup their losses. The drive for aftermarket marketability in turn dictates the kinds of films studios are willing to invest in (Hansen & Garcia-Meyers).

Rising Costs and Big Budget Movies

In the days of the vertically integrated studio system, filmmaking was a streamlined process, neither as risky nor as expensive as it is today. When producers, directors, screenwriters, art directors, actors, cinematographers, and other technical staff were all under contract with one studio, turnaround time for the casting and production of a film was often as little as 3 to 4 months. Beginning in the 1970s, after the decline of the studio system, the production costs for films increased dramatically, forcing the studios to invest more of their budgets in marketing efforts that could generate presales—that is, sales of distribution rights for a film in different sectors before the movie's release (Hansen & Garcia-Meyers). This is still true of filmmaking today. With contracts that must be negotiated with actors, directors, and screenwriters, and with extended production times, costs are exponentially higher than they were in the 1930s—when a film could be made for around $300,000 (Schaefer, 1999). By contrast, today's average production budget, not including marketing expenses, is close to $65 million today (Nash Information Services).

Consider James Cameron's *Avatar*, released in 2009, which cost close to $340 million, making it one of the most expensive films of all time. Where does such an astronomical budget go? When weighing the total costs of producing and releasing a film, about half of the money goes to advertising. In the case of *Avatar*, the film cost $190 million to make and around $150 million to market (Sherkat-Massoom, 2010; Keegan, 2009). Of that $190 million production budget, part goes toward above-the-line costs, those that are negotiated before filming begins, and part to below-the-line costs, those that are generally fixed. Above-the-line costs include screenplay rights; salaries for the writer, producer, director, and leading actors; and salaries for directors', actors', and producers' assistants. Below-the-line costs include the salaries for nonstarring cast members and technical crew, use of technical equipment, travel, locations, studio rental, and catering (Tirelli). For *Avatar*, the reported $190 million doesn't include money for research and development of 3-D filming and computer-modeling technologies required to put the film together. If these costs are factored in, the total movie budget may be closer to $500 million (Keegan). Fortunately for 20th Century Fox, *Avatar* made a profit over these expenses in box-office sales alone, raking in $750 million domestically (to make it the highest-grossing movie of all time) in the first 6 months after its release (Box Office Mojo, 2010). However, one thing you should keep in mind is that *Avatar* was released in both 2-D and 3-D. Because 3-D ticket prices are more expensive than traditional 2-D theaters, the box-office returns are inflated.

The Big Budget Flop

However, for every expensive film that has made out well at the box office, there are a handful of others that have tanked. Back in 1980, when United Artists (UA) was a major Hollywood studio, its epic western *Heaven's Gate* cost nearly six times its original budget: $44 million instead of the proposed $7.6 million. The movie, which bombed at the box office, was the largest failure in film history at the time, losing at least $40 million, and forcing the studio to be bought out by MGM (Hall & Neale, 2010). Since then, *Heaven's Gate* has become synonymous with commercial failure in the film industry (Dirks).

More recently, the 2005 movie *Sahara* lost $78 million, making it one of the biggest financial flops in film history. The film's initial production budget of $80 million eventually doubled to $160 million, due to complications with filming in Morocco and to numerous problems with the script (Bunting, 2007).

Piracy

Movie piracy used to be perpetrated in two ways: Either someone snuck into a theater with a video camera, turning out blurred, wobbly, off-colored copies of the original film, or somebody close to the film leaked a private copy intended for reviewers. In the digital age, however, crystal-clear bootlegs of movies on DVD and the Internet are increasingly likely to appear illegally, posing a much greater threat to a film's profitability. Even safeguard techniques like digital watermarks are frequently sidestepped by tech-savvy pirates (France, 2009).

In 2009, an unfinished copy of 20th Century Fox's *X-Men Origins: Wolverine* appeared online 1 month before the movie's release date in theaters. Within a week, more than 1 million people had downloaded the pirated film. Similar situations have occurred in recent years with other major movies, including *The Hulk* (2003) and *Star Wars Episode III: Revenge of the Sith* (2005) (France, 2009). According to a 2006 study sponsored by the MPAA, Internet piracy and other methods of illegal copying cost major Hollywood studios $6.1 billion in the previous year (Hiestand, 2006). The findings of this report have since been called into question, with investigators claiming that there was no clear methodology for how researchers estimated those figures (Sandoval, 2010). Nonetheless, the ease of theft made possible by the digitization of film and improved file-sharing technologies like BitTorrent software, a peer-to-peer protocol for transferring large quantities of information between users, have put increased financial strain on the movie industry.

Key Takeaways

- A film's performance at the box office is often directly related to the studio marketing budget that backs it.

- Because of high marketing and production costs, the major studios have increasingly come to rely on blockbuster films to keep themselves profitable.

- Independent films found increased popularity in the 1990s and 2000s, in part because they represented a break from the predictable material often released by studios.

- With the rise of digital filming technology and online movies, movie piracy has become an increasing concern for Hollywood.

Exercises

In Section 8.3 "Issues and Trends in Film", you learned that blockbuster films rely on certain predictable elements to attract audiences. Think about recent blockbusters like *Alice in Wonderland*, *Avatar*, and *Pirates of the Caribbean* and consider the following:

1. What elements do these films have in common? Why do you think these elements help to sell movies?

2. How have the big Hollywood studios shaped these elements?

3. How do economic concerns, like box-office totals, promote predictable elements?

4. Have these movies been affected by piracy? If so, how? If not, why?

References

Apted, Michael. "Film's New Anxiety of Influence," *Newsweek*, December 28, 2007. http://www.newsweek.com/2007/12/27/film-s-new-anxiety-of-influence.html.

Belton, *American Cinema/American Culture*, 61–62.

Bergan, *Film*, 60.

Bergan, Ronald. *Film* (New York: Dorling Kindersley, 2006), 84.

Box Office Mojo, "Avatar," May 31, 2010, http://boxofficemojo.com/movies/?id=avatar.htm.

Bunting, Glenn F. "$78 Million of Red Ink?" *Los Angeles Times*, April 15, 2007, http://articles.latimes.com/2007/apr/15/business/fi-movie15/4.

Busis, Hillary. "How Do Movie Theaters Decide Which Trailers to Show?" *Slate*, April 15, 2010, http://www.slate.com/id/2246166/.

Dick, Kirby. interview, *Fresh Air*.

Dirks, "The History of Film: the 1980s."

Epstein, Edward Jay. "Neither the Power nor the Glory: Why Hollywood Leaves Originality to the Indies," *Slate*, October 17, 2005, http://www.slate.com/id/2128200.

France, Lisa Respers. "In Digital Age, Can Movie Piracy Be Stopped?" *CNN*, May 2, 2009, http://www.cnn.com/2009/TECH/05/01/wolverine.movie.piracy/.

Gienow-Hecht, Jessica C. E. "A European Considers the Influence of American Culture," *eJournal USA*, February 1, 2006, http://www.america.gov/st/econenglish/2008/June/20080608094132xjyrreP0.2717859.html.

Hall, Sheldon and Stephen Neale, "Super Blockbusters: 1976–1985," in *Epics, Spectacles, and Blockbusters: A Hollywood History* (Detroit: Wayne State Univ. Press, 2010), 231.

Hansen and Garcia-Meyers, "Blockbusters," 283.

Hiestand, Jesse. "MPAA Study: '05 Piracy Cost $6.1 Bil.," *Hollywood Reporter*, May 3, 2006. http://business.highbeam.com/2012/article-1G1-146544812/mpaa-study-05-piracy-cost-61-bil.

James, Caryn. "Critic's Notebook: Romanticizing Hollywood's Dream Factory," *New York Times*, November 7, 1989, http://www.nytimes.com/1989/11/07/movies/critic-s-notebook-romanticizing-hollywood-s-dream-factory.html.

Keegan, "How Much Did Avatar Really Cost?"

Keegan, Rebecca. "How Much Did Avatar Really Cost?" *Vanity Fair*, December 2009, http://www.vanityfair.com/online/oscars/2009/12/how-much-did-avatar-really-cost.html.

Lee, Diana. "Hollywood's Interest in Asian Films Leads to Globalization," UniOrb.com, December 1, 2005, http://uniorb.com/ATREND/movie.htm.

Nash Information Services, "Glossary of Movie Business Terms," The Numbers, http://www.the-numbers.com/glossary.php.

Nash Information Services, "The Million Dollar Hotel," *The Numbers: Box Office Data, Movie Stars, Idle Speculation*, http://www.the-numbers.com/2001/BHOTL.php.

Nash Information Services, "What Women Want," *The Numbers: Box Office Data, Movie Stars, Idle Speculation*, http://www.the-numbers.com/2000/WWWNT.php.

New World Encyclopedia, s.v. "Film Industry," www.newworldencyclopedia.org/entry/Hollywood.

Pells, Richard. "Is American Culture 'American'?" *eJournal USA*, February 1, 2006, http://www.america.gov/st/econ-english/2008/June/20080608102136xjyrreP0.3622858.html.

Powdermaker, Hortense. "Hollywood, the Dream Factory," http://astro.temple.edu/~ruby/wava/powder/intro.html.

Sandoval, Greg. "Feds Hampered by Incomplete MPAA Piracy Data," *CNET News*, April 19, 2010, http://news.cnet.com/8301-31001_3-20002837-261.html.

Schaefer, Eric. *"Bold! Daring! Shocking! True!": A History of Exploitation Films, 1919–1959* (Durham, NC: Duke University Press, 1999), 50.

Sherkat-Massoom, Mojgan. "10 Most Expensive Movies Ever Made," *Access Hollywood*, 2010, http://today.msnbc.msn.com/id/34368822/ns/entertainment-access_hollywood/?pg=2#ENT_AH_MostExpensiveMovies.

Tirelli, Aldo-Vincenzo "Production Budget Breakdown: The Scoop on Film Financing," *Helium*, http://www.helium.com/items/936661-production-budget-breakdown-the-scoop-on-film-financing.

8.5 The Influence of New Technology

Learning Objectives

1. Identify the impact of home-entertainment technology on the motion picture industry.

2. Recognize the role the DVD market plays in the economics of moviemaking.

3. Describe the impact of digital cinematography on the film industry.

New technologies have a profound impact, not only on the way films are made, but also on the economic structure of the film industry. When VCR technology made on-demand home movie viewing possible for the first time, filmmakers had to adapt to a changing market. The recent switch to digital technology also represents a turning point for film. In this section, you will learn how these and other technologies have changed the face of cinema.

Effects of Home Entertainment Technology

The first technology for home video recording, Sony's Betamax cassettes, hit the market in 1975. The device, a combined television set and videocassette recorder (VCR), came with the high price tag of $2,495, making it a luxury still too expensive for the average American home. Two years later, RCA released the vertical helical scan (VHS) system of recording, which would eventually outsell Betamax, though neither device was yet a popular consumer product. Within several years however, the concept of home movie recording and viewing was beginning to catch on. In 1979, Columbia Pictures released 20 films for home viewing, and a year later Disney entered the market with the first authorized video rental plan for retail stores. By 1983, VCRs were still relatively uncommon, found in just 10 percent of American homes, but within 2 years the device had found a place in nearly one-third of U.S. households (Entertainment Merchant Association).

At the same time, video rental stores began to spring up across the country. In 1985, three major video rental chains—Blockbuster, Hastings, and Movie Gallery—opened their doors. The video rental market took off between 1983 and 1986, reaching $3.37 billion in 1986. Video sales that year came to $1 billion, for total revenue of more than $4 billion, marking the first time in history that video would eclipse box-office revenues ($3.78 billion that year) (Entertainment Merchant Association).

Video sales and rentals opened a new mass market in the entertainment industry—the home movie viewer—and offered Hollywood an extended source of income from its films. On the other hand, the VCR also introduced the problem of piracy.

VCRs Legal, Just Barely

In an age when Hollywood was already struggling financially because of increased production costs, Sony's release of home video recording technology became a major source of anxiety for Hollywood studios. If people could watch movies in their own homes, would they stop going to the movies altogether? In the 1976 case *Sony Corp. of America v. Universal City Studios*, Universal Studios, and the Walt Disney Company sued Sony in the U.S. District Court for the Central District of California. The suit argued that because Sony was manufacturing a technology that could potentially be used to break copyright law, the company was therefore liable for any copyright infringement committed by VCR purchasers. The District Court struggled with the case, eventually ruling against Sony. However, Sony appealed to the Supreme Court, where the case was again highly debated. Part of the struggle was the recognition that the case had wider implications: Does a device with recording capabilities conflict with copyright law? Is an individual guilty of copyright infringement if she records a single movie in her own home for her own private use?

Eventually the Supreme Court ruled that Sony and other VCR manufacturers could not be held liable for copyright infringement. This case represented an important milestone for two reasons. It opened up a new market in the entertainment sector, enabling video rental and home movie sales. Additionally, the case set a standard for determining whether a device with copying or recording capability violated copyright law. The court ruled that because nonprofit, noncommercial home recording did not constitute copyright violation, VCR technology did have legitimate legal uses, and Sony and other companies could not be held liable for any misuse of their devices. Recently, this case has posed interpretive challenges in legal battles and in debates over file sharing through the Internet (Spruill & Adler, 2009).

The Optical Disc System

In 1980, around the time when consumers were just beginning to purchase VCRs for home use, Pioneer Electronics introduced another technology, the LaserDisc, an optical storage disc that produced higher quality images than did VHS tapes. Nonetheless, because of its large size (12 inches in diameter) and lack of recording capabilities, this early disc system never became popular in the U.S. market. However, the LaserDisc's successor, the digital versatile disc (DVD) was a different story. Like LaserDisc, the DVD is an optical storage disc—that is, a device whose encoded information follows a spiral pattern on the disc's surface and can be read when illuminated by a laser diode. However, unlike the analog-formatted LaserDisc, the DVD's information storage is entirely digital, allowing for a smaller, lighter, more compressed medium.

The first DVDs were released in stores in 1997, impressing consumers and distributers with their numerous advantages over the VHS tape: sharper-resolution images, compactness, higher durability, interactive special features, and better copy protection. In only a few years, sales of DVD players and discs surpassed those of VCRs and videos, making the DVD the most rapidly adopted consumer electronics product of all time (Entertainment Merchant Association).

In 1999, the movie rental market was revolutionized by Netflix. Netflix began in 1997 as a video rental store in California. In 1999, the company began offering a subscription service online. Subscribers would select movies that they wanted to see on Netflix's website, and the movies would arrive in their mailbox a few days later, along with a prepaid return envelope. This allowed users to select from thousands of movies and television shows in the privacy of their own home.

More recently, DVD technology has been surpassed by the Blu-ray Disc format, intended for storing and producing high-definition video. Released in 2006, the Blu-ray Disc technology has the same physical dimensions as DVDs, but because they are encoded to be read by lasers with a shorter wavelength, the discs have more than five times the storage capacity of the DVD (Blu Ray). By 2009 there were 10.9 million Blu-ray Disc players in U.S. homes (Molbaek, 2009). However, the technology has yet to replace the DVD in rental stores and among the majority of U.S. consumers.

DVD Revenues and Decline

DVD rentals and sales make up a major source of revenue for the movie industry, accounting for nearly half of the returns on feature films. In fact, for some time the industry has been exploiting the profitability of releasing some films directly to DVD without ever premiering them in theaters or of releasing films on DVD simultaneously with their theater releases. According to one estimate, for every movie that appears in theaters, there are three that go straight to DVD (Court, 2006). While *direct-to-DVD* has become synonymous with poor production values and ill-conceived sequels, there are a number of reasons why a studio might bypass the multiplexes. Prequels and sequels of box-office hits, shot on a lower production budget, are often released this way and can generate considerable income from the niche market of hard-core fans. The fourth *American Pie* film, *Bring It On: In It to Win It*, and *Ace Ventura Pet Detective, Jr.* are all examples of successful direct-to-DVD films. However, in other cases, the costs of theatrical promotion and release may simply be too high for a studio to back. This is especially true among independently produced films that lack the big-studio marketing budgets. *Slumdog Millionaire* (2009) was almost one of these cases. However, the film did make it to theaters, going on to win eight Academy Awards in 2009, including Best Picture (Charity, 2009). Finally, a film may go straight to DVD when its content is too controversial to be released in theaters. For example, almost all porn films are direct-to-DVD releases.

Between 2005 and 2008, the number of direct-to-DVD releases grew 36 percent as studios began to see the profitability of the strategy (Barnes, 2008). After a movie's success at the box office, a prequel, sequel, or related movie might earn the same profit pound-for-pound at the rental store if filmmakers slash the production budget, often replacing the original celebrity actors with less expensive talent. In 2008, direct-to-DVD brought in around $1 billion in sales (Barnes, 2008).

Despite the profitability of the DVD market, the economic downturn that began in 2007, along with the concurrent release of Blu-ray Disc technology and online digital downloads, have brought about a decline in DVD sales among U.S. consumers (Garrett, 2008). With the rise in digital downloads, Netflix broadened its appeal in 2007 by offering subscribers live-streaming movies and TV shows. This allowed viewers to watch programs on their computers, handheld devices, the Nintendo Wii game system, the Sony PlayStation 3 game system, and the Microsoft Xbox 360 game system without ever having the disc itself.

Additionally, by late 2007 film studios also became anxious over another trend: the Redbox rental system. Redbox, an American company that places DVD rental vending machines in pharmacies, grocery stores, and fast-food chains around the country, had placed a kiosk in approximately 22,000 locations by 2009 (Barnes, 2009). For the movie industry, the trouble isn't the widespread availability of Redbox rentals, it's the price. As of March

2001, customers can rent DVDs from a Redbox kiosk for only $1 per day, which has already led to a severe decline in rental revenue for the film industry (Diorio, 2009). According to the traditional pricing model, prices for rentals are based on a release window; newly released films cost more to rent for a specified period of time after their release. When customers can rent both older and newly released movies at the same low price, rentals don't produce the same returns (Hiestand, 2006).

Hollywood has also suffered major losses from online piracy. Since 2007, studios have been teaming up to turn this potential threat into a source of income. Now, instead of illegally downloading their favorite movies from file-sharing sites, fans can go to legal, commercial-supported sites like Hulu.com, where they can access a selected variety of popular movies and TV shows for the same price as accessing NBC, ABC, and CBS—free. In April 2010, Hulu announced it had already launched a fee-based service, Hulu Plus, in addition to its free service, for users who want access to even more programs, such as *Glee* (Reuters, 2010). Hulu doesn't allow viewers to download the films to their home computers, but it does provide a home-viewing experience through online streaming of content (Hulu, 2010).

The Industry Goes Digital

In an industry where technological innovations can transform production or distribution methods over the course of a few years, it's incredible to think that most movies are still captured on celluloid film, the same material that Thomas Edison used to capture his kinetoscope images well over a century ago. In 2002, George Lucas's *Star Wars Episode II: Attack of the Clones* became the first major Hollywood movie filmed on high-definition digital video. However, the move to digitally filmed movies has been gradual; much of the movie industry—including directors, producers, studios, and major movie theater chains—has been slow to embrace this major change in filming technology. At the time that Lucas filmed *Attack of the Clones*, only 18 theaters in the country were equipped with digital projectors (Kirsner, 2006).

However, digital cinematography has become an increasingly attractive, and increasingly popular, option for a number of reasons. For one thing, during production, it eliminates the need to reload film. A scene filmed in the traditional method, requiring multiple takes, can now be filmed in one continuous take because no raw material is being used in the process (Kirsner, 2006). The digital format streamlines the editing process as well. Rather than scanning the images into a computer before adding digital special effects and color adjustments, companies with digitally filmed material can send it electronically to the editing suite. Additionally, digital film files aren't susceptible to scratching or wear over time, and they are capable of producing crystal-clear, high-resolution images (Taub, 2009).

Figure 8.9

Attack of the Clones was the first film to be made with digital cinematography.

Wikimedia Commons – public domain.

For distributers and production companies, digitally recorded images eliminate the costs of purchasing, developing, and printing film. Studios spend around $800 million each year making prints of the films they distribute to theaters and additional money on top of that to ship the heavy reels (Burr, 2002). For a film like *Attack of the Clones*, widely released in 3,000 theaters, printing and shipping costs for 35-mm film would be around $20 million (Burr, 2002). On the other hand, with digital format, which requires no printing and can be sent to theaters on a single hard drive, or, as the system develops, over cable or satellite, these costs are virtually eliminated (Carvajal, 2005; Burr).

In part, the change has been gradual because, for theaters, the costs of making the digital switch (at around $125,000 for a high-quality digital projector) (Reuters, 2003) is high, and the transformation offers them fewer short-term incentives than it does for distributors, who could save a significant amount of money with digital technology. Furthermore, theaters have already heavily invested in their current projection equipment for 35-mm film (Carvajal). In the long run, the high-definition picture capabilities of digital movies might boost profits as more moviegoers turn out at the theaters, but there are no guarantees. In the meantime, the major studios are negotiating with leading theater chains to underwrite some of the conversion expenses (McCarthy, 2009).

Another financial pitfall of digital film is, surprisingly, the cost of storage once the film is out of major circulation. For major studios, a significant portion of revenues—around one-third—comes from the rerelease of old films. Studios invest an annual budget of just over $1,000 per film to keep their 35-millimeter masters in archival storage (Cieply, 2007). Keeping the film stock at controlled temperature and moisture levels prevents degradation, so masters are often stored in mines, where these conditions can be met most optimally (Cieply, 2007).

Digital data however, for all of its sophistication, is actually less likely to last than traditional film is; DVDs can degrade rapidly, with only a 50 percent chance of lasting up to 15 years (Cieply, 2007), while hard drives must be operated occasionally to prevent them from locking up. As a result, the storage cost for digital originals comes closer to $12,500 per film per year (Cieply, 2007). Moreover, as one generation of digital technology gives way to another, files have to be migrated to newer formats to prevent originals from becoming unreadable.

The Resurgence of 3-D

After World War II, as movie attendance began to decline, the motion picture industry experimented with new technologies to entice audiences back into increasingly empty theaters. One such gimmick, the 3-D picture, offered the novel experience of increased audience "participation" as monsters, flying objects, and obstacles appeared to invade the theater space, threatening to collide with spectators. The effect was achieved by manipulating filming equipment to work like a pair of human eyes, mimicking the depth of field produced through binocular vision. By joining two cameras together and spacing them slightly apart with their lenses angled fractionally toward one another, filmmakers could achieve an effect similar to that created by the overlapping fields of vision of the right and left eye. In theaters, the resulting images were played simultaneously on two separate projectors. The 3-D glasses spectators wore were polarized to filter the images so that the left eye received only "left eye" projections and the right eye received only "right eye" projections (Buchanan, 2008).

3-D was an instant sensation. *House of Wax*, the first big-budget 3-D movie, released in 1953, brought in over $1 million during its first 3 weeks in theaters, making it one of the most successful films of the year. Best of all for investors, 3-D could be created with fairly inexpensive equipment. For this reason, a boom of 3-D development soon occurred nationwide. Forty-six 3-D movies were filmed in a span of 2 years. However, 3-D proved to be a brief success, with its popularity already beginning to wane by the end of 1953 (Hayes, 2009).

Figure 8.10

Resurgence of 3-D.

J Mark Dodds – PopCorn Culture – CC BY-NC-ND 2.0.

3-D soon migrated from the realm of common popular entertainment to novelty attraction, appearing in IMAX cinemas, as an occasional marketing draw for kids' movies, and in theme-park classics like *Captain Eo* and *Honey, I Shrunk the Audience*. *Captain Eo*, a Disneyland attraction from 1986 to 1993, featured pop sensation

Michael Jackson in his heyday. Following Jackson's death, the film was rereleased for a limited time in 2010 (Rivera, 2009).

Despite the marginal role 3-D has played since the midcentury fad died out, new technologies have brought about a resurgence in the trend, and the contemporary 3-D experience seems less like a gimmick and more like a serious development in the industry. DreamWorks animation CEO Jeffrey Katzenberg, for one, likened the new 3-D to the introduction of color (McCarthy). One of the downfalls that led to the decline of 3-D in the 1950s was the "3-D headache" phenomenon audiences began to experience as a result of technical problems with filming (Hayes). To create the 3-D effect, filmmakers need to calculate the point where the overlapping images converge, an alignment that had to be performed by hand in those early years. And for the resulting image to come through clearly, the parallel cameras must run in perfect sync with one another—another impossibility with 35-millimeter film, which causes some distortion by the very fact of its motion through the filming camera.

Today the 3-D headache is a thing of the past, as computerized calibration makes perfect camera alignment a reality and as the digital recording format eliminates the celluloid-produced distortion. Finally, a single digital projector equipped with a photo-optical device can now perform the work of the two synchronized projectors of the past. For the theater chains, 3-D provides the first real incentive to make the conversion to digital. Not only do audiences turn out in greater numbers for an experience they can't reproduce at home, even on their HD television sets, but theaters are also able to charge more for tickets to see 3-D films. In 2008, for example, *Journey to the Center of the Earth*, which grossed $102 million, earned 60 percent of that money through 3-D ticket sales, even though it played in 3-D on only 30 percent of its screens (McCarthy). Two of the top-grossing movies of all time, *Avatar* (2009) and *Alice in Wonderland* (2010), were both released in 3-D.

Key Takeaways

- The introduction of the VCR in the late 1970s made home movie viewing easy. The VCR was replaced by DVD technology in the late 1990s, which is currently being replaced by Blu-ray Disc technology.

- DVD sales and rentals account for about a third of film revenues. Some films are released straight to DVD without ever appearing in theaters.

- *Star Wars Episode II: Attack of the Clones* (2002) was the first big-budget film to be recorded digitally. Since then, many more films have been made with digital cinematography. However a full-scale industry change has been gradual, mainly because of the costs of conversion.

- Three-dimensional movies were a fad in the 1950s. In recent years, because of improved technologies, 3-D movies have seen a resurgence.

Exercises

Imagine you work for a major Hollywood studio and you are negotiating a contract with a large theater chain to switch to a digital projection system. Consider the following:

1. What are the pros and cons of this switch?

2. How have digital projection systems affected the motion picture industry?

3. How has digital film affected the DVD market?

End-of-Chapter Assessment

Review Questions

1.
Section 1

   a. Explain the importance of Georges Méliès's work in the development of cinematography?

   b. Why was the MPPC formed?

   c. What caused the movie industry to move to Hollywood?

   d. Describe the factors that led to the rise and fall of the Hollywood studio system.

   e. What impact did the HUAC investigations have on Hollywood?

2.
Section 2

   a. Explain audience reactions to *The Birth of a Nation*. How did this film reflect the culture of its time?

   b. Explain the role Frank Capra's *Why We Fight* films played in World War II cinema.

   c. What does *The Graduate* reflect about the culture of the late 1960s?

   d. Explain how American individualism is reinforced in popular films.

   e. Name some films that have had an impact on social issues.

3.
Section 3

   a. Why might studios invest nearly half of their budgets in marketing efforts?

   b. List the six major Hollywood studios today and explain their influence on the film industry.

   c. What economic factors have led to the blockbuster standard?

   d. Explain the influence of foreign films on American cinema.

   e. What factors have led to the increase of film piracy?

4.
Section 4

   a. Explain the significance of the *Sony Corp. of America v. Universal City Studios* case.

b. Why are some movies released direct-to-DVD?

c. Explain the reluctance of major theater chains to switch to the digital system.

d. What are some advantages of digital cinematography?

e. Why did the 3-D movie trend fizzle out in the 1950s?

Critical Thinking Questions

1. Imagine you are a film studies teacher and you choose to show excerpts from *The Birth of a Nation* in your class to illustrate its significance in film history. One student is highly offended by the film and stops to voice her concerns to you after class. Taking into consideration the things you have learned about the history of cinema and the relationship between film and culture, how would you explain your choice to this student?

2. Assume you want to create a documentary to raise awareness about a social issue that concerns you. What issue would you address and what would you choose to document? Whom would you interview, where would you go, and so on?

3. How would you respond to a visitor from another country who accuses the United States of cultural imperialism through the export of American movies?

4. Imagine you want to produce a remake of a movie from the 1980s. Choose a movie that you think would be a blockbuster. Create a marketing plan that includes merchandise tie-ins and sources of revenue beyond the box office.

5. After its decline in the 1950s, 3-D experienced a brief comeback in the 1980s. Based on what you know about the movie industry of the time and the culture of the 1980s, why might this have occurred?

Career Connection

Research the career of a Hollywood producer. In this career, identify the different types of producers involved in a production. What tasks are these producers expected to perform? Do people in this career specialize in a certain genre of film? If so, which genre would you specialize in and why?

References

Barnes, Brookes. "Movie Studios see a Threat in Growth of Redbox," *New York Times*, September 6, 2009, http://www.nytimes.com/2009/09/07/business/media/07redbox.html.

Barnes, Brooks. "Direct-to-DVD Releases Shed Their Loser Label," *New York Times*, January 28, 2008, http://www.nytimes.com/2008/01/28/business/media/28dvd.html.

Blu-Ray.com, "Blu-Ray Disc," http://www.blu-ray.com/info/.

Buchanan, Matt. "Giz Explains 3D Technologies," *Gizmodo* (blog), November 12, 2008, http://gizmodo.com/5084121/giz-explains-3d-technologies.

Burr, Ty. "Will the 'Star Wars' Digital Gamble Pay Off?"

Burr, Ty. "Will the 'Star Wars' Digital Gamble Pay Off?" *Entertainment Weekly*, April 19, 2002, http://archives.cnn.com/2002/SHOWBIZ/Movies/04/19/ew.hot.star.wars/.

Carvajal, "Nurturing Digital Cinema."

Carvajal, Doreen. "Nurturing Digital Cinema," *New York Times*, May 23, 2005, http://www.nytimes.com/2005/05/22/technology/22iht-movies23.html.

Charity, Tom. "Review: Why Some Films Go Straight to DVD," *CNN*, February 27, 2009, http://www.cnn.com/2009/SHOWBIZ/Movies/02/27/review.humboldt.
/index.html.

Cieply, Michael. "The Afterlife is Expensive for Digital Movies," *New York Times*, December 23, 2007, http://www.nytimes.com/2007/12/23/business/media/23steal.html.

Court, Robert W. "Straight to DVD," *New York Times*, May 6, 2006, Opinion section, http://www.nytimes.com/2006/05/06/opinion/06cort.html.

Diorio, Carl. "$1 DVD Rentals Costing Biz $1 Bil: Study," *Hollywood Reporter*, December 7, 2009, http://www.hollywoodreporter.com/news/1-dvd-rentals-costing-biz-92098.

Entertainment Merchant Association, "A History of Home Video and Video Game Retailing," http://www.entmerch.org/industry_history.html.

Entertainment Merchant Association, "History of Home Video"; Dirks, "History of Film: the 1990s," *Filmsite*.

Garrett, Dianne. "DVD Sales Down 3.6% in '07," January 7, 2008, www.variety.com/article/VR1117978576?refCatId=20.

Hayes, "Short History of 3D Movies."

Hayes, John. "'You See Them WITH Glasses!' A Short History of 3D Movies," *Wide Screen Movies Magazine*, 2009, http://widescreenmovies.org/wsm11/3D.htm.

Hiestand, Jesse. "MPAA Study: '05 Piracy Cost $6.1 Bil.," *Hollywood Reporter*, May 3, 2006. http://business.highbeam.com/2012/article-1G1-146544812/mpaa-study-05-piracy-cost-61-bil.

Hulu, "Media Info," 2010, http://www.hulu.com/about.

Kirsner, Scott. "Studios Shift to Digital Movies, but Not Without Resistance," *New York Times*, July 4, 2006, http://www.nytimes.com/2005/05/22/technology/22iht-movies23.html?scp=15&sq=digital%20movie&st=cse.

McCarthy, "Tech Behind 3D's Big Revival."

McCarthy, Erin. "The Tech Behind 3D's Big Revival," *Popular Mechanics*, April 1, 2009, http://www.popularmechanics.com/technology/digital/3d/4310810.

Molbaek, Henning. "10.7 Million Blu-Ray Players in U.S. Homes," DVDTown.com, Jan 9, 2009, http://www.dvdtown.com/news/107-million-blu-ray-players-in-us-homes/6288.

Reuters, "Hulu Launches Paid Subscription TV Service," *Fox News*, June 30, 2010, http://www.foxnews.com/scitech/2010/06/30/hulu-starts-paid-subscription-tv-service/.

Reuters, "Movie Theaters Going Digital," *CNN*, December 24, 2003, http://www.cnn.com/2003/TECH/ptech/12/24/digital.movietheater.reut/index.html.

Rivera, Heather Hust. "Captain EO Returns to Disneyland Resort." *Disney Parks Blog*, December 18, 2009. http://disneyparks.disney.go.com/blog/2009/12/captain-eo-returns-to-disneyland-resort/.

Spruill, Willie and Derek Adler, "Sony Corp. of America v. Universal City Studios," Downloading & Piracy project for Laura N. Gasaway's Cyberspace Law Seminar, University of North Carolina School of Law, 2009, http://www.unc.edu/courses/2009spring/law/357c/001/Piracy/cases.htm.

Taub, Eric A. "More Digital Projectors, Coming to a Theater Near You," *Gadgetwise* (blog), *New York Times*, June 18, 2009, http://gadgetwise.blogs.nytimes.com/2009/06/18/its-a-4k-world-after-all/.

Chapter 9: Television

9.1 The Evolution of Television

Learning Objectives

1. Identify two technological developments that paved the way for the evolution of television.

2. Explain why electronic television prevailed over mechanical television.

3. Identify three important developments in the history of television since 1960.

Since replacing radio as the most popular mass medium in the 1950s, television has played such an integral role in modern life that, for some, it is difficult to imagine being without it. Both reflecting and shaping cultural values, television has at times been criticized for its alleged negative influences on children and young people and at other times lauded for its ability to create a common experience for all its viewers. Major world events such as the John F. Kennedy and Martin Luther King assassinations and the Vietnam War in the 1960s, the *Challenger* shuttle explosion in 1986, the 2001 terrorist attacks on the World Trade Center, and the impact and aftermath of Hurricane Katrina in 2005 have all played out on television, uniting millions of people in shared tragedy and hope. Today, as Internet technology and satellite broadcasting change the way people watch television, the medium continues to evolve, solidifying its position as one of the most important inventions of the 20th century.

The Origins of Television

Inventors conceived the idea of television long before the technology to create it appeared. Early pioneers speculated that if audio waves could be separated from the electromagnetic spectrum to create radio, so too could TV waves be separated to transmit visual images. As early as 1876, Boston civil servant George Carey envisioned complete television systems, putting forward drawings for a "selenium camera" that would enable people to "see by electricity" a year later (Federal Communications Commission, 2005).

During the late 1800s, several technological developments set the stage for television. The invention of the cathode ray tube (CRT) by German physicist Karl Ferdinand Braun in 1897 played a vital role as the forerunner of the TV picture tube. Initially created as a scanning device known as the cathode ray oscilloscope, the CRT effectively combined the principles of the camera and electricity. It had a fluorescent screen that emitted a visible light (in the form of images) when struck by a beam of electrons. The other key invention during the 1880s was the mechanical scanner system. Created by German inventor Paul Nipkow, the scanning disk was a large, flat metal disk with a series of small perforations arranged in a spiral pattern. As the disk rotated, light passed through the holes, separating pictures into pinpoints of light that could be transmitted as a series of electronic lines. The number of scanned lines equaled the number of perforations, and each rotation of the disk produced a television frame. Nipkow's mechanical disk served as the foundation for experiments on the transmission of visual images for several decades.

In 1907, Russian scientist Boris Rosing used both the CRT and the mechanical scanner system in an experimental television system. With the CRT in the receiver, he used focused electron beams to display images, transmitting crude geometrical patterns onto the television screen. The mechanical disk system was used as a camera, creating a primitive television system.

Figure 9.1

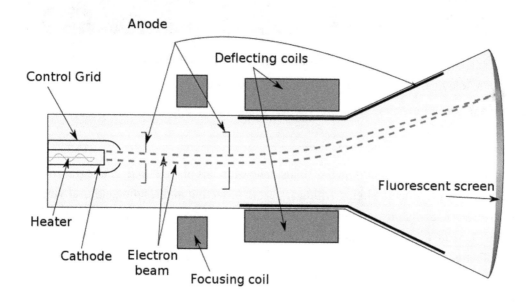

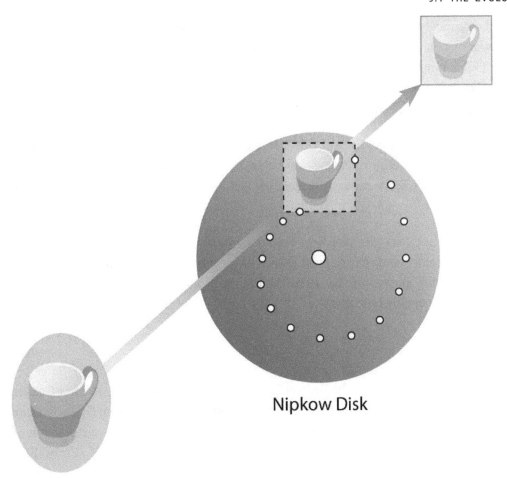

Nipkow Disk

Two key inventions in the 1880s paved the way for television to emerge: the cathode ray tube and the mechanical disk system.

Mechanical Television versus Electronic Television

From the early experiments with visual transmissions, two types of television systems came into existence: mechanical television and electronic television. Mechanical television developed out of Nipkow's disk system and was pioneered by British inventor John Logie Baird. In 1926, Baird gave the world's first public demonstration of a television system at Selfridge's department store in London. He used mechanical rotating disks to scan moving images into electrical impulses, which were transmitted by cable to a screen. Here they showed up as a low-resolution pattern of light and dark. Baird's first television program showed the heads of two ventriloquist dummies, which he operated in front of the camera apparatus out of the audience's sight. In 1928, Baird extended his system by transmitting a signal between London and New York. The following year, the British Broadcasting Corporation (BBC) adopted his mechanical system, and by 1932, Baird had developed the first commercially viable television system and sold 10,000 sets. Despite its initial success, mechanical television had several technical limitations. Engineers could get no more than about 240 lines of resolution, meaning images would always be slightly fuzzy (most modern televisions produce images of more than 600 lines of resolution). The use of a spinning disk also limited the number of new pictures that could be seen per second, resulting in excessive flickering. The mechanical aspect of television proved to be a disadvantage that required fixing in order for the technology to move forward.

At the same time Baird (and, separately, American inventor Charles Jenkins) was developing the mechanical model, other inventors were working on an electronic television system based on the CRT. While working on his father's farm, Idaho teenager Philo Farnsworth realized that an electronic beam could scan a picture in horizontal lines, reproducing the image almost instantaneously. In 1927, Farnsworth transmitted the first all-electronic TV picture by rotating a single straight line scratched onto a square piece of painted glass by 90 degrees.

Farnsworth barely profited from his invention; during World War II, the government suspended sales of TV sets, and by the time the war ended, Farnsworth's original patents were close to expiring. However, following the war, many of his key patents were modified by RCA and were widely applied in broadcasting to improve television picture quality.

Having coexisted for several years, electronic television sets eventually began to replace mechanical systems. With better picture quality, no noise, a more compact size, and fewer visual limitations, the electronic system was far superior to its predecessor and rapidly improving. By 1939, the last mechanical television broadcasts in the United States had been replaced with electronic broadcasts.

Early Broadcasting

Television broadcasting began as early as 1928, when the Federal Radio Commission authorized inventor Charles Jenkins to broadcast from W3XK, an experimental station in the Maryland suburbs of Washington, DC. Silhouette images from motion picture films were broadcast to the general public on a regular basis, at a resolution of just 48 lines. Similar experimental stations ran broadcasts throughout the early 1930s. In 1939, RCA subsidiary NBC (National Broadcasting Company) became the first network to introduce regular television broadcasts, transmitting its inaugural telecast of the opening ceremonies at the New York World's Fair. The station's initial broadcasts transmitted to just 400 television sets in the New York area, with an audience of 5,000 to 8,000 people (Lohr, 1940).

Television was initially available only to the privileged few, with sets ranging from $200 to $600—a hefty sum in the 1930s, when the average annual salary was $1,368 (KC Library). RCA offered four types of television receivers, which were sold in high-end department stores such as Macy's and Bloomingdale's, and received channels 1 through 5. Early receivers were a fraction of the size of modern TV sets, featuring 5-, 9-, or 12-inch screens. Television sales prior to World War II were disappointing—an uncertain economic climate, the threat of war, the high cost of a television receiver, and the limited number of programs on offer deterred numerous prospective buyers. Many unsold television sets were put into storage and sold after the war.

NBC was not the only commercial network to emerge in the 1930s. RCA radio rival CBS (Columbia Broadcasting System) also began broadcasting regular programs. So that viewers would not need a separate television set for each individual network, the Federal Communications Commission (FCC) outlined a single technical standard. In 1941, the panel recommended a 525-line system and an image rate of 30 frames per second. It also recommended that all U.S. television sets operate using analog signals (broadcast signals made of varying radio waves). Analog signals were replaced by digital signals (signals transmitted as binary code) in 2009.

With the outbreak of World War II, many companies, including RCA and General Electric, turned their attention to military production. Instead of commercial television sets, they began to churn out military electronic equipment.

In addition, the war halted nearly all television broadcasting; many TV stations reduced their schedules to around 4 hours per week or went off the air altogether.

Color Technology

Although it did not become available until the 1950s or popular until the 1960s, the technology for producing color television was proposed as early as 1904, and was demonstrated by John Logie Baird in 1928. As with his black-and-white television system, Baird adopted the mechanical method, using a Nipkow scanning disk with three spirals, one for each primary color (red, green, and blue). In 1940, CBS researchers, led by Hungarian television engineer Peter Goldmark, used Baird's 1928 designs to develop a concept of mechanical color television that could reproduce the color seen by a camera lens.

Following World War II, the National Television System Committee (NTSC) worked to develop an all-electronic color system that was compatible with black-and-white TV sets, gaining FCC approval in 1953. A year later, NBC made the first national color broadcast when it telecast the Tournament of Roses Parade. Despite the television industry's support for the new technology, it would be another 10 years before color television gained widespread popularity in the United States, and black-and-white TV sets outnumbered color TV sets until 1972 (Klooster, 2009).

The Golden Age of Television

Figure 9.3

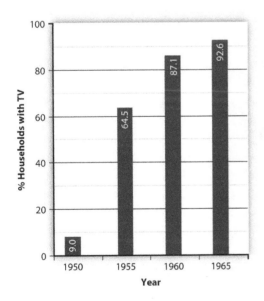

During the so-called "golden age" of television, the percentage of U.S. households that owned a television set rose from 9 percent in 1950 to 95.3 percent in 1970.

The 1950s proved to be the golden age of television, during which the medium experienced massive growth in popularity. Mass-production advances made during World War II substantially lowered the cost of purchasing a set, making television accessible to the masses. In 1945, there were fewer than 10,000 TV sets in the United States. By 1950, this figure had soared to around 6 million, and by 1960 more than 60 million television sets had been sold (World Book Encyclopedia, 2003). Many of the early television program formats were based on network radio shows and did not take advantage of the potential offered by the new medium. For example, newscasters simply read the news as they would have during a radio broadcast, and the network relied on newsreel companies to provide footage of news events. However, during the early 1950s, television programming began to branch out from radio broadcasting, borrowing from theater to create acclaimed dramatic anthologies such as *Playhouse 90* (1956) and *The U.S. Steel Hour* (1953) and producing quality news film to accompany coverage of daily events.

Two new types of programs—the magazine format and the TV spectacular—played an important role in helping the networks gain control over the content of their broadcasts. Early television programs were developed and produced by a single sponsor, which gave the sponsor a large amount of control over the content of the show. By increasing program length from the standard 15-minute radio show to 30 minutes or longer, the networks substantially increased advertising costs for program sponsors, making it prohibitive for a single sponsor. Magazine programs such as the *Today* show and *The Tonight Show*, which premiered in the early 1950s, featured multiple segments and ran for several hours. They were also screened on a daily, rather than weekly, basis, drastically increasing advertising costs. As a result, the networks began to sell spot advertisements that ran for 30 or 60 seconds. Similarly, the television spectacular (now known as the television special) featured lengthy music-variety shows that were sponsored by multiple advertisers.

Figure 9.4

ABC's *Who Wants to Be a Millionaire* brought the quiz show back to prime-time television after a 40-year absence.

sonicwwtbamfangamer2 – millionaire – CC BY-SA 2.0.

In the mid-1950s, the networks brought back the radio quiz-show genre. Inexpensive and easy to produce, the trend caught on, and by the end of the 1957–1958 season, 22 quiz shows were being aired on network television, including CBS's *$64,000 Question*. Shorter than some of the new types of programs, quiz shows enabled single corporate sponsors to have their names displayed on the set throughout the show. The popularity of the quiz-show genre plunged at the end of the decade, however, when it was discovered that most of the shows were rigged. Producers provided some contestants with the answers to the questions in order to pick and choose the most likable or controversial candidates. When a slew of contestants accused the show *Dotto* of being fixed in 1958, the networks rapidly dropped 20 quiz shows. A New York grand jury probe and a 1959 congressional investigation effectively ended prime-time quiz shows for 40 years, until ABC revived the genre with its launch of *Who Wants to Be a Millionaire* in 1999 (Boddy, 1990).

The Rise of Cable Television

Formerly known as Community Antenna Television, or CATV, cable television was originally developed in the 1940s in remote or mountainous areas, including in Arkansas, Oregon, and Pennsylvania, to enhance poor reception of regular television signals. Cable antennas were erected on mountains or other high points, and homes connected to the towers would receive broadcast signals.

In the late 1950s, cable operators began to experiment with microwave to bring signals from distant cities. Taking advantage of their ability to receive long-distance broadcast signals, operators branched out from providing a local community service and began focusing on offering consumers more extensive programming choices. Rural parts of Pennsylvania, which had only three channels (one for each network), soon had more than double the original number of channels as operators began to import programs from independent stations in New York and Philadelphia. The wider variety of channels and clearer reception the service offered soon attracted viewers from urban areas. By 1962, nearly 800 cable systems were operational, serving 850,000 subscribers.

Figure 9.5

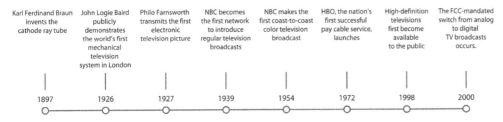

The Evolution of Television

Cable's exponential growth was viewed as competition by local TV stations, and broadcasters campaigned for the FCC to step in. The FCC responded by placing restrictions on the ability of cable systems to import signals from distant stations, which froze the development of cable television in major markets until the early 1970s. When gradual deregulation began to loosen the restrictions, cable operator Service Electric launched the service that would change the face of the cable television industry—pay TV. The 1972 Home Box Office (HBO) venture, in which customers paid a subscription fee to access premium cable television shows and video-on-demand products, was the nation's first successful pay cable service. HBO's use of a satellite to distribute its programming made the network available throughout the United States. This gave it an advantage over the microwave-distributed services, and other cable providers quickly followed suit. Further deregulation provided by the 1984 Cable Act enabled the industry to expand even further, and by the end of the 1980s, nearly 53 million households subscribed to cable television (see Section 6.3 "Current Popular Trends in the Music Industry"). In the 1990s, cable operators upgraded their systems by building higher-capacity hybrid networks of fiber-optic and coaxial cable. These broadband networks provide a multichannel television service, along with telephone, high-speed Internet, and advanced digital video services, using a single wire.

The Emergence of Digital Television

Following the FCC standards set out during the early 1940s, television sets received programs via analog signals made of radio waves. The analog signal reached TV sets through three different methods: over the airwaves, through a cable wire, or by satellite transmission. Although the system remained in place for more than 60 years, it had several disadvantages. Analog systems were prone to static and distortion, resulting in a far poorer picture quality than films shown in movie theaters. As television sets grew increasingly larger, the limited resolution made scan lines painfully obvious, reducing the clarity of the image. Companies around the world, most notably in Japan, began to develop technology that provided newer, better-quality television formats, and the broadcasting industry began to lobby the FCC to create a committee to study the desirability and impact of switching to digital television. A more efficient and flexible form of broadcast technology, digital television uses signals that translate TV images and sounds into binary code, working in much the same way as a computer. This means they require much less frequency space and also provide a far higher quality picture. In 1987, the Advisory Committee on Advanced Television Services began meeting to test various TV systems, both analog and digital. The committee ultimately agreed to switch from analog to digital format in 2009, allowing a transition period in which broadcasters could send their signal on both an analog and a digital channel. Once the switch took place, many older analog TV sets were unusable without a cable or satellite service or a digital converter. To retain consumers' access to free over-the-air television, the federal government offered $40 gift cards to people who needed to buy a digital converter, expecting to recoup its costs by auctioning off the old analog broadcast spectrum to wireless companies (Steinberg, 2007). These companies were eager to gain access to the analog spectrum for mobile broadband projects because this frequency band allows signals to travel greater distances and penetrate buildings more easily.

The Era of High-Definition Television

Around the same time the U.S. government was reviewing the options for analog and digital television systems, companies in Japan were developing technology that worked in conjunction with digital signals to create crystal-clear pictures in a wide-screen format. High-definition television, or HDTV, attempts to create a heightened sense of realism by providing the viewer with an almost three-dimensional experience. It has a much higher resolution than standard television systems, using around five times as many pixels per frame. First available in 1998, HDTV products were initially extremely expensive, priced between $5,000 and $10,000 per set. However, as with most new technology, prices dropped considerably over the next few years, making HDTV affordable for mainstream shoppers.

Figure 9.6

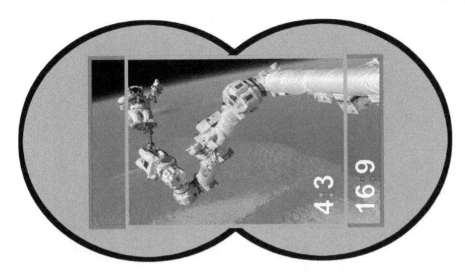

HDTV uses a wide-screen format with a different aspect ratio (the ratio of the width of the image to its height) than standard-definition TV. The wide-screen format of HDTV is similar to that of movies, allowing for a more authentic film-viewing experience at home.

Wikimedia Commons – CC BY-SA 3.0.

As of 2010, nearly half of American viewers are watching television in high definition, the fastest adoption of TV technology since the introduction of the VCR in the 1980s (Stelter, 2010). The new technology is attracting viewers to watch television for longer periods of time. According to the Nielsen Company, a company that measures TV viewership, households with HDTV watch 3 percent more prime-time television—programming screened between 7 and 11 p.m., when the largest audience is available—than their standard-definition counterparts (Stelter, 2010). The same report claims that the cinematic experience of HDTV is bringing families back together in the living room in front of the large wide-screen TV and out of the kitchen and bedroom, where individuals tend to watch television alone on smaller screens. However, these viewing patterns may change again soon as the Internet plays an increasingly larger role in how people view TV programs. The impact of new technologies on television is discussed in much greater detail in Section 9.4 "Influence of New Technologies" of this chapter.

Figure 9.7

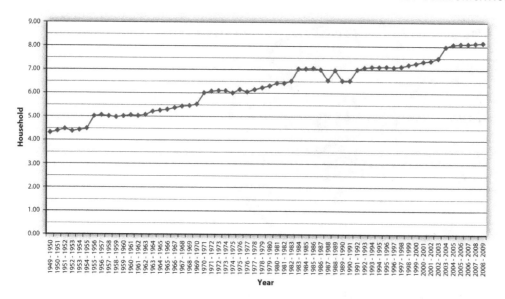

Since 1950, the amount of time the average household spends watching television has almost doubled.

Key Takeaways

- Two key technological developments in the late 1800s played a vital role in the evolution of television: the cathode ray tube and the scanning disk. The cathode ray tube, invented by German physicist Karl Ferdinand Braun in 1897, was the forerunner of the TV picture tube. It had a fluorescent screen that emitted a visible light (in the form of images) when struck by a beam of electrons. The scanning disk, invented by German inventor Paul Nipkow, was a large, flat metal disk that could be used as a rotating camera. It served as the foundation for experiments on the transmission of visual images for several decades.

- Out of the cathode ray tube and the scanning disk, two types of primitive television systems evolved: mechanical systems and electronic systems. Mechanical television systems had several technical disadvantages: Low resolution caused fuzzy images, and the use of a spinning disk limited the number of new pictures that could be seen per second, resulting in excessive flickering. By 1939, all mechanical television broadcasts in the United States had been replaced by electronic broadcasts.

- Early televisions were expensive, and the technology was slow to catch on because development was delayed during World War II. Color technology was delayed even further because early color systems were incompatible with black-and-white television sets. Following the war, television rapidly replaced radio as the new mass medium. During the "golden age" of television in the 1950s, television moved away from radio formats and developed new types of shows, including the magazine-style variety show and the television spectacular.

- Since 1960, several key technological developments have taken place in the television industry. Color television gained popularity in the late 1960s and began to replace black-and-white television in the 1970s. Cable television, initially developed in the 1940s to cater to viewers in rural areas, switched its focus from local to national television, offering an extensive number of channels. In 2009, the traditional analog system, which had been in place for 60 years, was replaced with digital television, giving viewers a higher-quality picture and freeing up frequency space. As of 2010, nearly half of American viewers have high-definition television, which offers a crystal-clear picture in wide-screen to provide a cinematic experience at home.

Exercises

Please respond to the following writing prompts. Each response should be a minimum of one paragraph.

1. Prior to World War II, television was in the early stages of development. In the years following the war, the technical development and growth in popularity of the medium were exponential. Identify two ways television evolved after World War II. How did these changes make postwar television superior to its predecessor?

2. Compare the television you use now with the television from your childhood. How have TV sets changed in your lifetime?

3. What do you consider the most important technological development in television since the 1960s? Why?

References

Boddy, William. "The Seven Dwarfs and the Money Grubbers," in *Logics of Television: Essays in Cultural Criticism*, ed. Patricia Mellencamp (Bloomington, IN: Indiana University Press, 1990), 98–116.

Federal Communications Commission, "Visionary Period, 1880's Through 1920's," *Federal Communications Commission*, November 21, 2005, http://www.fcc.gov/omd/history/tv/1880-1929.html.

KC Library, Lone Star College: Kinwood, "American Cultural History 1930–1939," http://kclibrary.lonestar.edu/decade30.html.

Klooster, John. *Icons of Invention: The Makers of the Modern World from Gutenberg to Gates* (Santa Barbara, CA: ABC-CLIO, 2009), 442.

Lohr, Lenox. *Television Broadcasting* (New York: McGraw Hill, 1940).

Steinberg, Jacques. "Converters Signal a New Era for TVs," *New York Times*, June 7, 2007, http://www.nytimes.com/2007/06/07/technology/07digital.html.

Stelter, Brian. "Crystal-Clear, Maybe Mesmerizing," *New York Times*, May 23, 2010, http://www.nytimes.com/2010/05/24/business/media/24def.html.

World Book Encyclopedia (2003), s.v. "Television."

9.2 The Relationship Between Television and Culture

Learning Objectives

1. Identify ways in which American culture is reflected on television.
2. Identify ways in which television affects the development of American culture.

Since its inception as an integral part of American life in the 1950s, television has both reflected and nurtured cultural mores and values. From the escapist dramas of the 1960s, which consciously avoided controversial issues and glossed over life's harsher realities in favor of an idealized portrayal, to the copious reality TV shows in recent years, on which participants discuss even the most personal and taboo issues, television has held up a mirror to society. But the relationship between social attitudes and television is reciprocal; broadcasters have often demonstrated their power to influence viewers, either consciously through slanted political commentary, or subtly, by portraying controversial relationships (such as single parenthood, same-sex marriages, or interracial couplings) as socially acceptable. The symbiotic nature of television and culture is exemplified in every broadcast, from family sitcoms to serious news reports.

Cultural Influences on Television

In the 1950s, most television entertainment programs ignored current events and political issues. Instead, the three major networks (ABC, NBC, and CBS) developed prime-time shows that would appeal to a general family audience. Chief among these types of shows was the domestic comedy—a generic family comedy that was identified by its character-based humor and usually set within the home. Seminal examples included popular 1950s shows such as *Leave It to Beaver, The Donna Reed Show,* and *The Adventures of Ozzie and Harriet.* Presenting a standardized version of the White middle-class suburban family, domestic comedies portrayed the conservative values of an idealized American life. Studiously avoiding prevalent social issues such as racial discrimination and civil rights, the shows focused on mostly White middle-class families with traditional nuclear roles (mother in the home, father in the office) and implied that most domestic problems could be solved within a 30-minute time slot, always ending with a strong moral lesson.

Although these shows depicted an idealized version of American family life, many families in the 1950s were traditional nuclear families. Following the widespread poverty, political uncertainty, and physical separation of the war years, many Americans wanted to settle down, have children, and enjoy the peace and security that family life appeared to offer. During the booming postwar era, a period of optimism and prosperity, the traditional nuclear family flourished. However, the families and lifestyles presented in domestic comedies did not encompass the overall American experience by any stretch of the imagination. As historian Stephanie Coontz points out, "the June Cleaver or Donna Stone homemaker role was not available to the more than 40 percent of black women with small children who worked outside the home (Coontz, 1992)." Although nearly 60 percent of the U.S. population was labeled middle class by the mid-1950s, 25 percent of all families and more than 50 percent of two-parent Black families were poor. Migrant workers suffered horrific deprivations, and racial tensions were rife. None of this was reflected in the world of domestic comedies, where even the Hispanic gardener in *Father Knows Best* was named Frank Smith (Coontz, 1992).

Figure 9.8

Most domestic comedies in the 1950s portrayed an idealized version of family life and ignored social and political events.

Dennis S. Hurd – The Cleavers – CC BY-NC-ND 2.0.

Not all programs in the 1950s were afraid to tackle controversial social or political issues. In March 1954, journalist Edward R. Murrow broadcast an unflattering portrait of U.S. Senator Joseph McCarthy on his show *See It Now*. McCarthy, a member of the Senate Investigation Committee, had launched inquiries regarding potential Communist infiltration in U.S. institutions. Murrow thought that McCarthy's aggressive tactics were a potential threat to civil liberties. His portrait cast the senator from Wisconsin in an unflattering light by pointing out contradictions in his speeches. This led to such an uproar that McCarthy was formally reprimanded by the U.S. Senate (Friedman, 2008).

Entertainment programs also tackled controversial issues. The long-running television western *Gunsmoke*, which aired on CBS from 1955 to 1975, flourished in a Cold War society, where U.S. Marshal Matt Dillon (James Arness) stood up to lawlessness in defense of civilization. The characters and community in *Gunsmoke* faced relevant social issues, including the treatment of minority groups, the meaning of family, the legitimacy of violence, and the strength of religious belief. During the 1960s, the show adapted to the desires of its viewing audience, becoming increasingly aware of and sympathetic to ethnic minorities, in tune with the national mood during the civil rights era. This adaptability helped the show to become the longest-running western in TV history.

Violence and Escapism in the 1960s

During the 1960s, television news broadcasts brought the realities of real-world events into people's living rooms in vivid detail. *The CBS Evening News with Walter Cronkite,* which debuted in 1962, quickly became the country's most popular newscast, and by the end of the decade, journalist Walter Cronkite was known as the most trusted man in America. Following John F. Kennedy's election to the presidency at the beginning of the decade, the 1960s took an ominous turn. Shocked viewers tuned into Cronkite's broadcast on November 22, 1963, to learn about the assassination of their president. During the next few days, viewers followed every aspect of the tragedy on television, from the tremor in Cronkite's voice as he removed his glasses and announced the news of Kennedy's death, to the frantic scenes from Dallas police headquarters where the assassin, Lee Harvey Oswald, was gunned down by nightclub owner Jack Ruby, to the thousands of mourners lining up next to the president's flag-draped coffin.

Figure 9.9

Television began to play a major role in U.S. politics during the presidency of John. F. Kennedy.

Around the same time as Kennedy's assassination, horrific images from Vietnam were streaming into people's living rooms during the nation's first televised war. With five camera crews on duty in the Saigon bureau, news crews captured vivid details of the war in progress. Although graphic images were rarely shown on network TV, several instances of violence reached the screen, including a CBS report in 1965 that showed Marines lighting the thatched roofs of the village of Cam Ne with Zippo lighters and an NBC news report in 1968 that aired a shot of South Vietnamese General Nguyen Ngoc Loan executing a captive on a Saigon street. Further images, of children being burned and scarred by napalm and prisoners being tortured, fueled the antiwar sentiments of many Americans. In addition to the devastation caused by the president's death and the Vietnam War, Americans were also feeling the pressure of the Cold War—the clash between the United States and the Soviet Union in the years following World War II. This pressure was especially great during periods of tension throughout the 1950s and 1960s, such as the 1962 Cuban Missile Crisis, a confrontation that caused many people to fear nuclear war.

As a result of the intense stress faced by many Americans during the 1960s, broadcasters and viewers turned to escapist programs such as *I Dream of Jeannie,* a fantasy show about a 2,000-year-old genie who marries an astronaut, and *Bewitched*, a supernatural-themed show about a witch who tries to live as a suburban housewife. Both shows typified the situation comedy, or sitcom, a comedy genre featuring a recurring cast of characters who resolve zany situations based on their everyday lives. Other popular sitcoms in the 1960s included *The Beverly Hillbillies*, a show about a poor backwoods family who move to Beverly Hills, California, after finding oil on their land, and *Gilligan's Island*, the ultimate escapist comedy about seven characters shipwrecked on an uncharted island. None of the 1960s sitcoms mentioned any of the political unease that was taking place in the outside world, providing audiences with a welcome diversion from real life. Other than an occasional documentary, TV programming in the 1960s consisted of a sharp dichotomy between prime-time escapist comedy and hard news.

Figure 9.10

Escapist sitcoms like *I Dream of Jeannie* provided Americans with a much-needed diversion from the stressful events of the 1960s.

Wikimedia Commons – public domain.

Diversity and Politics in the 1970s

During the 1970s, broadcasters began to diversify families on their shows to reflect changing social attitudes toward formerly controversial issues such as single parenthood and divorce. Feminist groups including the National Organization for Women (NOW), the National Women's Political Caucus, and the Coalition of Labor Union Women pushed for equality on issues such as pay and encouraged women to enter the workforce. In 1972, the U.S. Supreme Court sanctioned women's right to abortion, giving them control over their reproductive rights. Divorce rates skyrocketed during the 1970s, as states adopted no-fault divorce laws, and the change in family dynamics was reflected on television. Between 1972 and 1978, CBS aired the socially controversial sitcom *Maude*. Featuring a middle-aged feminist living with her fourth husband and divorced daughter, the show exploded the dominant values of the White middle-class domestic sitcom and its traditional gender roles. Throughout its 7-year run, *Maude* tackled social and political issues such as abortion, menopause, birth control, alcoholism, and depression. During its first four seasons, the show was in the top 10 in Nielsen ratings, illustrating the changing tastes of the viewing audience, who had come of age during the era of civil rights and Vietnam protests and developed a taste for socially conscious television. Other 1970s sitcoms took the same approach, including *Maude*'s CBS predecessor, *All in the Family*, which covered issues ranging from racism and homophobia to rape and miscarriage, and *The Mary Tyler Moore Show*, which reflected changing attitudes toward women's rights by featuring television's first never-married independent career woman as the central character. Even wholesome family favorite *The Brady Bunch*, which ran from 1969 to 1974, featured a non-nuclear family, reflecting the rising rates of blended families in American society.

Figure 9.11

The popularity of controversial shows like *Maude* reflected the changing cultural and social values of the 1970s.

Wikimedia Commons – public domain.

In addition to changing family dynamics on sitcoms and other prime-time shows, variety and comedy sketch shows developed a political awareness in the 1970s that reflected audiences' growing appetite for social and political commentary. Sketch comedy show *Saturday Night Live* (*SNL*) premiered on NBC in 1975 and has remained on air ever since. Featuring a different celebrity guest host every week and relatively unknown comedy regulars, the show parodies contemporary popular culture and politics, lambasting presidential candidates and pop stars alike. Earlier NBC sketch comedy show *Laugh-In*, which ran from 1968 to 1973, also featured politically charged material, though it lacked the satirical bite of later series such as *SNL*. By the end of the decade, television broadcasting reflected a far more politically conscious and socially aware viewing audience.

The Influence of Cable Television in the 1980s

Until the mid-1980s, the top three networks (ABC, NBC, and CBS) dominated television broadcasting in the United States. However, as cable services gained popularity following the deregulation of the industry in 1984, viewers found themselves with a multitude of options. Services such as Cable News Network (CNN), Entertainment and Sports Programming Network (ESPN), and Music Television (MTV) profoundly altered the television landscape in the world of news, sports, and music. New markets opened up for these innovative program types, as well as for older genres such as the sitcom. During the 1980s, a revival of family sitcoms took place with two enormous hits: *The Cosby Show* and *Family Ties*. Both featured a new take on modern family life, with the mothers working outside of the home and the fathers pitching in with housework and parental duties. Despite their success on network television, sitcoms faced stiff competition from cable's variety of choices. Between 1983 and 1994, weekly broadcast audience shares (a measure of the number of televisions in use that are tuned to a particular show) for network television dropped from 69 to 52, while cable networks' shares rose from 9 to 26 (Newcomb, 2004).

With a growing number of households subscribing to cable TV, concern began to grow about the levels of violence to which children were becoming exposed. In addition to regularly broadcast network programs, cable offered viewers the chance to watch films and adult-themed shows during all hours, many of which had far more violent content than normal network programming. One study found that by the time an average child leaves elementary school, he or she has witnessed 8,000 murders and more than 100,000 other acts of violence on television (Blakey, 2002). Although no conclusive links have been drawn between witnessing violence on television and carrying out violence in real life, the loosening boundaries regarding sexual and violent content on television is a persistent cause for concern for many parents. For more information on the social effects of violence in the media, please refer to Chapter 2 "Media Effects".

Specialization in the 1990s and 2000s

Although TV viewership is growing, the vast number of cable channels and other, newer content delivery platforms means that audiences are thinly stretched. In recent years, broadcasters have been narrowing the focus of their programming to meet the needs and interests of an increasingly fragmented audience. Entire cable channels devoted to cooking, music, news, African American interests (see sidebar below), weather, and courtroom drama enable viewers to choose exactly what type of show they want to watch, and many news channels are further specialized according to viewers' political opinions. This trend toward specialization reflects a more general shift within society, as companies cater increasingly to smaller, more targeted consumer bases. Business magazine editor Chris Anderson explains, "We're leaving the watercooler era, when most of us listened, watched and read from the same relatively small pool of mostly hit content. And we're entering the microculture era, when we are all into different things (Gunther, 2006)." Just as cable broadcasters are catering to niche markets, Internet-based companies such as Amazon.com and Netflix are taking advantage of this concept by selling large numbers of books, DVDs, and music albums with narrow appeal. Section 9.3 "Issues and Trends in the Television Industry" and Section 9.4 "Influence of New Technologies" of this chapter will cover the recent trends and issues of this era in television.

Black Entertainment Television (BET)

Launched in 1980, Black Entertainment Television (BET) was the first television network in the United States dedicated to the interests of African American viewers. The basic-cable franchise was created in Washington, DC, by media entrepreneur Robert Johnson, who initially invested $15,000 in the venture. Within a decade, he had turned the company into a multimillion-dollar enterprise, and in 1991 it became the first Black-controlled company on the New York Stock Exchange. The company was sold to Viacom in 2003 for $3 billion.

Pre-dating MTV by a year, BET initially focused on Black-oriented music videos but soon diversified into original urban-oriented programs and public affairs shows. Although BET compensated somewhat for the underrepresentation of Blacks on television (African Americans made up 8 percent of the prime-time characters on television in 1980 but made up 12 percent of the population), viewers complained about the portrayal of stereotypical images and inappropriate violent or sexual behavior in many of the rap videos shown by the network. In a 2004 interview with BET vice president of communications Michael Lewellen, former BET talk show host Bev Smith said, "We had videos on BET in those days that were graphic but didn't proliferate as they seem to be doing now. That's all you do seem to see are scantily dressed women who a lot of African American women are upset about in those videos (Fox News, 2004)." Despite the criticisms, BET remained the No. 1 cable network among Blacks 18 to 34 in 2010 and retained an average audience of 524,000 total viewers during the first quarter of the year (Forbes, 2010).

Television's Influence on Culture

Despite entering a microculture era with a variety of niche markets, television remains the most important unifying cultural presence in the United States. During times of national crises, television news broadcasts have galvanized the country by providing real-time coverage of major events. When terrorists crashed planes into the World Trade Center towers in 2001, 24-hour TV news crews provided stunned viewers around the world with continuous updates about the attack and its aftermath. Meanwhile, network blockbusters such as *Lost* and *24* have united viewers in shared anticipation, launching numerous blogs, fan sites, and speculative workplace discussions about characters' fates.

Televised coverage of the news has had several cultural effects since the 1950s. Providing viewers with footage of the most intense human experiences, televised news has been able to reach people in a way that radio and newspapers cannot. The images themselves have played an important role in influencing viewer opinion. During the coverage of the civil rights movement, for example, footage of a 1963 attack on civil rights protesters in Birmingham, Alabama, showed police blasting African American demonstrators—many of them children—with fire hoses. Coupled with images of angry White segregationist mobs squaring off against Black students, the news footage did much to sway public opinion in favor of liberal legislation such as the 1964 Voting Rights Act. Conversely, when volatile pictures of the race riots in Detroit and other cities in the late 1960s hit the airwaves, horrified viewers saw the need for a return to law and order. The footage helped create an anti-civil-rights backlash that encouraged many viewers to vote for conservative Republican Richard Nixon during the 1968 presidential election.

During the past few decades, mass-media news coverage has gone beyond swaying public opinion through mere imagery. Trusted centrist voices such as that of Walter Cronkite, who was known for his impartial reporting of some of the biggest news stories in the 1960s, have been replaced by highly politicized news coverage on cable channels such as conservative Fox News and liberal MSNBC. As broadcasters narrow their focus to cater to more specialized audiences, viewers choose to watch the networks that suit their political bias. Middle-of-the-road network CNN, which aims for nonpartisanship, frequently loses out in the ratings wars against Fox and MSNBC, both of which have fierce groups of supporters. As one reporter put it, "A small partisan base is enough for big ratings; the mildly interested middle might rather watch *Grey's Anatomy* (Poniewozik, 2010)." Critics argue that partisan news networks cause viewers to have less understanding of opposing political opinions, making them more polarized.

Table 9.1 Partisan Profile of TV News Audiences in 2008

News Channel	Republican (%)	Democratic (%)	Independent (%)
Fox News	39	33	22
Nightly Network	22	45	26
MSNBC	18	45	27
CNN	18	51	23
NewsHour	21	46	23

Source: "Partisanship and Cable News Audiences," Oct. 30, 2009, Pew Research Center for the People & the Press, a project of the Pew Research Center

Social Controversy

The issue of whether television producers have a responsibility to promote particular social values continues to generate heated discussion. When the unmarried title character in the CBS series *Murphy Brown*—a comedy show about a divorced anchorwoman—got pregnant and chose to have the baby without any involvement from the father, then–Vice President Dan Quayle referenced the show as an example of degenerating family values. Linking the 1992 Los Angeles riots to a breakdown of family structure and social order, Quayle lambasted producers' poor judgment, saying, "It doesn't help matters when prime-time TV has Murphy Brown, a character who supposedly epitomizes today's intelligent, highly paid professional woman, mocking the importance of fathers by bearing a child alone, and calling it just another 'lifestyle choice (Time, 1992).'" Quayle's outburst sparked lively debate between supporters and opponents of his viewpoint, with some praising his outspoken social commentary and others dismissing him as out of touch with America and its growing number of single mothers.

Similar controversy arose with the portrayal of openly gay characters on prime-time television shows. When the lead character on the ABC sitcom *Ellen* came out in 1997 (2 weeks after Ellen DeGeneres, the actress who played the role, announced that she was gay), she became the first leading gay character on both broadcast and cable networks. The show proved to be a test case for the nation's tolerance of openly gay characters on prime-time TV and became the subject of much debate. Embraced by liberal supporters and lambasted by conservative objectors (evangelical Baptist minister Jerry Falwell infamously dubbed her "Ellen DeGenerate"), both the actress and the show furthered the quest to make homosexuality acceptable to mainstream audiences. Although *Ellen* was canceled the following year (amid disagreements with producers about whether it should contain a parental advisory warning), DeGeneres successfully returned to television in 2003 with her own talk show. Subsequent shows with prominent gay characters were quick to follow in *Ellen*'s footsteps. According to the Gay & Lesbian Alliance Against Defamation (GLAAD), 18 lesbian, gay, bisexual, or transgender characters accounted for 3 percent of scripted series regulars in the 2009–2010 broadcast television schedule, up from 1.3 percent in 2006 (Mitchell, 2009).

Creating Stars via Reality Television

Emerging out of the 1948 TV series *Candid Camera*, in which people were secretly filmed responding to elaborate practical jokes, reality television aimed to capture real, unscripted life on camera. The genre developed in several different directions, from home-video clip shows (*America's Funniest Home Videos*, *America's Funniest People*) to true-crime reenactment shows (*America's Most Wanted*, *Unsolved Mysteries*) to thematic shows based on professions of interest (*Project Runway*, *Police Women of Broward County*, *Top Chef*). Near the turn of the millennium, the genre began to lean toward more voyeuristic shows, such as MTV's *The Real World*, an unscripted "documentary" that followed the lives of seven strangers selected to live together in a large house or apartment in a major city. The show drew criticisms for glamorizing bad behavior and encouraging excessive drinking and casual sex, although its ratings soared with each successive controversy (a trend that critics claim encouraged producers to actively stage rating-grabbing scenarios). During the late 1990s and 2000s, a wave of copycat reality TV shows emerged, including the voyeuristic series *Big Brother*, which filmed a group of strangers living together in an isolated house full of cameras in an attempt to win large amounts of cash, and *Survivor*, a game show in which participants competed against each other by performing endurance challenges on an uninhabited island. *Survivor*'s success as the most popular show on television in the summer of 2000 ensured the continued growth of the reality television genre, and producers turned their attention to reality dating shows such as *The Bachelor*, *Temptation Island*, and *Dating in the Dark*. Cheap to produce, with a seemingly never-ending supply of willing contestants and eager advertising sponsors, reality TV shows continue to bring in big ratings. As of 2010, singing talent competition *American Idol* is television's biggest revenue generator, pulling in $8.1 million in advertising sales every 30 minutes it is on the air (Bond, 2010).

Figure 9.12

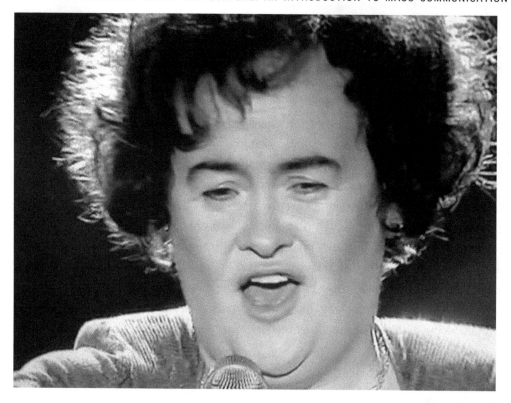

The stress of appearing on reality television shows has proved detrimental to some contestants' health. *Britain's Got Talent* star Susan Boyle suffered a nervous breakdown in 2009.

Banalities – SuBo Dreamed a Dream – CC BY 2.0.

Reality TV has created the cultural phenomenon of the instant celebrity. Famous for simply being on the air, reality show contestants are extending their 15 minutes in the spotlight. Kate Gosselin, star of *Jon & Kate Plus 8*, a cable TV show about a couple who have eight children, has since appeared in numerous magazine articles, and in 2010 she starred on celebrity reality dance show *Dancing with the Stars*. *Survivor* contestant Elisabeth Hasselbeck became a co-host on TV talk show *The View*, and several *American Idol* contestants (including Kelly Clarkson and Carrie Underwood) have become household names. The genre has drawn criticism for creating a generation that expects to achieve instant wealth without having to try very hard and also for preying on vulnerable people whom critics call "disposable." When *Britain's Got Talent* star Susan Boyle suffered a public meltdown in 2009 after the stress of transitioning from obscurity to stardom in an extremely short time period, the media began to point out the dangers of reality television. In 2009, TheWrap.com investigated the current lives of former stars of reality shows such as *The Contender*, *Paradise Hotel*, *Wife Swap*, and *Extreme Makeover*, and found that at least 11 participants had committed suicide as an apparent result of their appearances on screen (Adams, 2009; Feldlinger).

Key Takeaways

- Television has been reflecting changing cultural values since it first gained popularity after World War II. During the 1950s, most programs ignored current events and political issues in favor of family-friendly domestic comedies, which featured White suburban middle-class families. Extreme stress during the 1960s, caused by political events such as the Vietnam War and the Cuban Missile Crisis, led people to turn to escapist television offered by fantasy sitcoms. These provided a sharp dichotomy with the hard-news shows of the era. Social consciousness during the 1970s prompted television producers to reflect changing social attitudes regarding single parenthood, women's roles, and divorce, and sitcom families began to reflect the increasing number of non-nuclear families in society. The increasing popularity of cable TV in the 1980s led to an explosion of news and entertainment channels, some of which raised concerns about the levels of violence on television. During the 1990s and 2000s, TV networks became more specialized, catering to niche markets in order to meet the needs of an increasingly fragmented audience.

- Television reflects cultural values, and it also influences culture. One example of this is the polarization of cable TV news, which is no longer centrist but caters to individual political tastes. Critics argue that this influences cable news viewers' opinions and makes them less open to opposing political viewpoints. Entertainment programs also play an influential role within society. By portraying controversial relationships such as single parents or gay couples as acceptable, TV shows have the power to shape viewers' attitudes. In recent years, broadcasters have created the concept of the instant celebrity through the genre of reality television. Contestants on reality TV shows now permeate every aspect of culture and the media, from the music charts to popular magazines and newspapers.

Exercises

Please respond to the following short-answer writing prompts. Each response should be a minimum of one paragraph.

1. Choose a popular sitcom from the past 50 years you are familiar with (you can view episodes on Hulu.com to refamiliarize yourself if necessary). Using the ideas in this section as a starting point, identify three ways in which your chosen sitcom reflects or reflected American culture.

2. Spend a few days reviewing news coverage on Fox News and MSNBC. How is coverage of similar news stories different? Do you think partisan news networks can affect public opinion? Why or why not?

References

Adams, Guy. "Lessons From America on the Dangers of Reality Television," *Independent* (London), June 6, 2009, http://www.independent.co.uk/news/world/americas/lessons-from-america-on-the-dangers-of-reality-television-1698165.html.

Blakey, Rea. "Study Links TV Viewing Among Kids to Later Violence," *CNN Health*, March 28, 2002, http://archives.cnn.com/2002/HEALTH/parenting/03/28/kids.tv.violence/index.html.

Bond, Paul. "'Idol' Listed as TV's Biggest Revenue Generator," *Hollywood Reporter*, May 5, 2010, http://www.hollywoodreporter.com/hr/content_display/news/e3i8f1f42046a622bda2d602430b16d3ed9.

Coontz, Stephanie. "'Leave It to Beaver' and 'Ozzie and Harriet': American Families in the 1950s," in *The Way We Never Were: American Families and the Nostalgia Trip* (New York: BasicBooks, 1992), 28.

Forbes, "BET Networks Unveils New African American Consumer Market Research and New Programming at 2010 Upfront Presentation," April 14, 2010, http://www.forbes.com/feeds/prnewswire/2010/04/14/prnewswire201004141601PR_NEWS_USPR_____NE86679.html.

Fox News, The O'Reilly Factor, "Is Black Entertainment Television Taking a Disturbing Turn?" *Fox News*, May 26, 2004, http://www.foxnews.com/story/0,2933,120993,00.html.

Frank Feldlinger, "TheWrap Investigates: 11 Players Have Committed Suicide," TheWrap, http://www.thewrap.com/television/article/thewrap-investigates-11-players-have-committed-suicide-3409.

Friedman, Michael J. "'See It Now': Murrow vs. McCarthy," in *Edward R. Murrow: Journalism at Its Best*, publication of U.S. Department of State, June 1, 2008, http://www.america.gov/st/democracyhr-english/2008/June/20080601110244eaifas8.602542e-02.html.

Gunther, Marc. "The Extinction of Mass Culture, *CNN Money*, July 12, 2006, http://money.cnn.com/2006/07/11/news/economy/pluggedin_gunther.fortune/index.htm.

Mitchell, Wendy. "GLAAD Report: Gay Characters on Network TV Still on the Rise," *Entertainment Weekly*, September 30, 2009, http://hollywoodinsider.ew.com/2009/09/30/glaad-report-gay-characters-on-rise/.

Newcomb, Horace. ed., *Encyclopedia of Television* (New York: Fitzroy Dearborn, 2004), 389.

Poniewozik, James. "CNN: Can a Mainstream News Outlet Survive?" *Time*, May 3, 2010, http://www.time.com/time/magazine/article/0,9171,1983901,00.html.

Time, "Dan Quayle vs. Murphy Brown," June 1, 1992, http://www.time.com/time/magazine/article/0,9171,975627,00.html.

9.3 Issues and Trends in the Television Industry

Learning Objectives

1. Explain the influence of sponsors on program content.
2. Describe the major trends among the broadcasting and cable networks.

When television was in its infancy, producers modeled the new medium on radio. Popular radio shows such as police drama *Dragnet* and western cowboy series *Gunsmoke* were adapted for television, and new TV shows were sponsored by single advertisers, just as radio shows had been. Television was dominated by three major networks—NBC, ABC, and CBS—and these networks accounted for more than 95 percent of all prime-time viewing until the late 1970s. Today, the television industry is far more complex. Programs are sponsored by multiple advertisers; programming is controlled by major media conglomerates; and the three major networks no longer dominate the airwaves but instead share their viewers with numerous cable channels. Several factors account for these trends within the industry, including technological developments, government regulations, and the creation of new networks.

The Influence of Corporate Sponsorship

Early television programs were often developed, produced, and supported by a single sponsor, which sometimes reaped the benefits of having its name inserted into the program's title—*Colgate Comedy Hour*, *Camel Newsreel*, *Goodyear TV Playhouse*. However, as production costs soared during the 1950s (a single one-hour TV show cost a sponsor about $35,000 in 1952 compared with $90,000 at the end of the decade), sponsors became increasingly unable to bear the financial burden of promoting a show single-handedly. This suited the broadcast networks, which disliked the influence sponsors exerted over program content. Television executives, in particular NBC's Sylvester L. "Pat" Weaver, advocated the magazine concept, in which advertisers purchased one- or two-minute blocks rather than the entire program, just as magazines contained multiple advertisements from different sponsors. The presence of multiple sponsors meant that no one advertiser controlled the entire program.

Figure 9.13

Many sponsors believed that if viewers identified their favorite shows, such as the *Colgate Comedy Hour*, with a sponsor, they would be more likely to purchase the product being advertised.

Although advertising agencies relinquished control of production to the networks, they retained some influence over the content of the programs they sponsored. As one executive commented, "If my client sells peanut butter and the script calls for a guy to be poisoned eating a peanut butter sandwich, you can bet we're going to switch that poison to a martini (Newcomb)." Sponsors continue to influence program content indirectly by financially supporting shows they support and pulling funding from those they do not. For example, in 1995, pharmaceutical giant Procter & Gamble, the largest television advertiser, announced it would no longer sponsor salacious daytime talk shows. The company provided producers with details about its guidelines, pulling out of shows it deemed offensive and supporting shows that dealt with controversial subject matter responsibly. Communications heavyweight AT&T took a similar path, reviewing shows after they were taped but before they aired in order to make decisions about corporate sponsorship on an individual basis (Advertising Age, 1995). In 2009, advertisers used their financial might to take a stand against Fox News host Glenn Beck, who offended viewers and sponsors alike with his incendiary comments that President Obama was a "racist" and had a "deep-seated hatred for white people." Sponsors of the *Glenn Beck* TV talk show began to remove advertising spots from the program in protest of Beck's comments. A spokeswoman for Progressive car insurance said, "We place advertising on a variety of programming with the goal of reaching a broad range of insurance consumers who might be interested in our products. We also seek to avoid advertising on programming that our customers or potential customers may find extremely offensive (Spain, 2009)." Other shows whose advertisers have pulled ads include NBC's long-running sketch comedy show *Saturday Night Live*, BET's *Hot Ghetto Mess*, and ABC's *Ellen* sitcom.

Public Television and Corporate Sponsorship

Corporate sponsorship does not just affect network television. Even public television has become subject to the influence of advertising. Established in 1969, Public Broadcasting Service (PBS) developed out of a report by the Carnegie Commission on Educational Television, which examined the role of educational, noncommercial television on society. The report recommended that the government finance public television in order to provide diversity of programming during the network era—a service created "not to sell products" but to "enhance citizenship and public service (McCauley, 2003)." Public television was also intended to provide universal access to television for viewers in rural areas or viewers who could not afford to pay for private television services. PBS focused on educational program content, targeting viewers who were less appealing to the commercial networks and advertisers, such as the over-50 age demographic and children under 12.

The original Carnegie Commission report recommended that Congress create a federal trust fund based on a manufacturer's excise tax on the sale of TV sets to finance public television. Following intense lobbying by the National Association of Broadcasters, the proposal was removed from the legislation that established the service. As a result, public television subsists on viewer contributions and federal funding and the latter has been drastically reduced in recent years. Although a 2007 proposal by President George W. Bush to eliminate more than half of the federal allocation to public broadcasting ($420 million out of $820 million) was overturned, PBS has become increasingly dependent on corporate sponsorship to stay afloat. By 2006, corporate sponsors funded more than 25 percent of all public television. Sponsorship has saved many programs that would otherwise have been lost, but critics have bemoaned the creeping commercialism of public television. When PBS began selling banner advertisements on its website in 2006, Gary Ruskin, executive director of consumer group Commercial Alert, commented, "It's just one more intrusion of the commercial ethos into an organization that was supposed to be firmly noncommercial. The line between them and the commercial networks is getting fuzzier and fuzzier (Gold, 2006)." Despite such criticisms, the drop in federal funding has forced public television executives to seek more creative ways of obtaining financial backing—for example, through online banner ads. In 2009, PBS shortened the length of time companies were required to sponsor some programs in an effort to encourage advertisers (Stelter, 2009). As of 2010, the future of PBS remained uncertain. With better-funded cable channels offering niche-interest shows that were traditionally public television's domain (BBC nature series *Planet Earth* was shown on the Discovery Channel, while historical dramas *John Adams* and *The Tudors* are shown on premium cable channels HBO and Showtime), PBS is left to rely on shows that have been around for decades, such as *Nova* and *Nature*, to attract audiences (McGrath, 2008). Only time will tell how PBS fares in the face of competition.

The Rise and Fall of the Network

The period between 1950 and 1970 is historically recognized as the network era. Aside from a small portion of airtime controlled by public television, the three major networks (known as the Big Three) dominated the television industry, collectively accounting for more than 95 percent of prime-time viewing. In 1986, Rupert Murdoch, the head of multinational company News Corp, launched the Fox network, challenging the dominance of the Big Three. In its infancy, Fox was at best a minor irritation to the other networks. With fewer than 100 affiliated stations (the other networks all had more than 200 affiliates each), reaching just 80 percent of the nation's households (compared with the Big Three's 97 percent coverage rate), and broadcasting just one show (*The Late Show Starring Joan Rivers*), Fox was barely a consideration in the ratings war. During the early 1990s, these dynamics began to change. Targeting young viewers and Black audiences with shows such as *Beverly*

Hills 90210, Melrose Place, In Living Color, and *The Simpsons,* Fox began to establish itself as an edgy, youth-oriented network. Luring affiliates away from other networks to increase its viewership, Fox also extended its programming schedule beyond the initial 2-night-a-week broadcasts. By the time the fledgling network acquired the rights to National Football League (NFL) games with its $1.58 billion NFL deal in 1994, entitling it to 4 years of NFL games, Fox was a worthy rival to the other three broadcast networks. Its success turned the Big Three into the Big Four. In the 1994–1995 television season, 43 percent of U.S. households were watching the Big Four at any given moment during prime time (Poniewozik, 2009).

Fox's success prompted the launch of several smaller networks in the mid-1990s. UPN (owned by Paramount, recently acquired by Viacom) and WB (owned by media giant Time Warner) both debuted in January 1995. Using strategies similar to Fox, the networks initially began broadcasting programs 2 nights a week, expanding to a 6-day schedule by 2000. Targeting young and minority audiences with shows such as *Buffy the Vampire Slayer, Moesha, Dawson's Creek,* and *The Wayans Bros.,* the new networks hoped to draw stations away from their old network affiliations. However, rather than repeating the success of Fox, UPN and WB struggled to make an impact. Unable to attract many affiliate stations, the two fledgling networks reached fewer households than their larger rivals because they were unobtainable in some smaller cities. High start-up costs, relatively low audience ratings, and increasing production expenses spelled the end of the "netlets," a term coined by *Variety* magazine for minor-league networks that lacked a full week's worth of programming. After losing $1 billion each, parent companies CBS (having split from Viacom) and Time Warner agreed to merge UPN and WB, resulting in the creation of the CW network in 2006. Targeting the desirable 18–34 age group, the network retained the most popular shows from before the merger—*America's Next Top Model* and *Veronica Mars* from UPN and *Beauty and the Geek* and *Smallville* from WB—as well as launching new shows such as *Gossip Girl* and *The Vampire Diaries.* Despite its cofounders' claims that the CW would be the "fifth great broadcast network," the collaboration got off to a shaky start. Frequently outperformed by Spanish-language television network Univision in 2008 and with declining ratings among its target audience, critics began to question the future of the CW network (Grego, 2010). However, the relative success of shows such as *Gossip Girl* and *90210* in 2009 gave the network a foothold on its intended demographic, quashing rumors that co-owners CBS Corporation and Warner Bros. might disband the network. Warner Bros. Television Group President Bruce Rosenblum said, "I think the built-in assumption and the expectation is that the CW is here to stay (Collins, 2009)."

Figure 9.14

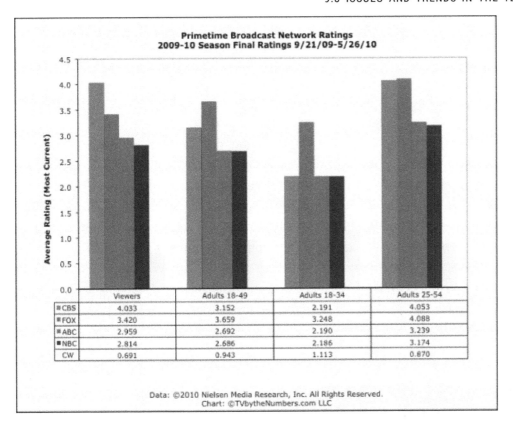

Despite launching several new shows geared toward its target demographic, the CW remains fifth in the network rankings.

Cable Challenges the Networks

A far greater challenge to network television than the emergence of smaller competitors was the increasing dominance of cable television. Between 1994 and 2009, the percentage of U.S. households watching the Big Four networks during prime time plummeted from 43 percent to 27 percent (Poniewozik, 2009). Two key factors influenced the rapid growth of cable television networks: industry deregulation and the use of satellites to distribute local TV stations around the country.

During the 1970s, the growth of cable television was restricted by FCC regulations, which protected broadcasters by establishing franchising standards and enforcing anti-siphoning rules that prevented cable from taking sports and movie programming away from the networks. However, during the late 1970s, a court ruled that the FCC had exceeded its authority, and the anti-siphoning rules were repealed. This decision paved the way for the development of cable movie channels, contributing to the exponential growth of cable in the 1980s and 1990s. Further deregulation of cable in the 1984 Cable Communications Policy Act removed restrictions on cable rates, enabling operators to charge what they wanted for cable services as long as there was effective competition to the service (a standard that over 90 percent of all cable markets could meet). Other deregulatory policies during the 1980s included the eradication of public-service requirements and the elimination of regulated amounts of advertising in children's programming, expanding the scope of cable channel stations. Deregulation was intended to encourage competition within the industry but instead enabled local cable companies to establish monopolies all over the country. In 1989, U.S. Senator Al Gore of Tennessee commented, "Precipitous rate hikes of 100 percent or more in one year have not been unusual since cable was given total freedom to charge whatever the market will bear…. Since cable was deregulated, we have also witnessed an extraordinary concentration of control and integration by cable operators and program services, manifesting itself in blatantly anticompetitive behavior toward those who would compete with existing cable operators for the right to distribute services (Zaretsky, 1995)." The FCC reintroduced regulations for basic cable rates in 1992, by which time more than 56 million households (over 60 percent of the households with televisions) subscribed to a cable service.

The growth of cable TV was also assisted by a national satellite distribution system. Pioneered by Time Inc., which founded cable network company HBO, the corporation used satellite transmission in 1975 to beam the "Thrilla from Manila"—the historic heavyweight boxing match between Muhammad Ali and Joe Frazier—into people's homes. Shortly afterward, entrepreneur Ted Turner, owner of independent Atlanta-based station WTBS, uplinked his station's signal onto the same satellite as HBO, enabling cable operators to downlink the station on one of their channels. Initially provided free to subscribers to encourage interest, the station offered TV reruns, wrestling, and live sports from Atlanta. Having created the first "superstation," Turner expanded his realm by founding 24-hour news network CNN in 1980. At the end of the year, 28 national programming services were available, and the cable revolution had begun. Over the next decade, the industry underwent a period of rapid growth and popularity, and by 1994 viewers could choose from 94 basic and 20 premium cable services.

Figure 9.15

The 1975 "Thrilla from Manila" was one of the first offerings by HBO.

benyupp – muhammad ali – CC BY 2.0.

Narrowcasting

Because the proliferation of cable channels provided viewers with so many choices, broadcasters began to move away from mass-oriented programming in favor of more targeted shows. Whereas the broadcast networks sought to obtain the widest audience possible by avoiding programs that might only appeal to a small minority of viewers, cable channels sought out niche audiences within specific demographic groups—a process known as narrowcasting. In much the same way that specialist magazines target readers interested in a particular sport or hobby, cable channels emphasize one topic, or group of related topics, that appeal to specific viewers (often those who have been neglected by broadcast television). People interested in current affairs can tune into CNN, MSNBC, Fox News, or any number of other news channels, while those interested in sports can switch on ESPN or TSN (The Sports Network). Other channels focus on music, shopping, comedy, science fiction, or programs aimed at specific cultural or gender groups. Narrowcasting has proved beneficial for advertisers and marketers, who no longer need to time their communications based on the groups of people who are most likely to watch television at certain times of the day. Instead, they concentrate their approach on subscription channels that appeal directly to their target consumers.

Impact on Networks

The popularity of cable television has forced the Big Four networks to rethink their approach to programming over the past three decades. Because of the narrowcasting mode of distribution and exhibition, cable TV has offered more explicit sexual and violent content than broadcast television does. To compete for cable channels' viewing audience, broadcast networks have loosened restrictions on graphic material and now frequently feature partial nudity, violence, and coarse language. This has increased viewership of mildly controversial shows such as *CSI*, *NCIS*, *Grey's Anatomy*, and *Private Practice*, while opening the networks to attacks from conservative advocacy groups that object to extreme content.

The broadcast networks are increasingly adapting narrowcasting as a programming strategy. Newer networks, such as the CW, deliberately target the 18–34 age group (women in particular). Since its inception, the CW has replaced urban comedies such as *Everybody Hates Chris* with female-oriented series such as *Gossip Girl* and *The Vampire Diaries*. Older networks group similar programs that appeal to specific groups in adjacent time slots to retain viewers for as long as possible. For example, ABC sitcoms *Modern Family* and *Cougar Town* run back to back, while Fox follows reality police series *Cops* with crime-fighting show *America's Most Wanted*.

Despite responding to challenges from cable, the broadcast networks' share of the total audience has declined each year. Between 2000 and 2009, the networks saw their numbers drop by around 8 million viewers (Bianco, 2009).

Figure 9.16

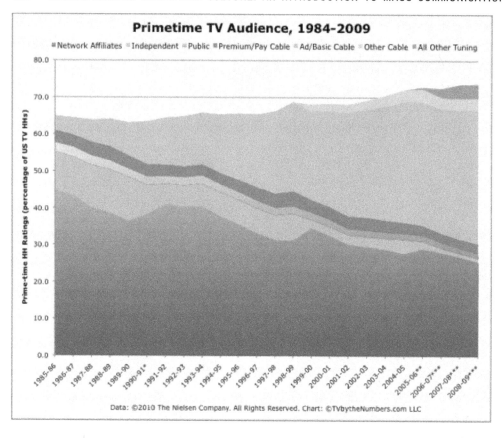

Primetime TV Audience, 1984-2009

Network Affiliates ■ Independent ■ Public ■ Premium/Pay Cable ■ Ad/Basic Cable ■ Other Cable ■ All Other Tuning

Data: ©2010 The Nielsen Company. All Rights Reserved. Chart: ©TVbytheNumbers.com LLC

Increased competition from cable channels has caused a steady decline in the networks' audience ratings.

Key Takeaways

- During the 1950s, the cost of producing a single television show increased as shows became longer and production costs soared. Sponsorship on network television shifted from single sponsorship, in which a program was entirely supported and produced by one advertiser, to multiple sponsorship, in which advertisers bought 1- or 2-minute spots on the show. Although no one advertiser controlled the content of the show, sponsors had some say in the program's subject matter. Sponsors have retained some control over program content by withdrawing funding from shows that are deemed to have offensive or inappropriate content.

- Public television was created to enhance citizenship and also to provide a television service for people in rural areas or those who could not afford to pay for a private television service. Despite its origins as a noncommercial entity, public television has increasingly had to turn to commercial sponsorship to stay afloat. Government funding for public television has declined over the years, and competition from niche cable channels has rendered its future uncertain.

- Between 1950 and 1970, the Big Three networks (ABC, CBS, and NBC) accounted for around 95 percent of prime-time viewing. The addition of Fox in 1986 created the Big Four; however, attempts to create an additional major network have been unsuccessful. CBS-owned UPN and Time Warner-owned WB merged in 2006 to create the CW. Targeted at women aged 18–34, the CW consistently ranks a low fifth in the ratings.

- The primary challenge to network television has been the rapid growth of cable, which grew exponentially in the 1980s and 1990s as a result of industry deregulation and the use of satellites to distribute local channels to a national audience (pioneered by HBO in the 1970s). Cable broadcasters use a process known as narrowcasting to target niche audiences for their shows. Channels usually focus on a single topic, such as news, weather, shopping, or comedy. Competition from cable has forced network television to loosen its restrictions regarding sex and violence on shows, and the networks have turned increasingly to narrowcasting in an effort to retain audiences. Despite its efforts, competition from cable and other sources has caused prime-time viewing audiences of the Big Four networks to drop from 43 percent in 1994 to 27 percent in 2009.

Exercises

Please respond to the following short-answer writing prompts. Each response should be a minimum of one paragraph.

1.
Choose one of the Big Four networks and print out its weekly programming schedule. Watch the network's prime-time programs over the course of a week, noting the target demographic for each show. Observe the advertising sponsors that support each show and compare how the products and services fit with the intended audience.

- Does the network make use of narrowcasting to air shows with the same demographic in adjacent time slots?

- How do the types of products and services advertised during each show change depending on the content and target audience?

- Does the network cater to one target audience in particular?

2. How has the rise of cable television affected the Big Four networks? What trends have emerged out of this competition?

References

Advertising Age, "Speak Up About Talk Shows," November 27, 1995, http://adage.com/article?article_id=84233.

Bianco, Robert. "The Decade in Television: Cable, the Internet Become Players," *USA Today*, December 29, 2009, http://www.usatoday.com/life/television/news/2009-12-28-decadeTV28_CV_N.htm.

Collins, Scott. "With Ratings Comeback, has CW Finally Turned the Corner?" *Los Angeles Times*, April 7, 2009, http://latimesblogs.latimes.com/showtracker/2009/04/last-week-the-cw-scored-its-best-ratings-in-nearly-five-months-ordinarily-this-might-not -sound-like-huge-news-but-cw-is-a.html.

Gold, Matea. "Marketing Tie-ins Finding Their Way to PBS Sponsors," *Baltimore Sun*, October 23, 2006, http://articles.baltimoresun.com/2006-10-23/features/0610230151_1_pbs-corporate-underwriters-public-television.

Grego, Melissa. "How The CW Stays Undead," *Broadcasting and Cable*, February 1, 2010, http://www.broadcastingcable.com/article/446733-How_The_CW_Stays_Undead.php.

McCauley, Michael P. *Public Broadcasting and the Public Interest* (Armonk, NY: M. E. Sharpe, 2003), 239.

McGrath, Charles. "Is PBS Still Necessary?" *New York Times*, February 17, 2008, http://www.nytimes.com/2008/02/17/arts/television/17mcgr.html.

Newcomb, *Encyclopedia of Television*, 2170.

Poniewozik, James. "Here's to the Death of Broadcast," *Time*, March 26, 2009, http://www.time.com/time/magazine/article/0,9171,1887840,00.html.

Spain, William. "Advertisers Deserting Fox News' Glenn Beck," *MarketWatch*, August 14, 2009, http://www.marketwatch.com/story/advertisers-deserting-fox-news-glenn-beck-2009-08-14.

Stelter, Brian. "PBS to Shorten Time Commitments for Sponsorships," *New York Times*, May 7, 2009, http://www.nytimes.com/2009/05/08/business/media/08adco.html.

Zaretsky, Adam M. "The Cable TV Industry and Regulation," *Regional Economist*, July 1995, http://research.stlouisfed.org/publications/regional/95/07/CableTV.pdf.

9.4 Influence of New Technologies

Learning Objectives

1. Describe the difference between satellite television and cable television.

2. Identify two of the major satellite companies in today's market.

3. Identify ways in which the Internet has affected content delivery and viewing patterns.

The experience of watching television is rapidly changing with the progression of technology. No longer restricted to a limited number of channels on network television, or even to a TV schedule, viewers are now able to watch exactly what they want to watch, when they want to watch it. Nontelevision delivery systems such as the Internet, which enables viewers to download traditional TV shows onto a computer, laptop, iPod, or smartphone, are changing the way people watch television. Meanwhile, cable and satellite providers are enabling viewers to purchase TV shows to watch at their convenience through the use of video-on-demand services, changing the concept of prime-time viewing. Digital video recording (DVR) systems such as TiVo, which enable users to record particular shows onto the system's computer memory, are having a similar effect.

Although TV audiences are becoming increasingly fragmented, they are also growing because of the convenience and availability of new technology. In 2009, Nielsen's Three Screen Report, which encompassed television, cell phone, and computer usage, reported that the average viewer watched more than 151 hours of television per month, up 3.6 percent from the previous year (Semuels, 2009). Viewers might not all be sitting together in the family room watching prime-time shows on network TV between 7 and 11 p.m., but they are watching.

The War Between Satellite and Cable Television

The origins of satellite television can be traced to the space race of the 1950s, when the United States and the Soviet Union were competing to put the first satellite into space. Soviet scientists accomplished the goal first with the launch of *Sputnik* in 1957, galvanizing Americans (who were fearful of falling behind in space technology during the Cold War era) into intensifying their efforts and resulting in the creation of the National Aeronautics and Space Administration (NASA) in 1958. AT&T launched *Telstar*, the first active communications satellite, on July 10, 1962, and the first transatlantic television signal—a black-and-white image of a U.S. flag waving in front of the Andover Earth Station in western Maine—transmitted that same day. However, the television industry did not utilize satellites for broadcasting purposes until the late 1970s when PBS introduced Public Television Satellite Service. Satellite communication technology caught on and was used by broadcasters as a distribution method between 1978 and 1984 by pioneering cable channels such as HBO, TBS (Turner Broadcasting System), and CBN (Christian Broadcasting Network, later the Family Channel).

The trouble with early satellite television systems was that once people purchased a satellite system, they had free access to every basic and premium cable service that was broadcasting via satellite signals. The FCC had an "open skies" policy, under which users had as much right to receive signals as broadcasters had the right to transmit them. Initially, the satellite receiver systems were prohibitively expensive for most families, costing more than $10,000. However, as the price of a satellite dish dropped toward the $3,000 mark in the mid-1980s, consumers began to view satellite TV as a cheaper, higher-quality alternative to cable. Following the initial purchase of a dish system, the actual programming—consisting of more than 100 cable channels—was free. Cable broadcasters lobbied the government for legal assistance and, under the 1984 Cable Act, were allowed to encrypt their satellite feeds so that only people who purchased a decoder from a satellite provider could receive the channel.

Following the passing of the Cable Act, the satellite industry took a dramatic hit. Sales of the popular direct-to-home (DTH) systems (precursors to the smaller, more powerful direct broadcast satellite systems introduced in the 1990s) that had offered free cable programming slumped from 735,000 units in 1985 to 225,000 units a year later, and around 60 percent of satellite retailers went out of business. The satellite industry's sudden drop in popularity was exacerbated by large-scale antidish advertising campaigns by cable operators, depicting satellite dishes as unsightly. Although sales picked up in the late 1980s with the introduction of integrated receiving and decoding units and the arrival of program packages, which saved consumers the time and effort of signing up for individual programming services, the growth of the satellite industry was stunted by piracy—the theft of satellite signals. Of the 1.9 million units manufactured between 1986 and 1990, fewer than 500,000 were receiving signals legally (Thibedeau, 2000). The problem was ultimately solved by the actions of the Satellite Broadcasting and Communications Association (SBCA), an association created in 1986 by the merger of two trade organizations—the Society of Private and Commercial Earth Stations (SPACE) and the Direct Broadcast Satellite Association (DBSA). SPACE was composed of manufacturers, distributors, and retailers of direct-to-home systems, and DBSA represented companies interested in direct broadcast satellite systems. The SBCA set up an antipiracy task force, aggressively pursuing illegal hackers with the FBI's help.

Once the piracy problem was under control, the satellite industry could move forward. In 1994, four major cable companies launched a first-generation direct broadcast satellite (DBS) system called PrimeStar. The system, a small-dish satellite-delivered program service specifically intended for home reception, was the first successful attempt to enter the market in the United States. Within a year, PrimeStar was beaming 67 channels into 70,000 homes for a monthly fee of $25 to $35 (in addition to a hardware installation fee of $100 to $200). By 1996, competing companies DirecTV and the EchoStar Dish Network had entered the industry, and Dish Network's cheaper prices were forcing its competitors to drop their fees. DirecTV acquired PrimeStar's assets in 1999 for around $1.82 billion, absorbing its rival's 2.3 million subscribers (Junnarker, 1999).

Figure 9.17

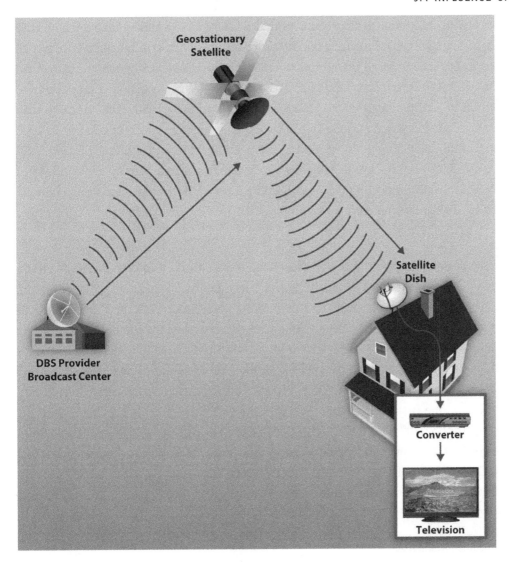

Subscribers of DBS receive signals from geostationary satellites that are broadcast in digital format at microwave frequency and intercepted by a satellite dish. A converter next to the television produces output that can be viewed on the television receiver.

The Current Satellite Market: DirecTV versus Dish Network

As of 2010, the two biggest players in the satellite TV industry are DirecTV and Dish Network. Assisted by the passing of the Satellite Television Home Viewers Act in 1999, which enabled satellite providers to carry local TV stations (putting them on equal footing with cable television), both companies have grown rapidly over the past decade. In the first quarter of 2010, DirecTV boasted 18.6 million subscribers, placing it ahead of its rival, Dish Network, which reported a total of 14.3 million subscribers (Paul, 2010). Dish courts customers who have been hit by the economic downturn, aggressively cutting its prices and emphasizing its low rates. Conversely, DirecTV targets affluent consumers, emphasizing quality and choice in its advertising campaigns and investing in advanced services and products such as multiroom viewing (enabling a subscriber to watch a show in one room, pause it, and continue watching the same show in another room) to differentiate itself from rival satellite and cable companies.

Since the 1999 legislation put satellite television in direct competition with cable, the major satellite companies have increasingly pitted themselves against cable broadcasters, offering consumers numerous incentives to switch providers. One of these incentives is the addition of premium networks for satellite subscribers in the same vein as premium cable channel HBO. In 2005, DirecTV expanded its 101 Network channel to include original shows, becoming the first satellite station to air first episodes of a broadcast television series with NBC daytime soap opera *Passions* in 2007. The station aired first-run episodes of football drama series *Friday Night Lights* in 2008 and set its sights on the male over-35 demographic by obtaining syndication rights to popular HBO series *Oz* and *Deadwood* a year later. Commenting on the satellite company's programming plans, executive vice president for entertainment for DirecTV Eric Shanks said, "We'd like to become a pre-cable window for these premium channels (Carter, 2009)." In other words, the company hopes to purchase HBO shows such as *Sex and the City* before HBO sells the series to basic-cable channels like TBS.

In another overt bid to lure cable customers over to satellite television, both DirecTV and Dish Network offer a number of comprehensive movies and sports packages, benefiting from their additional channel capacity (satellite TV providers typically offer around 350 channels, compared with 180 channels on cable) and their ability to receive international channels often unavailable on cable. In the mid-2000s, the satellite companies also began encroaching on cable TV's domination of bundled packages, by offering all-in-one phone, Internet, and television services. Despite being ideally suited to offering such packages with their single telecommunications pipe into the house, cable companies such as Comcast, Cox, and Time Warner had developed a reputation for offering poor service at extortionate prices. In the first three quarters of 2004, the eight largest cable providers (with the exception of bankrupt Adelphia) lost 552,000 basic-cable subscribers. Between 2000 and 2004, cable's share of the TV market fell from 66 percent to 62 percent, while the number of U.S. households with satellite TV increased from 12 percent to 19 percent (Belson, 2004). Despite reports that cash-strapped consumers are switching off pay-TV services to save money during strained economic times, satellite industry revenues have risen steadily over the past decade.

The Impact of DVRs and the Internet: Changing Content Delivery

Over the past two decades, the viewing public has become increasingly fragmented as a result of growing competition between cable and satellite channels and traditional network television stations. Now, TV audiences are being presented with even more options. Digital video recorders (DVRs) like TiVo allow viewers to select and record shows they can watch at a later time. For example, viewers can set their DVRs to record all new (or old) episodes of the show *Deadliest Catch* and then watch the recorded episodes whenever they have free time.

DVRs can be used by advertisers to track which shows are being viewed. DVRs are even capable of targeting viewers with specific ads when they decide to watch their recorded program. In 2008, consumer groups battled with cable companies and lawmakers to protect the privacy of viewers who did not wish to be tracked this way, causing Nielsen to make tracking optional.

Nontelevision delivery systems such as the Internet allow viewers to download their favorite shows at any time, on several different media. The Internet has typically been bad news for traditional forms of media; newspapers, magazines, the music industry, video rental companies, and bookstores have all suffered from the introduction of the Internet. However, unlike other media, television has so far survived the Internet's effects. Television remains the dominant source of entertainment for most Americans, who are using new media in conjunction with traditional TV viewing, watching vast quantities of television in addition to streaming numerous YouTube videos and catching up on missed episodes via the networks' web pages. In the third quarter of 2008, the average American watched 142 hours of television per month, an increase of 5 hours per month from the same quarter the previous year. Internet use averaged 27 hours per month, an increase of an hour and a half between 2007 and 2008 (Stross, 2009).

New Viewing Outlets: YouTube and Hulu

Of the many recent Internet phenomena, few have made as big an impact as video-sharing website YouTube. Created by three PayPal engineers in 2005, the site enables users to upload personal videos, television clips, music videos, and snippets of movies that can be watched by other users worldwide. Although it initially drew unfavorable comparisons with the original music-sharing site Napster (see Chapter 6 "Music"), which was buried under an avalanche of copyright infringement lawsuits, YouTube managed to survive the controversy by forming agreements with media corporations, such as NBC Universal Television, to legally broadcast video clips from shows such as *The Office*. In 2006, the company, which showed more than 100 million video clips per day, was purchased by Google for $1.65 billion (MSNBC, 2006). Correctly predicting that the site was the "next step in the evolution of the Internet," Google CEO Eric Schmidt has watched YouTube's popularity explode since the takeover. As of 2010, YouTube shows more than 2 billion clips per day and allows people to upload 24 hours of video every single minute (Youtube). To secure its place as the go-to entertainment website, YouTube is expanding its boundaries by developing a movie rental service and showing live music concerts and sporting events in real time. In January 2010, Google signed a deal with the Indian Premier League, making 60 league cricket matches available on YouTube's IPL channel and attracting 50 million viewers worldwide (Timmons, 2010).

Figure 9.18

Agreements between YouTube and media corporations allow viewers to watch clips of their favorite shows on YouTube for free.

andresmh – Homeless on YouTube – CC BY-SA 2.0.

While YouTube remains focused on user-generated material, viewers looking for commercial videos of movies and TV shows are increasingly turning to Hulu. Established in 2007 following a deal between NBC Universal, News Corporation, and a number of leading Internet companies (including Yahoo!, AOL, MSN, and MySpace), the site gives users access to an entire library of video clips without charge and syndicates its material to partner distribution sites. The videos include full episodes of current hit shows such as *House, Saturday Night Live,* and *The Simpsons,* as well as older hits from the studios' television libraries. Supported through advertising, the venture, which is only available to viewers in the United States, became the premier video broadcast site on the web within 2 years. In July 2009, the site received more than 38 million viewers and delivered more videos than any site except YouTube (Salter, 2009). Throughout the entire year, Hulu generated an estimated $120 million in revenue and increased its advertiser base to 250 sponsors (Salter, 2009). Its advertising model appeals to viewers, who need only watch two minutes of promotion in 22 minutes of programming, compared with 8 minutes on television. Limiting sponsorship to one advertiser per show has helped make recall rates twice as high as those for the same advertisements on television, benefiting the sponsors as well as the viewers.

Some critics and television executives claim that the Hulu model has been too successful for its own good, threatening the financial underpinnings of cable TV by reducing DVD sales and avoiding carriage fees—in 2009, Fox pulled most of the episodes of *It's Always Sunny in Philadelphia* from Hulu's site. Per the networks' request, Hulu also shut off access to its programming from Boxee, a fledgling service that enabled viewers to stream online video to their TV sets. "We have to find ways to advance the business rather than cannibalize it," stated the distribution chief at TNT, a network that refused to stream episodes of shows such as *The Closer* on Hulu's site (Rose, 2009). However, many television executives realize that if they do not cannibalize their own material, others will. When a viral video of *Saturday Night Live* short "Lazy Sunday" hit the web in 2005, generating millions of hits on YouTube, NBC did not earn a dime. Broadcast networks—the Big Four and the CW—have also begun streaming shows for free in an effort to stop viewers from watching episodes on other websites.

Video-on-Demand

Originally introduced in the early 1990s, the concept of video on demand (VOD)—a pay-per-view system that allows viewers to order or download a film via television or the Internet and watch it at their convenience—was not immediately successful because of the prohibitive cost of ordering a movie compared to buying or renting it from a store. Another early complaint about the service was that studios withheld movies until long after they were available on DVD, by which time most people who wanted to view the film had already seen it. Both of these disadvantages have since been remedied, with movies now released at the same time on VOD as they are on DVD at competitive rental prices. Currently, most cable and satellite TV providers offer some form of on-demand service, either VOD, which provides movies 24 hours a day and enables viewers all the functionality of a DVD player (such as the ability to pause, rewind, or fast forward films), or near video on demand (NVOD), which broadcasts multiple copies of a film or program over short time intervals but does not allow viewers to control the video.

As an alternative to cable or satellite VOD, viewers can also readily obtain movies and television shows over the

Internet, via free services such as YouTube and Hulu or through paid subscriptions to sites that stream movies to a computer. Online DVD rental service Netflix started giving subscribers instant access to its catalog of older TV programs and films in 2007, while Internet giant Amazon.com set up a rival service resembling the pay-per-view model in 2008. Viewers can also stream free episodes of their favorite shows via cable and broadcast networks' websites. With the increasing popularity of smartphones—cell phones that contain built-in applications and Internet access—viewers are using VOD as a way of watching television while they are out of the house. Having discovered that consumers are willing to watch entire TV episodes or even films on their smartphones, industry executives are looking for ways to capitalize on smartphone technology. In 2010, News Corporation's Fox Mobile Group was planning to launch Bitbop, a service that will stream TV episodes to smartphones for $9.99 a month. Discussing the project, Bitbop architect Joe Bilman said that "the marriage of on-demand content and mobility has the power to light a fire in the smartphone space (Stelter, 2010)." The shift from traditional television viewing to online viewing is making a small but noticeable dent in the $84 billion cable and satellite industry. Between the beginning of 2008 and the end of 2009, an estimated 800,000 U.S. households cut the cable cord in favor of web viewing (Schonfeld, 2010).

Interactive Television

Moving a step beyond VOD, cable and satellite TV providers are combining aspects of traditional television viewing with online content to create an entirely new way of watching shows—interactive television (iTV). Using an additional set-top box and their remote control, viewers can utilize several different features that go beyond simply watching a television show. For example, interactive television enables users to take part in quiz shows, vote for a favorite contestant on a game show, view highlights or look up statistics during sports matches, create a music playlist or photo slideshow, and view local information such as weather and traffic through a ticker under a current TV program. Software such as Microsoft's UltimateTV, released in 2001, even brought interactivity to individual television shows. For example, a viewer watching CBS crime series *CSI* can click on the interactive icon in the corner of the screen and obtain instant information about forensic analysis techniques, along with an episode guide, character biographies, and a map of the show's Las Vegas setting.

Interactive television is beginning to take on the social format of the web, linking viewers with online communities who use communication tools such as Twitter and Skype IM to discuss what they just saw on television in real time. When popular musical comedy show *Glee* hit the screens in 2009, marketing experts at Fox pushed for a strong online presence, airing the pilot episode well in advance of the actual season debut and generating buzz on social networking sites such as Twitter and Facebook. Once the show gained widespread popularity, Fox launched an interactive hypertrailer on its website, allowing viewers to click on and "like" the show's cast members on Facebook. The *Glee* cast also participates in weekly "tweet-peats," which feature live Twitter feeds that scroll across the bottom of the screen during reruns of the show, providing behind-the-scenes details and answering fan questions. The CW network uses a similar technique with its "TV to Talk About" campaign, a tagline that changes from ad to ad to include iterations such as "TV to text about," "blog about," or "tweet about." Its website offers forums where viewers can discuss episodes and interact with video extras, photos, and background clips about various shows. Online television forum Television Without Pity provides viewers with an alternative place for discussion that is not affiliated with any one network.

Figure 9.19

A Nielsen report found that during the fourth quarter of 2009, 60 percent of Americans spent up to 3.5 hours every month going online and watching TV simultaneously.

Christopher Bowns – My desk – CC BY-SA 2.0.

Despite the shift toward interactive television, one barrier that manufacturers seem to be unwilling to cross is the addition of Internet to people's TV sets. Although Internet-enabled televisions began trickling into the market in 2008 and 2009, many industry executives remained skeptical of their potential. In February 2009, Sony spokesman Greg Belloni said, "Sony's stance is that consumers don't want an Internet-like experience with their TVs, and we're really not focused on bringing anything other than Internet video or widgets to our sets right now (Richtel, 2009)." Although some analysts predict that up to 20 percent of televisions will be Internet-enabled by 2012, consulting firm Deloitte anticipates the continued concurrent use of TV sets with laptops, MP3 players, and other browser-enabled devices (Deloitte, 2010).

Key Takeaways

- The first satellite television signal was broadcast in 1962; however, the television industry did not begin utilizing satellites for broadcasting purposes until the late 1970s. Early problems with satellite TV included the high cost of a satellite dish and the theft of satellite signals following the passing of the Cable Act in 1984. Once piracy was under control, satellite television companies began to emerge and become profitable. The two biggest current satellite television providers are DirecTV, which targets its services toward affluent consumers, and Dish Network, which targets lower-earning consumers. Since the 1999 legislation enabled satellite companies to broadcast local channels, satellite TV has become a viable threat to cable. Satellite companies attempt to lure cable customers by offering premium channels, sports and movie packages, and competitive prices.

- Unlike some other forms of media, television is so far surviving the impact of the Internet. However, the World Wide Web is changing content delivery methods and the way people conceive television and program scheduling. New viewing outlets such as YouTube and Hulu enable viewers to watch online video clips, entire episodes of TV shows, and movies free of charge (although Hulu also offers paid content with a wider selection of programs to offset the losses in network advertising revenue). Video-on-demand services, now available through most cable and satellite providers, allow viewers to order movies or TV programs at their convenience, rather than having to adhere to a fixed programming schedule. VOD is also available through Internet sites such as Amazon.com and Netflix, allowing people to stream shows and video clips to their smartphones and watch television while on the go. Thanks to the influence of the Internet, television is becoming more interactive, with providers combining aspects of traditional viewing and online content. This is manifested in two ways: new features that provide viewers with hundreds of additional options while they watch their favorite shows (for example, the ability to look up a news story or get a weather update), and social television, which encourages viewers to combine TV viewing with social networking (for example, by blogging or joining an online chat forum about the show).

Exercises

Please respond to the following short-answer writing prompts. Each response should be a minimum of one paragraph.

1. What is the difference between satellite and cable television? In today's market, who is winning the battle for consumers?

2. Aside from DirecTV and Dish Network, what other satellite options do consumers have? How do these options differ from DirecTV and Dish Network?

3. How have the Internet and DVRs affected your television-viewing habits?

End-of-Chapter Assessment

Review Questions

1.
Section 1

a. What were some of the technological developments that paved the way for the evolution of television, and what role did they play?

b. What factors contributed to the dominance of electronic television over mechanical television?

c. Why was color technology slow to gain popularity following its development?

d. What were some of the important landmarks in the history of television after 1960?

2.
Section 2

a. What cultural factors influenced television programming between 1950 and 2010?

b. How did television influence culture between 1950 and 2010? How are television and culture interrelated?

3.
Section 3

a. How can corporate sponsors influence television programming?

b. What factors have influenced the decline of the major networks since 1970? How have the networks adapted to changes in the industry?

c. How does cable television differ from network television? How has the growth of cable been influenced by industry legislation?

4.
Section 4

a. What are the main differences between satellite television and cable television? What factors influenced the growing popularity of satellite television in the 1980s and 1990s?

b. Who are the two main competitors in the satellite television industry? How do they differ?

c. How is the Internet changing content delivery methods and viewing patterns?

Critical Thinking Questions

1. Do television programs just reflect cultural and social change, or do they influence it?

2. Television audiences are becoming increasingly fragmented as a result of competition from cable and satellite companies and nontelevision delivery systems such as the Internet. What are the potential social implications of this trend?

3. How can broadcast networks compete against satellite and cable operators?

4. Critics frequently blame television for increasing levels of violence and aggression in children. Do broadcasters have a social responsibility to their viewers, and if so, how can they fulfill it?

5. Supporters of public television argue that it serves a valuable role in the community, whereas opponents believe it is outdated. Is public television still relevant in today's society, or should funding be cut completely?

Career Connection

Whether online viewing outlets continue to grow in popularity or viewers return to more traditional methods of watching television, broadcasters are likely to remain dependent on advertising sponsors to fund their programming. Advertising sales executives work for a specific network and sell TV time to agencies and companies, working within budgets to ensure that clients make effective use of their advertising time.

Read through the U.S. Bureau of Labor Statistics overview of a career in advertising sales. You can find it at: http://www.bls.gov/oco/ocos297.htm.

Then, read BNET's analysis of the television advertising industry at http://industry.bnet.com/media/10008136/truth-in-network-tv-advertising-and-what-to-do-about-it/. Once you have looked at both sites, use the information to answer these questions:

1. According to the Bureau of Labor Statistics website, the employment rate for advertising sales agents is expected to increase by 7 percent between 2010 and 2018, about average for all professions. What reasons does the site give for this increase? How will the growth be offset?

2. What predictions does the BNET article make about future trends in the Big Four networks' advertising sales? How might this affect career prospects?

3. Based on the analysis in the BNET article and the information on the Bureau of Labor Statistics website, how is the advertising sales industry likely to change and develop?

4. As the Bureau of Labor Statistics website points out, creativity is an invaluable trait for advertising sales executives. Using the information on both sites, think of a list of creative ways to attract new clients to the ailing broadcast networks.

References

Belson, Ken. "Cable's Rivals Lure Customers With Packages," *New York Times*, November 22, 2004, http://www.nytimes.com/2004/11/22/technology/22satellite.html.

Carter, Bill. "DirecTV Raises Its Sights for a Channel," *New York Times*, January 23, 2009, http://www.nytimes.com/2009/01/24/business/media/24direct.html.

Deloitte, "Deloitte Analyses Top Trends for the Media Industry for 2010," news release, http://www.deloitte.com/view/en_GB/uk/industries/tmt/press-release/37df818581646210VgnVCM100000ba42f00aRCRD.htm.

Junnarker, Sandeep. "DirecTV to Buy Rival PrimeStar's Assets," *CNET*, January 22, 1999, http://news.cnet.com/DirecTV-to-buy-rival-Primestars-assets/2100-1033_3-220509.html.

MSNBC, Associated Press, "Google Buys YouTube for $1.65 Billion," *MSNBC*, October 10, 2006, http://www.msnbc.msn.com/id/15196982/ns/business-us_business/.

Paul, Franklin. "Dish Network Subscriber Gain, Profit Beat Street," *Reuters*, May 10, 2010, http://www.reuters.com/article/idUSTRE6492MW20100510.

Richtel, Matt. "What Convergence? TV's Hesitant March to the Net," *New York Times*, February 15, 2009, http://www.nytimes.com/2009/02/16/technology/internet/16chip.html.

Rose, Frank. "Hulu, a Victim of Its Own Success?" *Wired*, May 12, 2009, http://www.wired.com/epicenter/2009/05/hulu-victim-success/.

Salter, Chuck. "Can Hulu Save Traditional TV?" *Fast Company*, November 1, 2009, http://www.fastcompany.com/magazine/140/the-unlikely-mogul.html.

Schonfeld, Erick. "Estimate: 800,000 U.S. Households Abandoned Their TVs for the Web," *TechCrunch*, April 13, 2010, http://techcrunch.com/2010/04/13/800000-households-abandoned-tvs-web/.

Semuels, Alana. "Television Viewing at All-Time High," *Los Angeles Times*, February 24, 2009, http://articles.latimes.com/2009/feb/24/business/fi-tvwatching24.

Stelter, Brian. "Audiences, and Hollywood, Flock to Smartphones," *New York Times*, May 2, 2010, http://www.nytimes.com/2010/05/03/business/media/03mobile.html.

Stross, Randall. "Why Television Still Shines in a World of Screens," *New York Times*, February 7, 2009, http://www.nytimes.com/2009/02/08/business/media/08digi.html.

Thibedeau, Harry W. "DTH Satellite TV: Timelines to the Future," Satellite Broadcasting & Communications Association, 2000, http://satelliteretailers.com/dish_installation.html.

Timmons, Heather. "Google Sees a New Role for YouTube: An Outlet for Live Sports," *New York Times*, May 2, 2010, http://www.nytimes.com/2010/05/03/business/media/03cricket.html.

YouTube, "YouTube Fact Sheet," http://www.youtube.com/t/fact_sheet.

Chapter 10: Electronic Games and Entertainment

10.1 Electronic Games and Entertainment

Want to Get Away?

Figure 10.1

Anders Adermark – Playing – CC BY-NC-ND 2.0.

Video games have come a long way from using a simple joystick to guide Pac-Man on his mission to find food and avoid ghosts. This is illustrated by a 2007 Southwest Airlines commercial in which two friends are playing a baseball video game on a Nintendo Wii–like console. The batting friend tells the other to throw his pitch—and he does, excitedly firing his controller into the middle of the plasma TV, which then falls off the wall. Both friends stare in shock at the shattered flat screen as the narrator asks, "Want to get away?"

Such a scene is unlikely to have taken place in the early days of video games when Atari reigned supreme and the action of playing solely centered on hand–eye coordination. The learning curve was relatively nonexistent;

players maneuvered a joystick to shoot lines of aliens in the sky, or they turned the wheel on a paddle to play a virtual game of table tennis.

But as video games became increasingly popular, they also became increasingly complex. Consoles upgraded and evolved on a regular basis, and the games kept up. Players called each other with loopholes and tips on how to get Mario and Luigi onto the next level, and now they exchange their tricks on gaming blogs. Games like *The Legend of Zelda* and *Final Fantasy* created alternate worlds and intricate story lines, providing multiple-hour epic adventures.

Long criticized for taking kids out of the backyard and into a sedentary spot in front of the TV, many video games have circled back to their simpler origins and, in doing so, have made players more active. Casual gamers who could quickly figure out how to put together puzzle pieces in *Tetris* can now just as easily figure out how to "swing" a tennis racket with a Wiimote. Video games are no longer a convenient scapegoat for America's obesity problems; *Wii Fit* offers everything from yoga to boxing, and *Dance Dance Revolution* estimates calories burned while players dance.

The logistics of video games continue to change, and as they do, gaming has begun to intersect with every other part of culture. Players can learn how to "perform" their favorite songs with *Guitar Hero* and *Rock Band*. Product placement akin to what is seen in movies and on TV is equally prevalent in video games such as the popular *Forza Motorsport* or *FIFA* series. As the Internet allows for players across the world to participate simultaneously, video games have the potential to one day look like competitive reality shows (Dolan). Arguably, video games even hold a place in the art world, with the increasing complexity of animation and story lines (Tres Kap).

And now, with endless possibilities for the future, video games are attracting new and different demographics. Avid players who grew up with video games may be the first ones to purchase 3-D televisions for the 3-D games of the future (Williams, 2010). But casual players, perhaps of an older demographic, will be drawn to the simplicity of a game like *Wii Bowling*. Video games have become more accessible than ever. Social media websites like Facebook offer free video game applications, and smartphone users can download apps for as little as a dollar, literally putting video games in one's back pocket. Who needs a cumbersome Scrabble board when it's available on a touch screen anytime, anywhere?

Video games have become ubiquitous in modern culture. Understanding them as a medium allows a fuller understanding of their implications in the realms of entertainment, information, and communication. Studying their history reveals new perspectives on the ways video games have affected mainstream culture.

References

Dolan, Michael. "The Video Game Revolution: The Future of Video Gaming," *PBS,* http://www.pbs.org/kcts/videogamerevolution/impact/future.html.

Tres Kap, Jona. "The Video Game Revolution: But is it Art?" *PBS,* http://www.pbs.org/kcts/videogamerevolution/impact/art.html.

Williams, M. H. "Study Shows Casual and Core Gamers Are Ready for 3-D Gaming," Industry Gamers, June 15, 2010, http://www.industrygamers.com/news/study-shows-casual-and-core-gamers-are-ready-for-3d-gaming/.

10.2 The Evolution of Electronic Games

Learning Objectives

1. Identify the major companies involved in video game production.

2. Explain the important innovations that drove the acceptance of video games by mainstream culture.

3. Determine major technological developments that influenced the evolution of video games.

Pong, the electronic table-tennis simulation game, was the first video game for many people who grew up in the 1970s and is now a famous symbol of early video games. However, the precursors to modern video games were created as early as the 1950s. In 1952 a computer simulation of tic-tac-toe was developed for the Electronic Delay Storage Automatic Calculator (EDSAC), one of the first stored-information computers, and in 1958 a game called *Tennis for Two* was developed at Brookhaven National Laboratory as a way to entertain people coming through the laboratory on tours (Egenfeldt-Nielsen, 2008).

Figure 10.2

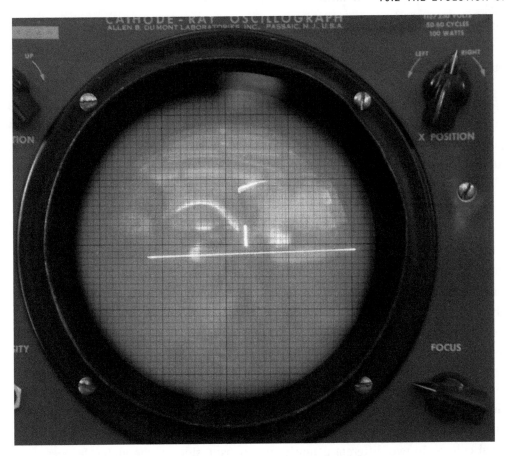

Tennis for Two was a rudimentary game designed to entertain visitors to the Brookhaven National Laboratory.

These games would generate little interest among the modern game-playing public, but at the time they enthralled their users and introduced the basic elements of the cultural video game experience. In a time before personal computers, these games allowed the general public to access technology that had been restricted to the realm of abstract science. *Tennis for Two* created an interface where anyone with basic motor skills could use a complex machine. The first video games functioned early on as a form of media by essentially disseminating the experience of computer technology to those who did not have access to it.

As video games evolved, their role as a form of media grew as well. Video games have grown from simple tools that made computing technology understandable to forms of media that can communicate cultural values and human relationships.

The 1970s: The Rise of the Video Game

The 1970s saw the rise of video games as a cultural phenomenon. A 1972 article in *Rolling Stone* describes the early days of computer gaming:

Reliably, at any nighttime moment (i.e. non-business hours) in North America hundreds of computer technicians are effectively out of their bodies, locked in life-or-death space combat computer-projected onto cathode ray tube display screens, for hours at a time, ruining their eyes, numbing their fingers in frenzied mashing of control buttons, joyously slaying their friend and wasting their employers' valuable computer time. Something basic is going on (Brand, 1972).

This scene was describing *Spacewar!*, a game developed in the 1960s at the Massachusetts Institute of Technology (MIT) that spread to other college campuses and computing centers. In the early '70s, very few people owned computers. Most computer users worked or studied at university, business, or government facilities. Those with access to computers were quick to utilize them for gaming purposes.

Arcade Games

The first coin-operated arcade game was modeled on *Spacewar!* It was called *Computer Space*, and it fared poorly among the general public because of its difficult controls. In 1972, *Pong*, the table-tennis simulator that has come to symbolize early computer games, was created by the fledgling company Atari, and it was immediately successful. *Pong* was initially placed in bars with pinball machines and other games of chance, but as video games grew in popularity, they were placed in any establishment that would take them. By the end of the 1970s, so many video arcades were being built that some towns passed zoning laws limiting them (Kent, 1997).

The end of the 1970s ushered in a new era—what some call the golden age of video games—with the game *Space Invaders*, an international phenomenon that exceeded all expectations. In Japan, the game was so popular that it caused a national coin shortage. Games like *Space Invaders* illustrate both the effect of arcade games and their influence on international culture. In two different countries on opposite sides of the globe, Japanese and American teenagers, although they could not speak to one another, were having the same experiences thanks to a video game.

Video Game Consoles

The first video game console for the home began selling in 1972. It was the Magnavox Odyssey, and it was based on prototypes built by Ralph Behr in the late 1960s. This system included a *Pong*-type game, and when the arcade version of *Pong* became popular, the Odyssey began to sell well. Atari, which was making arcade games at the time, decided to produce a home version of *Pong* and released it in 1974. Although this system could only play one game, its graphics and controls were superior to the Odyssey, and it was sold through a major department store, Sears. Because of these advantages, the Atari home version of *Pong* sold well, and a host of other companies began producing and selling their own versions of *Pong* (Herman, 2008).

A major step forward in the evolution of video games was the development of game cartridges that stored the games and could be interchanged in the console. With this technology, users were no longer limited to a set number of games, leading many video game console makers to switch their emphasis to producing games. Several groups, such as Magnavox, Coleco, and Fairchild, released versions of cartridge-type consoles, but Atari's 2600 console had the upper hand because of the company's work on arcade games. Atari capitalized off of its arcade successes by releasing games that were well known to a public that was frequenting arcades. The popularity of games such as *Space Invaders* and *Pac-Man* made the Atari 2600 a successful system. The late 1970s also saw the birth of companies such as Activision, which developed third-party games for the Atari 2600 (Wolf).

Home Computers

The birth of the home computer market in the 1970s paralleled the emergence of video game consoles. The first computer designed and sold for the home consumer was the Altair. It was first sold in 1975, several years after video game consoles had been selling, and it sold mainly to a hobbyist market. During this period, people such as Steve Jobs, the founder of Apple, were building computers by hand and selling them to get their start-up businesses going. In 1977, three important computers—Radio Shack's TRS-80, the Commodore PET, and the Apple II—were produced and began selling to the home market (Reimer, 2005).

The rise of personal computers allowed for the development of more complex games. Designers of games such as *Mystery House*, developed in 1979 for the Apple II, and *Rogue*, developed in 1980 and played on IBM PCs, used the processing power of early home computers to develop video games that had extended plots and story lines. In these games, players moved through landscapes composed of basic graphics, solving problems and working through an involved narrative. The development of video games for the personal computer platform expanded the ability of video games to act as media by allowing complex stories to be told and new forms of interaction to take place between players.

The 1980s: The Crash

Atari's success in the home console market was due in large part to its ownership of already-popular arcade games and the large number of game cartridges available for the system. These strengths, however, eventually proved detrimental to the company and led to what is now known as the video game crash of 1983. Atari bet heavily on its past successes with popular arcade games by releasing *Pac-Man* for the Atari 2600. *Pac-Man* was a successful arcade game that did not translate well to the home console, leading to disappointed consumers and lower-than-expected sales. Additionally, Atari produced 10 million of the lackluster *Pac-Man* games on its first run, despite the fact that active consoles were only estimated at 10 million. Similar mistakes were made with a game based on the movie *E.T.: The Extra-Terrestrial*, which has gained notoriety as one of the worst games in Atari's history. It was not received well by consumers despite the success of the movie, and Atari had again bet heavily on its success. Piles of unsold *E.T.* game cartridges were reportedly buried in the New Mexico desert under a veil of secrecy (Monfort & Bogost, 2009).

As retail outlets became increasingly wary of home console failures, they began stocking fewer games on shelves. This action, combined with an increasing number of companies producing games, led to overproduction and a resulting fallout in the video game market in 1983. Many smaller game developers did not have the capacity to withstand this downturn and went out of business. Although Coleco and Atari were able to make it through the crash, neither company regained its former share of the video game market. It was 1985 when the video game market picked up again.

The Rise of Nintendo

Nintendo, a Japanese card and novelty producer that had begun to produce electronic games in the 1970s, was responsible for arcade games such as *Donkey Kong* in the early 1980s. Its first home console, developed in 1984 for sale in Japan, tried to succeed where Atari had failed. The Nintendo system used newer, better microchips, bought in large quantities, to ensure high-quality graphics at a price consumers could afford. Keeping console prices low meant Nintendo had to rely on games for most of its profits and maintain control of game production. This was something Atari had failed to do, and it led to a glut of low-priced games that caused the crash of 1983. Nintendo got around this problem with proprietary circuits that would not allow unlicensed games to be played on the console. This allowed Nintendo to dominate the home video game market through the end of the decade, when one-third of homes in the United States had a Nintendo system (Cross & Smits, 2005).

Nintendo introduced its Nintendo Entertainment System (NES) in the United States in 1985. The game *Super Mario Brothers*, released with the system, was also a landmark in video game development. The game employed a narrative in the same manner as more complicated computer games, but its controls were accessible and its objectives simple. The game appealed to a younger demographic, generally boys in the 8–14 range, than the one targeted by Atari (Kline, et. al., 2003). Its designer, Shigeru Miyamoto, tried to mimic the experiences of childhood adventures, creating a fantasy world not based on previous models of science fiction or other literary genres (McLaughlin, 2007). *Super Mario Brothers* also gave Nintendo an iconic character who has been used in numerous other games, television shows, and even a movie. The development of this type of character and fantasy world became the norm for video game makers. Games such as *The Legend of Zelda* became franchises with film and television possibilities rather than simply one-off games.

As video games developed as a form of media, the public struggled to come to grips with the kind of messages this medium was passing on to children. These were no longer simple games of reflex that could be compared to similar nonvideo games or sports; these were forms of media that included stories and messages that concerned parents and children's advocates. Arguments about the larger meaning of the games became common, with some seeing the games as driven by ideas of conquest and gender stereotypes, whereas others saw basic stories about traveling and exploration (Fuller & Jenkins, 1995).

Other Home Console Systems

Other software companies were still interested in the home console market in the mid-1980s. Atari released the 2600jr and the 7800 in 1986 after Nintendo's success, but the consoles could not compete with Nintendo. The Sega Corporation, which had been involved with arcade video game production, released its Sega Master System in 1986. Although the system had more graphics possibilities than the NES, Sega failed to make a dent in Nintendo's market share until the early 1990s, with the release of Sega Genesis (Kerr, 2005).

Computer Games Flourish and Innovate

The enormous number of games available for Atari consoles in the early 1980s took its toll on video arcades. In 1983, arcade revenues had fallen to a 3-year low, leading game makers to turn to newer technologies that could not be replicated by home consoles. This included arcade games powered by laser discs, such as *Dragon's Lair* and *Space Ace*, but their novelty soon wore off, and laser-disc games became museum pieces (Harmetz, 1984). In 1989, museums were already putting on exhibitions of early arcade games that included ones from the early 1980s. Although newer games continued to come out on arcade platforms, they could not compete with the home console market and never achieved their previous successes from the early 1980s. Increasingly, arcade gamers chose to stay at home to play games on computers and consoles. Today, dedicated arcades are a dying breed. Most that remain, like the Dave & Buster's and Chuck E. Cheese's chains, offer full-service restaurants and other entertainment attractions to draw in business.

Home games fared better than arcades because they could ride the wave of personal computer purchases that occurred in the 1980s. Some important developments in video games occurred in the mid-1980s with the development of online games. Multiuser dungeons, or MUDs, were role-playing games played online by multiple users at once. The games were generally text-based, describing the world of the MUD through text rather than illustrating it through graphics. The games allowed users to create a character and move through different worlds, accomplishing goals that awarded them with new skills. If characters attained a certain level of proficiency, they could then design their own area of the world. *Habitat,* a game developed in 1986 for the Commodore 64, was a graphic version of this type of game. Users dialed up on modems to a central host server and then controlled characters on screen, interacting with other users (Reimer, 2005).

During the mid-1980s, a demographic shift occurred. Between 1985 and 1987, games designed to run on business computers rose from 15 percent to 40 percent of games sold (Elmer-Dewitt, et. al., 1987). This trend meant that game makers could use the increased processing power of business computers to create more complex games. It also meant adults were interested in computer games and could become a profitable market.

The 1990s: The Rapid Evolution of Video Games

Video games evolved at a rapid rate throughout the 1990s, moving from the first 16-bit systems (named for the amount of data they could process and store) in the early 1990s to the first Internet-enabled home console in 1999. As companies focused on new marketing strategies, wider audiences were targeted, and video games' influence on culture began to be felt.

Console Wars

Nintendo's dominance of the home console market throughout the late 1980s allowed it to build a large library of games for use on the NES. This also proved to be a weakness, however, because Nintendo was reluctant to improve or change its system for fear of making its game library obsolete. Technology had changed in the years since the introduction of the NES, and companies such as NEC and Sega were ready to challenge Nintendo with 16-bit systems (Slaven).

Figure 10.3

Sega's commercials suggested that it was a more violent version of Nintendo.

jeriaska – Splatterhouse – CC BY-NC 2.0.

The Sega Master System had failed to challenge the NES, but with the release of its 16-bit system, Sega Genesis, the company pursued a new marketing strategy. Whereas Nintendo targeted 8- to 14-year-olds, Sega's marketing plan targeted 15- to 17-year olds, making games that were more mature and advertising during programs such as the MTV Video Music Awards. The campaign successfully branded Sega as a cooler version of Nintendo and moved mainstream video games into a more mature arena. Nintendo responded to the Sega Genesis with its own 16-bit system, the Super NES, and began creating more mature games as well. Games such as Sega's *Mortal Kombat* and Nintendo's *Street Fighter* competed to raise the level of violence possible in a video game. Sega's advertisements even suggested that its game was better because of its more violent possibilities (Gamespot).

By 1994, companies such as 3DO, with its 32-bit system, and Atari, with its allegedly 64-bit Jaguar, attempted to get in on the home console market but failed to use effective marketing strategies to back up their products. Both systems fell out of production before the end of the decade. Sega, fearing that its system would become obsolete, released the 32-bit Saturn system in 1995. The system was rushed into production and did not have enough games available to ensure its success (Cyberia PC). Sony stepped in with its PlayStation console at a time when Sega's Saturn was floundering and before Nintendo's 64-bit system had been released. This system targeted an even older demographic of 14- to 24-year-olds and made a large effect on the market; by March of 2007, Sony had sold 102 million PlayStations (Edge Staff, 2009).

Computer Games Gain Mainstream Acceptance

Computer games had avid players, but they were still a niche market in the early 1990s. An important step in the mainstream acceptance of personal computer games was the development of the first-person shooter genre. First popularized by the 1992 game *Wolfenstein 3D*, these games put the player in the character's perspective, making it seem as if the player were firing weapons and being attacked. *Doom,* released in 1993, and *Quake,* released in 1996, used the increased processing power of personal computers to create vivid three-dimensional worlds that were impossible to fully replicate on video game consoles of the era. These games pushed realism to new heights and began attracting public attention for their graphic violence.

Figure 10.4

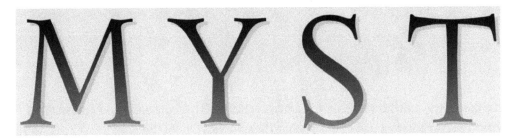

Myst challenged the notion that only violent games could be successful.

Wikimedia Commons – public domain.

Another trend was reaching out to audiences outside of the video-game-playing community. *Myst,* an adventure game where the player walked around an island solving a mystery, drove sales of CD-ROM drives for computers. *Myst,* its sequel *Riven,* and other nonviolent games such as *SimCity* actually outsold *Doom* and *Quake* in the 1990s (Miller, 1999). These nonviolent games appealed to people who did not generally play video games, increasing the form's audience and expanding the types of information that video games put across.

Online Gaming Gains Popularity

A major advance in game technology came with the increase in Internet use by the general public in the 1990s. A major feature of *Doom* was the ability to use multiplayer gaming through the Internet. Strategy games such as *Command and Conquer* and *Total Annihilation* also included options where players could play each other over the Internet. Other fantasy-inspired role-playing games, such as *Ultima Online,* used the Internet to initiate the massively multiplayer online role-playing game (MMORPG) genre (Reimer). These games used the Internet as their platform, much like the text-based MUDs, creating a space where individuals could play the game while socially interacting with one another.

Portable Game Systems

The development of portable game systems was another important aspect of video games during the 1990s. Handheld games had been in use since the 1970s, and a system with interchangeable cartridges had even been sold in the early 1980s. Nintendo released the Game Boy in 1989, using the same principles that made the NES dominate the handheld market throughout the 1990s. The Game Boy was released with the game *Tetris,* using the game's popularity to drive purchases of the unit. The unit's simple design meant users could get 20 hours of playing time on a set of batteries, and this basic design was left essentially unaltered for most of the decade. More advanced handheld systems, such as the Atari Lynx and Sega Game Gear, could not compete with the Game Boy despite their superior graphics and color displays (Hutsko, 2000).

The decade-long success of the Game Boy belies the conventional wisdom of the console wars that more advanced technology makes for a more popular system. The Game Boy's static, simple design was readily accessible, and its stability allowed for a large library of games to be developed for it. Despite using technology almost a decade old, the Game Boy accounted for 30 percent of Nintendo of America's overall revenues at the end of the 1990s (Hutsko, 2000).

The Early 2000s: 21st-Century Games

The Console Wars Continue

Sega gave its final effort in the console wars with the Sega Dreamcast in 1999. This console could connect to the Internet, emulating the sophisticated computer games of the 1990s. The new features of the Sega Dreamcast were not enough to save the brand, however, and Sega discontinued production in 2001, leaving the console market entirely (Business Week).

A major problem for Sega's Dreamcast was Sony's release of the PlayStation 2 (PS2) in 2000. The PS2 could function as a DVD player, expanding the role of the console into an entertainment device that did more than play video games. This console was incredibly successful, enjoying a long production run, with more than 106 million units sold worldwide by the end of the decade (A Brief History of Game Console Warfare).

In 2001, two major consoles were released to compete with the PS2: the Xbox and the Nintendo GameCube. The Xbox was an attempt by Microsoft to enter the market with a console that expanded on the functions of other game consoles. The unit had features similar to a PC, including a hard drive and an Ethernet port for online play through its service, Xbox Live. The popularity of the first-person shooter game *Halo*, an Xbox exclusive release, boosted sales as well. Nintendo's GameCube did not offer DVD playback capabilities, choosing instead to focus on gaming functions. Both of these consoles sold millions of units but did not come close to the sales of the PS2.

Computer Gaming Becomes a Niche Market

As consoles developed to rival the capabilities of personal computers, game developers began to focus more on games for consoles. From 2000 to the end of the decade, the popularity of personal computer games has gradually declined. The computer gaming community, while still significant, is focused on game players who are willing to pay a lot of money on personal computers that are designed specifically for gaming, often including multiple monitors and user modifications that allow personal computers to play newer games. This type of market, though profitable, is not large enough to compete with the audience for the much cheaper game consoles (Kalning, 2008).

The Evolution of Portable Gaming

Nintendo continued its control of the handheld game market into the 2000s with the 2001 release of the Game Boy Advance, a redesigned Game Boy that offered 32-bit processing and compatibility with older Game Boy games. In 2004, anticipating Sony's upcoming handheld console, Nintendo released the Nintendo DS, a handheld console that featured two screens and Wi-Fi capabilities for online gaming. Sony's PlayStation Portable (PSP) was released the following year and featured Wi-Fi capabilities as well as a flexible platform that could be used to play other media such as MP3s (Patsuris, 2004). These two consoles, along with their newer versions, continue to dominate the handheld market

One interesting innovation in mobile gaming occurred in 2003 with the release of the Nokia N-Gage. The N-Gage was a combination of a game console and mobile phone that, according to consumers, did not fill either role very well. The product line was discontinued in 2005, but the idea of playing games on phones persisted and has been developed on other platforms (Stone, 2007). Apple currently dominates the industry of mobile phone games; in 2008 and 2009 alone, iPhone games generated $615 million in revenue (Farago, 2010). As mobile phone gaming grows in popularity and as the supporting technology becomes increasingly more advanced, traditional portable gaming platforms like the DS and the PSP will need to evolve to compete. Nintendo is already planning a successor to the DS that features 3-D graphics without the use of 3-D glasses that it hopes will help the company retain and grow its share of the portable gaming market.

Video Games Today

The trends of the late 2000s have shown a steadily increasing market for video games. Newer control systems and family-oriented games have made it common for many families to engage in video game play as a group. Online games have continued to develop, gaining unprecedented numbers of players. The overall effect of these innovations has been the increasing acceptance of video game culture by the mainstream.

Home Consoles

The current state of the home console market still involves the three major companies of the past 10 years: Nintendo, Sony, and Microsoft. The release of Microsoft's Xbox 360 led this generation of consoles in 2005. The Xbox 360 featured expanded media capabilities and integrated access to Xbox Live, an online gaming service. Sony's PlayStation 3 (PS3) was released in 2006. It also featured enhanced online access as well as expanded multimedia functions, with the additional capacity to play Blu-ray discs. Nintendo released the Wii at the same time. This console featured a motion-sensitive controller that departed from previous controllers and focused on accessible, often family-oriented games. This combination successfully brought in large numbers of new game players, including many older adults. By June 2010, in the United States, the Wii had sold 71.9 million units, the Xbox 360 had sold 40.3 million, and the PS3 trailed at 35.4 million (VGChartz, 2010). In the wake of the Wii's success, Microsoft and Sony have introduced their own motion-sensitive systems (Mangalindan, 2010).

Key Takeaways

- In a time before personal computers, early video games allowed the general public to access technology that had been restricted to the realm of abstract science. *Tennis for Two* created an interface where anyone with basic motor skills could use a complex machine. The first video games functioned early on as a form of media by essentially disseminating the experience of computer technology to those without access to it.

- Video games reached wider audiences in the 1990s with the advent of the first-person shooter genre and popular nonaction games such as *Myst*. The games were marketed to older audiences, and their success increased demand for similar games.

- Online capabilities that developed in the 1990s and expanded in the 2000s allowed players to compete in teams. This innovation attracted larger audiences to gaming and led to new means of social communication.

- A new generation of accessible, family-oriented games in the late 2000s encouraged families to interact through video games. These games also brought in older demographics that had never used video games before.

Exercises

Video game marketing has changed to bring in more and more people to the video game audience. Think about the influence video games have had on you or people you know. If you have never played video games, then think about the ways your conceptions of video games have changed. Sketch out a timeline indicating the different occurrences that marked your experiences related to video games. Now compare this timeline to the history of video games from this section. Consider the following questions:

1. How did your own experiences line up with the history of video games?

2. Did you feel the effects of marketing campaigns directed at you or those around you?

3. Were you introduced to video games during a surge in popularity? What games appealed to you?

References

A Brief History of Game Console Warfare, "PlayStation 2," slide in "A Brief History of Game Console Warfare."

Brand, Stewart. "Space War," *Rolling Stone*, December 7, 1972.

Business Week, "Sega Dreamcast," slide in "A Brief History of Game Console Warfare," *Business Week*, http://images.businessweek.com/ss/06/10/game_consoles/.

Cross, Gary and Gregory Smits, "Japan, the U.S. and the Globalization of Children's Consumer Culture," *Journal of Social History* 38, no. 4 (2005).

CyberiaPC.com, "Sega Saturn (History, Specs, Pictures)," http://www.cyberiapc.com/vgg/sega_saturn.htm.

Edge staff, "The Making Of: Playstation," *Edge*, April 24, 2009, http://www.next-gen.biz/features/the-making-of-playstation.

Egenfeldt-Nielsen, Simon. *Understanding Video Games: The Essential Introduction* (New York: Taylor & Francis, 2008), 50.

Elmer-Dewitt, Philip and others, "Computers: Games that Grownups Play," *Time*, July 27, 1987, http://www.time.com/time/magazine/article/0,9171,965090,00.html.

Farago, Peter. "Apple iPhone and iPod Touch Capture U.S. Video Game Market Share," *Flurry* (blog), March 22, 2010, http://blog.flurry.com/bid/31566/Apple-iPhone-and-iPod-touch-Capture-U-S-Video-Game-Market-Share.

Fuller, Mary and Henry Jenkins, "Nintendo and New World Travel Writing: A Dialogue," *Cybersociety: Computer-Mediated Communication and Community*, ed. Steven G. Jones (Thousand Oaks, CA: Sage Publications, 1995), 57–72.

Gamespot, "When Two Tribes Go to War: A History of Video Game Controversy," http://www.gamespot.com/features/6090892/p-5.html.

Harmetz, Aljean. "Video Arcades Turn to Laser Technology as Queues Dwindle," *Morning Herald* (Sydney), February 2, 1984.

Herman, Leonard. "Early Home Video Game Systems," in *The Video Game Explosion: From Pong to PlayStation and Beyond*, ed. Mark Wolf (Westport, CT: Greenwood Press, 2008), 54.

Hutsko, Joe. "88 Million and Counting; Nintendo Remains King of the Handheld Game Players," *New York Times*, March 25, 2000, http://www.nytimes.com/2000/03/25/business/88-million-and-counting-nintendo-remains-king-of-the-handheld-game-players.html.

Kalning, Kristin. "Is PC Gaming Dying? Or Thriving?" *MSNBC*, March 26, 2008, http://www.msnbc.msn.com/id/23800152/wid/11915773/.

Kent, "Super Mario Nation."

Kent, Steven. "Super Mario Nation," *American Heritage*, September 1997, http://www.americanheritage.com/articles/magazine/ah/1997/5/1997_5_65.shtml.

Kerr, Aphra. "Spilling Hot Coffee? Grand Theft Auto as Contested Cultural Product," in *The Meaning and Culture of Grand Theft Auto: Critical Essays*, ed. Nate Garrelts (Jefferson, NC: McFarland, 2005), 17.

Kline, Stephen, Nick Dyer-Witheford, and Greig De Peuter, *Digital Play: The Interaction of Technology, Culture, and Marketing* (Montreal: McGill-Queen's University Press, 2003), 119.

Mangalindan, J. P. "Is Casual Gaming Destroying the Traditional Gaming Market?" *Fortune*, March 18, 2010, http://tech.fortune.cnn.com/2010/03/18/is-casual-gaming-destroying-the-traditional-gaming-market/.

McLaughlin, Rus. "IGN Presents the History of Super Mario Bros.," *IGN Retro*, November 8, 2007, http://games.ign.com/articles/833/833615p1.html.

Miller, Stephen C. "News Watch; Most-Violent Video Games Are Not Biggest Sellers," *New York Times*, July 29, 1999, http://www.nytimes.com/1999/07/29/technology/news-watch-most-violent-video-games-are-not-biggest-sellers.html.

Montfort, Nick and Ian Bogost, *Racing the Beam*: *The Atari Video Computer System* (Cambridge, MA: MIT Press, 2009), 127.

Patsuris, Penelope. "Sony PSP vs. Nintendo DS," *Forbes*, June 7, 2004, http://www.forbes.com/2004/06/07/cx_pp_0607mondaymatchup.html.

Reimer, "The Evolution of Gaming."

Reimer, Jeremy. "The Evolution of Gaming: Computers, Consoles, and Arcade," *Ars Technica* (blog), October 10, 2005, http://arstechnica.com/old/content/2005/10/gaming-evolution.ars/4.

Reimer, Jeremy. "Total share: 30 years of personal computer market share figures," *Ars Technica* (blog), December 14, 2005, http://arstechnica.com/old/content/2005/12/total-share.ars/2.

Slaven, Andy. *Video Game Bible, 1985–2002*, (Victoria, BC: Trafford), 70–71.

Stone, Brad. "Play It Again, Nokia. For the Third Time," *New York Times*, August 27, 2007, http://www.nytimes.com/2007/08/27/technology/27nokia.html.

VGChartz, "Weekly Hardware Chart: 19th June 2010," http://www.vgchartz.com.

Wolf, Mark J. P. "Arcade Games of the 1970s," in *The Video Game Explosion* (see note 7), 41.

10.3 Influential Contemporary Games

Learning Objectives

1. Identify the effect electronic games have on culture.

2. Select the most influential and important games released to the general public within the last few years.

3. Describe ways new games have changed the video game as a form of media.

With such a short history, the place of video games in culture is constantly changing and being redefined. Are video games entertainment or art? Should they focus on fostering real-life skills or developing virtual realities? Certain games have come to prominence in recent years for their innovations and genre-expanding attributes. These games are notable for not only great economic success and popularity but also for having a visible influence on culture.

Guitar Hero and *Rock Band*

The musical series *Guitar Hero*, based on a Japanese arcade game of the late '90s, was first launched in North America in 2005. In the game, the player uses a guitar-shaped controller to match the rhythms and notes of famous rock songs. The closer the player approximates the song, the better the score. This game introduced a new genre of games in which players simulate playing musical instruments. *Rock Band*, released in 2007, uses a similar format, including a microphone for singing, a drum set, and rhythm and bass guitars. These games are based on a similar premise as earlier rhythm-based games such as *Dance Dance Revolution*, in which players keep the rhythm on a dance pad. *Dance Dance Revolution*, which was introduced to North American audiences in 1999, was successful but not to the extent that the later band-oriented games were. In 2008, music-based games brought in an estimated $1.9 billion.

Figure 10.5

Rock Band includes a microphone and a drum set along with a guitar.

Guitar Hero and *Rock Band* brought new means of marketing and a kind of cross-media stimulus with them. The songs featured in the games experienced increased downloads and sales—as much as an 840 percent increase in some cases (Peckham, 2008). The potential of this type of game did not escape its developers or the music industry. Games dedicated solely to one band were developed, such as *Guitar Hero: Aerosmith* and *The Beatles: Rock Band*. These games were a mix of music documentary, greatest hits album, and game. They included footage from early concerts, interviews with band members, and, of course, songs that allowed users to play along. When *Guitar Hero: Aerosmith* was released, the band's catalog experienced a 40 percent increase in sales (Quan, 2008).

The rock band Metallica made its album *Death Magnetic* available for *Guitar Hero III* on the same day it was released as an album (Quan, 2008). Other innovations include Rock Band Network, a means for bands and individuals to create versions of their own songs for *Rock Band* that can be downloaded for a fee. The sporadic history of the video game industry makes it unclear if this type of game will maintain market share or even maintain its popularity, but it has clearly opened new avenues of expression as a form of media.

The *Grand Theft Auto* series

The first game in the *Grand Theft Auto (GTA)* series was released in 1997 for the PC and Sony PlayStation. The game had players stealing cars—not surprising given its title—and committing a variety of crimes to achieve specific goals. The game's extreme violence made it popular with players of the late 1990s, but its true draw was the variety of options that players could employ in the game. Specific narratives and goals could be pursued, but if players wanted to drive around and explore the city, they could do that as well. A large variety of cars, from sports cars to tractor trailers, were available depending on the player's goals. The violence could likewise be taken to any extreme the player wished, including stealing cars, killing pedestrians, and engaging the police in a shoot-out. This type of game is known as a sandbox game, or open world, and it is defined by the ability of users to freely pursue their own objectives (Donald, 2000).

The *GTA* series has evolved over the past decade by increasing the realism, options, and explicit content of the first game. *GTA III* and *GTA IV*, as well as a number of spin-off games, such as the recent addition *The Ballad of Gay Tony,* have made the franchise more profitable and more controversial. These newer games have expanded on the idea of an open video game world, allowing players to have their characters buy and manage businesses, play unrelated mini-games (such as bowling and darts), and listen to a wide variety of in-game music, talk shows, and even television programs. However, increasing freedom also results in increasing controversy, as players can choose to solicit prostitutes, visit strip clubs, perform murder sprees, and assault law enforcement agents. Lawsuits have attempted to tie the games to real-life instances of violence, and *GTA* games are routinely the target of political investigations into video game violence (Morales, 2005).

World of Warcraft

World of Warcraft (WoW), released in 2004, is a massively multiplayer online role-playing game (MMORPG) loosely based on the *Warcraft* strategy franchise of the 1990s. The game is conducted entirely online, though it is accessed through purchased software, and players purchase playing time. Each player chooses an avatar, or character, that belongs to one of several races, such as orcs, elves, and humans. These characters can spend their time on the game by completing quests, learning trades, or simply interacting with other characters. As characters gain experience, they obtain skills and earn virtual money. Players also choose whether they can attack other players without prior agreement by choosing a PvP (player versus player) server. The normal server allows players to fight each other, but it can only be done if both players consent. A third server is reserved for those players who want to role-play, or act in character.

Figure 10.6

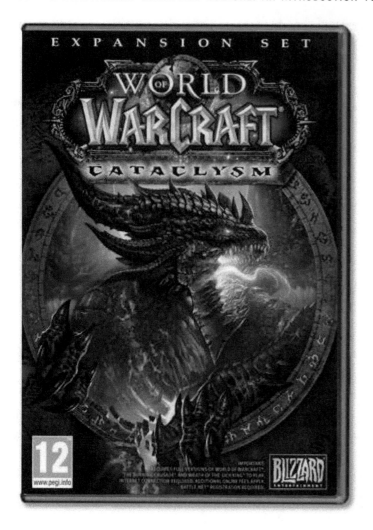

World of Warcraft allows players to team up with other avatars to go on quests or just socialize.

GAME Online – World of Warcraft: Cataclysm for PC – CC BY-NC-ND 2.0.

Various organizations have sprung up within the *WoW* universe. Guilds are groups that ascribe to specific codes of conduct and work together to complete tasks that cannot be accomplished by a lone individual. The guilds are organized by the players; they are not maintained by *WoW* developers. Each has its own unique identity and social rules, much like a college fraternity or social club. Voice communication technology allows players to speak to each other as they complete missions and increases the social bonding that holds such organizations together (Barker, 2006).

WoW has taken the medium of video games to unprecedented levels. Although series such as *Grand Theft Auto* allow players a great deal of freedom, everything done in the games was accounted for at some point. *WoW*, which depends on the actions of millions of players to drive the game, allows people to literally live their lives through a game. In the game, players can earn virtual gold by mining it, killing enemies, and killing other players. It takes a great deal of time to accumulate gold in this manner, so many wealthy players choose to buy this gold with actual dollars. This is technically against the rules of the game, but these rules are unenforceable. Entire real-world industries have developed from this trade in gold. Chinese companies employ workers, or "gold farmers," who work 10-hour shifts finding gold in *WoW* so that the company can sell it to clients. Other players make money by finding deals on virtual goods and then selling them for a profit. One *WoW* player even "traveled" to Asian servers to take advantage of cheap prices, conducting a virtual import–export business (Davis, 2009).

The unlimited possibilities in such a game expand the idea of what a game is. It is obvious that an individual who buys a video game, takes it home, and plays it during his or her leisure is, in fact, playing a game. But if that person is a "gold farmer" doing repetitive tasks in a virtual world to make a real-world living, the situation is not as clear. *WoW* challenges conventional notions of what a game is by allowing the players to create their own goals. To some players, the goal may be to gain a high level for their character; others may be interested in role-playing, whereas others are focused on making a profit. This kind of flexibility leads to the development of scenarios never before encountered in game-play, such as the development of economic classes.

Call of Duty: Modern Warfare

The *Call of Duty* series of first-person shooter games is notable for its record-breaking success in the video game market, generating more than $3 billion in retail sales through late 2009 (Ivan, 2009). *Call of Duty: Modern Warfare 2* was released in 2009 to critical acclaim and a great deal of controversy. The game included a 5-minute sequence in which the player, as a CIA agent infiltrating a terrorist cell, takes part in a massacre of innocent civilians. The player was not required to shoot civilians and could skip the sequence if desired, but these options did not stop international attention and calls to ban the game (Games Radar, 2009). Proponents of the series argue that *Call of Duty* has a Mature rating and is not meant to be played by minors. They also point out that the games are less violent than many modern movies. However, the debate has continued, escalating as far as the United Kingdom's House of Commons (Games Radar, 2009).

Wii Sports and Wii Fit

The Nintendo Wii, with its dedicated motion-sensitive controller, was sold starting in 2006. The company had attempted to implement similar controllers in the past, including the Power Glove in 1989, but it had never based an entire console around such a device. The Wii's simple design was combined with basic games such as *Wii Sports* to appeal to previously untapped audiences. *Wii Sports* was included with purchase of the Wii console and served as a means to demonstrate the new technology. It included five games: baseball, bowling, boxing, tennis, and golf. *Wii Sports* created a way for group play without the need for familiarity with video games. It was closer to outdoor social games such as horseshoes or croquet than it was to *Doom*. There was also nothing objectionable about it: no violence, no in-your-face intensity—just a game that even older people could access and enjoy. *Wii Bowling* tournaments were sometimes organized by retirement communities, and many people found the game to be a new way to socialize with their friends and families (Wischnowsky, 2007).

Wii Fit combined the previously incompatible terms "fitness" and "video games." Using a touch-sensitive platform, players could do aerobics, strength training, and yoga. The game kept track of players' weights, acting as a kind of virtual trainer (Vella, 2008).*Wii Fit* used the potential of video games to create an interactive version of an exercise machine, replacing workout videos and other forms of fitness that had never before considered Nintendo a competitor. This kind of design used the inherent strengths of video games to create a new kind of experience.

Nintendo found most of its past success marketing to younger demographics with games that were less controversial than the 1990s first-person shooters. *Wii Sports* and *Wii Fit* saw Nintendo playing to its strengths and expanding on them with family-friendly games that encouraged multiple generations to use video games as a social platform. This campaign was so successful that it is being imitated by rival companies Sony and Microsoft, which have released the Sony PlayStation Move and the Microsoft Kinect.

Key Takeaways

- *Guitar Hero* and *Rock Band* created a new means of marketing for the music industry. Music featured on the games experienced increased downloads and sales.

- The *Grand Theft Auto* series was revolutionary and controversial for its open-ended field. Players could choose from a number of different options, allowing them to set their own goals and create their own version of the game.

- *World of Warcraft* has brought the MMORPG genre to new heights of popularity. The large number of users has made the game evolve to a level of complexity unheard of in video games.

- *Wii Sports* and *Wii Fit* brought video games to audiences that had never been tapped by game makers. Older adults and families used *Wii Sports* as a means of family bonding, and *Wii Fit* took advantage of motion-controlled game playing to enter the fitness market.

Exercises

Think about the ways in which the games from this section were innovative and groundbreaking. Consider the following questions:

1. What new social, technological, or cultural areas did they explore?

2. Pick one of these areas—social, technological, or cultural—and write down ways in which video games could have a future influence in this area.

References

Barker, Carson. "Team Players: Guilds Take the Lonesome Gamer Out of Seclusion…Kind Of," *Austin Chronicle*, July 28, 2006, http://www.austinchronicle.com/gyrobase/Issue/story?oid=oid%3A390551.

Davis, Rowenna. "Welcome to the New Gold Mines," *Guardian* (London), March 5, 2009, http://www.guardian.co.uk/technology/2009/mar/05/virtual-world-china?intcmp=239.

Donald, Ryan. review of Grand Theft Auto (PlayStation), *CNET*, 28 April 2000, http://reviews.cnet.com/legacy-game-platforms/grand-theft-auto-playstation/4505-9882_7-30971409-2.html.

Games Radar, "The Decade in Gaming: The 10 Most Shocking Moments of the Decade," December 29, 2009, http://www.gamesradar.com/f/the-10-most-shocking-game-moments-of-the-decade/a-20091221122845427051/p-2.

Ivan, Tom. "Call of Duty Series Tops 55 Million Sales," *Edge*, November 27, 2009, http://www.edge-online.com/news/call-of-duty-series-tops-55-million-sales.

Morales, Tatiana. "Grand Theft Auto Under Fire," *CBS News*, July 14, 2005, http://www.cbsnews.com/stories/2005/07/13/earlyshow/living/parenting/main708794.shtml.

Peckham, Matt. Music Sales Rejuvenated by Rock Band, Guitar Hero," *PC World*, December 22, 2008, http://www.washingtonpost.com/wp-dyn/content/article/2008/12/22/AR2008122200798.html.

Quan, Denise. "Is 'Guitar Hero' Saving Rock 'n' Roll?" *CNN*, August 28, 2008, http://www.cnn.com/2008/SHOWBIZ/Music/08/20/videol.games.music/.

Vella, Matt. "Wii Fit Puts the Fun in Fitness," *Business Week*, May 21, 2008, http://www.businessweek.com/innovate/content/may2008/id20080520_180427.htm.

Wischnowsky, Dave. "Wii Bowling Knocks Over Retirement Home," *Chicago Tribune*, February 16, 2007, http://www.chicagotribune.com/news/local/chi-070216nintendo,0,2755896.story.

10.4 The Impact of Video Games on Culture

Learning Objectives

1. Describe gaming culture and how it has influenced mainstream culture.

2. Analyze the ways video games have affected other forms of media.

3. Describe how video games can be used for educational purposes.

4. Identify the arguments for and against the depiction of video games as an art.

An NPD poll conducted in 2007 found that 72 percent of the U.S. population had played a video game that year (Faylor, 2008). The increasing number of people playing video games means that video games are having an undeniable effect on culture. This effect is clearly visible in the increasing mainstream acceptance of aspects of gaming culture. Video games have also changed the way that many other forms of media, from music to film, are produced and consumed. Education has also been changed by video games through the use of new technologies that help teachers and students communicate in new ways through educational games such as *Brain Age*. As video games have an increasing influence on our culture, many have voiced their opinions on whether this form of media should be considered an art.

Game Culture

To fully understand the effects of video games on mainstream culture, it is important to understand the development of gaming culture, or the culture surrounding video games. Video games, like books or movies, have avid users who have made this form of media central to their lives. In the early 1970s, programmers got together in groups to play *Spacewar!*, spending a great deal of time competing in a game that was rudimentary compared to modern games (Brand). As video arcades and home video game consoles gained in popularity, youth culture quickly adapted to this type of media, engaging in competitions to gain high scores and spending hours at the arcade or with the home console.

In the 1980s, an increasing number of kids were spending time on consoles playing games and, more importantly, increasingly identifying with the characters and products associated with the games. Saturday morning cartoons were made out of the *Pac-Man* and *Super Mario Bros.* games, and an array of nongame merchandise was sold with video game logos and characters. The public recognition of some of these characters has made them into cultural icons. A poll taken in 2007 found that more Canadians surveyed could identify a photo of Mario, from *Super Mario Bros.*, than a photo of the current Canadian prime minister (Cohn & Toronto, 2007).

As the kids who first played *Super Mario Bros.* began to outgrow video games, companies such as Sega, and later Sony and Microsoft, began making games to appeal to older demographics. This has increased the average age of video game players, which was 35 in 2009 (Entertainment Software Association, 2009). The Nintendo Wii has even found a new demographic in retirement communities, where *Wii Bowling* has become a popular form of entertainment for the residents (Wischnowsky). The gradual increase in gaming age has led to an acceptance of video games as an acceptable form of mainstream entertainment.

The Subculture of Geeks

The acceptance of video games in mainstream culture has consequently changed the way that the culture views certain people. "Geek" was the name given to people who were adept at technology but lacking in the skills that tended to make one popular, like fashion sense or athletic ability. Many of these people, because they often did not fare well in society, favored imaginary worlds such as those found in the fantasy and science fiction genres. Video games were appealing because they were both a fantasy world and a means to excel at something. Jim Rossignol, in his 2008 book *This Gaming Life: Travels in Three Cities*, explained part of the lure of playing *Quake III* online:

Cold mornings, adolescent disinterest, and a nagging hip injury had meant that I was banished from the sports field for many years. I wasn't going to be able to indulge in the camaraderie that sports teams felt or in the extended buzz of victory through dedication and cooperation. That entire swathe of experience had been cut off from me by cruel circumstance and a good dose of self-defeating apathy. Now, however, there was a possibility for some kind of redemption: a sport for the quick-fingered and the computer-bound; a space of possibility in which I could mold friends and strangers into a proficient gaming team (Rossignol, 2008).

Video games gave a group of excluded people a way to gain proficiency in the social realm. As video games became more of a mainstream phenomenon and video game skills began to be desired by a large number of people, the popular idea of geeks changed. It is now common to see the term "geek" used to mean a person who understands computers and technology. This former slur is also prominent in the media, with headlines in 2010 such as "Geeks in Vogue: Top Ten Cinematic Nerds (Sharp, 2010)."

Many media stories focusing on geeks examine the ways in which this subculture has been accepted by the mainstream. Geeks may have become "cooler," but mainstream culture has also become "geekier." The acceptance of geek culture has led to acceptance of geek aesthetics. The mainstreaming of video games has led to acceptance of fantasy or virtual worlds. This is evident in the popularity of film/book series such as *The Lord of the Rings* and *Harry Potter*. Comic book characters, emblems of geek culture, have become the vehicles for blockbuster movies such as *Spider-Man* and *The Dark Knight*. The idea of a fantasy or virtual world has come to appeal to greater numbers of people. Virtual worlds such as those represented in the *Grand Theft Auto* and *Halo* series and online games such as *World of Warcraft* have expanded the idea of virtual worlds so that they are not mere means of escape but new ways to interact (Konzack, 2006).

The Effects of Video Games on Other Types of Media

Video games during the 1970s and '80s were often derivatives of other forms of media. *E.T.*, *Star Wars*, and a number of other games took their cues from movies, television shows, and books. This began to change in the 1980s with the development of cartoons based on video games, and in the 1990s and 2000s with live-action feature films based on video games.

Television

Television programs based on video games were an early phenomenon. *Pac-Man, Pole Position,* and *Q*bert* were among the animated programs that aired in the early 1980s. In the later 1980s, shows such as *The Super Mario Bros. Super Show!* and *The Legend of Zelda* promoted Nintendo games. In the 1990s, *Pokémon,* originally a game developed for the Nintendo Game Boy, was turned into a television series, a card game, several movies, and even a musical (Internet Movie Database). Recently, several programs have been developed that revolve entirely around video games—the web series *The Guild,* for instance, tells the story of a group of friends who interact through an unspecified MMORPG.

Nielsen, the company that tabulates television ratings, has begun rating video games in a similar fashion. In 2010, this information showed that video games, as a whole, could be considered a kind of fifth network, along with the television networks NBC, ABC, CBS, and Fox (Shields, 2009). Advertisers use Nielsen ratings to decide which programs to support. The use of this system is changing public perceptions to include video game playing as a habit similar to television watching.

Video games have also influenced the way that television is produced. The Rocket Racing League, scheduled to be launched in 2011, will feature a "virtual racetrack." Racing jets will travel along a virtual track that can only be seen by pilots and spectators with enabled equipment. Applications for mobile devices are being developed that will allow spectators to race virtual jets alongside the ones flying in real time (Hadhazy, 2010). This type of innovation is only possible with a public that has come to demand and rely on the kind of interactivity that video games provide.

Film

The rise in film adaptations of video games accompanies the increased age of video game users. In 1995, *Mortal Kombat,* a live-action movie based on the video game, grossed over $70 million at the box office, placing it 22nd in the rankings for that year (Box Office Mojo). *Lara Croft: Tomb Raider,* released in 2001, starred well-known actress Angelina Jolie and ranked No. 1 at the box office when it was released, and 15th overall for the year (Box Office Mojo). Films based on video games are an increasingly common sight at the box office, such as producer Jerry Bruckheimer's *Prince of Persia,* or the recent sequel to *Tron,* based on the idea of a virtual gaming arena.

Another aspect of video games' influence on films is how video game releases are marketed and perceived. The release date for anticipated game *Grand Theft Auto IV* was announced and marketed to compete with the release of the film *Iron Man. Grand Theft Auto IV* supposedly beat *Iron Man* by $300 million in sales. This kind of comparison is, in some ways, misleading. Video games cost much more than a ticket to a movie, so higher sales does not mean that more people bought the game than the movie. Also, the distribution apparatus for the two media is totally different. Movies can only be released in theaters, whereas video games can be sold at any retail outlet (Associated Press, 2008). What this kind of news story proves, however, is that the general public considers video games as something akin to a film. It is also important to realize that the scale of production and profit for video games is similar to that of films. Video games include music scores, actors, and directors in addition to the game designers, and the budgets for major games reflect this. *Grand Theft Auto IV* cost an estimated $100 million to produce (Bowditch, 2008).

Music

Video games have been accompanied by music ever since the days of the arcade. Video game music was originally limited to computer beeps turned into theme songs. The design of the Nintendo 64, Sega Saturn, and Sony PlayStation made it possible to use sampled audio on new games, meaning songs played on physical instruments could be recorded and used on video games. Beginning with the music of the *Final Fantasy* series, scored by famed composer Nobuo Uematsu, video game music took on film score quality, complete with full orchestral and vocal tracks. This innovation proved beneficial to the music industry. Well-known musicians such as Trent Reznor, Thomas Dolby, Steve Vai, and Joe Satriani were able to create the soundtracks for popular games, giving these artists exposure to new generations of potential fans (Video Games Music Big Hit, 1997). Composing music for video games has turned into a profitable means of employment for many musicians. Schools such as Berklee College of Music, Yale, and New York University have programs that focus on composing music for video games. The students are taught many of the same principles that are involved in film scoring (Khan, 2010).

Many rock bands have allowed their previously recorded songs to be used in video games, similar to a hit song being used on a movie soundtrack. The bands are paid for the rights to use the song, and their music is exposed to an audience that otherwise might not hear it. As mentioned earlier, games like *Rock Band* and *Guitar Hero* have been used to promote bands. The release of *The Beatles: Rock Band* was timed to coincide with the release of digitally remastered reissues of the Beatles' albums.

Another phenomenon relating to music and video games involves musicians covering video game music. A number of bands perform only video game covers in a variety of styles, such as the popular Japanese group the Black Mages, which performs rock versions of *Final Fantasy* music. Playing video game themes is not limited to rock bands, however. An orchestra and chorus called Video Games Live started a tour in 2005 dedicated to playing well-known video game music. Their performances are often accompanied by graphics projected onto a screen showing relevant sequences from the video games (Play Symphony).

Machinima

Recently, the connection between video games and other media has increased with the popularity of machinima, animated films and series created by recording character actions inside video games. Beginning with the short film "Diary of a Camper," filmed inside the game *Quake* in 1996, fans of video games have adopted the technique of machinima to tell their own stories. Although these early movies were released only online and targeted a select niche of gamers, professional filmmakers have since adopted the process, using machinima to storyboard scenes and to add a sense of individuality to computer-generated shots. This new form of media is increasingly becoming mainstream, as TV shows such as *South Park* and channels such as MTV2 have introduced machinima to a larger audience (Strickland).

Video Games and Education

Figure 10.7

Educational video games have proven to be useful tools for educators.

One sign of the mainstreaming of video games is the increase of educational institutions that embrace them. As early as the 1980s, games such as *Number Munchers* and *Word Munchers* were designed to help children develop basic math and grammar skills. In 2006, the Federation of American Scientists completed a study that approved of video game use in education. The study cited the fact that video game systems were present in most households, kids favored learning through video games, and games could be used to facilitate analytical skills (Feller, 2006). Another study, published in the science journal *Nature* in 2002, found that regular video game players had better developed visual-processing skills than people who did not play video games. Participants in the test were asked to play a first-person shooter game for 1 hour a day for 10 days, and were then tested for specific visual attention skills. The playing improved these skills in all participants, but the regular video game players had a greater skill level than the non–game players. According to the study, "Although video-game playing may seem to be rather mindless, it is capable of radically altering visual attention processing (Green & Bavelier, 2003)."

Other educational institutions have begun to embrace video games as well. The Boy Scouts of America have created a "belt loop," something akin to a merit badge, for tasks including learning to play a parent-approved game and developing a schedule to balance video game time with homework (Murphy, 2010). The federal government has also seen the educational potential of video games. A commission on balancing the federal budget suggested a video game that would educate Americans about the necessary costs of balancing the federal budget (Wolf, 2010). The military has similarly embraced video games as training simulators for new soldiers. These simulators, working off of newer game technologies, present several different realistic options that soldiers could face on the field. The games have also been used as recruiting tools by the U.S. Army and the Army National Guard (Associated Press, 2003).

The ultimate effect of video game use for education, whether in schools or in the public arena, means that video games have been validated by established cultural authorities. Many individuals still resist the idea that video games can be beneficial or have a positive cultural influence, but their embrace by educational institutions has given video games validation.

Video Games as Art

While universally accepted as a form of media, a debate has recently arisen over whether video games can be considered a form of art. Roger Ebert, the well-known film critic, has historically argued that "video games can never be art," citing the fact that video games are meant to be won, whereas art is meant to be experienced (Ebert, 2010).

His remarks have generated an outcry from both video gamers and developers. Many point to games such as 2009's *Flower*, in which players control the flow of flower petals in the wind, as examples of video games developing into art. *Flower* avoids specific plot and characters to allow the player to focus on interaction with the landscape and the emotion of the game-play (That Game Company). Likewise, more mainstream games such as the popular *Katamari* series, released in 2004, are built around the idea of creation, requiring players to pull together a massive clump of objects in order to create a star.

Video games, once viewed as a mindless source of entertainment, are now being featured in publications such as *The New Yorker* magazine and *The New York Times* (Fisher, 2010). With the development of increasingly complex musical scores and the advent of machinima, the boundaries between video games and other forms of media are slowly blurring. While they may not be considered art by everyone, video games have contributed significantly to modern artistic culture.

Key Takeaways

- The aesthetics and principles of gaming culture have had an increasing effect on mainstream culture. This has led to the gradual acceptance of marginalized social groups and increased comfort with virtual worlds and the pursuit of new means of interaction.

- Video games have gone from being a derivative medium that took its cues from other media, such as books, films, and music, to being a form of media that other types derive new ideas from. Video games have also interacted with older forms of media to change them and create new means of entertainment and interaction.

- Educational institutions have embraced the use of video games as valuable tools for teaching. These tools include simulated worlds in which important life skills can be learned and improved.

- While video games may not be accepted by everyone as a form of art, there is no doubt that they contribute greatly to artistic media such as music and film.

Exercises

Think about the ways in which video games have influenced and affected other forms of media. Then consider the following questions:

1. Are there things video games will never be able to offer?

2. Write down several examples of ways in which other forms of media are not replicated by video games. Then speculate on ways video games could eventually emulate these forms.

References

Associated Press, "'Grand Theft Auto IV' Beats 'Iron Man' by $300 Million," *Fox News*, May 9, 2008, http://www.foxnews.com/story/0,2933,354711,00.html.

Associated Press, "Military Training Is Just a Game," *Wired*, October 3, 2003, http://www.wired.com/gaming/gamingreviews/news/2003/10/60688.

Bowditch, Gillian. "Grand Theft Auto Producer is Godfather of Gaming," *Times* (London), April 27, 2008, http://www.timesonline.co.uk/tol/news/uk/scotland/article3821838.ece.

Box Office Mojo, "Lara Croft: Tomb Raider," http://www.boxofficemojo.com/movies/?id=tombraider.htm.

Box Office Mojo, "Mortal Kombat," http://boxofficemojo.com/movies/?id=mortalkombat.htm.

Brand, "Space War."

Cohn & Wolfe Toronto, "Italian Plumber More Memorable Than Harper, Dion," news release, November 13, 2007, http://www.newswire.ca/en/releases/mmnr/Super_Mario_Galaxy/index.html.

Ebert, Roger. "Video Games Can Never Be Art," *Chicago Sun-Times*, April 16, 2010, http://blogs.suntimes.com/ebert/2010/04/video_games_can_never_be_art.html.

Entertainment Software Association, *Essential Facts About the Computer and Video Game Industry: 2009 Sales, Demographic, and Usage Data*, 2009, http://www.theesa.com/facts/pdfs/ESA_EF_2009.pdf.

Faylor, Chris. "NPD: 72% of U.S. Population Played Games in 2007; PC Named "Driving Force in Online Gaming," Shack News, April 2, 2008, http://www.shacknews.com/onearticle.x/52025.

Feller, Ben. "Group: Video Games Can Reshape Education," *MSNBC*, October 18, 2006, http://www.msnbc.msn.com/id/15309615/from/ET/.

Fisher, Max. "Are Video Games Art?" *Atlantic Wire*, April 19, 2010, http://www.theatlanticwire.com/features/view/feature/Are-Video-Games-Art-1085/.

Green, C. Shawn. and Daphne Bavelier, "Action Video Game Modifies Visual Selective Attention," *Nature* 423, no. 6939 (2003): 534–537.

Hadhazy, Adam. "'NASCAR of the Skies' to Feature Video Game-Like Interactivity," *TechNewsDaily*, April 26, 2010, http://www.technewsdaily.com/nascar-of-the-skies-to-feature-video-game-like-interactivity–0475/.

Internet Movie Database, "Pokémon," http://www.imdb.com/.

Khan, Joseph P. "Berklee is Teaching Its Students to Compose Scores for Video Games," *Boston Globe*, January 19, 2010, http://www.boston.com/news/education/higher/articles/2010/01/19/berklee_is_teaching_students_to_compose_scores_for_video_games/.

Konzack, Lars. "Geek Culture: The 3rd Counter-Culture," (paper, FNG2006, Preston, England, June 26–28, 2006), http://www.scribd.com/doc/270364/Geek-Culture-The-3rd-CounterCulture.

Murphy, David. "Boy Scouts Develop 'Vide Game' Merit Badge," *PC Magazine*, May 2, 2010, http://www.pcmag.com/article2/0,2817,2363331,00.asp.

Play Symphony, Jason Michael Paul Productions, "About," Play! A Video Game Symphony, http://www.play-symphony.com/about.php.

Rossignol, Jim. *This Gaming Life: Travels in Three Cities* (Ann Arbor, MI: University of Michigan Press, 2008), 17.

Sharp, Craig. "Geeks in Vogue: Top Ten Cinematic Nerds," *Film Shaft*, April 26, 2010, http://www.filmshaft.com/geeks-in-vogue-top-ten-cinematic-nerds/.

Shields, Mike. "Nielsen: Video Games Approach 5th Network Status," *Adweek*, March 25, 2009, http://www.adweek.com/aw/content_display/news/agency/e3i4f087b1aeac6f008d0ecadfeffe4a191.

Strickland, Jonathan. "How Machinima Works," HowStuffWorks.com, http://entertainment.howstuffworks.com/machinima3.htm.

That Game Company, "Flower," http://thatgamecompany.com/games/flower/.

Video Games Music Big Hit, "Video Games Music Big Hit," *Wilmington (NC) Morning Star*, February 1, 1997, 36.

Wischnowsky, "Wii Bowling."

Wolf, Richard. "Nation's Soaring Deficit Calls for Painful Choices," *USA Today*, April 14, 2010, http://www.usatoday.com/news/washington/2010-04-12-deficit_N.htm.

10.5 Controversial Issues

Learning Objectives

1. Describe controversial issues related to modern video games.
2. Analyze the issues and problems with rating electronic entertainment.
3. Discuss the effects of video game addiction.
4. Examine the gender issues surrounding video games.

The increasing realism and expanded possibilities of video games has inspired a great deal of controversy. However, even early games, though rudimentary and seemingly laughable nowadays, raised controversy over their depiction of adult themes. Although increased realism and graphics capabilities of contemporary video games have increased the shock value of in-game violence, international culture has been struggling to come to terms with video game violence since the dawn of video games.

Violence

Violence in video games has been controversial from their earliest days. *Death Race*, an arcade game released in 1976, encouraged drivers to run over stick figures, which then turned into *X*s. Although the programmers claimed that the stick figures were not human, the game was controversial, making national news on the TV talk show *Donahue* and the TV news magazine *60 Minutes*. Video games, regardless of their realism or lack thereof, had added a new potential to the world of games and entertainment: the ability to simulate murder.

The enhanced realism of video games in the 1990s accompanied a rise in violent games as companies expanded the market to target older demographics. A great deal of controversy exists over the influence of this kind of violence on children, and also over the rating system that is applied to video games. There are many stories of real-life violent acts involving video games. The 1999 Columbine High School massacre was quickly linked to the teenage perpetrators' enthusiasm for video games. The families of Columbine victims brought a lawsuit against 25 video game companies, claiming that if the games had not existed, the massacre would not have happened (Ward, 2001). In 2008, a 17-year-old boy shot his parents after they took away his video game system, killing his mother (Harvey, 2009). Also in 2008, when six teens were arrested for attempted carjacking and robbery, they stated that they were reenacting scenes from *Grand Theft Auto* (Cochran, 2008).

There is no shortage of news stories that involve young men committing crimes relating to an obsession with video games. The controversy has not been resolved regarding the influences behind these crimes. Many studies have linked aggression to video games; however, critics take issue with using the results of these studies to claim that the video games caused the aggression. They point out that people who enact video-game–related crimes already have psychopathic tendencies, and that the results of such research studies are correlational rather than causational—a naturally violent person is drawn to play violent video games (Adams, 2010). Other critics point out that violent games are designed for adults, just as violent movies are, and that parents should enforce stricter standards for their children.

The problem of children's access to violent games is a large and complex one. Video games present difficult issues for those who create the ratings. One problem is the inconsistency that seems to exist in rating video games and movies. Movies with violence or sexual themes are rated either R or NC-17. Filmmakers prefer the R rating over the NC-17 rating because NC-17 ratings hurt box office sales, and they will often heavily edit films to remove overly graphic content. The Entertainment Software Rating Board (ESRB), rates video games. The two most restrictive ratings the ESRB has put forth are "M" (for Mature; 17 and older; "may contain mature sexual themes, more intense violence, and/or strong language") and "AO" (for Adults Only; 18 and up; "may include graphic depictions of sex and/or violence"). If this rating system were applied to movies, a great deal of movies now rated R would be labeled AO. An AO label can have a devastating effect on game sales; in fact, many retail outlets will not sell games with an AO rating (Hyman, 2005). This creates a situation where a video game with a sexual or violent scene as graphic as the ones seen in R-rated movies is difficult to purchase, whereas a pornographic magazine can be bought at many convenience stores. This issue reveals a unique aspect of video games. Although many of them are designed for adults, the distribution system and culture surrounding video games is still largely youth-oriented.

Video Game Addiction

Another controversial issue is the problem of video game addiction. As of the print date, the American Medical Association (AMA) has not created an official diagnosis of video game addiction, citing the lack of long-term research. However, the AMA uses the term "video game overuse" to describe video game use that begins to affect other aspects of an individual's life, such as relationships and health. Studies have found that socially marginalized people have more of a tendency to overuse games, especially online role-playing games like *World of Warcraft*. Other studies have found that patterns of time usage and social dysfunction in players who overuse games are similar to those of other addictive disorders (Khan, 2007).

Figure 10.8

Video game use can become an obsession with some people.

Steven Andrew – Video Games – CC BY-NC 2.0.

Groups such as Online Gamers Anonymous have developed a 12-step program similar to that of Alcoholics Anonymous to help gamers deal with problems relating to game overuse. This group is run by former online gamers and family members of those affected by heavy game use (On-line Gamers Anonymous). This problem is not new, but it has become more prevalent. In the early 1990s, many stories surfaced of individuals dropping out of college or getting divorced because of addiction to MUDs (Greene, 1998). In addition, heavy video gaming, much like heavy computer use in an office setting, can result in painful repetitive stress injuries. Even worse are the rare, but serious, cases of death resulting from video game overuse. In the early '80s, two deaths were linked to the video game *Berzerk*. The players, both in their late teens, suffered fatal heart attacks while struggling to achieve top scores (Arcade History). The issue of video game addiction has become a larger one because of the ubiquity of video games and Internet technology. In countries that have a heavily wired infrastructure, such as South Korea, the problem is even bigger. In 2010, excessive game use was problematic enough that the South Korean government imposed an online gaming curfew for people under the age of 18 that would block certain sites after midnight. This decision followed the death of a 3-month-old baby from starvation while her parents played an online game at an Internet café (Cain, 2010).

Another side of video game addiction is told well by Jim Rossignol in his book *This Gaming Life: Travels in Three Cities*. The book describes Rossignol's job as a journalist for a financial company and his increasing involvement with *Quake III*. Rossignol trained a team of players to compete in virtual online tournaments, scheduling practices and spending the hours afterward analyzing strategies with his teammates. His intense involvement in the game led to poor performance at his job, and he was eventually fired. After being fired, he spent even more time on the game, not caring about his lack of a job or shrinking savings. The story up to this point sounds like a testimonial about the dangers of game addiction. However, because of his expertise in the game, he was hired by a games magazine and enjoyed full-time employment writing about what he loved doing. Rossignol does not gloss over the fact that games can have a negative influence, but his book speaks to the ways in which gaming—often what would be described as obsessive gaming—can cause positive change in people's lives (Rossignol).

Sexism

Figure 10.9

Games such as *Tomb Raider* and *Dead or Alive Xtreme* have been criticized for their demeaning depiction of women.

Joshua | Ezzell – TOMB RAIDER 2013 | Simplified – CC BY 2.0.

It is no secret that young adult men make up the majority of video gamers. A study in 2009 found that 60 percent of gamers were male, and the average age of players was 35 (Entertainment Software Association, 2009). While the gender gap has certainly narrowed in the past 30 years, video gaming is still in many ways a male-dominated medium.

Male influence can be seen throughout the industry. Women make up less than 12 percent of game designers and programmers, and those who do enter the field often find themselves facing subtle—and not so subtle—sexism (Media Awareness Network). When *Game Developer* magazine released its list of top 50 people in the video game industry for 2010, bloggers were quick to note that no female developers appeared in the list (Doctorow, 2010). In 2007, scandal erupted over a pornographic comic featuring Jade Raymond, current managing director of the French video game publisher Ubisoft, that surfaced on an online forum. The motivation behind the comic was to allege that Raymond did not deserve her position at Ubisoft because she earned it based on her looks, rather than on her abilities and experience.

Sexism in video games has existed since the early days of the medium. The plot of the infamous *Custer's Revenge*, released for the Atari 2600 in 1982, centered on the rape of a Native American woman. Popular NES games such as *Super Mario Bros.* and *The Legend of Zelda* featured a male figure rescuing a damsel in distress. Both the protagonist and antagonist in the original *Tomb Raider* game had hourglass figures with prominent busts and nonexistent waists, a trend that continues in the franchise today. In 2003, the fighting series *Dead or Alive* released a spin-off game titled *Dead or Alive Xtreme Beach Volleyball* that existed to showcase the well-endowed female characters in swim attire (Strauss, 2010). The spin-off was so popular that two more similar games were released.

Some note that video games are not unique in their demeaning portrayal of women. Like movies, television, and other media forms, video games often fall back on gender stereotyping in order to engage consumers. Defenders point out that many male video game characters are also depicted lewdly. Games such as *God of War* and *Mortal Kombat* feature hypersexualized men with bulging muscles and aggressive personalities who rely on their brawn rather than their brains. How are men affected by these stereotypes? Laboratory studies have shown that violence and aggression in video games affect men more than women, leading to higher levels of male aggression (Bartholow & Anderson, 2002). While sexism is certainly present in video games, it seems sexual stereotyping affects both genders negatively.

In recent years, game designers have sought to move away from these clichéd representations of gender. The popular game *Portal*, released in 2007, features a female protagonist clad in a simple orange jumpsuit who relies on her wits to solve logic puzzles. Series such as *Half-Life* and *Phoenix Wright: Ace Attorney* star male heroes who are intellectuals instead of warriors. Other games, like the *Mass Effect* series and *Halo: Reach*, allow gamers to choose the gender of the main character without altering elements of the plot or game-play. However, despite recent strides forward, there is no doubt that as the video game industry continues to evolve, so too will the issue of gender.

Key Takeaways

- Video game violence has been an issue since the 1976 game *Death Race*. The potential of video games to simulate murder created a new issue in entertainment media.

- A great number of news stories link video games with violent crimes. Studies have found a correlation between aggressive behavior and video games, but critics claim that these studies do not prove that video games cause violent acts.

- The video game rating system informs purchasers about the content of a game. The highest rating, Adults Only, hurts video game sales, so companies try to make games that are rated Mature. Critics charge that video game ratings are inconsistent with other schemes, such as the movie rating system.

- Video game addiction is associated more with online games, although many instances of single-player obsessions exist as well. It has become a high-profile issue with the rise in popularity of online gaming.

- The American Medical Association has not developed a diagnosis for video game addiction. Instead, it uses the term "video game overuse" to describe a state where an individual's gaming habits have a detrimental effect on his or her personal life.

- Sexism and gender issues are hot topics in the video game industry, as female gamers and developers often struggle for equal footing. Controversy has arisen over character stereotypes; however, modern games are beginning to break through conventional barriers of gender.

Exercises

Choose video game violence or video game addiction and search for it on the Internet. Examine the research that is associated with the issue you chose. Then consider the following questions:

1. What is your opinion of the issue in light of the research?

2. Has your issue been researched thoroughly?

3. Visit message boards and forums and search for journal articles related to video game addiction or

violence. What actions would you suggest to research these issues more fully?

References

Adams, Jill U. "A Closer Look: Effects of Violent Video Games," *Los Angeles Times*, May 3, 2010, http://www.latimes.com/news/health/la-he-closer-20100503,0,5586471.story.

Arcade History, "Berzerk, the Video Game," http://www.arcade-history.com/?n=berzerk&page=detail&id=236.

Bartholow, Bruce D. and Craig A. Anderson, "Effects of Violent Video Games on Aggressive Behavior: Potential Sex Differences," *Journal of Experimental Social Psychology* 38, no. 3 (2002): 283–290.

Cain, Geoffrey. "South Korea Cracks Down on Gaming Addiction," *Time*, April 20, 2010, http://www.time.com/time/world/article/0,8599,1983234,00.html.

Cochran, Lee. "Teens Say: Video Game Made Them Do It," *ABC News*, June 27, 2008, http://abcnews.go.com/TheLaw/story?id=5262689.

Doctorow, Cory. "Gamasutra's Most Important Gamers List Is a Boy's Club," *BoingBoing* (blog), April 14, 2010, http://boingboing.net/2010/04/14/gamasutras-most-impo.html.

Entertainment Software Association, *Essential Facts About the Computer and Video Game Industry: 2009*.

Greene, R. W. "Is Internet Addiction for Worrywarts or a Genuine Problem?" *CNN*, September 23, 1998, http://www.cnn.com/TECH/computing/9809/23/netaddict.idg/index.html.

Harvey, Mike. "Teenager Daniel Petric Shot Parents Who Took Away Xbox," *Times* (London), January 13, 2009, http://www.timesonline.co.uk/tol/news/world/us_and_americas/article5512446.ece.

Hyman, Paul. "Video Game Rating Board Don't Get No Respect," *Hollywood Reporter*, April 8, 2005, http://www.hollywoodreporter.com/hr/search/article_display.jsp?vnu_content_id=1000874859.

Khan, Mohamed. *Emotional and Behavioral Effects of Video Games and Internet Overuse*, American Medical Association, Council on Science and Public Health, 2007, http://www.ama-assn.org/ama1/pub/upload/mm/443/csaph12a07-fulltext.pdf.

Media Awareness Network, "Gender Stereotyping," http://www.media-awareness.ca/english/parents/video_games/concerns/gender_videogames.cfm.

On-line Gamers Anonymous, "About OLGA & OLG-Anon," http://www.olganon.org.

Rossignol, *This Gaming Life*, 4–11.

Strauss, Michael. "A Look at Female Characters in Video Games," Associated Content, July 16, 2010, http://www.associatedcontent.com/article/5487226/a_look_at_female_characters_in_video_pg2.html?cat=19.

Ward, Mark. "Columbine Families Sue Computer Game Makers," *BBC News*, May 1, 2001, http://news.bbc.co.uk/2/hi/science/nature/1295920.stm.

10.6 Blurring the Boundaries Between Video Games, Information, Entertainment, and Communication

Learning Objectives

1. Identify how video games allow previously marginalized groups to enjoy new social experiences.
2. Explain how virtual worlds can be used to facilitate learning.
3. Describe the different ways video games have been used to communicate messages.

Early video games were easily identifiable as games. They had basic goals and set rules of play. As games have developed in complexity, they have allowed for newer options and an expanded idea of what constitutes a game. At the same time, the aesthetics and design of game culture have been applied to tools and entertainment phenomena that are not technically games. The result is a blurring of the lines between games and other forms of communication, and the creation of new means of mixing information, entertainment, and communication.

Video Games and the Social World of Sports

Figure 10.10

Team video games can provide many of the benefits of physical sports.

Fabio Hofnik – New Super Mario Bros. – CC BY-NC 2.0.

Video games have developed in complexity and flexibility to the point that they are providing new kinds of social interactions. This is perhaps clearest when games are compared to physical sports. Most of the abstract reasons for involvement in sports—things like teamwork, problem solving, and leadership—are also reasons to play video games that allow online team interaction. Sports are often portrayed as a social platform where people can learn new skills. Amateur sports teams provide an important means of socialization and communication for many people, allowing individuals from different gender, ethnic, and class backgrounds to find a common forum for communication. Video games have similar capacities; players who engage in online team battles must communicate with one another effectively and learn to collectively solve problems. In fact, video games could arguably provide a more inclusive platform for socializing because they do not exclude most socially or physically challenged individuals. The social platform of online games is certainly no utopia, as competitive endeavors of any sort inevitably create opportunities for negative communication, but it allows people of different genders, races, and nationalities to play on equal footing, a feat that is difficult, if not impossible, in the physical realm.

Virtual Worlds and Societal Interaction

Massively multiplayer online role-playing games (MMORPGs) such as *World of Warcraft*, *EverQuest*, and *EVE Online* allow for an unprecedented variety of goals to be pursued. According to one study on online communities,

that means games are no longer meant to be a solitary activity played by a single individual. Instead, the player is expected to join a virtual community that is parallel with the physical world, in which societal, cultural, and economical systems arise (Zaphiris, et. al., 2008).

MMORPGs can function as a kind of hybrid of social media and video games in this respect. In some instances, these games could function entirely as social media, and not as games. Consider a player who has no desire to achieve any of the prescribed goals of a game, such as going on quests or accomplishing tasks. This individual could simply walk around in social areas and talk to new people. Is the player still playing a game at this point, or has the game turned into a type of social media?

Virtual worlds such as *Second Life* are good examples of the thin line between games and social media. In this virtual world, users create avatars to represent themselves. They can then explore the world and take part in the culture that characterizes it. The *Second Life* website FAQ (frequently asked questions) tries to illustrate the differences between a virtual world and a video game:

While the Second Life interface and display are similar to most popular massively multiplayer online role playing games (or MMORPGs), there are two key, unique differences:

Creativity: The Second Life virtual world provides almost unlimited freedom to its Residents. This world really is whatever you make it. If you want to hang out with your friends in a garden or nightclub, you can. If you want to go shopping or fight dragons, you can. If you want to start a business, create a game or build a skyscraper you can. It's up to you.

Ownership: Instead of paying a monthly subscription fee, Residents can start a Basic account for FREE. Additional Basic accounts cost a one-time flat fee of just $9.95. If you choose to get land to live, work and build on, you pay a monthly lease fee based on the amount of land you have. You also own anything you create—Residents retain intellectual property rights over their in-world creations (Second Life).

Virtual worlds may differ from traditional video games in key ways, but these differences will likely be further blurred as games develop. Regardless of the way these worlds are classified, they are based heavily on the aesthetics and design of video games.

Virtual worlds are societies in which communication can be expanded to relay information in ways that cannot be done with other forms of media. Universities have set up virtual classrooms in *Second Life* that employ techniques for teaching that are otherwise impossible. Curriculum can be set up to take advantage of the virtual world's creative capacity (Kluge & Riley, 2008). For example, a class on architecture could lead students through a three-dimensional recreation of a Gothic cathedral, a history class could rely on an interactive battlefield simulation to explain the mechanics of a famous battle, or a physics class could use simulations to demonstrate important principles.

Figure 10.11

Virtual classrooms have been used in *Second Life* as new teaching tools.

Virtual worlds have been used to relay new kinds of information as well. In 2007, specialists developed virtual-reality simulations to help patients with Asperger's syndrome navigate through social situations. Individuals with Asperger's syndrome have difficulty recognizing nonverbal cues and adapting to change. The simulations allowed these patients to create avatars that then played out social situations such as job interviews. The simulations could be adjusted to allow for more complicated interactions, and the users could replay their own performances to better understand the simulation (University of Texas at Dallas News Center, 2008). The creation of avatars and the ability to replay scenes until the user improves performance is a direct influence of video games.

Social Media and Games

Figure 10.12

FarmVille is integrated with Facebook and lets players grow and harvest crops to expand their farms.

tarikgore1 – farmville – CC BY 2.0.

Social media outlets such as Facebook have also used video games to expand their communication platforms. *FarmVille*, a game in which players plant, harvest, and sell crops and expand their farm plots with the profits, is integrated with Facebook so that all users can connect with their real-life friends in the game. The game adds another aspect of communication—one centered on competition, strategy, and the aesthetics of game-play—to the Facebook platform. In 2010, *FarmVille* had 80 million users, an unprecedented number of people playing a single game. Other games for Facebook include *Lexulous* (formerly *Scrabulous*), a game that mimicked the board game *Scrabble* closely enough that it had to be changed, and *Pet Society*, a game that allows users to raise virtual animals as pets. These games are unique in their demographic scope; they seek to engage literally anyone. By coupling games with social media sites, game designers have pushed the influence of video games to unprecedented levels (Walker, 2010).

Due to the increasing popularity of video games, many social networking websites have emerged in recent years that target hard-core gamers and casual gamers alike. The website GamingPassions.com describes itself as a "free online dating and social networking site for the Video Gaming community" that "allows you to meet other video game lovers who 'get it (Gaming Passions).'" Others, such as DateCraft, target players who share a love of specific games, such as *World of Warcraft*. These websites allow players to socialize outside of the confines of a video game and provide a way for fans of any game to connect (Fawkes, 2010).

Mobile Phones and Gaming

The maker of *FarmVille*, a company called Zynga, has released a number of social networking games that can be played via Internet-enabled mobile phones. *Mafia Wars*, a simulated version of organized crime that originated as an online game, lets users manage their money and complete jobs from their mobile phones. This innovation is only a change of platform from the computer to the phone, but it promises to make gaming a common means of social interaction.

Phones are used to communicate directly with another person, whether through text messages, Facebook posts, or phone calls. Adding games to phones creates a new language that people can use to communicate with each other. One can imagine the ways in which a spat between friends or a couple hooking up could be communicated through this medium. During the week of Valentine's Day in 2010, the creators of *FarmVille* reported that users sent more than 500 million copies of virtual gifts to each other (Ingram, 2010). Competition, aggression, hostility, as well as generosity and general friendliness are given new means of expression with the addition of video games to the mobile platform.

Video Games and Their Messages

An important genre of games is often overlooked when focusing on the overall history and effect of video games. These games are created to get a specific point across to the player, and are generally low-budget efforts by individuals or small groups. The group Molleindustria puts out a host of these games, including *Oligarchy*, a game in which the player is an oil-drilling business executive who pursues corruption to gain profits, or *Faith Fighter*, in which religious icons fight each other (Industria). *Downing Street Fighter* is a similar game, designed as a satirical representation of the United Kingdom's 2010 elections (Verjee, 2010).

Other games in this genre include a great deal of content that informs players about current events. One example is *Cutthroat Capitalism*, where users play the part of Somali pirates who are carrying out kidnapping and piracy missions. The player must weigh the risks and rewards of their exploits given a variety of economic factors (Carney, 2009). This game allows players to understand the forces at work behind international phenomena such as piracy. Other games include the *Redistricting Game*, a game aimed at encouraging congressional redistricting reform, and *Planet Green Game*, in which players find ways to conserve energy (McGervan, 2007). These games' publishers have used their medium to transmit information in new ways. Political satire in the medium of the video game allows the player to, in effect, play a satirical joke to its logical conclusion, exploring the entire scope of the joke. Advocacy games engage players with an interactive political message, rather than sending out traditional media ads. Mainstream groups such as PETA have also turned to video games to convey messages. During the 2008 Thanksgiving season, the animal-rights group released a parody of the popular *Cooking Mama* games to demonstrate the cruelty of eating meat (Sliwinski, 2008).

Figure 10.13

The unauthorized PETA edition of *Cooking Mama* tackles the issue of animal cruelty.

Shahab Zargari – Evil Cooking Mama – CC BY 2.0.

Although games of this type are not in a league with game series like *Halo*—either in design or in popularity—they are pushing the boundaries of the video game as a form of media. Political pamphlets were a major source of information and political discourse during the American Revolution. Video games may well come to serve a similar informational function.

Key Takeaways

- Team-oriented video games have allowed new groups to learn skills similar to those learned in physical sports. Team building, competition, and problem solving are all major components of playing on a virtual team.
- Virtual worlds, though not video games in themselves, use the design and principles of video games to create new social spaces. These spaces are being used to create new social platforms and new ways of communicating complex ideas.
- Video games have been added to social networking sites to expand the ways in which people can communicate with each other. The medium of the game allows players to interact with their friends in new ways.

Exercises

Several examples of the ways in which virtual worlds could be used for education were mentioned in this section.

1. Think of ways in which this course could be taught in a virtual world. What advantages would this kind of teaching bring to a course like this?

2. What disadvantages does it carry with it?

End-of-Chapter Assessment

Review Questions

1.
Section 1

   a. Identify the companies that headed the video game industry in the 1970s, '80s, '90s, and 2000s.

   b. Name three important innovations in video games that appealed to new audiences.

   c. Name three technologies that were fundamental to the evolution of video games.

   d. Explain the importance of the Internet in the evolution of video games.

2.
Section 2

   a. Name three of the games listed in this section and explain how they were innovative.

   b. Explain how *World of Warcraft* expanded the video game as a form of media.

   c. How are the latest trends in video games expanding the video game?

   d. Compare music releases on *Guitar Hero* or *Rock Band* with traditional music releases such as MP3s or physical albums. What are the advantages and disadvantages of these forms?

3.
Section 3

   a. Describe some of the aesthetics and ideas of gaming culture.

   b. Pick a type of media, such as film or books, and analyze the ways that video games have affected it.

   c. Describe one response of mainstream culture to the influence of video games.

4.
Section 4

   a. Summarize the points in the public debate over video game violence.

   b. When do you think video game use becomes an addiction?

   c. Name one way that the controversy over video game violence could be addressed.

   d. Explain the ways in which video game and movie ratings differ.

5.
Section 5

a. Give an example of the ways in which video games have allowed people to experience new things.

b. Give an example of the ways in which virtual worlds can be used in education.

c. Compare games that advocate political messages with other forms of political persuasion.

Critical Thinking Questions

1. How has youth culture been influenced and even manipulated by the makers of video games?

2. How have video games influenced your communication or learning?

3. Should video games be rated in a different way than movies? Explain your answer.

4. What are the limitations of video games when compared to other forms of media?

5. Do you think the overall influence of video games on culture has been positive or negative? Explain your answer.

Career Connection

Video games are a growing industry, and the budgets to create them are increasing every year. Video games require large production teams. The following jobs are important aspects of video game production:

- Game developer
- Art director
- Programmer
- Sound designer
- Producer
- Game tester
- Animator

Choose one of the jobs listed here or find a different job associated with the games industry and research the requirements for it online. When you have researched your job, answer the following questions:

1. What made you choose this job?

2. What strengths do you have that would help you excel at this job?

3. List the steps that you would take if you were to pursue this job.

References

Carney, Scott. "An Economic Analysis of the Somali Pirate Business Model," *Wired*, July 13, 2009, http://www.wired.com/politics/security/magazine/17-07/ff_somali_pirates.

Fawkes, Guy. "Online Dating for Video Gamers," Associated Content, March 19, 2010, http://www.associatedcontent.com/article/2806686/online_dating_for_video_game_players.html?cat=41.

Gaming Passions, "Welcome to Gaming Passions," http://www.gamingpassions.com/.

Industria, Molle. http://www.molleindustria.org/en/home.

Ingram, Mathew. "Farmville Users Send 500M Valentines in 48 Hours," GigaOM, February 10, 2010, http://gigaom.com/2010/02/10/farmville-users-send-500m-valentines-in-48-hours/.

Kluge, Stacy. and Liz Riley, "Teaching in Virtual Worlds: Issues and Challenges," *Issues in Informing Science and Information Technology* 5 (2008): 128.

McGeveran, William. "Video Games With a Message," *Info/Law* (blog), June 18, 2007, http://blogs.law.harvard.edu/infolaw/2007/06/18/video-games-with-a-message/.

Second Life, "Frequently Asked Questions: Is Second Life a game?" http://secondlife.com/whatis/faq.php#02.

Sliwinski, Alexander. "PETA Parody Grills Cooking Mama," *Joystiq*, November 17 2008, http://www.joystiq.com/2008/11/17/peta-parody-grills-cooking-mama/.

University of Texas at Dallas News Center, "Avatars Help Asperger Syndrome Patients Learn to Play the Game of Life," news release, University of Texas at Dallas News Center, November 18, 2007, http://www.utdallas.edu/news/2007/11/18-003.html.

Verjee, Zain. "Will There Be a Knockout Blow?" *CNN*, May 3, 2010, http://ukelection.blogs.cnn.com/2010/05/03/will-there-be-a-knock-out-blow/.

Walker, Tim. "Welcome to FarmVille: Population 80 million," *Independent* (London), February 22, 2010, http://www.independent.co.uk/life-style/gadgets-and-tech/features/welcome-to-farmville-population-80-million-1906260.html.

Zaphiris, Panayiotis, Chee Siang Ang, and Andrew Laghos, "Online Communities," in *The Human-Computer Interaction Handbook: Fundamentals, Evolving Technologies, and Emerging Applications*, ed. Andrew Sears and Julie Jacko (New York: Taylor & Francis Group, 2008), 607.

Chapter 11: The Internet and Social Media

11.1 The Internet and Social Media

Cleaning Up Your Online Act

Figure 11.1

Brian Rosner – New Friends at CU – CC BY 2.0.

It used to be that applying for a job was fairly simple: send in a resume, write a cover letter, and call a few references to make sure they will say positive things. The hiring manager understands that this is a biased view, designed to make the applicant look good, but that is all forgivable. After all, everyone applying for a particular job is going through this same process, and barring great disasters, the chances of something particularly negative reaching the desk of a hiring manager are not that great.

However, there is a new step that is now an integral part of this application process—hiding (or at least cleaning up) the applicants' virtual selves. This could entail "Googling"—shorthand for searching on Google—their own name to see the search results. If the first thing that comes up is a Flickr album (an online photo album from the photo-sharing site Flickr) from last month's Olympian-themed cocktail party, it may be a good idea to make that album private to ensure that only friends can view the album.

The ubiquity of Web 2.0 social media like Facebook and Twitter allows anyone to easily start developing an online persona from as early as birth (depending on the openness of one's parents)—and although this online persona may not accurately reflect the individual, it may be one of the first things a stranger sees. Those online photos may not look bad to friends and family, but one's online persona may be a hiring manager's first impression of a prospective employee. Someone in charge of hiring could search the Internet for information on potential new hires even before calling references.

First impressions are an important thing to keep in mind when making an online persona professionally acceptable. Your presence online can be the equivalent of your first words to a brand-new acquaintance. Instead of showing a complete stranger your pictures from a recent party, it might be a better idea to hide those pictures and replace them with a well-written blog—or a professional-looking website.

The content on social networking sites like Facebook, where people use the Internet to meet new people and maintain old friendships, is nearly indestructible and may not actually belong to the user. In 2008, as Facebook was quickly gaining momentum, *The New York Times* ran an article, "How Sticky Is Membership on Facebook? Just Try Breaking Free"—a title that seems at once like a warning and a big-brother taunt. The website does allow the option of deactivating one's account, but "Facebook servers keep copies of the information in those accounts indefinitely (Aspan, 2008)." It is a double-edged sword: On one hand, users who become disillusioned and quit Facebook can come back at any time and resume their activity; on the other, one's information is never fully deleted. If a job application might be compromised by the presence of a Facebook profile, clearing the slate is possible, albeit with some hard labor. The user must delete, item by item, every individual wall post, every group membership, every photo, and everything else.

Not all social networks are like this—MySpace and Friendster still require users who want to delete their accounts to confirm this several times, but they offer a clear-cut "delete" option—but the sticky nature of Facebook information is nothing new (Aspan, 2008). Google even keeps a cache of deleted web pages, and the Internet Archive keeps decades-old historical records. This transition from ephemeral media—TV and radio, practically over as quickly as they are broadcast—to the enduring permanence of the Internet may seem strange, but in some ways it is built into the very structure of the system. Understanding how the Internet was conceived may help elucidate the ways in which the Internet functions today—from the difficulties of deleting an online persona to the speedy and near-universal access to the world's information.

References

Aspan, Maria. "How Sticky Is Membership on Facebook? Just Try Breaking Free," *New York Times*, February 11, 2008, http://www.nytimes.com/2008/02/11/technology/11facebook.html.

11.2 The Evolution of the Internet

Learning Objectives

1. Define *protocol* and *decentralization* as they relate to the early Internet.
2. Identify technologies that made the Internet accessible.
3. Explain the causes and effects of the dot-com boom and crash.

From its early days as a military-only network to its current status as one of the developed world's primary sources of information and communication, the Internet has come a long way in a short period of time. Yet there are a few elements that have stayed constant and that provide a coherent thread for examining the origins of the now-pervasive medium. The first is the persistence of the Internet—its Cold War beginnings necessarily influencing its design as a decentralized, indestructible communication network.

The second element is the development of rules of communication for computers that enable the machines to turn raw data into useful information. These rules, or protocols, have been developed through consensus by computer scientists to facilitate and control online communication and have shaped the way the Internet works. Facebook is a simple example of a protocol: Users can easily communicate with one another, but only through acceptance of protocols that include wall posts, comments, and messages. Facebook's protocols make communication possible and control that communication.

These two elements connect the Internet's origins to its present-day incarnation. Keeping them in mind as you read will help you comprehend the history of the Internet, from the Cold War to the Facebook era.

The History of the Internet

The near indestructibility of information on the Internet derives from a military principle used in secure voice transmission: decentralization. In the early 1970s, the RAND Corporation developed a technology (later called "packet switching") that allowed users to send secure voice messages. In contrast to a system known as the hub-and-spoke model, where the telephone operator (the "hub") would patch two people (the "spokes") through directly, this new system allowed for a voice message to be sent through an entire network, or web, of carrier lines, without the need to travel through a central hub, allowing for many different possible paths to the destination.

During the Cold War, the U.S. military was concerned about a nuclear attack destroying the hub in its hub-and-spoke model; with this new web-like model, a secure voice transmission would be more likely to endure a large-scale attack. A web of data pathways would still be able to transmit secure voice "packets," even if a few of the nodes—places where the web of connections intersected—were destroyed. Only through the destruction of all the nodes in the web could the data traveling along it be completely wiped out—an unlikely event in the case of a highly decentralized network.

This decentralized network could only function through common communication protocols. Just as we use certain protocols when communicating over a telephone—"hello," "goodbye," and "hold on for a minute" are three examples—any sort of machine-to-machine communication must also use protocols. These protocols constitute a shared language enabling computers to understand each other clearly and easily.

The Building Blocks of the Internet

In 1973, the U.S. Defense Advanced Research Projects Agency (DARPA) began research on protocols to allow computers to communicate over a distributed network. This work paralleled work done by the RAND Corporation, particularly in the realm of a web-based network model of communication. Instead of using electronic signals to send an unending stream of ones and zeros over a line (the equivalent of a direct voice connection), DARPA used this new packet-switching technology to send small bundles of data. This way, a message that would have been an unbroken stream of binary data—extremely vulnerable to errors and corruption—could be packaged as only a few hundred numbers.

Figure 11.2

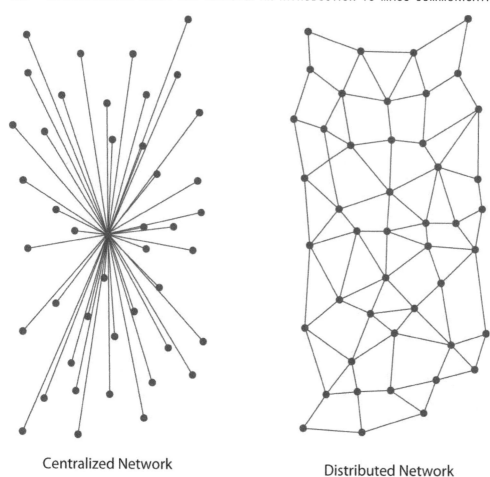

Centralized Network

Distributed Network

Centralized versus distributed communication networks

Imagine a telephone conversation in which any static in the signal would make the message incomprehensible. Whereas humans can infer meaning from "Meet me [static] the restaurant at 8:30" (we replace the static with the word *at*), computers do not necessarily have that logical linguistic capability. To a computer, this constant stream of data is incomplete—or "corrupted," in technological terminology—and confusing. Considering the susceptibility of electronic communication to noise or other forms of disruption, it would seem like computer-to-computer transmission would be nearly impossible.

However, the packets in this packet-switching technology have something that allows the receiving computer to make sure the packet has arrived uncorrupted. Because of this new technology and the shared protocols that made computer-to-computer transmission possible, a single large message could be broken into many pieces and sent through an entire web of connections, speeding up transmission and making that transmission more secure.

One of the necessary parts of a network is a host. A host is a physical node that is directly connected to the Internet and "directs traffic" by routing packets of data to and from other computers connected to it. In a normal network, a specific computer is usually not directly connected to the Internet; it is connected through a host. A host in this case is identified by an Internet protocol, or IP, address (a concept that is explained in greater detail later). Each unique IP address refers to a single location on the global Internet, but that IP address can serve as a gateway for many different computers. For example, a college campus may have one global IP address for all of its students' computers, and each student's computer might then have its own local IP address on the school's network. This nested structure allows billions of different global hosts, each with any number of computers connected within their internal networks. Think of a campus postal system: All students share the same global address (1000 College Drive, Anywhere, VT 08759, for example), but they each have an internal mailbox within that system.

The early Internet was called ARPANET, after the U.S. Advanced Research Projects Agency (which added "Defense" to its name and became DARPA in 1973), and consisted of just four hosts: UCLA, Stanford, UC Santa Barbara, and the University of Utah. Now there are over half a million hosts, and each of those hosts likely serves thousands of people (Central Intelligence Agency). Each host uses protocols to connect to an ever-growing network of computers. Because of this, the Internet does not exist in any one place in particular; rather, it is the name we give to the huge network of interconnected computers that collectively form the entity that we think of as the Internet. The Internet is not a physical structure; it is the protocols that make this communication possible.

Figure 11.3

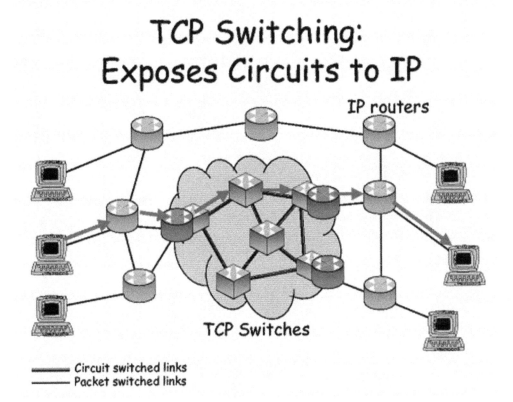

A TCP gateway is like a post office because of the way that it directs information to the correct location.

One of the other core components of the Internet is the Transmission Control Protocol (TCP) gateway. Proposed in a 1974 paper, the TCP gateway acts "like a postal service (Cerf, et. al., 1974)." Without knowing a specific physical address, any computer on the network can ask for the owner of any IP address, and the TCP gateway will consult its directory of IP address listings to determine exactly which computer the requester is trying to contact. The development of this technology was an essential building block in the interlinking of networks, as computers could now communicate with each other without knowing the specific address of a recipient; the TCP gateway would figure it all out. In addition, the TCP gateway checks for errors and ensures that data reaches its destination uncorrupted. Today, this combination of TCP gateways and IP addresses is called TCP/IP and is essentially a worldwide phone book for every host on the Internet.

You've Got Mail: The Beginnings of the Electronic Mailbox

E-mail has, in one sense or another, been around for quite a while. Originally, electronic messages were recorded within a single mainframe computer system. Each person working on the computer would have a personal folder, so sending that person a message required nothing more than creating a new document in that person's folder. It was just like leaving a note on someone's desk (Peter, 2004), so that the person would see it when he or she logged onto the computer.

However, once networks began to develop, things became slightly more complicated. Computer programmer Ray Tomlinson is credited with inventing the naming system we have today, using the @ symbol to denote the server (or host, from the previous section). In other words, name@gmail.com tells the host "gmail.com" (Google's e-mail server) to drop the message into the folder belonging to "name." Tomlinson is credited with writing the first network e-mail using his program SNDMSG in 1971. This invention of a simple standard for e-mail is often cited as one of the most important factors in the rapid spread of the Internet, and is still one of the most widely used Internet services.

The use of e-mail grew in large part because of later commercial developments, especially America Online, that made connecting to e-mail much easier than it had been at its inception. Internet service providers (ISPs) packaged e-mail accounts with Internet access, and almost all web browsers (such as Netscape, discussed later in the section) included a form of e-mail service. In addition to the ISPs, e-mail services like Hotmail and Yahoo! Mail provided free e-mail addresses paid for by small text ads at the bottom of every e-mail message sent. These free "webmail" services soon expanded to comprise a large part of the e-mail services that are available today. Far from the original maximum inbox sizes of a few megabytes, today's e-mail services, like Google's Gmail service, generally provide gigabytes of free storage space.

E-mail has revolutionized written communication. The speed and relatively inexpensive nature of e-mail makes it a prime competitor of postal services—including FedEx and UPS—that pride themselves on speed. Communicating via e-mail with someone on the other end of the world is just as quick and inexpensive as communicating with a next-door neighbor. However, the growth of Internet shopping and online companies such as Amazon.com has in many ways made the postal service and shipping companies more prominent—not necessarily for communication, but for delivery and remote business operations.

Hypertext: Web 1.0

In 1989, Tim Berners-Lee, a graduate of Oxford University and software engineer at CERN (the European particle physics laboratory), had the idea of using a new kind of protocol to share documents and information throughout the local CERN network. Instead of transferring regular text-based documents, he created a new language called hypertext markup language (HTML). *Hypertext* was a new word for text that goes beyond the boundaries of a single document. Hypertext can include links to other documents (hyperlinks), text-style formatting, images, and a wide variety of other components. The basic idea is that documents can be constructed out of a variety of links and can be viewed just as if they are on the user's computer.

This new language required a new communication protocol so that computers could interpret it, and Berners-Lee decided on the name hypertext transfer protocol (HTTP). Through HTTP, hypertext documents can be sent from computer to computer and can then be interpreted by a browser, which turns the HTML files into readable web pages. The browser that Berners-Lee created, called World Wide Web, was a combination browser-editor, allowing users to view other HTML documents and create their own (Berners-Lee, 2009).

Figure 11.4

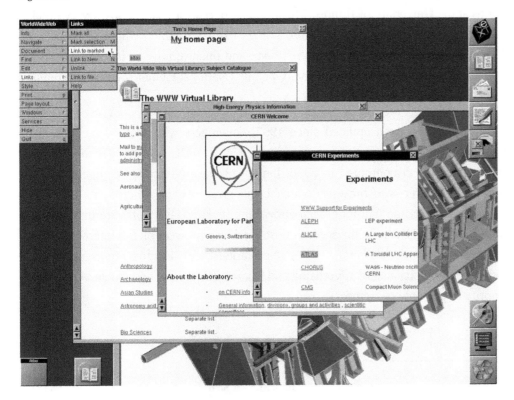

Tim Berners-Lee's first web browser was also a web page editor.

Modern browsers, like Microsoft Internet Explorer and Mozilla Firefox, only allow for the viewing of web pages; other increasingly complicated tools are now marketed for creating web pages, although even the most complicated page can be written entirely from a program like Windows Notepad. The reason web pages can be created with the simplest tools is the adoption of certain protocols by the most common browsers. Because Internet Explorer, Firefox, Apple Safari, Google Chrome, and other browsers all interpret the same code in more or less the same way, creating web pages is as simple as learning how to speak the language of these browsers.

In 1991, the same year that Berners-Lee created his web browser, the Internet connection service Q-Link was renamed America Online, or AOL for short. This service would eventually grow to employ over 20,000 people, on the basis of making Internet access available (and, critically, simple) for anyone with a telephone line. Although the web in 1991 was not what it is today, AOL's software allowed its users to create communities based on just about any subject, and it only required a dial-up modem—a device that connects any computer to the Internet via a telephone line—and the telephone line itself.

In addition, AOL incorporated two technologies—chat rooms and Instant Messenger—into a single program (along with a web browser). Chat rooms allowed many users to type live messages to a "room" full of people, while Instant Messenger allowed two users to communicate privately via text-based messages. The most important aspect of AOL was its encapsulation of all these once-disparate programs into a single user-friendly bundle. Although AOL was later disparaged for customer service issues like its users' inability to deactivate their service, its role in bringing the Internet to mainstream users was instrumental (Zeller Jr., 2005).

In contrast to AOL's proprietary services, the World Wide Web had to be viewed through a standalone web browser. The first of these browsers to make its mark was the program Mosaic, released by the National Center for Supercomputing Applications at the University of Illinois. Mosaic was offered for free and grew very quickly in popularity due to features that now seem integral to the web. Things like bookmarks, which allow users to save the location of particular pages without having to remember them, and images, now an integral part of the web, were all inventions that made the web more usable for many people (National Center for Supercomputing Appliances).

Although the web browser Mosaic has not been updated since 1997, developers who worked on it went on to create Netscape Navigator, an extremely popular browser during the 1990s. AOL later bought the Netscape company, and the Navigator browser was discontinued in 2008, largely because Netscape Navigator had lost the market to Microsoft's Internet Explorer web browser, which came preloaded on Microsoft's ubiquitous Windows operating system. However, Netscape had long been converting its Navigator software into an open-source program called Mozilla Firefox, which is now the second-most-used web browser on the Internet (detailed in Table 11.1 "Browser Market Share (as of February 2010)") (NetMarketshare). Firefox represents about a quarter of the market—not bad, considering its lack of advertising and Microsoft's natural advantage of packaging Internet Explorer with the majority of personal computers.

Table 11.1 Browser Market Share (as of February 2010)

Browser	Total Market Share
Microsoft Internet Explorer	62.12%
Firefox	24.43%
Chrome	5.22%
Safari	4.53%
Opera	2.38%

Source: Courtesy Net Applications.com http://www.netapplications.com/

For Sale: The Web

As web browsers became more available as a less-moderated alternative to AOL's proprietary service, the web became something like a free-for-all of startup companies. The web of this period, often referred to as Web 1.0, featured many specialty sites that used the Internet's ability for global, instantaneous communication to create a new type of business. Another name for this free-for-all of the 1990s is the "dot-com boom." During the boom, it seemed as if almost anyone could build a website and sell it for millions of dollars. However, the "dot-com crash" that occurred later that decade seemed to say otherwise. Quite a few of these Internet startup companies went bankrupt, taking their shareholders down with them. Alan Greenspan, then the chairman of the U.S. Federal Reserve, called this phenomenon "irrational exuberance (Greenspan, 1996)," in large part because investors did not necessarily know how to analyze these particular business plans, and companies that had never turned a profit could be sold for millions. The new business models of the Internet may have done well in the stock market, but they were not necessarily sustainable. In many ways, investors collectively failed to analyze the business prospects of these companies, and once they realized their mistakes (and the companies went bankrupt), much of the recent market growth evaporated. The invention of new technologies can bring with it the belief that old business tenets no longer apply, but this dangerous belief—the "irrational exuberance" Greenspan spoke of—is not necessarily conducive to long-term growth.

Some lucky dot-com businesses formed during the boom survived the crash and are still around today. For example, eBay, with its online auctions, turned what seemed like a dangerous practice (sending money to a stranger you met over the Internet) into a daily occurrence. A less-fortunate company, eToys.com, got off to a promising start—its stock quadrupled on the day it went public in 1999—but then filed for Chapter 11 "The Internet and Social Media" bankruptcy in 2001 (Barnes, 2001).

One of these startups, theGlobe.com, provided one of the earliest social networking services that exploded in popularity. When theGlobe.com went public, its stock shot from a target price of $9 to a close of $63.50 a share (Kawamoto, 1998). The site itself was started in 1995, building its business on advertising. As skepticism about the dot-com boom grew and advertisers became increasingly skittish about the value of online ads, theGlobe.com ceased to be profitable and shut its doors as a social networking site (The Globe, 2009). Although advertising is pervasive on the Internet today, the current model—largely based on the highly targeted Google AdSense service—did not come around until much later. In the earlier dot-com years, the same ad might be shown on thousands of different web pages, whereas now advertising is often specifically targeted to the content of an individual page.

However, that did not spell the end of social networking on the Internet. Social networking had been going on since at least the invention of Usenet in 1979 (detailed later in the chapter), but the recurring problem was always the same: profitability. This model of free access to user-generated content departed from almost anything previously seen in media, and revenue streams would have to be just as radical.

The Early Days of Social Media

The shared, generalized protocols of the Internet have allowed it to be easily adapted and extended into many different facets of our lives. The Internet shapes everything, from our day-to-day routine—the ability to read newspapers from around the world, for example—to the way research and collaboration are conducted. There are three important aspects of communication that the Internet has changed, and these have instigated profound changes in the way we connect with one another socially: the speed of information, the volume of information, and the "democratization" of publishing, or the ability of anyone to publish ideas on the web.

One of the Internet's largest and most revolutionary changes has come about through social networking. Because of Twitter, we can now see what all our friends are doing in real time; because of blogs, we can consider the opinions of complete strangers who may never write in traditional print; and because of Facebook, we can find people we haven't talked to for decades, all without making a single awkward telephone call.

Recent years have seen an explosion of new content and services; although the phrase "social media" now seems to be synonymous with websites like Facebook and Twitter, it is worthwhile to consider all the ways a social media platform affects the Internet experience.

How Did We Get Here? The Late 1970s, Early 1980s, and Usenet

Almost as soon as TCP stitched the various networks together, a former DARPA scientist named Larry Roberts founded the company Telnet, the first commercial packet-switching company. Two years later, in 1977, the invention of the dial-up modem (in combination with the wider availability of personal computers like the Apple II) made it possible for anyone around the world to access the Internet. With availability extended beyond purely academic and military circles, the Internet quickly became a staple for computer hobbyists.

One of the consequences of the spread of the Internet to hobbyists was the founding of Usenet. In 1979, University of North Carolina graduate students Tom Truscott and Jim Ellis connected three computers in a small network and used a series of programming scripts to post and receive messages. In a very short span of time, this system spread all over the burgeoning Internet. Much like an electronic version of community bulletin boards, anyone with a computer could post a topic or reply on Usenet.

The group was fundamentally and explicitly anarchic, as outlined by the posting "What is Usenet?" This document says, "Usenet is not a democracy…there is no person or group in charge of Usenet …Usenet cannot be a democracy, autocracy, or any other kind of '-acy (Moraes, et. al., 1998).'" Usenet was not used only for socializing, however, but also for collaboration. In some ways, the service allowed a new kind of collaboration that seemed like the start of a revolution: "I was able to join rec.kites and collectively people in Australia and New Zealand helped me solve a problem and get a circular two-line kite to fly," one user told the United Kingdom's *Guardian* (Jeffery, et. al., 2009).

GeoCities: Yahoo! Pioneers

Fast-forward to 1995: The president and founder of Beverly Hills Internet, David Bohnett, announces that the name of his company is now "GeoCities." GeoCities built its business by allowing users ("homesteaders") to create web pages in "communities" for free, with the stipulation that the company placed a small advertising banner at the top of each page. Anyone could register a GeoCities site and subsequently build a web page about a topic. Almost all of the community names, like Broadway (live theater) and Athens (philosophy and education), were centered on specific topics (Archive, 1996).

This idea of centering communities on specific topics may have come from Usenet. In Usenet, the domain alt.rec.kites refers to a specific topic (kites) within a category (recreation) within a larger community (alternative topics). This hierarchical model allowed users to organize themselves across the vastness of the Internet, even on a large site like GeoCities. The difference with GeoCities was that it allowed users to do much more than post only text (the limitation of Usenet), while constraining them to a relatively small pool of resources. Although each GeoCities user had only a few megabytes of web space, standardized pictures—like mailbox icons and back buttons—were hosted on GeoCities's main server. GeoCities was such a large part of the Internet, and these standard icons were so ubiquitous, that they have now become a veritable part of the Internet's cultural history. The Web Elements category of the site Internet Archaeology is a good example of how pervasive GeoCities graphics became (Internet Archaeology, 2010).

GeoCities built its business on a freemium model, where basic services are free but subscribers pay extra for things like commercial pages or shopping carts. Other Internet businesses, like Skype and Flickr, use the same model to keep a vast user base while still profiting from frequent users. Since loss of online advertising revenue was seen as one of the main causes of the dot-com crash, many current web startups are turning toward this freemium model to diversify their income streams (Miller, 2009).

GeoCities's model was so successful that the company Yahoo! bought it for $3.6 billion at its peak in 1999. At the time, GeoCities was the third-most-visited site on the web (behind Yahoo! and AOL), so it seemed like a sure bet. A decade later, on October 26, 2009, Yahoo! closed GeoCities for good in every country except Japan.

Diversification of revenue has become one of the most crucial elements of Internet businesses; from *The Wall Street Journal* online to YouTube, almost every website is now looking for multiple income streams to support its services.

Key Takeaways

- The two primary characteristics of the original Internet were decentralization and free, open protocols that anyone could use. As a result of its decentralized "web" model of organization, the Internet can store data in many different places at once. This makes it very useful for backing up data and very difficult to destroy data that might be unwanted. Protocols play an important role in this, because they allow some degree of control to exist without a central command structure.

- Two of the most important technological developments were the personal computer (such as the Apple II) and the dial-up modem, which allowed anyone with a phone line to access the developing Internet. America Online also played an important role, making it very easy for practically anyone with a computer to use the Internet. Another development, the web browser, allowed for access to and creation of web pages all over the Internet.

- With the advent of the web browser, it seemed as if anyone could make a website that people wanted to use. The problem was that these sites were driven largely by venture capital and grossly inflated initial public offerings of their stock. After failing to secure any real revenue stream, their stock plummeted, the market crashed, and many of these companies went out of business. In later years, companies tried to diversify their investments, particularly by using a "freemium" model of revenue, in which a company would both sell premium services and advertise, while offering a free pared-down service to casual users.

Exercises

Websites have many different ways of paying for themselves, and this can say a lot about both the site and its audience. The business models of today's websites may also directly reflect the lessons learned during the early days of the Internet. Start this exercise by reviewing a list of common ways that websites pay for themselves, how they arrived at these methods, and what it might say about them:

- Advertising: The site probably has many casual viewers and may not necessarily be well established. If there are targeted ads (such as ads directed toward stay-at-home parents with children), then it is possible the site is successful with a small audience.

- Subscription option: The site may be a news site that prides itself on accuracy of information or lack of bias, whose regular readers are willing to pay a premium for the guarantee of quality material. Alternately, the site may cater to a small demographic of Internet users by providing them with exclusive, subscription-only content.

- Selling services: Online services, such as file hosting, or offline services and products are probably the clearest way to determine a site's revenue stream. However, these commercial sites often are not prized for their unbiased information, and their bias can greatly affect the content on the site.

Choose a website that you visit often, and list which of these revenue streams the site might have. How might this affect the content on the site? Is there a visible effect, or does the site try to hide it? Consider how events during the early history of the Internet may have affected the way the site operates now. Write down a revenue stream that the site does not currently have and how the site designers might implement such a revenue stream.

References

Archive, While GeoCities is no longer in business, the Internet Archive maintains the site at http://www.archive.org/web/geocities.php. Information taken from December 21, 1996.

Barnes, Cecily. "eToys files for Chapter 11," *CNET*, March 7, 2001, http://news.cnet.com/2100-1017-253706.html.

Berners-Lee, Tim. "The WorldWideWeb Browser," 2009, http://www.w3.org/People/Berners-Lee/WorldWideWeb.

Central Intelligence Agency, "Country Comparison: Internet Hosts," *World Factbook*, https://www.cia.gov/library/publications/the-world-factbook/rankorder/2184rank.html.

Cerf, Vincton, Yogen Dalal, and Carl Sunshine, "Specification of Internet Transmission Control Program," December 1974, http://tools.ietf.org/html/rfc675.

Greenspan, Alan. "The Challenge of Central Banking in a Democratic Society, " (lecture, American Enterprise Institute for Public Policy Research, Washington, DC, December 5, 1996), http://www.federalreserve.gov/boarddocs/speeches/1996/19961205.htm.

Internet Archaeology, 2010, http://www.internetarchaeology.org/swebelements.htm.

Jeffery, Simon and others, "A People's History of the Internet: From Arpanet in 1969 to Today," *Guardian* (London), October 23, 2009, http://www.guardian.co.uk/technology/interactive/2009/oct/23/internet-arpanet.

Kawamoto, Dawn. "TheGlobe.com's IPO one for the books," *CNET*, November 13, 1998, http://news.cnet.com/2100-1023-217913.html.

Miller, Claire Cain. "Ad Revenue on the Web? No Sure Bet," *New York Times*, May 24, 2009, http://www.nytimes.com/2009/05/25/technology/start-ups/25startup.html.

Moraes, Mark, Chip Salzenberg, and Gene Spafford, "What is Usenet?" December 28, 1999, http://www.faqs.org/faqs/usenet/what-is/part1/.

National Center for Supercomputing Appliances, "About NCSA Mosaic," 2010, http://www.ncsa.illinois.edu/Projects/mosaic.html.

NetMarketShare, "Browser Market Share," http://marketshare.hitslink.com/browser-market-share.aspx?qprid=0&qpcal=1&qptimeframe=M&qpsp=132.

Peter, Ian. "The History of Email," The Internet History Project, 2004, http://www.nethistory.info/History%20of%20the%20Internet/email.html.

The Globe, theglobe.com, "About Us," 2009, http://www.theglobe.com/.

Zeller, Jr., Tom. "Canceling AOL? Just Offer Your Firstborn," *New York Times*, August 29, 2005, allhttp://www.nytimes.com/2005/08/29/technology/29link.html.

11.3 Social Media and Web 2.0

Learning Objectives

1. Identify the major social networking sites, and give possible uses and demographics for each one.
2. Show the positive and negative effects of blogs on the distribution and creation of information.
3. Explain the ways privacy has been addressed on the Internet.
4. Identify new information that marketers can use because of social networking.

Although GeoCities lost market share, and although theGlobe.com never really made it to the 21st century, social networking has persisted. There are many different types of social media available today, from social networking sites like Facebook to blogging services like Blogger and WordPress.com. All these sites bring something different to the table, and a few of them even try to bring just about everything to the table at once.

Social Networking

Social networking services—like Facebook, Twitter, LinkedIn, Google Buzz, and MySpace—provide a limited but public platform for users to create a "profile." This can range anywhere from the 140-character (that's letters and spaces, not words) "tweets" on Twitter, to the highly customizable MySpace, which allows users to blog, customize color schemes, add background images, and play music. Each of these services has its key demographic—MySpace, for example, is particularly geared toward younger users. Its huge array of features made it attractive to this demographic at first, but eventually it was overrun with corporate marketing and solicitations for pornographic websites, leading many users to abandon the service. In addition, competing social networking sites like Facebook offer superior interfaces that have lured away many of MySpace's users. MySpace has attempted to catch up by upgrading its own interface, but it now faces the almost insurmountable obstacle of already-satisfied users of competing social networking services. As Internet technology evolves rapidly, most users have few qualms about moving to whichever site offers the better experience; most users have profiles and accounts on many services at once. But as relational networks become more and more established and concentrated on a few social media sites, it becomes increasingly difficult for newcomers and lagging challengers to offer the same rich networking experience. For a Facebook user with hundreds of friends in his or her social network, switching to MySpace and bringing along his or her entire network of friends is a daunting and infeasible prospect. Google has attempted to circumvent the problem of luring users to create new social networks by building its Buzz service into its popular Gmail, ensuring that Buzz has a built-in user base and lowering the social costs of joining a new social network by leveraging users' Gmail contact lists. It remains to be seen if Google will be truly successful in establishing a vital new social networking service, but its tactic of integrating Buzz into Gmail underscores how difficult it has become to compete with established social networks like Twitter and Facebook.

Whereas MySpace initially catered to a younger demographic, LinkedIn caters to business professionals looking for networking opportunities. LinkedIn is free to join and allows users to post resumes and job qualifications (rather than astrological signs and favorite TV shows). Its tagline, "Relationships matter," emphasizes the role of an increasingly networked world in business; just as a musician might use MySpace to promote a new band, a LinkedIn user can use the site to promote professional services. While these two sites have basically the same structure, they fulfill different purposes for different social groups; the character of social networking is highly dependent on the type of social circle.

Twitter offers a different approach to social networking, allowing users to "tweet" 140-character messages to their "followers," making it something of a hybrid of instant messaging and blogging. Twitter is openly searchable, meaning that anyone can visit the site and quickly find out what other Twitter users are saying about any subject. Twitter has proved useful for journalists reporting on breaking news, as well as highlighting the "best of" the Internet. Twitter has also been useful for marketers looking for a free public forum to disseminate marketing messages. It became profitable in December 2009 through a $25 million deal allowing Google and Microsoft to display its users' 140-character messages in their search results (Van Buskirk, 2009). Facebook, originally deployed exclusively to Ivy League schools, has since opened its doors to anyone over 13 with an e-mail account. With the explosion of the service and its huge growth among older demographics, "My parents joined Facebook" has become a common complaint (My Parents Joined Facebook).

Another category of social media, blogs began as an online, public version of a diary or journal. Short for "web logs," these personal sites give anyone a platform to write about anything they want to. Posting tweets on the Twitter service is considered micro-blogging (because of the extremely short length of the posts). Some services, like LiveJournal, highlight their ability to provide up-to-date reports on personal feelings, even going so far as to add a "mood" shorthand at the end of every post. The Blogger service (now owned by Google) allows users with Google accounts to follow friends' blogs and post comments. WordPress.com, the company that created the open-source blogging platform WordPress.org, and LiveJournal both follow the freemium model by allowing a basic selection of settings for free, with the option to pay for things like custom styles and photo hosting space. What these all have in common, however, is their bundling of social networking (such as the ability to easily link to and comment on friends' blogs) with an expanded platform for self-expression. At this point, most traditional media companies have incorporated blogs, Twitter, and other social media as a way to allow their reporters to update instantly and often. This form of media convergence, discussed in detail in Section 11.3 "The Effects of the Internet and Globalization on Popular Culture and Interpersonal Communication" of this chapter, is now a necessary part of doing business.

There are many other types of social media out there, many of which can be called to mind with a single name: YouTube (video sharing), *Wikipedia* (open-source encyclopedia composed of "wikis" editable by any user), Flickr (photo sharing), and Digg (content sharing). Traditional media outlets have begun referring to these social media services and others like them as "Web 2.0." Web 2.0 is not a new version of the web; rather, the term is a reference to the increased focus on user-generated content and social interaction on the web, as well as the evolution of online tools to facilitate that focus. Instead of relying on professional reporters to get information about a protest in Iran, a person could just search for "Iran" on Twitter and likely end up with hundreds of tweets linking to everything from blogs to CNN.com to YouTube videos from Iranian citizens themselves. In addition, many of these tweets may actually be instant updates from people using Twitter in Iran. This allows people to receive information straight from the source, without being filtered through news organizations or censored by governments.

Going Viral

In 2009, Susan Boyle, an unemployed middle-aged Scottish woman, appeared on *Britain's Got Talent* and sang "I Dreamed a Dream" from the musical *Les Miserables*, becoming an international star almost overnight. It was not her performance itself that catapulted her to fame and sent her subsequently released album to the top of the UK Billboard charts and kept it there for 6 weeks. What did it was a YouTube video of her performance, viewed by 87,000,000 people and counting (Youtube, 2009).

Figure 11.5

Susan Boyle turned from a successful TV contestant into an international celebrity when the YouTube video of her performance went viral.

Youtube.

Media that is spread from person to person when, for example, a friend sends you a link saying "You've got to see this!" is said to have "gone viral." Marketing and advertising agencies have deemed advertising that makes use of this phenomenon as "viral marketing." Yet many YouTube sensations have not come from large marketing firms. For instance, the four-piece pop-punk band OK Go filmed a music video on a tiny budget for their song "Here

It Goes Again" and released it exclusively on YouTube in 2006. Featuring a choreographed dance done on eight separate treadmills, the video quickly became a viral sensation and, as of May 2011, has over 7,265,825 views. The video helped OK Go attract millions of new fans and earned them a Grammy award in 2007, making it one of the most notable successes of viral Internet marketing. Viral marketing is, however, notoriously unpredictable and is liable to spawn remixes, spinoffs, and spoofs that can dilute or damage the messages that marketers intend to spread. Yet, when it is successful, viral marketing can reach millions of people for very little money and can even make it into the mainstream news.

Recent successes and failures in viral marketing demonstrate how difficult it is for marketers to control their message as it is unleashed virally. In 2007, the band Radiohead released their album *In Rainbows* online, allowing fans to download it for any amount of money they chose—including for free. Despite practically giving the album away, the digital release of *In Rainbows* still pulled in more money than Radiohead's previous album, *Hail to the Thief*, while the band simultaneously sold a huge number of $80 collector editions and still sold physical CDs months after the digital release became available (New Musical Express, 2008). In contrast, the food giant Healthy Choice enlisted Classymommy.com blogger Colleen Padilla to write a sponsored review of its product, leading to a featured *New York Times* article on the blogger (not the product), which gave the product only a passing mention (Joshi, 2009). Often, a successfully marketed product will reach some people through the Internet and then break through into the mainstream media. Yet as the article about Padilla shows, sometimes the person writing about the product overshadows the product itself.

Not all viral media is marketing, however. In 2007, someone posted a link to a new trailer for *Grand Theft Auto IV* on the video games message board of the web forum 4chan.org. When users followed the link, they were greeted not with a video game trailer but with Rick Astley singing his 1987 hit "Never Gonna Give You Up." This technique—redirecting someone to that particular music video—became known as Rickrolling and quickly became one of the most well-known Internet memes of all time (Fox News, 2008). An Internet meme is a concept that quickly replicates itself throughout the Internet, and it is often nonsensical and absurd. Another meme, "Lolcats," consists of misspelled captions—"I can has cheezburger?" is a classic example—over pictures of cats. Often, these memes take on a metatextual quality, such as the meme "Milhouse is not a meme," in which the character Milhouse (from the TV show *The Simpsons*) is told that he is not a meme. Chronicling memes is notoriously difficult, because they typically spring into existence seemingly overnight, propagate rapidly, and disappear before ever making it onto the radar of mainstream media—or even the mainstream Internet user.

Benefits and Problems of Social Media

Social media allows an unprecedented volume of personal, informal communication in real time from anywhere in the world. It allows users to keep in touch with friends on other continents, yet keeps the conversation as casual as a Facebook wall post. In addition, blogs allow us to gauge a wide variety of opinions and have given "breaking news" a whole new meaning. Now, news can be distributed through many major outlets almost instantaneously, and different perspectives on any one event can be aired concurrently. In addition, news organizations can harness bloggers as sources of real-time news, in effect outsourcing some of their news-gathering efforts to bystanders on the scene. This practice of harnessing the efforts of several individuals online to solve a problem is known as crowdsourcing.

The downside of the seemingly infinite breadth of online information is that there is often not much depth to the coverage of any given topic. The superficiality of information on the Internet is a common gripe among many journalists who are now rushed to file news reports several times a day in an effort to complete with the "blogosphere," or the crowd of bloggers who post both original news stories and aggregate previously published news from other sources. Whereas traditional print organizations at least had the "luxury" of the daily print deadline, now journalists are expected to blog or tweet every story and file reports with little or no analysis, often without adequate time to confirm the reliability of their sources (Auletta, 2010).

Additionally, news aggregators like Google News profit from linking to journalists' stories at major newspapers and selling advertising, but these profits are not shared with the news organizations and journalists who created the stories. It is often difficult for journalists to keep up with the immediacy of the nonstop news cycle, and with revenues for their efforts being diverted to news aggregators, journalists and news organizations increasingly lack the resources to keep up this fast pace. Twitter presents a similar problem: Instead of getting news from a specific newspaper, many people simply read the articles that are linked from a Twitter feed. As a result, the news cycle leaves journalists no time for analysis or cross-examination. Increasingly, they will simply report, for example, on what a politician or public relations representative says without following up on these comments or fact-checking them. This further shortens the news cycle and makes it much easier for journalists to be exploited as the mouthpieces of propaganda.

Consequently, the very presence of blogs and their seeming importance even among mainstream media has made some critics wary. Internet entrepreneur Andrew Keen is one of these people, and his book *The Cult of the Amateur* follows up on the famous thought experiment suggesting that infinite monkeys, given infinite typewriters, will one day randomly produce a great work of literature (Huxley): "In our Web 2.0 world, the typewriters aren't quite typewriters, but rather networked personal computers, and the monkeys aren't quite monkeys, but rather Internet users (Keen, 2007)." Keen also suggests that the Internet is really just a case of my-word-against-yours, where bloggers are not required to back up their arguments with credible sources. "These days, kids can't tell the difference between credible news by objective professional journalists and what they read on [a random website] (Keen, 2007)." Commentators like Keen worry that this trend will lead to young people's inability to distinguish credible information from a mass of sources, eventually leading to a sharp decrease in credible sources of information.

For defenders of the Internet, this argument seems a bit overwrought: "A legitimate interest in the possible effects of significant technological change in our daily lives can inadvertently dovetail seamlessly into a 'kids these days' curmudgeonly sense of generational degeneration, which is hardly new (Downey, 2009)." Greg Downey, who runs the collaborative blog Neuroanthropology, says that fear of kids on the Internet—and on social media in particular—can slip into "a 'one-paranoia-fits-all' approach to technological change." For the argument that online experiences are "devoid of cohesive narrative and long-term significance," Downey offers that, on the contrary, "far from evacuating narrative, some social networking sites might be said to cause users to 'narrativize' their experience, engaging with everyday life already with an eye toward how they will represent it on their personal pages."

Another argument in favor of social media defies the warning that time spent on social networking sites is destroying the social skills of young people. "The debasement of the word 'friend' by [Facebook's] use of it should not make us assume that users can't tell the difference between friends and Facebook 'friends,'" writes Downey. On the contrary, social networks (like the Usenet of the past) can even provide a place for people with more obscure interests to meet one another and share commonalities. In addition, marketing through social media is completely free—making it a valuable tool for small businesses with tight marketing budgets. A community theater can invite all of its "fans" to a new play for less money than putting an ad in the newspaper, and this direct invitation is far more personal and specific. Many people see services like Twitter, with its "followers," as more semantically appropriate than the "friends" found on Facebook and MySpace, and because of this Twitter has, in many ways, changed yet again the way social media is conceived. Rather than connecting with "friends," Twitter allows social media to be purely a source of information, thereby making it far more appealing to adults. In addition, while 140 characters may seem like a constraint to some, it can be remarkably useful to the time-strapped user looking to catch up on recent news.

Social media's detractors also point to the sheer banality of much of the conversation on the Internet. Again, Downey keeps this in perspective: "The banality of most conversation is also pretty frustrating," he says. Downey suggests that many of the young people using social networking tools see them as just another aspect of communication. However, Downey warns that online bullying has the potential to pervade larger social networks while shielding perpetrators through anonymity.

Another downside of many of the Internet's segmented communities is that users tend to be exposed only to information they are interested in and opinions they agree with. This lack of exposure to novel ideas and contrary opinions can create or reinforce a lack of understanding among people with different beliefs, and make political and social compromise more difficult to come by.

While the situation may not be as dire as Keen suggests in his book, there are clearly some important arguments to consider regarding the effects of the web and social media in particular. The main concerns come down to two things: the possibility that the volume of amateur, user-generated content online is overshadowing better-researched sources, and the questionable ability of users to tell the difference between the two.

Education, the Internet, and Social Media

Although Facebook began at Harvard University and quickly became popular among the Ivy League colleges, the social network has since been lambasted as a distraction for students. Instead of studying, the argument claims, students will sit in the library and browse Facebook, messaging their friends and getting nothing done. Two doctoral candidates, Aryn Karpinski (Ohio State University) and Adam Duberstein (Ohio Dominican University), studied the effects of Facebook use on college students and found that students who use Facebook generally receive a full grade lower—a half point on the GPA scale—than students who do not (Hamilton, 2009). Correlation does not imply causation, though, as Karpinski said that Facebook users may just be "prone to distraction."

On the other hand, students' access to technology and the Internet may allow them to pursue their education to a greater degree than they could otherwise. At a school in Arizona, students are issued laptops instead of textbooks, and some of their school buses have Wi-Fi Internet access. As a result, bus rides, including the long trips that are often a requirement of high school sports, are spent studying. Of course, the students had laptops long before their bus rides were connected to the Internet, but the Wi-Fi technology has "transformed what was often a boisterous bus ride into a rolling study hall (Dillon, 2010)." Even though not all students studied all the time, enabling students to work on bus rides fulfilled the school's goal of extending the educational hours beyond the usual 8 a.m. to 3 p.m.

Privacy Issues With Social Networking

Social networking provides unprecedented ways to keep in touch with friends, but that ability can sometimes be a double-edged sword. Users can update friends with every latest achievement—"[your name here] just won three straight games of solitaire!"—but may also unwittingly be updating bosses and others from whom particular bits of information should be hidden.

The shrinking of privacy online has been rapidly exacerbated by social networks, and for a surprising reason: conscious decisions made by participants. Putting personal information online—even if it is set to be viewed by only select friends—has become fairly standard. Dr. Kieron O'Hara studies privacy in social media and calls this era "intimacy 2.0 (Kleinman, 2010)," a riff on the buzzword "Web 2.0." One of O'Hara's arguments is that legal issues of privacy are based on what is called a "reasonable standard." According to O'Hara, the excessive sharing of personal information on the Internet by *some* constitutes an offense to the privacy of *all*, because it lowers the "reasonable standard" that can be legally enforced. In other words, as cultural tendencies toward privacy degrade on the Internet, it affects not only the privacy of those who choose to share their information, but also the privacy of those who do not.

Privacy Settings on Facebook

With over 500 million users, it is no surprise that Facebook is one of the upcoming battlegrounds for privacy on the Internet. When Facebook updated its privacy settings in 2009 for these people, "privacy groups including the American Civil Liberties Union…[called] the developments 'flawed' and 'worrisome,'" reported *The Guardian* in late 2009 (Johnson, 2009).

Mark Zuckerberg, the founder of Facebook, discusses privacy issues on a regular basis in forums ranging from his official Facebook blog to conferences. At the Crunchies Awards in San Francisco in early 2010, Zuckerberg claimed that privacy was no longer a "social norm (Johnson, 2010)." This statement follows from his company's late-2009 decision to make public information sharing the default setting on Facebook. Whereas users were previously able to restrict public access to basic profile information like their names and friends, the new settings make this information publicly available with no option to make it private. Although Facebook publicly announced the changes, many outraged users first learned of the updates to the default privacy settings when they discovered—too late—that they had inadvertently broadcast private information. Facebook argues that the added complexity of the privacy settings gives users more control over their information. However, opponents counter that adding more complex privacy controls while simultaneously making public sharing the default setting for those controls is a blatant ploy to push casual users into sharing more of their information publicly—information that Facebook will then use to offer more targeted advertising (Bankston, 2009).

In response to the privacy policy, many users have formed their own grassroots protest groups within Facebook. In response to critiques, Facebook changed its privacy policy again in May 2010 with three primary changes. First, privacy controls are simpler. Instead of various controls on multiple pages, there is now one main control users can use to determine who can see their information. Second, Facebook made less information publicly available. Public information is now limited to basic information, such as a user's name and profile picture. Finally, it is now easier to block applications and third-party websites from accessing user information (Lake, 2010).

Similar to the Facebook controversy, Google's social networking Gmail add-on called Buzz automatically signed up Gmail users to "follow" the most e-mailed Gmail users in their address book. Because all of these lists were public by default, users' most e-mailed contacts were made available for anyone to see. This was especially alarming for people like journalists who potentially had confidential sources exposed to a public audience. However, even though this mistake—which Google quickly corrected—created a lot of controversy around Buzz, it did not stop users from creating over 9 million posts in the first 2 days of the service (Jackson, 2010). Google's integration of Buzz into its Gmail service may have been upsetting to users not accustomed to the pitfalls of social networking, but Google's misstep has not discouraged millions of others from trying the service, perhaps due to their experience dealing with Facebook's ongoing issues with privacy infringement.

For example, Facebook's old privacy settings integrated a collection of applications (written by third-party developers) that included everything from "Which *American Idol* Contestant Are You?" to an "Honesty Box" that allows friends to send anonymous criticism. "Allowing Honesty Box access will let it pull your profile information, photos, your friends' info, and other content that it requires to work," reads the disclaimer on the application installation page. The ACLU drew particular attention to the "app gap" that allowed "any quiz or application run by you to access information about you and your friends (Ozer, 2009)." In other words, merely using someone else's Honesty Box gave the program information about your "religion, sexual orientation, political affiliation, pictures, and groups (Ozer, 2009)." There are many reasons that unrelated applications may want to collect this information, but one of the most prominent is, by now, a very old story: selling products. The more information a marketer has, the better he or she can target a message, and the more likely it is that the recipient will buy something.

Figure 11.6

Zynga, one of the top social game developers on Facebook, created the game *FarmVille*. Because *FarmVille* is ad-supported and gives users the option to purchase Farmville virtual currency with actual money, the game is free and accessible for everyone to play.

Rachel – My Farmville farm – CC BY-NC-ND 2.0.

Social Media's Effect on Commerce

Social media on the Internet has been around for a while, and it has always been of some interest to marketers. The ability to target advertising based on demographic information given willingly to the service—age, political preference, gender, and location—allows marketers to target advertising extremely efficiently. However, by the time Facebook's population passed the 350-million mark, marketers were scrambling to harness social media. The increasingly difficult-to-reach younger demographic has been rejecting radios for Apple's iPod mobile digital devices and TV for YouTube. Increasingly, marketers are turning to social networks as a way to reach these consumers. Culturally, these developments indicate a mistrust among consumers of traditional marketing techniques; marketers must now use new and more personalized ways of reaching consumers if they are going to sell their products.

The attempts of marketers to harness the viral spread of media on the Internet have already been discussed earlier in the chapter. Marketers try to determine the trend of things "going viral," with the goal of getting millions of YouTube views; becoming a hot topic on Google Trends, a website that measures the most frequently searched topics on the web; or even just being the subject of a post on a well-known blog. For example, Procter & Gamble sent free samples of its Swiffer dust mop to stay-at-home-mom bloggers with a large online audience. And in 2008, the movie *College* (or *College: The Movie*) used its tagline "Best.Weekend.Ever." as the prompt for a YouTube video contest. Contestants were invited to submit videos of their best college weekend ever, and the winner received a monetary prize (Hickey, 2008).

What these two instances of marketing have in common is that they approach people who are already doing something they enjoy doing—blogging or making movies—and give them a relatively small amount of compensation for providing advertising. This differs from methods of traditional advertising because marketers seek to bridge a credibility gap with consumers. Marketers have been doing this for ages—long before breakfast cereal slogans like "Kid Tested, Mother Approved" or "Mikey likes it" ever hit the airwaves. The difference is that now the people pushing the products can be friends or family members, all via social networks.

For instance, in 2007, a program called Beacon was launched as part of Facebook. With Beacon, a Facebook user is confronted with the option to "share" an online purchase from partnering sites. For example, a user might buy a book from Amazon.com and check the corresponding "share" box in the checkout process, and all of his or her friends will receive a message notifying them that this person purchased and recommends this particular product. Explaining the reason for this shift in a *New York Times* article, Mark Zuckerberg said, "Nothing influences a person more than a trusted friend (Story, 2007)." However, many Facebook users did not want their purchasing information shared with other Facebookers, and the service was shut down in 2009 and subsequently became the subject of a class action lawsuit. Facebook's troubles with Beacon illustrate the thin line between taking advantage of the tremendous marketing potential of social media and violating the privacy of users.

Facebook's questionable alliance with marketers through Beacon was driven by a need to create reliable revenue streams. One of the most crucial aspects of social media is the profitability factor. In the 1990s, theGlobe.com was one of the promising new startups, but almost as quickly, it went under due to lack of funds. The lesson of theGlobe.com has not gone unheeded by today's social media services. For example, Twitter has sold access to its content to Google and Microsoft to make users' tweets searchable for $25 million.

Google's Buzz is one of the most interesting services in this respect, because Google's main business is advertising—and it is a highly successful business. Google's search algorithms allow it to target advertising to a user's specific tastes. As Google enters the social media world, its advertising capabilities will only be compounded as users reveal more information about themselves via Buzz. Although it does not seem that users choose their social media services based on how the services generate their revenue streams, the issue of privacy in social media is in large part an issue of how much information users are willing to share with advertisers. For example, using Google's search engine, Buzz, Gmail, and Blogger give that single company an immense amount of information and a historically unsurpassed ability to market to specific groups. At this relatively early stage of the fledgling online social media business—both Twitter and Facebook only very recently turned a profit, so commerce has only recently come into play—it is impossible to say whether the commerce side of things will transform the way people use the services. If the uproar over Facebook's Beacon is any lesson, however, the relationship between social media and advertising is ripe for controversy.

Social Media as a Tool for Social Change

The use of Facebook and Twitter in the recent political uprisings in the Middle East has brought to the fore the question whether social media can be an effective tool for social change.

On January 14, 2011, after month-long protests against fraud, economic crisis, and lack of political freedom, the Tunisian public ousted President Zine El Abidine Ben Ali. Soon after the Tunisian rebellion, the Egyptian public expelled President Hosni Mubarak, who had ruled the country for 30 years. Nearly immediately, other Middle Eastern countries such as Algeria, Libya, Yemen, and Bahrain also erupted against their oppressive governments in the hopes of obtaining political freedom (Gamba, 2011).

What is common among all these uprisings is the role played by social media. In nearly all of these countries, restrictions were imposed on the media and government resistance was brutally discouraged (Beaumont, 2011). This seems to have inspired the entire Middle East to organize online to rebel against tyrannical rule (Taylor, 2011). Protesters used social media not only to organize against their governments but also to share their struggles with the rest of the world (Gamba).

In Tunisia, protesters filled the streets by sharing information on Twitter (Taylor). Egypt's protests were organized on Facebook pages. Details of the demonstrations were circulated by both Facebook and Twitter. E-mail was used to distribute the activists' guide to challenging the regime (Beaumont). Libyan dissenters too spread the word about their demonstrations similarly (Taylor).

Owing to the role played by Twitter and Facebook in helping protesters organize and communicate with each other, many have termed these rebellions as "Twitter Revolutions (Morozov, 2011)" or "Facebook Revolutions (Davis, 2011)" and have credited social media for helping to bring down these regimes (Beardsley, 2011).

During the unrest, social media outlets such as Facebook and Twitter helped protesters share information by communicating ideas continuously and instantaneously. Users took advantage of these unrestricted vehicles to share the most graphic details and images of the attacks on protesters, and to rally demonstrators (Beaumont). In other words, use of social media was about the ability to communicate across borders and barriers. It gave common people a voice and an opportunity to express their opinions.

Critics of social media, however, say that those calling the Middle East movements Facebook or Twitter revolutions are not giving credit where it is due (Villarreal, 2011). It is true that social media provided vital assistance during the unrest in the Middle East. But technology alone could not have brought about the revolutions. The resolve of the people to bring about change was most important, and this fact should be recognized, say the critics (Taylor).

Key Takeaways

- Social networking sites often encompass many aspects of other social media. For example, Facebook began as a collection of profile pictures with very little information, but soon expanded to include photo albums (like Flickr) and micro-blogging (like Twitter). Other sites, like MySpace, emphasize connections to music and customizable pages, catering to a younger demographic. LinkedIn specifically caters to a professional demographic by allowing only certain kinds of information that is professionally relevant.

- Blogs speed the flow of information around the Internet and provide a critical way for nonprofessionals with adequate time to investigate sources and news stories without the necessary platform of a well-known publication. On the other hand, they can lead to an "echo chamber" effect, where they simply repeat one another and add nothing new. Often, the analysis is wide ranging, but it can also be shallow and lack the depth and knowledge of good critical journalism.

- Facebook has been the leader in privacy-related controversy, with its seemingly constant issues with privacy settings. One of the critical things to keep in mind is that as more people become comfortable with more information out in the open, the "reasonable standard" of privacy is lowered. This affects even people who would rather keep more things private.

- Social networking allows marketers to reach consumers directly and to know more about each specific consumer than ever before. Search algorithms allow marketers to place advertisements in areas that get the most traffic from targeted consumers. Whereas putting an ad on TV reaches all demographics, online advertisements can now be targeted specifically to different groups.

Exercises

1. Draw a Venn diagram of two social networking sites mentioned in this chapter. Sign up for both of them (if you're not signed up already) and make a list of their features and their interfaces. How do they differ? How are they the same?

2. Write a few sentences about how a marketer might use these tools to reach different demographics.

References

Auletta, Ken. "Non-Stop News," Annals of Communications, *New Yorker*, January 25, 2010, http://www.newyorker.com/reporting/2010/01/25/100125fa_fact_auletta.

Bankston, Kevin. "Facebook's New Privacy Changes: The Good, the Bad, and the Ugly," *Deeplinks Blog*,

Electronic Frontier Foundation, December 9, 2009, http://www.eff.org/deeplinks/2009/12/facebooks-new-privacy-changes-good-bad-and-ugly.

Beardsley, Eleanor. "Social Media Gets Credit for Tunisian Overthrow," *NPR*, January 16, 2011, http://www.npr.org/2011/01/16/132975274/Social-Media-Gets-Credit-For-Tunisian-Overthrow.

Beaumont, "Can Social Networking Overthrow a Government?"

Beaumont, Peter. "Can Social Networking Overthrow a Government?" *Morning Herald* (Sydney), February 25, 2011, http://www.smh.com.au/technology/technology-news/can-social-networking-overthrow-a-government-20110225-1b7u6.html.

Davis, Eric. "Social Media: A Force for Political Change in Egypt," April 13, 2011, http://new-middle-east.blogspot.com/2011/04/social-media-force-for-political-change.html.

Dillon, Sam. "Wi-Fi Turns Rowdy Bus Into Rolling Study Hall," *New York Times*, February 11, 2010, http://www.nytimes.com/2010/02/12/education/12bus.html.

Downey, Greg. "Is Facebook Rotting Our Children's Brains?" Neuroanthropology.net, March 2, 2009, http://neuroanthropology.net/2009/03/02/is-facebook-rotting-our-childrens-brains/.

Fox News, "The Biggest Little Internet Hoax on Wheels Hits Mainstream," April 22, 2008, http://www.foxnews.com/story/0,2933,352010,00.html.

Gamba, "Facebook Topples Governments in Middle East."

Gamba, Grace. "Facebook Topples Governments in Middle East," *Brimstone Online*, March 18, 2011, http://www.gshsbrimstone.com/news/2011/03/18/facebook-topples-governments-in-middle-east.

Hamilton, Anita. "What Facebook Users Share: Lower Grades," *Time*, April 14, 2009, http://www.time.com/time/business/article/0,8599,1891111,00.html.

Hickey, Jon. "Best Weekend Ever," 2008, http://www.youtube.com/watch?v=pldG8MdEIOA.

Huxley, T. H. (the father of Aldous Huxley), this thought experiment suggests that infinite monkeys given infinite typewriters would, given infinite time, eventually write *Hamlet*.

Jackson, Todd. "Millions of Buzz users, and improvements based on your feedback," *Official Gmail Blog*, February 11, 2010, http://gmailblog.blogspot.com/2010/02/millions-of-buzz-users-and-improvements.html.

Johnson, Bobbie. "Facebook Privacy Change Angers Campaigners," *Guardian* (London), December 10, 2009, http://www.guardian.co.uk/technology/2009/dec/10/facebook-privacy.

Johnson, Bobbie. "Privacy No Longer a Social Norm, Says Facebook Founder," *Guardian* (London), January 11, 2010, http://www.guardian.co.uk/technology/2010/jan/11/facebook-privacy.

Joshi, Pradnya. "Approval by a Blogger May Please a Sponsor," *New York Times*, July 12, 2009, http://www.nytimes.com/2009/07/13/technology/internet/13blog.html.

Keen, Andrew. *The Cult of the Amateur: How Today's Internet Is Killing Our Culture* (New York: Doubleday, 2007).

Kleinman, Zoe. "How Online Life Distorts Privacy Rights for All," *BBC News*, January 8, 2010, http://news.bbc.co.uk/2/hi/technology/8446649.stm.

Lake, Maggie. "Facebook's privacy changes," *CNN*, June 2, 2010, http://www.cnn.com/video/#/video/tech/2010/05/27/lake.facebook.pr.

Morozov, Evgeny. "How Much Did Social Media Contribute to Revolution in the Middle East?" *Bookforum*, April/May 2011, http://www.bookforum.com/inprint/018_01/7222.

My Parents Joined Facebook, http://myparentsjoinedfacebook.com/ for examples on the subject.
New Musical Express, "Radiohead Reveal How Successful 'In Rainbows' Download Really Was," October 15, 2008, http://www.nme.com/news/radiohead/40444.

Ozer, Nicole. "Facebook Privacy in Transition – But Where Is It Heading?" ACLU of Northern California, December 9, 2009, http://www.aclunc.org/issues/technology/blog/facebook_privacy_in_transition_-_but_where_is_it_heading.shtml.

Story, Louise. "Facebook Is Marketing Your Brand Preferences (With Your Permission)," *New York Times*, November 7, 2007, http://www.nytimes.com/2007/11/07/technology/07adco.html.

Taylor, "Why Not Call It a Facebook Revolution?"

Taylor, Chris. "Why Not Call It a Facebook Revolution?" *CNN*, February 24, 2011, http://edition.cnn.com/2011/TECH/social.media/02/24/facebook.revolution.

Van Buskirk, Eliot. "Twitter Earns First Profit Selling Search to Google, Microsoft," *Wired*, December 21, 2009, http://www.wired.com/epicenter/2009/12/twitter-earns-first-profit-selling-search-to-google-microsoft.

Villarreal, Alex. "Social Media A Critical Tool for Middle East Protesters," *Voice of America*, March 1, 2011, http://www.voanews.com/english/news/middle-east/Social-Media-a-Critical-Tool-for-Middle-East-Protesters-117202583.html.

Youtube, BritainsSoTalented, "Susan Boyle – Singer – Britains Got Talent 2009," 2009, http://www.youtube.com/watch?v=9lp0IWv8QZY.

11.4 The Effects of the Internet and Globalization on Popular Culture and Interpersonal Communication

Learning Objectives

1. Describe the effects of globalization on culture.
2. Identify the possible effects of news migrating to the Internet.
3. Define the Internet paradox.

It's in the name: *World Wide Web*. The Internet has broken down communication barriers between cultures in a way that could only be dreamed of in earlier generations. Now, almost any news service across the globe can be accessed on the Internet and, with the various translation services available (like Babelfish and Google Translate), be relatively understandable. In addition to the spread of American culture throughout the world, smaller countries are now able to cheaply export culture, news, entertainment, and even propaganda.

The Internet has been a key factor in driving globalization in recent years. Many jobs can now be outsourced entirely via the Internet. Teams of software programmers in India can have a website up and running in very little time, for far less money than it would take to hire American counterparts. Communicating with these teams is now as simple as sending e-mails and instant messages back and forth, and often the most difficult aspect of setting up an international video conference online is figuring out the time difference. Especially for electronic services such as software, outsourcing over the Internet has greatly reduced the cost to develop a professionally coded site.

Electronic Media and the Globalization of Culture

The increase of globalization has been an economic force throughout the last century, but economic interdependency is not its only by-product. At its core, globalization is the lowering of economic and cultural impediments to communication between countries all over the globe. Globalization in the sphere of culture and communication can take the form of access to foreign newspapers (without the difficulty of procuring a printed copy) or, conversely, the ability of people living in previously closed countries to communicate experiences to the outside world relatively cheaply.

TV, especially satellite TV, has been one of the primary ways for American entertainment to reach foreign shores. This trend has been going on for some time now, for example, with the launch of MTV Arabia (Arango, 2008). American popular culture is, and has been, a crucial export.

At the Eisenhower Fellowship Conference in Singapore in 2005, U.S. ambassador Frank Lavin gave a defense of American culture that differed somewhat from previous arguments. It would not be all Starbucks, MTV, or *Baywatch*, he said, because American culture is more diverse than that. Instead, he said that "America is a nation of immigrants," and asked, "When Mel Gibson or Jackie Chan come to the United States to produce a movie, whose culture is being exported (Lavin, 2005)?" This idea of a truly globalized culture—one in which content can be distributed as easily as it can be received—now has the potential to be realized through the Internet. While some political and social barriers still remain, from a technological standpoint there is nothing to stop the two-way flow of information and culture across the globe.

China, Globalization, and the Internet

The scarcity of artistic resources, the time lag of transmission to a foreign country, and censorship by the host government are a few of the possible impediments to transmission of entertainment and culture. China provides a valuable example of the ways the Internet has helped to overcome (or highlight) all three of these hurdles.

China, as the world's most populous country and one of its leading economic powers, has considerable clout when it comes to the Internet. In addition, the country is ruled by a single political party that uses censorship extensively in an effort to maintain control. Because the Internet is an open resource by nature, and because China is an extremely well-connected country—with 22.5 percent (roughly 300 million people, or the population of the entire United States) of the country online as of 2008 (Google, 2010)—China has been a case study in how the Internet makes resistance to globalization increasingly difficult.

Figure 11.7

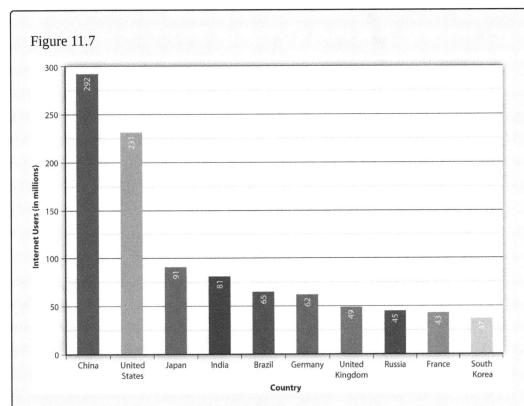

China has more Internet users than any other country.

On January 21, 2010, Hillary Clinton gave a speech in front of the Newseum in Washington, DC, where she said, "We stand for a single Internet where all of humanity has equal access to knowledge and ideas (Ryan & Halper, 2010)." That same month, Google decided it would stop censoring search results on Google.cn, its Chinese-language search engine, as a result of a serious cyber-attack on the company originating in China. In addition, Google stated that if an agreement with the Chinese government could not be reached over the censorship of search results, Google would pull out of China completely. Because Google has complied (albeit uneasily) with the Chinese government in the past, this change in policy was a major reversal.

Withdrawing from one of the largest expanding markets in the world is shocking coming from a company that has been aggressively expanding into foreign markets. This move highlights the fundamental tension between China's censorship policy and Google's core values. Google's company motto, "Don't be evil," had long been at odds with its decision to censor search results in China. Google's compliance with the Chinese government did not help it make inroads into the Chinese Internet search market—although Google held about a quarter of the market in China, most of the search traffic went to the tightly controlled Chinese search engine Baidu. However, Google's departure from China would be a blow to antigovernment forces in the country. Since Baidu has a closer relationship with the Chinese government, political dissidents tend to use Google's Gmail, which uses encrypted servers based in the United States. Google's threat to withdraw from China raises the possibility that globalization could indeed hit roadblocks due to the ways that foreign governments may choose to censor the Internet.

New Media: Internet Convergence and American Society

One only needs to go to CNN's official Twitter feed and begin to click random faces in the "Following" column to see the effect of **media convergence** through the Internet. Hundreds of different options abound, many of them individual journalists' Twitter feeds, and many of those following other journalists. Considering CNN's motto, "The most trusted name in network news," its presence on Twitter might seem at odds with providing in-depth, reliable coverage. After all, how in-depth can 140 characters get?

The truth is that many of these traditional media outlets use Twitter not as a communication tool in itself, but as a way to allow viewers to aggregate a large amount of information they may have missed. Instead of visiting multiple home pages to see the day's top stories from multiple viewpoints, Twitter users only have to check their own Twitter pages to get updates from all the organizations they "follow." Media conglomerates then use Twitter as part of an overall integration of media outlets; the Twitter feed is there to support the news content, not to report the content itself.

Internet-Only Sources

The threshold was crossed in 2008: The Internet overtook print media as a primary source of information for national and international news in the U.S. Television is still far in the lead, but especially among younger demographics, the Internet is quickly catching up as a way to learn about the day's news. With 40 percent of the public receiving their news from the Internet (see Figure 11.8) (Pew Research Center for the People, 2008), media outlets have been scrambling to set up large presences on the web. Yet one of the most remarkable shifts has been in the establishment of online-only news sources.

Figure 11.8

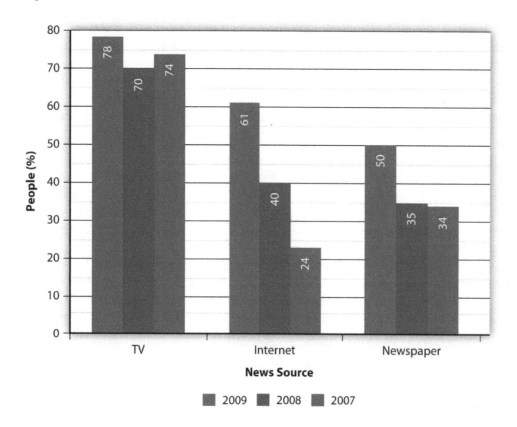

Americans now receive more national and international news from the Internet than they do from newspapers.

The conventional argument claims that the anonymity and the echo chamber of the Internet undermine worthwhile news reporting, especially for topics that are expensive to report on. The ability of large news organizations to put reporters in the field is one of their most important contributions and (because of its cost) is often one of the first things to be cut back during times of budget problems. However, as the Internet has become a primary news source for more and more people, new media outlets—publications existing entirely online—have begun to appear.

In 2006, two reporters for the *Washington Post*, John F. Harris and Jim VandeHei, left the newspaper to start a politically centered website called Politico. Rather than simply repeating the day's news in a blog, they were determined to start a journalistically viable news organization on the web. Four years later, the site has over 6,000,000 unique monthly visitors and about a hundred staff members, and there is now a Politico reporter on almost every White House trip (Wolff, 2009).

Far from being a collection of amateurs trying to make it big on the Internet, Politico's senior White House correspondent is Mike Allen, who previously wrote for *The New York Times, Washington Post*, and *Time*. His daily Playbook column appears at around 7 a.m. each morning and is read by much of the politically centered media. The different ways that Politico reaches out to its supporters—blogs, Twitter feeds, regular news articles, and now even a print edition—show how media convergence has even occurred within the Internet itself. The interactive nature of its services and the active comment boards on the site also show how the media have become a two-way street: more of a public forum than a straight news service.

"Live" From New York ...

Top-notch political content is not the only medium moving to the Internet, however. *Saturday Night Live* (*SNL*) has built an entire entertainment model around its broadcast time slot. Every weekend, around 11:40 p.m. on Saturday, someone interrupts a skit, turns toward the camera, shouts "Live from New York, it's Saturday Night!" and the band starts playing. Yet the show's sketch comedy style also seems to lend itself to the watch-anytime convenience of the Internet. In fact, the online TV service Hulu carries a full eight episodes of *SNL* at any given time, with regular 3.5-minute commercial breaks replaced by Hulu-specific minute-long advertisements. The time listed for an *SNL* episode on Hulu is just over an hour—a full half-hour less than the time it takes to watch it live on Saturday night.

Hulu calls its product "online premium video," primarily because of its desire to attract not the YouTube amateur, but rather a partnership of large media organizations. Although many networks, like NBC and Comedy Central, stream video on their websites, Hulu builds its business by offering a legal way to see all these shows on the same site; a user can switch from *South Park* to *SNL* with a single click, rather than having to move to a different website.

Premium Online Video Content

Hulu's success points to a high demand among Internet users for a wide variety of content collected and packaged in one easy-to-use interface. Hulu was rated the Website of the Year by the Associated Press (Coyle, 2008) and even received an Emmy nomination for a commercial featuring Alec Baldwin and Tina Fey, the stars of the NBC comedy *30 Rock* (Neil, 2009). Hulu's success has not been the product of the usual dot-com underdog startup, however. Its two parent companies, News Corporation and NBC Universal, are two of the world's media giants. In many ways, this was a logical step for these companies to take after fighting online video for so long. In December 2005, the video "Lazy Sunday," an *SNL* digital short featuring Andy Samberg and Chris Parnell, went viral with over 5,000,000 views on YouTube before February 2006, when NBC demanded that YouTube take down the video (Biggs, 2006). NBC later posted the video on Hulu, where it could sell advertising for it.

Hulu allows users to break out of programming models controlled by broadcast and cable TV providers and choose freely what shows to watch and when to watch them. This seems to work especially well for cult programs that are no longer available on TV. In 2008, the show *Arrested Development*, which was canceled in 2006 after repeated time slot shifts, was Hulu's second-most-popular program.

Hulu certainly seems to have leveled the playing field for some shows that have had difficulty finding an audience through traditional means. *30 Rock*, much like *Arrested Development*, suffered from a lack of viewers in its early years. In 2008, *New York Magazine* described the show as a "fragile suckling that critics coddle but that America never quite warms up to (Sternbergh, 2008)." However, even as *30 Rock* shifted time slots mid-season, its viewer base continued to grow through the NBC partner of Hulu. The nontraditional media approach of NBC's programming culminated in October 2008, when NBC decided to launch the new season of *30 Rock* on Hulu a full week before it was broadcast over the airwaves (Wortham, 2008). Hulu's strategy of providing premium online content seems to have paid off: As of March 2011, Hulu provided 143,673,000 viewing sessions to more than 27 million unique visitors, according to Nielsen (ComScore, 2011).

Unlike other "premium" services, Hulu does not charge for its content; rather, the word *premium* in its slogan seems to imply that it *could* charge for content if it wanted to. Other platforms, like Sony's PlayStation 3, block Hulu for this very reason—Sony's online store sells the products that Hulu gives away for free. However, Hulu has been considering moving to a paid subscription model that would allow users to access its entire back catalog of shows. Like many other fledgling web enterprises, Hulu seeks to create reliable revenue streams to avoid the fate of many of the companies that folded during the dot-com crash (Sandoval, 2009).

Like Politico, Hulu has packaged professionally produced content into an on-demand web service that can be used without the normal constraints of traditional media. Just as users can comment on Politico articles (and now, on most newspapers' articles), they can rate Hulu videos, and Hulu will take this into account. Even when users do not produce the content themselves, they still want this same "two-way street" service.

Table 11.2 Top 10 U.S. Online Video Brands, Home and Work

Rank	Parent	Total Streams (in Millions)	Unique Viewers (in Millions)
1	YouTube	6,622,374	112,642
2	Hulu	635,546	15,256
3	Yahoo!	221,355	26,081
4	MSN	179,741	15,645
5	Turner	137,311	5,343
6	MTV Networks	131,077	5,949
7	ABC TV	128,510	5,049
8	Fox Interactive	124,513	11,450
9	Nickelodeon	117,057	5,004
10	Megavideo	115,089	3,654

Source: The Nielsen Company

The Role of the Internet in Social Alienation

In the early years, the Internet was stigmatized as a tool for introverts to avoid "real" social interactions, thereby increasing their alienation from society. Yet the Internet was also seen as the potentially great connecting force between cultures all over the world. The idea that something that allowed communication across the globe could breed social alienation seemed counterintuitive. The American Psychological Association (APA) coined this concept the "Internet paradox."

Studies like the APA's "Internet paradox: A social technology that reduces social involvement and psychological well-being (Kraut, et. al., 1998)?" which came out in 1998, suggested that teens who spent lots of time on the Internet showed much greater rates of self-reported loneliness and other signs of psychological distress. Even though the Internet had been around for a while by 1998, the increasing concern among parents was that teenagers were spending all their time in chat rooms and online. The fact was that teenagers spent much more time on the Internet than adults, due to their increased free time, curiosity, and familiarity with technology.

However, this did not necessarily mean that "kids these days" were antisocial or that the Internet caused depression and loneliness. In his critical analysis "Deconstructing the Internet Paradox," computer scientist, writer, and PhD recipient from Carnegie Mellon University Joseph M. Newcomer points out that the APA study did not include a control group to adjust for what may be normal "lonely" feelings in teenagers. Again, he suggests that "involvement in any new, self-absorbing activity which has opportunity for failure can increase depression," seeing Internet use as just another time-consuming hobby, much like learning a musical instrument or playing chess (Newcomer, 2000).

The general concept that teenagers were spending all their time in chat rooms and online forums instead of hanging out with flesh-and-blood friends was not especially new; the same thing had generally been thought of the computer hobbyists who pioneered the esoteric Usenet. However, the concerns were amplified when a wider range of young people began using the Internet, and the trend was especially strong in the younger demographics.

The "Internet Paradox" and Facebook

As they developed, it became quickly apparent that the Internet generation did not suffer from perpetual loneliness as a rule. After all, the generation that was raised on instant messaging invented Facebook and still makes up most of Facebook's audience. As detailed earlier in the chapter, Facebook began as a service limited to college students—a requirement that practically excluded older participants. As a social tool and as a reflection of the way younger people now connect with each other over the Internet, Facebook has provided a comprehensive model for the Internet's effect on social skills and especially on education.

A study by the Michigan State University Department of Telecommunication, Information Studies, and Media has shown that college-age Facebook users connect with offline friends twice as often as they connect with purely online "friends (Ellison, et. al., 2007)." In fact, 90 percent of the participants in the study reported that high school friends, classmates, and other friends were the top three groups that their Facebook profiles were directed toward.

In 2007, when this study took place, one of Facebook's most remarkable tools for studying the ways that young people connect was its "networks" feature. Originally, a Facebook user's network consisted of all the people at his or her college e-mail domain: the "mycollege" portion of "me@mycollege.edu." The MSU study, performed in April 2006, just 6 months after Facebook opened its doors to high school students, found that first-year students met new people on Facebook 36 percent more often than seniors did. These freshmen, in April 2006, were not as active on Facebook as high schoolers (Facebook began allowing high schoolers on its site during these students' first semester in school) (Rosen, 2005). The study concluded that they could "definitively state that there is a positive relationship between certain kinds of Facebook use and the maintenance and creation of social capital (Ellison, et. al., 2007)." In other words, even though the study cannot show whether Facebook use causes or results from social connections, it can say that Facebook plays both an important and a nondestructive role in the forming of social bonds.

Although this study provides a complete and balanced picture of the role that Facebook played for college students in early 2006, there have been many changes in Facebook's design and in its popularity. In 2006, many of a user's "friends" were from the same college, and the whole college network might be mapped as a "friend-of-a-friend" web. If users allowed all people within a single network access to their profiles, it would create a voluntary school-wide directory of students. Since a university e-mail address was required for signup, there was a certain level of trust. The results of this Facebook study, still relatively current in terms of showing the Internet's effects on social capital, show that not only do social networking tools *not* lead to more isolation, but that they actually have become integral to some types of networking.

However, as Facebook began to grow and as high school and regional networks (such as "New York City" or "Ireland") were incorporated, users' networks of friends grew exponentially, and the networking feature became increasingly unwieldy for privacy purposes. In 2009, Facebook discontinued regional networks over concerns that networks consisting of millions of people were "no longer the best way for you to control your privacy (Zuckerberg, 2009)." Where privacy controls once consisted of allowing everyone at one's college access to specific information, Facebook now allows only three levels: friends, friends of friends, and everyone.

Meetup.com: Meeting Up "IRL"

Of course, not everyone on teenagers' online friends lists are actually their friends outside of the virtual world. In the parlance of the early days of the Internet, meeting up "IRL" (shorthand for "in real life") was one of the main reasons that many people got online. This practice was often looked at with suspicion by those not familiar with it, especially because of the anonymity of the Internet. The fear among many was that children would go into chat rooms and agree to meet up in person with a total stranger, and that stranger would turn out to have less-than-friendly motives. This fear led to law enforcement officers posing as underage girls in chat rooms, agreeing to meet for sex with older men (after the men brought up the topic—the other way around could be considered entrapment), and then arresting the men at the agreed-upon meeting spot.

In recent years, however, the Internet has become a hub of activity for all sorts of people. In 2002, Scott Heiferman started Meetup.com based on the "simple idea of using the Internet to get people off the Internet (Heiferman, 2009)." The entire purpose of Meetup.com is not to foster global interaction and collaboration (as is the purpose of something like Usenet,) but rather to allow people to organize locally. There are Meetups for politics (popular during Barack Obama's presidential campaign), for New Yorkers who own Boston terriers (Fairbanks, 2008), for vegan cooking, for board games, and for practically everything else. Essentially, the service (which charges a small fee to Meetup organizers) separates itself from other social networking sites by encouraging real-life interaction. Whereas a member of a Facebook group may never see or interact with fellow members, Meetup.com actually keeps track of the (self-reported) real-life activity of its groups—ideally, groups with more activity are more desirable to join. However much time these groups spend together on or off the Internet, one group of people undoubtedly has the upper hand when it comes to online interaction: *World of Warcraft* players.

World of Warcraft: Social Interaction Through Avatars

A writer for *Time* states the reasons for the massive popularity of online role-playing games quite well: "[My generation's] assumptions were based on the idea that video games would never grow up. But no genre has worked harder to disprove that maxim than MMORPGs—Massively Multiplayer Online Games (Coates, 2007)." *World of Warcraft (WoW*, for short) is the most popular MMORPG of all time, with over 11 million subscriptions and counting. The game is inherently social; players must complete "quests" in order to advance in the game, and many of the quests are significantly easier with multiple people. Players often form small, four-to five-person groups in the beginning of the game, but by the end of the game these larger groups (called "raiding parties") can reach up to 40 players.

In addition, *WoW* provides a highly developed social networking feature called "guilds." Players create or join a guild, which they can then use to band with other guilds in order to complete some of the toughest quests. "But once you've got a posse, the social dynamic just makes the game more addictive and time-consuming," writes Clive Thompson for *Slate* (Thompson, 2005). Although these guilds do occasionally meet up in real life, most of their time together is spent online for hours per day (which amounts to quite a bit of time together), and some of the guild leaders profess to seeing real-life improvements. Joi Ito, an Internet business and investment guru, joined *WoW* long after he had worked with some of the most successful Internet companies; he says he "definitely (Pinckard, 2006)" learned new lessons about leadership from playing the game. Writer Jane Pinckard, for video game blog *1UP*, lists some of Ito's favorite activities as "looking after newbs [lower-level players] and pleasing the veterans," which he calls a "delicate balancing act (Pinckard, 2006)," even for an ex-CEO.

Figure 11.9

Guilds often go on "raiding parties"—just one of the many semisocial activities in *World of Warcraft*.

monsieur paradis – gathering in Kargath before a raid – CC BY-NC 2.0.

With over 12 million subscribers, *WoW* necessarily breaks the boundaries of previous MMORPGs. The social nature of the game has attracted unprecedented numbers of female players (although men still make up the vast majority of players), and its players cannot easily be pegged as antisocial video game addicts. On the contrary, they may even be called *social* video game players, judging from the general responses given by players as to why they enjoy the game. This type of play certainly points to a new way of online interaction that may continue to grow in coming years.

Social Interaction on the Internet Among Low-Income Groups

In 2006, the journal *Developmental Psychology* published a study looking at the educational benefits of the Internet for teenagers in low-income households. It found that "children who used the Internet more had higher grade point averages (GPA) after one year and higher scores after standardized tests of reading achievement after six months than did children who used it less," and that continuing to use the Internet more as the study went on led to an even greater increase in GPA and standardized test scores in reading (there was no change in mathematics test scores) (Jackson, et. al., 2006).

One of the most interesting aspects of the study's results is the suggestion that the academic benefits may exclude low-performing children in low-income households. The reason for this, the study suggests, is that children in low-income households likely have a social circle consisting of other children from low-income households who are also unlikely to be connected to the Internet. As a result, after 16 months of Internet usage, only 16 percent of the participants were using e-mail and only 25 percent were using instant messaging services. Another reason researchers suggested was that because "African-American culture is historically an 'oral culture,'" and 83 percent of the participants were African American, the "impersonal nature of the Internet's typical communication tools" may have led participants to continue to prefer face-to-face contact. In other words, social interaction on the Internet can only happen if your friends are also on the Internet.

The Way Forward: Communication, Convergence, and Corporations

On February 15, 2010, the firm Compete, which analyzes Internet traffic, reported that Facebook surpassed Google as the No. 1 site to drive traffic toward news and entertainment media on both Yahoo! and MSN (Ingram, 2010). This statistic is a strong indicator that social networks are quickly becoming one of the most effective ways for people to sift through the ever-increasing amount of information on the Internet. It also suggests that people are content to get their news the way they did before the Internet or most other forms of mass media were invented—by word of mouth.

Many companies now use the Internet to leverage word-of-mouth social networking. The expansion of corporations into Facebook has given the service a big publicity boost, which has no doubt contributed to the growth of its user base, which in turn helps the corporations that put marketing efforts into the service. Putting a corporation on Facebook is not without risk; any corporation posting on Facebook runs the risk of being commented on by over 500 million users, and of course there is no way to ensure that those users will say positive things about the corporation. Good or bad, communicating with corporations is now a two-way street.

Key Takeaways

- The Internet has made pop culture transmission a two-way street. The power to influence popular culture no longer lies with the relative few with control over traditional forms of mass media; it is now available to the great mass of people with access to the Internet. As a result, the cross-fertilization of pop culture from around the world has become a commonplace occurrence.

- The Internet's key difference from traditional media is that it does not operate on a set intervallic time schedule. It is not "periodical" in the sense that it comes out in daily or weekly editions; it is always updated. As a result, many journalists file both "regular" news stories and blog posts that may be updated and that can come at varied intervals as necessary. This allows them to stay up-to-date with breaking news without necessarily sacrificing the next day's more in-depth story.

- The "Internet paradox" is the hypothesis that although the Internet is a tool for communication, many teenagers who use the Internet lack social interaction and become antisocial and depressed. It has been largely disproved, especially since the Internet has grown so drastically. Many sites, such as Meetup.com or even Facebook, work to allow users to organize for offline events. Other services, like the video game *World of Warcraft*, serve as an alternate social world.

Exercises

1. Make a list of ways you interact with friends, either in person or on the Internet. Are there particular methods of communication that only exist in person?

2. Are there methods that exist on the Internet that would be much more difficult to replicate in person?

3. How do these disprove the "Internet paradox" and contribute to the globalization of culture?

4. Pick a method of in-person communication and a method of Internet communication, and compare and contrast these using a Venn diagram.

References

Arango, Tim. "World Falls for American Media, Even as It Sours on America," *New York Times*, November 30, 2008, http://www.nytimes.com/2008/12/01/business/media/01soft.html.

Biggs, John. "A Video Clip Goes Viral, and a TV Network Wants to Control It," *New York Times*, February 20, 2006, http://www.nytimes.com/2006/02/20/business/media/20youtube.html.

Coates, Ta-Nehisi Paul. "Confessions of a 30-Year-Old Gamer," *Time*, January 12, 2007, http://www.time.com/time/arts/article/0,8599,1577502,00.html.

ComScore, "ComScore release March 2011 US Online Video Rankings," April 12, 2011, http://www.comscore.com/Press_Events/Press_Releases/2011/4/comScore_Releases_March_2011_U.S._Online_Video_Rankings.

Coyle, Jake. "On the Net: Hulu Is Web Site of the Year," *Seattle Times*, December 19, 2008, http://seattletimes.nwsource.com/html/entertainment/2008539776_aponthenetsiteoftheyear.html.

Ellison, Nicole B. Charles Steinfield, and Cliff Lampe, "The Benefits of Facebook 'Friends': Social Capital and

College Students' Use of Online Social Network Sites," *Journal of Computer-Mediated Communication* 14, no. 4 (2007).

Ellison, Nicole B. Charles Steinfield, and Cliff Lampe, "The Benefits of Facebook 'Friends': Social Capital and College Students' Use of Online Social Network Sites," *Journal of Computer-Mediated Communication* 14, no. 4 (2007).

Fairbanks, Amanda M. "Funny Thing Happened at the Dog Run," *New York Times*, August 23, 2008, csehttp://www.nytimes.com/2008/08/24/nyregion/24meetup.html.

Google, "Internet users as percentage of population: China," February 19, 2010, http://www.google.com/publicdata?ds=wb-wdi&met=it_net_user_p2&idim=country: CHN&dl=en&hl=en&q=china+internet+users.

Heiferman, Scott. "The Pursuit of Community," *New York Times*, September 5, 2009, csehttp://www.nytimes.com/2009/09/06/jobs/06boss.html.

Ingram, Mathew. "Facebook Driving More Traffic Than Google," *New York Times*, February 15, 2010, http://www.nytimes.com/external/gigaom/2010/02/15/15gigaom-facebook-driving-more-traffic-than-google-42970.html.

Jackson, Linda A. and others, "Does Home Internet Use Influence the Academic Performance of Low-Income Children?" *Developmental Psychology* 42, no. 3 (2006): 433–434.

Kraut, Robert and others, "Internet Paradox: A Social Technology That Reduces Social Involvement and Psychological Well-Being?" American Psychologist, September 1998, http://psycnet.apa.org/index.cfm?fa=buy.optionToBuy&id=1998-10886-001.

Lavin, Frank. "'Globalization and Culture': Remarks by Ambassador Frank Lavin at the Eisenhower Fellowship Conference in Singapore," U.S. Embassy in Singapore, June 28, 2005, http://singapore.usembassy.gov/062805.html.

Neil, Dan. "'30 Rock' Gets a Wink and a Nod From Two Emmy-Nominated Spots," *Los Angeles Times*, July 21, 2009, http://articles.latimes.com/2009/jul/21/business/fi-ct-neil21.

Newcomer, Joseph M. "Deconstructing the Internet Paradox," *Ubiquity*, Association for Computing Machinery, April 2000, http://ubiquity.acm.org/article.cfm?id=334533. (Originally published as an op-ed in the *Pittsburgh Post-Gazette*, September 27, 1998.).

Pew Research Center for the People & the Press, "Internet Overtakes Newspapers as News Outlet," December 23, 2008, http://people-press.org/report/479/internet-overtakes-newspapers-as-news-source.

Pinckard, Jane. "Is World of Warcraft the New Golf?" *1UP.com*, February 8, 2006, http://www.1up.com/news/world-warcraft-golf.

Rosen, Ellen. "THE INTERNET; Facebook.com Goes to High School," *New York Times*, October 16, 2005, http://query.nytimes.com/gst/fullpage.html?res=9C05EEDA173FF935A25753C1A9639C8B63&scp=5&sq=facebook&st=nyt.

Ryan, Johnny and Stefan Halper, "Google vs China: Capitalist Model, Virtual Wall," OpenDemocracy, January 22, 2010, http://www.opendemocracy.net/johnny-ryan-stefan-halper/google-vs-china-capitalist-model-virtual-wall.

Sandoval, Greg. "More Signs Hulu Subscription Service Is Coming," *CNET*, October 22, 2009, http://news.cnet.com/8301-31001_3-10381622-261.html.

Sternbergh, Adam. "'The Office' vs. '30 Rock': Comedy Goes Back to Work," *New York Magazine*, April 10, 2008, http://nymag.com/daily/entertainment/2008/04/the_office_vs_30_rock_comedy_g.html.

Thompson, Clive. "An Elf's Progress: Finally, Online Role-Playing Games That Won't Destroy Your Life," *Slate*, March 7, 2005, http://www.slate.com/id/2114354.

Wolff, Michael. "Politico's Washington Coup," *Vanity Fair*, August 2009, http://www.vanityfair.com/politics/features/2009/08/wolff200908.

Wortham, Jenna. "Hulu Airs Season Premiere of *30 Rock* a Week Early," *Wired*, October 23, 2008, http://www.wired.com/underwire/2008/10/hulu-airs-seaso/.

Zuckerberg, Mark. "An Open Letter from Facebook Founder Mark Zuckerberg," Facebook, December 1, 2009, http://blog.facebook.com/blog.php?post=190423927130.

11.5 Issues and Trends

Learning Objectives

1. Define *information superhighway* as it relates to the Internet.
2. Identify ways to identify credible sources online.
3. Define *net neutrality*.
4. Describe some of the effects of the Internet and social media on traditional media.

By 1994, the promise of the "information superhighway" had become so potent that it was given its own summit on the University of California Los Angeles campus. The country was quickly realizing that the spread of the web could be harnessed for educational purposes; more than just the diversion of computer hobbyists, this new vision of the web would be a constant learning resource that anyone could use.

The American video artist pioneer Nam June Paik takes credit for the term *information superhighway*, which he used during a study for the Rockefeller Foundation in 1974, long before the existence of Usenet. In 2001, he said, "If you create a highway, then people are going to invent cars. That's dialectics. If you create electronic highways, something has to happen (The Biz Media, 2010)." Paik's prediction proved to be startlingly prescient.

Al Gore's use of the term in the House of Representatives (and later as vice president) had a slightly different meaning and context. To Gore, the promise of the Interstate Highway System during the Eisenhower era was that the government would work to allow communication across natural barriers, and that citizens could then utilize these channels to conduct business and communicate with one another. Gore saw the government as playing an essential role in maintaining the pathways of electronic communication. Allowing business interests to get involved would compromise what he saw as a necessarily neutral purpose; a freeway doesn't judge or demand tolls—it is a public service—and neither should the Internet. During his 2000 presidential campaign, Gore was wrongly ridiculed for supposedly saying that he "invented the Internet," but in reality his work in the House of Representatives played a crucial part in developing the infrastructure required for Internet access.

Figure 11.10

Although Al Gore did not invent the Internet, he did popularize the term *information superhighway* in an effort to build support for Internet infrastructure and neutrality.

Dan Farber – Al Gore at Web 2.0 Summit – CC BY-NC 2.0.

However, a certain amount of money was necessary to get connected to the web. In this respect, AOL was like the Model T of the Internet—it put access to the information superhighway within reach of the average person. But despite the affordability of AOL and the services that succeeded it, certain demographics continued to go without access to the Internet, a problem known as the "digital divide," which you will learn more about in this section.

From speed of transportation, to credibility of information (don't trust the stranger at the roadside diner), to security of information (keep the car doors locked), to net neutrality (toll-free roads), to the possibility of piracy, the metaphor of the information superhighway has proved to be remarkably apt. All of these issues have played out in different ways, both positive and negative, and they continue to develop to this day.

Information Access Like Never Before

In December 2002, a survey by the Pew Internet & American Life Project found that 84 percent of Americans believed that they could find information on health care, government, news, or shopping on the Internet (Jesdanun, 2002). This belief in a decade-old system of interconnected web pages would in itself be remarkable, but taking into account that 37 percent of respondents were not even connected to the Internet, it becomes even more fantastic. In other words, of the percentage of Americans without Internet connections, 64 percent still believed that it could be a source of information about these crucial topics. In addition, of those who expect to find such information, at least 70 percent of them succeed; news and shopping were the most successful topics, government was the least. This survey shows that most Americans believed that the Internet was indeed an effective source of information. Again, the role of the Internet in education was heralded as a new future, and technology was seen to level the playing field for all students.

Nowhere was this more apparent than in the Bush administration's 2004 report, "Toward a New Golden Age in Education: How the Internet, the Law, and Today's Students Are Revolutionizing Expectations." By this time, the term *digital divide* was already widely used and the goal of "bridging" it took everything from putting computers in classrooms to giving personal computers to some high-need students to use at home.

The report stated that an "explosive growth" in sectors such as e-learning and virtual schools allowed each student "individual online instruction (U.S. Department of Education, 2004)." More than just being able to find information online, people expected the Internet to provide virtually unlimited access to educational opportunities. To make this expectation a reality, one of the main investments that the paper called for was increased broadband Internet access. As Nam June Paik predicted, stringing fiber optics around the world would allow for seamless video communication, a development that the Department of Education saw as integral to its vision of educating through technology. The report called for broadband access "24 hours a day, seven days a week, 365 days a year," saying that it could "help teachers and students realize the full potential of this technology (U.S. Department of Education, 2004)."

Rural Areas and Access to Information

One of the founding principles of many public library systems is to allow for free and open access to information. Historically, one of the major roadblocks to achieving this goal has been a simple one: location. Those living in rural areas or those with limited access to transportation simply could not get to a library. But with the spread of the Internet, the hope was that a global library would be created—an essential prospect for rural areas.

One of the most remarkable educational success stories in the Department of Education's study is that of the Chugach School District in Alaska. In 1994, this district was the lowest performing in the state: over 50 percent staff turnover, the lowest standardized test scores, and only one student in 26 years graduating from college (U.S. Department of Education, 2004). The school board instituted drastic measures, amounting to a complete overhaul of the system. They abolished grade levels, focusing instead on achievement, and by 2001 had increased Internet usage from 5 percent to 93 percent.

The Department of Education study emphasizes these numbers, and with good reason: The standardized test percentile scores rose from the 1920s to the 1970s in a period of 4 years, in both math and language arts. Yet these advances were not exclusive to low-performing rural students. In Florida, the Florida Virtual School system allowed rural school districts to offer advanced-placement coursework. Students excelling in rural areas could now study topics that were previously limited to districts that could fill (and fund) an entire classroom. Just as the Interstate Highway System commercially connected the most remote rural communities to large cities, the Internet has brought rural areas even further into the global world, especially in regard to the sharing of information and knowledge.

The Cloud: Instant Updates, Instant Access

As technology has improved, it has become possible to provide software to users as a service that resides entirely online, rather than on a person's personal computer. Since people can now be connected to the Internet constantly, they can use online programs to do all of their computing. It is no longer absolutely necessary to have, for example, a program like Microsoft Word to compose documents; this can be done through an online service like Google Docs or Zoho Writer.

"Cloud computing" is the process of outsourcing common computing tasks to a remote server. The actual work is not done by the computer attached to the user's monitor, but by other (maybe many other) computers in the "cloud." As a result, the computer itself does not actually need that much processing power; instead of calculating "1 + 1 = 2," the user's computer asks the cloud, "What does 1 + 1 equal?" and receives the answer. Meanwhile, the system resources that a computer would normally devote to completing these tasks are freed up to be used for other things. An additional advantage of cloud computing is that data can be stored in the cloud and retrieved from any computer, making a user's files more conveniently portable and less vulnerable to hardware failures like a hard drive crash. Of course, it can require quite a bit of bandwidth to send these messages back and forth to a remote server in the cloud, and in the absence of a reliable, always-on Internet connection, the usefulness of these services can be somewhat limited.

Figure 11.11

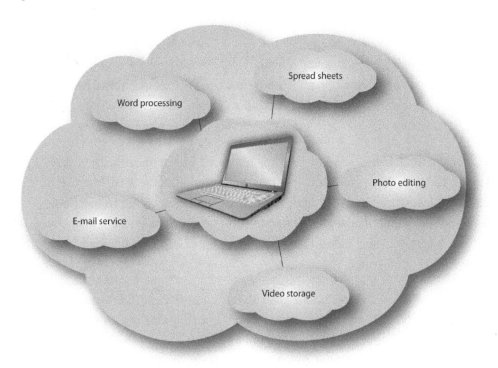

Cloud computing allows a computer to contain very little actual information. Many of the programs used by the now-popular "netbooks" are stored online.

The concept of the cloud takes into account all the applications that are hosted on external machines and viewed on a user's computer. Google Docs, which provides word processors, spreadsheets, and other tools, and Microsoft's Hotmail, which provides e-mail access, both constitute aspects of the "cloud." These services are becoming even more popular with the onset of mobile applications and netbooks, which are small laptops with relatively little processing power and storage space that rely on cloud computing. A netbook does not need the processing power required to run Microsoft Word; as long as it has a web browser, it can run the Google Docs word processor and leave (almost) all of the processing to the cloud. Because of this evolution of the Internet, computers can be built less like stand-alone machines and more like interfaces for interacting with the larger system in the cloud.

One result of cloud computing has been the rise in web applications for mobile devices, such as the iPhone, BlackBerry, and devices that use Google's Android operating system. 3G networks, which are cell phone networks capable of high-speed data transfer, can augment the computing power of phones just by giving the phones the ability to send data somewhere else to be processed. For example, a Google Maps application does not actually calculate the shortest route between two places (taking into account how highways are quicker than side roads, and numerous other computational difficulties) but rather just asks Google to do the calculation and send over the result. 3G networks have made this possible in large part because the speed of data transfer has now surpassed the speed of cell phones' calculation abilities. As cellular transmission technology continues to improve with the rollout of the next-generation 4G networks (the successors to 3G networks), connectivity speeds will further increase and allow for a focus on ever-more-comprehensive provisions for multimedia.

Credibility Issues: (Dis)information Superhighway?

The Internet has undoubtedly been a boon for researchers and writers everywhere. Online services range from up-to-date news and media to vast archives of past writing and scholarship. However, since the Internet is open to any user, anyone with a few dollars can set up a credible-sounding website and begin to disseminate false information.

This is not necessarily a problem with the Internet specifically; any traditional medium can—knowingly or unknowingly—publish unreliable or outright false information. But the explosion of available sources on the Internet has caused a bit of a dilemma for information seekers. The difference is that much of the information on the Internet is not the work of professional authors, but of amateurs who have questionable expertise. On the Internet, anyone can self-publish, so the vetting that usually occurs in a traditional medium—for example, by a magazine's editorial department—rarely happens online.

That said, if an author who is recognizable from elsewhere writes something online, it may point to more reliable information (Kirk, 1996). In addition, looking for a trusted name on the website could lead to more assurance of reliability. For example, the site krugmanonline.com, the official site of Princeton economist Paul Krugman, does not have any authorial data. Even statements like "Nobel Prize Winner and Op-Ed Columnist for the *New York Times*" do not actually say anything about the author of the website. Much of the content is aggregated from the web as well. However, the bottom-left corner of the page has the mark "© 2009 W. W. Norton & Company, Inc." (Krugman's publisher). Therefore, a visitor might decide to pick and choose which information to trust. The author is clearly concerned with selling Krugman's books, so the glowing reviews may need to be verified elsewhere; on the other hand, the author biography is probably fairly accurate, since the publishing company has direct access to Krugman, and Krugman himself probably looked it over to make sure it was valid. Taking the authorship of a site into account is a necessary step when judging information; more than just hunting down untrue statements, it can give insight into subtle bias that may arise and point to further research that needs to be done.

Just Trust Me: Bias on the web

One noticeable thing on Paul Krugman's site is that all of his book reviews are positive. Although these are probably real reviews, they may not be representative of his critical reception at large. Mainstream journalistic sources usually attempt to achieve some sort of balance in their reporting; given reasonable access, they will interview opposing viewpoints and reserve judgment for the editorial page. Corporate sources, like on Krugman's site, will instead tilt the information toward their product.

Often, the web is viewed as a source of entertainment, even in its informational capacity. Because of this, sites that rely on advertising may choose to publish something more inflammatory that will be linked to and forwarded more for its entertainment value than for its informational qualities.

On the other hand, a website might attempt to present itself as a credible source of information about a particular product or topic, with the end goal of selling something. A website that gives advice on how to protect against bedbugs that includes a direct link to its product may not be the best source of information on the topic. While so much on the web is free, it is worthwhile looking into how websites actually maintain their services. If a website is giving something away for free, the information might be biased, because it must be getting its money from somewhere. The online archive of *Consumer Reports* requires a subscription to access it. Ostensibly, this subscription revenue allows the service to exist as an impartial judge, serving the users rather than the advertisers.

Occasionally, corporations may set up "credible" fronts to disseminate information. Because sources may look reliable, it is always important to investigate further. Global warming is a contentious topic, and websites about the issue often represent the bias of their owners. For example, the Cato Institute publishes anti-global-warming theory columns in many newspapers, including well-respected ones such as the *Washington Times*. Patrick Basham, an adjunct scholar at the Cato Institute, published the article "Live Earth's Inconvenient Truths" in the *Washington Times* on July 11, 2007. Basham writes, "Using normal scientific standards, there is no proof we are causing the Earth to warm, let alone that such warming will cause an environmental catastrophe (Basham, 2007)."

However, the website ExxposeExxon.com states that the Cato Institute received $125,000 from the oil giant ExxonMobil, possibly tainting its data with bias (Exxon, 2006). In addition, ExxposeExxon.com is run as a side project of the international environmental nonprofit Greenpeace, which may have its own reasons for producing this particular report. The document available on Greenpeace's site (a scanned version of Exxon's printout) states that in 2006, the corporation gave $20,000 to the Cato Institute (Greenpeace, 2007) (the other $105,000 was given over the previous decade).

This back-and-forth highlights the difficulty of finding credible information online, especially when money is at stake. In addition, it shows how conflicting sources may go to great lengths—sorting through a company's corporate financial reports—in order to expose what they see as falsehoods. What is the upside to all of this required fact-checking and cross-examination? Before the Internet, this probably would have required multiple telephone calls and plenty of time waiting on hold. While the Internet has made false information more widely available, it has also made checking that information incredibly easy.

Wikipedia: The Internet's Precocious Problem Child

Nowhere has this cross-examination and cross-listing of sources been more widespread than with *Wikipedia*. Information free and available to all? That sounds like a dream come true—a dream that *Wikipedia* founder Jimmy Wales was ready to pursue. Since the site began in 2001, the Wikimedia Foundation (which hosts all of the *Wikipedia* pages) has become the sixth-most-visited site on the web, barely behind eBay in terms of its unique page views.

Table 11.3 Top 10 Global Web Parent Companies, Home and Work

Rank	Parent	Unique Audience (Millions)	Active Reach %	Time
1	Google	362,006	84.29	2:27:15
2	Microsoft	322,352	75.06	2:53:48
3	Yahoo!	238,035	55.43	1:57:26
4	Facebook	218,861	50.96	6:22:24
5	eBay	163,325	38.03	1:42:46
6	Wikimedia	154,905	36.07	0:15:14
7	AOL LLC	128,147	29.84	2:08:32
8	Amazon	128,071	29.82	0:23:24
9	News Corp.	125,898	29.31	0:53:53
10	InterActiveCorp	122,029	28.41	0:10:52

Source: The Nielsen Company

Organizations had long been trying to develop factual content for the web but *Wikipedia* went for something else: verifiability. The guidelines for editing *Wikipedia* state: "What counts is whether readers can verify that material added to *Wikipedia* has already been published by a reliable source, not whether editors think it is true (Wikipedia)." The benchmark for inclusion on *Wikipedia* includes outside citations for any content "likely to be challenged" and for "all quotations."

While this may seem like it's a step ahead of many other sources on the Internet, there is a catch: Anyone can edit *Wikipedia*. This has a positive and negative side—though anyone can vandalize the site, anyone can also fix it. In addition, calling a particularly contentious page to attention can result in one of the site's administrators placing a warning at the top of the page stating that the information is not necessarily verified. Other warnings include notices on articles about living persons, which are given special attention, and articles that may violate *Wikipedia*'s neutrality policy. This neutrality policy is a way to mitigate the extreme views that may be posted on a page with open access, allowing the community to decide what constitutes a "significant" view that should be represented (Wikipedia).

As long as users do not take the facts on *Wikipedia* at face value and make sure to follow up on the relevant sources linked in the articles they read, the site is an extremely useful reference tool that gives users quick access to a wide range of subjects. However, articles on esoteric subjects can be especially prone to vandalism or poorly researched information. Since every reader is a potential editor, a lack of readers can lead to a poorly edited page because errors, whether deliberate or not, go uncorrected. In short, the lack of authorial credit can lead to problems with judging bias and relevance of information, so the same precautions must be taken with *Wikipedia* as with any other online source, primarily in checking references. The advantage of *Wikipedia* is its openness and freedom—if you find a problem, you can either fix it (with your own verifiable sources) or flag it on the message boards. Culturally, there has been a shift from valuing a few reliable sources to valuing a multiplicity of competing sources. However, weighing these sources against one another has become easier than ever before.

Security of Information on the Internet

As the Internet has grown in scope and the amount of personal information online has proliferated, securing this information has become a major issue. The Internet now houses everything from online banking systems to highly personal e-mail messages, and even though security is constantly improving, this information is not invulnerable.

An example of this vulnerability is the Climategate scandal in late 2009. A collection of private e-mail messages were hacked from a server at the University of East Anglia, where much of the Intergovernmental Panel on Climate Change research takes place. These e-mails show internal debates among the scientists regarding which pieces of data should be released and which are not relevant (or helpful) to their case (Revkin, 2009). In these e-mails, the scientists sometimes talk about colleagues—especially those skeptical of climate change—in a derisive way. Of course, these e-mails were never meant to become public.

This scandal demonstrates how easy it can be to lose control of private information on the Internet. In previous decades, hard copies of these letters would have to be found, and the theft could probably be traced back to a specific culprit. With the Internet, it is much more difficult to tell who is doing the snooping, especially if it is done on a public network. The same protocols that allow for open access and communication also allow for possible exploitation. Like the Interstate Highway System, the Internet is impartial to its users. In other words: If you're going to ride, lock your doors.

Hacking E-mail: From LOVE-LETTER-FOR-YOU to Google in China

Another explosive scandal involving e-mail account hacking also occurred in late 2009, when Google's Gmail service was hacked by IP addresses originating in China. Gmail was one of the primary services used by human rights activists due to its location in the United States and its extra encryption. To understand the magnitude of this, it is important to understand the history of e-mail hacking and the importance of physical server location and local laws.

In 2000, a computer virus was unleashed by a student in the Philippines that simply sent a message with the subject line "I Love You." The e-mail had a file attached, called LOVE-LETTER-FOR-YOU.TXT.vbs. The suffix

".txt" is generally used for text files and was meant, in this case, as a distraction; the file's real suffix was ".vbs," which means that the file is a script. When run, this script ran and e-mailed itself across the user's entire address book, before sending any available passwords to an e-mail address in the Philippines. One of the key aspects of this case, however, was a matter of simple jurisdiction: The student was not prosecuted, due to the lack of computer crime laws in the Philippines (Zetter, 1983).

The encryption that Gmail uses resulted in only two of the accounts being successfully hacked, and hackers were only able to see e-mail subject lines and timestamps—no message content was available (Zetter, 2010). Since the chaos that ensued after the "I Love You" virus, e-mail users and service providers have become more vigilant in their defensive techniques. However, the increased reliance on e-mail for daily communication makes it an attractive target for hackers. The development of cloud computing will likely lead to entirely new problems with Internet security; just as a highway brings two communities together, it can also cause these communities to share problems.

Can't Wait: Denial of Service

Although many people increasingly rely on the Internet for communication and access to information, this reliance has come with a hefty price. Most critically, a simple exploit can cause massive roadblocks to Internet traffic, leading to disruptions in commerce, communication, and, as the military continues to rely on the Internet, national security.

Distributed denial-of-service (DDoS) attacks work like cloud computing, but in reverse. Instead of a single computer going out to retrieve data from many different sources, DDoS is a coordinated effort by many different computers to bring down (or overwhelm) a specific website. Essentially, any web server can only handle a certain amount of information at once. While the largest and most stable web servers can talk to a huge number of computers simultaneously, even these can be overwhelmed.

During a DDoS attack on government servers belonging to both the United States and South Korea in July 2009, many U.S. government sites were rendered unavailable to users in Asia for a short time (Gorman & Ramstad, 2009). Although this did not have a major effect on U.S. cyber-security, the ease with which these servers could be exploited was troubling. In this case, the DDoS attacks were perpetuated by an e-mail virus known as MyDoom, which essentially turned users' computers into server-attacking "zombies." This exploit—coupling an e-mail scam with a larger attack—is difficult to trace, partly because the culprit is likely not one of the original attackers, but rather the victim of a virus used to turn vulnerable computers into an automated hacker army. Since the attack, President Barack Obama has committed to creating a new post for a head of cyber-security in the government.

Net Neutrality

Most Internet users in the United States connect through a commercial Internet service provider (ISP). The major players—Comcast, Verizon, Time Warner Cable, AT&T, and others—are portals to the larger Internet, serving as a way for anyone with a cable line or phone line to receive broadband Internet access through a dedicated data line.

Ideally, ISPs treat all content impartially; any two websites will load at the same speed if they have adequate server capabilities. Service providers are not entirely happy with this arrangement. ISPs have proposed a new service model that would allow corporations to pay for a "higher tier" service. For example, this would allow AOL Time Warner to deliver its Hulu service (which Time Warner co-owns with NBC) faster than all other video services, leading to partnerships between Internet content providers and Internet service providers. The service providers also often foot the bill for expanding high-speed Internet access, and they see this new two-tiered service as a way to cash in on some of that investment (and, presumably, to reinvest the funds received).

The main fear—and the reason the FCC introduced net neutrality rules—is that such a service would hamper the ability of an Internet startup to grow its business. Defenders of net neutrality contend that small businesses (those without the ability to forge partnerships with the service providers) would be forced onto a "second-tier" Internet service, and their content would naturally suffer, decreasing inventiveness and competition among Internet content providers.

Net Neutrality Legislation: The FCC and AT&T

One of the key roadblocks to Internet legislation is the difficulty of describing the Internet and the Internet's place among communication bills of the past. First of all, it is important to realize that legislation relating to the impartiality of service providers is not unheard-of. Before the 1960s, AT&T was allowed to restrict its customers to using only its own telephones on its networks. In the 1960s, the FCC launched a series of "Computer Inquiries," stating, in effect, that any customer could use any device on the network, as long as it did not actually harm the network. This led to inventions such as the fax machine, which would not have been possible under AT&T's previous agreement.

A key point today is that these proto–net neutrality rules protected innovation even when they "threatened to be a substitute for regulated services (Cannon, 2003)." This is directly relevant to a controversy involving Apple's iPhone that culminated in October 2009 when AT&T agreed to allow VoIP (voice over Internet protocol) on its 3G data networks. VoIP services, like the program Skype, allow a user to place a telephone call from an Internet data line to a traditional telephone line. In the case of the iPhone, AT&T did not actually block the transmission of data—it just had Apple block the app from its App Store. Since AT&T runs the phone service as well as the data lines, and since many users have plans with unlimited data connections, AT&T could see its phone profits cut drastically if all its users suddenly switched to using Skype to place all their telephone calls.

Misleading Metaphors: It's Not a Big Truck

Senator Ted Stevens, the former head of the committee in charge of regulating the Internet, said on the floor of the Senate that the Internet is "not a big truck…it's a series of tubes (Curtis, 2006)." According to this metaphor, an e-mail can get "stuck in the tubes" for days behind someone else's material, leading to poorer service for the customer. In reality, service providers sell data-usage plans that only set a *cap* on the amount of data that someone can send over the Internet (measured in bits per second, where a bit is the smallest measurement of data). If a service is rated at 1.5 million bits per second (megabits per second, or 1.5 Mbps), it may only reach this once in a while—no one can "clog the tubes" without paying massive amounts of money for the service. Theoretically, the company will then invest this service fee in building more robust "tubes."

Net neutrality is difficult to legislate in part because it can be confusing: It relies on understanding how the Internet works and how communications are regulated. Stevens's metaphor is misleading because it assumes that Internet capacity is not already regulated in some natural way. To use the superhighway analogy, Stevens is suggesting that the highways are congested, and his solution is to allow companies to dedicate express lanes for high-paying customers (it should be noted that the revenue would go to the service providers, even though the government has chipped in quite a bit for information superhighway construction). The danger of this is that it would be very difficult for a small business or personal site to afford express-lane access. Worse yet, the pro–net neutrality organization Save the Internet says that a lack of legislation would allow companies to "discriminate in favor of their own search engines" and "leave the rest of us on a winding dirt road (Save the Internet, 2010)." For areas that only have access to one Internet service, this would amount to a lack of access to all the available content.

Digital Technology and Electronic Media

Content on the Internet competes with content from other media outlets. Unlimited and cheap digital duplication of content removes the concept of scarcity from the economic model of media; it is no longer necessary to buy a physical CD fabricated by a company in order to play music, and digital words on a screen convey the news just as well as words printed on physical newspaper. Media companies have been forced to reinvent themselves as listeners, readers, and watchers have divided into smaller and smaller subcategories.

Traditional media companies have had to evolve to adapt to the changes wrought by the Internet revolution, but these media are far from obsolete in an online world. For example, social media can provide a very inexpensive and reliable model for maintaining a band's following. A record company (or the band itself) can start a Facebook page, through which it can notify all its fans about new albums and tour dates—or even just remind fans that it still exists. MySpace has been (and still is, to an extent) one of the main musical outlets on the Internet. This free service comes with a small web-based music player that allows people interested in the band to listen to samples of its music. Coupling free samples with social networking allows anyone to discover a band from anywhere in the world, leading to the possibility of varying and eclectic tastes not bound by geography.

Key Takeaways

- On one hand, the information superhighway has opened up rural areas to global connections and made communication and trade much easier. One downside, however, is that illicit and unwanted information can move just as quickly as positive information—it is up to the recipient to decide.

- The lack of authorial attribution on many online forums can make it difficult to find credible information. However, *Wikipedia*'s concept of "verifiability," or citing verified sources, has provided a good check to what can become a matter of mere my-word-against-yours. It is important to gauge possible bias in a source and to judge whether the author has an economic interest in the information.

- Net neutrality is a general category of laws that seek to make it illegal for service providers to discriminate among types of Internet content. One downside of content discrimination is that a service provider could potentially make competitors' sites load much more slowly than their own.

Exercises

1. Find a website about a single product, musician, or author. Does the site have a stated or strongly implied author?

2. Look for a copyright notice and a date, usually at the bottom of the page. How might that author's point of view bias the information on the site?

3. How can one determine the author's credibility?

End-of-Chapter Assessment

Review Questions

1.
Section 1

a. What are two of the original characteristics of the Internet, and how do they continue to affect it?

b. What were some of the technological developments that had a part in the "democratization" of the Internet, or the spread of the Internet to more people?

c. What were the causes and effects of the dot-com boom and crash? How did the dot-com boom and crash influence the Internet in later years, particularly with regards to content providers' income streams?

2.
Section 2

a. What are some of the differences between social networking sites, and how do they reflect a tendency to cater to a specific demographic?

b. How might blogs help the flow of information around the world? How might they damage that information?

c. How has privacy been treated on social networking sites, and how does this affect the culture?

d. How have marketers tried to use social networking to their advantage?

3.
Section 3

a. How has globalization on the Internet changed the way culture is distributed?

b. What are the implications of the Internet overtaking print media as a primary source for news, and how might that affect the public discourse?

c. What is the "Internet paradox," and how have various websites and services tried to combat it? How do Internet users socialize on the Internet?

4.
Section 4

a. How does the metaphor of an "information superhighway" relate to both the positive and negative aspects of the Internet?

b. What are some threats to credibility online, and how can users proactively seek only credible sources?

c. What is net neutrality, and how could it change the way we access information on the Internet?

d. How has the Internet affected the music business? How has the Internet affected the music from an artistic perspective?

Critical Thinking Questions

1. One of the repeated promises of the Internet is that it is truly democratic and that anyone can have a voice. Has this played out in a viable way, or was that a naive assumption that never really came to fruition?

2. How do the concepts of decentralization and protocol play a part in the way the Internet works?

3. How have social networks transformed marketing? What are some of the new ways that marketers can target specific people?

4. How has the Internet changed the way people socialize online? Are there entirely new forms of socializing that did not exist before the Internet?

5. How has the concept of *verifiability* changed the way that "truth" is regarded on the Internet—even in the culture at large? Has the speed and volume with which new information becomes available on the Internet made verifiable information more difficult to come by?

Career Connection

There is a constantly growing market for people who know how to use social media effectively. Often, companies will hire someone specifically to manage their Facebook and Twitter feeds as another aspect of public relations and traditional marketing.

Read the article "5 True Things Social Media Experts Do Online," written by social media writer Glen Allsopp. You can find it at http://www.techipedia.com/2010/social-media-expert-skills/.

Then, explore the site of Jonathan Fields, located at http://www.jonathanfields.com/blog/. After exploring for a bit, read the "About" section (the link is at the top). These two sites will help you answer the following questions:

1. How has Jonathan Fields made "everything else irrelevant"? What are some of the indications that he gives in his biography that he is passionate about his industry doing well?

2. Review Jonathan's Twitter feed on the right column of his site. Who are some of the other people he features, and how might this relate to Glen Allsopp's advice to "highlight others"?

3. Also look at Jonathan's "Small Business Marketing" section. What are some of the things he does to help businesses reach customers? How might this be potentially rewarding?

4. Think about the ways that you may use social media in your own life, and how you might be able to use those skills to help a business. Pick an activity that you might (or do) participate in online and write down how you might do the same thing from the perspective of a company. For example, how would you write the "About Me" section of a company's Facebook profile? How could you start turning this skill into a career?

References

Basham, Patrick. "Live Earth's Inconvenient Truths," Cato Institute, July 11, 2007, http://www.cato.org/pub_display.php?pub_id=8497.

Cannon, Robert. "The Legacy of the Federal Communications Commission's Computer Inquiries," *Federal Communication Law Journal* 55, no. 2 (2003): 170.

Curtis, Alex. "Senator Stevens Speaks on Net Neutrality," Public Knowledge, June 28, 2006, http://www.publicknowledge.org/node/497.

Exxon, Exxpose. "Global Warming Deniers and ExxonMobil," 2006, http://www.exxposeexxon.com/facts/gwdeniers.html.

Gorman, Siobhan and Evan Ramstad, "Cyber Blitz Hits U.S., Korea," *Wall Street Journal*, July 9, 2009, http://online.wsj.com/article/SB124701806176209691.html.

Greenpeace, *ExxonMobil 2006 Contributions and Community Investments*, October 5, 2007, http://research.greenpeaceusa.org/?a=view&d=4381.

Jesdanun, Anick. "High Expectations for the Internet," December 30, 2002, http://www.crn.com/it-channel/18822182;jsessionid=3Z2ILJNFKM1FZQE1GHPCKH4ATMY32JVN.

Kirk, Elizabeth E. "Evaluating Information Found on the Internet," Sheridan Libraries, Johns Hopkins University, 1996, http://www.library.jhu.edu/researchhelp/general/evaluating/.

Revkin, Andrew C. "Hacked E-Mail Is New Fodder for Climate Dispute," *New York Times*, November 20, 2009, http://www.nytimes.com/2009/11/21/science/earth/21climate.html.

Save the Internet, "FAQs," 2010, http://www.savetheinternet.com/faq.

The Biz Media, "Video and the Information Superhighway: An Artist's Perspective," *The Biz Media*, May 3, 2010, http://blog.thebizmedia.com/video-and-the-information-superhighway/.

U.S. Department of Education, *Toward a New Golden Age in American Education: How the Internet, the Law and Today's Students Are Revolutionizing Expectations*, National Education Technology Plan, 2004, http://www2.ed.gov/about/offices/list/os/technology/plan/2004/site/theplan/edlite-intro.html.

Wikipedia, s.v. "Wikipedia:Neutral point of view," http://en.wikipedia.org/wiki/Wikipedia:Neutral_point_of_view.

Wikipedia, s.v. "Wikipedia:Verifiability," http://en.wikipedia.org/wiki/Wikipedia:Verifiability.

Zetter, Kim. "Google to Stop Censoring Search Results in China After Hack Attack," *Wired*, January 12, 2010, http://www.wired.com/threatlevel/2010/01/google-censorship-china/.

Zetter, Kim. "Nov. 10, 1983: Computer 'Virus' Is Born," *Wired*, November 10, 2009, http://www.wired.com/thisdayintech/2009/11/1110fred-cohen-first-computer-virus/.

Chapter 12: Advertising and Public Relations

12.1 Advertising

Learning Objectives

1. Describe important eras in the history of American advertising.

2. Analyze the overall effects of government regulation on advertising.

3. Identify the types of advertising used today.

4. Describe the impact of advertising on American consumerism and cultural values.

Advertising is defined as promoting a product or service through the use of paid announcements (Dictionary). These announcements have had an enormous effect on modern culture, and thus deserve a great deal of attention in any treatment of the media's influence on culture.

History of Advertising

Figure 12.1

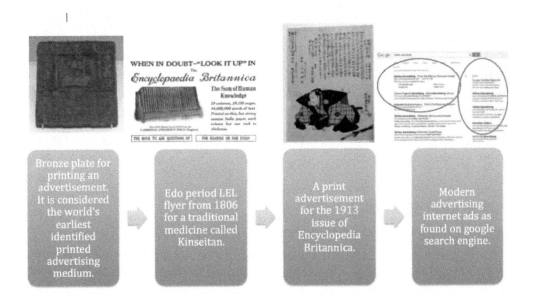

History of Advertising

Advertising dates back to ancient Rome's public markets and forums and continues into the modern era in most homes around the world. Contemporary consumers relate to and identify with brands and products. Advertising has inspired an independent press and conspired to encourage carcinogenic addictions. An exceedingly human invention, advertising is an unavoidable aspect of the shared modern experience.

Ancient and Medieval Advertising

In 79 CE, the eruption of Italy's Mount Vesuvius destroyed and, ultimately, preserved the ancient city of Pompeii. Historians have used the city's archaeological evidence to piece together many aspects of ancient life. Pompeii's ruins reveal a world in which the fundamental tenets of commerce and advertising were already in place. Merchants offered different brands of fish sauces identified by various names such as "Scaurus' tunny jelly." Wines were branded as well, and their manufacturers sought to position them by making claims about their prestige and quality. Toys and other merchandise found in the city bear the names of famous athletes, providing, perhaps, the first example of endorsement techniques (Hood, 2005).

The invention of the printing press in 1440 made it possible to print advertisements that could be put up on walls and handed out to individuals. By the 1600s, newspapers had begun to include advertisements on their pages. Advertising revenue allowed newspapers to print independently of secular or clerical authority, eventually achieving daily circulation. By the end of the 16th century, most newspapers contained at least some advertisements (O'Barr, 2005).

Selling the New World

European colonization of the Americas during the 1600s brought about one of the first large-scale advertising campaigns. When European trading companies realized that the Americas held economic potential as a source of natural resources such as timber, fur, and tobacco, they attempted to convince others to cross the Atlantic Ocean and work to harvest this bounty. The advertisements for this venture described a paradise without beggars and with plenty of land for those who made the trip. The advertisements convinced many poor Europeans to become indentured servants to pay for the voyage (Mierau, 2000).

Nineteenth-Century Roots of Modern Advertising

Figure 12.2

Early penny press papers such as the *New York Sun* took advantage of advertisements, which allowed them to sell their issues for a penny or two.

The rise of the penny press during the 1800s had a profound effect on advertising. The *New York Sun* embraced a novel advertising model in 1833 that allowed it to sell issues of the paper for a trifling amount of money, ensuring a higher circulation and a wider audience. This larger audience in turn justified greater prices for advertisements, allowing the paper to make a profit from its ads rather than from direct sales (Vance).

P. T. Barnum and Advertising

The career of P. T. Barnum, cofounder of the famed Barnum & Bailey circus, gives a sense of the uncontrolled nature of advertising during the 1800s. He began his career in the 1840s writing ads for a theater, and soon after, he began promoting his own shows. He advertised these shows any way he could, using not only interesting newspaper ads but also bands of musicians, paintings on the outside of his buildings, and street-spanning banners.

Barnum also learned the effectiveness of using the media to gain attention. In an early publicity stunt, Barnum hired a man to wordlessly stack bricks at various corners near his museum during the hours preceding a show. When this activity drew a crowd, the man went to the museum and bought a ticket for the show. This stunt drew such large crowds over the next 2 days, that the police made Barnum put a halt to it, gaining it even wider media attention. Barnum was sued for fraud over a bearded woman featured in one of his shows; the plaintiffs claimed that she was, in fact, a man. Rather than trying to keep the trial quiet, Barnum drew attention to it by parading a crowd of witnesses attesting to the bearded woman's gender, drawing more media attention—and more customers.

Figure 12.3

P. T. Barnum used the press to spark interest in his shows.

trialsanderrors – The marvelous foot-ball dogs, poster for Barnum & Bailey, 1900 – CC
BY 2.0.

Barnum aimed to make his audience think about what they had seen for an extended time. His Feejee
mermaid—actually a mummified monkey and fish sewn together—was not necessarily interesting because
viewers thought the creation was really a mermaid, but because they weren't sure if it was or not. Such
marketing tactics brought Barnum's shows out of his establishments and into social conversations and
newspapers (Applegate, 1998). Although most companies today would eschew Barnum's outrageous style,
many have used the media and a similar sense of mystery to promote their products. Apple, for example,

famously keeps its products such as the iPhone and iPad under wraps, building media anticipation and coverage.

In 1843, a salesman named Volney Palmer founded the first U.S. advertising agency in Philadelphia. The agency made money by linking potential advertisers with newspapers. By 1867, other agencies had formed, and advertisements were being marketed at the national level. During this time, George Rowell, who made a living buying bulk advertising space in newspapers to subdivide and sell to advertisers, began conducting market research in its modern recognizable form. He used surveys and circulation counts to estimate numbers of readers and anticipate effective advertising techniques. His agency gained an advantage over other agencies by offering advertising space most suited for a particular product. This trend quickly caught on with other agencies. In 1888, Rowell started the first advertising trade magazine, *Printers' Ink* (Gartrell).

In Chapter 5 "Magazines", you read about *McClure's* success in 1893 thanks to an advertising model: selling issues for nearly half the price of other magazines and depending on advertising revenues to make up the difference between cost and sales price. Magazines such as *Ladies' Home Journal* focused on specific audiences, so they allowed advertisers to market products designed for a specific demographic. By 1900, *Harper's Weekly*, once known for refusing advertising, featured ads on half of its pages (All Classic Ads).

The Rise of Brand Names

Figure 12.4

In the early 1900s, brand-name food items, such as this one, began making a household name for themselves.

Stuart Rankin – Payn's Sure-Raising Flour – CC BY-NC 2.0.

Another ubiquitous aspect of advertising developed around this time: brands. During most of the 19th century, consumers purchased goods in bulk, weighing out scoops of flour or sugar from large store barrels and paying for them by the pound. Innovations in industrial packaging allowed companies to mass produce bags, tins, and cartons with brand names on them. Although brands existed before this time, they were generally reserved for goods that were inherently recognizable, such as china or furniture. Advertising a particular kind of honey or flour made it possible for customers to ask for that product by name, giving it an edge over the unnamed competition.[1]

Figure 12.5

Department stores such as Sears, Roebuck and Co. reached consumers outside of the city through mail-order catalogs.

Nesster – 1961 Sears: Mail Order Envelope – CC BY 2.0.

The rise of department stores during the late 1800s also gave brands a push. Nationwide outlets such as Sears, Roebuck & Company and Montgomery Ward sold many of the same items to consumers all over the country. A particular item spotted in a big-city storefront could come to a small-town shopper's home thanks to mail-order catalogs. Customers made associations with the stores, trusting them to have a particular kind of item and to provide quality wares. Essentially, consumers came to trust the store's name rather than its specific products.[2]

Advertising Gains Stature During the 20th Century

Although advertising was becoming increasingly accepted as an element of mass media, many still regarded it as an unseemly occupation. This attitude began to change during the early 20th century. As magazines—widely considered a highbrow medium—began using more advertising, the advertising profession began attracting more artists and writers. Writers used verse and artists produced illustrations to embellish advertisements. Not surprisingly, this era gave rise to commercial jingles and iconic brand characters such as the Jolly Green Giant and the Pillsbury Doughboy.

The household cleaner Sapolio produced advertisements that made the most of the artistic advertising trend. Sapolio's ads featured various drawings of the residents of "Spotless Town" along with a rhymed verse celebrating the virtues of this fictional haven of cleanliness. The public anticipated each new ad in much the same way people today anticipate new TV episodes. In fact, the ads became so popular that citizens passed "Spotless Town" resolutions to clean up their own jurisdictions. Advertising trends later moved away from flowery writing and artistry, but the lessons of those memorable campaigns continued to influence the advertising profession for years to come (Fox, 1984).

Advertising Makes Itself Useful

World War I fueled an advertising and propaganda boom. Corporations that had switched to manufacturing wartime goods wanted to stay in the public eye by advertising their patriotism. Equally, the government needed to encourage public support for the war, employing such techniques as the famous Uncle Sam recruiting poster. President Woodrow Wilson established the advertiser-run Committee on Public Information to make movies and posters, write speeches, and generally sell the war to the public. Advertising helped popularize World War I on the home front, and the war in turn gave advertising a much-needed boost in stature. The postwar return to regular manufacturing initiated the 1920s as an era of unprecedented advertising.[3]

New Media

The rising film industry made celebrity testimonials, or product endorsements, an important aspect of advertising during the 1920s. Film stars including Clara Bow and Joan Crawford endorsed products such as Lux toilet soap. In these early days of mass-media consumer culture, film actors and actresses gave the public figures to emulate as they began participating in popular culture.[4]

As discussed in Chapter 7 "Radio", radio became an accepted commercial medium during the 1920s. Although many initially thought radio was too intrusive a medium to allow advertising, as it entered people's homes by the end of the decade, advertising had become an integral aspect of programming. Advertising agencies often created their own programs that networks then distributed. As advertisers conducted surveys and researched prime time slots, radio programming changed to appeal to their target demographics. The famous *Lux Radio Theater*, for example, was named for and sponsored by a brand of soap. Product placement was an important part of these early radio programs. Ads for Jell-O appeared during the course of the *Jack Benny Show* (JackBennyShow.com), and *Fibber McGee and Molly* scripts often involved their sponsor's floor wax (Burgan, 1996). The relationship between a sponsor and a show's producers was not always harmonious; the producers of radio programs were constrained from broadcasting any content that might reflect badly on their sponsor.

The Great Depression and Backlash

Unsurprisingly, the Great Depression, with its widespread decreases in levels of income and buying power, had a negative effect on advertising. Spending on ads dropped to a mere 38 percent of its previous level. Social reformers added to revenue woes by again questioning the moral standing of the advertising profession. Books such as *Through Many Windows* and *Our Master's Voice* portrayed advertisers as dishonest and cynical, willing to say anything to make a profit and unconcerned about their influence on society. Humorists also questioned advertising's authority. The Depression-era magazine *Ballyhoo* regularly featured parodies of ads, similar to those seen later on *Saturday Night Live* or in *The Onion*. These ads mocked the claims that had been made throughout the 1920s, further reducing advertising's public standing.[5]

This advertising downturn lasted only as long as the Depression. As the United States entered World War II, advertising again returned to encourage public support and improve the image of businesses.[6] However, there was one lasting effect of the Depression. The rising consumer movement made false and misleading advertising a major public policy issue. At the time, companies such as Fleischmann's (which claimed its yeast could cure crooked teeth) were using advertisements to pitch misleading assertions. Only business owners' personal morals stood in the way of such claims until 1938, when the federal government created the Federal Trade Commission (FTC) and gave it the authority to halt false advertising.

In 1955, TV outpaced all other media for advertising. TV provided advertisers with unique, geographically oriented mass markets that could be targeted with regionally appropriate ads (Samuel, 2006). The 1950s saw a 75 percent increase in advertising spending, faster than any other economic indicator at the time.[7]

Single sponsors created early TV programs. These sponsors had total control over programs such as *Goodyear TV Playhouse* and *Kraft Television Theatre*. Some sponsors went as far as to manipulate various aspects of the programs. In one instance, a program run by the DeSoto car company asked a contestant to use a false name rather than his given name, Ford. The present-day network model of TV advertising took hold during the 1950s as the costs of TV production made sole sponsorship of a show prohibitive for most companies. Rather than having a single sponsor, the networks began producing their own shows, paying for them through ads sold to a number of different sponsors.[8] Under the new model of advertising, TV producers had much more creative control than they had under the sole-sponsorship model.

The quiz shows of the 1950s were the last of the single-sponsor–produced programs. In 1958, when allegations of quiz show fraud became national news, advertisers moved out of programming entirely. The quiz show scandals also added to an increasing skepticism of ads and consumer culture (Boddy, 1990).

Advertising research during the 1950s had used scientifically driven techniques to attempt to influence consumer opinion. Although the effectiveness of this type of advertising is questionable, the idea of consumer manipulation through scientific methods became an issue for many Americans. Vance Packard's best-selling 1957 book *The Hidden Persuaders* targeted this style of advertising. *The Hidden Persuaders* and other books like it were part of a growing critique of 1950s consumer culture. The U.S. public was becoming increasingly wary of advertising claims—not to mention increasingly weary of ads themselves. A few adventurous ad agencies used this consumer fatigue to usher in a new era of advertising and American culture (Frank, 1998).

The Creative Revolution

Burdened by association with Nazi Germany, where the company had originated, Volkswagen took a daring risk during the 1950s. In 1959, the Doyle Dane Bernbach (DDB) agency initiated an ad campaign for the company that targeted skeptics of contemporary culture. Using a frank personal tone with the audience and making fun of the planned obsolescence that was the hallmark of Detroit automakers, the campaign stood apart from other advertisements of the time. It used many of the consumer icons of the 1950s, such as suburbia and game shows, in a satirical way, pitting Volkswagen against mainstream conformity and placing it strongly on the side of the consumer. By the end of the 1960s, the campaign had become an icon of American anticonformity. In fact, it was such a success that other automakers quickly emulated it. Ads for the Dodge Fever, for example, mocked corporate values and championed rebellion.[9]

This era of advertising became known as the **creative revolution** for its emphasis on creativity over straight salesmanship. The creative revolution reflected the values of the growing anticonformist movement that culminated in the countercultural revolution of the 1960s. The creativity and anticonformity of 1960s advertising quickly gave way to more product-oriented conventional ads during the 1970s. Agency conglomeration, a recession, and cultural fallout were all factors in the recycling of older ad techniques. Major TV networks dropped their long-standing ban on comparative advertising early in the decade, leading to a new trend in positioning ads that compared products. Advertising wars such as Coke versus Pepsi and, later, Microsoft versus Apple were products of this trend.[10]

Innovations in the 1980s stemmed from a new TV channel: MTV. Producers of youth-oriented products created ads featuring music and focusing on stylistic effects, mirroring the look and feel of music videos. By the end of the decade, this style had extended to more mainstream products. Campaigns for the pain reliever Nuprin featured black-and-white footage with bright yellow pills, whereas ads for Michelob used grainy atmospheric effects (New York Times, 1989).

Advertising Stumbles

During the late 1980s, studies showed that consumers were trending away from brands and brand loyalty. A recession coupled with general consumer fatigue led to an increase in generic brand purchases and a decrease in advertising. In 1983, marketing budgets allocated 70 percent of their expenditures to ads and the remaining 30 percent to other forms of promotion. By 1993, only 25 percent of marketing budgets were dedicated to ads (Klein, 2002).

These developments resulted in the rise of big-box stores such as Wal-Mart that focused on low prices rather than expensive name brands. Large brands remade themselves during this period to focus less on their products and more on the ideas behind the brand. Nike's "Just Do It" campaign, endorsed by basketball star Michael Jordan, gave the company a new direction and a new means of promotion. Nike representatives have stated they have become more of a "marketing-oriented company" as opposed to a product manufacturer.[11]

Figure 12.7

In the 1990s, Nike was the target of protests due to its questionable labor practices.

WBUR Boston's NPR News Station – Protest – CC BY-NC-ND 2.0.

As large brands became more popular, they also attracted the attention of reformers. Companies such as Starbucks and Nike bore the brunt of late 1990s sweatshop and labor protests. As these brands attempted to incorporate ideas outside of the scope of their products, they also came to represent larger global commerce forces (Hornblower, 2000). This type of branding increasingly incorporated public relations techniques that will be discussed later in this chapter.

The Rise of Digital Media

Twenty-first-century advertising has adapted to new forms of digital media. Internet outlets such as blogs, social media forums, and other online spaces have created new possibilities for advertisers, and shifts in broadcasting toward Internet formats have threatened older forms of advertising. Video games, smartphones, and other technologies also present new possibilities. Specific new media advertising techniques will be covered in the next section.

Types of Advertising

Despite the rise of digital media, many types of traditional advertising have proven their enduring effectiveness. Local advertisers and large corporations continue to rely on billboards and direct-mail fliers. In 2009, Google initiated a billboard campaign for its Google Apps products that targeted business commuters. The billboards featured a different message every day for an entire month, using simple computer text messages portraying a fictitious executive learning about the product. Although this campaign was integrated with social media sites such as Twitter, its main thrust employed the basic billboard (Ionescu, 2009).

Figure 12.8

Google billboards targeted commuters, creating a story that spanned the course of a month.

Danny Sullivan – Ask Versus Google In Billboards – CC BY 2.0.

Newspapers and Magazines

Although print ads have been around for centuries, Internet growth has hit newspaper advertising hard. A 45 percent drop in ad revenue between 2007 and 2010 signaled a catastrophic decline for the newspaper industry (Sterling, 2010). Traditionally, newspapers have made money through commercial and classified advertising. Commercial advertisers, however, have moved to electronic media forms, and classified ad websites such as Craigslist offer greater geographic coverage for free. The future of newspaper advertising—and of the newspaper industry as a whole—is up in the air.

Print magazines have suffered from many of the same difficulties as newspapers. Declining advertising revenue has contributed to the end of popular magazines such as *Gourmet* and to the introduction of new magazines that cross over into other media formats, such as *Food Network Magazine*. Until a new, effective model is developed, the future of magazine advertising will continue to be in doubt.

Radio

Compared to newspapers and magazines, radio's advertising revenue has done well. Radio's easy adaptation to new forms of communication has made it an easy sell to advertisers. Unlike newspapers, radio ads target specific consumers. Advertisers can also pay to have radio personalities read their ads live in the studio, adding a sense of personal endorsement to the business or product. Because newer forms of radio such as satellite and Internet stations have continued to use this model, the industry has not had as much trouble adapting as print media have.

Television

TV advertisement relies on verbal as well as visual cues to sell items. Promotional ad time is purchased by the advertiser, and a spot usually runs 15 to 30 seconds. Longer ads, known as infomercials, run like a TV show and usually aim for direct viewer response. New technologies such as DVR allow TV watchers to skip through commercials; however, studies have shown that these technologies do not have a negative effect on advertising (Gallagher, 2010). This is partly due to product placement. Product placement is an important aspect of TV advertising, because it incorporates products into the plots of shows. Although product placement has been around since the 1890s, when the Lumière brothers first placed Lever soap in their movies, the big boom in product placement began with the reality TV show *Survivor* in 2000 (Anderson, 2006). Since then, product placement has been a staple of prime-time entertainment. Reality TV shows such as *Project Runway* and *American Idol* are known for exhibiting products on screen, and talk-show host Oprah Winfrey made news in 2004 when she gave away new Pontiacs to her audience members (Stansky, 2008). Even children's shows are known to hock products; a new cartoon series recently began on Nickelodeon featuring characters that represent different Sketchers sneakers (Freidman, 2010).

Digital Media

Emerging digital media platforms such as the Internet and mobile phones have created many new advertising possibilities. The Internet, like TV and radio, offers free services in exchange for advertising exposure. However, unlike radio or TV, the Internet is a highly personalized experience that shares private information.

Viral Ads

As you read in Chapter 11 "The Internet and Social Media", new advertising techniques have become popular on the Internet. Advertisers have tried to capitalize on the shared-media phenomenon by creating viral ads that achieve spontaneous success online. Fewer than one in six ads that are intended to go viral actually succeed, so marketers have developed strategies to encourage an advertisement's viral potential. Successful spots focus on creativity rather than a hard-selling strategy and generally target a specific audience (Fox Business, 2010). Recent Old Spice ads featured former NFL player Isaiah Mustafa in a set of continuous scenes, from a shower room to a yacht. The commercial ends with the actor on horseback, a theatrical trick that left viewers wondering how the stunt was pulled off. As of July 2010, the ad was the most popular video on YouTube with more than 94 million views, and Old Spice sales had risen 106 percent (Neff, 2010).

Social Media

Social media sites such as Facebook use the information users provide on their profiles to generate targeted advertisements. For instance, if a person is a fan of Mariah Carey or joined a group associated with the singer, he or she might see announcements advertising her new CD or a local concert. While this may seem harmless, clicking on an ad sends user data to the advertising company, including name and user ID. Many people have raised privacy concerns over this practice, yet it remains in use. Free e-mail services such as Gmail also depend on targeted advertising for their survival. Indeed, advertising is the only way such services could continue. Given the ongoing privacy debates concerning targeted Internet advertising, a balance between a user's privacy and accessibility of services will have to be settled in the near future.

Mobile Phones

Mobile phones provide several different avenues for advertisers. The growing use of Internet radio through mobile-phone platforms has created a market for advertisements tapped by radio advertising networks such as TargetSpot. By using the radio advertising model for mobile phones, users receive increased radio broadcast options and advertisers reach new targeted markets (Marketwire, 2010).

Another development in the mobile-phone market is the use of advertising in smartphone apps. Free versions of mobile-phone applications often include advertising to pay for the service. Popular apps such as WeatherBug and Angry Birds offer free versions with ads in the margins; however, users can avoid these ads by paying a few dollars to upgrade to "Pro" versions. Other apps such as Foursquare access a user's geographic location and offer ads for businesses within walking distance (Fairlee, 2010).

Figure 12.9

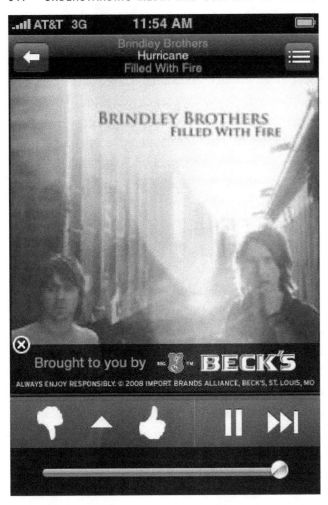

Free smartphone apps often contain ads to help pay for the service.

David Berkowitz – Beck's Campaign on Pandora iPhone App – Music Screen – CC BY 2.0.

Government Regulation of Advertising

Advertising regulation has played an important role in advertising's history and cultural influence. One of the earliest federal laws addressing advertising was the Pure Food and Drug Law of 1906. A reaction to public outcry over the false claims of patent medicines, this law required informational labels to be placed on these products. It did not, however, address the questionable aspects of the advertisements, so it did not truly delve into the issue of false advertising.[12]

The Formation of the FTC

Founded in 1914, the Federal Trade Commission (FTC) became responsible for regulating false advertising claims. Although federal laws concerning these practices made plaintiffs prove that actual harm was done by the advertisement, state laws passed during the early 1920s allowed prosecution of misleading advertisements regardless of harm done.[13] The National Association of Attorneys General has helped states remain an important part of advertising regulation. In 1995, 13 states passed laws that required sweepstakes companies to provide full disclosure of rules and details of contests (O'Guinn, et. al., 2009).

During the Great Depression, New Deal legislation threatened to outlaw any misleading advertising, a result of the burgeoning consumer movement and the public outcry against advertising during the period (Time, 1941). The reformers did not fully achieve their goals, but they did make a permanent mark on advertising history. The 1938 Wheeler-Lea Amendment expanded the FTC's role to protect consumers from deceptive advertising. Until this point, the FTC was responsible for addressing false advertising complaints from competitors. With this legislation, the agency also became an important resource for the consumer movement.

Truth in Advertising

In 1971, the FTC began the Advertising Substantiation Program to force advertisers to provide evidence for the claims in their advertisements. Under this program, the FTC gained the power to issue cease-and-desist orders to advertisers regarding specific ads in question and to order corrective advertising. Under this provision, the FTC can force a company to issue an advertisement acknowledging and correcting an earlier misleading ad. Regulations under this program established that supposed experts used in advertisements must be qualified experts in their field, and celebrities must actually use the products they endorse.[14] In 2006, Sunny Health Nutrition was brought to court for advertising height-enhancing pills called HeightMax. The FTC found the company had hired an actor to appear as an expert in its ads, and that the pills did not live up to their claim. Sunny Health Nutrition was forced to pay $375,000 to consumers for misrepresenting its product (Consumer Affairs, 2006).

In 1992, the FTC introduced guidelines defining terms such as *biodegradable* and *recyclable*. The growth of the environmental movement in the early 1990s led to an upsurge in environmental claims by manufacturers and advertisers. For example, Mobil Oil claimed their Hefty trash bags were biodegradable. While technically this statement is true, a 500- to 1,000-year decomposition cycle does not meet most people's definitions of the term (Lapidos, 2007). The FTC guidelines made such claims false by law (Schneider, 1992).

Regulation of the Internet

The FTC has also turned its attention to online advertising. The Children's Online Privacy Act of 1998 was passed to prohibit companies from obtaining the personal information of children who access websites or other online resources. Because of the youth orientation of the Internet, newer advertising techniques have drawn increasing criticism. Alcohol companies in particular have come under scrutiny. Beer manufacturer Heineken's online presence includes a virtual city in which users can own an apartment and use services such as e-mail. This practice mirrors that of children's advertising, in which companies often create virtual worlds to immerse children in their products. However, the age-verification requirements to participate in this type of environment are easily falsified and can lead to young children being exposed to more mature content (Gardner, 2010).

Consumer and privacy advocates who are concerned over privacy intrusions by advertisers have also called for Internet ad regulation. In 2009, the FTC acted on complaints against Sears that resulted in an injunction against the company for not providing sufficient disclosure. Sears offered $10 to consumers to download a program that tracked their Internet browsing. The FTC came down on Sears because the downloaded software tracked sensitive information that was not fully disclosed to the consumer. Similar consumer complaints against Facebook and

Google for their consumer tracking have, at present, not resulted in FTC actions; however, the growing outcry makes new regulation of Internet advertising likely (Shields, 2010).

Advertising's Influence on Culture

Discussing advertising's influence on culture raises a long-standing debate. One opinion states that advertising simply reflects the trends inherent in a culture, the other claims advertising takes an active role in shaping culture. Both ideas have merit and are most likely true to varying degrees.

Advertising and the Rise of Consumer Culture

George Babbitt, the protagonist of Sinclair Lewis's 1922 novel *Babbitt*, was a true believer in the growing American consumer culture:

Just as the priests of the Presbyterian Church determined his every religious belief…so did the national advertisers fix the surface of his life, fix what he believed to be his individuality. These standard advertised wares—toothpastes, socks, tires, cameras, instantaneous hot-water heaters—were his symbols and proofs of excellence; at first the signs, and then the substitutes, for joy and passion and wisdom (Lewis, 1922).

Although Lewis's fictional representation of a 1920s-era consumer may not be an actual person, it indicates the national consumer culture that was taking shape at the time. As it had always done, advertising sought to attach products to larger ideas and symbols of worth and cultural values. However, the rise of mass media and of the advertising models that these media embraced made advertising take on an increasingly influential cultural role.

Automobile ads of the 1920s portrayed cars as a new, free way of life rather than simply a means of transportation. Advertisers used new ideas about personal hygiene to sell products and ended up breaking taboos about public discussion of the body. The newly acknowledged epidemics of halitosis and body odor brought about products such as mouthwash and deodorant. A Listerine campaign of the era transformed bad breath from a nuisance into the mark of a sociopath (Ashenburg, 2008). Women's underwear and menstruation went from being topics unsuitable for most family conversations to being fodder for the pages of national magazines.[15]

Figure 12.10

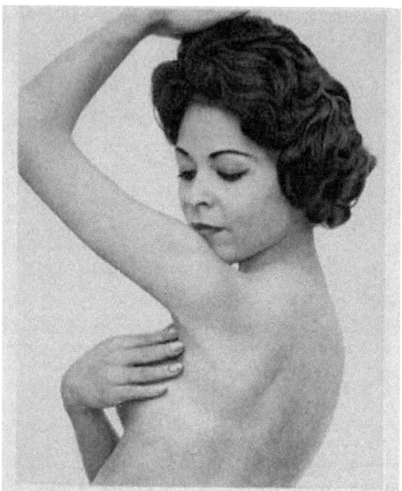

New Yodora helps keep you <u>bath-fresh</u> around the clock.

You are never daintier than when you step out of your bath or shower. Now a remarkably pure white deodorant helps you stay that way all day long. It's new Yodora—with hexachlorophene, world's number one deodorant. With Yodora's protection, you never need doubt you are at your fresh and dainty best all day long—the woman you want to be, the woman others expect you to be. Get new Yodora. It's gentle, but it works.

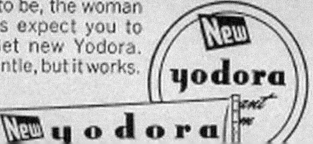

Advertisements for deodorants and other hygiene products broke social taboos about public discussion of hygiene.

Classic Film – 1964 Beauty Ad, Yodora Deodorant – CC BY-NC 2.0.

Creating the Modern World

World War I bond campaigns had made it clear that advertising could be used to influence public beliefs and values. Advertising focused on the new—making new products and ideas seem better than older ones and ushering in a sense of the modernity. In an address to the American Association of Advertising Agencies in 1926, President Coolidge went as far as to hold advertisers responsible for the "regeneration and redemption of mankind (Marchand, 1985)."

Up through the 1960s, most advertising agencies were owned and staffed by affluent white men, and advertising's portrayals of typical American families reflected this status quo. Mainstream culture as propagated by magazine, radio, and newspaper advertising was that of middle- or upper-class White suburban families (Marchand, 1985). This sanitized image of the suburban family, popularized in such TV programs as *Leave It to Beaver*, has been mercilessly satirized since the cultural backlash of the 1960s.

A great deal of that era's cultural criticism targeted the image of the advertiser as a manipulator and promulgator of superficial consumerism. When advertisers for Volkswagen picked up on this criticism, turned it to their advantage, and created a new set of consumer symbols that would come to represent an age of rebellion, they neatly co-opted the arguments against advertising for their own purposes. In many instances, advertising has functioned as a codifier of its own ideals by taking new cultural values and turning them into symbols of a new phase of consumerism. This is the goal of effective advertising.

Apple's 1984 campaign is one of the most well-known examples of defining a product in terms of new cultural trends. A fledgling company compared to computer giants IBM and Xerox, Apple spent nearly $2 million on a commercial that would end up only being aired once (McAloney, 1984). During the third quarter of the 1984 Super Bowl, viewers across the United States watched in amazement as an ad unlike any other at the time appeared on their TV screens. The commercial showed a drab gray auditorium where identical individuals sat in front of a large screen. On the screen was a man, addressing the audience with an eerily captivating voice. "We are one people, with one will," he droned. "Our enemies shall talk themselves to death. And we will bury them with their own confusion. We shall prevail (McAloney, 1984)!" While the audience sat motionlessly, one woman ran forward with a sledgehammer and threw it at the screen, causing it to explode in a flash of light and smoke. As the scene faded out, a narrator announced the product. "On January 24, Apple Computer will introduce the Macintosh. And you'll see why 1984 won't be like *1984* (Freidman, 1984)." With this commercial, Apple defined itself as a pioneer of the new generation. Instead of marketing its products as utilitarian tools, it advertised them as devices for combating conformity (Freidman, 1984). Over the next few decades, other companies imitated this approach, presenting their products as symbols of cultural values.

In his study of advertising's cultural impact, *The Conquest of Cool*, Thomas Frank compares the advertising of the 1960s with that of the early 1990s:

How [advertisers] must have rejoiced when the leading minds of the culture industry announced the discovery of an all-new angry generation, the "Twenty-Somethings," complete with a panoply of musical styles, hairdos, and verbal signifiers ready-made to rejuvenate advertising's sagging credibility.... The strangest aspect of what followed wasn't the immediate onslaught of even hipper advertising, but that the entire "Generation X" discourse repeated...the discussions of youth culture that had appeared in *Advertising Age, Madison Avenue*, and on all those youth-market panel discussions back in the sixties.[16]

To be clear, advertisers have not set out to consciously manipulate the public in the name of consumer culture. Rather, advertisers are simply doing their job—one that has had an enormous influence on culture.

Advertising Stereotypes

The White, middle-class composition of ad agencies contributed to advertisements' rare depictions of minority populations. DDB—the agency responsible for the Volkswagen ads of the 1960s—was an anomaly in this regard. One of its more popular ads was for Levy's rye bread. Most conventional advertisers would have ignored the ethnic aspects of this product and simply marketed it to a mainstream White audience. Instead, the innovative agency created an ad campaign that made ethnic diversity a selling point, with spots featuring individuals from a variety of racial backgrounds eating the bread with the headline "You don't have to be Jewish to love Levy's."

During the 1950s, stereotypical images of African Americans promulgated by advertisers began to draw criticism from civil rights leaders. Icons such as Aunt Jemima, the Cream of Wheat chef, and the Hiram Walker butler were some of the most recognizable black figures in U.S. culture. Unlike the African Americans who had gained fame through their artistry, scholarship, and athleticism, however, these advertising characters were famous for being domestic servants.

During the 1960s, meetings of the American Association of Advertising Agencies (AAAA) hosted civil rights leaders, and agencies began to respond to the criticisms of bias. A New York survey in the mid-1960s discovered that Blacks were underrepresented at advertising agencies. Many agencies responded by hiring new African American employees, and a number of Black-owned agencies started in the 1970s.[17]

Early advertising frequently reached out to women because they made approximately 80 percent of all consumer purchases. Thus, women were well represented in advertising. However, those depictions presented women in extremely narrow roles. Through the 1960s, ads targeting women generally showed them performing domestic duties such as cooking or cleaning, whereas ads targeting men often placed women in a submissive sexual role even if the product lacked any overt sexual connotation. A National Car Rental ad from the early 1970s featured a disheveled female employee in a chair with the headline "Go Ahead, Take Advantage of Us." Another ad from the 1970s pictured a man with new Dacron slacks standing on top of a woman, proclaiming, "It's nice to have a girl around the house (Frauenfelder, 2008)."

An advertising profile printed in *Advertising Age* magazine gave a typical advertiser's understanding of the housewife at the time:

She likes to watch TV and she does not enjoy reading a great deal. She is most easily reached through TV and the simple down-to-earth magazines.... Mental activity is arduous for her.... She is a person who wants to have things she can believe in rather than things she can think about (Rodnitzky, 1999).

The National Organization for Women (NOW) created a campaign during the early 1970s targeting the role of women in advertisements. Participants complained about the ads to networks and companies and even spray-painted slogans on offensive billboards in protest.

Representation of minorities and women in advertising has improved since the 1960s and '70s, but it still remains a problem. The 2010 Super Bowl drew one of the most diverse audiences ever recorded for the event, including a 45 percent female audience. Yet the commercials remained focused strictly on men. And of 67 ads shown during the game, only four showed minority actors in a lead role. Despite the obvious economic benefit of diversity in marketing, advertising practices have resisted change (Ali, 2010).

Advertising to Children

The majority of advertisements that target children feature either toys or junk food. Children under the age of eight typically lack the ability to distinguish between fantasy and reality, and many advertisers use this to their advantage. Studies have shown that most children-focused food advertisements feature high-calorie, low-nutrition foods such as sugary cereals. Although the government regulates advertising to children to a degree, the Internet has introduced new means of marketing to youth that have not been addressed. Online video games called advergames feature famous child-oriented products. The games differ from traditional advertising, however, because the children playing them will experience a much longer period of product exposure than they do from the typical 30-second TV commercial. Child advocacy groups have been pushing for increased regulation of advertising to children, but it remains to be seen whether this will take place (Calvert, 2008).

Positive Effects of Advertising

Although many people focus on advertising's negative outcomes, the medium has provided unique benefits over time. Early newspaper advertising allowed newspapers to become independent of church and government control, encouraging the development of a free press with the ability to criticize powerful interests. When newspapers and magazines moved to an advertising model, these publications became accessible to large groups of people who previously could not afford them. Advertising also contributed to radio's and TV's most successful eras. Radio's golden age in the 1940s and TV's golden age in the 1950s both took place when advertisers were creating or heavily involved with the production of most of the programs.

Advertising also makes newer forms of media both useful and accessible. Many Internet services, such as e-mail and smartphone applications, are only free because they feature advertising. Advertising allows promoters and service providers to reduce and sometimes eliminate the upfront purchase price, making these services available to a greater number of people and allowing lower economic classes to take part in mass culture.

Advertising has also been a longtime promoter of the arts. During the Renaissance, painters and composers often relied on wealthy patrons or governments to promote their work. Corporate advertising has given artists new means to fund their creative efforts. In addition, many artists and writers have been able to support themselves by working for advertisers. The use of music in commercials, particularly in recent years, has provided musicians with notoriety and income. Indeed, it is hard to imagine the cultural landscape of the United States without advertising.

Key Takeaways

- Advertising has existed since ancient times but began to take on its modern form during the Age of Exploration. By the 19th century, newspapers and magazines had begun printing advertising to generate needed revenues.

- Although many considered advertising to be lowbrow or immoral up to the early 20th century, it saw greater acceptance after its use during World War I to encourage support for the war.

- Up to the mid-20th century, advertising featured stereotypical affluent White families and was sale driven. Criticism of advertiser manipulation became the basis of a new style of advertising during the creative revolution of the 1960s.

- The rise of the Internet has caused print advertising revenues to decline but allows for personally targeted ads. Such tracking practices have aroused concern from privacy groups.

- The Federal Trade Commission is charged with ensuring that advertisements make verifiable claims and do not overtly mislead consumers.

- Advertising has infused American culture with mass images and ideas, creating a nation of consumers and shaping how people view themselves and others.

Exercises

Please answer the following short-answer questions. Each response should be a minimum of one paragraph.

1. What are the important eras in the history of American advertising?
2. How does government regulation affect advertising?
3. What types of advertising are in use today?
4. What influence does advertising have on American consumerism and culture?
5. How has advertising affected newspapers?

[1]Mierau, 42.

[2]Hood, 28–51.

[3]Fox, 74–77.

[4]Fox, 89.

[5]Fox, 121–124.

[6]Fox, 168.

[7]Fox, 173.

[8]Fox, 210–215.

[9]Frank, 60–67, 159.

[10]Fox, 324–325.

[11]Klein, 12–22.

[12]Fox, 65–66.

[13]Hood, 74–75.

[14]O'Guinn, Allen, and Semenik, 131–137.

[15]Fox, 95–96.

[16]Frank, 233–235.

[17]Fox, 278–284.

References

Ali, Sam. "New Study: Super Bowl Ads Created by White Men," *DiversityInc.com*, May 10, 2010., http://www.diversityinc.com/article/7566/New-Study-Super-Bowl-Ads-Created-by-White-Men/.

All Classic Ads, "Advertising Timeline," Vintage Collection, All Classic Ads, http://www.allclassicads.com/advertising-timeline.html.

Anderson, Nate. "Product placement in the DVR era," *Ars Technica* (blog), March 19, 2006, http://arstechnica.com/gadgets/news/2006/03/productplacement.ars.

Applegate, Edd. *Personalities and Products: A Historical Perspective on Advertising in America* (Westport, CT: Greenwood Press, 1998), 57–64.

Ashenburg, Katherine. *The Dirt on Clean: An Unsanitized History* (Toronto: Vintage Canada, 2008), 245–247.

Boddy, William. "The Seven Dwarfs and the Money Grubbers: The Public Relations Crisis of US Television in the Late 1950s," in *Logics of Television: Essays in Cultural Criticism*, ed. Patricia Mellencamp (Bloomington, IN: Indiana University Press, 1990), 110.

Burgan, Read G. "Radio Fun with Fibber McGee and Molly," RGB Digital Audio, January 24, 1996, http://www.rgbdigitalaudio.com/OTR_Reviews/Fibber_McGee_OTRArticle.htm.

Calvert, Sandra. "Children as Consumers: Advertising and Marketing," *The Future of Children* 18, no. 1 (Spring 2008): 205–211.

ConsumerAffairs.com, "Feds Slam 'Height-Enhancing' Pills," November 29, 2006, http://www.consumeraffairs.com/news04/2006/11/ftc_chitosan.html.

Dictionary.com, s.v. "Advertising," http://dictionary.reference.com/browse/advertising.

Fairlee, Rik. "Smartphone Users Go for Location-Based Apps," *PC Magazine*, May 18, 2010, http://www.pcmag.com/article2/0,2817,2363899,00.asp.

Fox Business, "Old Spice and E*TRADE Ads Provide Lessons in Viral Marketing," March 17, 2010, http://www.foxbusiness.com/story/markets/industries/finance/old-spice-etrade-ads-provide-lessons-viral-marketing/.

Fox, Stephen. *The Mirror Makers* (New York: William Morrow, 1984), 41–46.

Frank, Thomas. *The Conquest of Cool* (Chicago: University of Chicago Press, 1998), 41.

Frauenfelder, Mark. "Creepy Slacks Ad From 1970," *Boing Boing*, (blog), May 12, 2008, http://boingboing.net/2008/05/12/creepy-slacks-ad-fro.html.

Friedman, Ted. "Apple's *1984*: The Introduction of the Macintosh in the Cultural History of Personal Computers," http://www.duke.edu/~tlove/mac.htm.

Friedman, Wayne. "Product Placement in Kids' TV Programs: Stuff Your Footwear Can Slip On," TV Watch, September 16, 2010, http://www.mediapost.com/publications/?fa=Articles.showArticle&art_aid=135873.

Gallagher, James. "Duke Study: TiVo Doesn't Hurt TV Advertising," *Triangle Business Journal*, May 3, 2010, 20advertisinghttp://www.bizjournals.com/triangle/stories/2010/05/03/daily6.html.

Gardner, Amanda. "Alcohol Companies Use New Media to Lure Young Drinkers: Report," *Bloomberg BusinessWeek*, May 19, 2010, http://www.businessweek.com/lifestyle/content/healthday/639266.html.

Gartrell, Ellen. "More About Early Advertising Publications," Digital Collections, Duke University Libraries, http://library.duke.edu/digitalcollections/eaa/printlit.html.

Hood, John. *Selling the Dream: Why Advertising Is Good Business* (Westport, CT: Praeger, 2005), 12–13.

Hornblower, Margot. "Wake Up and Smell the Protest," *Time*, April 17, 2000.

Ionescu, Daniel. "Google Billboard Ads Gun for Microsoft and Promote Google Apps," *PC World*, August 3, 2009, http://www.pcworld.com/article/169475/google_billboard_ads_gun_for_microsoft_and_promote_google_apps.html.

JackBennyShow.com, "Jell-O," Jack Benny Show, http://jackbennyshow.com/index_090.htm.

Klein, Naomi. *No Logo* (New York: Picador, 2002), 14.

Lapidos, Juliet. "Will My Plastic Bag Still Be Here in 2507?" *Slate*, June 27, 2007, http://www.slate.com/id/2169287.

Lewis, Sinclair. *Babbitt* (New York: Harcourt, Brace, and Co., 1922), 95.

Marchand, Roland. *Advertising the American Dream: Making Way for Modernity, 1920–1940* (Berkeley: University of California Press, 1985), 7–9.

Marketwire, "TargetSpot Enters the Mobile Advertising Market," news release, *SmartBrief*, February 23, 2010, http://www.smartbrief.com/news/aaaa/industryMW-detail.jsp?id=4217DD5E-932F-460E-BE30-4988E17DEFEC.

McAloney, Curt. "The 1984 Apple Commercial: The Making of a Legend," Curt's Media, http://www.curtsmedia.com/cine/1984.html.

Mierau, Christina B. *Accept No Substitutes: The History of American Advertising* (Minneapolis, MN: Lerner, 2000), 7–8.

Neff, Jack. "How Much Old Spice Body Wash Has the Old Spice Guy Sold?" *AdvertisingAge*, July 26, 2010, http://adage.com/article?article_id=145096.

New York Times, "How MTV Has Rocked Television Commercials," October 9, 1989, http://www.nytimes.com/1989/10/09/business/the-media-business-how-mtv-has-rocked-television-commercials.html.

O'Barr, William M. "A Brief History of Advertising in America," *Advertising & Society Review* 6, no. 3 (2005), http://muse.jhu.edu/journals/asr/v006/6.3unit02.html.

O'Guinn, Thomas, Chris Allen, and Richard Semenik, *Advertising and Integrated Brand Promotion* (Mason, OH: Cengage Learning, 2009), 133.

Rodnitzky, Jerome. *Feminist Phoenix: The Rise and Fall of a Feminist Counterculture* (Westport, CT: Praeger, 1999), 114–115.

Samuel, Lawrence. *Brought to You By: Postwar Television Advertising and the American Dream* (Austin, TX: University of Texas Press, 2001), 88–94.

Schneider, Keith. "Guides on Environmental Ad Claims," *New York Times*, July 29, 1992, http://www.nytimes.com/1992/07/29/business/guides-on-environmental-ad-claims.html.

Shields, Mike. "Pitching Self-Regulation," *Adweek*, February 15, 2010.

Stansky, Tanner. "14 Milestones in TV Product Placement," *Entertainment Weekly*, July 28, 2008, http://www.ew.com/ew/article/0,,20215225,00.html.

Sterling, Bruce. "More Newspaper Calamity," *Wired*, March 15, 2010, http://www.wired.com/beyond_the_beyond/2010/03/more-newspaper-calamity/.

Time, "The Press: Advertising v. New Deal," September 1, 1941, http://www.time.com/time/magazine/article/0,9171,850703,00.html.

Vance, Jennifer. "Extra, Extra, Read All About It!" *Penny Press*, http://iml.jou.efl.edu/projects/Spring04/vance/pennypress.html.

12.2 Public Relations

Whereas advertising is the paid use of media space to sell something, public relations (PR) is the attempt to establish and maintain good relations between an organization and its constituents (Theaker, 2004). Practically, PR campaigns strive to use the free press to encourage favorable coverage. In their book *The Fall of Advertising and the Rise of PR*, Al and Laura Ries make the point that the public trusts the press far more than they trust advertisements. Because of this, PR efforts that get products and brands into the press are far more valuable than a simple advertisement. Their book details the ways in which modern companies use public relations to far greater benefit than they use advertising (Ries & Ries, 2004). Regardless of the fate of advertising, PR has clearly come to have an increasing role in marketing and ad campaigns.

The Four Models of PR

Table 12.1 Grunig and Hunt's Four PR Models

Type of Model	Description	Example
Traditional publicity model (the press agentry model)	Professional agents seek media coverage for a client, product, or event.	Thong-clad actor Sacha Baron Cohen promotes *Bruno* by landing in Eminem's lap at the 2009 MTV Video Music Awards.
Public information model	Businesses communicate information to gain desired results.	Colleges send informational brochures to potential students; a company includes an "about" section on its website.
Persuasive communication model (the two-way asymmetric model)	Organizations attempt to persuade an audience to take a certain point of view.	Public service announcements like the one that shows "your brain" and "your brain on drugs."
Two-way symmetric model	Both parties make use of a back-and-forth discussion.	A company sends out customer satisfaction surveys; company Facebook groups and message boards.

Source: James E. Grunig and Todd Hunt, Managing Public Relations (Belmont, CA: Wadsworth Publishing, 1984).

Todd Hunt and James Grunig developed a theory of four models of PR. This model has held up in the years since its development and is a good introduction to PR concepts (Grunig & Hunt, 1984).

Traditional Publicity Model

Under the traditional publicity model, PR professionals seek to create media coverage for a client, product, or event. These efforts can range from wild publicity stunts to simple news conferences to celebrity interviews in fashion magazines. P. T. Barnum was an early American practitioner of this kind of PR. His outrageous attempts at publicity worked because he was not worried about receiving negative press; instead, he believed that any coverage was a valuable asset. More recent examples of this style of extreme publicity include controversy-courting musicians such as Lady Gaga and Marilyn Manson. More restrained examples of this type of PR include the modern phenomenon of faded celebrities appearing on TV shows, such as Paula Abdul's long-running appearances on *American Idol*.

Public Information Model

The goal of the public information model is to release information to a constituency. This model is less concerned with obtaining dramatic, extensive media coverage than with disseminating information in a way that ensures adequate reception. For example, utility companies often include fliers about energy efficiency with customers' bills, and government agencies such as the IRS issue press releases to explain changes to existing codes. In addition, public interest groups release the results of research studies for use by policy makers and the public.

Persuasive Communication: Two-Way Asymmetric

The persuasive communication model, or the two-way asymmetric, works to persuade a specific audience to adopt a certain behavior or point of view. To be considered effective, this model requires a measured response from its intended audience.

Figure 12.12

Edward Bernays created campaigns using the persuasive communication model.

chrisch_ – Rule the World! – CC BY-NC 2.0.

Government propaganda is a good example of this model. Propaganda is the organized spreading of information to assist or weaken a cause (Dictionary). Edward Bernays has been called the founder of modern PR for his work during World War I promoting the sale of war bonds. One of the first professional PR experts, Bernays made the two-way asymmetric model his early hallmark. In a famous campaign for Lucky Strike cigarettes, he convinced a group of well-known celebrities to walk in the New York Easter parade smoking Lucky Strikes. Most modern corporations employ the persuasive communication model.

Two-Way Symmetric Model

The two-way symmetric model requires true communication between the parties involved. By facilitating a back-and-forth discussion that results in mutual understanding and an agreement that respects the wishes of both parties, this PR model is often practiced in town hall meetings and other public forums in which the public has a real effect on the results. In an ideal republic, Congressional representatives strictly employ this model. Many nonprofit groups that are run by boards and have public service mandates use this model to ensure continued public support.

Commercial ventures also rely on this model. PR can generate media attention or attract customers, and it can also ease communication between a company and its investors, partners, and employees. The two-way symmetric model is useful in communicating within an organization because it helps employees feel they are an important part of the company. Investor relations are also often carried out under this model.

PR Functions

Either private PR companies or in-house communications staffers carry out PR functions. A PR group generally handles all aspects of an organization's or individual's media presence, including company publications and press releases. Such a group can range from just one person to dozens of employees depending on the size and scope of the organization.

PR functions include the following:

- Media relations: takes place with media outlets
- Internal communications: occurs within a company between management and employees, and among subsidiaries of the same company
- Business-to-business: happens between businesses that are in partnership
- Public affairs: takes place with community leaders, opinion formers, and those involved in public issues
- Investor relations: occurs with investors and shareholders
- Strategic communication: intended to accomplish a specific goal
- Issues management: keeping tabs on public issues important to the organization
- Crisis management: handling events that could damage an organization's image[1]

Anatomy of a PR Campaign

Figure 12.13

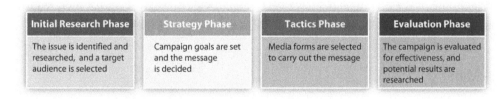

Anatomy of a PR campaign

PR campaigns occur for any number of reasons. They can be a quick response to a crisis or emerging issue, or they can stem from a long-term strategy tied in with other marketing efforts. Regardless of its purpose, a typical campaign often involves four phases.

Initial Research Phase

The first step of many PR campaigns is the initial research phase. First, practitioners identify and qualify the issue to be addressed. Then, they research the organization itself to clarify issues of public perception, positioning, and internal dynamics. Strategists can also research the potential audience of the campaign. This audience may include media outlets, constituents, consumers, and competitors. Finally, the context of the campaign is often researched, including the possible consequences of the campaign and the potential effects on the organization. After considering all of these factors, practitioners are better educated to select the best type of campaign.

Strategy Phase

During the strategy phase, PR professionals usually determine objectives focused on the desired goal of the campaign and formulate strategies to meet those objectives. Broad strategies such as deciding on the overall message of a campaign and the best way to communicate the message can be finalized at this time.

Tactics Phase

During the tactics phase, the PR group decides on the means to implement the strategies they formulated during the strategy phase. This process can involve devising specific communication techniques and selecting the forms of media that suit the message best. This phase may also address budgetary restrictions and possibilities.

Evaluation Phase

After the overall campaign has been determined, PR practitioners enter the evaluation phase. The group can review their campaign plan and evaluate its potential effectiveness. They may also conduct research on the potential results to better understand the cost and benefits of the campaign. Specific criteria for evaluating the campaign when it is completed are also established at this time (Smith, 2002).

Examples of PR Campaigns

Since its modern inception in the early 20th century, PR has turned out countless campaigns—some highly successful, others dismal failures. Some of these campaigns have become particularly significant for their lasting influence or creative execution. This section describes a few notable PR campaigns over the years.

Diamonds for the Common Man

During the 1930s, the De Beers company had an enormous amount of diamonds and a relatively small market of luxury buyers. They launched a PR campaign to change the image of diamonds from a luxury good into an accessible and essential aspect of American life. The campaign began by giving diamonds to famous movie stars, using their built-in publicity networks to promote De Beers. The company created stories about celebrity proposals and gifts between lovers that stressed the size of the diamonds given. These stories were then given out to selected fashion magazines. The result of this campaign was the popularization of diamonds as one of the necessary aspects of a marriage proposal (Reid, 2006).

Big Tobacco Aids Researchers

Figure 12.14

Grimault's Indian Cigarettes for asthma

Recommended by Medical Authorities for the immediate relief of Asthma and Bronchial trouble, Hay Fever, Laryngitis and Irritation of the air passages.

GRIMAULT'S CIGARETTES

ease the feeling of tightness across the chest and give a relief from gasping for breath.

GRIMAULT & Cⁱᵉ, 8, r. Vivienne, Paris.

In response to the increasing number of health concerns surrounding smoking, tobacco companies began
running ads that argued the benefits of smoking their brand.

In 1953, studies showing the detrimental health effects of smoking caused a drop in cigarette sales. An alliance of
tobacco manufacturers hired the PR group Hill & Knowlton to develop a campaign to deal with this problem. The
first step of the campaign Hill & Knowlton devised was the creation of the Tobacco Industry Research Committee
(TIRC) to promote studies that questioned the health effects of tobacco use. The TIRC ran advertisements
featuring the results of these studies, giving journalists who were addressing the subject an easy source to quote.
The groups working against smoking were not familiar with media relations, making it harder for journalists to
quote them and use their arguments.

The campaign was effective, however, not because it denied the harmful effects of smoking but because it
stressed the disagreements between researchers. By providing the press with information favorable to the tobacco
manufacturers and publicly promoting new filtered cigarettes, the campaign aimed to replace the idea that
smoking was undeniably bad with the idea that there was disagreement over the effects of smoking. This strategy
served tobacco companies well up through the 1980s.

Taco Bell Targets *Mir*

When the Russian space station *Mir* was set to crash land in the Pacific Ocean in 2001, Taco Bell created a floating
vinyl target that the company placed in the Pacific. Taco Bell promised to give every American a free taco if the
space station hit the target. This simple PR stunt gave all the journalists covering the *Mir* crash landing a few lines
to add to their stories. Scientists even speculated on the chances of the station hitting the target—slim to none.
Ultimately, the stunt gained Taco Bell global advertising (BBC World, 2001).

PR as a Replacement for Advertising

In some cases, PR has begun overtaking advertising as the preferred way of promoting a particular company or
product. For example, the tobacco industry offers a good case study of the migration from advertising to PR.
Regulations prohibiting radio and TV cigarette advertisements had an enormous effect on sales. In response, the
tobacco industry began using PR techniques to increase brand presence.

Tobacco company Philip Morris started underwriting cultural institutions and causes as diverse as the Joffrey
Ballet, the Smithsonian, environmental awareness, and health concerns. Marlboro sponsored events that brought a
great deal of media attention to the brand. For example, during the 1980s, the Marlboro Country Music Tour took
famous country stars to major coliseums throughout the country and featured talent contests that brought local
bands up on stage, increasing the audience even further. Favorable reviews of the shows generated positive press
for Marlboro. Later interviews with country artists and books on country music history have also mentioned this
tour.

On the fifth anniversary of the Vietnam Veterans Memorial in 1987, Marlboro's PR groups organized a celebration
hosted by comedian Bob Hope. Country music legends the Judds and Alabama headlined the show, and Marlboro
paid for new names inscribed on the memorial. By attaching the Marlboro brand to such an important cultural

event, the company gained an enormous amount of publicity. Just as importantly, these efforts at least partially restored the stature that the brand lost due to health concerns (Saffir, 2000).

Branding

While advertising is an essential aspect of initial brand creation, PR campaigns are vital to developing the more abstract aspects of a brand. These campaigns work to position a brand in the public arena in order to give it a sense of cultural importance.

Shift From Advertising to PR

Pioneered by such companies as Procter & Gamble during the 1930s, the older, advertising-centric model of branding focused on the product, using advertisements to associate a particular branded good with quality or some other positive cultural value. Yet, as consumers became exposed to ever-increasing numbers of advertisements, traditional advertising's effectiveness dwindled. The ubiquity of modern advertising means the public is skeptical of—or even ignores—claims advertisers make about their products. This credibility gap can be overcome, however, when PR professionals using good promotional strategies step in.

The new PR-oriented model of branding focuses on the overall image of the company rather than on the specific merits of the product. This branding model seeks to associate a company with specific personal and cultural values that hold meaning for consumers. In the early 1990s, for example, car company Saturn marketed its automobiles not as a means of transportation but as a form of culture. PR campaigns promoted the image of the Saturn family, associating the company with powerful American values and giving Saturn owners a sense of community. Events such as the 1994 Saturn homecoming sought to encourage this sense of belonging. Some 45,000 people turned out for this event; families gave up their beach holidays simply to come to a Saturn manufacturing plant in Tennessee to socialize with other Saturn owners and tour the facility.

Recently Toyota faced a marketing crisis when it instituted a massive recall based on safety issues. To counter the bad press, the company launched a series of commercials featuring top Toyota executives, urging the public to keep their faith in the brand (Bernstein, 2010). Much like the Volkswagen ads half a century before, Toyota used a style of self-awareness to market its automobiles. The positive PR campaign presented Toyotas as cars with a high standard of excellence, backed by a company striving to meet customers' needs.

Studies in Success: Apple and Nike

Apple has also employed this type of branding with great effectiveness. By focusing on a consistent design style in which every product reinforces the Apple experience, the computer company has managed to position itself as a mark of individuality. Despite the cynical outlook of many Americans regarding commercial claims, the notion that Apple is a symbol of individualism has been adopted with very little irony. Douglas Atkin, who has written about brands as a form of cult, readily admits and embraces his own brand loyalty to Apple:

I'm a self-confessed Apple loyalist. I go to a cafe around the corner to do some thinking and writing, away from the hurly-burly of the office, and everyone in that cafe has a Mac. We never mention the fact that we all have Macs. The other people in the cafe are writers and professors and in the media, and the feeling of cohesion and community in that cafe becomes very apparent if someone comes in with a PC. There's almost an observable shiver of consternation in the cafe, and it must be discernable to the person with the PC, because they never come back.

Brand managers that once focused on the product now find themselves in the role of community leaders, responsible for the well-being of a cultural image (Atkin, 2004).

Kevin Roberts, the current CEO of Saatchi & Saatchi Worldwide, a branding-focused creative organization, has used the term "lovemark" as an alternative to trademark. This term encompasses brands that have created "loyalty beyond reason," meaning that consumers feel loyal to a brand in much the same way they would toward friends or family members. Creating a sense of mystery around a brand generates an aura that bypasses the usual cynical take on commercial icons. A great deal of Apple's success comes from the company's mystique. Apple has successfully developed PR campaigns surrounding product releases that leak selected rumors to various press outlets but maintain secrecy over essential details, encouraging speculation by bloggers and mainstream journalists on the next product. All this combines to create a sense of mystery and an emotional anticipation for the product's release.

Emotional connections are crucial to building a brand or lovemark. An early example of this kind of branding was Nike's product endorsement deal with Michael Jordan during the 1990s. Jordan's amazing, seemingly magical performances on the basketball court created his immense popularity, which was then further built up by a host of press outlets and fans who developed an emotional attachment to Jordan. As this connection spread throughout the country, Nike associated itself with Jordan and also with the emotional reaction he inspired in people. Essentially, the company inherited a PR machine that had been built around Jordan and that continued to function until his retirement (Roberts, 2003).

Branding Backlashes

An important part of maintaining a consistent brand is preserving the emotional attachment consumers have to that brand. Just as PR campaigns build brands, PR crises can damage them. For example, the massive Gulf of Mexico oil spill in 2010 became a PR nightmare for BP, an oil company that had been using PR to rebrand itself as an environmentally friendly energy company.

In 2000, BP began a campaign presenting itself as "Beyond Petroleum," rather than British Petroleum, the company's original name. By acquiring a major solar company, BP became the world leader in solar production and in 2005 announced it would invest $8 billion in alternative energy over the following 10 years. BP's marketing firm developed a PR campaign that, at least on the surface, emulated the forward-looking two-way symmetric PR model. The campaign conducted interviews with consumers, giving them an opportunity to air their grievances and publicize energy policy issues. BP's website featured a carbon footprint calculator consumers could use to calculate the size of their environmental impact (Solman, 2008). The single explosion on BP's deep-water oil rig in the Gulf of Mexico essentially nullified the PR work of the previous 10 years, immediately putting BP at the bottom of the list of environmentally concerned companies.

A company's control over what its brand symbolizes can also lead to branding issues. The Body Shop, a cosmetics company that gained popularity during the 1980s and early 1990s, used PR to build its image as a company that created natural products and took a stand on issues of corporate ethics. The company teamed up with Greenpeace and other environmental groups to promote green issues and increase its natural image.

By the mid-1990s, however, revelations about the unethical treatment of franchise owners called this image into serious question. The Body Shop had spent a great deal of time and money creating its progressive, spontaneous image. Stories of travels to exotic locations to research and develop cosmetics were completely fabricated, as was the company's reputation for charitable contributions. Even the origins of the company had been made up as a PR tool: The idea, name, and even product list had been ripped off from a small California chain called the Body Shop that was later given a settlement to keep quiet. The PR campaign of the Body Shop made it one of the great success stories of the early 1990s, but the unfounded nature of its PR claims undermined its image dramatically. Competitor L'Oréal eventually bought the Body Shop for a fraction of its previous value (Entine, 2007).

Other branding backlashes have plagued companies such as Nike and Starbucks. By building their brands into global symbols, both companies also came to represent unfettered capitalist greed to those who opposed them. During the 1999 World Trade Organization protests in Seattle, activists targeted Starbucks and Nike stores for physical attacks such as window smashing. Labor activists have also condemned Nike over the company's use of sweatshops to manufacture shoes. Eventually, Nike created a vice president for corporate responsibility to deal with sweatshop issues.[2]

Blackspot: The Antibrand Brand

Adbusters, a publication devoted to reducing advertising's influence on global culture, added action to its criticisms of Nike by creating its own shoe. Manufactured in union shops, Blackspot shoes contain recycled tire rubber and hemp fabric. The Blackspot logo is a simple round dot that looks like it has been scribbled with white paint, as if a typical logo had been covered over. The shoes also include a symbolic red dot on the toe with which to kick Nike. Blackspot shoes use the Nike brand to create their own antibrand, symbolizing progressive labor reform and environmentally sustainable business practices (New York Times, 2004).

Figure 12.16

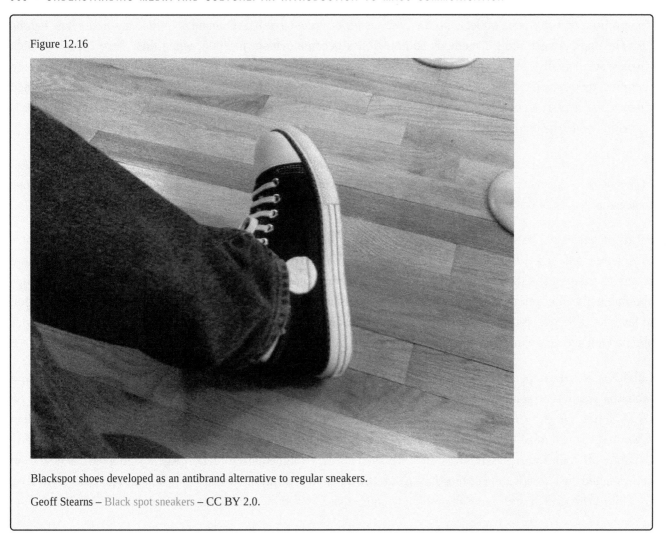

Blackspot shoes developed as an antibrand alternative to regular sneakers.

Geoff Stearns – Black spot sneakers – CC BY 2.0.

Relationship With Politics and Government

Politics and PR have gone hand in hand since the dawn of political activity. Politicians communicate with their constituents and make their message known using PR strategies. Benjamin Franklin's trip as ambassador to France during the American Revolution stands as an early example of political PR that followed the publicity model. At the time of his trip, Franklin was an international celebrity, and the fashionable society of Paris celebrated his arrival; his choice of a symbolic American-style fur cap immediately inspired a new style of women's wigs. Franklin also took a printing press with him to produce leaflets and publicity notices that circulated through Paris's intellectual and fashionable circles. Such PR efforts eventually led to a treaty with France that helped the colonists win their freedom from Great Britain (Isaacson, 2003).

Famous 20th-century PR campaigns include President Franklin D. Roosevelt's Fireside Chats, a series of radio addresses that explained aspects of the New Deal. Roosevelt's personal tone and his familiarity with the medium of radio helped the Fireside Chats become an important promotional tool for his administration and its programs. These chats aimed to justify many New Deal policies, and they helped the president bypass the press and speak directly to the people. More recently, Blackwater Worldwide, a private military company, dealt with criticisms of its actions in Iraq by changing its name. The new name, Xe Services, was the result of a large-scale PR campaign to distance the company from associations with civilian violence (Associated Press, 2009).

The proliferation of media outlets and the 24-hour news cycle have led to changes in the way politicians handle PR. The gap between old PR methods and new ones became evident in 2006, when then–Vice President Dick Cheney accidentally shot a friend during a hunting trip. Cheney, who had been criticized in the past for being secretive, did not make a statement about the accident for three days. Republican consultant Rich Galen explained Cheney's silence as an older PR tactic that tries to keep the discussion out of the media. However, the old trick is less effective in the modern digital world.

That entire doctrine has come and gone. Now the doctrine is you respond instantaneously, and where possible with a strong counterattack. A lot of that is because of the Internet, a lot of that is because of cable TV news (Associated Press, 2006).

PR techniques have been used in propaganda efforts throughout the 20th century. During the 1990s, the country of Kuwait employed Hill & Knowlton to encourage U.S. involvement in the Persian Gulf region. One of the more infamous examples of their campaign was a heavily reported account by a Kuwaiti girl testifying that Iraqi troops had dumped babies out of incubators in Kuwaiti hospitals. Outrage over this testimony helped galvanize opinion in favor of U.S. involvement. As it turned out, the Kuwaiti girl was really the daughter of the Kuwaiti ambassador and had not actually witnessed any of the alleged atrocities (Parsons, 2005).

Lobbyists also attempt to influence public policy using PR campaigns. The Water Environment Federation, a lobbying group representing the sewage industry, initiated a campaign to promote the application of sewage on farms during the early 1990s. The campaign came up with the word *biosolids* to replace the term *sludge*. Then it worked to encourage the use of this term as a way to popularize sewage as a fertilizer, providing information to public officials and representatives. In 1992, the U.S. Environmental Protection Agency adopted the new term and changed the classification of biosolids to a fertilizer from a hazardous waste. This renaming helped New York City eliminate tons of sewage by shipping it to states that allowed biosolids (Stauber & Rampton, 1995).

Political Branding

Politics has also embraced branding. Former President Bill Clinton described his political battles in terms of a brand war:

[The Republicans] were brilliant at branding. They said they were about values…. Everybody is a values voter, but they got the brand…they said they were against the death tax…what a great brand…. I did a disservice to the American people not by putting forth a bad plan, but by not being a better brander, not being able to explain it better (Kiley, 2008).

Branding has been used to great effect in recent elections. A consistently popular political brand is that of the outsider, or reform-minded politician. Despite his many years of service in the U.S. Senate, John McCain famously adopted this brand during the 2008 presidential election. McCain's competitor, Barack Obama, also employed branding strategies. The Obama campaign featured several iconic portraits and slogans that made for a consistent brand and encouraged his victory in 2008. Before Obama's inauguration in January 2009, an unprecedented amount of merchandise was sold, a further testament to the power of branding (Alberts, 2009).

Figure 12.17

The 2008 Obama campaign used logos as a way to publicize Obama's brand.

Phillip Jeffrey – Obama '08 Logo – CC BY-NC-ND 2.0.

Branding as a New Form of Communication

That so many different groups have adopted branding as a means of communication is a testament to its ubiquity. Even anticommercial, antibrand groups such as *Adbusters* have created brands to send messages. Social media sites have also encouraged branding techniques by allowing users to create profiles of themselves that they use to communicate their core values. This personal application is perhaps the greatest evidence of the impact of advertising and PR on modern culture. Branding, once a technique used by companies to sell their products, has become an everyday means of communication.

Key Takeaways

- The four models of PR include traditional publicity, public information, persuasive communication, and two-way symmetrical models.
- PR campaigns begin with a research phase, develop objectives during a strategy phase, formulate ways to meet objectives during the tactics phase, and assess the proposed campaign during the evaluation phase.
- Branding focuses on the lifestyles and values inherent in a brand's image as opposed to the products that are manufactured. It can be quickly undone by PR crises such as the BP oil spill.
- PR has always been an important part of political campaigning and activity. In recent years, branding has become an important part of national political campaigns.

Exercises

Please answer the following short-answer questions. Each response should be a minimum of one paragraph.

1. What are the four models of PR and the four stages of a typical PR campaign?

2. Analyze the role (or roles) of PR in media and culture.

3. In what ways is PR taking the place of traditional advertising?

4. What is branding and how is it important to PR?

5. How is PR used in the news media?

6. In which ways is PR used in politics?

End-of-Chapter Assessment

Review Questions

1.
Section 1

a. How did advertising shape early consumer culture during the 1920s?

b. Explain how government legislation has regulated advertisements and their claims.

c. How did the creative revolution of the 1960s change advertising?

d. How did the multiple-sponsor format change TV?

e. Give an example of a digital media format and explain how it has incorporated advertising.

2.
Section 2

a. What PR model did P. T. Barnum utilize the most?

b. Which phase of a PR campaign involves creating objectives?

c. What was the focus of BP's PR campaign before the 2010 oil spill?

d. What are some of the key components of Apple's branding strategy?

e. How would you describe Barack Obama's brand during the 2008 presidential campaign?

Critical Thinking Questions

1. Do you think that government regulation of advertising is justified? Explain your answer.

2. In your opinion, would most Americans give up their privacy in order to retain free, advertiser-supported services such as e-mail? Explain your answer.

3. Do you think that print media can survive without traditional forms of advertising? Explain your answer.

4. How do you think branding has affected American culture?

5. How has branding affected political discourse in the United States?

Career Connection

Advertising has had an enormous influence on the ways that people present and imagine themselves. Personal branding has become an industry, with consultants and coaches ready to help anyone find his or her own brand. Creating a personal brand is a useful way to assess your skills and feelings about the advertising or PR professions.

Research the term *personal brand* using a search engine. Look for strategies that would help you construct your own brand. Imagine that you are a brand and describe what that brand offers. This does not need to be limited to professional capacities, but should represent your personal philosophy and life experiences. In 15 words or less, write a description of your brand.

Answer the following questions about your brand description:

1. How well does the brand description capture your personality?

2. How appealing do you think this brand would be to potential employers?

3. How appealing do you think this brand would be to potential friends?

4. Are you comfortable with the idea of promoting your own brand? Explain your answer.

5. How do you think the personal branding process is different from or similar to the corporate branding process?

[1] Theaker, 7.

[2] Klein, 366.

References

Alberts, Sheldon. "Brand Obama," *Financial Post*, January 17, 2009, http://www.financialpost.com/m/story.html?id=1191405.

Associated Press, "Blackwater Ditches Tarnished Brand Name," *USA Today*, February 13, 2009, http://www.usatoday.com/news/military/2009-02-13-blackwater_N.htm.

Associated Press, "Cheney Hunting Accident Seen as P.R. Disaster," *MSNBC*, February 16, 2006, http://www.msnbc.msn.com/id/11396608/ns/politics/.

Atkin, Douglas. interview, *Frontline, PBS*, February 2, 2004, http://www.pbs.org/wgbh/pages/frontline/shows/persuaders/interviews/atkin.html.

BBC World, "Taco Bell Cashes in on Mir," March 20, 2001, http://news.bbc.co.uk/2/hi/americas/1231447.stm.

Bernstein, Sharon. "Toyota faces a massive marketing challenge," *Los Angeles Times*, February 9, 2010, http://articles.latimes.com/2010/feb/09/business/la-fi-toyota-marketing10-2010feb10.

Dictionary.com, s.v. "Propaganda," http://dictionary.reference.com/browse/propaganda.

Entine, Jon. "Queen of Green Roddick's 'Unfair Trade' Started When She Copied Body Shop Formula," *Daily Mail (London)*, September 15, 2007, http://www.dailymail.co.uk/femail/article-482012/Queen-Green-Roddicks-unfair-trade-started-copied-Body-Shop-formula.html.

Grunig, James E. and Todd Hunt, *Managing Public Relations*, 1984 (Belmont, CA: Wadsworth Publishing).

Isaacson, Walter. *Benjamin Franklin: An American Life* (New York: Simon & Schuster, 2003), 325–349.

Kiley, David. "How Will Bill Clinton Manage His Brand?" *BusinessWeek*, June 10, 2008, analysishttp://www.businessweek.com/bwdaily/dnflash/content/jun2008/db2008069_046398.htm.

New York Times, "Nat Ives, "Anti-Ad Group Tries Advertising," *New York Times*, September 21, 2004, http://www.nytimes.com/2004/09/21/business/media/21adco.html.

Parsons, Patricia. *Ethics in Public Relations* (Sterling, VA: Chartered Institute of Public Relations, 2005), 7.

Reid, Stuart. "The Diamond Myth," *Atlantic*, http://www.theatlantic.com/magazine/archive/2006/12/the-diamond-myth/5491/.

Ries, Al and Laura Ries, *The Fall of Advertising and the Rise of PR* (New York: HarperBusiness, 2004), 90.

Roberts, Kevin. interview, *Frontline, PBS*, December 15, 2003, http://www.pbs.org/wgbh/pages/frontline/shows/persuaders/interviews/roberts.html.

Saffir, Leonard. *Power Public Relations: How to Master the New PR* (Lincolnwood, IL: NTC Contemporary, 2000), 77–88.

Smith, Ronald. *Strategic Planning for Public Relations* (Mahwah, NJ: Erlbaum Associates, 2002), 9–11.

Solman, Gregory. "BP: Coloring Public Opinion?" *Adweek*, January 14, 2008, 1http://www.adweek.com/aw/content_display/news/strategy/e3i9ec32f006d17a91cd72d6192b9f7599a.

Stauber, John and Sheldon Rampton, *Toxic Sludge is Good for You!* (Monroe, ME: Common Courage Press, 1995), 105–119.

Theaker, Alison. *The Public Relations Handbook* (Oxfordshire, England: Routledge, 2004), 4.

Chapter 13: Economics of Mass Media

13.1 Economics of Mass Media

Media Conglomerate or Monopoly?

Figure 13.1

Mike Mozart – Comcast – CC BY 2.0.

In the late 19th century, Andrew Carnegie had a brilliant idea. Instead of buying materials and manufacturing steel, Carnegie bought up mines, railways, and all other aspects of the industry, pioneering a business model that later became known as vertical integration, in which a company owns both its suppliers and buyers. Gathering, manufacturing, and delivering raw materials and finished goods all under the control of a single corporation allowed Carnegie's profits to soar by cutting out the middleman and allowing him to drive the competition out of certain markets. A century later, this same strategy still works; it may not drive industrialization, but its effects are just as powerful.

In late 2009, cable company Comcast announced a plan to purchase a controlling ownership stake in NBC Universal to allow Comcast to join with NBC (Arango, 2009). This multibillion-dollar deal would give Comcast a 51 percent stake in the company, with present owners General Electric (GE) retaining control of the other 49 percent. The proposed venture brought together all NBC Universal content—including Universal Pictures and Focus Features; Spanish-language network Telemundo and the cable networks USA, Bravo, CNBC, and MSNBC—with Comcast's cable channels, which include E! Entertainment, the Golf Channel, and the sports network Versus. Already one of the nation's largest cable and broadband Internet providers, Comcast would then conceivably have the power to restrict these hugely popular NBC-owned networks to its own cable service, thus forcing consumers to adopt Comcast in order to watch them, or to charge huge premiums to competitors' cable subscribers for the channels, thereby making their own cable service more desirable.

The most concerning—or beneficial, for Comcast—aspect of this merger is how it may integrate online content with traditional cable media. NBC Universal cofounded Hulu, the second-largest online video channel in the United States. If Comcast sees ad-driven sites such as Hulu as a threat to its cable business, then ownership over the online video portal would allow Comcast to restrict the site and all of NBC's online content to its own cable subscribers. In effect, Comcast would be allowed to create a subscription model for Internet content, just as it sells subscriptions for cable content. For years, viewers have been able to pick and choose from a wide variety of sources, selecting only the online content that they want; now, some fear that Comcast could bring the problems of a cable subscription—hundreds of channels but only some worth watching—to the Internet (Chasick, 2009).

This merger has the potential to reshape the way that mass media is produced and distributed to consumers. When most Internet users subscribed to America Online (AOL), the company set up its own site simply as a portal to other companies' content. The proposed integration of content producers and service providers, however, allows for unprecedented control of Internet content. Net neutrality poses another problem; Comcast could potentially grant its own content channels—such as a subscription-only version of Hulu—privileges over competing channels. While this does not necessarily pose a problem when there is healthy competition, in many regions Comcast is the only provider of broadband Internet, thus raising concerns of a potential monopoly. No matter what happens with this particular merger, it seems that the economics of mass media are becoming even more tangled as the rapid rise of new technology threatens to transform or replace traditional media outlets.

References

Arango, Tim. "G.E. Makes It Official: NBC Will Go to Comcast," *New York Times*, December 4, 2009, http://www.nytimes.com/2009/12/04/business/media/04nbc.html.

Chasick, Alex. "Why a Comcast/NBC Merger Is Bad News," *Consumerist* (blog), December 3, 2009, http://consumerist.com/2009/12/why-a-comcastnbc-merger-is-bad-news.html.

13.2 Characteristics of Media Industries

Learning Objectives

1. Identify the three basic media business models.
2. Identify the business models of several media industries.
3. Describe the differences between the two ways in which media receives revenue.

The merger of Comcast and NBC is just one example of the myriad ways media companies do business. Television, print publishing, radio broadcasting, music, and film all have their own economic nuances and distinct models. However, these business models fall into three general categories: monopoly, oligopoly, and monopolistic competition.

Of these three basic media business models, monopoly is probably the most familiar. A monopoly occurs when one controls a product or service—for example, a small town with only one major newspaper. Oligopoly, or the control of a product or service by just a few companies, commonly occurs in publishing; a few major publishers put out most best-selling books, and relatively few companies control many of the nation's highest-circulating magazines. Television is much the same way, as the major broadcast networks—Comcast and GE's NBC, Disney's ABC, National Amusements's CBS, and News Corporation's Fox—own nearly all broadcast and cable outlets. Finally, monopolistic competition takes place when multiple companies offer essentially the same product or service. For example, Ticketmaster and Live Nation were longtime competitors until they merged in 2010, with both providing basically the same set of event-management services for music and other live entertainment industries.

The last few decades have seen increasing conglomeration of media ownership, allowing for economies of scale that previously could not be achieved. Instead of individual local radio stations competing for advertising revenue among a range of local companies, for example, large corporations can now buy wholesale advertising for any or all of their brands on a dozen different radio stations in a single media market all owned by a conglomerate such as Clear Channel. The economics of mass media has become a matter of macroeconomic proportions: GE now makes everything from jet engines to cable news. The implications of this go beyond advertising. Because major corporations now own nearly every media outlet, ongoing fears of corporate control of media messaging have intensified.

However, these fears are often channeled into productive enterprises. In many media industries, an ongoing countercurrent exists to provide diversity not found in many corporate-owned models. Independent radio stations such as those affiliated with nonprofit organizations and colleges provide news and in-depth analysis as well as a variety of musical and entertainment programs that are not found on corporate stations. Likewise, small music labels have had recent success promoting and distributing music through online CD sales or digital distribution services such as iTunes appliance program. YouTube makes it easier for videographers to reach a surprisingly large market, often surpassing even professional sites such as Hulu.

Raising Revenue

Companies employ many different ways to raise revenue for their services, but all boil down to two fundamental ideas: The money comes either from consumers or from advertising. In practice, many outlets combine the two to give themselves a flexible stream of income. Equally, consumers may be willing to pay slightly more for fewer ads, or to sit through more advertising in exchange for free content.

Traditional book publishers, which make practically all of their money by selling their products directly to consumers, lie on one extreme end of the spectrum. In some respects, cable companies use a related model under which they directly sell consumers the delivery and subscription of a bundled package of programming channels. However, cable channels primarily rely on a mix of media revenue models, receiving funding from advertising along with subscription fees. Magazines and newspapers may fall into this middle-ground category as well, although online classified advertising has caused print publications to lose this important revenue stream in recent years. Broadcast television is the clearest example of advertising-driven income, as there are no subscription fees for these channels. Because this lack of direct fees increases the potential audience for the network, networks can sell their advertising time at a premium, as opposed to a cable channel with a more limited and likely more narrow viewership.

Print Media

Print media fall into three basic categories: books, newspapers, and magazines. The book publishing industry is basically an oligopoly; the top 10 trade publishers made up 72 percent of the total market in 2009, with the top 5 alone comprising 58 percent of this (Hyatt, 2010). Newspapers tend toward local monopolies and oligopolies, as there are generally few local news sources. In the past classified advertising made up a substantial portion of newspaper revenue. However, the advent of the Internet—particularly free classified services such as Craigslist—has weakened the newspaper industry through dwindling classified advertising revenues.

Newspapers

The newspaper industry also entails a mix of initial, or first copy costs, and relatively low marginal costs. Journalistic and editorial costs are relatively high, whereas the costs of newsprint and distribution are fairly low. The transition from the labor-intensive process of mechanical typesetting to modern electronic printing greatly reduced the marginal costs of producing newspapers. However, the price of newsprint still goes through cyclical ups and downs, making it difficult to price a newspaper in the long run.

The highest costs of publishing a paper remain the editorial and administrative overheads. Back-office activities such as administration and finance can often be combined if a company owns more than one paper. Unlike the historical restrictions on broadcast media that limited the number of stations owned by a single network, print media has faced no such ownership limits. Because of this, a company such as Gannett has come to own *USA Today* as well as mostly local newspapers in 33 states, Guam, and the United Kingdom (Columbia Journalism Review, 2008). Other companies, such as McClatchy, also run their own wire services, partly as a way of reducing the costs of providing national journalism to many local markets.

Magazines

Like newspapers, magazines are largely owned by just a few companies. However, unlike newspapers, many magazine chains are themselves owned by much larger media conglomerates. Time Warner—the highest-ranking media company in 2003—owns numerous magazines, including *Time, Fortune,* and *Sports Illustrated.* Taking all of its publications into account, Time Warner controls a 20 percent share of all magazine advertising in the United States. However, many smaller publishers produce niche publications, many of which do not aspire to a wider market. In all, magazines seem to be undergoing a period of economic decline, with a net loss of some 120 publications in 2009 alone (Flamm, 2009).

Television and Radio

As discussed in Chapter 9 "Television", large media conglomerates own nearly all television networks. Both national networks and local affiliates are typically owned by conglomerates; however, stations such as Fox-owned WNYW in New York or CBS-owned KCNC in Denver are able to mix local content with national reporting and programming, much as large newspaper companies do.

In a local market, one cable company usually dominates the cable service market. In many places, one cable company, such as Comcast—the largest of the cable companies—is the only option. Over the past several years, however, satellite companies such as Dish Network and DirecTV, which are able to reach any number of consumers with limited local infrastructure, have introduced increased, albeit limited, levels of competition.

Even as cable is expanding, radio has become heavily consolidated. Since the 1990s, massive radio networks such as Clear Channel Communications have bought up many local stations in an effort to control every radio station in a given media market. However, the FCC has designated the lower part of the FM radio band for noncommercial purposes, including nonprofit programming such as educational, religious, or public radio stations—and continues to hold public discussion on frequency allocations. These practices help retain a certain level of programming diversity in the face of increased homogenization, largely because such stations are not supported through advertising. Because they are funded by donations or nonprofit institutions, these stations benefit economically from catering to a minority of listeners who may support the station directly, rather than a larger majority that has other options for entertainment.

Music and Film

Because both the music and film industries face unique business opportunities and challenges, each operates on an economic model unlike either print or broadcast media. Just like those forms of media, however, music and film have undergone significant changes due to consolidation and technological and consumer shifts in recent years.

The Big Four

The music industry is closely related to the radio industry, and the two have a high degree of codependence. Without music, radio would not be quite as lively or nearly as popular; without radio, music would be more difficult for listeners to discover, and perhaps be limited to a local consumer base.

As radio companies have consolidated, so has the music industry. A total of four record companies, popularly called the "Big Four" within the industry, dominate the recorded music business and thus most mainstream radio airwaves. Because a conglomerate such as Clear Channel is ill-equipped to handle local tastes and musical acts—and because it tends to be easier to manage programming across a large regional area than on a station-by-station basis—the Big Four record companies tend to focus on national and international acts. After all, if a label can convince a single radio conglomerate to play a particular act's music, that performer instantly gains access to a broad national market.

Music is therefore widely considered an oligopoly, despite the presence of countless small, independent companies. A handful of major record labels dominate the market, and they are all basically structured the same way. Universal is owned by NBC, which was in turn owned by GE and now Comcast; Sony Music is owned by the eponymous Japanese technology giant; Warner Music Group, although now its own entity, was previously under the umbrella of Time Warner; and the EMI Group is owned by a private investment firm.

Consolidation and Ticketing

Although the Big Four dominate the recorded music industry, they have surprisingly little to do with live performances. Traditionally, musicians have toured to promote their albums—and sell enough copies to pay off their advances—and the live show was a combination of self-promotion and income. An artist's record company provided financial support, but a concert ticket generated significantly more income per sale than a CD. Since the merger of ticketing companies Ticketmaster and Live Nation, the ticketing services for large venues have practically been monopolized. For example, Madison Square Garden, one of the largest venues in New York City, does not handle its booking in-house, and with good reason; the technology to manage tens of thousands of fans trying to buy tickets to a soon-to-be-sold-out concert the day they go on sale would likely break the system. Instead, Ticketmaster handles all of the ticketing for Madison Square Garden, adding a 10 percent to 20 percent fee to the face value of the ticket for its exclusive service, depending on the venue and price of the show.

Film

Because of the nature of film, the economics of the medium are slightly different from those of music. The absence of film in broadcasting, the lack of a live performance, and the exponentially higher budgets are just some of its unique facets. As with music, however, large companies tend to dominate the market. These massive studios are now connected corporately with other media outlets. For example, Sony and Universal both have partners in the music industry, while Fox and Disney control major television broadcast and cable networks as well as film studios.

Just as record labels do with radio conglomerates, film distribution companies tend to sell to large chains, such as the over 6,000-screens-strong Regal Entertainment Group and the over 4,000-screens-strong AMC Entertainment, which have national reach (National Association of Theater Owners, 2009). However, independent filmmakers still provide limited competition to these larger studios.

From Miramax to the Weinstein Company

Figure 13.2

The founders of Miramax, brothers Bob and Harvey Weinstein, had a messy breakup with major studio Disney.

Wikimedia Commons – public domain.

Brothers Bob and Harvey Weinstein founded Miramax in 1979 with the intention of independence. Over the ensuing years, they released films that were off-limits to major distributors, such as Quentin Tarantino's violent *Reservoir Dogs* and Steven Soderbergh's controversial *Sex, Lies, and Videotape*. After Disney bought the smaller studio in 1993, Miramax gained access to even larger financial backing, albeit somewhat begrudgingly. Miramax had cultivated relationships with the now-blockbuster directors Tarantino and Kevin Smith—the director of *Clerks*, *Dogma*, and *Jay and Silent Bob Strike Back*—and when Tarantino's *Pulp Fiction* made more than $100 million at the box office within 2 years of Disney's purchase of Miramax, it seemed like a good deal. As a result, Disney signed the Weinsteins to a new contract, giving them an annual budget of $700 million, and in 2003 Disney gave the Weinsteins permission to raise additional hundreds of millions of dollars from Goldman Sachs in order to make even more expensive movies (New York Times, 2005).

By 2004, however, relations between Miramax and Disney were turning sour. In May of that year, Disney would not allow Miramax to release Michael Moore's incendiary documentary *Fahrenheit 9/11*. In response, the Weinsteins sought outside funding and released it themselves to great success; the film became the highest-grossing documentary of all time, with revenue of $222 million on a mere $6 million budget (Box Office Mojo). A year later, the Weinsteins dissolved their relationship with Disney. Disney, however, kept the Miramax brand and the entire Miramax library of films.

Yet this fissure did not end the Weinsteins' careers. In 2005, the brothers founded a new independent film company, the Weinstein Co., which has had some success with films including *Vicky Cristina Barcelona* and *The Queen*, as well as the Michael Moore documentaries *Sicko* and *Capitalism: A Love Story*. However, when even independent film legends such as the Weinsteins have only limited success, it's clear that success is hard to come by. The *A.V. Club*—a companion to the satirical newspaper *The Onion*—asked in January 2010, just after Disney closed Miramax for good, "How much longer will the studio 'indie' model be viable at all (Tobias, 2010)?" Today, there are few true "indie" studios left, and several major studios have closed their boutique studios, such as Warner Independent and Paramount Vantage. But even if some are questioning the economics of the indie-studio models of the 1980s and 1990s, it seems that there will always be an artistic drive for independent film—and, eventually, someone's bound to make the economics of it work again.

New Media, Old Models

In many ways, the Internet has been a game-changer throughout the media industry. However, a few things have stayed the same; major media companies own popular media content sites such as Hulu and YouTube and control access to a great deal of online information. Even bloggers, who have found a new role as drivers of the media cycle, are at a disadvantage when it comes to the ability to generate original content. They tend to drive much of their traffic by reposting and adding commentary to news stories from established media outlets. One large and relatively influential outlet, the *Drudge Report*, is mainly composed of links to outside news organizations rather than original journalism. It gained fame during the late 1990s for breaking the Bill Clinton and Monica Lewinsky scandal—albeit by posting about how *Newsweek* killed reporter Michael Isikoff's story on the matter (BBC News, 1998). Still, the economic complications of the Internet have changed the calculus of media permanently, a status made clear by the drastic increase in free content over the past decade.

Key Takeaways

- The three main media business models are monopoly, oligopoly, and monopolistic competition.
- The print, recorded music, and film industries are generally oligopolies; television is generally monopolistic competition; and live event ticketing is essentially a monopoly.
- Media companies employ two main methods of generating revenue. Advertising builds income by selling time or space where a viewer will see it. Consumers may also provide a direct revenue stream by purchasing a good or service.

Exercises

Choose a media outlet such as the *Washington Post* or CNN and visit its website to determine its parent company. Often this will be in the *"Corporate"* or *"About Us"* sections. Then visit the *Columbia Journalism Review*'s resource "Who Owns What?" at http://www.cjr.org/resources/index.php. Consider and respond to the following questions:

1. Into which of the three basic media business models does this media outlet fall?

2. How does this media outlet employ each of the two ways that media receives revenue? Does it exclusively use one way or does it use a blend of the two?

3. How large is the parent company of this media outlet? Does it own any other outlets?

4. How might the parent company be using vertical integration to its advantage?

5. Were there any surprises to what you found? Were there any corporate connections that you did not expect to see? Explain.

References

BBC News, "Scandalous Scoop Breaks Online," January 25, 1998, http://news.bbc.co.uk/2/hi/special_report/1998/clinton_scandal/50031.stm.

Box Office Mojo, "Fahrenheit 9/11," http://boxofficemojo.com/movies/?id=fahrenheit911.htm.

Columbia Journalism Review, "Who Owns What," August 13, 2008, http://www.cjr.org/resources/index.php.

Flamm, Matthew. "367 Magazines Shuttered in 2009," *Crain's New York Business*, December 11, 2009, http://www.crainsnewyork.com/article/20091211/FREE/912119988.

Hyatt, Michael. "Top Ten U.S. Book Publishers for 2009," January 15, 2010, http://michaelhyatt.com/2010/01/top-ten-u-s-book-publishers-for-2009.html.

National Association of Theater Owners, "Top Ten Circuits," July 1, 2009, http://www.natoonline.org/statisticscircuits.htm.

New York Times, "Significant Events in Disney's Ownership of Miramax," *New York Times*, March 5, 2005, http://www.nytimes.com/imagepages/2005/03/06/movies/20050306_MIRAMAX.html.

Tobias, Scott. "R.I.P. (Companies Are People, Too, Division): Miramax 1979–2010," *A.V. Club*, January 28, 2010, http://www.avclub.com/articles/rip-companies-are-people-too-division-miramax-1979,37639/.

13.3 The Internet's Effects on Media Economies

Learning Objectives

1. Recognize the ways synergy is used on the Internet.
2. Summarize the purpose and impact of the Digital Millennium Copyright Act.

The challenge to media economics is one of production. When print media was the only widely available media, the concept was simple: Sell newspapers, magazines, and books. Sales of these goods could be gauged like any other product, although in media's case, the good was intangible—information—rather than the physical paper and ink. The transition from physical media to broadcast media presented a new challenge, because consumers did not pay money for radio and, later, television programming; instead, the price was an interruption every so often by a "word from our sponsors." However, even this practice hearkened back to the world of print media; just as newspapers and magazines sell advertising space, radio and television networks sell space on their airwaves.

The fundamental shift in Internet economics has been the miniscule price of online space compared to that in print or broadcast media. Combined with the instantaneous proliferation of information, the Internet seems to pose a grave threat to traditional media. Media outlets have responded by establishing themselves online, and it is now practically unheard of for any media company to lack an Internet presence. Companies' archives have opened up, and aside from a few holdouts such as *The Wall Street Journal*, nearly every newspaper allows free online access, although some papers, like *The New York Times*, are going to experiment with a paid subscription model to solve the problem of dwindling revenues. Newspapers now offer video content online, and radio and television networks have published traditional text-and-photo stories. Through Internet portals, media companies have synergized their content; they are no longer merely television networks or local newspapers but instead are quickly moving to become a little bit of everything.

Online Synergy

Although the Internet has had many effects on media economics, ranging from media piracy to the lowered costs of distribution, arguably the greatest effect has been the synergy of different forms of media. For example, the front page of *The New York Times* website contains multiple short video clips, and the front page of Fox News' website contains clips from the cable television network along with relevant articles written by FoxNews.com staff. Media outlets offer many of these services for free to consumers, if for no other reason than because consumers have become accustomed to getting this content for free elsewhere on the Internet.

The Internet has also drastically changed the way that companies' advertising models operate. During the early years of the Internet, many web ads were geared toward sites such as Amazon and eBay, where consumers purchased products or services. Today, however, many ads—particularly on sites for high-profile media outlets such as Fox News and *The New York Times*—are for products that are not typically bought online, such as cars or major credit cards. However, another category of advertising that is tailored toward individual web pages has also gained prominence on the Internet. In this form of advertising, marketers match advertisers with particular keywords on particular web pages. For example, if the page is a how-to guide for fixing a refrigerator, some of the targeted ads might be for local refrigerator repair shops.

Internet by Google

Figure 13.3

Google makes almost all of its money through advertising, allowing it to provide many services such as e-mail and document sharing for free.

search-engine-land – Google Ads – CC BY 2.0.

Search-engine company Google has been working to perfect this type of targeted advertising search. Low-cost text ads may appear next to its search results, on various web pages, and in the sidebar of its free web-based e-mail service, Gmail. More than just using algorithms to sort through massive amounts of data and matching advertising to content, Google has lowered the cost barrier to advertising, as well as the volume barrier to hosting advertising. Because Google automatically matches sites with advertisers, an independent site can sign up for its advertising service and get paid for each person who follows the text links. Likewise, relatively small companies can buy advertising space in specialized niches without having to go through a large-volume ad buyer. This business has proven extremely productive; the bulk of Google's revenue comes from advertising even as it gives away services such as e-mail and document sharing.

Problems of Digital Delivery

Search engines like Google and video-sharing sites like YouTube (which is owned by Google) allow access to online information, but they do not actually produce that information themselves. Thus, the propensity of these sites to gather information and then make it available to consumers free of charge does not necessarily sit well with those who financially depend on the sale of this information.

Google News

One of Google's more controversial projects is Google News, a news aggregator that automatically collects news stories from various sources on the Internet. This service allows users to view the latest news from many different sources conveniently in one location. However, the project has been met with opposition from a number of those news sources, who contend that Google has infringed on their copyrights and cost them revenue. The *Wall Street Journal* has been one of the more vocal critics of Google News. In April 2009, editor Robert Thomson said that news aggregators are "best described as parasites (Schulze, 2009)." In December 2009, Google responded to these complaints by allowing publishers to set a limit on the number of articles per day a reader can view for free through Google.

Music and File Sharing

The recent confrontation between Google and the traditional news media is only one of many problems resulting from digital technology. Digital technology can create exact copies of data so that one copy cannot be distinguished from the other. In other words, although a printed book might be nicer than a photocopy of that book, a digitization of the book is exactly the same as all other digitized copies and can be transmitted almost instantly. Similarly, although cassette tape copies of recorded music offered lower sound fidelity than the originals, the emergence of writable CD technology during the 1990s allowed for the creation of a copy of a digital audio CD that was identical to the original.

As data storage and transmission costs dropped, CDs no longer had to be physically copied to other CDs. With the advent of MP3 digital encoding, the music information on a CD could be compressed into a relatively small, portable format that could be transmitted easily over the Internet, and music file sharing took off. Although these recordings were not exactly the same as their CD-quality counterparts, most listeners could not tell the difference—or they just didn't care, because they were now able to share music files conveniently and for free. The practice of transmitting music over the Internet through services such as Napster quickly ballooned.

Video Streaming

As high-bandwidth Internet connections proliferated, video-sharing and streaming sites such as YouTube started up. Although these sites were supposedly intended for users to upload and share their own amateur videos, one of the big draws of the site was the high quantity of television show episodes, music videos, and other commercial content that has been posted illegally. The replication potential inherent in digital technology combined with online transmission has caused a sea change in media industries that rely on income directly from consumers, such as books and recorded music. However, as the next section will show, the shift of media and information to the Internet can pose the risk of a digital divide, where those without Internet access are at an even greater disadvantage than they were before.

Digital Millennium Copyright Act (DMCA)

Producers of content are not without protection under the law. In 1998, Congress enacted the Digital Millennium Copyright Act (DMCA) in an effort to stop the illegal copying and distribution of copyrighted material. The legislation defined many digital gray areas that previously may not have been explicitly covered, such as circumventing antipiracy measures in commercial software; requiring webcasters to pay licensing fees to record companies; and exempting libraries, archives, and some other nonprofit institutions from some of these rules under certain circumstances. Since 1998, this legislation has been the bedrock of a variety of claims against sites such as YouTube. Under the law, copyright holders may send letters to Internet hosts distributing their copyrighted material. Certifying that they have a good-faith belief that the host does not have prior permission to distribute the content, copyright holders may request a removal of that material from the site (U.S. Copyright Office, 1998).

Although much of the law has to do with the rights of copyright holders to request the removal of their works from unlicensed sites, much of the DMCA also enacts protections for Internet service providers (ISPs). Although before there had been some question as to whether ISPs could be charged with copyright infringement merely for allowing reproducers to use their bandwidth, the DMCA made it clear that ISPs are not expected to police their own bandwidth for illegal use and are therefore not liable. Although the DMCA is not necessarily to everyone's liking—requiring individual takedown notices is time-consuming for corporations, and the relative lack of safeguards can allow large companies to bully ISPs into shutting down smaller sites, given a good-faith notice—the protections and clarifications that it has created have cleared up some of the confusion surrounding digital media (Vance, 2003). However, as the price of bandwidth drastically drops and as more media goes digital, copyright laws will inevitably need to be amended again.

Key Takeaways

- The Internet has allowed media companies to synergize their content, broadcasting the same ideas and products across multiple platforms. This significantly helps with reducing relative first copy costs because the Internet's marginal costs are minimal.

- The DMCA exempts Internet service providers from liability in policing their own services for illegal downloads. However, it also enacts copyright protection for digital media, thereby allowing copyright holders to send takedown notices. As long as they profess a good-faith belief that the works were not used with permission, the recipient is generally required to take them down.

Exercises

Navigate to a traditional media outlet's online portal, such as NYTtimes.com or FoxNews.com. Print out a hard copy of the home page and write on it, or save it to your computer and open it in a document editor such as Microsoft Word to annotate it. Note items such as these:

1. Are there any media formats on the page aside from the outlet's normal ones? Why might this traditional media outlet choose to produce different media formats on the Internet?

2. Does the media outlet promote its other products? If so, how? How does the Internet enable this type of synergy?

3. What types of personalization options are there? Does social networking show any influence?

4. Under the DMCA, what recourse would this media outlet have if its copyrighted content were being hosted elsewhere without its permission?

References

Schulze, Jane. "Google Dubbed Internet Parasite by WSJ Editor," *Australian* (Sydney), April 6, 2009, http://www.theaustralian.com.au/business/media/google-dubbed-internet-parasite/story-e6frg996-1225696931547.

U.S. Copyright Office, "Copyright Law: Chapter 5," 1998, http://www.copyright.gov/title17/92chap5.html.

Vance, Ashlee. "Court Confirms DMCA 'Good Faith' Web Site Shut Down Rights," *Register*, May 30, 2003, http://www.theregister.co.uk/2003/05/30/court_confirms_dmca_good_faith/.

13.4 Digital Divide in a Global Economy

Learning Objectives

1. Identify ways that digital communication is changing international economics, particularly in developing countries.

2. Identify difficulties that face those without adequate Internet access in developed countries.

3. Evaluate the relative success of various plans for closing the "digital divide."

More than just a tool for information transfer, the Internet has become a conduit for a globalized workforce. A corporation in New York can outsource electronically based work to a highly connected developing country like India without incurring the sort of shipping charges or communication delays that previously impeded such efforts. Internet access, particularly for business, has made development possible in remote areas, allowing corporations access to less expensive labor and allowing money to flow into developing countries. However, as the Internet has become integrated into daily business life, a digital divide has emerged: Some derive the benefits from Internet access, but many others do not.

Many U.S. and international leaders and nongovernmental organizations have identified the digital divide as an area of concern. A globalized workforce does not separate the world into easily divisible political territories but rather into those that have useful access to technology to reach a wider market and those that do not. As the 21st century develops, worldwide communication has become increasingly imperative for a healthy economy, creating a new challenge to make sure that rapid technological changes do not preclude economic success for less developed economies.

However, the problem extends beyond simple access or even competency. The 80/20 effect, under which 80 percent of profit is created for the most affluent 20 percent, exacerbates the digital divide. In other words, the Internet—created in large part by and for the rich—is practically useless for the poor, particularly in developing countries. Thus, bridging the digital divide is about helping those with little or no access to the digital world gain the ability to use technology in economically advantageous ways.

The Informational Shift

As information and media move online, those without ready access to the Internet are increasingly being left behind. Even in developed countries such as the United States, the digital divide is readily apparent. Often, older and less educated workers do not have computer skills or home Internet access. In June 2009, the Pew Research Center studied the demographic differences in broadband Internet adoption and found that 45 percent of those without Internet access were age 65 and over (Horrigan, 2009). Even more significantly, a quarter of the unconnected were between the ages of 50 and 64. These workers are at a distinct disadvantage when it comes to finding and being hired for jobs.

As classified advertisements and job postings have left newspapers for the web, Internet access has become vital to even finding a job to apply for. In the above-mentioned Pew survey, 20 percent of respondents had incomes of less than $20,000 per year. However, these 20 percent made up a disproportionately high 48 percent of the survey's non-Internet users; a full 64 percent of low-income survey participants did not have access to the Internet. These numbers drastically dropped as wages increased—while those making under $40,000 per year made up 80 percent of non-Internet users, those making over $50,000 made up 50 percent of high-speed Internet users. As the Internet is becoming an integral part of our daily lives, a lack of access among certain groups could severely hamper upward economic mobility.

Computer Skills and Older Workers

Access to the Internet is an essential aspect of many successful job hunts, but it is also important to consider computer skills themselves. Many older adults who grew up without the Internet lack the computer and technology skills that contemporary jobs require. MSNBC reported in October 2009 that unemployment rates for older workers were at a 60-year high, having doubled in the period between late 2007 and the fall of 2009 (Johnson, 2009). While the overall unemployment rate at that time had reached a 26-year high, older workers who lacked the skills of younger, computer-savvy adults were suffering disproportionately. Lack of computer skills can be a crippling impediment to job success, even if a person can find a job in difficult economic times.

In response to these challenges, libraries and other nonprofit groups have taken on the task of training older unemployed workers to effectively use the Internet for job-related needs. These training courses, beginning with turning on a computer and using the mouse and ranging into advanced office program use, seek to provide skills necessary to allow older workers to reenter the work force. These organizations also aim to show users that they can increase their quality of life by setting up e-mail for communication with friends and family members.

The Digital Divide Abroad

While the digital divide in the United States is largely a matter of education, cost barrier, and lack of adoption of new technology, the digital divide in economically underdeveloped countries adds the complication of infrastructure. Internet service requires the existence of widespread stable networks to handle large computer centers, and electronic access to the outside world needs a constant data connection. Therefore, in many developing countries, practically no residents have access to computers and the Internet; this cuts them off not only from information but from the entire global economy.

Table 13.1 Internet Connectivity by Country

Country	Population (Millions)	Internet Users (Millions)	Percent Connected
China	1,330	298	22
India	1,173	81	7
United States	310	231	75
Indonesia	243	30	12
Brazil	201	65	32
Japan	127	91	72
Afghanistan	29	0.5	2
Mongolia	3.1	0.3	10

Source: *CIA World Factbook,* https://www.cia.gov/library/publications/the-world-factbook/ **(accessed July 27, 2011).**

The Digital Divide Institute has launched a campaign to integrate Indonesia into the global digital network as a representative solution to this problem. Indonesia is the world's fourth-largest country in terms of population and already has wide cell-phone coverage—a significant advantage when it comes to rural information access (Digital Divide Institute, 2010). The organization claims that by expanding these wireless communication networks to encompass 3G and high-speed Internet access, access to the Internet could rise so much that Indonesia could become a fully emerging market for global services. To put this in perspective, connecting 20 percent of Indonesians to the Internet brings the total connected population of Indonesia to 48 million users, equivalent to all of South Korea, one of the most connected countries in the world (Central Intelligence Agency). The economic and political benefits of widespread Internet connectivity to nations like Indonesia are huge. The Digital Divide Institute points to Ireland as an example of how increasingly high-tech jobs can accompany the decline of terrorism—evidence that bridging the digital divide can be an issue of international security as well as global prosperity.

The Bottom Billion

One contentious issue in bridging the digital divide is which billion to focus on—of the 6.8 billion people in the world, only an estimated 1.6 billion are connected to the Internet (Central Intelligence Agency). Therefore, the discussion of bridging the digital divide is quickly complicated by this question: To whom should we build the bridge? While some organizations such as the Digital Divide Institute suggest that the global "pyramid" should focus on the next billion—countries such as Indonesia with wide cell-phone coverage but little access to useful, global digital technology. Other organizations see it differently.

Figure 13.4

The One Laptop per Child project aims to put one of these XO computers in the hands of many children in developing countries.

One Laptop per Child – Papau New Guinea: Gaire #5 – CC BY 2.0.

Many believe that everyone in the world can benefit from technology if it is deployed properly. The organization One Laptop per Child (OLPC) seeks to achieve exactly what its name implies with a low-cost design that runs on free software and requires very little energy (Labtop). Central to OLPC's goal is the idea that learning to use technology needs to be recalibrated toward learning through technology. Another crucial idea is the organization's conception of networks as essentially localized with the potential to be expanded. OLPC's XO laptop connects to its neighbors, creating many small networks through a fairly wide wireless range. In addition, its ability to access the Internet through this wide wireless range allows remote educational opportunities for children in developing countries. Although it may seem to leap directly from no communication access to wireless Internet video streaming, this program has shown that it may even be more cost effective than traditional connective technologies like phone lines.

Key Takeaways

- Digital communication allows workers in developing countries with adequate infrastructure to perform remote computer tasks.

- Those without Internet access are essentially left out of much of the new economy. A lack of computer skills or Internet access can make it very difficult to find jobs. Computer skills are required for many jobs, so a lack of those skills may restrict someone to low-paying work.

- The plan to close the digital divide for the next billion people unconnected to the Internet effectively capitalizes on existing resources; however, plans such as the One Laptop per Child project work to provide a comprehensive hardware and software solution for everyone who lacks Internet access.

Exercises

Please respond to the following short-answer writing prompts. Each response should be a minimum of one paragraph.

1. Consider trying to search for a job without digital technology. How many newspapers would you need to buy? What would you have to do to actually get your application to the company?

2. What barriers exist that make it difficult to close the digital divide in developing economies like India and China?

3. What efforts have been made to spread Internet access to more parts of the world? How successful have these efforts been?

References

Central Intelligence Agency, "Country Comparison: Population," *World Factbook*, https://www.cia.gov/library/publications/the-world-factbook/rankorder/2119rank.html.

Central Intelligence Agency, "World," *World Factbook*, https://www.cia.gov/library/publications/the-world-factbook/geos/xx.html.

Digital Divide Institute, "Indonesia," 2010, http://www.digitaldivide.org/indonesia.html.

Horrigan, John. "Home Broadband Adoption 2009," *Pew Internet & American Life Project*, June 17, 2009, http://www.pewinternet.org/Reports/2009/10-Home-Broadband-Adoption-2009.aspx.

Johnson, Alex. "Lack of Computer Skills Foils Many Job-Seekers," *MSNBC*, October 2, 2009, http://www.msnbc.msn.com/id/33106445.

Labtop, One Laptop per Child Association, "One Laptop per Child (OLPC): Laptop." http://laptop.org/en/laptop/index.shtml.

13.5 Information Economy

The modern theory of the information economy was expressed in the 1998 publication of *Information Rules: A Strategic Guide to the Network Economy*, written by Cal Shapiro, an economics professor at the University of California, Berkeley, and Hal Varian, now chief economist at Google. Their fundamental argument was simple: "Technology changes. Economic laws do not (Shapiro & Varian, 1998)."

While economic laws may not change, the fundamentals of the business of information are far different from the fundamentals of most traditional businesses. For example, the cost of producing a single sandwich is relatively consistent, per sandwich, with the cost of producing multiple sandwiches. As discussed in the first section of this chapter, information works differently. With a newspaper, the first copy costs are far higher than the marginal costs of secondary copies. The high first costs and low marginal costs of the information economy contribute very heavily to the potential for large corporations gaining dominance. The confluence of these two costs creates a potential economy of scale, favoring the larger of the competitors.

In addition, information is what economists refer to as an experience good, meaning that consumers must actually experience the good to judge its value. The problem with information is that the experience is the good; how do you know, for example, that a movie has high-quality acting and an interesting plot before you've watched it? The solution to this is branding, which was discussed in the previous chapter. Although it may be difficult to judge a movie before watching, knowing that a given film was made by a certain director or stars an actor you like increases its value. Marketers use movie trailers, press coverage, and other marketing tools to communicate this branding message in the hopes of convincing you to watch the films they are promoting.

Another important facet of information technology is the associated switching costs. When economists consider switching costs, they take into account the difference between the cost of one technology and the cost of another. If this difference is less than the cost it would take to switch—for information, the cost of moving all of the relevant data to the new technology—then it is deemed possible to switch. A classic example is moving a music collection from vinyl LPs to CDs. For a consumer to switch systems—that is, to buy a CD player and stereo—that person would also have to rebuild his or her entire music collection with the new format. Luckily for the CD player, the increase in convenience and quality was great enough that most consumers were inclined to switch technologies; however, as is apparent to anyone going to a thrift store or garage sale, old technologies are still being used because the information on the records was important enough for some people to keep them around.

Regulation of the Information Economy

Although Chapter 15 "Media and Government" will discuss government regulation in greater depth, a basic understanding of the interaction between government and media over time is essential to understanding the modern information economy. Public policy and governmental intervention exacerbate an already complicated system of information economics, but for good reason—unlike typical goods and services, the information economy has many significant side effects. The consequences of one hamburger chain outcompeting or buying up all other hamburger chains would surely be fairly drastic for the hamburger-loving world, but not altogether disastrous; there would be only one type of hamburger, but there would still be many other types of fast food remaining. On the contrary, the consequences of monopolization by one media company could be alarming. Because distributed information can influence public policy and public opinion, those in charge of the government have an interest in ensuring fair distribution of that information. The bias toward free markets has been mitigated—even in the United States—when it comes to the information economy.

The Federal Communications Commission (FCC) is largely responsible for this regulation. Established by the Communications Act of 1934, the FCC is charged with "regulating interstate and international communications" for nearly every medium except for print (Federal Communications Commission). The FCC also attempts to maintain a nonpartisan, or at least bipartisan, outlook, with a maximum of three of its five commissioners belonging to the same political party. Although the FCC controls many important things—making sure that electronic devices don't emit radio waves that interfere with other important tools, for example—some of its most important and most contentious responsibilities relate to the media.

As the guardian of the public interest, the FCC has called for more competition among media companies; for example, the ongoing litigation of the merger between Comcast and NBC is not concerned with whether consumers will like streaming Hulu over the Internet, but rather whether one company should own both the content and the mode of distribution. The public good is not served if consumers' ability to choose is taken away when a service provider like Comcast restricts access to only the content that the provider owns, especially if that service provider is the consumers' only choice. In other words, the idea of public good is concerned not with the end result of competition, but with its process. The FCC protects consumers' ability to choose from a wide variety of media products, and the competition among media producers hopefully results in better products for consumers. If the end result is that all customers choose Hulu anyway, either because it has the shows they like or because it offers the best video-streaming capability, then the process has worked to create the best possible model; there was a winner, and it was a fair fight.

A Brief History of Antitrust Legislation

The main tool that the government employs to keep healthy competition in the information marketplace is antitrust legislation. The seminal Sherman Antitrust Act of 1890 helped establish modern U.S. antitrust legislation. Although originally intended to dissolve the monopolistic enterprises of late-19th-century industrialists such as Andrew Carnegie and John D. Rockefeller, the law's basic principles have applied to media companies as well. The antitrust office has also grown since the original Sherman Act; although the Office of the Attorney General originally brought antitrust lawsuits after the act's passage, this responsibility shifted to its own Antitrust Division in 1933 under President Franklin D. Roosevelt.

The Sherman Antitrust Act of 1890 outlined many propositions and goals that legislators deemed necessary to foster a competitive marketplace. For example, Chapter 1 "Media and Culture", Section 13.2 "The Internet's Effects on Media Economies", of the act states that "Every person who shall monopolize, or attempt to monopolize, or combine or conspire with any other person or persons, to monopolize any part of the trade or commerce among the several States…shall be deemed guilty of a felony (Cornell University Law School, 2009)." This establishment of monopolization as a felony was remarkable; before, free-market capitalism was the rule regardless of the public good, making the Sherman Antitrust Act an early proponent of the welfare of people at large.

Two additional pieces of legislation, the Clayton Antitrust Act of 1911 and the Celler-Kefauver Act of 1950, refined the Sherman Antitrust Act in order to make the system of antitrust suits work more effectively. For instance, the Clayton Act makes it unlawful for one company to "acquire…the whole or any part of the stock" of another company when the result would encourage the development of a monopoly (Legal Information Institute, 2009). More than just busting trusts, the Clayton Act thus seeks to stop anticompetitive practices before they take hold. The Celler-Kefauver Act made it more difficult for corporations to get around antitrust legislation; while the Clayton Act allowed the government to regulate the purchase of a competitor's stock, the Celler-Kefauver Act extended this to include the competitor's assets.

Deregulation and the Telecommunications Act of 1996

Although the early part of the 20th century seemed to be devoted to breaking up trusts and keeping monopolies in check, the media—particularly in the latter part of the century—was still able to move steadily toward conglomeration (companies joining together to form a larger, more diversified corporation). Widespread deregulation (the removal of legal regulations on an industry) took place during the 1980s, in large part through the efforts of free-market economists who argued that deregulation would foster more competition in the information marketplace. However, possibly due in large part to the media economy's focus on economies of scale, this was not the case in practice. Companies became increasingly conglomerated, and corporations such as Comcast and Time Warner came to dominate the marketplace. The Telecommunications Act of 1996 helped solidify this trend. Although touted as a way to let "any communications business compete in any market against any other" and to foster competition, this act in practice sped up the conglomeration of media (Federal Communications Commission, 2008).

Media Conglomerates and Vertical Integration

The extension of the Telecommunications Act of 1996 of corporate abilities to vertically integrate was a primary driving factor behind this increased conglomeration. Vertical integration has proven particularly useful for media companies due to their high first costs and low marginal costs. For example, a television company that both produces and distributes content can run the same program on two different channels for nearly the same cost as only broadcasting it on one. Because of the localized nature of broadcast media, two broadcast television channels will likely reach different geographical areas. This results in cost savings for the company, but also somewhat decreases local diversity in media broadcasting.

In fact, the Telecommunications Act made some changes in authority for these local markets. The concept of Section 253 is that no state may prohibit "the ability of any entity to provide any interstate or intrastate telecommunications service (Federal Communications Commission, 1996)." Thus, since state and local governments cannot prohibit any company from entering into a marketplace, there are checks on the amount of a local market that any one company can reach. In addition, the Telecommunications Act capped the share of U.S. television audience for any one company at 35 percent. However, the passage of additional legislation in 1999 allowing any one company to own two television stations in a single market greatly diluted the effect of this initial ruling. Although CBS, NBC, and ABC may be declining in popularity, they "still offer the only means of reaching a genuinely mass television audience" in the country (Doyle, 2002).

Corporate Advantages of Vertical Integration

Almost all of the major media players in today's market practice extensive vertical integration through either administrative management or content integration. Administrative management refers to the potential for divisions of a single company to share the same higher-level management structure, which presents opportunities for increased operational efficiency. For example, Disney manages theme parks and movie studios. Although these two industries are not very closely connected through content, both are large, multinational ventures. Placing both of these divisions under a single corporation allows them to share certain structural similarities, accounting practices, and any other administrative resources that may be helpful across multiple industries.

Content integration—an important practice for media industries—is the ability of these companies to use the same content across multiple platforms. Disney's theme parks would lose much of their charm and meaning without Mickey Mouse and Cinderella's castle; the integration of these two industries—Disney's theme parks and Disney's animated characters—proves profitable for both. Behind the scenes, Disney is also able to reap some excellent benefits from their consolidation. For example, Disney could release a movie through its studio, and then immediately book the stars on news programs that air on Disney-owned broadcast television network ABC. Beyond just the ABC broadcast network, Disney also has many cable channels that it can use to directly market its movies and products to the targeted demographics. Unlike a competitor that might be wary of promoting a Disney movie, Disney's ownership of many different media outlets allows it to single-handedly reach a large audience.

Ethical Issues of Vertical Integration

However, this high level of vertical integration raises several ethical concerns. In the above situation, for example, Disney could entice reviewers on its television outlets to give positive reviews to a Disney studio movie. Therefore, this potential for misused trust and erroneous information could be harmful.

In many ways, the conglomeration of media companies takes place behind the scenes, with only a minority of consumers aware of vertically integrated holdings. Media companies often try to foster a sense of independence from a larger corporation. Of course, there are exceptions to this rule; the NBC sitcom *30 Rock* often delves into the troubles of running a satirical sketch-comedy show (a parody of NBC's *Saturday Night Live*) under the ownership of GE, NBC's real-life owner.

The Issues of the Internet

Although media companies are steadily turning into larger businesses than ever before, many of them have nevertheless fallen on hard times. The instant, free content of the Internet is largely blamed for this decline. From the shift of classified advertising from newspapers to free online services to the decline in physical music sales in favor of digital downloads, the Internet has transformed traditional media economics.

One of the main issues with an unregulated Internet is that it allows digital files to be replicated and sent anywhere else in the world. Large music companies, which traditionally made almost all of their money from selling physical music formats such as vinyl records or compact discs, find themselves at a disadvantage. Consumers can share and distribute music files to anyone, and Internet service providers are exempted from liability under the DMCA. With providers freed of liability and media consumption a driving factor in the rise of high-speed Internet services, ISPs have no incentive to deter illegal sharing along with legal downloads.

Digital Downloads and DRM

Although music companies have had some success selling music through digital outlets, they have not been pioneers in online music sales. Rather, technology companies such as Apple and Amazon.com, sensing a large market for digital downloads coupled with a sleek delivery system, have led the way. Already accustomed to downloading MP3s, consumers readily adopted the model. However, record companies believed that the lack of digital rights management (DRM) protection offered by MP3s represented a major downside.

Apple provided a way to strike a compromise between accessibility and rights control. Having already captured much of the personal digital audio player market with the iPod, which uses other Apple products, Apple has also long prided itself on creating highly integrated systems of both software and hardware. Because so many people were already using the iPod, Apple had a huge potential market for a music store even if it offered DRM-locked tracks that would only play on Apple devices. This inflexibility even offered a small benefit for consumers; Apple succeeded in convincing companies to price their digital downloads lower than CDs.

This compromise may have sold a lot of iPods and MP3s, but it did not satisfy the record companies. When consumers started to download one hit single for 99 cents—rather than buying the whole album for $15 on CD—the music industry felt the pain. Still, huge monetary advances in digital music have taken place. Between 2004 and 2008, digital music sales increased from $187 million to $1.8 billion.

Piracy

The music industry has wasted no amount of firepower to blame piracy for the decline in album sales: "There's no minimizing the impact of illegal file-sharing. It robs songwriters and recording artists of their livelihoods, and it ultimately undermines the future of music itself," said Cary Sherman, president of the Recording Industry Association of America (Sherman, 2003). However, economists see the truth of the matter as significantly more ambiguous. Analyzing over 10,000 weeks of data distributed over many albums, a pair of economists at the

Harvard Business School and University of North Carolina found that "Downloads have an effect on sales which is statistically indistinguishable from zero (Oberholzer-Gee & Strumpf, 2007)." Either way, two things are clear: Consumers are willing to pay for digital music, and digital downloads are on the market to stay for the foreseeable future.

Key Takeaways

- Switching costs and economies of scale play major roles in the information economy. The former helps determine whether a new technological format will take hold, and the latter encourages the growth of large media conglomerates.

- The three founding pieces of antitrust legislation were the Sherman Antitrust Act (1890), which laid the foundation of antitrust legislation; the Clayton Antitrust Act (1911), which allowed the government to regulate the purchase of a company's stock; and the Celler-Kefauver Act (1950), which allowed the government to regulate the purchase of another company's assets.

- Vertical integration occurs when a company controls all aspects of an industry: procuring raw materials, manufacturing, and delivering. Media companies benefit from vertical integration, but the practice raises numerous ethical issues.

Exercises

Visit the *Columbia Journalism Review*'s "Who Owns What?" web page at http://www.cjr.org/resources/index.php. Choose a company from the drop-down menu. Make a chart of all the company's different media outlets and complete the following activities:

1. Choose two subsidiaries of the parent company and discuss how they might be able to use vertical integration to their advantage.

2. How might the larger corporation be using an economy of scale?

3. How might the company be attempting to lessen switching costs? For example, does the company offer the same content on multiple platforms in order to reach customers who may have only one of these platforms? Give an example.

4. How might the three founding pieces of antitrust legislation affect the company's decisions?

References

Cornell University Law School, Legal Information Institute, "Monopolizing trade a felony; penalty," *Cornell University Law School*, January 5, 2009, http://www.law.cornell.edu/uscode/html/uscode15/usc_sec_15_00000002—000-.html.

Doyle, Gillian. *Understanding Media Economics* (Thousand Oaks, CA: Sage, 2002).

Federal Communications Commission, "About the Federal Communications Commission," http://www.fcc.gov/aboutus.html.

Federal Communications Commission, "FCC—Telecommunications Act of 1996," November 15, 2008, http://www.fcc.gov/telecom.html.

Federal Communications Commission, "Telecommunications Act of 1996, Section 253 (a)," January 3, 1996, http://www.fcc.gov/Reports/tcom1996.pdf.

Legal Information Institute, "Acquisition by one corporation of stock of another," Cornell University Law School, January 5, 2009, http://www.law.cornell.edu/uscode/html/uscode15/usc_sec_15_00000018——000-.html.

Oberholzer-Gee, Felix and Koleman Strumpf, "The Effect of File Sharing on Record Sales: An Empirical Analysis," *Journal of Political Economy* 115, no. 1 (February 2007): 1–42.

Shapiro, Carl. and Hal R. Varian, *Information Rules: A Strategic Guide to the Network Economy* (Cambridge, MA: Harvard Business School Press, 1998).

Sherman, Cary. "File-Sharing Is Illegal. Period," *USA Today*, September 18, 2003.

13.6 Globalization of Media

The media industry is, in many ways, perfect for globalization, or the spread of global trade without regard for traditional political borders. As discussed above, the low marginal costs of media mean that reaching a wider market creates much larger profit margins for media companies. Because information is not a physical good, shipping costs are generally inconsequential. Finally, the global reach of media allows it to be relevant in many different countries.

However, some have argued that media is actually a partial cause of globalization, rather than just another globalized industry. Media is largely a cultural product, and the transfer of such a product is likely to have an influence on the recipient's culture. Increasingly, technology has also been propelling globalization. Technology allows for quick communication, fast and coordinated transport, and efficient mass marketing, all of which have allowed globalization—especially globalized media—to take hold.

Globalized Culture, Globalized Markets

Much globalized media content comes from the West, particularly from the United States. Driven by advertising, U.S. culture and media have a strong consumerist bent (meaning that the ever-increasing consumption of goods is encouraged as an economic virtue), thereby possibly causing foreign cultures to increasingly develop consumerist ideals. Therefore, the globalization of media could not only provide content to a foreign country, but may also create demand for U.S. products. Some believe that this will "contribute to a one-way transmission of ideas and values that result in the displacement of indigenous cultures (Santos, 2001)."

Globalization as a world economic trend generally refers to the lowering of economic trade borders, but it has much to do with culture as well. Just as transfer of industry and technology often encourages outside influence through the influx of foreign money into the economy, the transfer of culture opens up these same markets.

As globalization takes hold and a particular community becomes more like the United States economically, this community may also come to adopt and personalize U.S. cultural values. The outcome of this spread can be homogenization (the local culture becomes more like the culture of the United States) or heterogenization (aspects of U.S. culture come to exist alongside local culture, causing the culture to become more diverse), or even both, depending on the specific situation (Rantanen, 2005).

Making sense of this range of possibilities can be difficult, but it helps to realize that a mix of many different factors is involved. Because of cultural differences, globalization of media follows a model unlike that of the globalization of other products. On the most basic level, much of media is language and culture based and, as such, does not necessarily translate well to foreign countries. Thus, media globalization often occurs on a more structural level, following broader "ways of organizing and creating media (Mirza, 2009)." In this sense, a media company can have many different culturally specific brands and still maintain an economically globalized corporate structure.

Vertical Integration and Globalization

Because globalization has as much to do with the corporate structure of a media company as with the products that a media company produces, vertical integration in multinational media companies becomes a necessary aspect of studying globalized media. Many large media companies practice vertical integration: Newspaper chains take care of their own reporting, printing, and distribution; television companies control their own production and broadcasting; and even small film studios often have parent companies that handle international distribution.

A media company often benefits greatly from vertical integration and globalization. Because of the proliferation of U.S. culture abroad, media outlets are able to use many of the same distribution structures with few changes. Because media rely on the speedy ability to react to current events and trends, a vertically integrated company can do all of this in a globalized rather than a localized marketplace; different branches of the company are readily able to handle different markets. Further, production values for single-country distribution are basically the same as those for multiple countries, so vertical integration allows, for example, a single film studio to make higher-budget movies than it may otherwise be able to produce without a distribution company that has as a global reach.

Foreign Markets and *Titanic*

Figure 13.5

The movie *Titanic*, which became the highest-grossing movie of all time, made twice as much internationally as it did domestically.

Worth considering is the reciprocal influence of foreign culture on American culture. Certainly, American culture is increasingly exported around the world thanks to globalization, and many U.S. media outlets count strongly on their ability to sell their product in foreign markets. But what Americans consider their own culture has in fact been tailored to the tastes not only of U.S. citizens but also to those of worldwide audiences. The profit potential of foreign markets is enormous: If a movie does well abroad, for example, it might make up for a weak stateside showing, and may even drive interest in the movie in the United States.

One prime example of this phenomenon of global culture and marketing is James Cameron's 1997 film *Titanic*. One of the most expensive movies ever produced up to that point, with an official budget of around $200 million, *Titanic* was not anticipated to perform particularly well at the U.S. box office. Rather, predictions of foreign box-office receipts allowed the movie to be made. Of the total box-office receipts of *Titanic*, only about one-third came from the domestic market. Although *Titanic* became the highest-grossing film up to that point, it grossed just $140 million more domestically than *Star Wars* did 20 years earlier (Box Office Mojo). The difference was in the foreign market. While *Star Wars* made about the same amount—$300 million—in both the domestic and foreign markets, *Titanic* grossed $1.2 billion in foreign box-office receipts. In all, the movie came close to hitting the $2 billion mark, and now sits in the No. 2 position behind Cameron's 2009 blockbuster, *Avatar*.

One reason that U.S. studios can make these kinds of arrangements is their well-developed ties with the worldwide movie industry. Hollywood studios have agreements with theaters all over the world to show their films. By contrast, the foreign market for French films is not nearly as established, as the industry tends to be partially subsidized by the French government. Theaters showing Hollywood studio films in France funnel portions of their box-office receipts to fund French films. However, Hollywood has lobbied the World Trade Organization—a largely pro-globalization group that pushes for fewer market restrictions—to rule that this French subsidy is an unfair restriction on trade (Terrill, 1999).

In many ways, globalization presents legitimate concerns about the endangerment of indigenous culture. Yet simple concerns over the transfer of culture are not the only or even the biggest worries caused by the spread of American culture and values.

Key Takeaways

- Technology allows for quick communication, transport, and mass marketing, greatly contributing to a globalized marketplace.

- Media economies of scale achieve much larger profit margins by using digital technology to sell information instantly over a global market.

- Foreign markets offer excellent profit potential as they contribute to media companies' economies of scale. The addition of new audiences and consumer markets may help a company build a global following in the long run.

Exercises

Think of a U.S. product that is available throughout the world, such as an athletic brand like Nike or a food product like Pepsi or Coca-Cola. Now go online to the different country-specific branches of the company's web site.

1. What differences are there?

2. How might the company be attempting to tailor its globalized product to a specific culture?

3. What advances into the foreign market does this use of the Internet allow the company to make?

4. What advantages does this globalization of its products give the company?

5. In what other ways has technology helped speed this globalization?

References

Box Office Mojo, "All Time Domestic Box Office Results," http://boxofficemojo.com/alltime/domestic.htm.

Mirza, Jan. "Globalization of Media: Key Issues and Dimensions," *European Journal of Scientific Research* 29, no. 1 (2009): 66–75.

Rantanen, Terhi. *The Media and Globalization* (Thousand Oaks, CA: Sage, 2005).

Santos, Josefina M. C. "Globalisation and Tradition: Paradoxes in Philippine Television and Culture," *Media Development*, no. 3 (2001): 43–48.

Terrill, Roman. "Globalization in the 1990s," *University of Iowa Center for International Finance and Development*, 1999, http://www.uiowa.edu/ifdebook/ebook2/contents/part3-I.shtml#B.

13.7 Cultural Imperialism

Learning Objectives

1. Describe how hegemony applies to different aspects of global culture.
2. Identify the attributes of McDonaldization.
3. Analyze the ways that local cultures respond to outside forces.

Cultural imperialism was around long before the United States became a world power. In its broadest strokes, imperialism describes the ways that one nation asserts its power over another. Just as imperial Britain economically ruled the American colonists, so did Britain strongly influence the culture of the colonies. The culture was still a mix of nationalities—many Dutch and Germans settled as well—but the ruling majority of ex-Britons led British culture to generally take over.

Today, cultural imperialism tends to describe the United States' role as a cultural superpower throughout the world. American movie studios are generally much more successful than their foreign counterparts not only because of their business models but also because the concept of Hollywood has become one of the modern worldwide movie business's defining traits. Multinational, nongovernmental corporations can now drive global culture. This is neither entirely good nor entirely bad. On one hand, foreign cultural institutions can adopt successful American business models, and corporations are largely willing to do whatever makes them the most money in a particular market—whether that means giving local people a shot at making movies, or making multicultural films such as 2008's *Slumdog Millionaire*. However, cultural imperialism has potential negative effects as well. From a spread of Western ideals of beauty to the possible decline of local cultures around the world, cultural imperialism can have a quick and devastating effect.

Cultural Hegemony

To begin discussing the topic of cultural imperialism, it is important to look at the ideas of one of its founding theorists, Antonio Gramsci. Strongly influenced by the theories and writings of Karl Marx, Italian philosopher and critic Gramsci originated the idea of cultural hegemony to describe the power of one group over another. Unlike Marx, who believed that the workers of the world would eventually unite and overthrow capitalism, Gramsci instead argued that culture and the media exert such a powerful influence on society that they can actually influence workers to buy into a system that is not economically advantageous to them. This argument that media can influence culture and politics is typified in the notion of the American Dream. In this rags-to-riches tale, hard work and talent can lead to a successful life no matter where one starts. Of course, there is some truth to this, but it is by far the exception rather than the rule.

Marx's ideas remained at the heart of Gramsci's beliefs. According to Gramsci's notion, the **hegemons** of capitalism—those who control the capital—can assert economic power, while the hegemons of culture can assert cultural power. This concept of culture is rooted in Marxist class struggle, in which one group is dominated by another and conflict arises. Gramsci's concept of cultural hegemony is pertinent in the modern day not because of the likelihood of a local property-owning class oppressing the poor, but because of concern that rising globalization will permit one culture to so completely assert its power that it drives out all competitors.

Spreading American Tastes Through McDonaldization

A key danger of cultural imperialism is the possibility that American tastes will crowd out local cultures around the globe. The McDonaldization of the globe applies not just to its namesake, McDonald's, with its franchises in seemingly every country, but to any industry that applies the technique of McDonald's on a large scale. Coined by George Ritzer in his book *The McDonaldization of Society* (1993), the concept is rooted in the process of rationalization. With McDonaldization, four aspects of the business are taken to the extreme: efficiency, calculability, predictability, and control. These four things are four of the main aspects of free markets. Applying the concepts of an optimized financial market to cultural and human items such as food, McDonaldization enforces general standards and consistency throughout a global industry.

Figure 13.6

McDonald's has opened up many culturally specific versions of its chain, all employing its famous Golden Arches.

Mike Mozart – McDonald's – CC BY 2.0.

Unsurprisingly, McDonald's is the prime example of this concept. Although the fast-food restaurant is somewhat different in every country—for example, Indian restaurants offer a pork-free, beef-free menu to accommodate regional religious practices—the same fundamental principles apply in a culturally specific way. The branding of the company is the same wherever it is; the "I'm lovin' it" slogan is inescapable, and the Golden Arches are, according to Eric Schlosser in *Fast Food Nation*, "more widely recognized than the Christian cross (Schlosser, 2001)." Yet, more importantly, the business model of McDonald's stays relatively the same from country to country. Although culturally specific variations exist, any McDonald's in a particular area has basically the same menu as any other. In other words, wherever a consumer is likely to travel within a reasonable range, the menu options and the resulting product remain consistent.

McDonaldizing Media

Media works in an uncannily similar way to fast food. Just as the automation of fast food—from freeze-dried french fries to prewrapped salads—attempts to lower a product's marginal costs, thus increasing profits, media outlets seek to achieve a certain degree of consistency that allows them to broadcast and sell the same product throughout the world with minimal changes. The idea that media actually spreads a culture, however, is controversial. In his book *Cultural Imperialism*, John Tomlinson argues that exported American culture is not necessarily imperialist because it does not push a cultural agenda; it seeks to make money from whatever cultural elements it can throughout the world. According to Tomlinson, "No one really disputes the dominant presence of Western multinational, and particularly American, media in the world: what is doubted is the cultural implications of this presence (Tomlinson, 2001)."

There are, of course, by-products of American cultural exports throughout the world. American cultural mores, such as the Western standard of beauty, have increasingly made it into global media. As early as 1987, Nicholas Kristof wrote in *The New York Times* about a young Chinese woman who was planning to have an operation to make her eyes look rounder, more like the eyes of Caucasian women. Western styles—"newfangled delights like nylon stockings, pierced ears and eye shadow"—also began to replace the austere blue tunics of Mao-era China. The pervasiveness of cultural influence is difficult to track, however, as the young Chinese woman says that she wanted to have the surgery not because of Western looks but because "she thinks they are pretty (Kristof, 1987)."

Cultural Imperialism, Resentment, and Terrorism

Figure 13.7

After September 11, 2001, President George W. Bush framed the issue of terrorism as a cultural conflict as much as a military one.

Wikimedia Commons – public domain.

Not everyone views the spread of American tastes as a negative occurrence. During the early 21st century, much of the United States's foreign policy stemmed from the idea that spreading freedom, democracy, and free-market capitalism through cultural influence around the world could cause hostile countries such as Iraq to adopt American ways of living and join the United States in the fight against global terrorism and tyranny. Although this plan did not succeed as hoped, it raises the question of whether Americans should truly be concerned about spreading their cultural system if they believe that it is an ideal one.

Speaking after the attacks of September 11, 2001, then-President George W. Bush presented two simple ideas to the U.S. populace: "They [terrorists] hate our freedoms," and "Go shopping (Bush, 2001)." These twin ideals of personal freedom and economic activity are often held up as the prime exports of American culture. However, the idea that other local beliefs need to change may threaten people of other cultures.

Freedom, Democracy, and Rock 'n' Roll

The spread of culture works in mysterious ways. Hollywood probably does not actually have a master plan to export the American way of life around the globe and displace local culture, just as American music may not necessarily be a progenitor of democratic government and economic cooperation. Rather, local cultures respond to the outside culture of U.S. media and democracy in many different ways. First of all, media are often much more flexible than believed; the successful exportation of the film *Titanic* was not an accident in which everyone in the world suddenly wanted to experience movies like an American. Rather, the film's producers had judged that it would succeed on a world stage just as on a domestic stage. Therefore, in some ways U.S. media have become more widespread, and also more worldwide in focus. It could even be argued that American cultural exports promote intercultural understanding; after all, to sell to a culture, a business must first understand that culture.

By contrast, some local cultures around the world have taken to Western-style business models so greatly that they have created their own hybrid cultures. One well-known example of this is India's Bollywood film industry. Combining traditional Indian music and dance with American-style filmmaking, Bollywood studios release around 700 major films each year, three times the rate of the major Hollywood studios. India's largest film industry mixes melodrama with musical interludes, lip-synced by actors but sung by pop stars. These pop songs are disseminated well before a movie's release, both to build up hype and to enter multiple media markets. Although similar marketing tactics have been employed in the United States, Bollywood seems to have mastered the art of cross-media integration. The music and dance numbers are essentially cinematic forms of music videos, both promoting the soundtrack and adding variety to the film. The numbers also feature many different Indian national languages and a hybrid of Western dance music and Indian classical singing, a certain departure from conventional Western media (Corliss, 1996).

While cultural imperialism might cause resentment in many parts of the world, the idea that local cultures are helpless under the crushing power of American cultural imposition is clearly too simplistic to hold water. Instead, local cultures seem to adopt American-style media models, changing their methods to fit the corporate structures rather than just the aesthetics of U.S. media. These two economic and cultural aspects are clearly intertwined, but the idea of a foreign power unilaterally crushing a native culture does not seem to be entirely true.

Key Takeaways

- Cultural hegemony refers to the power of the dominant culture to overshadow and even overtake local cultures.

- McDonaldization is characterized by efficiency, calculability, predictability, and control. These four attributes—more than any specific cultural ideas—are the primary features of globalized American businesses.

- Local cultures can respond to outside forces in many ways. In some circumstances, there may be a backlash against what can be seen as a hostile culture. However, cultures such as India have adopted American cultural and economic ideas to create a hybrid of foreign business models and local cultures.

Exercises

Please respond to the following short-answer writing prompts. Each response should be a minimum of one paragraph.

1. Pick a media company that interests you, such as a magazine, a television station, or a record label. In what ways has this company undergone the process of McDonaldization throughout its history? Has this process made the company more efficient? How so? What, if anything, has been

lost because of this process? Why?

2. In what ways does the United States act as a cultural hegemon?

3. How do local cultures respond to the influence of foreign culture? What are some examples of local cultures resisting the influence of foreign culture? What are some examples where local cultures have embraced foreign culture?

End-of-Chapter Assessment

Review Questions

1.
Section 1

    a. What are the three basic business models of media?

    b. Using the models you listed above, classify the following media industries: book publishing, television broadcasting, and live-event ticketing.

    c. What are the two ways that media companies make money?

2.
Section 2

    a. What is synergy, and how can media companies use it?

    b. Explain the purpose and influence of the Digital Millennium Copyright Act.

3.
Section 3

    a. What is the effect of digital communication in developing countries?

    b. How are citizens of developed countries who lack useful Internet access affected?

    c. What is the digital divide, and who is trying to close it? How?

4.
Section 4

    a. How does the information economy differ from the traditional economy?

    b. What are switching costs?

    c. How does vertical integration relate to globalized media?

5.
Section 5

    a. What effects has technology had on international economics?

b. What is globalization, and how does it affect the media?

c. How do the media increase profit margins in foreign countries?

6.
Section 6

a. What is hegemony?

b. What are the main traits of media McDonaldization?

c. Name a positive and a negative way in which culture may respond to an outside force.

Critical Thinking Questions

1. How do vertical integration, first copy costs, and the information economy relate to one another?

2. How does the digital divide affect developed and developing countries differently? What predictions can you make about its effects in the future?

3. How has the Internet changed the value of experience goods?

4. Is the application of antitrust legislation to media companies positive or negative? How does having a larger, more efficient media company help society? How does it damage society?

5. What is the effect of globalized media on world cultures? Do you think that the current trends will continue, or do you see local cultures reasserting their power? Give examples.

Career Connection

Media now rely heavily on synergy, or cross-platform media distribution. Because of this, one of the industry's quickly expanding career fields employs people who manage the online outlets of a more traditional media outlet such as radio or television. Although such jobs used to require extensive technological knowledge, modern online project managers, online media editors, and web producers spend much of their time determining how best to display the content online.

In this activity, you will research a media outlet and then answer questions about the choices that the web producer, editor, or manager made regarding its content. Some possible websites to research include the following:

- *Time,* http://www.time.com/
- *Adult Swim,* http://www.adultswim.com/
- *MSNBC,* http://www.msnbc.msn.com/
- *BBC,* http://www.bbc.co.uk/

Now answer the following questions regarding the site that you picked:

1. What sort of multimedia content does the site use that might relate to its main product?

2. Is there anything that might not relate to its main product? What might its purpose be?

3. How do the editorial decisions of the site reflect the influence of the Internet?

4. Are there any online-only content sections of the site? How might these relate to the corporation's main purpose?

References

Bush, President George W. address on terrorism before a joint meeting of Congress, *New York Times*, September 21, 2001, http://www.nytimes.com/2001/09/21/us/nation-challenged-president-bush-s-address-terrorism-before-joint-meeting.html.

Corliss, Richard. "Hooray for Bollywood!" *Time*, September 16, 1996, http://www.time.com/time/magazine/article/0,9171,985129,00.html.

Kristof, Nicholas D. "In China, Beauty Is a Big Western Nose," *New York Times*, April 29, 1987, http://www.nytimes.com/1987/04/29/garden/in-china-beauty-is-a-big-western-nose.html.

Schlosser, Eric, *Fast Food Nation: The Dark Side of the All-American Meal* (Boston: Houghton Mifflin, 2001), 4.

Tomlinson, John. *Cultural Imperialism: A Critical Introduction* (London: Continuum, 2001).

Chapter 14: Ethics of Mass Media

14.1 Ethics of Mass Media

TMZ, Tabloids, and Celebrity Gossip: Freedom of the Press or Invasion of Privacy?

Figure 14.1

Maryland GovPics – Press Gaggle – CC BY 2.0.

The U.S. Constitution's First Amendment guarantees Americans freedom of the press, which many would agree is an important ingredient in upholding democratic principles. Freedom from government censorship allows the news media to keep citizens informed about the state of their society. But when does the press take this freedom from censorship and restriction too far? The death of Princess Diana in 1997 brought fierce criticism against the paparazzi, and tabloid reporting in general, when it was found that the princess's car had been pursued by paparazzi vehicles before the crash that caused her death. Since then, the public's interest in celebrity gossip has not diminished; rather, the growth of online news sources has led to a proliferation of celebrity gossip websites.

A potential concern regarding this trend is that tabloid-style gossip is not confined to public figures in the entertainment industry; it can have far-reaching consequences. The firing of General Stanley McChrystal from his post as commander of all U.S. and NATO forces in Afghanistan in June 2010 was nearly the direct result of an article in *Rolling Stone*, in which he made less-than-flattering comments about Vice President Joe Biden

(Hastings, 2010). McChrystal himself did not directly criticize the president or the administration's policies; instead, his views were inferred from comments made by his aides (MSNBC, 2010). However, this was sufficient to cost him his job. In recent years, tabloid reporting has become increasingly invasive and sometimes dangerous.

Should the government begin placing stronger regulations on tabloid reporting as privacy advocates have argued? The Constitution, after all, while guaranteeing freedom of the press, also guarantees individuals certain rights to privacy, and most journalists would agree that standards of ethical journalism include efforts to protect these rights. However, some paparazzi photographers and celebrity journalists disregard journalistic codes of ethics in their efforts to get a story (Alach, 2008). Many argue that because celebrities are "public figures," the same privacy rights that protect the general public don't apply. *Us Weekly*'s editor in chief, Janice Min, has argued, "A celebrity is like an elected official. If you're getting paid $20 million a movie, you have to rely on public goodwill to stay in office. You have to accept the fact that you're a public commodity (Freydkin, 2004)." Harvey Levin, editor in chief for the popular celebrity gossip blog TMZ, would agree. When discussing invasions into the private lives of stars like Britney Spears, Levin proclaimed that "Britney is gold; she is crack to our readers. Her life is a complete train-wreck and I thank God for her every day (New York Times, 2009)."

On the other side of the debate, many argue that the public-figure limitation should be balanced with the consideration of a story's newsworthiness. As law professor Patrick J. Alack has argued, "If 'social value' is what constitutes newsworthiness, it is hard to imagine a more perverse concept of social value that incorporates…Paris Hilton's late-night dining preferences or Lindsay Lohan's driving habits."[1]

TMZ, a website that publishes celebrity news in real time, was launched in 2005, and since its creation the site has received numerous criticisms from more prestigious news sources like *The Washington Post* and ABC News. Yet Thane Burnett, reporter for *The Toronto Sun*, admits that "despite the sideways glances, mainstream news services prowl TMZ's site for coverage (Burnett, 2009)." With the immediacy of Internet news coverage, mainstream media outlets face increasing pressure to release major news while it is still fresh. That pressure is compounded by celebrity gossip sites like TMZ that may resort to unorthodox methods to gather information; the shelf life of breaking news is growing increasingly shorter.

[1]Alach, "Paparazzi and Privacy," 237.

References

Alach, Patrick J. "Paparazzi and Privacy," *Loyola of Los Angeles Entertainment Law Review* 28, no. 3 (2008): 205.

Burnett, Thane. "Caught on Camera," *Toronto Sun*, May 12, 2009, http://www.torontosun.com/entertainment/celebrities/2009/05/12/9429036-sun.html.

Freydkin, Donna. "Celebrities Fight for Privacy," *USA Today*, July 6, 2004, http://www.usatoday.com/life/people/2004-07-06-celeb-privacy_x.htm.

Hastings, Michael. "The Runaway General," *Rolling Stone*, June 25, 2010, http://www.rollingstone.com/politics/news/17390/119236.

MSNBC, "Obama, McCain, Kerry Comment on McChrystal," June 22, 2010, http://www.msnbc.msn.com/id/37850711/ns/us_news-military/.

New York Times, "TMZ Productions," Times Topics, July 7, 2009, http://topics.nytimes.com/top/news/business/companies/tmz_productions/index.html?scp=1-spot&sq=tmz&st=cse.

14.2 Ethical Issues in Mass Media

Learning Objectives

1. Explain the importance of racial and gender diversity in mass media.
2. Identify the ethical concerns associated with race and gender stereotypes.
3. List some common concerns about sexual content in the media.

In the competitive and rapidly changing world of mass-media communications, media professionals—overcome by deadlines, bottom-line imperatives, and corporate interests—can easily lose sight of the ethical implications of their work. However, as entertainment law specialist Sherri Burr points out, "Because network television is an audiovisual medium that is piped free into ninety-nine percent of American homes, it is one of the most important vehicles for depicting cultural images to our population (Burr, 2001)." Considering the profound influence mass media like television have on cultural perceptions and attitudes, it is important for the creators of media content to grapple with ethical issues.

Stereotypes, Prescribed Roles, and Public Perception

The U.S. population is becoming increasingly diverse. According to U.S. Census statistics from 2010, 27.6 percent of the population identifies its race as non-White (U.S. Census Bureau, 2010). Yet in network television broadcasts, major publications, and other forms of mass media and entertainment, minorities are often either absent or presented as heavily stereotyped, two-dimensional characters. Rarely are minorities depicted as complex characters with the full range of human emotions, motivations, and behaviors. Meanwhile, the stereotyping of women, gays and lesbians, and individuals with disabilities in mass media has also been a source of concern.

The word *stereotype* originated in the printing industry as a method of making identical copies, and the practice of stereotyping people is much the same: a system of identically replicating an image of an "other." As related in Chapter 8 "Movies" about D. W. Griffith's *The Birth of a Nation*, a film that relied on racial stereotypes to portray Southern Whites as victims in the American Civil War, stereotypes—especially those disseminated through mass media—become a form of social control, shaping collective perceptions and individual identities. In American mass media, the White man is still shown as the standard: the central figure of TV narratives and the dominant perspective on everything from trends, to current events, to politics. White maleness becomes an invisible category because it gives the impression of being the norm (Hearne).

Minority Exclusion and Stereotypes

In the fall of 1999, when the major television networks released their schedules for the upcoming programming season, a startling trend became clear. Of the 26 newly released TV programs, none depicted an African American in a leading role, and even the secondary roles on these shows included almost no racial minorities. In response to this omission, the National Association for the Advancement of Colored People (NAACP) and the National Council of La Raza (NCLR), an advocacy group for Hispanic Americans, organized protests and boycotts. Pressured—and embarrassed—into action, the executives from the major networks made a fast dash to add racial minorities to their prime-time shows, not only among actors, but also among producers, writers, and directors. Four of the networks—ABC, CBS, NBC, and Fox—added a vice president of diversity position to help oversee the networks' progress toward creating more diverse programming (Baynes, 2003).

Despite these changes and greater public attention regarding diversity issues, minority underrepresentation is still an issue in all areas of mass media. In fact, the trend in recent years has been regressive. In a recent study, the NAACP reported that the number of minority actors on network television has actually decreased, from 333 during the 2002–2003 season to 307 four years later (WWAY, 2009). Racial minorities are often absent, peripheral, or take on stereotyped roles in film, television, print media, advertising, and even in video games. Additionally, according to a 2002 study by the University of California, Los Angeles, the problem is not only a visible one, but also one that extends behind the scenes. The study found that minorities are even more underrepresented in creative and decision-making positions than they are on screen (Media Awareness Network, 2010). This lack of representation among producers, writers, and directors often directly affects the way minorities are portrayed in film and television, leading to racial stereotypes.

Though advocacy groups like the NCLR and the NAACP have often been at the forefront of protests against minority stereotypes in the media, experts are quick to point out that the issue is one everyone should be concerned about. As media ethicist Leonard M. Baynes argues, "Since we live in a relatively segregated country…broadcast television and its images and representations are very important because television can be the common meeting ground for all Americans."[1] There are clear correlations between mass media portrayals of minority groups and public perceptions. In 1999, after hundreds of complaints by African Americans that they were unable to get taxis to pick them up, the city of New York launched a crackdown, threatening to revoke the licenses of cab drivers who refused to stop for African American customers. When interviewed by reporters, many cab drivers blamed their actions on fears they would be robbed or asked to drive to dangerous neighborhoods.[2]

Racial stereotypes are not only an issue in entertainment media; they also find their way into news reporting, which is a form of storytelling. Journalists, editors, and reporters are still predominately White. According to a 2000 survey, only 11.6 percent of newsroom staff in the United States were racial and ethnic minorities (Media Awareness Network, 2010). The situation has not improved dramatically during the past decade. According to a 2008 newsroom census released by the American Society of Newspaper Editors, the percentage of minority journalists working at daily newspapers was a scant 13.52 percent (National Association of Hispanic Journalists, 2010). Because of this underrepresentation behind the scenes, the news media is led by those whose perspective is already privileged, who create the narratives about those without privilege. In the news media, racial minorities are often cast in the role of villains or troublemakers, which in turn shapes public perceptions about these groups. Media critics Robert Entman and Andrew Rojecki point out that images of African Americans on welfare, African American violence, and urban crime in African American communities "facilitate the construction of menacing imagery (Christians, 2005)." Similarly, a study by the National Association of Hispanic Journalists found that only 1 percent of the evening news stories aired by the three major U.S. television networks cover Latinos or Latino issues, and that when Latinos are featured, they are portrayed negatively 80 percent of the time.[3] Still others have criticized journalists and reporters for a tendency toward reductive presentations of complex issues involving minorities, such as the religious and racial tensions fueled by the September 11 attacks. By reducing these conflicts to "opposing frames"—that is, by oversimplifying them as two-sided struggles so that they can be quickly and easily understood—the news media helped create a greater sense of separation between Islamic Americans and the dominant culture after September 11, 2001 (Whitehouse, 2009).

Since the late 1970s, the major professional journalism organizations in the United States—Associated Press Managing Editors (APME), Newspaper Association of America (NAA), American Society of Newspaper Editors (ASNE), Society for Professional Journalists (SPJ), Radio and Television News Directors Association (RTNDA), and others—have included greater ethnic diversity as a primary goal or ethic. However, progress has been slow. ASNE has set 2025 as a target date to have minority representation in newsrooms match U.S. demographics.[4]

Because the programming about, by, and for ethnic minorities in the mainstream media is disproportionately low, many turn to niche publications and channels such as BET, Univision, Telemundo, *Essence, Jet*, and others for sources of information and entertainment. In fact, 45 percent of ethnic-minority adults prefer these niche media sources to mainstream television, radio programs, and newspapers.(Whitehouse, 2009) These sources cover stories about racial minorities that are generally ignored by the mainstream press and offer ethnic-minority perspectives on more widely covered issues in the news (State of the Media, 2010). Entertainment channels like BET (a 24-hour cable television station that offers music videos, dramas featuring predominately Black casts, and other original programming created by African Americans) provide the diverse programming that mainstream TV networks often drop (Zellars, 2006). Print sources like *Vista*, a bilingual magazine targeting U.S. Hispanics, and *Vivid*, the most widely circulated African American periodical, appeal to ethnic minority groups because they are controlled and created by individuals within these groups. Though some criticize ethnic niche media, claiming that they erode common ground or, in some instances, perpetuate stereotypes, the popularity of these media has only grown in recent years and will likely continue in the absence of more diverse perspectives in mainstream media sources (Tran; Flint, 2010).

Femininity in Mass Media

In the ABC sitcom *The Donna Reed Show* (1958–1966), actress Donna Reed plays a stay-at-home mother who fills her days with housework, cooking for her husband and children, decorating, and participating in community organizations, all while wearing pearls, heels, and stylish dresses. Such a traditional portrayal of femininity no doubt sounds dated to modern audiences, but stereotyped gender roles continue to thrive in the mass media. Women are still often represented as subordinate to their male counterparts—emotional, noncompetitive, domestic, and sweet natured. In contrast to these types, other women are represented as unattractively masculine, crazy, or cruel. In TV dramas and sitcoms, women continue to fill traditional roles such as mothers, nurses, secretaries, and housewives. By contrast, men in film and television are less likely to be shown in the home, and male characters are generally characterized by dominance, aggression, action, physical strength, and ambition

(Chandler). In the mainstream news media, men are predominately featured as authorities on specialized issues like business, politics, and economics, while women are more likely to report on stories about natural disasters or domestic violence—coverage that does not require expertise (Media Awareness Network).

Not only is the White male perspective still presented as the standard, authoritative one, but also the media itself often comes to embody the male gaze. Media commentator Nancy Hass notes that "shows that don't focus on men have to feature the sort of women that guys might watch (Media Awareness Network)." Feminist critics have long been concerned by the way women in film, television, and print media are defined by their sexuality. Few female role models exist in the media who are valued primarily for qualities like intelligence or leadership. Inundated by images that conform to unrealistic beauty standards, women come to believe at an early age that their value depends on their physical attractiveness. According to one *Newsweek* article, eating disorders in girls are now routinely being diagnosed at younger ages, sometimes as early as eight or nine. The models who appear in magazines and print advertising are unrealistically skinny (23 percent thinner than the average woman), and their photographs are further enhanced to hide flaws and blemishes. Meanwhile, the majority of women appearing on television are under the age of 30, and many older actresses, facing the pressure to embody the youthful ideal, undergo surgical enhancements to appear younger (Derenne & Beresin, 2006). One recent example is TV news host Greta Van Susteren, a respected legal analyst who moved from CNN to Fox in 2002. At the debut of her show, *On the Record*, Van Susteren, sitting behind a table that allowed viewers to see her short skirt, had undergone not only a hair and wardrobe makeover, but also surgical enhancement to make her appear younger and more attractive.[5]

In addition to the prevalence of gender stereotypes, the ratio of men to women in the mass media, in and behind the scenes, is also disproportionate. Surprisingly, though women slightly outnumber men in the general population, over two-thirds of TV sitcoms feature men in the starring role (Media Awareness Network). Among writers, producers, directors, and editors, the number of women lags far behind. In Hollywood, for instance, only 17 percent of behind-the-scenes creative talent is represented by women. Communications researcher Martha Lauzen argues that "when women have more powerful roles in the making of a movie or TV show, we know that we also get more powerful female characters on-screen, women who are more real and more multi-dimensional (Media Awareness Network)."

Sexual Content in Public Communication

Creators of all forms of media know that sex—named, innuendoed, or overtly displayed—is a surefire way to grab an audience's attention. "Sex sells" is an advertising cliché; the list of products that advertisers have linked to erotic imagery or innuendo, from cosmetics and cars to vacation packages and beer, is nearly inexhaustible. Most often, sexualized advertising content is served up in the form of the female body, in part or in whole, featured in provocative or suggestive poses beside a product that may have nothing to do with sexuality. However, by linking these two things, advertisers are marketing desire itself.

Figure 14.2

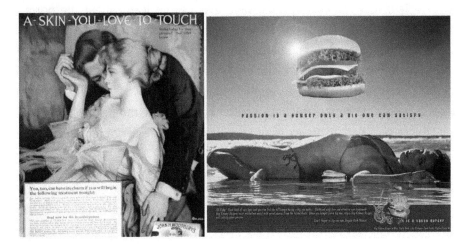

Sex Sells: Commodifying Desire, Past and Present

Sex is used to sell not just consumer goods; it sells media, too. Music videos on MTV and VH1, which promote artists and their music, capture audience attention with highly suggestive dance moves, often performed by scantily clad women. Movie trailers may flash brief images of nudity or passionate kissing to suggest more to come in the movie. Video games feature female characters like Lara Croft of *Tomb Raider*, whose tightly fitted clothes reveal all the curves of her Barbie-doll figure. And partially nude models grace the cover of men's and women's magazines like *Maxim*, *Cosmopolitan*, and *Vogue* where cover lines promise titillating tips, gossip, and advice on bedroom behavior (Reichert & Lambiase, 2005).

In the 1920s and 1930s, filmmakers attracted audiences to the silver screen with the promise of what was then considered scandalous content. Prior to the 1934 Hays Code, which placed restrictions on "indecent" content in movies, films featured erotic dances, male and female nudity, references to homosexuality, and sexual violence (for more information on the Hays Code, see Chapter 8 "Movies" and Chapter 15 "Media and Government"). D. W. Griffith's *Intolerance* (1916) includes scenes with topless actresses, as does *Ben Hur* (1925). In Warner Bros.' *Female* (1933), the leading lady, the head of a major car company, spends her evenings in sexual exploits with her male employees, a story line that would never have passed the Hays Code a year later (Morris, 1996). *Trouble in Paradise*, a 1932 romantic comedy, was withdrawn from circulation after the institution of the Hays Code because of its frank discussion of sexuality. Similarly, *Dr. Jekyll and Mr. Hyde* (1931), which featured a prostitute as one of the main characters, was also banned under the code (Hauesser, 2007).

In the 1960s, when the sexual revolution led to increasingly permissive attitudes toward sexuality in American culture, the Hays Code was replaced with the MPAA rating system. The rating system, designed to warn parents about potentially objectionable material in films, allowed filmmakers to include sexually explicit content without fear of public protest. Since the replacement of the Hays Code, sexual content has been featured in movies with much greater frequency.

The problem, according to many media critics, is not that sex now appears more often, but that it is almost always portrayed unrealistically in American mass media (Galician, 2004). This can be harmful, they say, because the mass media are important socialization agents; that is, ways that people learn about the norms, expectations, and values of their society.[6] Sex, as many films, TV shows, music videos, and song lyrics present it, is frequent and casual. Rarely do these media point out the potential emotional and physical consequences of sexual behavior. According to one study, portrayals of sex that include possible risks like sexually transmitted diseases or pregnancy only occur in 15 percent of the sexually explicit material on TV (Parents Television Council). Additionally, actors and models depicted in sexual relationships in the media are thinner, younger, and more attractive than the average adult. This creates unrealistic expectations about the necessary ingredients for a satisfying sexual relationship.

Social psychologists are particularly concerned with the negative effects these unrealistic portrayals have on women, as women's bodies are the primary means of introducing sexual content into media targeted at both men and women. Media activist Jean Kilbourne points out that "women's bodies are often dismembered into legs, breasts or thighs, reinforcing the message that women are objects rather than whole human beings." *Adbusters*, a magazine that critiques mass media, particularly advertising, points out the sexual objectification of women's bodies in a number of its spoof advertisements, such as the one in Figure 14.3, bringing home the message that advertising often sends unrealistic and harmful messages about women's bodies and sexuality. Additionally, many researchers note that in women's magazines, advertising, and music videos, women are often implicitly—and sometimes explicitly—given the message that a primary concern should be attracting and sexually satisfying men (Parents Televison Council). Furthermore, the recent increase in entertainment featuring sexual violence may, according to some studies, negatively affect the way young men behave toward women (Gunter, 2002).

Figure 14.3

Sexual objectification: Women's bodies are often headless or dismembered into legs, breasts, or thighs in media portrayals (Adbusters).

Chelsea K – Adbust – CC BY-NC 2.0.

Young women and men are especially vulnerable to the effects of media portrayals of sexuality. Psychologists have long noted that teens and children get much of their information and many of their opinions about sex through TV, film, and online media. In fact, two-thirds of adolescents turn to the media first when they want to learn about sexuality.[7] The media may help shape teenage and adolescent attitudes toward sex, but they can also lead young people to engage in sexual activity before they are prepared to handle the consequences. According to one study, kids with high exposure to sex on television were almost twice as likely to initiate sexual activity compared to kids without exposure (Collins, et. al., 2004).

Cultural critics have noted that sexually explicit themes in mass media are generally more widely accepted in European nations than they are in the United States. However, the increased concern and debates over censorship of sexual content in the United States may in fact be linked to the way sex is portrayed in American media rather than to the presence of the sexual content in and of itself. Unrealistic portrayals that fail to take into account the actual complexity of sexual relationships seem to be a primary concern. As Jean Kilbourne has argued, sex in the American media "has far more to do with trivializing sex than with promoting it. We are offered a pseudo-sexuality that makes it far more difficult to discover our own unique and authentic sexuality."[8] However, despite these criticisms, it is likely that unrealistic portrayals of sexual content will continue to be the norm in mass media unless the general public stops consuming these images.

Key Takeaways

- In American mass media, where the White male perspective is still presented as the standard, stereotypes of those who differ—women, ethnic minorities, and gays and lesbians—are an issue of ethical concern.

- Racial minorities are often absent, peripheral, or stereotyped in film, television, print media, advertising, and video games.

- Racial stereotypes occur in news reporting, where they influence public perceptions.

- Underrepresentation of women and racial and ethnic minorities is also a problem in the hiring of creative talent behind the scenes.

- The media still often subordinate women to traditional roles, where they serve as support for their male counterparts.

- The objectification of women in various visual media has particularly led to concerns about body image, unrealistic social expectations, and negative influences on children and adolescent girls.

- "Sex sells" consumer products and media such as movies and music videos.

- The issue of sexual content in the media has become a source of concern to media critics because of the frequency with which it occurs and also because of the unrealistic way it is portrayed.

Exercises

Choose a television show or movie you are familiar with and consider the characters in terms of racial and gender diversity. Then answer the following short-answer questions. Each response should be one to two paragraphs.

1. Does the show or movie you've chosen reflect racial and gender diversity? Why or why not? Explain why this kind of diversity is important in media.

2. Are there any racial or gender stereotypes present in the show or movie you've chosen? If so, identify them and describe how they are stereotypical. If not, describe what elements would prevent the portrayal of a female or ethnic minority characters from being stereotypical.

3. Does the show or movie you've selected feature any sexual content? If so, do you think that the content is gratuitous or unrealistic, or does it serve the story? Explain your answer. Then explain why the use of sexual content in media is a concern for many media critics.

[1]Baynes, "White Out," 293.

[2]Burr, "Television and Societal Effects," 159.

[3]Media Awareness Network, "Ethnic and Visible Minorities in the News."

[4]Whitehouse, "Why Diversity Is an Ethical Issue," 102.

[5]Media Awareness Network, "Media Coverage."

[6]Galician, *Sex, Love & Romance*, 82.

[7]Media Awareness Network, "Sex and Relationships in the Media."

[8]Media Awareness Network, "Sex and Relationships in the Media."

References

Adbusters, "Spoof Ads," https://www.adbusters.org/gallery/spoofads.

Baynes, Leonard M. "White Out: The Absence and Stereotyping of People of Color by the Broadcast Networks in Prime Time Entertainment Programming," *Arizona Law Review* 45 (2003): 293.

Burr, Sherri. "Television and Societal Effects: An Analysis of Media Images of African-Americans in Historical Context," *Journal of Gender, Race and Justice* 4 (2001): 159.

Chandler, Daniel. "Television and Gender Roles" http://www.aber.ac.uk/media/Modules/TF33120/gendertv.html#E.

Christians, Clifford G. "Communication Ethics," in *Encyclopedia of Science, Technology, and Ethics*, ed. Carl Mitchum (Detroit: Macmillan Reference USA, 2005), 1:366.

Collins, Rebecca L. and others, "Watching Sex on Television Predicts Adolescent Initiation of Sexual Behavior," *Pediatrics* 114, no. 3 (2004), http://pediatrics.aappublications.org/cgi/content/full/114/3/e280.

Derenne, Jennifer L. and Eugene V. Beresin, "Body Image, Media, and Eating Disorders," *Academic Psychiatry* 30 (2006), http://ap.psychiatryonline.org/cgi/content/full/30/3/257.

Flint, Joe. "No Black-and-White Answer for the Lack of Diversity on Television," *Company Town* (blog), *Los Angeles Times*, June 11, 2010, http://latimesblogs.latimes.com/entertainmentnewsbuzz/2010/06/diversity-television.html.

Galician, Mary Lou. *Sex, Love & Romance in the Mass Media* (New York: Routledge, 2004), 5; Media Awareness Network, "Sex and Relationships in the Media," *Media Awareness Network*, http://www.media-awareness.ca/english/issues/stereotyping/women_and_girls/women_sex.cfm.

Gunter, Barrie. *Media Sex: What Are the Issues?* (Mahwah, NJ: Lawrence Erlbaum Associates, 2002), 8.

Hauesser, Daniel P. "Indecent and Deviant: Pre-Hays Code Films You Should See," *indieWIRE*, 2007, http://www.spout.com/groups/Top_5/Re_5_Pre_Hays_Code_Films/190/19210/1/ShowPost.aspx.

Hearne, Joanna. "Hollywood Whiteness and Stereotypes," Film Reference, http://www.filmreference.com/encyclopedia/Independent-Film-Road-Movies/Race-and-Ethnicity-HOLLYWOOD-WHITENESS-AND-STEREOTYPES.html.

Media Awareness Network, "Ethnic and Visible Minorities in Entertainment Media," 2010, http://www.media-awareness.ca/english/issues/stereotyping/ethnics_and_minorities/minorities_entertainment.cfm.

Media Awareness Network, "Ethnic and Visible Minorities in the News," 2010, http://www.media-awareness.ca/english/issues/stereotyping/ethnics_and_minorities/minorities_news.cfm.

Media Awareness Network, "Media Coverage of Women and Women's Issues," http://www.media-awareness.ca/english/issues/stereotyping/women_and_girls/women_working.cfm.

Media Awareness Network, "The Economics of Gender Stereotyping," http://www.media-awareness.ca/english/issues/stereotyping/women_and_girls/women_economics.cfm.

Media Awareness Network, "Women Working in the Media," http://www.media-awareness.ca/english/issues/stereotyping/women_and_girls/women_working.cfm.

Morris, Gary. "Public Enemy: Warner Brothers in the Pre-Code Era," *Bright Lights Film Journal*, September 1996, http://www.brightlightsfilm.com/17/04b_warner.php.

National Association of Hispanic Journalists, "NAHJ Disturbed by Figures That Mask Decline in Newsroom Diversity," news release, 2010, http://www.nahj.org/nahjnews/articles/2008/April/ASNE.shtml.

Parents Television Council, "Facts and TV Statistics," http://www.parentstv.org/ptc/facts/mediafacts.asp.

Reichert, Tom and Jacqueline Lambiase, "Peddling Desire: Sex and the Marketing of Media and Consumer Goods," *Sex in Consumer Culture: The Erotic Content of Media and Marketing*, ed. Tom Reichert and Jacqueline Lambiase (New York: Routledge, 2005), 3.

State of the Media, Pew Project for Excellence in Journalism, "Ethnic," in *The State of the News Media 2010*, http://www.stateofthemedia.org/2010/ethnic_summary_essay.php.

Tran, Can. "TV Network Reviews: Black Entertainment Television (BET)," *Helium*, http://www.helium.com/items/884989-tv-network-reviews-black-entertainment-television-bet.

U.S. Census Bureau, "2010 Census Data," http://2010.census.gov/2010census/data/.

Whitehouse, Ginny. "Why Diversity Is an Ethical Issue," *The Handbook of Mass Media Ethics*, ed. Lee Wilkins and Clifford G. Christians (New York: Routledge, 2009), 101.

WWAY, "NAACP Not Pleased With the Diversity on Television," January 12, 2009, http://www.wwaytv3.com/ naacp_not_pleased_diversity_television/01/2009.

Zellars, Rachel. "Black Entertainment Television (BET)," in *Encyclopedia of African-American Culture and History*, 2nd ed., ed. Colin A. Palmer (Detroit: Macmillan Reference USA, 2006.) 1:259.

14.3 News Media and Ethics

Learning Objectives

1. Describe the role of media in delivering news to the public.

2. Identify the important characteristics of reliable journalism.

3. Summarize the effects of bias in news presentations.

Now more than ever, with the presence of online news sources, news delivery is expected to be instantaneous, and journalists and news agencies face pressure to release stories rapidly to keep up with competing media sources. With this added pressure, standards of accuracy and fairness become more difficult to uphold. What wins when ethical responsibility and bottom-line concerns are at odds? Columnist Ellen Goodman notes that there has always been a tension in journalism between being first and being right. She argues, "In today's amphetamine world of news junkies, speed trumps thoughtfulness too often (Goodman, 1993)." As you read the following sections, decide if you agree with Goodman's assessment of the state of the news media today.

Immediate News Delivery

In 1916, audiences across America tuned in to their radios to hear the first-ever breaking-news coverage of an event as the results of the presidential election between Woodrow Wilson and Charles Evans Hughes were announced from the offices of *The New York American*. Until that broadcast, news was delivered to American homes once per day in the form of a newspaper, and often this coverage lagged a day or more behind the actual incidents it reported. Whereas much of radio news coverage even into the 1930s involved the reading of newspaper stories and news wires on the air, radio offered something that the newspapers could not: live coverage of special events (Govier, 2007).

For decades, the public turned to the family radio when they wanted to hear the most recent coverage of important news. All of that changed, however, in 1963 with the assassination of President John F. Kennedy. CBS correspondent Dan Rather took television audiences live to "the corner window just below the top floor, where the assassin stuck out his 30 caliber rifle," and for the first time, people were able to see an event nearly as it occurred. This was the beginning of round-the-clock news coverage, and the American public, while still relying on print news for detailed coverage, came to expect greater immediacy of major event reporting through TV and radio broadcasts (Holguin, 2005).

Today, with the widespread availability of Internet news, instant coverage is the norm rather than the exception, and the Internet has generally replaced TV and radio as the source of immediate information. Visitors to ABCNews.com can watch an evening newscast three and a half hours before it airs on television (Sullivan, 2006). RSS (which stands for *Really Simple Syndication,* a standard for the easy syndication of online content) feeds, home pages for major news-delivery sites like Yahoo! News and CNN.com, news tickers, live video streams, blogs, Twitter, and a host of other media outlets ensure that news—and rumors of news—circulates within minutes of its occurrence. Additionally, with smartphone applications like those for *The New York Times* and *USA Today,* people can access the latest news coverage from almost anywhere.

The development of the Internet as a source of free and immediate access to information has forever changed the structure of the news media. Newspaper, television, and radio news programs have all had to adapt and diversify to compete for a share of the market. As Jeffrey Cole, director of the Center for Digital Communication put it, "For the first time in 60 years, newspapers are back in the breaking news business." Online, newspapers can compete with broadcast media for immediate coverage, posting articles on their home pages as soon as the stories are written, and supplementing the articles on their websites with audiovisual content. Gone is the era of single-medium newsrooms with predictable deadlines (USC Annenberg School for Communication and Journalism, 2009).

Not only are traditional news media restructuring, but news consumers are also changing the way they access information. Increasingly, audiences want news on demand; they want to get news when they want it, and they want to be able to gather it from a variety of sources. This is having a significant effect on media revenues. News aggregators, websites like Yahoo! News and Google News that compile news headlines from an array of legacy news organizations to display on their pages, have become popular information outlets. Although these websites don't hire reporters to produce news stories themselves, they get about the same amount of online traffic as websites for legacy news organizations like CNN and *The Wall Street Journal*. Moreover, many subscribers to print newspapers and magazines are canceling their subscriptions because they can get more current information online at no cost (State of the Media, 2010). Print advertising is down as well. In 2004, *The San Francisco Chronicle* reported losing $50 million in classified advertising to free online options like Craigslist.[1]

This loss of revenue has become a problem in recent years because while newspapers and magazines generate some income from advertisements on their websites, the money is not enough to compensate for lost readership and print ads. Subscriptions and advertising in traditional print media still account for 90 percent of industry funds, which means with less revenue in these areas, the support base for news organizations is dwindling. Newspapers and magazines across the country have had to restructure and scale down. Newspapers now spend $1.6 billion less annually on reporting and editing than they did 10 years ago (State of the Media, 2010).

Additionally, reduced budgets combined with greater pressure for immediacy have changed the way information gets reported and disseminated. Newsrooms are asking their staffs to focus on producing first accounts more quickly to feed multiple platforms. This often means that more resources go into distributing information than gathering it. Once news is released online by one source, it spreads rapidly, and other organizations scramble to release accounts, too, in order to keep up, often leaving staff less time for fact-checking and editing. The initial story is then followed quickly by commentary from both professional news organizations and nonprofessional sources on blogs, Twitter, and other social networks.

As a result of this restructuring, certain stories may get distributed, replayed, and commented on almost excessively, while other stories go unnoticed and in-depth coverage that would unearth more facts and context gets neglected. This has led a number of industry professionals to become anxious over the future of the news industry. The Center for Excellence in Journalism has called the news industry today "more reactive than proactive (State of the Media, 2010)." Journalist Patricia Sullivan complains, "Right now, almost no online news sites invest in original, in-depth and scrupulously edited news reporting."[2] While some may disagree with Sullivan, in-depth journalism remains an expensive and time-consuming venture that many online news sites, faced with uncertain revenue streams and a growing consumer demand for real-time news updates, are reluctant to bankroll extensively.

Already strapped for funds, news organizations know they have to cater to public demands, and foremost among these demands is speed. When pop-music icon Michael Jackson died on June 26, 2009, at 2:26 p.m., news of his death hit cyberspace by 2:44 p.m. and soon spread nationwide via Twitter. Surprisingly, the initial report of Jackson's death was released by celebrity gossip website TMZ. Legacy news sources were slower to publish accounts. The *Los Angeles Times*, wary of the sourcing of the story, waited to confirm the news and didn't publish the story on its website until 3:15 p.m., by which time, thanks to the speed of social media, the star's death was already "old news (Collins & Braxton, 2009)."

Figure 14.4

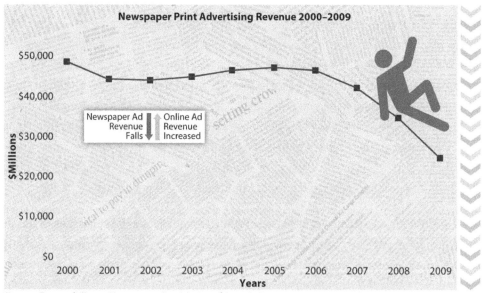

Source: Research Dept., Newspaper Association of America

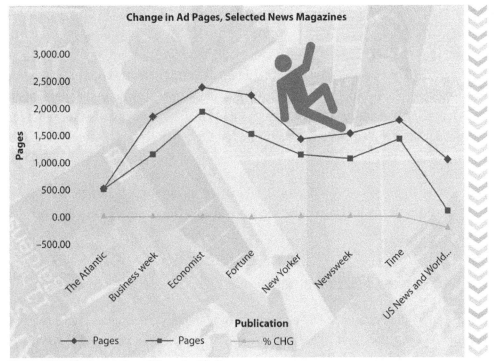

Source: MPA, The Association of Magazine Media.

American news organizations are losing their audiences to online media and have lost billions in advertising income.

Social Responsibility of News Media

In the preamble to its statement of purpose, the Committee of Concerned Journalists lists as the central purpose of journalism "to provide citizens with accurate and reliable information they need to function in a free society (Committee of Concerned Journalists)." This theory of the social responsibility of the press is often referred to as the vital information premise. Though sometimes worded differently by different organizations, it is widely accepted in the journalism community as the foundation for any principles of media ethics (Iggers, 1999). What are those specific principles? Here are some that are particularly important for journalists in the current media climate.

Present News Stories That Inform and Serve the Needs of Citizens

If the basis for the principles of ethical news reporting is giving citizens the information they need to function in a democratic society, then that information must be presented accurately. Journalists should be careful to verify the facts before they report them. As the Committee of Concerned Journalists asserts, "Accuracy is the foundation upon which everything else is built—context, interpretation, comment, criticism, analysis and debate," so reliable news sources are essential if citizens are to have a clear understanding of the society in which they live.[3] Furthermore, although news organizations have a professional responsibility toward advertisers and shareholders, their commitment is always to citizens first. This means that journalists must report the facts truthfully and without omission, even if they are not in the best interest of advertisers, shareholders, or friends.

Present Issues Fairly

Reporting issues fairly requires not only factual accuracy, but also lack of favoritism toward any organization, political group, ideology, or other agenda. The Society of Professional Journalists stipulates that journalists should refuse gifts and favors and avoid political involvement or public office if these things compromise journalistic integrity (Society of Professional Journalists). Additionally, journalists should avoid inflating stories for sensation and be as transparent as possible about their sources of information so that the public can investigate the issues further on their own.[4]

All sides of an issue should be presented in a news story. Of course, all journalists have a perspective from which they write, but a clear distinction should be made between news reports and editorial content (American Society of News Editors, 2009).

Present Stories in a Way That Addresses Their Complexity

Many issues in the news are layered and highly complex. Developing a thorough understanding of issues requires dedication and a sometimes lengthy investigation, and, especially in a world where rapid reporting is the norm, there can be a temptation to gloss over the finer points of an issue for the sake of efficiency. Additionally, most consumers of news, increasingly busy and overwhelmed by the amount of information available, want stories that can be quickly digested and easily comprehended. However, as the Committee of Concerned Journalists points out, the media must balance what readers want with what they need but cannot anticipate.[5] Oversimplifying issues, whether for the sake of a quick story or to satisfy public tastes, becomes a violation of the vital information premise.[6]

Present Diverse Perspectives

When discussing what he considers to be one of the key issues in professional journalism, media ethicist Jeremy Iggers points out that because democracy means the widest possible participation of citizens in public life, diversity in journalism is of fundamental importance.[7] Not only should newsroom staff represent a diversity of gender and races, but journalists should also speak for all groups in society—"not just those with attractive demographics," as the Committee for Concerned Journalists puts it. Journalists should represent the underrepresented because ignoring citizens is a form of disenfranchisement.[8]

Monitor Government and Corporations

When the framers of the U.S. Constitution guaranteed freedom of the press, one of the things they had in mind was the ability of the news media to serve as a watchdog over those in positions of power (Committee of Concerned Journalists). It is the duty of the press to ensure that business is conducted in the open and that government actions are public. One famous example of the media fulfilling its watchdog role was *The Washington Post*'s investigation of the 1972 Watergate scandal. During Richard Nixon's presidency, journalists at the *Post* uncovered information linking government agencies and officials to the break-in at the Democratic National Committee headquarters at the Watergate complex as part of an attempt to sabotage the Democratic campaign and guarantee Nixon's reelection (Flanagan & Koenig, 2003). Media coverage of the scandal increased publicity and ultimately put pressure on the government that led to an investigation and the prosecution of many who were involved (Baughman, et. al., 2001).

Characteristics of Reliable Journalism

While CNN and other news networks took some criticism for their delay in reporting Michael Jackson's death in 2009, others commended the news organizations for waiting for official confirmation. For many journalists and members of the public, ensuring accuracy, even when it means delays, is a hallmark of responsible journalism.

More than 400 journalistic codes of ethics have been produced by various unions and associations worldwide (White, 2008). Where they may differ on specifics, these codes of ethics agree that the news media's top obligation is to report the truth. When journalists say this, of course, they don't mean truth in an absolute, philosophical sense; they mean practical truth, the truth that involves reporting the facts as faithfully and accurately as possible. This notion of truth includes an accurate representation of information from reliable sources, but it also includes a complete representation, one that presents multiple perspectives on an issue and does not suppress vital information.

Many codes of ethics stress that the press has a duty to continue its investigation of the facts, even after initially reporting them, and to rectify any inaccuracies that may have occurred in the initial coverage of an issue (White). One example is *The Huffington Post*, a news website that, with over 2,000 bloggers, has the world's most linked-to blog. Blogging is sometimes criticized by more traditional journalists for the tendency, among some blogs, to include biases, unreliable information, and unfounded opinions—in other words, for instances of violating journalistic codes of ethics. However, *The Huffington Post* requires all of its pass-holding writers to fact check and to correct any factual errors within 24 hours or lose their privileges.[9]

Along with an emphasis on the truth, codes of ethics stress loyalty to citizens as a standard of primary importance. Of course, truth telling is an essential component of this loyalty, but additionally, the concern here is in reminding journalists whom their work serves. Especially in the current environment, in which media outlets face increased financial pressure, there is a tension between responsible journalism and the demands for profit. Aiden White notes that corporate and political influences are of increasing concern in this environment, but he reminds journalists that while they have duties to other constituencies, "media products are not just economic." Journalists must hold the larger public interest above other interests (White).

Another challenge often posed by bottom-line concerns and the pressure for a good story is sensitivity toward, and protection of, those involved in the news. Responsible journalists should strive to balance disclosure of the news with a respect for individual privacy. Finding this balance can sometimes be a challenge. On one hand, journalists should never expose private information that could be harmful to individuals for the sake of sensationalizing a story. Issues like family life, sexual behavior, sexual orientation, or medical conditions, for instance, are generally considered tabloid material that would violate the privacy of those involved.

On the other hand, there are times when the private lives of individuals must be made public in the interests of serving the common good. One example was the 2009 media scandal surrounding South Carolina Governor Mark Sanford, who, after media investigations over his weeklong disappearance in June of that year, admitted to flying to Argentina to visit his mistress. After it was revealed that Sanford had used public funds for his private travel, he resigned from his office as the chairman of the Republican Governors' Association (Associated

Press, 2009). Although the publicity surrounding this private matter was clearly painful for the governor and his family, releasing information about the incident, particularly regarding the misuse of public funds, was in the best interest of the citizens. The International Federation of Journalists offers three factors as a rough guideline in cases where privacy is in danger of being violated: the nature of the individual's place in society, the individual's reputation, and his or her place in public life. Politicians, judges, and others in elected office often must forgo their expectations of privacy for reasons of democracy and accountability—the public's right to know if their elected officials are engaged in unethical or criminal conduct generally trumps an individual's right to privacy.[10]

Figure 14.5

As shown in the scandal surrounding former South Carolina Governor Mark Sanford, drawing the line between exploiting individuals' private lives to sell stories and disclosing information in the public interest is not always clear.

Because the press has a duty to serve the best interests of the citizens in a democracy, it is important that journalists act independently and that they remain neutral in their presentation of information. *Objectivity* was once the common term used to support this notion. More recently, however, there has been wider acceptance of the fact that reporting always occurs through a lens of personal experience, culture, beliefs, and background that ultimately all influence the way any individual perceives a situation (Myrick, 2002). If this were not the case—if there were only one standard way everyone perceived, investigated, and reported on a story—what would be the value of including racial and gender diversity in the newsroom? Nevertheless, responsible journalism requires journalists to avoid favoritism and to present news that is fair and offers a complete picture of the issue.

The principle of journalistic independence is an important component of the news media's watchdog role. Journalists should avoid conflicts of interest—financial, political, or otherwise—and, when conflicts of interest are unavoidable, it is a journalist's ethical responsibility to disclose those.[11] One example involving conflict of interest centers on recent talk of government bailouts for the news media, similar to the bailouts for the auto and banking industries. However, many journalists are concerned that government support of this kind would present a conflict of interest and interfere with the media's watchdog role (Nicklaus, 2010).

In addition to maintaining independence, the news media should allow for commentary and opposition. Leaving space for citizens to voice concerns about journalistic conduct is an important part of serving the public interest and keeping the public's trust.

The Effects of Bias in News Presentations

While principles of ethical journalism require journalists to remain neutral in their reporting, there is, as previously mentioned, always a degree of bias that will be present in any news reporting due to the element of personal perspective that any journalist will naturally bring to his or her work. A 2005 in-depth study by political scientists at UCLA found that, of 20 media outlets, 18 had a perspective in their news reporting that was left of the national average. Of those 20, only Fox News and *The Washington Times* scored to the right of the average U.S. voter (Sullivan, 2005).

What, exactly, does political bias in the media look like? In the UCLA study, news sources were scored based on their sources of information and expert opinion. The news outlets with the most liberal slant—CBS News and *The New York Times*—cited liberal think tanks and policy groups with a much greater frequency than they cited conservative ones (Groseclose & Milyo, 2005). Political bias can also be observed by examining which stories a network or newspaper chooses to report. According to media analyst Seth Ackerman, the right-leaning Fox News network reports news stories that favor the Republican Party or show the Democratic Party in a negative light. Additionally, Fox's panels of pundits who offer commentary after the news tend to be politically conservative or moderate far more often than liberal (Ackerman, 2001).

Figure 14.6

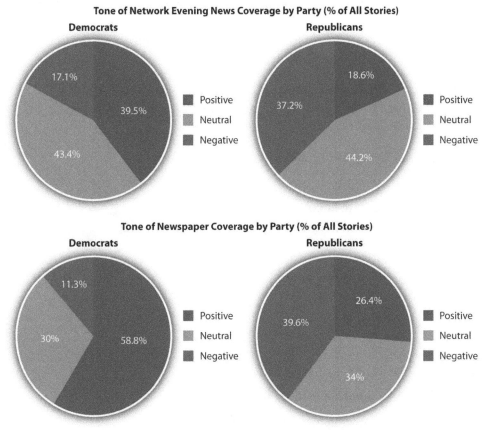

Source: Pew Research Center's Project for Excellence in Journalism

Some argue that there is a politically left bias in the news media.

Of course, such biases in news media have an effect on public opinion. However, while the picture a journalist or particular news outlet creates may not be entirely objective, journalists with integrity will strive to be fair and comprehensive, offering opposing views and citing their sources of information. Members of the public should remember that they also have a responsibility to be active, rather than passive, consumers of information. Good media consumers use critical analysis skills while reading news reports. If a story is presented conscientiously in the news, a reader or viewer will have the resources he or she needs to research an issue further and draw his or her own conclusions. As you continue reading the chapter, keep in mind the ethical obligations of those who work in mass media and the potential consequences of their failure to uphold them.

Key Takeaways

- The Internet has brought about profound and rapid changes in the structuring, delivery, and economics of news media.

  - Immediate news delivery has become the norm.

  - The pressure for immediate delivery increases the tension between factual accuracy and "getting there first" in news reporting.

- Because people can get instant news for free online, subscriptions to print media are down, and so are advertising revenues.

- Most journalistic codes of ethics are based on the premise that the news media exists to provide citizens with the information they need to function in a free and democratic society. Journalists should conform to several ethical obligations:

    - Present news stories that inform and serve the needs of citizens.

    - Present issues fairly.

    - Present stories in a way that addresses their complexity.

    - Present diverse perspectives.

    - Monitor government and corporations.

- Responsible journalism

    - ensures accuracy (even if it means causing delays);

    - reports the truth;

    - stays loyal to citizens by putting the public interest above all else;

    - is protective and sensitive to those involved in the news;

    - remains objective and presents information in a neutral way; and

    - allows for commentary and opposition.

- All news stories contain some bias because of the diversity of journalists' perspectives. While the news media is often criticized for representing a political bias in reporting, ethical journalists always strive to present issues in a fair and comprehensive way.

Exercises

Conduct your own survey of political bias in the news. Choose either a television network or newspaper known for more liberal tendencies, such as CNN or *The New York Times*, and a network or newspaper known for more conservative reporting, such as Fox News or *The Washington Times*. Examine both sources' coverage of the same news story (*not* a column or editorial). Then answer the following short-answer questions. Each response should be one to two paragraphs.

1. What differences do you notice between the two sources' news coverage?

2. What evidence, if any, do you find of political bias? If it does exist, what effect do you think this bias has on readers?

3. Consider the role of the media in delivering news to the public. In your opinion, can both sources' coverage still be characterized as fair and accurate? Why or why not?

[1]Sullivan, "As the Internet Grows Up."

[2]Sullivan, "As the Internet Grows Up."

[3]Committee of Concerned Journalists, "Statement of Shared Purpose."

[4]Committee of Concerned Journalists, "Statement of Shared Purpose."

[5]Committee of Concerned Journalists, "Statement of Shared Purpose."

[6]Society of Professional Journalists, "SPJ Code of Ethics."

[7]Iggers, *Good News, Bad News*, 138.

[8]Committee of Concerned Journalists, "Statement of Shared Purpose."

[9]White, *To Tell You the Truth*, 76.

[10]White, *To Tell You the Truth*, 136.

[11]Society of Professional Journalists, "SPJ Code of Ethics."

References

Ackerman, Seth. "The Most Biased Name in the News," *FAIR: Fairness and Accuracy in Reporting*, July/August 2001, http://www.fair.org/index.php?page=1067.

American Society of News Editors, "ASNE's Statement of Principles," August 2009, http://asne.org/article_view/articleid/325/asnes-statement-of-principles.aspx.

Associated Press, "Sanford Took Personal Trips on Plane," *CBS News*, August 9, 2009, http://www.cbsnews.com/stories/2009/08/09/politics/main5228211.shtml.

Baughman, Judith S. and others, "The Government and Watergate," in *American Decades*, ed. Judith S. Baughman and others (Detroit: Gale, 2001), vol. 8.

Collins, Scott and Greg Braxton, "TV Misses Out as Gossip Website TMZ Reports Michael Jackson's Death First," *Los Angeles Times*, June 26, 2009, http://articles.latimes.com/2009/jun/26/local/me-jackson-media26.

Committee of Concerned Journalists, "Statement of Shared Purpose," Pew Project for Excellence in Journalism, http://www.journalism.org/resources/principles.

Flanagan, Richard M. and Louis W. Koenig, "Watergate," in *Dictionary of American History*, ed. Stanley I. Kutler, 3rd ed. (New York: Charles Scribner's Sons, 2003), 8:425.

Goodman, Ellen. "Temper 'Instant' News Coverage," *Gainesville (FL) Sun*, February 7, 1993, http://news.google.com/newspapers?nid=1320&dat=19930207&id=vt4RAAAAIBAJ&sjid=XuoDAAAAIBAJ&pg=5028,1856837.

Govier, Gordon. "The Living Room Fixture," The Evolution of Radio News, 2007, http://www.radioscribe.com/formats.html.

Groseclose, Tim and Jeffrey Milyo, "A Measure of Media Bias," *Quarterly Journal of Economics* 120, no. 4 (2005), http://www.sscnet.ucla.edu/polisci/faculty/groseclose/pdfs/MediaBias.pdf.

Holguin, Jaime. "Rather Recalls JFK Assassination," *CBS News*, February 28, 2005, http://www.cbsnews.com/stories/2005/02/28/eveningnews/main677096.shtml.

Iggers, Jeremy.*Good News, Bad News: Journalism Ethics and the Public Interest* (Boulder, CO: Westview Press, 1999), 46.

Myrick, Howard A. "The Search for Objectivity in Journalism," *USA Today* (Society for the Advancement of Education), November 2002, http://findarticles.com/p/articles/mi_m1272/is_2690_131/ai_94384327/?tag=content;col1.

Nicklaus, David. "Bailing Out Journalism Would Threaten Its Independence," *St. Louis Post-Dispatch*, June 8, 2010, http://more.stltoday.com/stltoday/business/columnists.nsf/davidnicklaus/story/7db2f5de844ed63f8625773c000da74b?OpenDocument.

Society of Professional Journalists, "SPJ Code of Ethics," http://www.spj.org/ethicscode.asp.

State of the Media, Pew Project for Excellence in Journalism, *The State of the News Media 2010*, http://www.stateofthemedia.org/2010/overview_intro.php.

Sullivan, Meg. "Media Bias is Real, Finds UCLA Political Scientist," news release, UCLA, December 14, 2005, http://newsroom.ucla.edu/portal/ucla/Media-Bias-Is-Real-Finds-UCLA-6664.aspx.

Sullivan, Patricia. "As the Internet Grows Up, the News Industry Is Forever Changed," *Washington Post*, June 19, 2006, http://www.washingtonpost.com/wp-dyn/content/article/2006/06/13/AR2006061300929.html.

USC Annenberg School for Communication and Journalism, "Annual Internet Survey by Center for the Digital Future Finds Large Increases in Use of Online Newspapers," news release, Center for Digital Future, April 2009, http://annenberg.usc.edu/News%20and%20Events/News/090429CDF.aspx.

White, *To Tell You the Truth*, ii; Committee of Concerned Journalists, "Statement of Shared Purpose."

White, Aidan. *To Tell You the Truth: The Ethical Journalist Initiative* (Brussels: International Federation of Journalists, 2008), iii.

14.4 Ethical Considerations of the Online World

Learning Objectives

1. Explain concerns related to surveillance and personal privacy rights introduced by the Internet.

2. Differentiate between copyright infringement and fair use.

3. Identify plagiarism and copyright concerns introduced by the Internet.

Online media has developed rapidly, with technology advancing at a rate that often surpasses the ability of legislation and policy to keep up with it. As a result, issues like individuals' rights to privacy, copyright protections, and fair use restrictions have become the subject of numerous court cases and public debates as lawmakers, judges, and civil liberties organizations struggle to define the limits of technology and the access it provides to previously restricted information. In the following section you will look at some of the most prominent issues in today's online media environment. You should reflect on the ethical issues in mass media raised in the two preceding sections and how they are manifested in the areas of personal privacy, copyright law, and plagiarism.

Privacy and Surveillance

Concerns about online privacy issues in recent years have led some people to wonder whether the collection of personal information on websites has begun to infringe on individuals' constitutional rights. While the U.S. Constitution does not explicitly guarantee a general right to privacy, the Bill of Rights establishes privacy of beliefs, privacy of the home, and privacy of person and possessions from unreasonable searches. Additionally, in a number of court cases, the "right to liberty" clause has also been read as a guarantee of personal privacy (Linder, 2010). What do these constitutional rights mean when it comes to storing a person's credit card data online, or tracking his or her Internet searches, or using cookies to collect information about his or her purchasing habits? Because online media is developing so rapidly, many of these issues have not been settled by federal legislation and remain the source of numerous courtroom battles. Consider the 2010 case in which the online services company Yahoo! entered into a legal struggle with government officials who wanted to search the e-mail account of a Yahoo! user for incriminating evidence. While Yahoo! claimed the government would need a search warrant to access a user's e-mail, the government investigators claimed the Fourth Amendment does not apply in the case of an e-mail account (Electronic Frontier Foundation, 2010).

In defense of information collection and surveillance, many websites argue that, by using their services, individuals are agreeing to make their personal information available. However, many people don't realize the extent of surveillance capabilities or know how to protect certain personal information while using online tools. The more people rely on the Internet for shopping, communication, social networking, and media consumption, the more their personal data is stored online. Every time a person subscribes to a magazine, joins an organization, donates money to charity, gives to a political cause, or searches the pages of a government agency, that information is stored in a computer (Privacy Rights Clearinghouse, 2010). For example, cookies, text files that web page servers embed in users' hard drives, help search engines like Google and Yahoo! track their customers' search histories, buying habits, and browsing patterns. Cookies stored by Google last for 30 years (Godoy, 2006). These search engine cookies are used to customize users' searches and to deliver customized third-party ads based on a particular user's demographics and behavior. However, privacy advocates claim this practice fosters predatory advertising (Spring, 2010). Additionally, considering that search engines receive multiple requests per day for specific information on their users (requests that are often tied to criminal investigations and lawsuits), there is a growing concern that unfair or even erroneous profiling may result.[1] Much of this information is stored without users' knowledge or informed consent—although agreements for most software inform users when their data is being collected, few people have the patience or time to read and understand the dense legalistic language of these agreements. And even when users invest the time and effort to understand the agreements, they are left with the difficult choice of either agreeing to have their data recorded or going without useful software.

Internet users concerned about their privacy may also be unaware of another growing trend: the combination of online data with offline information to build profiles of web surfers. Data providers like BlueKai, Datalogic, and Nielsen are now able to pool offline data and demographics to create "digital dossiers" (detailed digital records of a particular subject or market) for online advertisers who want to reach a target market.[2] This combination of online and offline information provides a nearly complete picture of someone's life. If advertisers are looking for a 56-year-old retired female educator who is divorced, owns a home and a dog, suffers from arthritis, and plays tennis at the local fitness club, they can now find her. While advertisers have been careful to point out that people are identified by demographic subgroup but never by name, many organizations that advocate for privacy, such as the Electronic Frontier Foundation, believe that protections and greater transparency should be enforced (Spring, 2010).

Figure 14.7

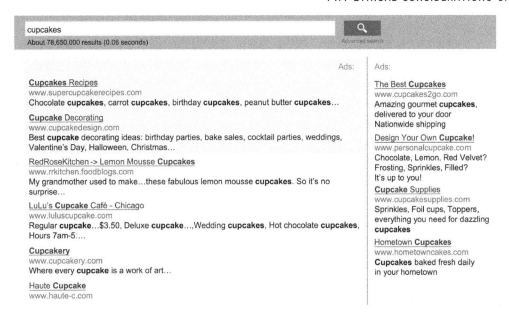

Online ads like these target users based on pools of very specific information.

Users also supply a wide range of information about themselves through online social networks that are connected with their names, contact information, and photographs. Creditors now look at individuals' social networks to determine whether they would be good credit customers, and banks may access social network information to make loan decisions (Mies, 2010). If users aren't careful about their privacy settings on MySpace, Twitter, or Facebook, photographs and other private information may be easily accessible to anyone performing a Google search. Of even greater concern is the growing trend to publicize information that was previously private as the networking sites evolve and change their interfaces.

Surveillance can range from the monitoring of online activity by employers and other institutions that want to make sure users are following guidelines, to high-level government investigations of terrorist activity. The USA PATRIOT Act, passed just 6 weeks after the September 11, 2001, terrorist attacks, expanded the federal government's rights to access citizens' personal information. Under the Patriot Act, authorities have access to personal records held by Internet service providers and other third parties, and government officials can tap in to an individual's e-mail communications and web searches if he or she is suspected of terrorist activity or of having connections to terrorist activity (American Civil Liberties Union, 2003; Olsen, 2001). One concern among civil liberties organizations is that the Patriot Act might become a back door for the government to conduct undisclosed surveillance that doesn't necessarily involve the threat of terrorism. For instance, under the Patriot Act the government can wiretap Internet communications even if the primary purpose is a criminal investigation, as long as intelligence gathering is a significant purpose of the investigation (Harvard Law School).

Fair Use and Plagiarism

Now that a large amount of research can easily be conducted online, and content can be copied and pasted from one platform to another with no more than the click of a button, concerns about plagiarism and copyright infringement are more relevant than ever. The concepts of copyright infringement and plagiarism can easily be confused with each other. The following provides an overview of copyright, its issues and limitations, and its distinction from plagiarism.

Copyright Infringement

Copyright is a form of protection provided by U.S. law, under which the creator of an original artistic or intellectual work is automatically granted certain rights, including the right to distribute, copy, and modify the work (U.S. Copyright Office). If someone rents a movie from Netflix, for example, and watches it with his friends, he hasn't violated any copyright laws because Netflix has paid for a license to loan the movie to its customers. However, if the same person rents a movie and burns himself a copy to watch later, he has violated copyright law because he has not paid for nor obtained the film creators' permission to copy the movie. Copyright law applies to most books, songs, movies, art, essays, and other pieces of creative work. However, after a certain length of time (70 to 120 years depending on the publication circumstances), creative and intellectual works enter the public domain; that is, they are free to be used and copied without permission.

Google Books: Turning Copyright Law on Its Head?

In 2002, Google began scanning millions of books in academic libraries to make them available online in digital format. Of the more than 12 million books Google has digitized since then—and made searchable through Google Book Search—2 million are in the public domain. Those 2 million books are available in "full view" and free for users to download, while books still under copyright are available as limited previews, where users can access about 20 percent of the texts. According to Google, the project will pave the way for greater democratization of knowledge, making texts available to readers who formerly wouldn't have had access to them. However, many authors, publishers, and legal authorities claim the project represents a massive copyright violation. In 2005, the Authors Guild and the Association of American Publishers filed class-action lawsuits against Google (Newitz, 2010).

William Cavanaugh, a lawyer with the U.S. Department of Justice, claims that the Google Books Settlement, an agreement partially reached in 2008, "turns copyright law on its head." According to the settlement agreement, in exchange for $125 million, part of which would go to authors and publishers, Google was released from liability for copying the books and was granted the right to charge money for individual and institutional subscriptions to its Google Books service (which gives subscribers full access to the copied books—even those under copyright). Authors have the choice to opt out of the agreement, asking to have their books removed from Google's servers. However, more than 30,000 publishers have already made deals with Google, which override the authors' rights to opt out (Oder, 2010).

Some works are in the public domain because the creator has chosen to make them available to anyone without requiring permission. However, most works are in the public domain because their copyright has expired; in the United States, anything published before 1923 is automatically in the public domain. Additionally, there have been changes to U.S. copyright law over the years that caused some works to enter the public domain earlier. Before 1964, for instance, any published work had to have its copyright renewed during the 28th year after its publication. If no renewal was filed, the copyright was lost. Figure 14.8 shows significant changes to U.S. copyright law since 1790 (Press, 2007).

Figure 14.8

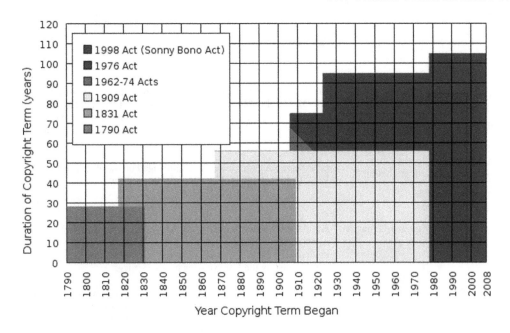

Changes to U.S. Copyright Law

While it is illegal to violate the rights granted by copyright law, the copyright holder's rights are not unlimited. One of the significant limitations is the policy of "fair use," under which the public is entitled to freely use copyrighted information for purposes such as criticism, commentary, news reporting, teaching, scholarship, research, or parody (U.S. Copyright Office, 2009). If a critic were writing a book review for a magazine, for instance, according to fair use, she would be allowed to summarize and quote from the book she wanted to review, whether or not the author of the book agreed to this use. According to the U.S. government, there are four issues to consider when determining fair use:

1. The purpose and character of the use, including whether such use is of commercial nature or is for nonprofit educational purposes

2. The nature of the copyrighted work

3. The amount and substantiality of the portion used in relation to the copyrighted work as a whole

4. The effect of the use on the potential market for, or value of, the copyrighted work (U.S. Copyright Office, 2009)

The distinction between what is considered fair and what constitutes copyright infringement is not always clearly defined. For one thing, there are no guidelines that specify a number of words, lines, or notes that can be taken without permission. Table 14.1 "Cases Involving Fair Use" provides some examples of distinctions between fair use and copyright infringement.

Table 14.1 Cases Involving Fair Use

Fair Use	Not Fair Use
Wright v. Warner Books Inc. **(1991):** In a biography of Richard Wright the biographer quoted from six of Wright's unpublished letters and 10 unpublished journal entries. CONSIDERATIONS: The copied letters amounted to less than 1 percent of Wright's total letter material. Additionally, the biographer's purpose in copying the documents was informational.	***Castle Rock Entertainment Inc. v. Carol Publication Group*** **(1998):** Carol Publication published a book of trivia questions about the TV series *Seinfeld*. The book included direct quotes from the show and based its questions on characters and events in the series. CONSIDERATIONS: The book infringed on the ability of Castle Rock (the copyright holder) to make its own trivia books.
Perfect 10 Inc. v. *Amazon.com* ***Inc.*** **(2007):** A Google search engine displayed thumbnail-sized photos of nude models from a subscription-only website. CONSIDERATIONS: The search engine's use of the photos transformed them into "pointers," directing users to the photos' original source. The transformative use was more important than any factors that would allow Google to make money from displaying the images.	***Los Angeles News Service v. KCAL-TV Channel 9*** **(1997):** A TV news station used a 30-second segment of a four-minute video that depicted the beating of a Los Angeles man. The video was copyrighted by the Los Angeles News Service. CONSIDERATIONS: The segment used by the news station was a significant portion of the total video. Additionally, the use was for commercial reasons and infringed on the Los Angeles News Service's ability to market the video.

Source: Stanford University Libraries. "Copyright & Fair Use." http://fairuse.stanford.edu/Copyright_and_Fair_Use_Overview/chapter9/9-c.html

Plagiarism

Sometimes plagiarism becomes confused with copyright violation. However, the two words are not synonymous; while there can be some overlap between them, not every instance of plagiarism involves copyright violation, and not every instance of copyright violation is an act of plagiarism. For one thing, while copyright violation can involve a wide range of acts, plagiarism is defined more narrowly as using someone else's information, writing, or speech without properly documenting or citing the source. In other words, plagiarism involves representing another person's work as one's own.

As the U.S. Copyright Office points out, it is possible to cite a copyrighted source of information without obtaining permission to reproduce that information.[3] In such a case, the user has violated copyright law even though she has not plagiarized the material. Similarly, a student writing a paper could copy sections of a document that is in the public domain without properly citing his sources, in which case he would not have broken any copyright laws. However, representing the information as his own work would be an instance of plagiarism.

Plagiarism, a perennially serious problem at academic institutions, has recently become even more prevalent. The ease of copying and pasting online content into a word-processing document can make it highly tempting for students to plagiarize material for research projects and critical papers. Additionally, a number of online "paper mills" contain archives where students can download papers for free or, in some cases, purchase them (Denhart, 1999). In 2003, *The New York Times* surveyed students at 23 college campuses and reported that 38 percent of students admitted to having committed copy-and-paste plagiarism within the previous year (De Leon, 2007).

To combat the rise in plagiarism, many schools and universities now subscribe to services that allow instructors to check students' work for plagiarized material. Plagiarism.org, for instance, offers an analytics tool that compares student writing against a database that includes work from online paper mills, academic databases, documents available through major search engines, and other student papers submitted to Plagiarism.org.[4] According to many researchers, part of the issue may be that students don't understand what constitutes plagiarism. Some students, for instance, claim they think information available online is in the public domain (Auer & Krupar, 2001). The following list offers suggestions for ways to avoid plagiarism in your own work.

- Don't procrastinate.

- Avoid taking shortcuts.

- Take thorough notes and keep accurate records.

- Rephrase ideas in your own words.

- Provide citations or attributions for all sources.

- Ask your instructor when in doubt (Longman Publishers).

While plagiarism is an issue of concern in academia, it occurs in print media as well. Writers, whether through carelessness or laziness, may lift content from existing materials without properly citing or reinterpreting them. In an academic setting, plagiarism may lead to consequences as severe as failure or even expulsion from an institution. However, outside of academia the consequences may be even more damaging. Writers have lost publishing contracts, permanently damaged their reputations, and even ruined their careers over instances of plagiarism. For example, the late George Harrison, of the Beatles, was successfully sued by Ronald Mack for copyright infringement of his song "He's So Fine."[5] It was determined by the court that Harrison unconsciously plagiarized the musical essence of Mack's song for his composition "My Sweet Lord."

You should now have an understanding of the key issues in media ethics, particularly as they relate to privacy rights, plagiarism, and copyright laws. Please ensure you understand the key concepts listed below.

Key Takeaways

- Concerns about the public's right to privacy have increased in recent years, as more personal information has become available online.

  - Every time someone makes a purchase, performs a web search, accesses a web page, downloads files, sends an e-mail, or engages in social networking, that information is stored in a computer and may be accessed by third parties under certain conditions.

  - The USA PATRIOT Act, passed after the September 11, 2001, attacks, has broadened the federal government's rights to access individuals' personal records.

  - Civil liberties organizations are concerned about clauses of the Patriot Act, such as the one that stipulates that the government can wiretap Internet communications as long as intelligence gathering is a significant purpose of the investigation.

- Rules that distinguish copyright violation from fair use are not always entirely clear and have been the subject of debate now that a greater amount of copyrighted work is easily accessible via the Internet.

- ◦ Works enter the public domain once their copyright has expired, at which point they can be altered, copied, and distributed freely.

- ◦ Because of numerous changes in U.S. copyright laws, some works have entered the public domain earlier than others.

- ◦ According to the U.S. government, when distinguishing between fair use and copyright infringement, there are four things to consider: whether or not the use is for profit, the nature of the copyrighted work, the percentage of the copyrighted material being used, and the effect of that use on the value of the copyrighted work.

- Plagiarism is also a growing concern because of the ease of copying and pasting texts from online sources into computer documents. It is important to keep in mind that plagiarism and copyright infringement are different issues: Plagiarism involves not giving credit to a work's creator, whereas copyright deals with the legality of using a created work.

Exercises

You will now examine several cases in detail to further explore your understanding of the concepts and key ideas covered in this chapter. Respond to the questions asked, and provide evidence or examples to defend and support your answer. Each response should be one or two paragraphs.

Case 1. Research the USA PATRIOT Act. You can read what the American Civil Liberties Union (ACLU) has to say about the act here: http://www.aclu.org/pdfs/safefree/patriot_report_20090310.pdf. You can read what the federal government has to say about the act here: http://www.justice.gov/archive/ll/highlights.htm

- What are its major stipulations?

- What are some major concerns of civil liberties advocates?

- Do you agree with the ACLU that "the Patriot Act eroded our most basic right—the freedom from unwarranted government intrusion into our private lives?" Or do you agree with the acronym the federal government created to explain the act: Uniting and Strengthening America by Providing Appropriate Tools Required to Intercept and Obstruct Terrorism? Explain your reasons.

Case 2. Consider the following case:

After the publication of author J. K. Rowling's popular *Harry Potter* novels, one fan created an elaborate website for Harry Potter enthusiasts. The website includes an encyclopedia of information about the books; indexed lists of people, places, and things; fan art; discussion forums; essays; timelines; and other features. Much of the content of the website's encyclopedia entries comes directly from the books. Use of the website is free and unrestricted, and while the site includes some ads, the income they generate only goes to offset the site's operating costs.

- Decide whether you believe the website represents an instance of fair use or whether the action was a copyright violation. Defend your response.

End-of-Chapter Assessment

Review Questions

1.
Section 1

 a. Why was the NAACP unhappy with the schedule of programs for the 1999 season of major television network entertainment?

 b. List at least four common characteristics of the way women are often presented in TV and movie entertainment.

 c. Why is it considered problematic that so few women and ethnic minorities are represented "behind the scenes" in the creation of mass-media products?

 d. Explain how mass media as a socialization agent relates to public attitudes toward sexual behavior.

2.
Section 2

 a. How does online news content put added pressure on news organizations?

 b. Explain the media's watchdog role.

 c. When is it considered acceptable for journalists to expose details about an individual's private life?

 d. How does political bias influence the way news gets presented?

3.
Section 3

 a. Identify cookies. Why are cookies a concern for privacy advocates?

 b. What are some reasons a created work might be in the public domain?

 c. List the four considerations the federal government lists for determining whether an action is fair use or copyright violation.

 d. Give an example of an act that could be considered plagiarism but not copyright violation.

Critical Thinking Questions

Answer the following critical thinking questions. Your responses should be one to two pages for each prompt.

1. Watch segments of the evening news on three of the major television networks. Based on the information presented here about representations of women and racial minorities, what do you observe? Do your observations corroborate claims of stereotyping and underrepresentation? Do you

notice important differences among the three networks where these issues are concerned?

2. Create a mock advertisement that breaks with common racial stereotypes, gender myths, or media representations of sexuality.

3. A number of prominent journalists and news experts have argued that the newspaper industry must find a new model for generating revenue if it hopes to survive. Create a short proposal in which you outline a plan for newspaper agencies to earn money from sources other than subscriptions and print advertising.

4. Develop an argument in which you defend the use of information gathering and profiling for the placement of Internet ads and the creation of customized web pages.

5. What might be some implications of the Google Books settlement? Why do you think William Cavanaugh claimed that it "turns copyright law on its head"?

Career Connection: Political Blogger

Research what it takes to be a professional political blogger for a news site like CNN.com or *The Huffington Post*. Then answer the following short-answer questions. Each response should be one to two paragraphs.

1. How much and what kind of research would you need to perform on a daily basis?

2. Where would you go for your information?

3. What are some elements that make for a successful blog?

4. What are some particular ethical concerns surrounding this form of journalism?

[1]Godoy, "Google Records Subpoena."

[2]Spring, "Good-Bye to Privacy?"

[3]U.S. Copyright Office, "Fair Use."

[4]Denhart, "The Web's Plagiarism Police."

[5]Bright Tunes Music v. Harrisongs Music, 420 F. Supp. 177 (S.D.N.Y. 1976).

References

American Civil Liberties Union, "Surveillance Under the USA PATRIOT Act," April 3, 2003, http://www.aclu.org/national-security/surveillance-under-usa-patriot-act.

Auer, Nicole J. and Ellen M. Krupar, "Mouse Click Plagiarism: The Role of Technology in Plagiarism and the Librarian's Role in Combating It," *Library Trends*, Winter 2001, http://findarticles.com/p/articles/mi_m1387/is_3_49/ai_75278304/.

De Leon, Michelle. "Internet Plagiarism on the Rise in Colleges," *Lehigh University Brown and White*, November 12, 2007, http://media.www.thebrownandwhite.com/media/storage/paper1233/news/2007/11/12/News/Internet.Plagiarism.On.The.Rise.In.Colleges-3094622.shtml.

Denhart, Andy. "The Web's Plagiarism Police," *Salon*, June 14, 1999, http://www.salon.com/technology/feature/1999/06/14/plagiarism.

Electronic Frontier Foundation, "EFF Backs Yahoo! to Protect User from Warrantless Email Search," news release, April 14, 2010, http://www.eff.org/press/archives/2010/04/13.

Godoy, Maria. "Google Records Subpoena Raises Privacy Fears," *NPR*, January 20, 2006, http://www.npr.org/templates/story/story.php?storyId=5165854.

Harvard Law School, Berkman Center for Internet and Society, "The USA Patriot Act, Foreign Intelligence Surveillance, and Cyberspace Privacy," Harvard Law School, http://cyber.law.harvard.edu/privacy/module5.html.

Linder, Doug. "The Right of Privacy," Exploring Constitutional Law, 2010, http://www.law.umkc.edu/faculty/projects/ftrials/conlaw/rightofprivacy.html.

Longman Publishers, "Avoiding Plagiarism," Pearson Education, http://wps.pearsoncustom.com/pcp_longman_ap_2/32/8420/2155775.cw/content/index.html.

Mies, Ginny. "Skeptical Shopper: Can Your Online Life Ruin Your Credit?" *PC World*, March 23, 2010,. http://www.pcworld.com/article/192207/skeptical_shopper_can_your_online_life_ruin_your_credit.html.

Newitz, Annalee. "5 Ways the Google Books Settlement Will Change the Future of Reading," *io9* (blog).April 2, 2010, http://io9.com/5501426/5-ways-the-google-book-settlement-will-change-the-future-of-reading.

Oder, Norman. "Google Settlement Fairness Hearing, Part Two: DOJ Expresses Opposition; Parties Mount Vigorous Defense," *Library Journal*, February 18, 2010, http://www.libraryjournal.com/article/CA6719808.html.

Olsen, Stephanie. "Patriot Act Draws Privacy Concerns," *CNET*, October 26, 2001, http://news.cnet.com/2100-1023-275026.html.

Press, Nolo. "Chapter 8: The Public Domain," Stanford University Libraries and Academic Information Resources, 2007, http://fairuse.stanford.edu/Copyright_and_Fair_Use_Overview/chapter8/index.html.

Privacy Rights Clearinghouse, "Privacy Today: A Review of Current Issues," March 2010, http://www.privacyrights.org/ar/Privacy-IssuesList.htm#publicrecords.

Spring, Tom. "Good-Bye to Privacy?" *PC World*, May 23, 2010, http://www.pcworld.com/article/196787/goodbye_to_privacy.html.

U.S. Copyright Office, "Copyright Basics," http://www.copyright.gov/.

U.S. Copyright Office, "Fair Use," May 2009, http://www.copyright.gov/fls/fl102.html.

Chapter 15: Media and Government

15.1 Media and Government

Facebook Versus the FTC

Figure 15.1

In May 2010, the social networking website Facebook was thrown into the news when its chief executive officer, Mark Zuckerberg, announced new changes to the site's privacy policy. Although the announcement alone did not necessarily garner heavy attention from the news media, the involvement of the Federal Trade Commission (FTC) ramped up public interest.

The previous month, several watchdog groups had sent letters to Congress and the FTC asking for an investigation of Facebook's privacy policy. The letters attacked the site's privacy policies, which dated from December 2009 and had been designed to provide users more control over privacy settings. However, *PC Magazine* noted, "given Facebook's move toward a more open format as it integrates status updates with search engines like Google and

Bing, the site encouraged its users to make more of their data public, and made some of the default settings more open (Albanesius, 2010)."

Essentially, Facebook provides three default options for sharing information: with "everyone," "friends of friends," or "friends only." Zuckerberg explained the privacy policy by saying,

We recommended that there be large pieces of information in each of these buckets. For friends only, that's all of the really sensitive stuff. For friends of friends, it could be who can see the photos and videos of you, which is actually the majority of the content people share on the site. And then for everyone, it's basic information and status updates and posts like that (Fletcher, 2010).

Concern grew that some of Facebook's default privacy settings allowed everyone, regardless of their level of connection to a user, to access some personal information. In their open letter to Congress, privacy watchdog groups addressed these concerns by stating, "Facebook continues to manipulate the privacy settings of users and its own policy so that it can take personal information provided by users for a limited purpose and make it widely available for commercial purposes…. The company has done this repeatedly and users are becoming increasingly angry and frustrated (Hachman, 2010)." In light of users' outrage, the letter asked the FTC to get involved.

The FTC is a congressional commission designed to oversee and enforce consumer protections. Despite—or perhaps because of—this stated goal, the FTC's lack of involvement in Facebook's privacy settings frustrated many individuals; one letter to Congress "openly worried that the FTC either lacked the power or the motivation to pursue questions of privacy at Facebook (Hachman, 2010)." The FTC responded that the issue was of "particular interest" to them, but as of this writing, no official action has been taken.

The issue has prompted a broader discussion of the government's role in regulating information disseminated on the Internet. *The New York Times* articulated the discussion's central questions: "What can government do to ensure that users have control of their own information, which might live on indefinitely on the web? Would regulation work? Or should government stay out of this arena (New York Times, 2010)?" Facebook stands by the rights of its users, arguing that "adult users should be free to publish information about their lives if they choose to do so (New York Times, 2010)." However, Facebook did respond to the open letter and modified its privacy settings to make it easier for individuals to control their online identities. Yet the debate continues over online privacy and the government's role in maintaining this privacy. The recent buzz over Facebook's privacy policies is just one of many examples of the debate over government's place in the world of media. How is copyright protected across different media outlets? What material is considered appropriate for broadcast? Does the U.S. government have the right to censor information? This chapter explores these and other questions regarding the long and complex relationship between media and the government.

References

Albanesius, Chloe. "Facebook Prepping Changes to Privacy Policy," *PC Magazine*, May 21, 2010, http://www.pcmag.com/article2/0,2817,2364063,00.asp.

Fletcher, Dan. "*Time*'s Q&A With Facebook CEO Mark Zuckerberg," *Time NewsFeed* (blog), *Time*, May 27, 2010, http://newsfeed.time.com/2010/05/27/times-qa-with-facebook-ceo-mark-zuckerberg/.

Hachman, Mark. "Facebook Targeted by New FTC Privacy Complaint," *PC Magazine*, May 7, 2010, http://www.pcmag.com/article2/0,2817,2363518,00.asp.

New York Times, "Should Government Take On Facebook?" *Room for Debate* (blog), May 25, 2010, http://roomfordebate.blogs.nytimes.com/2010/05/25/should-government-take-on-facebook/.

15.2 Government Regulation of Media

Learning Objectives

1. Describe the role of the FTC.
2. Explain the major duties of the Federal Communications Commission (FCC).
3. Describe deregulation and its effect on the media landscape.

The U.S. federal government has long had its hand in media regulation. Media in all their forms have been under governmental jurisdiction since the early 1900s. Since that time, regulatory efforts have transformed as new forms of media have emerged and expanded their markets to larger audiences.

Major Regulatory Agencies

Throughout the 20th century, three important U.S. regulatory agencies appeared. Under the auspices of the federal government, these agencies—the FTC, the Federal Radio Commission (FRC), and the FCC—have shaped American media and their interactions with both the government and audiences.

Federal Trade Commission

The first stirrings of the FTC date from 1903, when President Theodore Roosevelt created the Bureau of Corporations to investigate the practices of increasingly larger American businesses. In time, authorities determined that an agency with more sweeping powers was necessary. Founded on September 26, 1914, the FTC came into being when President Woodrow Wilson signed the FTC Act into law, creating an agency designed to "prevent unfair methods of competition in commerce (Federal Trade Commission)." From the beginning, the FTC absorbed the work and staff of the Bureau of Corporations, operating in a similar manner, but with additional regulatory authorization. In the words of the FTC,

Like the Bureau of Corporations, the FTC could conduct investigations, gather information, and publish reports. The early Commission reported on export trade, resale price maintenance, and other general issues, as well as meat packing and other specific industries. Unlike the Bureau, though, the Commission could…challenge "unfair methods of competition" under Section 5 of the FTC Act, and it could enforce…more specific prohibitions against certain price discriminations, vertical arrangements, interlocking directorships, and stock acquisitions (Federal Trade Commission).

Although its primary focus was on the prevention of anticompetitive business practices, in its early years, the FTC also provided oversight on wartime economic practices. During World War I, for example, President Wilson frequently turned to the FTC for advice on exports and trading with foreign nations, resulting in the Trading with the Enemy Act, which restricted trade with countries in conflict with the United States.

Federal Radio Commission

First established with the passage of the Radio Act of 1927, the FRC was intended to "bring order to the chaotic situation that developed as a result of the breakdown of earlier wireless acts passed during the formative years of wireless radio communication (Messere)." The FRC comprised five employees who were authorized to grant and deny broadcasting licenses and assign frequency ranges and power levels to each radio station.

In its early years, the FRC struggled to find its role and responsibility in regulating the radio airwaves. With no clear breakdown of what could or could not be aired, nearly everything was allowed to play. As you learned in Chapter 7 "Radio", the FRC lasted only until 1934, when it was absorbed by the FCC.

Federal Communications Commission

Figure 15.2

President Franklin D. Roosevelt established the Federal Communications Commission in 1934 as part of
the New Deal.

Since its creation by the Communications Act in 1934, the FCC has been "charged with regulating interstate
and international communications by radio, television, wire, satellite and cable (Federal Communications
Commission)." Part of the New Deal—President Franklin D. Roosevelt's Great Depression–era suite of federal
programs and agencies—the commission worked to establish "a rapid, efficient, Nation-wide, and world-wide
wire and radio communication service (Museum of Broadcast Communications)."

The responsibilities of the FCC are broad, and throughout its long history the agency has enforced several laws
that regulate media. A selection of these laws include the 1941 National TV Ownership Rule, which states that a
broadcaster cannot own television stations that reach more than 35 percent of the nation's homes; the 1970 Radio/
TV Cross-Ownership Restriction, which prohibits a broadcaster from owning a radio station and a TV station in
the same market; and the 1975 Newspaper/Broadcast Cross-Ownership Prohibition, which discourages ownership
of a newspaper and a TV station in the same market (PBS, 2004).

Regulation Today

Today, the FCC continues to hold the primary responsibility for regulating media outlets, with the FTC taking on
a smaller role. Although each commission holds different roles and duties, the overall purpose of governmental
control remains to establish and bring order to the media industry while ensuring the promulgation of the public
good. This section examines the modern duties of both commissions.

The Structure and Purposes of the FCC

The FCC contains three major divisions: broadcast, telegraph, and telephone. Within these branches, subdivisions
allow the agency to more efficiently carry out its tasks. Presently, the FCC houses 7 operating bureaus and 10
staff offices. Although the bureaus and offices have varying specialties, the bureaus' general responsibilities
include "processing applications for licenses and other filings; analyzing complaints; conducting investigations;
developing and implementing regulatory programs; and taking part in hearings (Federal Communications
Commission)." Four key bureaus are the Media Bureau, the Wireline Competition Bureau, the Wireless
Telecommunications Bureau, and the International Bureau.

The Media Bureau oversees licensing and regulation of broadcasting services. Specifically, the Media Bureau
"develops, recommends and administers the policy and licensing programs relating to electronic media, including
cable television, broadcast television, and radio in the United States and its territories (Federal Communications
Commission)." Because it aids the FCC in its decisions to grant or withhold licenses from broadcast stations,
the Media Bureau plays a particularly important role within the organization. Such decisions are based on the
"commission's own evaluation of whether the station has served in the public interest," and come primarily from
the Media Bureau's recommendations.[1] The Media Bureau has been central to rulings on children's programming
and mandatory closed captioning.

The Wireline Competition Bureau (WCB) is primarily responsible for "rules and policies concerning telephone companies that provide interstate—and, under certain circumstances, intrastate—telecommunications services to the public through the use of wire-based transmission facilities (i.e. corded/cordless telephones) (Federal Communications Commission)." Despite the increasing market for wireless-based communications in the United States, the WCB maintains its large presence in the FCC by "ensuring choice, opportunity, and fairness in the development of wireline telecommunications services and markets (Federal Communications Commission)." In addition to this primary goal, the bureau's objectives include "developing deregulatory initiatives; promoting economically efficient investment in wireline telecommunications services; and fostering economic growth (Federal Communications Commission)." The WCB recently ruled against Comcast regarding blocked online content to the public, causing many to question the amount of authority that the government has over the public and big businesses.

Another prominent bureau within the FCC is the Wireless Telecommunications Bureau (WTB). The rough counterpart of the WCB, this bureau oversees mobile phones, pagers, and two-way radios, handling "all FCC domestic wireless telecommunications programs and policies, except those involving public safety, satellite communications or broadcasting, including licensing, enforcement, and regulatory functions (Federal Communications Commission)." The WTB balances the expansion and limitation of wireless networks, registers antenna and broadband use, and manages the radio frequencies for airplane, ship, and land communication. As U.S. wireless communication continues to grow, this bureau seems likely to continue to increase in both scope and importance.

Finally, the International Bureau is responsible for representing the FCC in all satellite and international matters. A larger organization, the International Bureau's goal is to "connect the globe for the good of consumers through prompt authorizations, innovative spectrum management and responsible global leadership (Federal Communications Commission)." In an effort to avoid international interference, the International Bureau coordinates with partners around the globe regarding frequency allocation and orbital assignments. It also concerns itself with foreign investment in the United States, ruling that outside governments, individuals, or corporations cannot own more than 20 percent of stock in a U.S. broadcast, telephone, or radio company.

The Structure and Purposes of the FTC

Although the FCC provides most of the nation's media regulations, the FTC also has a hand in the media industry. As previously discussed, the FTC primarily dedicates itself to eliminating unfair business practices; however, in the course of those duties it has limited contact with media outlets.

One example of the FTC's media regulatory responsibility is the National Do Not Call Registry. In 2004, the agency created this registry to prevent most telemarketing phone calls, exempting such groups as nonprofit charities and businesses with which a consumer has an existing relationship. Although originally intended for landline phones, the Do Not Call Registry allows individuals to register wireless telephones along with traditional wire-based numbers.

Role of Antitrust Legislation

As discussed in Chapter 13 "Economics of Mass Media", the federal government has long regulated companies' business practices. Over the years, several antitrust acts (law discouraging the formation of monopolies) have been passed into law.

During the 1880s, Standard Oil was the first company to form a trust (a unit of business made up of a board of trustees, formed to monopolize an industry), an "arrangement by which stockholders…transferred their shares to a single set of trustees (Our Documents, 1890)." With corporate trustees receiving profits from the component companies, Standard Oil functioned as a monopoly (a business that economically controls a product or a service). The Sherman Antitrust Act was put into place in 1890 to dissolve trusts such as these. The Act stated that any combination "in the form of trust or otherwise that was in restraint of trade or commerce among the several states, or with foreign nations" was illegal (Our Documents, 1890).

The Sherman Antitrust Act served as a precedent for future antitrust regulation. As discussed in Chapter 13 "Economics of Mass Media", the 1914 Clayton Antitrust Act and the 1950 Celler-Kefauver Act expanded on the principles laid out in the Sherman Act. The Clayton Act helped establish the foundation for many of today's business and media competition regulatory practices. Although the Sherman Act established regulations in the United States, the Clayton Act further developed the rules surrounding antitrust, giving businesses a "fair warning" about the dangers of anticompetitive practice (Gongol, 2005). Specifically, the Clayton Act prohibits actions that may "substantially lessen competition or tend to create a monopoly in any line of commerce (Gongol, 2005)."

The problem with the Clayton Act was that, while it prohibited mergers, it offered a loophole in that companies were allowed to buy individual assets of competitors (such as stocks or patents), which could still lead to monopolies. Established in 1950 and often referred to as the Antimerger Act, the Cellar-Kefauver Act closed that loophole by giving the government the power to stop vertical mergers. (Vertical mergers happen when two companies in the same business but on different levels—such as a tire company and a car company—combine.) The act also banned asset acquisitions that reduced competition (Financial Dictionary).

These laws reflected growing concerns in the early and mid-20th century that the trend toward monopolization could lead to the extinction of competition. Government regulation of businesses increased until the 1980s, when the United States experienced a shift in mind-set and citizens called for less governmental power. The U.S. government responded as deregulation became the norm.

Move Toward Deregulation

Media deregulation actually began during the 1970s as the FCC shifted its approach to radio and television regulation. Begun as a way of clearing laws to make the FCC run more efficiently and cost effectively, deregulation truly took off with the arrival of the Reagan administration and its new FCC chairman, Mark Fowler, in 1981. The FCC began overturning existing rules and experienced "an overall reduction in FCC oversight of station and network operations (Museum of Broadcast Communications)." Between 1981 and 1985, lawmakers dramatically altered laws and regulation to give more power to media licensees and to reduce that of the FCC. Television licenses were expanded from 3 years to 5, and corporations were now allowed to own up to 12 separate TV stations.

The shift in regulatory control had a powerful effect on the media landscape. Whereas initially laws had prohibited companies from owning media entities in more than one medium, consolidation created large mass-media companies that increasingly dominated the U.S. media system. Before the increase in deregulation, eight major companies controlled phone services to different regions of the United States. Today, however, there are four (Kimmelman). Companies such as Viacom and Disney own television stations, record companies, and magazines. Bertelsmann alone owns more than 30 radio stations, 280 publishing outlets, and 15 record companies (Columbia Journalism Review). Due to this rapid consolidation, Congress grew concerned about the costs of deregulation, and by the late 1980s, it began to slow the FCC's release of control.

Today, deregulation remains a hotly debated topic. Some favor deregulation, believing that the public benefits from less governmental control. Others, however, argue that excessive consolidation of media ownership threatens the system of checks and balances.[2] Proponents on both sides of the argument are equally vocal, and it is likely that regulation of media will ebb and flow over the years, as it has since regulation first came into practice.

Internet Censorship Around the World

Is what you see on the Internet being censored? In Chapter 11 "The Internet and Social Media", you read about the debate between the search engine Google and China. However, Internet censorship is much more widespread, affecting people from Germany to Thailand to the United States. And now, thanks to a new online service, you can see for yourself.

In September 2010, Google launched its new web tool, Google Transparency. This program allows users to see a map of online censorship around the world. With this tool, people can view the number of times a country requests data to be removed, what kind of data they request be removed, and the percentage of requests that Google complies with. In some cases, the content is minor—YouTube videos that violate copyright, for example, are frequent offenders. In other cases, the requests are more formidable; Iran blocked all of YouTube after the disputed 2009 elections, and Pakistan blocked the site for more than a week in response to a 2010 online protest. Perhaps most surprising is the amount of requests from countries not normally associated with strict censorship. Germany, for example, has banned content it deems to be affiliated with neo-Nazism, and Thailand refuses to allow videos of its king that it finds offensive. Between January and June 2010, the United States asked Google 4,287 times for information regarding its users, and sent 128 requests to the search engine to remove data. Eighty percent of the time, Google complied with the requests for data removal (Sutter, 2010).

What is the general trend in Internet censorship? According to Google, it's becoming more and more commonplace every year. However, the search engine hopes that its new tool will combat this trend. A spokesperson for the company said, "The openness and freedom that have shaped the internet as a powerful tool has come under threats from governments who want to control that technology." By giving users access to censorship numbers, Google allows them to witness the amount of Internet censorship that they are subject to in their everyday lives. As censorship increases, many predict that citizen outrage will increase as well. The future of Internet censorship may be unsure, but for now, at least, the numbers are visible to all (Sutter, 2010).

Key Takeaways

- The FTC was established in 1914 and is designed to "protect America's consumers" and "prevent unfair methods of competition in commerce."

- Established in 1934 as part of President Franklin D. Roosevelt's New Deal, the FCC is charged with regulating interstate and international communications.

- During the 1980s, the U.S. government began the process of deregulating many existing FCC radio and television laws, allowing the FCC to run more effectively but also setting the stage for increased media consolidation.

Exercises

Visit the FCC's web page (http://www.fcc.gov/) and explore some of the regulations that currently exist. Think about television or radio programs that you watch or listen to. Then write a one-page paper addressing the following:

1. Describe the role of the FTC.

2. Explain the major duties of the FCC.

3. Describe deregulation and its effect on the media landscape.

[1]Museum of Broadcast Communications, "Federal Communications Commission."

[2]Kimmelman, "Deregulation of Media."

References

Columbia Journalism Review, "Resources: Who Owns What," http://www.cjr.org/resources/?c=bertelsmann.

Federal Communications Commission, "About the FCC," http://www.fcc.gov/aboutus.html.

Federal Communications Commission, "About the WTB," http://wireless.fcc.gov/index.htm?job=about.

Federal Communications Commission, "International Bureau," http://www.fcc.gov/ib/.

Federal Communications Commission, "Media Bureau," http://www.fcc.gov/mb/.

Federal Communications Commission, "Wireline Competition Bureau," http://www.fcc.gov/wcb/.

Federal Trade Commission, "A Brief History of the Federal Trade Commission," program notes, Federal Trade Commission 90th Anniversary Symposium, 6.

Federal Trade Commission, "About the Federal Trade Commission," http://ftc.gov/ftc/about.shtm.

Financial Dictionary, "Celler-Kefauver Antimerger Act," http://financial-dictionary.thefreedictionary.com/Celler-Kefauver+Antimerger+Act.

Gongol, Brian. "The Clayton Antitrust Act," February 18, 2005, http://www.gongol.com/research/economics/claytonact/.

Kimmelman, Gene. "Deregulation of Media: Dangerous to Democracy," Consumers Union, http://www.consumersunion.org/telecom/kimmel-303.htm.

Messere, Fritz. "The Federal Radio Commission Archives," http://www.oswego.edu/~messere/FRCpage.html.

Museum of Broadcast Communications, "Deregulation," http://www.museum.tv/eotvsection.php?entrycode=deregulation.

Museum of Broadcast Communications, "Federal Communications Commission," http://www.museum.tv/eotvsection.php?entrycode=federalcommu.

Our Documents, "Sherman Antitrust Act (1890)," http://www.ourdocuments.gov/doc.php?flash=old&doc=51.

PBS, "Media Regulation Timeline," *NOW With Bill Moyers*, PBS, January 30, 2004, http://www.pbs.org/now/politics/mediatimeline.html.

Sutter, John D. "Google: Internet freedom is declining," *CNN*, September 21, 2010, http://articles.cnn.com/2010-09-21/tech/google.transparency_1_internet-censorship-google-maps-internet-freedom?_s=PM:TECH.

15.3 The Law and Mass Media Messages

Learning Objectives

1. Identify important laws that relate to different aspects of the media.
2. Explain the effects of important laws on media outlets and audiences.

Media law has been a much-debated topic ever since the first U.S. media industry laws appeared in the early 1900s. The contention surrounding media law largely stems from the liberties guaranteed under the First Amendment of the U.S. Constitution, which includes the freedom of the press.

Generally speaking, media law comprises two areas: telecommunications law, which regulates radio and television broadcasts, and print law, which addresses publications such as books, newspapers, and magazines. Despite differences between the two areas, many media laws involve First Amendment protections. This section explores several areas of media law: privacy, libel and slander, copyright and intellectual property, freedom of information, and equal time and coverage.

In 1974, Congress passed the Privacy Act, which "protects records that can be retrieved by personal identifiers such as a name, social security number, or other identifying number or symbol (U.S. Department of Health and Human Services)." This act also regulates how agencies can collect, store, and use information and requires agencies to tell individuals when they are collecting information about them. Designed to ensure that all First Amendment guarantees remain honored, the act requires all public and private agencies to function within its boundaries.

Under the Privacy Act, media personnel must be careful to avoid revealing certain information about an individual without his or her permission, even if that portrayal is factually accurate. Privacy laws, including the Privacy Act, "limit…your ability to publish private facts about someone and recognize…an individual's right to stop you from using his or her name, likeness, and other personal attributes for certain exploitative purposes (Citizen Media Law Project)." Members of the media can avoid the pitfalls of privacy laws by maintaining a professional relationship with a community. To avoid liability, journalists and other media professionals are encouraged to report or comment only on "matters of legitimate public interest and only portray people who have a reasonable relationship to [their] topic (Citizen Media Law Project)." In 2005, a legal dispute arose between congressional aides Robert Steinbuch and Jessica Cutler. Steinbuch sued Cutler for publishing information about their intimate relationship; however, the case was dismissed when the court decided that Cutler had only provided facts that were already publically known (Citizen Media Law Project).

Libel and Slander

Media outlets also must be wary of committing acts of defamation. These occur when false statements about an individual are printed, broadcast, spoken, or otherwise communicated to others. Two different types of legal protections, libel and slander laws, exist to prevent such defamation from taking place. Although defamation encompasses both categories, they are separate concepts. Libel refers to written statements or printed visual depictions, while slander refers to verbal statements and gestures (Media Law Resource Center). State jurisdiction largely covers libel and slander laws, but they are nearly identical throughout the United States.

As with privacy laws, print and broadcast journalists can protect themselves from defamation lawsuits by carrying out responsible reporting. Media personnel are legally protected when communicating a report outweighs any potential damage to a person's reputation. However, when journalists do not report responsibly, the legal and financial consequences can be devastating. In the 2007 case *Murphy vs. Boston Herald*, the *Boston Herald* newspaper was sued for misquoting Massachusetts Superior Court Judge Ernest Murphy. The court ruled that the false quote was published with a malicious intent and awarded Murphy $2.1 million in damages (Wall, 2005). In the more famous case of Linda Tripp in 1998, Tripp was charged with secretly recording phone conversations between President Bill Clinton and Monica Lewinsky. Tripp faced a prison sentence of 10 years for slander and illegal documentation; however, the case was dropped in early 2000 due to witness bias (Van Natta Jr., 2000).

Copyright and Intellectual Property

Copyright laws fall under federal jurisdiction and are, therefore, identical across the country. As you learned in Chapter 4 "Newspapers", Congress first established U.S. copyright and patent protections in 1790 and, despite revisions and updates, has maintained some form of copyright law to this day. With coverage of a wide range of materials, copyright law encompasses "almost all creative work that can be written down or otherwise captured in a tangible medium (Citizen Media Law Project)." This includes literary works; musical works; dramatic works; pictorial, graphic, and sculptural works; motion pictures and other audiovisual works; sound recordings; and even architectural works. Once a work has achieved copyright, the copyright owner must grant permission for that work to be legally reproduced. After a certain number of years, a copyright expires and the work enters the public domain.

Copyright does not, however, protect facts. This is of particular importance for news media. Despite the length of time it takes to uncover facts, no individual or company can own them. Anyone may repeat facts as long as that person does not copy the written story or broadcast in which those facts were communicated.

Intellectual property law protects "products of the mind," including copyrights, patents, open licenses, trademarks, trade secrets, URLs, domain names, and even components of television programs (as David Letterman found out when he moved from NBC to CBS, and was forced to leave certain aspects of his TV show behind). Intellectual property law generally follows the same guidelines as copyright law, and the associated legislation seeks "to encourage innovation and creativity, with an ultimate aim of promoting a general benefit to society (Citizen Media

Law Project)." The role of copyright and intellectual property in the mass media will be covered in greater detail later in this chapter.

Freedom of Information Act

President Lyndon B. Johnson first signed the Freedom of Information Act (FOIA) into law in 1966. By requiring full or partial disclosure of U.S. government information and documents, the act "helps the public keep track of its government's actions, from the campaign expenditures of city commission candidates to federal agencies' management of billions of dollars in tax revenues (Citizen Media Law Project)." Because it allows everyone access to federal documents and information that otherwise would go unreleased, FOIA is particularly important for those working in the news media.

Although the act covers a large range of agencies, some offices are exempt from FOIA. The act provides access to the public records of the executive branch of the U. S. government but does not include documents from the current president, Congress, or the judicial branch (Citizen Media Law Project). Because FOIA pertains to individuals and information in high levels of government, the process of accessing information can be complicated. Those who are interested must become skilled at navigating the complex set of procedures to offer citizens accurate information. Although FOIA allows any person for any reason access to the records, journalists who work for mainstream media organizations often receive perks such as the waiving of fees and expedited processing (Citizen Media Law Project).

The Equal Time Rule

Falling under broadcast regulations, the Communication Act's Section 315—also known as the Equal Time Rule—requires radio and television stations to give equal opportunity for airtime to all candidates. Essentially, Section 315 ensures that TV and radio stations cannot favor any one political candidate over another.

Passed by Congress in 1927, the equal opportunity requirement was the first major federal broadcasting law. Even then, legislators feared that broadcasters and stations would still be able to manipulate elections. Although candidates cannot receive free airtime unless their opponents do as well, the law doesn't take into consideration campaign funding. Well-funded candidates who can afford to pay for airtime still have an advantage over their poorly funded peers.

News programs, interviews, and documentaries are exempt from the requirements of Section 315. This allows media outlets to report on the activities of a candidate without also having to cover the activities of his or her opponent. Presidential debates fall under this exemption as well and are not required to include third-party candidates.

Section 315 also prohibits media from censoring what a candidate says or presents on air. Recently there has been controversy over campaign ads picturing aborted fetuses. Citing Section 315, the FCC allowed these television ads to continue to run (Museum of Broadcast Communications).

The Fairness Doctrine

As discussed in Chapter 7 "Radio", the Fairness Doctrine was enacted in 1949, when applications for radio broadcast licenses outpaced the number of available frequencies. At the time, concerns that broadcasters might use their stations to promote a particular perspective encouraged the creation of the radio-specific version of Section 315. The FCC thus instituted the Fairness Doctrine to "ensure that all coverage of controversial issues by a broadcast station be balanced and fair (Museum of Broadcast Communications)."

The FCC took the view…that station licensees were "public trustees," and as such had an obligation to afford reasonable opportunity for discussion of contrasting points of view on controversial issues. The commission later held that stations were also obligated to actively seek out issues of importance to their community and air programming that addressed those issues (Museum of Broadcast Communications).

The Fairness Doctrine was considered controversial among journalists who felt that it infringed on the rights of free speech and freedom of press granted in the First Amendment. The doctrine was dissolved during the 1980s with the Reagan administration's deregulatory efforts. We can see these effects today with the popularity of political talk radio.

The Digital Millennium Copyright Act

In 1998, Congress passed the Digital Millennium Copyright Act (DMCA) to bring order to the then-largely-unregulated online arena. As discussed in Chapter 13 "Economics of Mass Media", the DMCA prohibits individuals from either circumventing access-control measures or trafficking devices that may help others circumvent copyright measures. Under this act, it is illegal to use code-cracking devices to illegally copy software, and websites are required to take down material that infringes on copyrights. (You've experienced this regulation yourself if you've ever visited YouTube or Google Video and found that a video has been removed due to copyright claims.)

The DMCA does allow webcasting (the broadcasting of media over the Internet) as long as webcasters pay licensing fees to the companies that own the material. This allows sites such as Hulu to legally stream movies and TV shows to viewers. The DMCA also protects institutes of higher education, including distance-learning programs, from certain copyright liabilities (Online Institute for Cyberspace Law and Policy).

One of the most controversial aspects of the DMCA is that, while it requires websites to remove copyrighted material, it does not require websites to monitor their content. A 3-year-long court battle between media giant Viacom and the Google-owned website YouTube was recently waged over this factor. Viacom argued that YouTube infringed on its rights by hosting copyrighted videos. Google responded that while YouTube may include copyrighted material, it is not required to scan every user-uploaded video for copyright infringement. When a claim is brought against a YouTube video, the video is removed—beyond that, the website is not responsible for content. The judge ruled in favor of Google, stating that it was indeed protected under the DMCA. While many saw this as a victory for Internet freedom, others warned that it would have future consequences for the protection of copyright holders (Rosenbaum, 2010).

Key Takeaways

- The Privacy Act works to guarantee privacy to individuals and controls how personal information is used. Defamation in the written form (libel) or the spoken form (slander) is illegal in the United States.

- Section 315 (Equal Time Rule) ensures that broadcast media cannot favor any one candidate over another by granting one more time than another. The Fairness Doctrine ensured that radio stations offered equal time to opposing viewpoints.

- The Freedom of Information Act grants the public, including the news media, access to many government documents. The Digital Millennium Copyright Act, established in 1998, extended existing copyright laws to encompass and protect information online.

Exercises

Visit the website of a major media outlet and examine the coverage of a recent local, state, or national election. Compare the coverage of different candidates. Then write answers to the short-response questions below. Each response should be a minimum of one paragraph.

1. Identify and describe important laws that relate to different aspects of the media.

2. Explain the effects of the Privacy Act, Section 315, the Fairness Doctrine, and the Digital Millennium Copyright Act on media outlets and audiences.

3. Using information gathered from the media website, do you think there was equal coverage of candidates during the recent election? Why or why not? How do you think this balance would have differed if Section 315 were not in existence?

References

Citizen Media Law Project, "Access to Government Records," http://www.citmedialaw.org/legal-guide/access-government-records.

Citizen Media Law Project, "Access to Records from the Federal Government," http://www.citmedialaw.org/legal-guide/access-records-from-federal-government.

Citizen Media Law Project, "Copyright," http://www.citmedialaw.org/legal-guide/copyright.

Citizen Media Law Project, "Intellectual Property," http://www.citmedialaw.org/legal-guide/intellectual-property.

Citizen Media Law Project, "Publication of Private Facts," http://www.citmedialaw.org/legal-guide/publication-private-facts.

Citizen Media Law Project, "Publishing Personal and Private Information," http://www.citmedialaw.org/legal-guide/publishing-personal-and-private-information.

Citizen Media Law Project, "Who Can Request Records Under FOIA," http://www.citmedialaw.org/legal-guide/who-can-request-records-under-foia.

Media Law Resource Center, "Frequently Asked Media Law Questions," http://www.medialaw.org/Content/NavigationMenu/Public_Resources/Libel_FAQs/Libel_FAQs.htm.

Museum of Broadcast Communications, "Equal Time Rule: U.S. Broadcasting Regulatory Rule," http://www.museum.tv/eotvsection.php?entrycode=equaltimeru.

Museum of Broadcast Communications, "Fairness Doctrine," http://www.museum.tv/eotvsection.php?entrycode=fairnessdoct.

Online Institute for Cyberspace Law and Policy, "The Digital Millennium Copyright Act," UCLA, http://www.gseis.ucla.edu/iclp/dmca1.htm.

Rosenbaum, Steve. "Viacom vs. YouTube: What Was Won. What Was Lost," *Huffington Post*, July 9, 2010, http://www.huffingtonpost.com/steve-rosenbaum/viacom-vs-YouTube-what-wa_b_641489.html.

U.S. Department of Health and Human Services, "The Privacy Act," http://www.hhs.gov/foia/privacy/index.html.

Van Natta Jr., Don. "Maryland Is Dropping Wiretap Case Against Tripp," *New York Times*, http://www.nytimes.com/2000/05/25/us/maryland-is-dropping-wiretap-case-against-tripp.html.

Wall, Barbara W. "News Watch: Boston Newspapers Suffer Setbacks in Libel Cases," Gannett, http://159.54.227.112/go/newswatch/2005/april/nw0401-4.htm.

15.4 Censorship and Freedom of Speech

Figure 15.3

Attempts to censor material, such as banning books, typically attract a great deal of controversy and debate.

Timberland Regional Library – Banned Books Display At The Lacey Library – CC BY-NC-ND 2.0.

To fully understand the issues of censorship and freedom of speech and how they apply to modern media, we must first explore the terms themselves. Censorship is defined as suppressing or removing anything deemed objectionable. A common, everyday example can be found on the radio or television, where potentially offensive words are "bleeped" out. More controversial is censorship at a political or religious level. If you've ever been banned from reading a book in school, or watched a "clean" version of a movie on an airplane, you've experienced censorship.

Much as media legislation can be controversial due to First Amendment protections, censorship in the media is often hotly debated. The First Amendment states that "Congress shall make no law…abridging the freedom of speech, or of the press (Case Summaries)." Under this definition, the term "speech" extends to a broader sense of "expression," meaning verbal, nonverbal, visual, or symbolic expression. Historically, many individuals have cited the First Amendment when protesting FCC decisions to censor certain media products or programs. However, what many people do not realize is that U.S. law establishes several exceptions to free speech, including defamation, hate speech, breach of the peace, incitement to crime, sedition, and obscenity.

Classifying Material as Indecent, Obscene, or Profane

To comply with U.S. law, the FCC prohibits broadcasters from airing obscene programming. The FCC decides whether or not material is obscene by using a three-prong test.

Obscene material:

1. causes the average person to have lustful or sexual thoughts;

2. depicts lawfully offensive sexual conduct; and

3. lacks literary, artistic, political, or scientific value.

Material meeting all of these criteria is officially considered obscene and usually applies to hard-core pornography (Federal Communications Commission). "Indecent" material, on the other hand, is protected by the First Amendment and cannot be banned entirely.

Indecent material:

1. contains graphic sexual or excretory depictions;

2. dwells at length on depictions of sexual or excretory organs; and

3. is used simply to shock or arouse an audience.

Material deemed indecent cannot be broadcast between the hours of 6 a.m. and 10 p.m., to make it less likely that children will be exposed to it (Federal Communications Commission).

These classifications symbolize the media's long struggle with what is considered appropriate and inappropriate material. Despite the existence of the guidelines, however, the process of categorizing materials is a long and arduous one.

There is a formalized process for deciding what material falls into which category. First, the FCC relies on television audiences to alert the agency of potentially controversial material that may require classification. The commission asks the public to file a complaint via letter, e-mail, fax, telephone, or the agency's website, including the station, the community, and the date and time of the broadcast. The complaint should "contain enough detail about the material broadcast that the FCC can understand the exact words and language used (Federal Communications Commission)." Citizens are also allowed to submit tapes or transcripts of the aired material. Upon receiving a complaint, the FCC logs it in a database, which a staff member then accesses to perform an initial review. If necessary, the agency may contact either the station licensee or the individual who filed the complaint for further information.

Once the FCC has conducted a thorough investigation, it determines a final classification for the material. In the case of profane or indecent material, the agency may take further actions, including possibly fining the network or station (Federal Communications Commission). If the material is classified as obscene, the FCC will instead refer the matter to the U.S. Department of Justice, which has the authority to criminally prosecute the media outlet. If convicted in court, violators can be subject to criminal fines and/or imprisonment (Federal Communications Commission).

Each year, the FCC receives thousands of complaints regarding obscene, indecent, or profane programming. While the agency ultimately defines most programs cited in the complaints as appropriate, many complaints require in-depth investigation and may result in fines called notices of apparent liability (NAL) or federal investigation.

Table 15.1 FCC Indecency Complaints and NALs: 2000–2005

Year	Total Complaints Received	Radio Programs Complained About	Over-the-Air Television Programs Complained About	Cable Programs Complained About	Total Radio NALs	Total Television NALs	Total Cable NALs
2000	111	85	25	1	7	0	0
2001	346	113	33	6	6	1	0
2002	13,922	185	166	38	7	0	0
2003	166,683	122	217	36	3	0	0
2004	1,405,419	145	140	29	9	3	0
2005	233,531	488	707	355	0	0	0

Source

Violence and Sex: Taboos in Entertainment

Although popular memory thinks of old black-and-white movies as tame or sanitized, many early filmmakers filled their movies with sexual or violent content. Edwin S. Porter's 1903 silent film *The Great Train Robbery*, for example, is known for expressing "the appealing, deeply embedded nature of violence in the frontier experience and the American civilizing process," and showcases "the rather spontaneous way that the attendant violence appears in the earliest developments of cinema (Film Reference)." The film ends with an image of a gunman firing a revolver directly at the camera, demonstrating that cinema's fascination with violence was present even 100 years ago.

Porter was not the only U.S. filmmaker working during the early years of cinema to employ graphic violence. Films such as *Intolerance* (1916) and *The Birth of a Nation* (1915) are notorious for their overt portrayals of violent activities. The director of both films, D. W. Griffith, intentionally portrayed content graphically because he "believed that the portrayal of violence must be uncompromised to show its consequences for humanity (Film Reference)."

Hays Code

Although audiences responded eagerly to the new medium of film, some naysayers believed that Hollywood films and their associated hedonistic culture was a negative moral influence. As you read in Chapter 8 "Movies", this changed during the 1930s with the implementation of the Hays Code. Formally termed the Motion Picture Production Code of 1930, the code is popularly known by the name of its author, Will Hays, the chairman of the industry's self-regulatory Motion Picture Producers and Distributors Association (MPPDA), which was founded in 1922 to "police all in-house productions (Film Reference)." Created to forestall what was perceived to be looming governmental control over the industry, the Hays Code was, essentially, Hollywood self-censorship. The code displayed the motion picture industry's commitment to the public, stating:

Motion picture producers recognize the high trust and confidence which have been placed in them by the people of the world and which have made motion pictures a universal form of entertainment…. Hence, though regarding motion pictures primarily as entertainment without any explicit purposes of teaching or propaganda, they know that the motion picture within its own field of entertainment may be directly responsible for spiritual or moral progress, for higher types of social life, and for much correct thinking (Arts Reformation).

Among other requirements, the Hays Code enacted strict guidelines on the portrayal of violence. Crimes such as murder, theft, robbery, safecracking, and "dynamiting of trains, mines, buildings, etc." could not be presented in detail (Arts Reformation). The code also addressed the portrayals of sex, saying that "the sanctity of the institution of marriage and the home shall be upheld. Pictures shall not infer that low forms of sex relationship are the accepted or common thing (Arts Reformation)."

Figure 15.4

As the chairman of the Motion Picture Producers and Distributors Association, Will Hays oversaw the creation of the industry's self-censoring Hays Code.

Wikimedia Commons – public domain.

As television grew in popularity during the mid-1900s, the strict code placed on the film industry spread to other forms of visual media. Many early sitcoms, for example, showed married couples sleeping in separate twin beds to avoid suggesting sexual relations.

By the end of the 1940s, the MPPDA had begun to relax the rigid regulations of the Hays Code. Propelled by the changing moral standards of the 1950s and 1960s, this led to a gradual reintroduction of violence and sex into mass media.

Ratings Systems

As filmmakers began pushing the boundaries of acceptable visual content, the Hollywood studio industry scrambled to create a system to ensure appropriate audiences for films. In 1968, the successor of the MPPDA, the Motion Picture Association of America (MPAA), established the familiar film ratings system to help alert potential audiences to the type of content they could expect from a production.

Film Ratings

Although the ratings system changed slightly in its early years, by 1972 it seemed that the MPAA had settled on its ratings. These ratings consisted of G (general audiences), PG (parental guidance suggested), R (restricted to ages 17 or up unless accompanied by a parent), and X (completely restricted to ages 17 and up). The system worked until 1984, when several major battles took place over controversial material. During that year, the highly popular films *Indiana Jones and the Temple of Doom* and *Gremlins* both premiered with a PG rating. Both films—and subsequently the MPAA—received criticism for the explicit violence presented on screen, which many viewers considered too intense for the relatively mild PG rating. In response to the complaints, the MPAA introduced the PG-13 rating to indicate that some material may be inappropriate for children under the age of 13.

Another change came to the ratings system in 1990, with the introduction of the NC-17 rating. Carrying the same restrictions as the existing X rating, the new designation came at the behest of the film industry to distinguish mature films from pornographic ones. Despite the arguably milder format of the rating's name, many filmmakers find it too strict in practice; receiving an NC-17 rating often leads to a lack of promotion or distribution because numerous movie theaters and rental outlets refuse to carry films with this rating.

Television and Video Game Ratings

Regardless of these criticisms, most audience members find the rating system helpful, particularly when determining what is appropriate for children. The adoption of industry ratings for television programs and video games reflects the success of the film ratings system. During the 1990s, for example, the broadcasting industry introduced a voluntary rating system not unlike that used for films to accompany all TV shows. These ratings are displayed on screen during the first 15 seconds of a program and include TV-Y (all children), TV-Y7 (children ages 7 and up), TV-Y7-FV (older children—fantasy violence), TV-G (general audience), TV-PG (parental guidance suggested), TV-14 (parents strongly cautioned), and TV-MA (mature audiences only).

Table 15.2 Television Ratings System

Rating	Meaning	Examples of Programs
TV-Y	Appropriate for all children	*Sesame Street, Barney & Friends, Dora the Explorer*
TV-Y7	Designed for children ages 7 and up	*SpongeBob SquarePants, Captain Planet*
TV-Y7-FV	Directed toward older children; includes depictions of fantasy violence	*The Powerpuff Girls, Pokémon, Avatar: The Last Airbender*
TV-G	Suitable for general audiences; contains little or no violence, no strong language, and little or no sexual material	*Hannah Montana, The Price Is Right, American Idol*
TV-PG	Parental guidance suggested	*The Simpsons, Seinfeld, Tyler Perry's House of Payne*
TV-14	Parents strongly cautioned; contains suggestive dialogue, strong language, and sexual or violent situations	*Saturday Night Live, Keeping Up With the Kardashians, Jersey Shore*
TV-MA	Mature audiences only	*South Park, The Boondocks, The Shield*

Source: http://www.tvguidelines.org/ratings.htm

At about the same time that television ratings appeared, the Entertainment Software Rating Board was established to provide ratings on video games. Video game ratings include EC (early childhood), E (everyone), E 10+ (ages 10 and older), T (teen), M (mature), and AO (adults only).

Table 15.3 Video Game Ratings System

Rating	Meaning	Examples of Games
EC	Designed for early childhood, children ages 3 and older	*Nickelodeon BINGO, Winnie the Pooh ABC's, Elmo's World*
E	Suitable for everyone over the age of 6; contains minimal fantasy violence and mild language	*Tiger Woods PGA Tour, Little Big Planet, Frogger, Myst*
E 10+	Appropriate for ages 10 and older; may contain more violence and/or slightly suggestive themes	*Dance Dance Revolution, Tales of Monkey Island, Rock Band, Scribblenauts*
T	Content is appropriate for teens (ages 13 and older); may contain violence, crude humor, sexually suggestive themes, use of strong language, and/or simulated gambling	*Final Fantasy XIV, The Sims 3, Super Smash Bros. Brawl*
M	Mature content for ages 17 and older; includes intense violence and/or sexual content	*Quake, Grand Theft Auto IV, God of War, Fallout 3*
AO	Adults (18+) only; contains graphic sexual content and/or prolonged violence	*Playboy Mansion: Private Party, Manhunt 2*

Source: http://www.esrb.org/ratings/ratings_guide.jsp

Even with these ratings, the video game industry has long endured criticism over violence and sex in video games. One of the top-selling video game series in the world, *Grand Theft Auto,* is highly controversial because players have the option to solicit prostitution or murder civilians (Media Awareness). In 2010, a report claimed that "38 percent of the female characters in video games are scantily clad, 23 percent baring breasts or cleavage, 31 percent exposing thighs, another 31 percent exposing stomachs or midriffs, and 15 percent baring their behinds (Media Awareness)." Despite multiple lawsuits, some video game creators stand by their decisions to place graphic displays of violence and sex in their games on the grounds of freedom of speech.

Key Takeaways

- The U.S. Government devised the three-prong test to determine if material can be considered "obscene." The FCC applies these guidelines to determine whether broadcast content can be classified as profane, indecent, or obscene.

- Established during the 1930s, the Hays Code placed strict regulations on film, requiring that filmmakers avoid portraying violence and sex in films.

- After the decline of the Hays Code during the 1960s, the MPAA introduced a self-policed film ratings system. This system later inspired similar ratings for television and video game content.

Look over the MPAA's explanation of each film rating online at http://www.mpaa.org/ratings/what-each-rating-means. View a film with these requirements in mind and think about how the rating was selected. Then answer the following short-answer questions. Each response should be a minimum of one paragraph.

1. Would this material be considered "obscene" under the Hays Code criteria? Would it be considered obscene under the FCC's three-prong test? Explain why or why not. How would the film be different if it were released in accordance to the guidelines of the Hays Code?

2. Do you agree with the rating your chosen film was given? Why or why not?

References

Arts Reformation, "The Motion Picture Production Code of 1930 (Hays Code)," ArtsReformation, http://www.artsreformation.com/a001/hays-code.html.

Case Summaries, "First Amendment—Religion and Expression," http://caselaw.lp.findlaw.com/data/constitution/amendment01/.

Federal Communications Commission, "Obscenity, Indecency & Profanity: Frequently Asked Questions," http://www.fcc.gov/eb/oip/FAQ.html.

Film Reference, "Violence," Film Reference, http://www.filmreference.com/encyclopedia/Romantic-Comedy-Yugoslavia/Violence-BEGINNINGS.html.

Media Awareness, Media Issues, "Sex and Relationships in the Media," http://www.media-awareness.ca/english/issues/stereotyping/women_and_girls/women_sex.cfm.

Media Awareness, Media Issues, "Violence in Media Entertainment," http://www.media-awareness.ca/english/issues/violence/violence_entertainment.cfm.

15.5 Ownership Issues in the Mass Media

Learning Objectives

1. Determine the importance of ethical and legal compliance in online interactions.

2. Identify the role of copyright protection in cyberspace.

3. Describe the RIAA's antipiracy efforts.

4. Explain why complete privacy does not exist online.

Since its inception, the Internet has posed problems of ownership. Over the years, the government has struggled to find ways to introduce copyright protections into the online environment because, unlike other forms of media, the Internet enables users to make an unlimited number of copies of material and to transmit that information around the world (Rosenblatt, 1997). In this section, we explore the unique challenges presented in dealing with online copyright and intellectual property and the U.S. government's role in regulating those fields.

Online Creativity and Intellectual Property Rights

Congress passed the Digital Millennium Copyright Act (DMCA) in 1998 to establish a protocol for online copyright matters. Yet the nature of the Internet causes very different copyright and intellectual property issues than older forms of media do. Because of the ease of sharing information online, for example, the DMCA has not worked as Congress expected (Electronic Frontier Foundation). Copying and sharing materials online is relatively simple and, as such, piracy and rights infringement run rampant. In fact, many have argued that despite the DMCA's attempt to stop piracy, in practice, it has done nothing (Electronic Frontier Foundation). Additionally, because information is disseminated so rapidly online, piracy opponents struggle with determining the rightful owner of a particular copyright.

The DMCA and its role in Internet policing have frustrated many online users and watchdog groups. The Electronic Frontier Foundation (EFF) claims that "the DMCA has become a serious threat that jeopardizes fair use, impedes competition and innovation, chills free expression and scientific research, and interferes with computer intrusion laws (Electronic Frontier Foundation)." In 2004, comic book company Marvel Entertainment sued game publishers NCsoft and Cryptic for copyright infringement in their online game *City of Heroes*. Marvel argued that players could use the character customization system in *City of Heroes* to make characters look almost identical to Marvel characters (Jenkins, 2004). Situations like this led groups such as the EFF to publically call for DMCA reform. Such disputes serve as reminders of the challenges inherent in issuing copyrights and intellectual property rights for the online industry.

Copyright Protection in Cyberspace

Certainly, the DMCA brought about major transformations by establishing copyright protection guidelines for the digital arena. However, in 1996—prior to the passage of the DMCA—the World Intellectual Property Organization (WIPO) established two treaties designed to "update and supplement the major existing WIPO treaties on copyright and related rights, primarily in order to respond to developments in technology and in the marketplace (World Intellectual Property Organization)." The first of these, the WIPO Copyright Treaty (WCT), was created to protect authors of literary and artistic works, including computer programs, original databases, and fine art (World Intellectual Property Organization). The second, the WIPO Performances and Phonograms Treaty (WPPT), deals with "related rights," or rights connected to copyright. This law was created to protect the rights of performers and producers of sound recordings (World Intellectual Property Organization). These treaties both ensure basic rights, such as compensation and acknowledgement for those who create works, and extend further protections (World Intellectual Property Organization).

Supported by the WIPO and the DMCA, new forms of communication now enjoy copyright protections. Copyright laws cover blogs and website content, provided that these sites contain original writing (U.S. Copyright Office). Despite these developments, however, the Internet still poses challenges for copyrighted material. Because the web changes so quickly, maintaining copyright protection with the Copyright Office can be difficult. Presently, a work must be fixed and in a tangible form to be protected under copyright. Different, altered versions of the same work might not be covered under an original filed copyright claim. As such, authors publishing online must be careful to ensure that their work is protected.

The RIAA versus Piracy

Widespread piracy problems arose during the late 1990s with the popularization of technology allowing peer-to-peer (P2P) music sharing. Suddenly, software such as Napster, Scour, Aimster, AudioGalaxy, Morpheus, Grokster, Kazaa, iMesh, and LimeWire popped up on computers everywhere, allowing access to free music around the world—and fueling online piracy. However, in 2003, the Recording Industry Association of America (RIAA) put the laws established by the DMCA into practice and began a campaign to stop music piracy. In response to the growing number of users, the organization announced that it had been gathering evidence against users sharing music on P2P networks. Rather than go after the software engineers, "the RIAA investigators targeted 'uploaders'—individuals who were allowing others to copy music files from their 'shared' folders (U.S. Copyright Office)."

This data collection led to the RIAA filing more than 250 lawsuits against individuals in what has been called "an unprecedented legal campaign against its own customers (Electronic Frontier Foundation)." Among the first of these lawsuits was one against a 12-year-old girl who had to pay $2,000 and publicly apologize to settle her case. Since then, the recording industry has filed, settled, or threatened legal actions against over 28,000 individuals (Electronic Frontier Foundation). Recently, the popular torrent site The Pirate Bay found itself under attack for allowing users to search for pirated copies of material. This case mirrors the case of Viacom versus YouTube, because the prosecution argued that The Pirate Bay was responsible for the material its users posted and downloaded. These lawsuits raise the question of whether websites are responsible for the actions of their users, an issue that looks to be central to future Internet legislation (Masnick, 2009).

The Law and Online Interactions

Many Americans use the Internet on a regular basis. However, although the Internet is a relatively new form of media, it is not exempt from media laws. Terms of service agreements, as well as legislation such as the 1986 Computer Fraud and Abuse Act, regulate Internet use. As you will see in the following case studies, when it comes to criminal use, the Internet is not as anonymous as it seems.

TOS Agreements

All software and most Internet sites have a terms of service agreement to which its users must comply. Terms of Service (TOS) are legally binding rules that an individual must adhere to in order to use a particular piece of software or service. iTunes, for instance, makes users agree to use their downloadable material for noncommercial use only and states that Apple is not responsible for lost or corrupted files. Anyone who has installed a new piece of software or logged on to social networking sites has agreed to a TOS. Entrance into these sites or use of a program typically requires a user to read through legal guidelines and then click a box agreeing to abide by the stated rules.

Deterred by the length and legal jargon of the standard TOS, however, many people skip to the end and simply accept the terms without reading them carefully. iTunes, for instance, has a clause that states:

You may not use or otherwise export or re-export the Licensed Application [iTunes] except as authorized by United States law…the Licensed Application may not be exported or re-exported…into any U.S.-embargoed countries…You also agree that you will not use these products for any purposes prohibited by United States law, including, without limitation, the development, design, manufacture, or production of nuclear, missile, or chemical or biological weapons (Apple).

While not all Terms of Service are as extensive, an individual's breach of any TOS may result in suspension, restriction, or cancellation of account privileges, depending on the severity of the offense. As individuals become increasingly reliant on Internet services such as e-mail, calendars, and social networks, the potential for disruption is enormous.

The Case of Megan Meier

In 2008, a compelling court case arose regarding TOS violation. Lori Drew, a 49-year-old woman, was accused of using a fake MySpace account to convince 13-year-old Megan Meier to commit suicide. After Drew's daughter had a confrontation with Meier, Drew created an account pretending to be a teenage boy. At first she used the persona to flirt with Meier and uncover information about the teenager's social life and relationship to her daughter. Later, when Drew decided she had enough information, she broke off her friendship, telling Meier that the world would be better off without her. Later that day, a distraught Megan Meier hanged herself (Steinhauer,

2008). After Lori Drew's identity was revealed, Meier's shocked parents filed charges against her. Despite the tragic events, whether Drew had actually committed a crime remained questionable. Eventually, prosecutors decided that:

Since there were no laws that applied in Missouri, the state where this tragedy occurred, [Drew] will face trial in California (the home of MySpace) where she will be charged with—of all things—TOS violations. Creating a false identity goes against MySpace's terms of service and…as a result she will be facing 1 count of conspiracy and 3 counts of accessing a computer without authorization (Spalding, 2008).

The case is complicated and the charge unprecedented. As one author writes, "This raises the questions as to how much weight do online 'contracts' hold (Spalding, 2008)."

Prosecutors charged Drew under the Computer Fraud and Abuse Act (CFAA), although that law is designed primarily to reduce hacking into computer systems. In August 2009, a jury found Drew guilty of "misdemeanor counts of unauthorized access," but commented that "the CFAA was not devised as a vehicle for criminalizing simple contractual violations on the Internet (Paul, 2009)." Although many believe that prosecutors pushed the charge too far, the Drew case brought TOS agreements to the attention of the public, shedding light on the complicated laws associated with Internet use.

Crimes on the Internet

Although cases such as Drew's have brought about unexpected challenges, other online cases have had less ambiguous results. One newly clarified aspect of online law involves the use of the Internet to commit a crime. Regardless of the supposed anonymity of online use, law enforcement agencies and courts can requisition Internet protocol (IP) addresses of suspected lawbreakers and trace their computers to discover their identities. This practice has brought many individuals to trial for criminal offenses committed over the Internet.

Online Hate Crimes and Anonymity

In 1998, a federal court found a 21-year-old Los Angeles man, Richard Machado, guilty of sending racist death threats to 59 Asian students. This case set a precedent because Machado was the first person to be convicted of an online hate crime for sending the message via e-mail. Machado had used a campus computer to send an e-mail to a group of mostly Asian students at University of California, Irvine, saying, "I personally will make it my life career to find and kill every one of [you]." Machado, a former UC Irvine student, signed the e-mail "Asian Hater." Prosecutors charged Machado with sending the threat based on the recipients' race or ethnicity and interfering with their right to attend a public university (Macavinta, 1998).

The case signaled a new legal development because it was the first trial regarding hate crimes online. Prosecutor Michael Gennaco said of Machado's sentencing, "The jury has spoken that a line needs to be drawn in cyberspace. If you cross that line, you'll be subjected to the same criminal penalties you would be as if you use a telephone or post mail to do these kinds of acts (Macavinta, 1998)." Internet law specialists agree with Gennaco that the Internet is not and should not be treated differently from other communication methods; something posted online carries the same weight as a phone conversation or face-to-face interaction. This means that online anonymity is, in fact, not anonymous.

Despite the precedent of Machado's case, many people still mistakenly believe that the Internet will protect them from prosecution. Such was the case of Walter Edward Bagdasarian, who discovered that the government can trace supposedly anonymous posts using IP addresses. U.S. Secret Service agents arrested Bagdasarian, a Southern California man, in 2009 for "posting a racist note to a Yahoo message board in October [2008] expressing displeasure over Barack Obama's candidacy, and predicting 'he will have a 50 cal in the head soon (Poulsen, 2009).'" The case exemplifies both the ease with which authorities can and do trace criminal behavior online and their propensity to take such cases seriously.

What does the future hold for Internet legislation? Many say that it will closely mirror that of other media outlets. Already there have been cases regarding Internet monopolies, defamation of users, and copyright infringement on message boards and personal websites (Netlitigation). Others argue that Internet regulation should take into account the differences between the use of the Internet and the use of other media; for example, an Arizona radio station that violates broadcasting laws is tried in Arizona, but where should an Internet podcaster be charged? If a user posts information on a community forum, is it protected under copyright? Does e-mail spam fall under the same regulations as telemarketing? What privacy rights should Internet users have? As the Internet grows and more issues are taken to court, authorities must come to terms with media issues in a constantly changing digital landscape.

Key Takeaways

- The DMCA and the WIPO provide basic legal guidelines for copyright and intellectual property protections online. Nevertheless, regulating and enforcing such statutes remains a complicated, difficult process due to the rapid change and shared authorship inherent to online content.

- In 2003, the RIAA began a campaign against illegal peer-to-peer sharing of music. Its actions resulted in hundreds of lawsuits and greater awareness of issues pertaining to digital copyrights.

- Law enforcement agencies and courts can requisition IP addresses and trace computers to discover the identity of online users suspected of committing crimes. Seemingly anonymous Internet activities may be subject to severe legal consequences.

Exercises

Thoroughly read a terms of service agreement from a major website you use frequently, such as a social networking site. How do the terms fit with your expectations? Is there anything that you find surprising? Is there anything that causes any concerns? With this in mind, answer the short-answer questions below. Each response should be a minimum of one paragraph.

1. Describe the importance of ethical and legal compliance in online interactions. What would happen if you violated the terms of service that you read?

2. Describe the RIAA's antipiracy efforts.

3. Explain why complete privacy does not exist online.

References

Apple, "Terms and Conditions," http://www.apple.com/legal/itunes/us/terms.html.

Electronic Frontier Foundation, "Digital Millennium Copyright Act," http://www.eff.org/issues/dmca.

Electronic Frontier Foundation, "RIAA v. The People," http://www.eff.org/riaa-v-people.

Jenkins, David. "Marvel Sues *City Of Heroes* Creators," *Gamasutra*, November 12, 2004, http://www.gamasutra.com/php-bin/news_index.php?story=4548.

Macavinta, Courtney. "Conviction in Online Threat Case," *CNET*, February 11, 1998, http://news.cnet.com/Conviction-in-online-threat-case/2100-1023_3-208044.html.

Masnick, Mike. "Pirate Bay Loses a Lawsuit; Entertainment Industry Loses an Opportunity," *Techdirt*, April 17, 2009, http://www.techdirt.com/articles/20090417/0129274535.shtml.

Netlitigation, "Internet Law: News, Suits, and Discussion," http://www.netlitigation.com/netlitigation/.

Paul, Ryan. "Judge: TOS Violations Not a Crime in Teen Suicide Case," *Ars Technica* (blog), August 31, 2009, http://arstechnica.com/tech-policy/news/2009/08/judge-says-tos-violations-arent-a-crime-acquits-lori-drew.ars.

Poulsen, Kevin. "Online Threat to Kill Obama Leads to Arrest," *Wired*, January 9, 2009, http://www.wired.com/threatlevel/2009/01/threat/.

Rosenblatt, Bill. "The Digital Object Identifier: Solving the Dilemma of Copyright Protection Online," *Journal of Electronic Publishing* 3, no. 2 (1997), http://quod.lib.umich.edu/cgi/t/text/text-idx?c=jep;view=text;rgn=main;idno=3336451.0003.204.

Spalding, Steve. "Lori Drew Facing Trial for TOS Violation," *How to Split an Atom*, November 21, 2008, http://howtosplitanatom.com/the-news/lori-drew-facing-trial-for-tos-violation/.

Steinhauer, Jennifer. "Verdict in MySpace Suicide Case," *New York Times*, November 26, 2008, http://www.nytimes.com/2008/11/27/us/27myspace.html.

U.S. Copyright Office, "What Does Copyright Protect?" http://www.copyright.gov/help/faq/faq-protect.html#what_protect.

World Intellectual Property Organization, "Frequently Asked Questions," http://www.wipo.int/copyright/en/faq/faqs.htm#P7_220.

15.6 Digital Democracy and Its Possible Effects

Learning Objectives

1. Explain how the Internet has changed citizens' role in the political process.
2. Determine the differences between traditional campaigning and digital campaigning.

In an era when work, discourse, and play are increasingly experienced via the Internet, it is fitting that politics have surged online as well in a recent phenomenon known as digital democracy. Digital democracy—also known as e-democracy—engages citizens in government and civic action through online tools. This new form of democracy began as an effort to include larger numbers of citizens in the democratic process. Recent evidence seems to confirm a rising popular belief that the Internet is the most effective modern way to engage individuals in politics. "Online political organizations…have attracted millions of members, raised tens of millions of dollars, and become a key force in electoral politics. Even more important, the 2004 and 2008 election cycles show that candidates themselves can use the Internet to great effect (Hindman, 2008)."

President Obama's Digital Campaign

Figure 15.6

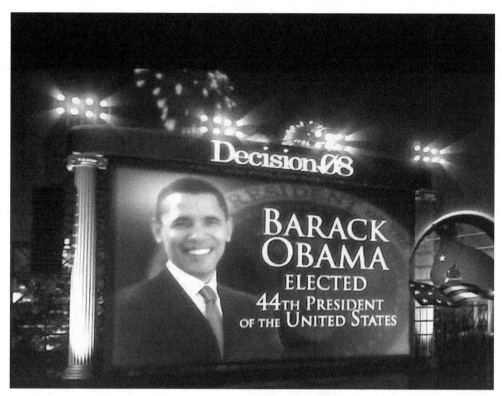

President Barack Obama has been called "the digital candidate" for his use of digital technology during his 2008 presidential campaign.

shutterblog – YES WE DID! – CC BY 2.0.

Perhaps the best example of a political candidate putting digital democracy to use is the successful 2008 presidential campaign of Barack Obama. On June 8, 2008, following Obama's victory in the Democratic presidential primaries, *The New York Times* published an article discussing the candidate's use of the Internet in his nomination bid. Titled "The Wiki-Way to the Nomination," the article credits Obama's success to his employment of digital technology: "Barack Obama is the victor, and the Internet is taking the bows (Cohen, 2008)."

Obama's campaign certainly is not the first to rely on the Internet. Another Democratic presidential hopeful, Howard Dean, famously built his campaign online during the 2004 election cycle. But the Obama campaign took full advantage of the possibilities of digital democracy and, ultimately, secured the Oval Office partially on the strength of that strategy. As one writer puts it, "What is interesting about the story of his digital campaign is the way in which digital was integrated fully into the Obama campaign, rather than [being] seen as an additional extra (Williams, 2009)." President Obama's successful campaign serves as an excellent example of the possibilities of digital democracy.

Traditional Websites

Several existing political websites proved beneficial to the Obama campaign. Founded in 1998, the liberal website MoveOn.org has long used its popularity and supporter base to mobilize citizens to vote, lobby, or donate funds to Democratic campaigns. With more than 4 million members, MoveOn.org plays a noticeable role in U.S. politics and serves as inspiration for other like-minded digital efforts.

The Obama campaign gave a nod to the success of such sites by building a significant web presence. Websites such as MyBarackObama.com formed the foundation of these online efforts. However, the success of the Obama digital campaign came from its use of online media in all its forms. The campaign turned not only to traditional websites but also to social networking sites, e-mail outreach, text messages, and viral videos.

Social Networking

More and more, digital democracy demands that its users rely on these alternative forms of Internet outreach. Social networking site Facebook was the hub of many digital outreach efforts during the 2008 campaign. As of 2010, Barack Obama's official Facebook page boasts more than 9 million fans, and the Obama administration uses the page to send messages about the current political climate.

Individuals not part of the official campaign also established Facebook pages supporting the candidate. Mamas for Obama emerged just prior to the election, as did Women for Obama and the Michelle Obama Fan Club. The groups range in size, but all speak to a new wave of digital democracy. Other political candidates, including 2008 Republican presidential contender John McCain, have also turned to Facebook, albeit in less comprehensive ways.

E-Mail Outreach

The Obama campaign also relied on e-mail. In 2009, an article was published titled "The Story Behind Obama's Digital Campaign" discussing the success of Obama's use of the Internet. According to the article, 13.5 million people signed up for updates on Obama's progress via the MyBarackObama.com website. The campaign regularly sent out e-mails to reach its audience.

Emails were short—never longer than 300 words—and never anonymous, there was always a consistency of voice and tone. Obama and other key figures in the campaign also contributed emails to be sent—"Michelle wrote her own emails…and more people opened those than her husband's"—giving the campaign a personal touch and authenticity, rather than the impression of being simply churned out by the PR machine (Williams, 2009).

A combination of message and financial appeal, the e-mails were successful not only in reaching target audiences but also in earning valuable campaign dollars.

Two billion emails were then sent out, although…this email content was carefully managed, with individuals targeted with different "tracks" depending on their circumstances and whether they had already donated to the campaign…. By the end of the campaign the website had mobilized over 3 million people to contribute over $500 million online (Williams, 2009).

Text Messaging

Additionally, Obama used text messaging to reach out to his supporters. During the campaign, supporters could sign up to receive text messages, and attendees at rallies and other events were asked to send text messages to friends or potential supporters to encourage them to participate in Obama's campaign. Members of MyBarackObama.com were the first to discover his running mate selection via text message (Organizing for

America). This tool proved helpful and demonstrated the Obama campaign's commitment to fully relying on the digital world.

E-Democracy

Perhaps even more impressive than the campaign's commitment to digital democracy were the e-democracy efforts of Obama's supporters. Websites such as Barackobamaisyournewbicycle.com, a gently mocking site "listing the many examples of Mr. Obama's magical compassion. ('Barack Obama carries a picture of you in his wallet'; 'Barack Obama thought you could use some chocolate'),"[1] emerged, but viral videos offered even stronger examples of Obama's grassroots campaign.

Figure 15.7

will.i.am #willpower Wrap Party at the Avalon in Hollywood, CA on August 13, 2012

The music video "Yes We Can," created by the Black Eyed Peas' will.i.am, was viewed more than 20 million times leading up to the 2008 presidential election. It is just one example of digital campaigning used by supporters of political candidates.

One example of a supporter-created video was "Barack Paper Scissors," an interactive game inspired by rock-paper-scissors. Posted on YouTube, the video logged some 600,000 views. The success of videos such as "Barack Paper Scissors" did not go unnoticed by the Obama campaign. The viral video "Yes We Can," in which Barack Obama's words were set to music by will.i.am (of the Black Eyed Peas), has been viewed more than 20 million times online. Capitalizing on the popularity of the clip, the campaign brought it from YouTube to its main website, thus generating even more views and greater exposure for its message.

Political Rumors Online

Although the Internet is a powerful tool for candidates, it also propagates rumors that can derail—or at least hinder—a politician's career. Blog posts and mass e-mails can be created within minutes and then reposted or forwarded in seconds. Thus, ideas spread like wildfire regardless of their relative truth. Snopes.com, a website dedicated to verifying or debunking urban legends and Internet rumors, has an entire search section dedicated to political rumors, ranging from shooting down a list of books supposedly banned by Sarah Palin to investigating whether actress Nancy Cartwright, best known as the voice of Bart Simpson, was once elected mayor of Northridge, California. The pages dedicated to major political figures such as President Obama can be huge; Obama's page, for example, lists more than 60 debunked rumors. Some of these rumors include the questioning of his U.S. citizenship, his decision to ban recreational fishing, and his refusal to sign Eagle Scout certificates.

Many of these online rumors are accompanied by "photographic evidence," thanks to technology such as Photoshop, which allows photographs to be manipulated with the click of a mouse. With such a spread of online rumors, savvy media consumers must be wary of what they read and seek out legitimate sources of information to verify the news that they receive.

Digital Democracy and the Digital Divide

Just as digital technology access issues can create the kinds of problems discussed in Chapter 13 "Economics of Mass Media", the digital divide can equally split the country's involvement with politics along tech-savvy lines. Certainly, the Obama campaign's reliance on modern technology allowed it to reach a large population of young voters; but in doing so, the campaign focused much of its attention in an area out of reach to other voters. In *The Myth of Digital Democracy*, author Matthew Hindman wonders, "Is the Internet making politics less exclusive?"[2] The answer is likely both yes and no. While the Internet certainly has the power to inform and mobilize many individuals, it also denies poorer citizens without digital access an opportunity to be part of the new wave of e-democracy.

Nevertheless, digital democracy will continue to play a large role in politics, particularly after the overwhelming success of President Obama's largely digital campaign. But politicians and their supporters must consider the digital divide and work to reach out to those who are not plugged in to the digital world.

Key Takeaways

- The Internet has dramatically changed citizens' involvement in the political process by giving them greater access to issues and candidates.
- Candidates can now communicate with individuals via websites, e-mail, text messages, and viral videos, offering citizens a more personal experience with the election process.
- Savvy consumers question the truth of unverified online information such as that contained in e-mails or blog posts.

Exercises

Visit YouTube and search for a local or national candidate with whom you are familiar. If possible, compare the video message to those available on a candidate's website. Then answer the following short-answer questions. Each response should be a minimum of one paragraph.

1. How does this video support the overall theme of the candidate's campaign?

2. How might access to videos such as these alter the way campaigns are run?

3. Explain how the growth of the Internet has changed citizens' roles in the political process.

[1]Cohen, "The Wiki-Way to the Nomination."

[2]Hindman, 4.

References

Cohen, Noam. "The Wiki-Way to the Nomination," *New York Times*, June 8, 2008, http://www.nytimes.com/2008/06/08/weekinreview/08cohen.html.

Hindman, Matthew. *The Myth of Digital Democracy* (Princeton, NJ: Princeton University Press, 2008), 4.

Organizing for America, BarackObama.com, "Be the First to Know," Organizing for America, http://my.barackobama.com/page/s/firsttoknow.

Williams, Eliza. "The Story Behind Obama's Digital Campaign," *Creative Review*, July 1, 2009, http://www.creativereview.co.uk/cr-blog/2009/june/the-story-behind-obamas-digital-campaign.

15.7 Media Influence on Laws and Government

Figure 15.8

In 2007, *The Washington Post* published a critical exposé on the Walter Reed Army Medical Center. In response to the public outcry, the U.S. Army launched an investigation and set about improving the facility. As demonstrated in this case, media coverage can directly influence people's lives.

Media have long had a voice and a role in politics. As you have read in earlier chapters, even some of the earliest newspapers and magazines used their pages as a forum for political discourse. When broadcast media emerged during the 20th century, radio briefs and television reports entered the conversation, bringing political stories to the public's living rooms.

In addition to acting as a watchdog, media provide readers and viewers with news coverage of issues and events, and also offer public forums for debate. Thus, media support—or lack thereof—can have a significant influence on public opinion and governmental action. In 2007, for example, *The Washington Post* conducted a 4-month investigation of the substandard medical treatment of wounded soldiers at Walter Reed Army Medical Center in Washington, DC. Because of the ensuing two-part feature, the Secretary of the Army and the two-star general in charge of the medical facility lost their jobs.

However, an ongoing debate exists over media's role in politics. Many individuals wonder who is really behind certain stories. William James Willis, author of *The Media Effect: How the News Influences Politics and Government* discusses this debate:

Sometimes the media appear willing or unwitting participants in chasing stories the government wants them to chase; other times politicians find themselves chasing issues that the media has enlarged by its coverage. Over the decades, political scientists, journalists, politicians, and political pundits have put forth many arguments about the media's power in influencing the government and politicians (Willis, 2007).

Regardless of who is encouraging whom, media coverage of politics certainly raises questions among the public. Despite laws put in place to prevent unbalanced political coverage, such as Section 315, a large majority of the public is still wary of the media's role in swaying political opinion. In a January 2010 survey, two-thirds of respondents said that the media has too much influence on the government. Additionally, 72 percent of respondents agreed that "most reporters try to help the candidate they want to win (Rasmussen Reports, 2010)." This statistic demonstrates the media's perceived political power along with the road the media must carefully navigate when dealing with political issues.

Politics, Broadcast Media, and the Internet

Throughout their respective histories, radio, television, and the Internet have played important roles in politics. As technology developed, citizens began demanding greater levels of information and analysis of media outlets and, in turn, politicians. Here we explore the transformation of politics with the development of media.

Radio

As discussed in Chapter 7 "Radio", radio was the first medium through which up-to-the-minute breaking news could be broadcast, with its popularization during the 1920s. On November 2, 1920, KDKA in East Pittsburgh, Pennsylvania, became the first station to broadcast election results from the Harding-Cox presidential race, "becoming a pioneer in a brand new technology (American History)." Suddenly, information that would previously have been available only later in the newspapers was transmitted directly into American living rooms. The public responded positively, wanting to be more involved in U.S. politics.

As radio technology developed, "Americans demanded participation in the political and cultural debates shaping their democratic republic (Jenkins)." Radio provided a way to hold these debates in a public forum; it also provided a venue for politicians to speak directly to the public, a phenomenon that had not been possible on a large scale prior to the invention of the radio. This dynamic changed politics. Suddenly, candidates and elected officials had to be able to effectively communicate their messages to a large audience. "Radio brought politicians into people's homes, and many politicians went to learn effective public-speaking for radio broadcasts (ThinkQuest)."

Television

Today, television remains Americans' chief source of political news, a relationship that dates back almost to the very beginning of the medium. Political candidates began using TV commercials to speak directly to the public as early as 1952. These "living room candidates," as they are often called, understood the power of the television screen and the importance of reaching viewers at home. In 1952, Dwight D. Eisenhower became the first candidate to harness television's popularity. Eisenhower stepped onto the television screen "when Madison Avenue advertising executive Rosser Reeves convinced [him] that short ads played during such popular TV programs as *I Love Lucy* would reach more voters than any other form of advertising. This innovation had a permanent effect on the way presidential campaigns are run (Living Room Candidate)."

Nixon–Kennedy Debates of 1960

The relationship between politics and television took a massive step forward in 1960 with a series of four televised "Great Debates" between presidential candidates John F. Kennedy and Richard Nixon. Seventy million U.S. viewers tuned into the first of these on September 26, 1960. The debates gave voters their first chance to see candidates debate, marking television's entry into politics.

Figure 15.9

In 1960, candidates John F. Kennedy and Richard Nixon brought presidential debating to television screens around the nation.

judy_and_ed – Replay – CC BY-NC 2.0.

Just as radio changed the way politicians thought about their speeches, television emphasized the importance of their appearance. Shortly before the first debate, Nixon had spent 2 weeks in the hospital with a knee injury. By the day of the debate he was extremely underweight. In addition, he wore an ill-fitting shirt and refused to wear makeup. Kennedy, however, was fit, tan, and confident. The visual difference between the two candidates was staggering; Kennedy appeared much more presidential. Indeed, those who watched the first broadcast declared that Kennedy had clearly won the debate, while those who listened by radio said that Nixon had won. A record number of viewers watched the debates, and many historians have attributed Kennedy's success at the polls that November to the public perception of the candidates formed during these debates (Mary Ferrell Foundation).

War and Television

Later in the decade, rising U.S. involvement in Vietnam brought television and public affairs together again in a significant way. The horrors of battle were broadcast directly into U.S. homes on a large scale for the first time; although television had been invented prior to the Korean War, "the medium was in its infancy…[and] its audience and technology [were] still too limited to play a major role (Museum of Broadcast Communications)." As such, in 1965 the Vietnam War became the first "living-room war."

Early in the war, the coverage was mostly upbeat:

It typically began with a battlefield roundup, written from wire reports based on the daily press briefing in Saigon…read by the anchor and illustrated with a battle map…. The battlefield roundup would normally be followed by a policy story from Washington, and then a film report from the field…. As with most television news, the emphasis was on the visual and above all the personal: "American boys in action" was the story, and reports emphasized their bravery and their skill in handling the technology of war (Museum of Broadcast Communications).

In 1969, however, television coverage began to change as journalists grew more and more skeptical of the government's claims of progress, and there was more emphasis on the human costs of war (Museum of Broadcast Communications). Although gore typically remained off screen, a few major violent moments were caught on film and broadcast into homes. In 1965, CBS aired footage of U.S. Marines setting village huts on fire, and in 1972, NBC audiences witnessed Vietnamese civilians fall victim to a napalm strike. Such scenes altered America's perspective of the war, generating antiwar sentiment.

Political News Programming

The way that news is televised has dramatically changed over the medium's history. For years, nightly news broadcasts dominated the political news cycle; then round-the-clock cable news channels appeared. Founded by Ted Turner in 1980, CNN (Cable News Network) was the first such network. Upon the launch of CNN, Turner stated, "We won't be signing off until the world ends. We'll be on, and we will cover the end of the world, live, and that will be our last event…and when the end of the world comes, we'll play 'Nearer, My God, to Thee' before we sign off (TV Tropes)."

Twenty-four-hour news stations such as CNN have become more popular, and nightly news programs have been forced to change their focus, now emphasizing more local stories that may not be covered by the major news programs. Additionally, the 21st century has seen the rise of the popularity and influence of satirical news shows such as *The Daily Show* and *The Colbert Report*. The comedic news programs have, in recent years, become major cultural arbiters and watchdogs of political issues thanks to the outspoken nature of their hosts and their frank coverage of political issues.

Online News and Politics

Finally, the Internet has become an increasingly important force in how Americans receive political information. Websites such as the Huffington Post, Daily Beast, and the Drudge Report are known for breaking news stories and political commentary. Additionally, political groups regularly use the Internet to organize supporters and influence political issues. Online petitions are available via the Internet, and individuals can use online resources to donate to political causes or connect with like-minded people.

Media and government have had a long and complicated history. Each influences the other through regulations and news cycles. As technology develops, the relationship between media and politics will likely become even more intermeshed. The hope is that the U.S. public will benefit from such developments, and both media and the government will seek out opportunities to involve the public in their decisions.

Key Takeaways

- Election results were broadcast on the radio in 1920, granting listeners access to political information as it was being made public and transforming the way that citizens viewed politics and political involvement.

- The televised Nixon–Kennedy debates of 1960 brought politics into the living rooms of Americans, forever changing U.S. citizens' understanding of the political process and making television a valuable platform for candidates and issues.

Exercises

Choose a political topic that interests you, such as conflict in the Middle East, the legalization of marijuana, or gay marriage. Find a radio story, a television story, and an Internet story about this topic. Then write a one-page paper answering the questions below.

1. Describe how radio transformed the political process. How was your topic presented differently on the radio than it was on television or the Internet?

2. Discuss the effect of televised debates on presidential campaigns. Was your issue addressed in the 2008 presidential campaign? Was it discussed on the televised debates?

3. How do different media tell the same story? Do any present a more balanced story? Which covered your topic the most in depth? Which covered it the least?

End-of-Chapter Assessment

Review Questions

1.
Section 1

a. What are the major duties of the FTC?

b. What are the major duties of the FCC?

c. Describe the effects of Reagan-era deregulation on the mass media.

2.
Section 2

a. Explain the difference between libel and slander.

b. What is Section 315, and how does it affect the media's relationship with politics?

c. What is the purpose and scope of the Freedom of Information Act?

3.
Section 3

a. Define censorship.

b. Briefly list the steps in the process that the FCC uses to classify materials as profane, indecent, or obscene.

c. How did the Hays Code affect mass media during the 20th century?

4.
Section 4

a. How and why has the RIAA worked to eliminate piracy?

b. What is a TOS and why is it important?

c. Why might authorities request personal information about an Internet user?

5.
Section 5

a. What is digital democracy?

b. List three ways that digital democracy affects modern political activity.

6.
Section 6

a. How did the invention of the radio transform politics?

b. What are two examples of the influence of television on government?

Critical Thinking Questions

1. Evaluate the role of the FCC in modern media. Do you think regulation should increase or decrease? Why?

2. Compare and contrast Section 315 and the Fairness Doctrine.

3. Discuss why profane and indecent material can be broadcast during certain time slots, but obscene material cannot be broadcast at all.

4. Explain the importance of compliance with terms of service agreements.

5. Describe the effects of the digital divide on political campaigning.

6. Discuss the role that television has played in swaying public opinion on issues of war.

Career Connection

Some media professionals work closely with political candidates to help them craft their public images and messages. Suppose that you were going to advise the campaign of a candidate for local, state, or national office. Choose a candidate who interests you and visit his or her existing website. Explore any other digital outreach efforts. Then answer the following questions to help you make recommendations for the campaign.

1. How does he or she employ social networking sites?

2. How does he or she target varying age groups on the Internet?

3. What could you do to strengthen his or her digital outreach?

References

American History, "History of the Radio," http://americanhistory.suite101.com/article.cfm/history_of_the_radio.

Jenkins, Henry. "Contacting the Past: Early Radio and the Digital Revolution," MIT Communications Forum, http://web.mit.edu/comm-forum/papers/jenkins_cp.html.

Living Room Candidate, Museum of the Moving Image, The Living Room Candidate, http://www.livingroomcandidate.org/.

Mary Ferrell Foundation, "Kennedy-Nixon Debates," *Mary Ferrell Foundation*, http://www.maryferrell.org/wiki/index.php/Kennedy-Nixon_Debates.

Museum of Broadcast Communications, "Vietnam on Television," http://www.museum.tv/eotvsection.php?entrycode=vietnamonte.

Rasmussen Reports, "67% Say News Media Have too Much Influence Over Government Decisions," news

release, January 14, 2010, http://www.rasmussenreports.com/public_content/politics/general_politics/january_2010
/67_say_news_media_have_too_much_influence_over_government_decisions.

ThinkQuest, "Radio's Emergence," http://library.thinkquest.org/27629/themes/media/md20s.html.

TV Tropes, "Twenty Four Hour News Networks," http://tvtropes.org/pmwiki/pmwiki.php/Main/TwentyFourHourNewsNetworks.

Willis, William James. *The Media Effect: How the News Influences Politics and Government* (Westport, CT: Praeger, 2007), 4.

Chapter 16: The Future of Mass Media

16.1 Changes in Media Over the Last Century

Learning Objectives

1. Describe the types of new media.
2. Identify how the Internet has affected media delivery.
3. Explain why new media is often more successful than traditional forms of media.

Life has changed dramatically over the past century, and a major reason for this is the progression of media technology. Compare a day in the life of a modern student—let's call her Katie—with a day in the life of someone from Katie's great-grandparents' generation. When Katie wakes up, she immediately checks her smartphone for text messages and finds out that her friend will not be able to give her a ride to class. Katie flips on the TV while she eats breakfast to check the news and learns it is supposed to rain that day. Before she leaves her apartment, Katie goes online to make sure she remembered the train times correctly. She grabs an umbrella and heads to the train station, listening to a music application on her smartphone on the way. After a busy day of classes, Katie heads home, occupying herself on the train ride by watching YouTube clips on her phone. That evening, she finishes her homework, e-mails the file to her instructor, and settles down to watch the TV show she digitally recorded the night before. While watching the show, Katie logs on to Facebook and chats with a few of her friends online to make plans for the weekend and then reads a book on her e-reader.

Katie's life today is vastly different from the life she would have led just a few generations ago. At the beginning of the 20th century, neither TV nor the Internet existed. There were no commercial radio stations, no roadside billboards, no feature films, and certainly no smartphones. People were dependent on newspapers and magazines for their knowledge of the outside world. An early-20th-century woman the same age as Katie—let's call her Elizabeth—wakes up to read the daily paper. Yellow journalism is rife, and the papers are full of lurid stories and sensational headlines about government corruption and the unfair treatment of factory workers. Full-color printing became available in the 1890s, and Elizabeth enjoys reading the Sunday comics. She also subscribes to *Good Housekeeping* magazine. Occasionally, Elizabeth and her husband enjoy visiting the local nickelodeon theater, where they watch short silent films accompanied by accordion music. They cannot afford to purchase a phonograph, but Elizabeth and her family often gather around a piano in the evening to sing songs to popular sheet music. Before she goes to sleep, Elizabeth reads a few pages of *The Strange Case of Dr. Jekyll and Mr. Hyde*. Separated by nearly a century of technology, Elizabeth's and Katie's lives are vastly different.

New Media

Traditional media encompasses all the means of communication that existed before the Internet and new media technology, including printed materials (books, magazines, and newspapers), broadcast communications (TV and radio), film, and music. New media, on the other hand, includes electronic video games and entertainment, and the Internet and social media. Although different forms of mass media rise and fall in popularity, it is worth noting that despite significant cultural and technological changes, none of the media discussed throughout this text has fallen out of use completely.

Electronic Games and Entertainment

First popularized in the 1970s with Atari's simple table-tennis simulator *Pong*, video games have come a long way over the past four decades. Early home game consoles could play only one game, a limitation solved by the development of interchangeable game cartridges. The rise of the personal computer in the 1980s enabled developers to create games with more complex story lines and to allow players to interact with each other via the computer. In the mid-1980s, online role-playing games developed, allowing multiple users to play at the same time. A dramatic increase in Internet use helped to popularize online games during the 1990s and 2000s, both on personal computers and via Internet-enabled home console systems such as the Microsoft Xbox and the Sony PlayStation. The Internet has added a social aspect to video gaming that has bridged the generation gap and opened up a whole new audience for video game companies. Senior citizens commonly gather in retirement communities to play Nintendo's Wii bowling and tennis games using a motion-sensitive controller, while young professionals and college students get together to play in virtual bands on games such as *Guitar Hero* and *Rock Band*. No longer associated with an isolated subculture, contemporary video games are bringing friends and families together via increasingly advanced gaming technology.

The Internet and Social Media

It is almost impossible to overstate the influence the Internet has had on media over the past two decades. Initially conceived as an attack-proof military network in the 1960s, the Internet has since become an integral part of daily life. With the development of the World Wide Web in the 1980s and the introduction of commercial browsers in the 1990s, users gained the ability to transmit pictures, sound, and video over the Internet. Companies quickly began to capitalize on the new technology, launching web browsers, offering free web-based e-mail accounts, and providing web directories and search engines. Internet usage grew rapidly, from 50 percent of American adults in 2000 to 75 percent of American adults in 2008 (Pew Research Center, 2010). Now that most of the industrialized world is online, the way we receive our news, do business, conduct research, contact friends and relatives, apply for jobs, and even watch TV has changed completely. To provide just one example, many jobs can now be performed entirely from home without the need to travel to a central office. Meetings can be conducted via videoconference, written communication can take place via e-mail, and employees can access company data via a server or file transfer protocol (FTP) site.

In addition to increasing the speed with which we can access information and the volume of information at our fingertips, the Internet has added a whole new democratic dimension to communication. Becoming the author of a printed book may take many years of frustrated effort, but becoming a publisher of online material requires little more than the click of a button. Thanks to social media such as blogs, social networking sites, wikis, and video-sharing websites, anyone can contribute ideas on the web. Social media has many advantages, including the instantaneous distribution of news, a variety of different perspectives on a single event, and the ability to communicate with people all over the globe. Although some industry analysts have long predicted that the Internet will render print media obsolete, mass-media executives believe newspapers will evolve with the times. Just as the radio industry had to rethink its commercial strategy during the rise of TV, newspaper professionals will need to rethink their methods of content delivery during the age of the Internet.

New Media versus Traditional Media

New technologies have developed so quickly that executives in traditional media companies often cannot retain control over their content. For example, when music-sharing website Napster began enabling users to exchange free music files over the Internet, peer-to-peer file sharing cost the music industry a fortune in lost CD sales. Rather than capitalize on the new technology, music industry executives sued Napster, ultimately shutting it down, but never quite managing to stamp out online music piracy. Even with legal digital music sales through online vendors such as Apple's iTunes Store, the music industry is still trying to determine how to make a large enough profit to stay in business.

The publishing industry has also suffered from the effects of new technology (although newspaper readership has been in decline since the introduction of TV and radio). When newspapers began developing online versions in response to competition from cable TV, they found themselves up against a new form of journalism: amateur blogging. Initially dismissed as unreliable and biased, blogs such as *Daily Kos* and *The Huffington Post* have gained credibility and large readerships over the past decade, forcing traditional journalists to blog and tweet in order to keep pace (which allows less time to check that sources are reliable or add in-depth analysis to a story). Traditional newspapers are also losing out to news aggregators such as Google News, which profit from providing links to journalists' stories at major newspapers without offering financial compensation to either the journalists or the news organizations. Many newspapers have adapted to the Internet out of necessity, fighting falling circulation figures and slumping advertising sales by offering websites, blogs, and podcasts and producing news stories in video form. Those that had the foresight to adapt to the new technology are breathing a sigh of relief; a 2010 Pew Research Center report found that more Americans receive their news via the Internet than from newspapers or radio sources, and that the Internet is the third most popular news source behind national and local TV news (see Section 6.3 "Current Popular Trends in the Music Industry") (Pew Research Center, 2010).

Pay-for-Content: Will It Work?

Critics of the pay-for-content model point to the failure of *Newsday*, a Long Island, New York, daily that was one of the first nonbusiness publications to use the pay-for-content model. In October 2009, *Newsday* began charging readers $5 a week ($260 a year) for unlimited access to its online content. Three months later, an analysis of the move indicated that it had been a total failure. Just 35 people had signed up to pay for access to the site. Having spent $4 million redesigning and relaunching the *Newsday* website in preparation for the new model, the owners grossed just $9,000 from their initial readership.

However, the lack of paying consumers may be partly accounted for by the number of exceptions granted by the company. Subscribers to the print version of the paper can access the site for free, as can those with

Optimum Cable. According to *Newsday* representatives, 75 percent of Long Island residents have either a newspaper subscription or Optimum Cable. "Given the number of households in our market that have access to *Newsday*'s website as a result of other subscriptions, it is no surprise that a relatively modest number have chosen the pay option," said a Cablevision spokeswoman (Koblin, 2010). Even though most Long Island residents have access to the site, traffic has dropped considerably. A Nielsen Online survey revealed that traffic fell from 2.2 million visits in October 2009 to 1.5 million visits in December 2009. Publishing executives will be watching closely to see whether *The New York Times* meets a similar fate when it adopts the pay-for-content model in 2011.

New media has three major advantages over traditional media. First, it is immediate, enabling consumers to find out the latest news, weather report, or stock prices at the touch of a button. Digital music can be downloaded instantly, movies can be ordered via cable or satellite on-demand services, and books can be read on e-readers. In an increasingly fast-paced world, there is little need to wait for anything. The second advantage is cost. Most online content is free, from blogs and social networking sites to news and entertainment sources. Whether readers are willing to pay for content once they are used to receiving it for free is something that the *The New York Times* set to find out in 2011, when it introduces a metered fee model for its online paper. Finally, new media is able to reach the most remote parts of the globe. For example, if a student is looking for information about day-to-day life in Iran, there is a high probability that a personal web page about living in that country exists somewhere on the Internet. Around three-fourths of Americans, half of Europeans, and just over one-fourth of the world's population overall have Internet access (Internet World Stats). This widespread reach makes the Internet an ideal target for advertisers, who can communicate with their desired niche audiences via tracking devices such as profile information on social networking sites.

Key Takeaways

- Traditional media includes printed materials (books, magazines, and newspapers), broadcast communications (TV and radio), film, and music. New media includes all forms of communication in the digital world, including electronic video games, the Internet, and social media. The Internet has added a social aspect to video gaming that has bridged the generation gap and opened up a whole new audience for video game companies, including senior citizens and families. The prevalence of the Internet in modern daily life affects us in nearly every way, from how we receive our news, to the way we do business, conduct research, contact friends and relatives, apply for jobs, and even how we watch TV.

- New media frequently trumps traditional media for three main reasons: It is more immediate, it is often free, and it can reach a wider number of people.

Exercises

Review the traditional and emerging forms of media. Then answer the following short-answer questions. Each response should be a minimum of one paragraph.

1. Think of three examples of traditional or new media. What are the advantages of each type of media? What are the disadvantages?

2. Which of these types of media has been around the longest? Which is the most modern?

3. How has the Internet affected the delivery of other types of media?

4. Do you believe that new media are more successful than traditional forms? Why or why not?

References

Internet World Stats, "Internet Usage Statistics," http://www.internetworldstats.com/stats.htm.

Koblin, John. "After 3 Months, Only 35 Subscriptions for *Newsday*'s Web Site," *New York Observer*, January 26, 2010, http://www.observer.com/2010/media/after-three-months-only-35-subscriptions-newsdays-web-site.

Pew Research Center, "The New News Landscape: Rise of the Internet," March 1, 2010, http://pewresearch.org/pubs/1508/internet-cell-phone-users-news-social-experience?src=prc-latest&proj=peoplepress.

Pew Research Center, *Internet User Profiles Reloaded*, January 5, 2010, http://pewresearch.org/pubs/1454/demographic-profiles-internet-broadband-cell-phone-wireless-users.

16.2 Information Delivery Methods

Figure 16.1

OLYMPUS DIGITAL CAMERA

Michael Jackson's death at age 50 caused a frenzy of media attention. Here, fans and the media have gathered at Jackson's mansion hoping to catch a glimpse of Jackson's family.

Wikimedia Commons – CC BY-SA 3.0.

When superstar Michael Jackson died of a cardiac arrest in June 2009, the news sent media outlets all over the world into a frenzy, providing journalists, bloggers, authors, and TV news anchors with months of material. The pop singer's death is a good example of how information is disseminated through the various media channels. Unafraid to publish unconfirmed rumors that may have to be retracted later, blogs and gossip websites are often first to produce celebrity news stories. Digital sources also have the advantage of immediacy—rather than waiting for a physical newspaper to be printed and delivered, a time-consuming process that occurs just once a day, bloggers and online reporters can publish a story on the Internet in the time it takes to type it out. Within 40 minutes after the Los Angeles Fire Department arrived at Jackson's home, a small entertainment website called X17online posted the news that Jackson had suffered a cardiac arrest. Twenty minutes later, larger entertainment site TMZ picked up the information and distributed it to hundreds of thousands of people via RSS (which stands for Really Simple Syndication)—a web publishing technology that enables users to automatically receive new digital content from the provider. Multiple *Wikipedia* members updated Jackson's biographical entry to include the news of his cardiac arrest before any major news networks or broadcasters had announced the news. By the time the cardiac arrest was reported on CNN's official Twitter account 2 hours after the 911 call, Twitter users and TMZ reporters were already posting reports of the star's death. The story created such a surge in online traffic that microblogging site Twitter temporarily shut down and Google returned an error message for searches of the singer's name because it assumed it was under attack. An hour after the news of Jackson's death hit the Internet, mainstream news sources such as *The Los Angeles Times*, MSNBC, and CNN confirmed the information, and it was immediately disseminated among local and national TV and radio stations.

The order in which the news broke among the major media outlets was a source of contention. Many outlets around the world were reluctant to rely on the TMZ report, because the website was primarily known for its frivolous content, aggressive paparazzi tactics, and embarrassing celebrity photographs. Many of the more reputable news sources, including CNN, waited until both the coroner's office and *The Los Angeles Times* had confirmed Jackson's death before announcing it as a fact to viewers, preferring to release an accurate story rather than to gain an edge over other news outlets (even though both TMZ and CNN are owned by Time Warner). "Given the nature of the story, we exercised caution," said CNN spokesman Nigel Pritchard (Collins & Braxton, 2009). However, Harvey Levin, managing editor of TMZ, denied that his site was less credible than any other news source. "TMZ is a news operation and we are fact based," he said. "Our goal is always to take stories and factually source them and present them. We're not a gossip site…. We have things researched, we have things lawyered, we make lots of phone calls…. I mean it's the same principle (Karlinsky & Harper, 2009)." Despite Levin's protests, it appears that, for now at least, old media stalwarts such as the Associated Press and *The LA Times* have the advantage of reliability over (sometimes) faster sources with less credibility. As Adam Fendelman, founder of entertainment news site HollywoodChicago.com, noted, "The Web and TV phenomenon that TMZ is is very good at fast-breaking and late-breaking news, but there's an inherent problem with trust in the everyday consumer's mind (Wong, 2009)" (see Section 6.4 "Influence of New Technology" for more advantages and disadvantages of new media).

Once news of Michael Jackson's death had been reported through all the major international media outlets, a tabloid war broke out, with newspapers and magazines determined to get the "story behind the story." Speculation about the cause of death and the role played by prescription drugs fed salacious media reports in the tabloids and news and gossip magazines long after the initial news story broke. Other newspapers and magazines, including *Time* and *Entertainment Weekly*, focused on tribute articles that reviewed Jackson's long list of accomplishments and reflected on his musical legacy, and the four major broadcast networks (ABC, NBC, Fox, and CBS) aired documentaries covering the pop star's life. In the days and weeks following Jackson's death, radio stations abandoned their playlists in favor of back-to-back Michael Jackson hits, contributing to a huge upswing in record sales. Media coverage continued for many months, saturating newspapers, magazines, and TV and radio stations—when the coroner's report ruled Jackson's death a homicide in August 2009, during the funeral service a month later, and again in February 2010 when Jackson's doctor was charged with involuntary manslaughter for administering a powerful sedative to help the star sleep.

Although the book-publishing industry was at a disadvantage because of the time delay between receiving news of Jackson's death and the ability to physically place books on shelves, many authors, agents, and publishers were able to capitalize on the star's tragic story. Numerous biographies were published in the months following Jackson's death, along with several explosive "tell-all" books by people close to the star that provided intimate details about his private life. To compensate for their lack of immediacy, books have several advantages over other print and web sources, primarily the ability to include greater depth of information on a subject than any other form of media. Fans eager for more information about their idol and his life eagerly purchased Jackson biographies, including his 1988 autobiography *Moonwalk*, which was re-released in October 2009.

Other, less immediate forms of media were also commercially successful, including a posthumous film titled *This Is It*, named after the much-anticipated comeback tour that was supposed to start just 3 weeks after Jackson's death. Composed of rehearsal footage from the concerts, the documentary was shown on more than 3,400 domestic screens during a sold-out 2-week run in October and November 2009. An accompanying two-disc soundtrack album, featuring classic Jackson hits along with new track "This Is It," topped the *Billboard* 200 chart upon its release in November 2009, selling 373,000 copies in its first week of release. A spin-off DVD also topped the U.S. sales chart in February 2010, selling more than 1.2 million copies the week of its release. Posthumous sales of Jackson's earlier material also generated huge amounts of revenue. In the first 4 months after Jackson's death, *Forbes* magazine estimated that his estate made $90 million in gross earnings. Music industry consultant Barry Massarsky commented, "Nothing increases the value of an artist's catalog [more] than death…an untimely death (Streib, 2009)." This cross-media approach is typical of every major news story, although the controversy surrounding Jackson throughout his life, the circumstances of his death, and the sheer magnitude of his contribution to pop history meant that the performer's demise had a particularly widespread effect.

Changing Delivery Methods

As the Michael Jackson example shows, the number of people receiving news from the Internet is rapidly growing, although TV remains the dominant source of information. Currently, most Americans use multiple resources for news. In a 2010 survey, 92 percent of people said they obtained their daily news from a variety of sources, including online news sites, blogs, social networking sites such as Twitter and Facebook, TV, newspapers, and radio (Choney, 2010). On a typical day, 6 in 10 American adults get their news online, placing the Internet third behind local TV news and national or cable TV news (Choney, 2010). The use of smartphone technology is contributing to the ease with which people can access online news; more than a third of cell phone owners use their phones to check for weather, news, sports, and traffic information (Choney, 2010).

For young people in particular, the rise in social networking use is transforming the news from a one-way passage of information into a social experience. People log on to their Facebook or Twitter accounts, post news stories to their friends' web pages, comment on stories that interest them, and react to stories they have recently read. During a survey of students at the University of Texas at Austin, senior Meg Scholz told researchers that she scanned news websites and blogs every time she went online to check her e-mail, eliminating the need to pick up a newspaper or watch TV news. "It's not that I have anything against a printed newspaper," she said. "But for my lifestyle the Internet is more accessible (Johnson, 2006)." Other Internet users appreciate the ability to filter news and information that is relevant to them; 28 percent of those surveyed said they customize their social networking home pages to include news from sources or on topics that interest them.[1] Researchers at the Pew Research Center's Internet & American Life Project, the organization that conducted the survey, speculate that this personalization of news is a result of the constant stream of information in modern life. Pew Research Center Director Lee Rainie commented, "People feel more and more pressed about the volume of information flowing into their lives. So, they customize the information flow in order to manage their lives well and in order to get the material that they feel is most relevant to them (Johnson, 2006)." Although TV remains the primary source of news for most Americans, Internet and mobile technology are changing the structure of information delivery methods to audiences, making it more portable, more personalized, and more participatory.

Key Takeaways

- Information delivery methods to audiences include print (newspapers, books, magazines), broadcast (radio, TV), new media (Internet, social media, blogs), and documentary films. When a big news story breaks, digital media sources have the advantage of speed over traditional media sources—but are not yet considered completely accurate or trustworthy. Established newspapers and magazines still have the advantage of credibility. A big news story passes through every media outlet, starting with the Internet and online newspapers, moving to print newspapers, magazines, TV, and radio, and finally on to slower, more detailed types of media such as books and documentaries.

- Information delivery methods are changing. Most people still get their news from local and national TV stations, but the Internet is the third most popular source of information, and its popularity is increasing. Smartphone technology is making Internet news more portable, while social networking sites provide a participatory aspect, enabling people to comment on or share news stories of interest. The ability to customize social networking home pages to filter news topics and sources is making news more personalized, allowing consumers to read only the information that interests them.

Exercises

Conduct a survey among your friends, family, and classmates to find out where they get their news on a regular basis. Then respond to the following short-answer questions. Each response should be a minimum of one paragraph.

1. What is the most common source of news among the population sample you surveyed?

2. Do most people obtain their news from a variety of sources or from a single source?

3. Does the main source of news vary according to age group? Create a line graph or bar graph to illustrate your results, and write a brief report of your findings.

4. Which group uses the Internet as a source of news and information the most? Why do you think this is?

[1]Choney, "Internet, TV Main News Sources for Americans."

References

Choney, Suzanne. "Internet, TV Main News Sources for Americans," *MSNBC*, March 1, 2010, http://www.msnbc.msn.com/id/35607411/ns/technology_and_science-tech_and_gadgets/.

Collins, Scott and Greg Braxton, "TV Misses Out as Gossip Website TMZ Reports Michael Jackson's Death First," *Los Angeles Times*, June 26, 2009, http://articles.latimes.com/2009/jun/26/local/me-jackson-media26.

Johnson, Peter. "Young People Turn to the Web for News," Media Mix, *USA Today*, March 22, 2006, http://www.usatoday.com/life/columnist/mediamix/2006-03-22-media-mix_x.htm.

Karlinsky, Neal and Eloise Harper, "Michael Jackson's Death Puts Us Weekly and TMZ at the Head of the Pack," *ABC News*, July 1, 2009, http://abcnews.go.com/Nightline/MichaelJackson/story?id=7971440&page=1.

Streib, Lauren. "Michael Jackson's Money Machine," *Forbes*, October 27, 2009, http://www.forbes.com/2009/10/27/michael-jackson-earnings-since-death-dead-celebs-09-business-entertainment-jackson.html.

Wong, Wailin. "Michael Jackson Death News: Online Activity Heats Up Twitter and Google, Slows Down Some Sites," *Chicago Tribune*, June 26, 2009, http://www.chicagotribune.com/topic/wghp-story-jackson-media-coverage-090625,0,4191041.story.

16.3 Modern Media Delivery: Pros and Cons

Learning Objectives

1. Describe the advantages of modern media delivery methods.
2. Describe the disadvantages of modern media delivery methods.

In October 2009, 17-year-old child-care student Ashleigh Hall made friends with a handsome 19-year-old man on Facebook. Ashleigh, from Darlington, England, and her new friend began chatting online and exchanged mobile phone numbers so they could text each other. The excited teenager soon told her friends that she was going on a date with her new boyfriend, Pete, and that his father would be picking her up in his car. Unfortunately, Pete and his "father" were one and the same person—convicted rapist Peter Chapman. The 33-year-old homeless sex offender used his Facebook alter ego (which included photographs of an unknown teenage boy) to lure Ashleigh to a secluded location, where he raped and murdered her. Chapman was arrested by chance shortly after the event, and in court he pleaded guilty to kidnap, rape, and murder.

Ashleigh's tragic story illustrates some disadvantages of modern media delivery: anonymity and unreliability. Although social networking sites such as Facebook are a convenient way to create new relationships and reconnect with old friends, there is no way of knowing whether users are who they claim to be, leaving people (particularly impressionable youths) vulnerable to online predators. Since much of the content on the Internet is unregulated, this lack of reliability spans the entire online spectrum, from news stories and *Wikipedia* articles to false advertising claims and unscrupulous con artists on websites such as Craigslist.

However, modern media can also work to mobilize efforts to stop crime. The popular NBC TV series *Dateline: To Catch a Predator* followed police investigators who used Internet chat rooms to identify potential child molesters. Posing as young teens, police officers entered chat rooms and participated in conversations with various users. If an adult user began a sexual dialogue and expressed interest in meeting the teen for sexual purposes, the police set up a sting operation, catching the would-be pedophile in the act. In cases such as these, the rapid transmission of information and the global nature of the Internet made it possible for criminals to be apprehended.

Advantages of Modern Media Delivery

If Ashleigh's story highlights some of the most negative aspects of modern media, the quick dissemination of news and information are some of the most beneficial aspects of the World Wide Web. As we noted earlier in the chapter, speed can be a huge advantage of online media delivery. When a news story breaks, it can be delivered almost instantaneously through RSS feeds and via many major outlets, enabling people all over the world to learn about a breaking news story mere minutes after it happens.

Once an Internet user has paid for a monthly service provider, most of the content on the web is free, allowing people access to an unlimited wealth of information via news websites, search engines, directories, and home pages for numerous topics ranging from cooking tips to sports trivia. When all this information became readily available at the touch of a button, many journalists and technology experts wrote articles claiming the information overload was bad for people's health. Fears that the new technology would cause attention deficit disorder, stunt people's reasoning, and damage their ability to empathize were raised by some highly respected publications, including *The Times* of London and the *The New York Times*. However, there is no consistent evidence that the Internet causes psychological problems; in fact, statistics show that people who use social networking sites have better offline social lives, and people who play computer games are better at absorbing and reacting to information than those who do not, and they experience no loss of accuracy or increased impulsiveness (Bell, 2010). As Vaughan Bell points out in his article about the history of media scares, "Worries about information overload are as old as information itself, with each generation reimagining the dangerous impacts of technology on mind and brain (Bell, 2010)."

In addition to speed, reach, and cost, online media delivery enables a wider range of voices and perspectives on any subject. Through nontraditional media such as blogs and Twitter, people can put their own personal slant on current events, popular culture, and issues that are important to them without feeling obliged to remain neutral. A study by the Pew Research Center found that nontraditional media sources report on a wider variety of stories than traditional media, enabling individual sites to develop their own personality and voice. The study also discovered that these online sources focus on highly emotional subject matter that can be personalized by the writers and shared in the social forum (Pew Research Center, 2010). By opening up blogs and social media sites to online discussion or debate, bloggers enable readers to generate their own content, turning audiences from passive consumers into active creators. In this way, knowledge becomes a social process rather than a one-way street—the blogger posts an opinion, a reader comments on the blogger's opinion, the blogger then evaluates the reader's comment and revises his or her perspective accordingly, and the process repeats itself until an issue has been thoroughly explored. Many bloggers also provide links to other blogs they support or enjoy reading, enabling ideas with merit to filter through various channels on the Internet.

Disadvantages of Modern Media Delivery

Along with a growing number of online predators misrepresenting themselves on social networking sites, the Internet is responsible for a lot of other types of misinformation circulating the web. Unless users are able to distinguish between reliable, unbiased sources and factual information, they may find themselves consuming inaccurate news reports or false encyclopedia entries. Even so-called reliable news sources are subject to occasional errors with their source material. When French composer Maurice Jarre died in 2009 at the age of 84, Irish sociology and economics student Shane Fitzgerald decided to try an experiment with Wikipedia. He added fictional quotes to Jarre's *Wikipedia* entry and then watched as newspapers worldwide (including reputable sources such as the *The Guardian*) copied his quotes word for word and attributed them to the composer. Red-faced journalists were later forced to correct their errors by retracting the quotes. Writing a follow-up report for *The Irish Times*, Fitzgerald commented, "If I could so easily falsify the news across the globe, even to this small extent, then it is unnerving to think about what other false information may be reported in the press (Lytle, 2009)."

Although most traditional media strive for nonpartisanship, many newer online sources are fervently right wing or left wing. With websites such as the *Huffington Post* on the left of the political spectrum and the *Drudge Report* on the right, consumers need to be aware when they are reading news with an ideological slant. Critics fear the trend toward social media sources may lead to the restriction of the movement of ideas. If consumers choose their media circle exclusively consistent with their own political biases, they will be limited to a narrow political viewpoint.

Along with practical disadvantages, the Internet also has several economic disadvantages. An increasing gap between people who can afford personal computers and access to the web and people who cannot, known as the digital divide, separates the haves and the have-nots. Although about 75 percent of U.S. households are connected to the Internet, there are gaps in access in terms of age, income, and education. For example, a recent study found that 93 percent of people aged 18–29 have Internet access, compared with 70 percent of people aged 50–64 and just 38 percent of people over 65 (Pew Research Center, 2010). Similar disparities occur with income and education (see Figure 16.2).

These disparities mean that people with lower incomes and educational levels are at a disadvantage when it comes to accessing online job listings, information, news, and computer-related skills that might help them in the workplace. The digital divide is even more prominent between developed and developing countries. In nations such as Jordan, Saudi Arabia, and Syria, the government permits little or no access to the Internet. In other countries, such as Mexico, Brazil, and Columbia, poor telecommunications infrastructure forces users to wait extremely inconvenient lengths of time to get online. And in many developing countries that have poor public utilities and intermittent electrical service, the Internet is almost unheard of. Despite its large population, the entire continent of Africa accounts for less than 5 percent of Internet usage worldwide.[1]

Figure 16.2

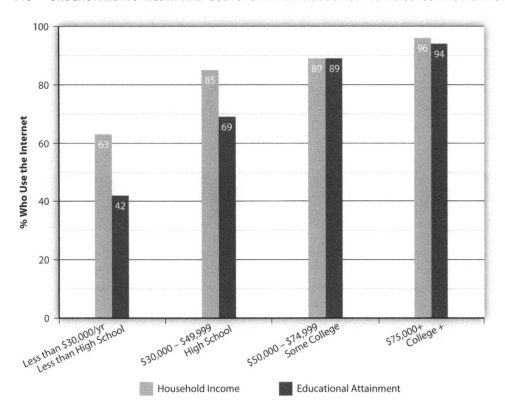

The digital divide places people with lower incomes and lower educational levels at a disadvantage when it comes to Internet access.

Traditional media also face economic disadvantages when it comes to profiting from the Internet. Having freely given away much of their online content, newspapers are struggling to transition to an entirely ad-based business model. Although publishers initially envisioned a digital future supported entirely by advertising, 2 years of plummeting ad revenue (the Newspaper Association of America reported that online advertising revenues fell 11.8 percent in 2009) has caused some papers to consider introducing online fees (see Section 6.5). Although modern media delivery is quick and efficient, companies are still trying to establish a successful economic model to keep them afloat in the long term.

Key Takeaways

- Modern media delivery has numerous advantages, including the speed at which content is delivered, the widespread reach of the Internet, and the low cost—most online content is free. The sheer amount of information available online has caused many critics to claim the information overload is bad for people's health; however, studies have not substantiated this theory. Online media delivery enables a wide range of voices and perspectives to be heard via blogs and social networking sites. These sites are also changing the way knowledge is consumed: from a one-way system (for example, through passively reading newspaper articles) to a dynamic process that involves an entire online community.

- Modern media delivery also has several disadvantages. Not all web pages are reliable sources of information; many are subject to user error (for example, on sites such as *Wikipedia*) or bias (for example, on partisan political blogs). The Internet also has economic disadvantages; it widens the digital divide between those who have access to the technology and those who do not (usually older people, people of lower economic means or educational status, or people in developing countries with poor infrastructure), and causes problems for traditional media, which are finding it difficult to profit from digital technology.

Exercises

Choose two online newspaper articles or blogs on the same subject, one from a liberal website such as the *Huffington Post* and one from a conservative website such as the *Drudge Report*. Read through both articles and underline examples of political bias or prejudice. Then answer the following short-answer questions. Each response should be a minimum of one paragraph.

1. How does each article use selective facts to support its argument?

2. What information is missing from each article?

3. How might reading just one of these articles unfairly sway someone looking for nonpartisan information on the topic you have chosen?

4. What are the advantages of modern media delivery methods? How might you have found both articles if the Internet did not exist?

[1]Internet World Stats, "Internet Usage Statistics."

References

Bell, Vaughan. "Don't Touch That Dial!" *Slate*, February 15, 2010, http://www.slate.com/id/2244198/pagenum/all/.

Lytle, J. Mark. "*Wikipedia* Hoax Shames Major Publishers," *TechRadar*, May 10, 2009, http://www.techradar.com/news/internet/web/wikipedia-hoax-shames-major-publishers-597729.

Pew Research Center, "Demographics of Internet Users," Pew Internet & American Life Project, January 6, 2010, http://www.pewinternet.org/Static-Pages/Trend-Data/Whos-Online.aspx.

Pew Research Center, "New Media, Old Media," May 23, 2010, http://pewresearch.org/pubs/1602/new-media-review-differences-from-traditional-press.

16.4 Current Trends in Electronic Media

Learning Objectives
1. Determine popular trends in social networking.
2. Describe the concept of membership-only websites that cater to specific audiences.
3. Explain the use and appeal of electronic applications.

What do your former high school classmates do for a living? What does your favorite celebrity think about the current administration? What do other professionals in your field think about industry trends? Which restaurant do your coworkers frequent? Five years ago, these questions would most likely have been met with blank stares, but thanks to the exponential growth of electronic media—social networking in particular—it is now possible to keep track of past and present contacts via the Internet, sometimes in exhaustive detail. As social media continues to grow in popularity, marketers, advertisers, and businesses are looking for ways to use the new technology to increase revenue and improve customer service. Meanwhile, social networking sites are expanding into commerce, connecting businesses and consumers via third-party sites so that people can bring a network of friends to partner websites. Facebook Connect, for example, enables a consumer to visit a partner site such as Forever 21, find a pair of jeans on sale, and broadcast the information to everyone on her Facebook network. If a few Facebook friends do the same thing, the information can create an effective viral marketing campaign for the partner site. A more secure version of the ill-fated Beacon (see Chapter 11 "The Internet and Social Media"), Facebook Connect extends the Facebook platform out of the social network's walls, creating one giant network on the web.

The current trend toward immediacy (instant Twitter updates, instant Google searches, instant driving directions from Yahoo! Maps) is compounded by the development of smartphone applications, which allow users to access or post information wherever they happen to be located. For example, a person shopping for a particular product can instantly compare the price of that product across an entire range of stores using the Android ShopSavvy app, while someone new to an area can immediately locate a gas station, park, or supermarket using iPhone's AroundMe app. Industry insiders have coined the term nowism to describe the instant gratification that can be achieved by real-time content on the web. Sparked by social networking sites such as Facebook and Twitter, the real-time trend looks set to continue, with companies from all types of industries jumping on the immediacy bandwagon.

Social Networking Continues to Grow

The growth of social media over the past few years has been exponential; according to Nielsen, Twitter alone grew 1,382 percent in February 2009, registering 7,000,000 unique visitors in the United States for the month. By February 2010, Twitter had 75,000,000 registered users and between 10,000,000 and 15,000,000 active tweeters (Gaudin, 2010). Meanwhile, Facebook has more than 400 million active users worldwide, according to its website, with each user averaging 130 Facebook friends. In February 2010, Facebook was declared the web's most popular site, with users spending an average of more than 7 hours a month on the site; more than the amount of time spent on Google, Yahoo!, YouTube, Amazon.com, *Wikipedia*, and MSN combined (Parr, 2010).

Figure 16.3

Rank	Brand	Unique Audience (000)	Time Per Person (hh:mm:ss)	MOM UA % Change	MOM Time % Change
		Top 10 Web Brands for January 2010 (U.S., Home and Work)			
1	Google	153,056	1:26:22	4.3%	-14.4%
2	Yahoo!	137,459	2:29:04	6.5%	-15.6%
3	MSN/WindowsLive/Bing	116,804	1:50:14	8.0%	-5.6%
4	Facebook	116,329	7:01:41	5.8%	9.7%
5	YouTube	99,525	1:02:27	7.6%	-10.3%
6	Microsoft	98,180	0:41:36	7.5%	-6.8%
7	AOL Media Network	87,629	2:14:12	-0.8%	-7.5%
8	Apple	68,877	1:18:58	7.9%	-10.0%
9	Wikipedia	64,917	0:15:59	10.7%	-2.7%
10	Fox Interactive Media	63,925	1:23:09	3.9%	-9.5%

Source: The Nielsen Company

The average U.S. user spends more than 7 hours a month on social networking site Facebook.

Initially conceived in 2004 as a website for students to keep in touch over the Internet and get to know each other better, Facebook has since developed into the world's largest social networking site. In addition to connecting friends and acquaintances and enabling users to share photos, links, and multimedia, the site (along with other social networking sites such as MySpace) has branched out into social gaming, a rapidly growing industry that allows users to download free games through the site and play online with friends and family members. Appealing to a wide demographic—including people who rarely play video games—social games such as FarmVille and Mafia Wars are free to play, but generate revenue for developers by offering additional bonuses or virtual goods for paying players. A recent survey found that most of the revenue generated by the social gaming audience comes from a small percentage of players (around 10 percent) who are willing to actually spend money on social networking games. Out of that 10 percent, just 2 percent of people, described as the "whales" of the social gaming industry, spend more than $25 a month on social games. Inside Network founder Justin Smith, who coauthored the survey, said, "It is clear that people either spend a lot of money or spend nothing (Takahashi, 2010)." The games, which primarily appeal to the female over-40 demographic, are designed so that Facebook users can spend a few minutes playing several times a day. In the United States, 55 percent of social network game players are women, and the average age is 48 (Johnson, 2010).

Other continuing trends in social networking include microblogging on sites such as Twitter, which is rapidly becoming the fastest source of news on the Internet. The site acts as a personal newswire, passing on information about shared world events as they affect people in real time. For example, when an earthquake shook Los Angeles in 2008, people began tweeting personal accounts from their homes 9 minutes before the Associated Press picked up the story. In 2009, citizens of Iran bypassed government censorship by tweeting news of the election results across the world. Organizations such as the Associated Press communicated with Twitter users to receive information about the resulting protests and demonstrations (Santana, 2009).

Business owners are also beginning to realize the power of Twitter; online shoe merchant Zappos.com provides more than 500 of its employees with Twitter accounts to humanize the people behind the sales and help them connect with their customers. Feedback from Twitter users provides companies with valuable information about how they can improve their products and services. Celebrities have also attached themselves to Twitter as a means of publicizing forthcoming projects and keeping in touch with fans. Actor Ashton Kutcher is particularly media savvy; beating news outlet CNN to become the first Twitter user with more than 1,000,000 followers in 2009, the star used his popularity to raise awareness for medical charity Malaria No More, donating 10,000 mosquito nets to the organization following his success as Twitter's first "millionaire." Kutcher's social media consultancy, Katalyst Films, maximizes the use of social networking technology by working with entertainment content, advertising, and online conversation in an effort to generate money from the web. "Entertainment, really, is a dying industry," Kutcher said in a 2009 interview. "We're a balanced social-media studio, with revenue streams from multiple sources—film, TV, and now digital. For the brand stuff, we're not replacing ad agencies but working with everyone to provide content and the monetization strategies to succeed on the Web (McGirt, 2009)."

In addition to brand marketing and cross-promotions infiltrating social networking sites, digital experts predict social media will become more exclusive, with people filtering out clutter from unwanted sources. David Armano, senior vice president of Edelman Digital, said, "Not everyone can fit on someone's newly created Twitter list and as networks begin to fill with noise, it's likely that user behavior such as 'hiding' the hyperactive updaters that appear in your Facebook news feed may become more common (Armano, 2009)."

Exclusivity on the Web

Armano's prediction for social networking sites may filter across other areas of the web. Membership-only sites that cater to a specific audience are becoming increasingly popular. Based on e-commerce models such as Gilt and Rue La La, which sell luxury brand clothing at below-retail prices by invitation only, websites such as Thrillist offer exclusive clothing deals in addition to providing information on food, drink, entertainment, nightlife, and gadgets by subscription newsletter. Aimed at young, affluent male professionals, Thrillist reaches more than 2,200,000 subscriptions across the United States and the United Kingdom, and has reached over $10,000,000 in revenue in 2010. Cofounder and CEO Ben Lerer believes that Thrillist represents the future of media. "It's what modern media looks like," he said. "Content plus commerce (McMahan, 2010)." In 2010, Thrillist acquired members-only online retailer JackThreads.com, enabling the company to offer its user base exclusive access to JackThreads' private shopping community as a benefit to subscribing.

Another highly targeted web trend is the emergence of micro magazines—digital publications aimed at a specific audience that attract advertisers wanting to reach a particular group of people. For example, the magazine *Fearless* is an online magazine entirely dedicated to stories of overcoming fear. Marketing expert Seth Godin believes that whereas publications such as *Newsweek* and *Time* are "slow and general, the world is fast and specific," which creates a need for online subscription magazines that can provide targeted material to interested individuals (Godin, 2010). "The big difference is that instead of paying for an office building and paper and overhead, the money for an ad in a micro-magazine can go directly to the people who write and promote it and the ad itself will be seen by exactly the right audience," Godin writes (Godin, 2010). The possibilities for micro magazines are endless, with focus topics covering every travel destination, interest group, and profession. Operating in a similar way to traditional subscription magazine models, micro magazines are distributed via e-mail or RSS and are supported by a forum or blog. This interactive aspect provides readers with a sense of community—rather than passive consumers of general-interest news, they are part of a network of readers who can communicate with others who have a shared interest.

Figure 16.4

The website Thrillist provides subscribers with a chic urban guide.

An Excess of Apps

In April 2009, Apple celebrated the 1 billionth download from its App Store. Launched in July 2008, the online venue for third-party iPhone and iPod Touch applications initially offered consumers 500 apps, ranging from shortcuts to websites such as Facebook and eBay to games and useful online services. Although competing smartphones such as the Treo and BlackBerry offered similar application facilities, Apple's App Store quickly became the most successful platform for mobile software, averaging around $1,000,000 a day in iPhone application sales during the first month of its existence (Morrison, 2008). Under a revenue-sharing agreement, the company keeps 30 percent of any income generated and gives the other 70 percent to third-party app developers. By April 2011, the App Store offered around 350,000 applications, aiding iPhone and iPad users with numerous daily activities, ranging from identifying an unknown song, to finding a nearby gas station, to matching the color of a photograph taken by the iPhone with a database of paint colors. Unlike many commercials that exaggerate a products' abilities, Apple's tagline "There's an app for that" is usually on the mark.

One recent trend in smartphone applications is the use of location-sharing services such as Foursquare, Gowalla, Brightkite, and Google Latitude. Utilizing the GPS function in modern smartphones, these apps enable users to "check in" to a venue so that friends can locate each other easily. The apps also encourage users to explore new places in their area by following other users' suggestions on places to go. Users have the option of automatically updating their Facebook and Twitter accounts when they check in, and are able to earn points or badges according to how many times they check into a location, adding a competitive element to the service. Users with the most check-ins at a location become the "mayor" of that place, and some businesses offer rewards to users who achieve this status.

Although many apps stand alone, some are tied to other forms of media. For example, popular musical-comedy TV show *Glee* has its own application that enables users to sing their favorite musical numbers from the show, upload their efforts to Facebook or MySpace, and invite friends to sing with them. The application also provides a voice-enhancing feature to correct users' pitch and harmonize their voices while they sing. Other cross-media applications include game versions of TV quiz shows *Are You Smarter Than a 5th Grader?* and *Who Wants to Be a Millionaire?*, apps for individual celebrities such as country singer Reba McEntire, and apps for TV news channels, including CNN and MSNBC. Making life easier for users while providing them with endless entertainment options, apps have become a huge part of everyday life for many people; by June 2010, Apple's App Store had generated total revenue of $1.4 billion (Elmer-DeWitt, 2010).

Key Takeaways

- Social networking sites continue to grow in popularity; Facebook is the largest social networking site on the web with more than 400 million users worldwide. Social gaming is a popular trend on networking sites, and many users are not typical video game players; instead, they fit the female over-40 demographic. Developers generate revenue from social networking sites by charging gamers real money for bonuses or virtual goods. Microblogging is another popular social networking trend. Key events around the world are often reported on microblog Twitter first by users who experience the events firsthand. Business owners use Twitter to connect with their customers more effectively. Celebrities such as Ashton Kutcher are media savvy and use Twitter to promote worthy causes. Digital experts predict social networking will become more exclusive in the future, with people filtering out clutter from unwanted sources.

- The Internet is moving in a more exclusive direction through membership-only sites such as Thrillist, which cater to specific audiences via subscription newsletters. Micro magazines such as *Fearless*, which target very specific audiences and are distributed via e-mail or RSS feed, are also becoming more popular.

- Applications for smartphones and tablet computers such as the iPad are hugely popular, offering consumers numerous shortcuts to their favorite websites in addition to games and services. Two current trends are location-sharing applications, facilitated by the GPS functionality on modern smartphones, and cross-media applications such as those that tie in with particular TV shows, celebrities, or music radio stations.

Exercises

Poll a group of friends or colleagues about the amount of time they spend on social networking sites, and write a one- to two-page report on the answers to the following questions.

1. How often do most people spend on each site at one time?

2. For what purpose do they primarily use social networking sites? Does this differ from the popular

trends in social networking that you read about in this section?

3. How many people play social networking games, and are they willing to spend money on them?

4. How many people use smartphone apps to connect to social networking sites? What is the appeal of such electronic applications?

5. Describe the concept of membership-only websites. Does anyone you interviewed subscribe to a membership-only website?

References

Armano, David. "Six Social Media Trends for 2010," *The Conversation* (blog), *Harvard Business Review*, November 2, 2009, http://blogs.hbr.org/cs/2009/11/six_social_media_trends.html.

Elmer-DeWitt, Philip. "App Store: 1% of Apple's Gross Profit," *Fortune*, CNN Money, June 23, 2010, http://tech.fortune.cnn.com/2010/06/23/app-store-1-of-apples-gross-profit/.

Gaudin, Sharon. "Twitter Users Send 50 Million Tweets a Day," *Computerworld*, February 23, 2010, http://www.computerworld.com/s/article/9161118/Twitter_users_send_50_million_tweets_a_day.

Godin, Seth. "Micro Magazines and a Future of Media," *Seth Godin's Blog*, May 6, 2010, http://sethgodin.typepad.com/seths_blog/2010/05/micro-magazines-and-a-future-of-media.html.

Johnson, Caleb. "Average Social Networking Gamer in the U.S.? Your Mom," *Switched*, February 17, 2010, http://www.switched.com/2010/02/17/average-social-networking-gamer-in-the-u-s-your-mom/.

McGirt, Ellen. "Mr. Social: Ashton Kutcher Plans to be the Next New-Media Mogul," *Fast Company*, December 1, 2009, http://www.fastcompany.com/magazine/141/want-a-piece-of-this.html.

McMahan, Ty. "Is Thrillist the Future of Media?" *Speakeasy* (blog), *Wall Street Journal*, May 13, 2010, http://blogs.wsj.com/speakeasy/2010/05/13/is-thrillist-the-future-of-media/.

Morrison, Dianne See. "Apple's App Store Sales Top $30 Million in First Month; Can Free Apps Make Developers Money?" *Washington Post*, August 11, 2008, http://www.washingtonpost.com/wp-dyn/content/article/2008/08/11/AR2008081100440.html.

Parr, Ben. "Facebook Is the Web's Ultimate Timesink," *Mashable* (blog), February 16, 2010, http://mashable.com/2010/02/16/facebook-nielsen-stats/.

Santana, Rebecca. "Twittering the election crisis in Iran," *USA Today*, June 16, 2009, http://www.usatoday.com/tech/world/2009-06-15-iran-twitter_N.htm.

Takahashi, Dean. "Social Game 'Whales' are Big Spenders on Facebook, Survey Says" *VentureBeat*, June 22, 2010, http://venturebeat.com/2010/06/22/social-game-whales-are-big-spenders-on-facebook-survey-says/.

16.5 Privacy Laws and the Impact of Digital Surveillance

Learning Objectives

1. Describe the impact of the USA PATRIOT Act on privacy.

2. Explain the consequences of social networking in terms of privacy and employment.

3. Describe current attempts to restore privacy at home and in the workplace.

When a young waitress named Ashley was having a tough time at work, she decided to vent about her job on Facebook. The 22-year-old had finished an overtime shift at a North Carolina pizza parlor and discovered that the demanding customer who had stayed late had left a meager tip. Feeling frustrated, Ashley posted a short status update on her Facebook profile, calling the anonymous customer an unflattering name. Unfortunately for Ashley, she had connected with her coworkers on the social networking site. Two days after her angry post, Ashley's manager called her in to show her a copy of her comments and promptly fired her (Lai, 2010). Ashley's story is one of many examples of employers terminating their employees as a result of inappropriate comments or photographs on social networking sites; a study by Internet security firm Proofpoint found that 8 percent of companies have dismissed an employee for his or her behavior on social networking sites (Ostrow, 2010). These cases highlight a blurring of personal and professional life in the Internet age, leaving many people uncomfortable with the notion that their employer can monitor what they say or do in their free time and use it as a reason for dismissal.

Since the passing of the USA PATRIOT Act, which extended the government's surveillance powers over communication devices, privacy has become a fiercely controversial issue in the United States, with supporters arguing the legal measures are necessary to prevent terrorist attacks, and opponents claiming that the act infringes on civil liberties. Privacy issues raised by the USA PATRIOT Act, combined with the growing problem of identity theft and increased monitoring in the workplace, make privacy a greater concern now than ever before.

The USA PATRIOT Act: Weakening Privacy Laws or Protecting Citizens?

Figure 16.5

President George W. Bush signs the USA PATRIOT Act.

http://georgewbush-whitehouse.archives.gov/news/releases/2001/10/images/20011026-5.html — public domain.

The USA PATRIOT Act has generated a huge amount of debate and controversy since its approval by President George W. Bush in October 2001. Signed into law with little debate or congressional review just 43 days after the September 11 attacks, the act's provisions enable the government, with permission from a special court, to obtain roving wiretaps over multiple communication devices, seize suspects' records without their knowledge, monitor an individual's web-surfing and library records, and conduct surveillance on a person deemed to be suspicious but without known ties to a terrorist group. Approving the House of Representatives' decision to renew 16 of the act's provisions in 2005, President Bush said, "The [USA] PATRIOT Act is essential to fighting the war on terror and preventing our enemies from striking America again. In the war on terror, we cannot afford to be without this law for a single moment (CNN, 2005)."

However, not everyone agrees with the former president's opinion. While proponents of the act cite the need to disrupt or prevent terrorist attacks, New York City Council member Bill Perkins, who sponsored a 2004 resolution condemning the law, says, "The [USA] PATRIOT Act is really unpatriotic, it undermines our civil rights and civil liberties. We never give up our rights, that's what makes us Americans (Garcia, 2004)." Opposition to the USA PATRIOT Act sparked a wave of protest across the United States. More than 330 communities in 41 states passed resolutions condemning the act (Egan, 2004). Librarians in Detroit reported that Muslim children had stopped checking out books on Islam out of fear they were being monitored, while librarians in New Jersey and California shredded records and computer sign-up sheets in an attempt to thwart the legislation. While citizens can protect against invasions of privacy on the Internet by limiting personal information and being careful about the information they share, the invasion of privacy through other lines of communication is more difficult to prevent. Despite fierce objections to the act, President Barack Obama signed an unamended 1-year extension of several key provisions of the PATRIOT Act (including the use of roving wire taps) in 2010. In the near future, politicians will have to decide whether citizen protection is worth the loss of liberties in the United States.

Social Networking: The Blurring of Personal and Professional

The privacy issue has strayed well beyond government legislation; it affects anyone who is currently employed or even just looking for a job. When employers consider whether or not to hire an individual, they no longer need to rely on just a résumé to obtain pertinent information. A simple Google search often reveals that a potential employee has a social networking site on the Internet, and unless privacy settings have been put in place, the employer can access everything the candidate has posted online. A 2010 survey by CareerBuilder.com revealed that 53 percent of companies check out candidates' profiles on social networking sites such as MySpace, Twitter, LinkedIn, and Facebook before deciding to employ them, and a further 12 percent of companies intend to review social networking sites of potential employees in the future (Skinner, 2010). Factors that affect an employer's decision whether or not to hire candidates based on their social networking page include the use of drugs or drinking, the posting of discriminatory comments, or the posting of photographs deemed to be inappropriate or provocative. The survey also revealed that some candidates posted information on their social networking page that proved they had lied on their résumé (Skinner, 2010).

Once employees are hired, they still need to be careful about what they post on social networking sites, particularly in relation to their jobs. Cheryl James, a hospital worker from Michigan, was fired in 2010 after she posted a message on Facebook describing a patient as a "cop killer" and hoping that he would "rot in hell (Dahl, 2010)." A few years earlier, Virgin Atlantic Airlines terminated 13 crew members for describing passengers as "chavs" (a derogatory British term similar to "white trash"). A Virgin spokesman commented, "There is a time and a place for Facebook. But there is no justification for it to be used as a sounding board for staff of any company to criticize the very passengers who pay their salaries (Conway, 2008)."

Although employees might reasonably expect to be disciplined for using social networking sites on company time—a 2009 study discovered that 54 percent of U.S. companies have banned workers from using social networks during work hours—the issue of whether companies can influence how their employees behave in their private lives is a little trickier (Gaudin, 2009). The outcome of a 2009 federal court case in New Jersey may have some bearing on whether companies have the right to spy on their employees while the employees are on password-protected sites using nonwork computers. The case, between restaurant employees Brian Pietrylo and Doreen Marino and managers at Houston's in Hackensack, New Jersey, centered on a forum set up by Pietrylo on MySpace. The forum, which was password-protected and required an e-mail invitation to join, made fun of the restaurant décor and patrons and included sexual jokes and negative comments about restaurant supervisors. Restaurant hostess Karen St. Jean, who had received an invitation to the forum, showed the supervisors the site and believed they found it amusing; however, the information was passed further up the management chain, and Pietrylo and Marino were fired. The restaurant claimed that the pair's online posts violated policies set out in the employee handbook, including professionalism and a positive attitude. Marino and Pietrylo filed for unfair dismissal, claiming that the restaurant managers had violated their privacy under New Jersey law. Following a trial in June 2009, a federal jury agreed that the restaurant had violated state and federal laws that protect the privacy of web communications. The jury awarded Pietrylo and Marino a total of $3,400 in back pay and $13,600 in punitive damages (Toutant, 2009).

Although the outcome of the New Jersey case may have some bearing on the use of social networking sites outside of work, employees should still exercise caution in the office. Companies are increasingly using technological advances to monitor Internet usage, track employees' whereabouts through GPS-enabled cell phones, and even film employees' movements via webcam or miniature video cameras. Lewis Maltby, author of workplace rights book *Can They Do That?*, says, "There are two trends driving the increase in monitoring. One is financial pressure. Everyone is trying to get leaner and meaner, and monitoring is one way to do it. The other reason is that it's easier than ever. It used to be difficult and expensive to monitor employees, and now, it's easy and cheap (Petrecca, 2010)." Whereas employees using their own equipment outside of work hours might have a reasonable expectation of privacy, the situation changes when using company property. Nancy Flynn, founder of training and consulting firm ePolicy Institute, said, "Federal law gives employers the legal right to monitor all computer activity. The computer system is the property of the employer, and the employee has absolutely no reasonable expectations of privacy when using that system (Petrecca, 2010)." Because this lack of privacy covers everything from instant messages sent to coworkers to e-mails sent from personal accounts when employees are logged onto the company network, the prudent action for employees to take is to separate their work life from their personal life as much as possible.

Restoration of Privacy

Social networking sites have come under fire in recent years for violating users' privacy. In 2009, Facebook simplified its settings to keep up with the popularity of microblogging sites such as Twitter. One consequence of this action was that the default setting enabled status updates and photos to be seen across the entire Internet (see Chapter 11 "The Internet and Social Media" for more information about Facebook privacy settings). The social networking site has also come under criticism for a temporary glitch that gave users unintended access to their friends' private instant messages, and for a new feature in 2010 that enabled the company to share private information with third-party websites. Although Facebook simplified its controls for sharing information by consolidating them on a single page and making it easier for users to opt out of sharing information with third-party applications, public concern prompted 14 privacy groups to file an unfair-trade complaint with the Federal Trade Commission (FTC) in May 2010 (Ashford, 2010). Congress is currently investigating whether more government regulation of social networking sites is necessary to protect people's privacy.

Figure 16.6

Google Street View cars breached privacy by inadvertently collecting private communications data from unsecured Wi-Fi networks.

Other companies, including Google, are actively attempting to restore users' privacy. In response to revelations that the company had accidentally captured and archived wireless data with its Google Street View cars (which are equipped with cameras to provide panoramic views along many streets around the world), Google announced in 2010 that it was launching an encrypted search facility. The technology uses SSL (secure sockets layer) to protect Internet searches from being intercepted while traveling across the web. Users can activate the secure search facility by typing "https" at the beginning of the URL instead of "http." Although the technology provides a measure of security—the search will not be archived in the computer's history or appear in the AutoFill during a subsequent search—it is not entirely private. Google maintains a record of what people search for, and Internet users will still need to rely on the company's promise not to abuse the data. However, if the encrypted search facility proves successful, it may become a role model for social networking sites, which could offer encryption for more than just log-ins.

Key Takeaways

- Privacy issues have become increasingly important in recent years with the rise of identity theft, workplace monitoring, and the passing of the USA PATRIOT Act in 2001. The PATRIOT Act was signed in the wake of the September 11, 2001, terrorist attacks. It gave the federal government extended surveillance rights, including the ability to obtain roving wiretaps over multiple communication devices, seize suspects' records without their knowledge, monitor an individual's web-surfing and library records, and conduct surveillance of a person deemed to be suspicious but without known ties to a terrorist group. Supporters of the act claimed the provisions were essential in the efforts to prevent further terrorist attacks; however, opponents claimed that the act breached civil liberties and unfairly infringed on people's privacy.

- Monitoring employees in the workplace has begun to stray outside of office hours, and employees are now finding their social networking sites being scanned by employers for offensive material. Inappropriate comments or photos on a social networking site may negatively affect a person's chance of finding a job if employers use sites such as Facebook and Twitter as a means of screening applicants. The issue of whether employers are allowed to discriminate against employees based on their out-of-work activities has not been fully decided; however, in general, anything that takes place on company property or on company time may be scrutinized and used as a reason for dismissal.

- Some websites are attempting to restore privacy settings in light of recent scandals in which personal information was divulged on the Internet. Google has established an encrypted search facility that enables users to browse the web without running the risk of sensitive information being intercepted. The encryption also prevents websites from being stored on the computer's history and stops them from appearing on the AutoFill function during future searches. However, the encryption is not entirely private because Google still retains a record of search information.

Exercises

Visit the website located at http://www.eff.org/wp/effs-top-12-ways-protect-your-online-privacy. Read through the 12 tips and use them to evaluate your security on the Internet. How many of the tips do you already follow? What can you do to protect your privacy further? Keep these answers in mind as you respond to the following short-answer questions. Each response should be a minimum of one paragraph.

1. How does the USA PATRIOT Act affect your privacy? Do you think your privacy is more secure on the Internet or through other lines of communication? Why?

2. Have you experienced one of the consequences of social networking discussed in this section? How might social networking sites affect your current or future employment?

3. What suggestions do you have for restoring privacy at home or in the workplace? What policies are already in effect?

References

Ashford, Warwick. "Facebook Stands Up to Privacy Coalition," *ComputerWeekly*, June 21, 2010, http://www.computerweekly.com/Articles/2010/06/21/241663/Facebook-stands-up-to-privacy-coalition.htm.

CNN, "Patriot Act's Fate Remains Uncertain," December 15, 2005, http://www.cnn.com/2005/POLITICS/12/14/patriot.act/.

Conway, Lawrence. "Virgin Atlantic Sacks 13 Staff for Calling its Flyers 'Chavs'," *Independent* (London), November 1, 2008, http://www.independent.co.uk/news/uk/home-news/virgin-atlantic-sacks-13-staff-for-calling-its-flyers-chavs-982192.html.

Dahl, Ronnie. "Oakwood Hospital Employee Fired for Facebook Posting," MyFOXDetroit.com, July 30, 2010, http://www.myfoxdetroit.com/dpp/news/local/oakwood-hospital-employee-fired-for-facebook-posting-20100730-wpms.

Egan, Timothy. "State of the Union: Opposing the Patriot Act," *BBC News*, September 13, 2004, http://news.bbc.co.uk/2/hi/programmes/3651542.stm.

Garcia, Michelle. "N.Y. City Council Passes Anti-Patriot Act Measure," *Washington Post*, February 5, 2004, http://www.washingtonpost.com/wp-dyn/articles/A13970-2004Feb4.html.

Gaudin, Sharon. "Study: 54% of Companies Ban Facebook, Twitter at Work," *Computerworld*, October 6, 2009, http://www.computerworld.com/s/article/9139020/Study_54_of_companies_ban_Facebook_Twitter_at_work.

Lai, Jodi. "Waitress Gets Fired After Facebook Rant About Bad Tipper," *National Post* (Don Mills, Toronto), May 17, 2010, http://news.nationalpost.com/2010/05/17/waitress-gets-fired-after-facebook-rant-about-bad-tipper/.

Ostrow, Adam. "Facebook Fired: 8% of US Companies Have Sacked Social Media Miscreants," *Mashable* (blog), August 10, 2009, http://mashable.com/2009/08/10/social-media-misuse/.

Petrecca, Laura. "More Employers Use Tech to Track Workers," *USA Today*, March 17, 2010, http://www.usatoday.com/money/workplace/2010-03-17-workplaceprivacy15_CV_N.htm.

Skinner, Carrie-Ann. "Job Seekers, Watch Your Walls – Employers Check Facebook," *PC World*, January 17, 2010, http://www.pcworld.com/article/186989/job_seekers_watch_your_walls_employers_check_facebook.html.

Toutant, Charles. "Restaurateurs Invade Waiters' MySpace," *New Jersey Law Journal*, June 19, 2009, http://www.law.com/jsp/lawtechnologynews/PubArticleLTN.jsp?id=1202431575049.

16.6 Mass Media, New Technology, and the Public

When the iPad went on sale in the United States in April 2010, 36-year-old graphic designer Josh Klenert described the device as "ridiculously expensive [and] way overpriced (Guglielmo, 2010)." The cost of the new technology, however, did not deter Klenert from purchasing an iPad; he preordered the tablet computer as soon as it was available and ventured down to Apple's SoHo store in New York on opening weekend to be one of the first to buy it. Klenert, and everyone else who stood in line at the Apple store during the initial launch of the iPad, is described by sociologists as an early adopter: a tech-loving pioneer who is among the first to embrace new technology as soon as it arrives on the market. What causes a person to be an early adopter or a late adopter? What are the benefits of each? In this section you will read about the cycle of technology and how it is diffused in a society. The process and factors influencing the diffusion of new technology is often discussed in the context of a diffusion model known as the technology adoption life cycle.

Diffusion of Technology: The Technology Adoption Life Cycle

Figure 16.7

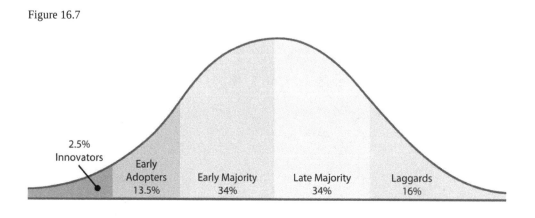

728

Like other cultural shifts, technological advances follow a fairly standard diffusion model.

The technology adoption life cycle was originally observed during the technology diffusion studies of rural sociologists during the 1950s. University researchers George Beal, Joe Bohlen, and Everett Rogers were looking at the adoption rate of hybrid seed among Iowa farmers in an attempt to draw conclusions about how farmers accept new ideas. They discovered that the process of adoption over time fit a normal growth curve pattern—there was a slow gradual rate of adoption, then quite a rapid rate of adoption, followed by a leveling off of the adoption rate. Personal and social characteristics influenced when farmers adopted the use of hybrid seed corn; younger, better-educated farmers tended to adapt to the new technology almost as soon as it became available, whereas older, less-educated farmers waited until most other farms were using hybrid seed before they adopted the process, or they resisted change altogether.

In 1962, Rogers generalized the technology diffusion model in his book *Diffusion of Innovations*, using the farming research to draw conclusions about the spread of new ideas and technology. Like his fellow farming model researchers, Rogers recognizes five categories of participants: innovators, who tend to be experimentalists and are interested in the technology itself; early adopters such as Josh Klenert, who are technically sophisticated and are interested in using the technology for solving professional and academic problems; early majority, who constitute the first part of the mainstream, bringing the new technology into common use; late majority, who are less comfortable with the technology and may be skeptical about its benefits; and laggards, who are resistant to the new technology and may be critical of its use by others (Rogers, 1995).

When new technology is successfully released in the market, it follows the technology adoption life cycle shown in Figure 16.7. Innovators and early adopters, attracted by something new, want to be the first to possess the innovation, sometimes even before discovering potential uses for it, and are unconcerned with the price. When the iPad hit stores in April 2010, 120,000 units were sold on the first day, primarily as a result of presales (Oliver, 2010). Sales dropped on days 2 and 3, suggesting that demand for the device dipped slightly after the initial first-day excitement. Within the first month, Apple had sold 1,000,000 iPads, exceeding industry expectations (Goldman, 2010). However, many mainstream consumers (the early majority) are waiting to find out just how popular the device will become before making a purchase. Research carried out in the United Kingdom suggests that many consumers are uncertain how the iPad will fit into their lives—the survey drew comments such as "Everything it does I can do on my PC or my phone right now" and "It's just a big iPod Touch…a big iPhone without the phone (O'Hear, 2010)." The report, by research group Simpson Carpenter, concludes that most consumers are "unable to find enough rational argument to justify taking the plunge (O'Hear, 2010)."

However, as with previous technological advances, the early adopters who have jumped on the iPad bandwagon may ultimately validate its potential, helping mainstream users make sense of the device and its uses. Forrester Research notes that much of the equipment acquired by early adopters—laptops, MP3 players, digital cameras, broadband Internet access at home, and mobile phones—is shifting into the mainstream. Analyst Jacqueline Anderson, who works for Forrester, said, "There's really no group out of the tech loop. America is becoming a digital nation. Technology adoption continues to roll along, picking up more and more mainstream consumers every year (Wortham, 2009)." To cite just one example, in 2008 nearly 10 million American households added HDTV, an increase of 27 percent over the previous year (Wortham, 2009). By the time most technology reaches mainstream consumers, it is more established, more user-friendly, and cheaper than earlier versions or prototypes. In June 2010, Amazon.com slashed the price of its Kindle e-reader from $259 to $189 in response to competition from Barnes & Noble's Nook (Bartash, 2010). Companies frequently reduce the price of technological devices once the initial novelty wears off, as a result of competition from other manufacturers or as a strategy to retain market share.

Although many people ultimately adapt to new technology, some are extremely resistant or unwilling to change at all. When Netscape web browser user John Uribe was repeatedly urged by a message from parent company AOL to switch to one of Netscape's successors, Firefox or Flock, he ignored the suggestions. Despite being informed that AOL would stop providing support for the web browser service in March 2008, Uribe continued to use it. "It's kind of irrational," Mr. Uribe said. "It worked for me, so I stuck with it. Until there is really some reason to totally abandon it, I won't (Helft, 2008)."Uribe is a self-confessed late adopter—he still uses dial-up Internet service and is happy to carry on using his aging Dell computer with its small amount of memory. Members of the late majority make up a large percentage of the U.S. population—a 2010 survey conducted by the U.S. Census Bureau found that despite the technology's widespread availability, 40 percent of households across the United States have no high-speed or broadband Internet connection, while 30 percent have no Internet at all (Whitney, 2010). Of 32.1 million households in urban areas, the most common reason for not having high-speed Internet was a lack of interest or a lack of need for the technology (Whitney, 2010).

Figure 16.8

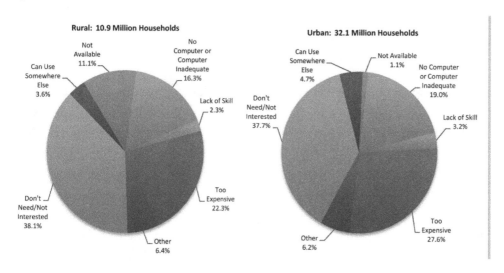

The most common reason that people in both rural and urban areas do not have high-speed Internet is a lack of interest in the technology.

Experts claim that, rather than slowing down the progression of new technological developments, laggards in the technology adoption life cycle may help to control the development of new technology. Paul Saffo, a technology forecaster, said, "Laggards have a bad rap, but they are crucial in pacing the nature of change. Innovation requires the push of early adopters and the pull of laypeople asking whether something really works. If this was a world in which only early adopters got to choose, we'd all be using CB radios and quadraphonic stereo."[1] He added that aspects of the laggard and early adopter coexist in most people. For example, many consumers buy the latest digital camera and end up using just a fraction of its functions. Technological laggards may be the reason that not every new technology becomes a mainstream trend (see sidebar).

Not Consumer-Approved: Technological Flops

Have you ever heard of the Apple Newton? How about Microsoft Bob? Or DIVX? For most people, the names probably mean very little because these were all flash-in-the-pan technologies that never caught on with mainstream consumers.

The Apple Newton was an early PDA, officially known as the MessagePad. Introduced by Apple in 1993, the Newton contained many of the features now popularized by modern smartphones, including personal information management and add-on storage slots. Despite clever advertising and relentless word-of-mouth campaigns, the Newton failed to achieve anything like the popularity enjoyed by most Apple products. Hampered by its large size compared to more recent equivalents (such as the PalmPilot) and its cost—basic models cost around $700, with more advanced models costing up to $1,000—the Newton was also ridiculed by talk show comedians and cartoonists because of the supposed inaccuracy of its handwriting-recognition function. By 1998, the Newton was no more. A prime example of an idea that was ahead of its time, the Newton was the forerunner to the smaller, cheaper, and more successful PalmPilot, which in turn paved the way for every successive mobile Internet device.

Even less successful in the late 1990s was DIVX, an attempt by electronics retailer Circuit City to create an alternative to video rental. Customers could rent movies on disposable DIVX discs that they could keep and watch for 2 days. They then had the choice of throwing away or recycling the disc or paying a continuation fee to keep watching it. Viewers who wanted to watch a disc an unlimited amount of times could pay to convert it into a "DIVX silver" disc for an additional fee. Launched in 1998, the DIVX system was promoted as an alternative to traditional rental systems with the promise of no returns and no late fees. However, its introduction coincided with the release of DVD technology, which was gaining traction over the DIVX format. Consumers feared that the choice between DIVX and DVD might turn into another Betamax versus VHS debacle, and by 1999 the technology was all but obsolete. The failure of DIVX cost Circuit City a reported $114,000,000 and left early enthusiasts of the scheme with worthless DIVX equipment (although vendors offered a $100 refund for people who bought a DIVX player) (Mokey, 2009).

Another catastrophic failure in the world of technology was Microsoft Bob, a mid-1990s attempt to provide a new, nontechnical interface to desktop computing operations. Bob, represented by a logo with a yellow smiley face that filled the *o* in its name, was supposed to make Windows more palatable to nontechnical users. With a cartoon-like interface that was meant to resemble the inside of a house, Bob helped users navigate their way around the desktop by having them click on objects in each room. Microsoft expected sales of Bob to skyrocket and held a big advertising campaign to celebrate its 1995 launch. Instead, the product failed dismally because of its high initial sale price, demanding hardware requirements, and tendency to patronize users. When Windows 95 was launched the same year, its new Windows Explorer interface required far less dumbing down than previous versions, and Microsoft Bob became irrelevant.

Technological failures such as the Apple Newton, DIVX, and Microsoft Bob prove that sometimes it is better to be a mainstream adopter than to jump on the new-product bandwagon before the technology has been fully tried and tested.

Mass Media Outlets and New Technology

As new technology reaches the shelves and the number of early majority consumers rushing to purchase it increases, mass media outlets are forced to adapt to the new medium. When the iPad's popularity continued to grow throughout 2010 (selling 3,000,000 units within 3 months of its launch date), traditional newspapers, magazines, and TV networks rushed to form partnerships with Apple, launching applications for the tablet so that consumers could directly access their content. Unconstrained by the limited amount of space available in a physical newspaper or magazine, publications such as *The New York Times* and *USA Today* are able to include more detailed reporting than they can fit in their traditional paper, as well as interactive features such as crossword puzzles and the use of video and sound. "Our iPad App is designed to take full advantage of the evolving capabilities offered by the Internet," said Arthur Sulzberger Jr., publisher of *The New York Times*. "We see our role on the iPad as being similar to our traditional print role—to act as a thoughtful, unbiased filter and to provide our customers with information they need and can trust (Brett, 2010)."

Because of Apple's decision to ban Flash (the dominant software for online video viewing) from the iPad, some traditional TV networks have been converting their video files to HTML5 in order to enable full TV episodes to be screened on the device. CBS and Disney were among the first networks to offer free TV content on the iPad in 2010 through the iPad's built-in web browser, while ABC streamed its shows via an iPad application. The iPad has even managed to revive forms of traditional media that had been discontinued; in June 2010, Condé Nast announced the restoration of *Gourmet* magazine as an iPad application called Gourmet Live. As more media content becomes available on new technology such as the iPad, the iPod, and the various e-readers available on the market, it appeals to a broader range of consumers, becoming a self-perpetuating model.

Key Takeaways

- The technology adoption life cycle offers a diffusion model of how people accept new ideas and new technology. The model recognizes five categories of participants: innovators, who tend to be experimentalists and are interested in the technology itself; early adopters, who are technically sophisticated and are interested in using the technology for solving professional and academic problems; early majority, who constitute the first part of the mainstream, bringing the new technology into common use; late majority, who are less comfortable with the technology and may be skeptical about its benefits; and laggards, who are resistant to the new technology and may be critical of its use by others.

- When new technology is released in the market, it follows the technology adoption life cycle. Innovators and early adopters want to be the first to own the technology and are unconcerned about the cost, whereas mainstream consumers wait to find out how popular or successful the technology will become before buying it. As the technology filters into the mainstream, it becomes cheaper and more user-friendly. Some people remain resistant to new technology, however, which helps to control its development. Technological flops such as Microsoft Bob and DIVX result from skeptical late adopters or laggards refusing to purchase innovations that appear unlikely to become commercially successful.

- As new technology transitions into the mainstream, traditional media outlets have to adapt to the new technology to reach consumers. Recent examples include the development of traditional media applications for the iPad, such as newspaper, magazine, and TV network apps.

Exercises

Choose a technological innovation from the past 50 years and research its diffusion into the mass market. Then respond to the following short-answer questions. Each response should be a minimum of one paragraph.

1. Does it fit the technology diffusion model?

2. How quickly did the technology reach the mass market? In what ways did mass media aid the spread of this technology?

3. Research similar inventions that never caught on. Why do you think this technology succeeded when so many others failed?

End-of-Chapter Assessment

Review Questions

1.
Section 1

a. What are the main types of traditional media, and what factors influenced their development?

b. What are the main types of new media and what factors influenced their development?

c. Why are new media often more successful than traditional media?

2.
Section 2

a. What were the main types of media used at the beginning of the 20th century?

b. What factors led to the rise of a national mass culture?

c. How has the Internet affected media delivery?

3.
Section 3

a. What are the main information delivery methods in modern media?

b. Why has the Internet become a primary source of news and information?

4.
Section 4

a. What are the main advantages of modern media delivery methods?

b. What are the main disadvantages of modern media delivery methods?

5.

Section 5

a. What factors influenced the development of the print industry? What factors contributed to its decline?

b. How has the Internet affected the print industry?

c. What is likely to happen to the print industry in the future? How is print media transitioning into the digital age?

6.
Section 6

a. What are the current trends in social networking?

b. How is the Internet becoming more exclusive?

c. What are the effects of smartphone applications on modern media?

7.
Section 7

a. What effects did the USA PATRIOT Act have on privacy in the United States?

b. What are some of the consequences of social networking sites in terms of privacy and employment?

c. How are some websites attempting to restore privacy?

8.
Section 8

a. What is the technology adoption life cycle and how does it relate to new media?

b. How do mass-media outlets respond to new technology?

Critical Thinking Questions

1. Is there a future for traditional media, or will it be consumed by digital technology?

2. Do employers have the right to use social networking sites as a method of selecting future employees? Are employees entitled to voice their opinion on the Internet even if it damages their company's reputation?

3. Did the USA PATRIOT Act make the country a safer place, or did it violate privacy laws and undermine civil liberties?

4. One of the disadvantages of modern media delivery is the lack of reliability of information on the Internet. Do you think online journalism (including blogging) will ultimately become a respected source of information, or will people continue to rely on traditional news media?

5. Will a pay-for-content model work for online newspapers and magazines, or have consumers

become too used to receiving their news for free?

Career Connection

As a result of rapid change in the digital age, careers in media are constantly shifting, and many people who work in the industry face an uncertain future. However, the Internet (and all the various technologies associated with it) has created numerous opportunities in the media field. Take a look at the following website and scroll down to the "Digital" section: http://www.getdegrees.com/articles/career-resources/top-60-jobs-that-will-rock-the-future/

The website lists several media careers that are on the rise, including the following:

- Media search consultant
- Interface designer
- Cloud computing engineer
- Integrated digital media specialist
- Casual game developer
- Mobile application developer

Read through the description of each career, including the links within each description. Choose one career that you are interested in pursuing, research the skills and qualifications it requires, and then write a one-page paper on what you found. Here are some other helpful websites you might like to use in your research:

- Digital Jobs of the Future: Integrated Digital Media Specialist: http://www.s2m.com.au/news/2009/11/26/digital-jobs-of-the-future-integrated-digital-media-specialist/?403
- Cloud Computing Jobs: http://cloudczar.com/
- Top Careers for College Graduates: Casual Game Development: http://www.examiner.com/x-11055-San-Diego-College-Life-Examiner~y2009m5d27-Top-careers-for-college-graduates-Casual-Game-Development
- How to Become a Mobile Application Developer: http://www.ehow.com/how_5638517_become-mobile-application-developer.html
- Mobile App Development: So Many Choices, So Few Guarantees: http://www.linuxinsider.com/story/70128.html?wlc=1277823391
- 20 Websites to Help You Master User Interface Design: http://sixrevisions.com/usabilityaccessibility/20-websites-to-help-you-master-user-interface-design/

[1]Helft, "Tech's Late Adapters."

References

Bartash, Jeffry. "Amazon Drops Kindle Price to $189," *MarketWatch*, June 21, 2010, http://www.marketwatch.com/story/amazon-drops-kindle-price-to-189-2010-06-21.

Brett, Andy. "The New York Times Introduces an iPad App," *TechCrunch*, April 1, 2010, http://techcrunch.com/2010/04/01/new-york-times-ipad/.

Goldman, Jim. "Apple Sells 1 Million iPads," *CNBC*, May 3, 2010, http://www.cnbc.com/id/36911690/Apple_Sells_1_Million_iPads.

Guglielmo, Connie. "Apple IPad's Debut Weekend Sales May Be Surpassing Estimates," *Businessweek*, April 4, 2010, http://www.businessweek.com/news/2010-04-04/apple-ipad-s-debut-weekend-sales-may-be-surpassing-estimates.html.

Helft, Miguel. "Tech's Late Adopters Prefer the Tried and True," *New York Times*, March 12, 2008, http://www.nytimes.com/2008/03/12/technology/12inertia.html.

Mokey, Nick. "Tech We Regret," *Digital Trends*, March 18, 2009, http://www.digitaltrends.com/how-to/tech-we-regret/.

O'Hear, Steve. "Report: The iPad Won't Go Mass Market Anytime Soon," *TechCrunch*, May 12, 2010, http://eu.techcrunch.com/2010/05/12/report-the-ipad-wont-go-mass-market-anytime-soon/.

Oliver, Sam. "Preorders for Apple iPad Slow After 120K First-Day Rush," *Apple Insider*, March 15, 2010, http://www.appleinsider.com/articles/10/03/15/preorders_for_apple_ipad_slow_after_120k_first_day_rush.html.

Rogers, Everett M. *Diffusion of Innovations*, 4th ed. (New York: The Free Press, 1995).

Whitney, Lance. "Survey: 40 Percent in U.S. Have No Broadband," *CNET*, February 16, 2010, http://news.cnet.com/8301-1035_3-10454133-94.html.

Wortham, Jenna. "The Race to Be an Early Adopter of Technologies Goes Mainstream, a Survey Finds," *New York Times*, September 1, 2009, http://www.nytimes.com/2009/09/02/technology/02survey.html.

CPSIA information can be obtained
at www.ICGtesting.com
Printed in the USA
BVHW01s0058310818
525954BV00016B/26/P